2nd International Conference on Technology, Innovation, Society and Science-to-Business (ICTIS 2018)

MATEC Web of Conferences Volume 215 (2018)

Padang, Indonesia
25 – 26 July 2018

Editors:

T. Baaken
P. van der Sijde
G. Maas
Zaidir M. Yahya

ISBN: 978-1-5108-7307-0

Printed from e-media with permission by:

Curran Associates, Inc.
57 Morehouse Lane
Red Hook, NY 12571

Some format issues inherent in the e-media version may also appear in this print version.

Printed by Curran Associates, Inc. (2018)

For additional information, please contact EDP Sciences – Web of Conferences at the address below.

EDP Sciences – Web of Conferences
17, Avenue du Hoggar
Parc d'Activité de Courtabœuf
BP 112
F-91944 Les Ulis Cedex A
France

Phone: +33 (0) 1 69 18 75 75
Fax: +33 (0) 1 69 28 84 91

contact-edps@webofconferences.org

Additional copies of this publication are available from:

Curran Associates, Inc.
57 Morehouse Lane
Red Hook, NY 12571 USA
Phone: 845-758-0400
Fax: 845-758-2633
Email: curran@proceedings.com
Web: www.proceedings.com

TABLE OF CONTENTS

EXPLORING AIR PROPERTIES FOR FMRI-COMPATIBLE INTERACTION DEVICES 1
Aulia Putra Handityo

OPTICAL SAR IMAGES FUSION: COMPARATIVE ANALYSIS OF RESULTING IMAGES DATA 8
Yuhendra, Minarni

COMPARISON ANALYSIS OF SIMPLE ADDITIVE WEIGHTING (SAW) AND WEIGTHED PRODUCT (WP) IN DECISION SUPPORT SYSTEMS 13
Wira Trise Putra Dede, Agustian Punggara Adrian

COMPARISON OF CASE-BASED REASONING AND DEMPSTER SHAFER ON EXPERT SYSTEM OF CASSAVA DISEASE IDENTIFICATION 18
Minarni, Warman Indra, Yuhendra, Handayani Wenda

QOS ANALYSIS ON OSPFV3 AND RIPNG USING GRE TUNNELING ON IPV6 INTEGRATED IPV4 NETWORK 23
Warman Indra, Franozal Alex

DECISION SUPPORT SYSTEM OF FRUIT CULTIVATION USING TECHNIQUE FOR OTHER REFERENCE METHOD BY SIMILARITY TO IDEAL SOLUTION (TOPSIS) 29
Yulianti Eva, Nanda Rahmat Rizki

DESIGN OF MULTICOLOUR LED WITH CONTROL AND MONITORING SYSTEM FOR PLANT GROWTH 36
Ng Wei Choon, Yunus Nurul Amziah Md, Halin Izhal Abdul

MOTORCYCLE PARKING DESIGN WITH SIMULATION APPROACH CASE STUDY: RUSUNAWA PENJARINGAN SARI 3, SURABAYA 40
Krisnanda Yohanes R., Hapsari Indri, Arlianto Jerry A., Tjahjoanggoro Anton J., Hartono Markus, Tondok Marselius S.

DEVELOPMENT AND DESIGNING SMART TRAFFIC LIGHT WITH XBEE PRO 45
Alfith Alfith, Kartiria Kartiria

DESIGN OF FUEL ANTI-THEFT BASED ON MICRO-CONTROLLERS USING SHORT MESSAGE SERVICE 49
Syofian Andi, Yultrisna

IDENTIFICATION OF NUMBER USING ARTIFICIAL NEURAL NETWORK BACKPROPAGATION 53
Amalia Sitti

A STUDY OF A CCD CAMERA FOR VIBRATION MEASUREMENT 59
Amin Zulkifli, Ikhsan Muhammad

THE LIFTING FORCE RELATIONSHIP OF A BLDC MOTOR ROTOR SYSTEM TO THE BLADE ROTATION SPEED 62
Al Al, Dewi Arfita Yuana, Hidayat Taufal

DATA LOGGER DEVELOPMENT TO EVALUATE POTENTIAL AREA OF SOLAR ENERGY 69
Effendi Asnal, Dewi Arfita Yuana, Ismail Fauzan

A TRUE HYBRID SOLAR WIND TURBINE ELECTRIC GENERATOR SYSTEM FOR SMALLER HYBRID RENEWABLE ENERGY POWER PLANTS 73
Al-Ajmi Mohammad Shafi, Mustapha Faizal, Mohd Ariffin Mohd. Khairol Anuar B., Md Yunus Nurul Amziah, Abdul Halin Izhal

IMPLEMENTATION OF MAXIMUM POWER POINT TRACKING TO IMPROVING THE SOLAR CELL EFFICIENCY 79
Bandri Sepannur, Zulkarnaini Zulkarnaini, Sofian Andi

EXPERIMENTAL STUDY TO PERFORMANCE IMPROVEMENT OF VAPOR COMPRESSION COOLING SYSTEM INTEGRATED DIRECT EVAPORATIVE COOLER AND CONDENSER 83
Rachman Arfidian, Nesti Lisa

METHODS OF CALCULATION OF ENERGY LOSSES OF THE REFRIGERATOR WHEN OPENING ITS DOORS 87
Petrosov S. P., Lemeshko M. A., Kozhemyachenko A. V., Bashnjak S. E.

PARTIAL DISCHARGE ANALYSIS ON ISOLATOR OF TRANSFORMER 94
Antonov Bachtiar, Thomas Thomas

STABILITY ANALYSIS OF 20 KV SYSTEM AT PT PLN (PERSERO) RAYON MUARALABUH BEFORE AND AFTER INTERCONECTION BY IPP (PLTMH PT. SKE) 98
Dewi Arfita Yuana, Effendi Asnal, Ridwan

STUDY OF COORDINATION ON PROTECTION RELAY IN HIGH VOLTAGE TRANSMISSION 150 KV (PAYAKUMBUH – KOTO PADANG, WEST SUMATRA) 105
Zulkarnaini Zulkarnaini, Rizki Muhammad

TOWER-FOOTING RESISTANCE AND LIGHTNING TRIP-OUTS OF 150 KV TRANSMISSION LINES IN WEST SUMATRA IN INDONESIA 112
Warmi Yusreni, Michishita Koji

WINDINGS DESIGN FOR SINGLE-PHASE INDUCTION MOTORS BASE ON 4-PHASE INDUCTION MOTOR (CASE STUDY: IDENTICAL WINDINGS DESIGN) 120
Anthony Zuriman, Erhaneli Erhaneli, Zulkarnaini Zulkarnaini

A DISCUSSION OF MAGNETOELECTRIC COMPOSITE DESIGN BY BONDING THE FERROMAGNETIC MATERIAL GRADED LAYERS IN INDUCTION MOTOR 124
Anthony Zuriman, Abral Hairul, Nazir Refdinal

OPTIMIZATION OF COMPACTION PRESSURE ON BRICK 128
Indra Ade, Edison Edison, Nofrianto Hendri

CRYSTAL STRUCTURE, THERMAL EXPANSION AND LONG-TERM BEHAVIORS OF SMBACOO$_{5+\delta}$ AS CATHODE FOR INTERMEDIATE-TEMPERATURE SOLID OXIDE FUEL CELLS 133
Subardi Adi, Fu Yen-Pei

SOLID-STATE FERMENTATION OF BANANA PEELS POTENTIAL STUDY FOR FEED ADDITIVE 138
Fatmawati Akbarningrum, Lidiawati Tuani, Hadinata Stephen, Adiarto Mikhael

EFFECT OF PH ON THE STABILITY OF W1/O/W2 DOUBLE EMULSION STABILIZED BY COMBINATION OF BIOSILICA AND TWEEN-20 143
Sapei Lanny, Adiarto Tokok, Handomo Roi, Chandra Sonny Hutomo

THE EFFECT OF FLY ASH COMPOSITION AND DRYING TIME CONCRETE BRICK IN DENSITY TEST 148
Nurzal, Perdana Mastaryanto, Putera Heru Pratama

EXPERIMENTAL TESTS AND ANALYTICAL STUDIES OF BEARING-TYPE AXIAL STEEL CONNECTION 152
Pranata Yosafat Aji, Sulandari Noek, Milyardi Roi

PROCUREMENT MANAGEMENT/ MATERIAL SUPPLY ON CONSTRUCTION PROJECTS 157
Tanubrata Maksum, Gunawan Ika

DESIGN OF STRUCTURAL DAMAGE IDENTIFICATION APPLICATIONS WEB-BASED 161
Anisya Anisya, Nugroho Fajar

THE RISK ANALYSIS OF ANDALAS UNIVERSITY HOSPITAL CONSTRUCTION PROJECT 165
Zaidir, Putri Melani Novia, Hasan Alizar

AN EVALUATION OF MECHANICAL PROPERTIES OF CLAY BRICK FOR MASONRY WALL IN INDONESIA 171
Ridwan Muhammad, Kurniawan Ruddy, Agus

SEISMIC PERFORMANCE OF EXISTING R/C BUILDING WITH IRREGULAR FLOOR PLAN SHAPE 177
Agus, Ridwan Muhammad, Ramadhana Febriyan

EFFECTS OF SINGLE AND MULTI OPENINGS IN BRICK INFILLS ON THE SEISMIC RESPONSE OF INFILLED RC FRAMES 182
Maidiawati, Tanjung Jafril, Medriosa Hamdeni, Hayati Yulia

DEVELOPMENT OF A RELATIVE VULNERABILITY INDEX (RVI) FOR ESTIMATION OF BUILDING VULNERABILITY TOWARDS TSUNAMI HAZARD 189
Honesti Leli, Majid Muhd Zaimi Abd, Djali Nazwar, Muchlian Meli, Syofyan Z

FEASIBILITY ANALYSIS OF SURFACE RAIL IN THE REVITALIZATION OF THE RAILWAY ROAD 193
Wahab Wilton

DIFFERENCE IN PRESS ANGLE TO THE QUALITY OF BRIQUETTES 197
Handra Nofriady, Hafni Hafni, Fahmi Hendriwan

ANALYSIS OF POWER LOSS OF 20 KV POWER DISTRIBUTION 201
Dasman Dasman

COLLECTIVE INTELLECTUAL RIGHT? A CASE ON PROTECTED GEOGRAPHY INDICATED 205
David Firmansyah, David Wahyudi

LITERATURE REVIEW ON RELATIONSHIP BUILDING FOR COMMUNITY-ACADEMIC COLLABORATION IN HEALTH RESEARCH AND INNOVATION 209
Chak Choiwai Maggie

LINKAGE BETWEEN FLEXIBILITY AND SMES PERFORMANCE: DOES IMPROVISATION MATTER? ... 218
Arshad Darwina, Zakaria Nazlina, Abdul-Kadir Kadzrina, Ahmad Norzieiriani

MULTI CRITERIA DECISIONS MAKING APPROACH TO CHOOSE 'INTEGRATORS' IN MALAYSIAN LOCAL BROILER INDUSTRY ... 224
Lamsali Hendrik, Ariffin Ahmad Shabudin

ABSORPTIVE CAPACITY IN LOW-TECH INDUSTRY: CASE STUDY OF INDONESIAN MANUFACTURING COMPANIES ... 231
Ariana Lutfah, Asmara Indri Juwita

INFLUENCE OF PRODUCT QUALITY, PRICE AND SUPPORTING INFRASTURCTURE TO PERCEIVED VALUE AND INTEREST IN BUYING OF ELECTRIC MOTORCYCLE ... 239
Rahmanullah Edwin Sholeh, Nurjanah Siti

INTERNAL FACTORS THAT AFFECT SMES TO EXPORT: A CASE STUDY OF FOOTWEAR CLUSTER ... 249
Dhewanto Wawan, Herliana Sri, Lantu Donald Crestofel, Lawiyah Nur

THE CONSTRAINTS OF AGRICULTURAL CREDIT AND GOVERNMENT POLICY STRATEGY ... 254
Herliana Sri, Sutardi Acip, Aina Qorri, Himmatul Aliya Qonita, Lawiyah Nur

THE FORMATION OF FOOD CLUSTER IN INDONESIA ... 261
Lantu Donald Crestofel, Herliana Sri, Rosmiati Mia, Aina Qorri, Lawiyah Nur

DETERMINANT FACTORS OF INFORMATION TECHNOLOGY ADOPTION IN CREATIVE BUSINESS AND THE RESULT OF ITS APPLICATION: CASE OF SMES CLUSTER IN SOUTH BANDUNG ... 265
Dhewanto Wawan, Lestari Yuliani Dwi, Heliana Sri, Aliya Qonita Himmatul, Lawiyah Nur

QUALITY ANALYSIS OF ORGANIC RICE VARIETY MENTIK SUSU AND SINTANUR NUTRITIONAL APPROACH ... 272
Handayani Sri, Affandi Muhammad Irfan, Astuti Sussi

INDONESIAN CULTURAL PREFERENCE IN DESIGNING USER INTERFACE ... 276
Persada Andhika Giri

MICRO IMAGINATION: IMAGINATION WITH AN ALTERNATIVE FRAMEWORK IN A CHEMISTRY CLASS ... 281
Abdullah Nurdiana, Wahab Nur Bahiyah Abdul, Wai Taufik Lock Kim, Surif Johari

Author Index

Exploring Air Properties for fMRI-Compatible Interaction Devices

Handityo Aulia Putra[1,2*]

[1]Keimyung University, Game and Mobile Engineering, Korea
[2]Kochi University of Technology, Information Engineering, Japan

Abstract. The strong magnetic field of functional magnetic resonance imaging (fMRI) and the supine position of participants in fMRI scanners severely limit how participants can interact during fMRI experiments. This paper explores the use of air properties to design interaction-device systems that allow various interaction styles inside a fMRI scanner. Airflow and air pressure are explored to design and develop the interaction system. A series of air-based devices are introduced and discussed to demonstrate the feasibility of an air-based approach. This includes soft tactile and conventional controls (e.g., button, slider, joystick, pedal). To achieve fMRI-compatibility, all parts used inside the scanner are built from non-ferromagnetic, off-the-shelf plastic, and/or 3D printed materials. The fMRI compatibility was evaluated on a 3.0 Tesla fMRI scanner. We conclude with example applications and thoughts on future avenues of research.

1 Introduction

Functional magnetic resonance imaging (fMRI) [1] enables medical doctors and researchers to study correlations between brain activation and tasks performed by participants during a brain scan. In addition to the scanned brain images, participants' responses and/or behavioral data while performing the tasks are required during post-processing of brain study to improve the detection of brain activity [2]. Furthermore, in a task that requires special stimulation other than visual stimulation, additional equipment is required to deliver the stimulation (signals) to the participants, such as haptic sensations and/or fragrance [3]. However, the strong magnetic field of fMRI limits the choice of response and/or stimulation device that can be used. Devices with traditional ferromagnetic materials and actuation/sensing methods are not permitted in the fMRI environment.

Optical fiber-based sensing has been used in various fMRI applications such as force measurement [4], motor response [5], and a musical instrument [6] because of its small size, it is not affected by electromagnetic interference (EMI), and presents no electromagnetic susceptibility (EMS). Due to its popularity, there are some commercial providers that offer fMRI-compatible fiber-optic devices for recording participant' responses during fMRI scans. However, these devices are typically expensive, requiring specialized control software, limited to recording response only and cannot be used to provide stimulation to the participants. Similarly, air-based (pneumatic) devices are invulnerable to EMI and lack of EMS. Pneumatic-based devices have also been used in various fMRI applications such as robot interaction [7-9], skin stimulation [10,11], haptic interface [12]. However, these devices are limited to one configuration and only provide stimulation to participants without sensing and/or recording participants' response information.

This paper proposes a complementary method for designing and developing fMRI-compatible devices that are able to both record participant responses and provide stimulation (such as soft tactile feedback and fragrance signal) to the participants in fMRI environment. This paper explores the use of air properties, especially air-flow and air-pressure (pneumatic) for designing and developing various interaction devices for use in the fMRI experiments (Figure 1). This paper also explores the use of the 3D printer, plastic pockets, and off-the-shelf materials to enable fast development and replication of various custom interaction devices for use in fMRI environment. We conducted informal interviews with several expert fMRI researchers who have been using fMRI to conduct experiments for more than 5 years to find out what possible interaction device functions may be required, which are currently unavailable and, which may be made possible by using the proposed air based interaction devices. We also conducted an evaluation experiment for fMRI-compatibility of the developed devices on a 3.0 Tesla fMRI scanner. The evaluation results show that air-based interaction devices are effective and that they comply with standards for the device in fMRI [13].

We envisioned that in the future these air-based devices will allow fMRI researchers to expand their choice of tools in experiments aimed at understanding human behavior using fMRI scanners. These devices could be selected from a standardized library, edited and then be

* Corresponding author: handityo@kmu.ac.kr

3D printed, allowing fast and inexpensive testing in pilot studies for new brain studies instead of directly purchasing expensive commercially available devices.

2 Related Work

The work presented in this paper builds on fMRI-compatible devices, pneumatic-based interaction devices, and device fabrication.

2.1 fMRI-compatible devices

Several researchers have developed various fMRI-compatible devices using pneumatics control [7-9] and optical-fiber [4-6]. However, fiber-optic-based devices are limited to only sensing and recording response information. Although pneumatic systems are able to record responses based on changes in air pressure, no previous work utilizes this capability to develop a response device using the pneumatic system. Also, there is no prior work that explores the use of air-flow to provide interaction inside the fMRI environment.

2.2 Pneumatic-based interaction devices

Utilizing pneumatics to develop interactive devices have been exemplified by several researchers, e.g., jamming interface [14], visual display with dynamic button [15], inflatable mouse [16], Pneui [17], robot interaction [18]. However, these devices were developed not to be used inside the fMRI environment, because they require additional components that may contain ferromagnetic materials. Our work is focused on allowing interaction by solely using air-properties and only components that can be put inside fMRI scanners i.e., made from plastic and/or non-ferromagnetic materials, and expanding our previous work [19]. Previous researchers demonstrated the flexibility of pneumatic control devices for interaction and the need to further expand the possible applications in different research areas such as fMRI.

2.3 Device fabrication

Pneumatic devices can be built using several methods such as 3D printing [20-21], manual construction [17], casting or molding [22]. Vazquez et al. [21] have shown that 3D printing is a unified and flexible approach to fabrication and customization of pneumatic devices. They also showed that it is possible to do multi-material 3D printing, however, the 3D printer that is capable of print using multiple materials is costly at present (Objet Eden260V, $19800 in 2016). Although manual construction such as plastic welding is considered cumbersome and error-prone compared to 3D printing, it is one of the fastest methods in fabricating air-pocket for using with pneumatic systems. In this paper, we explored a combination of plastic welding and 3D printing to develop various pneumatic chambers (air-pockets) to be used in our interaction devices. Fabricating using plastic welding to allow fast development which is used to provide proof-of-concept of the developed design then refined using 3D printing.

3 fMRI-compatible air-flow-based system

The air-flow-based system is designed to allow simple interactions with simultaneous soft air-tactile feedback to users. In this work, we used the air-flow-based system to allows users to have a soft air-flow sensation and a simple precise control over a levitated ball inside a transparent tube at the same time. Figure 2c shows a complete of the air-flow-based system. The air-flow-based system consists of a fan motor, a ball (diameter 8 mm) in a transparent tube (inner diameter of 1 cm, thickness 3 mm), an 8-meter long transparent tube (inner diameter of 1 cm, thickness 3 mm), a flow meter (range 100 mL/min to 1500 mL/min), an Arduino microcontroller and a 3D printed interaction device (Figure 1b). The Arduino controller turns on the fan-motor generating air-flow through the transparent tube to 3D the printed hand-nozzle device (Figure 3) which is held by the user. The hand-nozzle device was developed using a uPrint SE 3D printer with ivory color ABSplus material.

The strength of the air-tactile feedback is correlated with the strength of air-flow that is generated by the fan motor. Furthermore, in Figure 3, position control of the ball can be done in two different interactions, which are an on-off (open-close) interaction and a sliding interaction. Open-close interaction provides a digital-like control, while the slide interaction provides an analog-like control behavior.

Despite its simple setup, this system allows both soft tactile feedback (with just-noticeable differences (JND) in air flow pressure) while concurrently recording user behavior when precisely controlling the ball position, which normally could not be achieved with an optical-fiber-based system. By utilizing data recorded by a flow-sensor, the interaction enabled by this system can not only control the ball position (as shown in Figure 2) but also can be used to provide a single-button-like response or an analog slider response (Figure 3c).

4 fMRI-compatible pneumatic-based system

The main design consideration is that all components that will be put inside fMRI need to be non-ferromagnetic and/or contain no metal/electronic circuit. Thus we focus on utilizing air only without additional component such as a potentiometer or LED to our systems. In addition, the device should be able to be operated while the participant is lying down. The pneumatic-based systems that we explored in this work rely on changes in air pressure to record user response information, to generate tactile sensation to users or to send scented air to users inside fMRI scanner.

 https://doi.org/10.1051/matecconf/201821501001

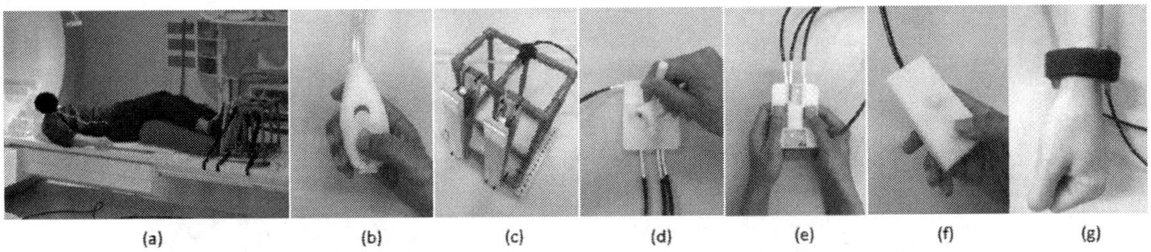

Fig. 1. Various air-based devices. (a) Pneumatic pedal set in fMRI scanner, (b) 3D printed air-flow based device for tap and slide interaction, (c) a pneumatic pedal device constructed from two pneumatic balls, wood, and PVC tube, (d) pneumatic joystick which can be used to manipulate x-y movements, (e) Pneumatic button with four pressure-sensitive buttons, constructed from four air pockets arranged in a 3D printed structure, (f) a two button pneumatic device, constructed using a single air pocket with 3D printed structure, (g) two 3D printed soft pneumatic button put together as wearable soft-haptic device.

Fig. 2. fMRI-Compatible air-flow-based system, (a) a participant uses an air-flow-based device to control the ball position located outside the fMRI room (b) from inside of the fMRI scanner, (b) air-flow-based system, consisted of a transparent tube and a ball, (c) Schematic diagram of air-flow-based system

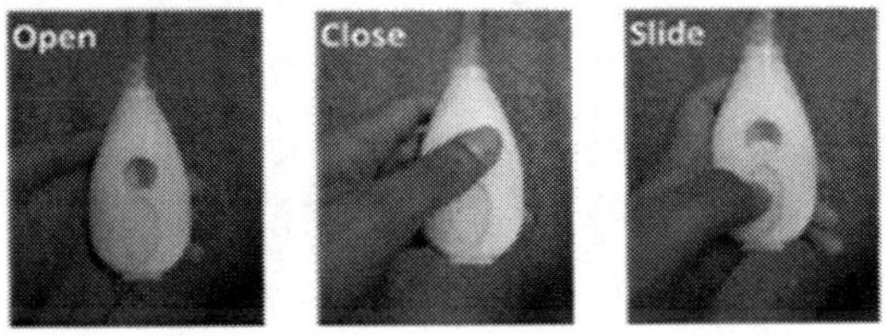

Fig. 3. Interaction for fMRI-Compatible air-flow based system, (a) open interaction to lift the ball by allowing air-flow, (b) close interaction to put the ball down by stopping air flow, and (c) slide interaction for precise control of ball position by controlling the amount of air-flow.

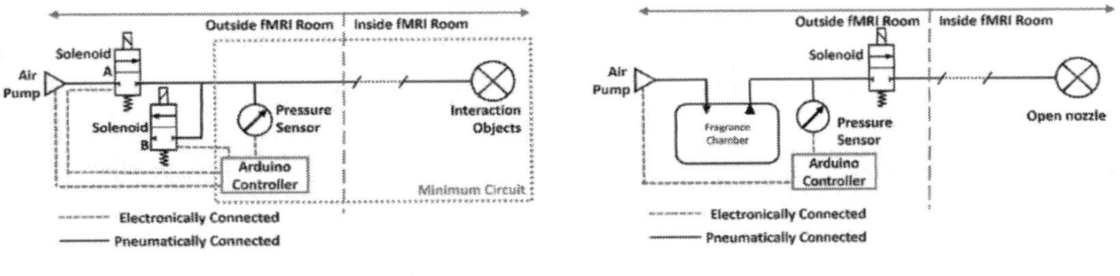

Fig. 4. Pneumatic diagram for (a) general design of pneumatic-based fMRI-compatible device and (b) fragrance delivery system

4.1 Design

In this work, we explored three designs to serve three different purposes. The first purpose is to dynamically change air pressure to alter the physical form of air pockets while the sensor continuously reads internal air pressure of the system to allows precise closed-loop control. The second purpose is to only sense user input with pressure sensors, thus further simplify the system. The third purpose is to deliver smell from fragrance chamber outside of fMRI room to users inside the fMRI room while air pressure sensor and solenoid control the air flow to the user to have a constant pressure.

Figure 4a shows the diagram for the first pneumatic design. This first design is for general use which contains an air-pump as a pressure source, two solenoid valves, a pressure sensor, and an interaction object (e.g., air pocket or 3D printed air chamber). In the rest state, both solenoids A and B are closed (no air in or out, both solenoids are normally closed). If solenoid A is actuated and B is at rest, the pressure source (air pump) can increase air pressure in the system. If solenoid B is actuated, the system is open, releasing air and thus decreasing the air pressure inside the system.

The second design is for recording air pressure information only. This design is the simplified version of the first design which consists only air pressure sensor and the interaction object as shown inside the minimum circuit part of Figure 4a. Assuming that there is no air-leakage in the system, this is useful to reduce the number of components in the system and to increase the scalability of the pneumatic system (e.g., although in a normal setup, a four-button variable sensing device would require four air pumps, eight solenoid valves, and four pressure sensors, in simplified design, the same device only require four pressure sensors to be functional). This design is limited to interaction objects that can return to its original shape after pressed or squeezed by users. Therefore, interaction object such as air pockets that need to be inflated first before can be used as an interaction device cannot use this design.

The last design is for delivering smell to users inside fMRI is shown in Figure 4a. By modifying the design in Figure 6, we can use the same components to allow different stimulation for the users. Air pressure sensor continuously reads internal air pressure of the system, if the internal air pressure is lower than the required threshold (air-flow that deliver the smell is weak), the solenoid valve is switched off and air-pump increases pressure for the fragrance chamber. If the internal air pressure is higher than the threshold (strong air-flow), the solenoid is activated allowing the smell to be delivered to the user. By monitoring the air pressure to be close to the threshold value, this system can maintain a stable flow of smell to the user. It is to be noted that the fragrance particle will diffuse over time and make the smell weaker if used for a long period of time.

4.2 Fabrication

We fabricated the pneumatic devices using plastic welding and two different 3D printers (one for rigid material and one for flexible material). The fabrication process using plastic welding is straightforward, affordable, and fast, but have low replicability. Fabricating using 3D printer takes a little bit longer time to design and print, but is very replicable when printing multiple custom devices.

4.2.1 Fabrication by plastic welding

In a condition where 3D printing is not available, plastic welding offers a fast way to develop a prototype for air-pocket used in pneumatic systems. We used plastic welding method to develop a simple air pocket by heat pressure molding off-the-shelf 0.3 mm thick polyethylene sheets (plastic) into a square and attaching a pneumatic tube on one end of the pocket. Although this method is error-prone (e.g., it is difficult to form an airtight pocket in single try), it is one of the fastest and most cost cost-effective ways to fabricate a custom-sized air-pocket. To ensure the air pocket was airtight, we used airtight tape (Teflon tape) and heated it with a heat gun to close any possible openings. Using this simple method, we were able to increase the fabrication success rate of this method. The fabricated air pocket can sustain internal air pressure of 4.5 PSI before breaking. One example of air-pocket that developed by this method is shown in Figure 5a. This air pocket can be used as an on-off button and also a pressure sensitive button.

4.2.2 Fabrication by 3D Printer

Although plastic welding can be used to fabricate air pockets, its choice of geometry and shape is limited and difficult to reproduce the same result multiple times. Therefore, we combined the air pocket that we fabricated using plastic welding with rigid 3D printed part to improve variation of a pneumatic device that we can develop.

In order to make the appearance of the air pocket more appealing, we 3D printed a case for four air pockets (Figure 1e) using a uPrint SE printer with ivory color ABSplus material. This allows the four air-pockets to work as a four-button pneumatic device. Using the same 3D printer, we also 3D printed a handle for the joystick device (Figure 1d). Since the 3D printed part is used only as a container, we designed so that it does not have any over-hanging geometry in order to reduce any support material in printing result. By avoiding over-hanging geometry, the fabrication process will become faster because it eliminates the need to remove the supporting material and cleaning process.

For soft and flexible parts of the system, we used a FORM2 printer with flexible resin, to fabricate soft and elastic part of our system, for example, a soft pneumatic button (Figure 5b). Although flexible resin from formLabs can not elongate as much as TangoPlus used in [21], it has a higher tensile strength which allows the printed parts to be more robust from breaking. Additionally, in this 3D printer, there is no supporting material. In order to print any overhanging geometry, FORM2 uses mesh-like supporting structure to hold the geometry (Figure 5d). One feature of this 3D printer is that it allows printing a hollow geometry without any internal support structure. Therefore, there is no need to clean the internal part of the printed result. However, naively printing hollow structure will result in failure of the 3D printed structure. In order to print overhanging and/or hollow geometry, the geometric should be tilted/positioned in such a way (around 15 to 20°) that each layer of the 3D printed structure can support the hollow part without any supporting structure.

5 Applications

In this section, we will illustrate some potential applications of fMRI-compatible pneumatic-based interaction devices. Figure 6 shows the pneumatic system that we used for all of the following application. The pneumatic system consists of an off-the-shelf MIS-2500-015G air pressure sensor from Metrodyne with a pressure range of 15 PSI (68.95 milli bar) (Metrodyne, 2012) to monitor the pressure levels, two 2-way solenoid valve (model EXA-C6-02C-3) to regulate the system pressure.

5.1 Pedal Simulation

Figure 1c shows a pedal interface constructed from woods, PVC tubes, and two lens blower which are the same items used for hand squeeze device shown in Figure 5c. With two pressure-sensitive input devices connected together, the pedal device can simulate interaction for acceleration and brake in car simulation. The pedal can detect when the user accelerates or brakes, or detect whether the user makes a slow acceleration/brake or fast. Currently, there is no pressure sensitive pedal device available commercially, thus this device open an opportunity for brain researchers, to better investigate human behavior when driving, i.e., not only investigate whether user press acceleration or brake, but also investigate how strong the user needs to press the pedals, or when the user makes a mistake, how much pressure the user already applied to pedal before realizing the mistake.

5.2 Game Interaction

Figure 7 shows two game interfaces that are controlled by the fMRI-compatible pneumatic devices. One game is a side-scrolling game, where the user controls the vertical position of red squares to avoid yellow bars. The control is done by pushing the pneumatic air-pocket (Figure 5a), pressing the pocket will move the red square up, and releasing it will move the red square down. The movement speed is controlled by how strong the user press the pocket in a short period of time. We also used two hand-squeeze devices to provide input for a simplified version of the guitar-hero-like game. The user needs to squeeze the right or left device when the red or green circle hit the target area.

5.3 Wearable Wrist Haptic Feedback

We develop two flexible pneumatic buttons (Figure 5b) and put them together to make a wearable wrist haptic device. Since the buttons are made from flexible material, increasing internal air pressure of the pneumatic system can elongate the button giving a soft pressure feedback. This wearable haptic device can be used by brain researchers to study human reaction to the haptic feedback that generated by smartwatch on the wrist. Since normal smartwatch cannot be used inside fMRI environment, this pneumatic wearable haptic device is a good alternative to reproduce smartwatch haptic feedback inside fMRI. The wearable wrist can be expanded by using more pneumatic buttons.

5.4 fMRI-compatibility Evaluation

We conducted an experiment to evaluate the fMRI-compatibility of the pneumatic device. A device needs to satisfy three characteristics to be called fMRI-compatible. First, it must be safe to use and not do any harm to the users in any way. Second, the device should not affect the scanned image of the fMRI. Third, the device must be able to work properly within a high magnetic field while the fMRI is running [6, 12].

The prototypes were designed to be compact, soft and free from any para-magnetic material so that they will not be affected by the magnetic field of fMRI. Even if the prototype hits the users in an accident, it will not harm the users in any way. In order to be used for fMRI environment, a minimum of 7 meters in tube length is needed as the participant needs to use the device from inside the fMRI room. Therefore we used a tube with 10 meters in length to allow more movement.

The experiment was supervised by a fMRI researcher/expert. As shown in Figure 8, we placed the pneumatic response device on the fMRI bed together with a fMRI phantom (an object used to evaluate the fMRI device that responds similarly to how human tissue and organs act) [23]. The fMRI has different scanning sequences for different purposes. We used a sequence that used the whole frequency range of the fMRI device so that if the device did not affect any of the readings, the device can be said to be fMRI-compatible with any scanning sequence.

We conducted the fMRI scanning sequence in three conditions. The first condition was scanning with the phantom only, this was to provide the baseline scanned image of the fMRI that is not affected by any device. The second condition was scanning with the phantom and the prototype in the off condition. This was done to investigate whether the prototype material affected the scanned image. The third condition was scanning with the phantom and the prototype in the running condition. This condition was done to test whether the prototype had any effect on the scanned image from the fMRI.

The scanned images from the three conditions are shown in Figure 8. One criterion to define that the scanned image is free from disturbance is that the image should show random noise. If there was any disturbance in the scanning process, the image should show a white line (vertical/horizontal) on the image. During scanning in the third condition, we also tested whether the scanning process affected the performance of the pneumatic response device by monitoring the pressure sensor reading. We found that during the scanning process the fMRI did not affect the pressure sensor reading (i.e., the sensor reading worked properly). Based on the resulting images and the sensor readings, the fMRI researcher concluded that the pneumatic response device has no effect on the scanned images and that it was fMRI-compatible.

6 Conclusion

We have described the process of developing air-flow based interaction devices and air-pressure-based (pneumatic) interaction devices for interaction in a fMRI environment. We have evaluated the interaction devices for their compatibility with the fMRI environment and its ability to provide continuous pressure value as an input parameter. We also have provided design considerations to develop air-based interaction device for use in fMRI environment. Furthermore, some applications of the interaction devices are presented. While many considerations were made for the pneumatic systems, we believe that our design rationale and fabrication approach can guide the fMRI researchers to develop interaction devices for fMRI experiments. The evaluation result suggested that the proposed method is promising and that the development of various types of fMRI response device can open up new research opportunities for fMRI researchers.

References

1. S. A. Huettel, A. W. Song, G. McCarthy, *Functional magnetic resonance imaging*, Sinauer Associates, Sunderland, (2004)
2. E. Amaro Jr., G.J. Barker, study design in fMRI: basic principles. *brain and cognition*, **60** (3), 220–232, (2006)
3. H. Matsukura, T. Nihei, H. Ishida, multi-sensorial field display: Presenting spatial distribution of air-flow and odor, In *Virtual Reality Conference* (VR), IEEE: 119–122, (2011)
4. M. Tada, T. Kanade, an mr-compatible optical force sensor for human function modeling. In *Medical Image Computing and Computer-Assisted Intervention–MICCAI*. Springer: 129–136, (2004)
5. J. Meinhardt, J. Muller, motor response detection using fiber optics during functional magnetic resonance imaging.' Behavior Research Methods, Instruments, & Computers, **33** (4), 556–558, (2001)
6. A. Hollinger, Design of fmri-compatible electronic musical interfaces. Master's thesis, McGill University, Motreal, Canada, (2008)
7. G. S. Fischer, I. Iordachita, C. Csoma, J. Tokuda, S.P. DiMaio, C.M. Tempany, N. Hata, G. Fichtinger, Mri-compatible pneumatic robot for transperineal prostate needle placement IEEE/ASME Trans. On Mechatronics, **13** (3), 295–305. (2008)
8. R. Gassert, R. Moser, E. Burdet, H. Bleuler, Mri/fmri-compatible robotic system with force feedback for interaction with human motion. IEEE ASME Trans. on Mechatronics, **11** (2), 216. (2006)
9. N. Yu, C. Hollnagel, A. Blickenstorfer, S. Kollias, R. Riener, fmri-compatible robotic interfaces with fluidic actuation. Robotics: Science and Systems, 25–28. (2008)
10. S.M. Golaszewski, F. Zschiegner, C.M. Siedentopf, J. Unterrainer, R.A. Sweeney, W. Eisner, S. Lechner-Steinleitner, F.M. Mottaghy, S. Felber, A new pneumatic vibrator for functional magnetic resonance imaging of the human sensorimotor cortex. Neuroscience letters, **324** (2), 125–128. (2002)
11. C. Wienbruch, V. Candia, J. Svensson, R. Kleiser, S.S. Kollias, A portable and low-cost fmri compatible pneumatic system for the investigation of the somatosensensory system in clinical and research environments. Neuroscience letters, **398** (3), 183–188. (2006)
12. N. Yu, W. Murr, A. Blickenstorfer, S. Kollias, R. Riener, An fmri compatible haptic interface with pneumatic actuation. In IEEE ICORR. IEEE: 714–720. (2007)
13. T.O. Woods, Standards for medical devices in mri: Present and future. Journal of Magnetic Resonance Imaging, **26** (5), 1186–1189. (2007)
14. S. Follmer, D. Leithinger, A. Olwal, N. Cheng, H. Ishii, Jamming user interfaces: Programmable particle stiffness and sensing for malleable and shape-changing devices. In Proc. of UIST 2012, ACM: 519–528. (2012)
15. C. Harrison, S.E. Hudson, Providing dynamically changeable physical buttons on a visual display. In Proc. CHI 2009, ACM: 299–308. (2009)
16. S. Kim, H. Kim, B. Lee, T.J. Nam, W. Lee, Inflatable mouse: volume-adjustable mouse with air-pressure-sensitive input and haptic feedback. In Proc. of CHI, ACM: 211–224. (2008)
17. L. Yao, R. Niiyama, J. Ou, S. Follmer, C. Della Silva, H. Ishii, Pneui: Pneumatically actuated soft composite materials for shape changing interfaces. In Proc. UIST, ACM: 13–22. (2013)
18. R. Slyper, J. Hodgins, Prototyping robot appearance, movement, and interactions using flexible 3d printing and air pressure sensors. In RO-MAN, IEEE: 6–11. (2012)

19. H.A. Putra, X. Ren, Developing fMRI-Compatible Interaction System through Air-Pressure. In Proc. Adj. UIST, ACM. (2016)
20. V. Savage, R. Schmidt, T. Grossman, G. Fitzmaurice, B. Hartmann, A series of tubes: Adding interactivity to 3d prints using internal pipes. In Proc. UIST, ACM: 3–12. (2014)
21. M. Vazquez, E. Brockmeyer, R. Desai, C. Harrison, S.E. Hudson, 3d printing pneumatic device controls with variable activation force capabilities. In Proc. CHI, ACM: 1295–1304. (2015)
22. B. Mosadegh, P. Polygerinos, C. Keplinger, S. Wennstedt, R.F. Shepherd, U. Gupta, J. Shim, K. Bertoldi, C.J. Walsh, G.M. Whitesides, Pneumatic networks for soft robotics that actuate rapidly. Advanced Functional Materials, **24** (15), 2163–2170. (2014)
23. V. Renvall, Functional magnetic resonance imaging reference phantom. Magnetic Resonance Imaging, **27** (5), 701 – 708. (2009)

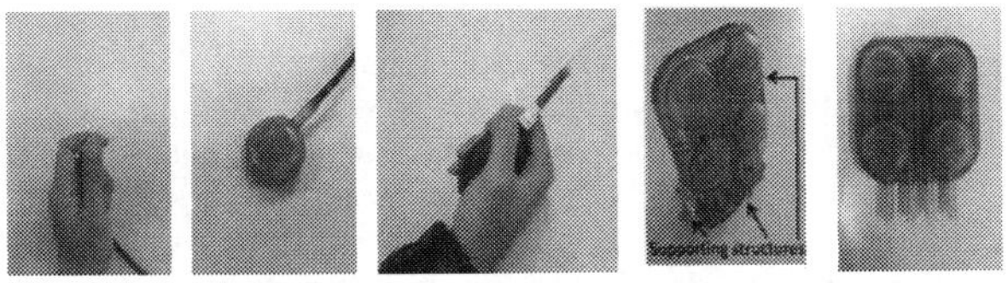

Fig. 5. (a) an air-pocket fabricated by plastic welding, (b) a soft button fabricated by 3D printer with flexible material, (c) a hand squeeze device built from off-the-shelf lens blower, (d) a freshly printed four-button flexible pneumatic device with mesh supporting structures, and (e) finished 3D printed four-button flexible pneumatic device

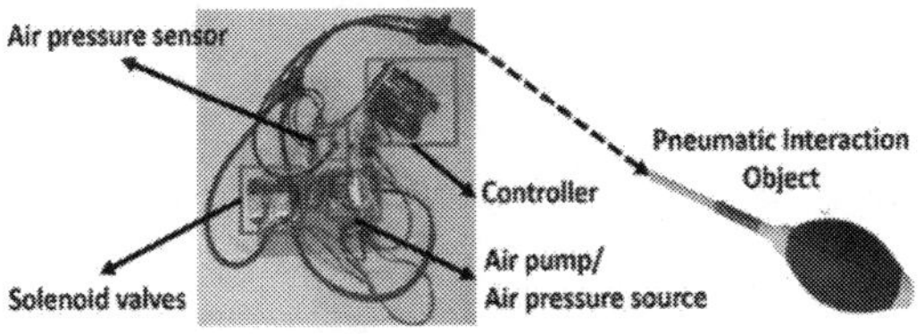

Fig. 4 Pneumatic-based interaction system used for application

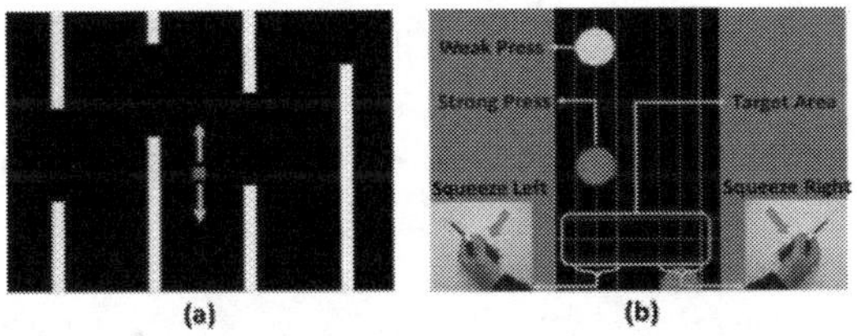

Fig. 7. Two game interfaces that are controlled by the fMRI-compatible pneumatic devices. (a) side scolling game and (b) a musical game

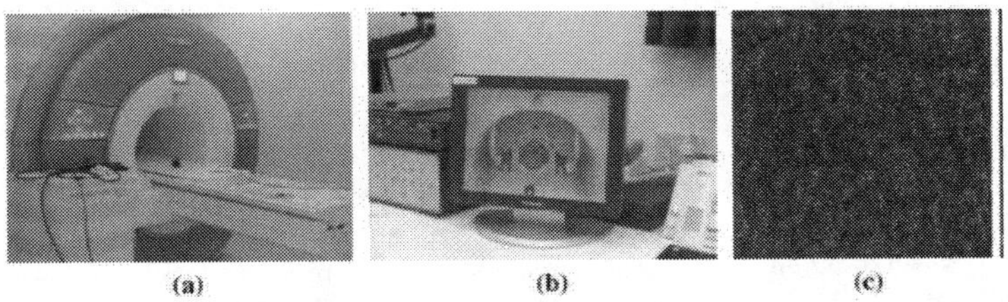

Fig. 8. Experimental setup for fMRI-compatibility test and result images. (a) The pneumatic device was put on the fMRI bed to be tested, (b) a view of the pneumatic device while the fMRI was running, (c) noise scan result for the normal condition without the one

Optical SAR Images Fusion: Comparative Analysis of Resulting Images Data

Yuhendra*, Minarni

Institut Teknologi Padang, Informatics Engineering Department, Padang, Indonesia,

Abstract. Image fusion is a useful tool for integrating low spatial resolution multispectral (MS) images with a high spatial resolution panchromatic (PAN) image, thus producing a high resolution multispectral image for better understanding of the observed earth surface. A main proposed the research were the effectiveness of different image fusion methods while filtering methods added to speckle suppression in synthetic aperture radar (SAR) images. The quality assessment of the filtering fused image implemented by statistical parameter namely mean, standard deviation, bias, universal index quality image (UIQI) and root mean squared error (RMSE). In order to test the robustness of the image quality, either speckle noise (Gamma map filter) is intentionally added to the fused image. When comparing and testing result, Gram Scmidth (GS) methods have shown better results for good colour reproduction, as compared with high pass filtering (HPF). And the other hands, GS, and wavelet intensity hue saturation (W-IHS) have shown the preserving good colour with original image for Landsat TM data.

1 Introduction

Currently, following with increasing the rapid advancements of new and greatly improved various space born imaging sensor systems in Remote Sensing (RS), it is can be done by both active (SAR, LiDAR) and passive (optical and thermal range, multispectral and hyper-spectral) devices and applied in many area studying Earth observational applications [1]. A lower spatial resolution multispectral (MS) image and high spatial resolution panchromatic (PAN) imaging sensors are the systems usually used for earth change observation phenomena, each one having its own specific advantage. Almost all of the operating earth observation very high resolution (VHR) imagery (Spot, Landsat, Ikonos, WorldView, QuicBird, GeoEye, and Orbview, etc), it was very important issues in various RS problems application in image sharpening, land classification, change detection, and object identification, visualization purposes etc. [2]. Otherwise, PAN imaging sensors provides an image in the visible band, which is characterized by high spatial information content well suited for intermediate scale mapping applications and urban analysis [2]. Considering image fusion observed scene analysis and RS application, the observed scene information fusion can be requirement in the following cases [3]; data recorded by different sensors (multi-sensor image fusion), data recorded by the same sensor scanning the same scene at different dates (multi-temporal image fusion), data recorded by the same sensor operating in different spectral bands (multi-frequency image fusion), data recorded by the same sensor at different polarizations (multi-polarization image fusion), and data recorded by the same sensor located on platforms flying at different heights (multi-resolution image fusion). A Multi-sensor, multi-temporal, multi-resolution and multi-parameter image data from operational Earth observation satellites are available and therefore possibly give a more complete view of observed objects [4]. Increasing the interest of area, some researcher has addressed multi-temporal data fusion problem. Some publication interest on the multi-sensor image fusion and application has reported [3-9]. The development of the multi-sensor information fusion is fundamental for change detection purpose but can be also valuable in image classification to improve the classification accuracy. The Principal study of fusing multiple images provided by heterogeneous image sensor has been addressed in many literatures with different methods, context and application [10].

In the synthetic aperture radar (SAR) images, speckle is coherent interference of waves scattered from terrain elements observed in each resolution cell with spatial resolution greater than the wavelength. It's can be reduced by incoherent processes. Due to the roughness of the imaged surface, each resolution cell will contain several scatterers, and the resulting image will have a granular appearance due to constructive and destructive interference. Speckle appears as spatially correlated, multiplicative noise that is statistically independent of the image intensity, although it is a radiometric feature of the imaged object.

Concerning used numerous methods and application for image fusion and filter fused in remotes sensing, it is

* Corresponding author: yuhendra@ieee.com

desirable to give a general assessment of the quality of the fused images filtering from the viewpoint of practical use. In this research, we use merging images fusion methods to assess the capability of fusion multi sensor using Wavelet-IHS (intensity-hue-saturation), HPF, and Grand Schmidt while image added to speckle noised, eg. Gamma Map filters (Figure 1) to observe of fused image for better spectral quality in object identification. Another commons investigation, we apply the following statistical parameter approaches for standardizing and automating the evaluation process of the fused images. First, we have examine the qualitative assessment is made with conventional visual inspection.

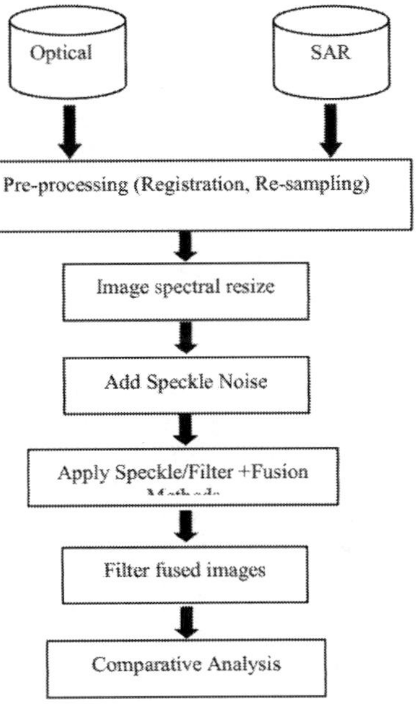

Fig. 1. Flowchart of filtering fused images

Table 1. Characteristics of Optical SAR Sensors

Sensor	Band Name	Wavelength (µm)	Resolution (m)
LANDSAT	B1	0.45-0.52	30 m
	B2	0.52-0.60	
	B3	0.63-0.69	
	B4	0.76-0.90	
	B5	1.55-1.75	
	B7	2.08- 2.35	
SAR	L	HH Polarization	12,5 m

2 Study Area and Satellite Imagey

2.1 Study Area

The study site for this work is located in the Sultan Hasanuddin International Airport in Makassar, South Sulawesi, Indonesia, see in Fig.2.

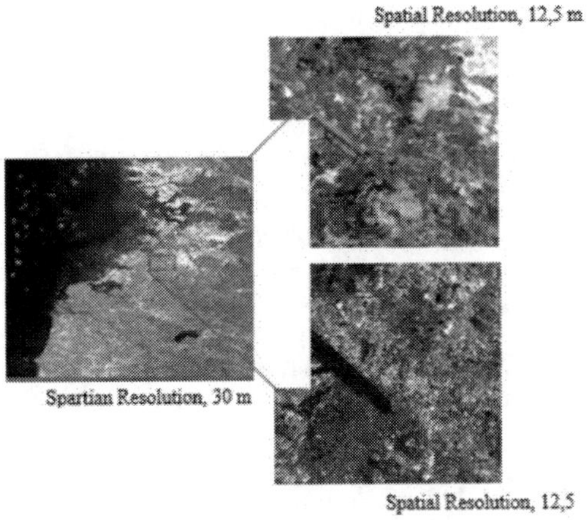

Fig. 2. Subset study area in South Sulawesi, Makasar

2.2 Satellite Imagery

For this work, two optical SAR images acquired by Lansat-5 TM and JERS-1 acquired on September 28, 2002 and August 18, 1998 with path row 116/64, 85/309 respectively, were used for investigating the performance of optical SAR image fusion analysis. A Lansat-5 images consists of one PAN and five MS with a spatial resolution of 30 m and SAR image has 2,5 spatial resolution with L Band, HH Polarization. The characteristics of both images are summarized in Table 1.

3 Methods

3.1 Pre-processing

3.1.1 Image correction and registration

The most important prerequisite for accurate data fusion is precise geometric correction. In image fusion needs commons control point on both the input images since different images of the same area used together. The common geometric correction is image to image registration. Registration can be done in various methods. A one of methods is image to image registration. An image to image registration is translation and rotation alignment process by which two images of like geometry on the same geographic area [12]. In registration processing, the most accurate way is to register the input images separately by establishing geometric relationship between the image and the ground using rigorous photogrammetric methods [13].

3.1.2. Re-sampling:

Next, we apply re-sampling, in which each data point (pixel) in the high-resolution base map is assigned with a value based on the MS image pixels. In order to achieve a good fusion result, low spatial spectral images should be re-sampled. At present, nearest neighbour re-sampling is often adopted which has some effects on the precision of new image. In this paper, an image fusion method is proposed with Cubic Convolution technique. In this way, Optical-SAR images with 30 m and 12,5 spatial resolutions are produced from original Landsat-TM and JERS-1 images, respectively (Figure 2).

3.1.3. Spatial resolution ratio:

The spatial resolution ratio improvement can make a sharpen image while preserving spectral information contained in the fused images. Since PAN images usually have a better spatial resolution than the multispectral images of the same sensor, while the MS images provide spectral properties of the objects. In image fusion, spatial resolution ratio plays an important role in image fusion.

3.1.4. Speckle (Image filtering):

Speckle is a scattering phenomenon and not a noise. The discrimination of different natural media by comparing intensity to a fixed threshold leads, in general to numerous errors due to the high variability of SAR speckled response. There are various speckle reduction filters available in image processing to process SAR images. Some give better visual interpretations while others have good noise reduction or smoothing capabilities. The use of each filter depends on the specification for a particular application. In image processing, the standard speckle filters like Median, Mean, Statistical Lee, Kuan, Frost, enhanced Frost and Gamma filters are generally used. Each of these speckle filters performs the filtering based on either local statistical data given in the filter window to determine the noise variance within the filter window. The analysis of image we used Gamma MAP filter. It was based on the assumption that the (un-speckled) intensity of the underlying scene is gamma distributed. The filter minimizes the loss of texture information better than the Frost and Lee filters within gamma distributed scenes. It is suitable for a wide range of gamma distributed scenes, such as forested areas, agriculture areas, and oceans.

3.2 Image Processing Using Fusion Algorithm

3.2.1 Gram-Schmidt (GS)

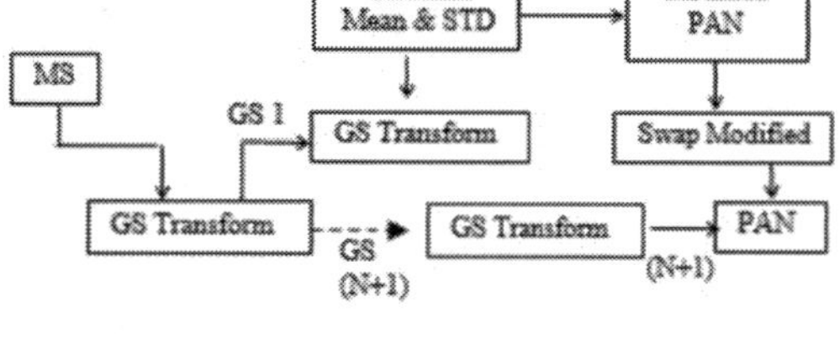

Fig. 3. GS Fusion Technique

3.2.1 High Pass Filter

The HPF technique is based on injecting spatial details taken from the PAN image onto the re-sampled MS images (Schowengerdt, 1998). The mathematical model can be given as

$$F_{i,j} = MS_{i,j} + [PAN_{i,j} - \overline{PAN_{i,j(w,h)}}] \quad (1)$$

where $F_{i,j}$ is the pixel of the fused image at coordinate (*i*, *j*), $MS_{i,j}$ and $PAN_{i,j}$ are corresponding pixel values in MS and PAN image, respectively; and $\overline{PAN_{i,j(w,h)}}$ stands for the local mean of high-resolution channel inside the window of *w* (width) × *h* (height) pixels centered at (*i*, *j*).

3.2.3. Wavelet-HIS

The Wavelet transform is a mathematical tool that is extensively used in image analysis and image fusion. The basic idea of image fusion, based on two-band wavelet transformation, is that a low-resolution image is replaced by the low frequency portion of the image in a two-band wavelet transformation. In W-PCA, the wavelet is transformed into principal components, and the first principal component is fused with the PI. Then, inverse wavelet transform is applied to the fused principal component and remaining principal components to obtain the fused image.

3.2.4. Statistical Parameter

Commonly used the statistical parameter, quality of fused image was assessed by means of some quality measures that can predict perceived image quality automatically. In this work, two types of quality assessment approaches are taken, namely qualitative (visual analysis and quantitative methods. The visual analysis is based on the visual comparison of the color between the original MIs and the fused image and that of the spatial details between the original PI and the fused image. These methods inevitably involve subjective factors and personal preference that can influence the result of evaluation. While visual inspection has limitation due to human judgment, quantitative approach based on the evaluation of "distortion" that is brought about by the noise added to the fused image is more desirable for mathematical modeling [18]. In this work, a validation method is proposed based on a quality criterion, namely, Mean, Standard Deviation, Bias, UIQI , Root mean squared error (RMSE) [6]] to estimation and chosen as a robustness criterion. This statistical parameter is often used for evaluation of fusion techniques. These parameters are defined as follows:

- Mean value refers to the gray level of pixels in an image. If the image size is *m*× *n*, the mean value is defined as

$$Mean = \frac{1}{mn}\sum_{i=j}^{m}\sum_{j=1}^{n} x_{ij}, \quad (2)$$

- *Standard deviation (STD)* reflects the deviation degree of values relative to the mean of the image. Normally, the STD is defined as

$$STD = \left[\frac{1}{n-1}\sum_{i=1}(MS_{i,j} - MS_{mean})^2\right]^{1/2} \quad (3)$$

Bias is the difference between the mean of the original image and that of the fused image. The ideal value is zero:

$$Bias = \frac{MS_{mean} - fused_{mean}}{MS_{mean}} = 1 - \frac{fused_{mean}}{MS_{mean}} \quad (4)$$

- *RMSE* is the root mean square error computed as

$$RMSE\ (B_i) = Bias^{2}(B_i) + STD^{2}(B_i) \quad (5)$$

- *Universal image quality index (UIQI)* is used to measure the similarity between two images.

$$UIQI = \frac{\sigma_{AB}}{\sigma_A \sigma_B} \cdot \frac{2\mu_A \mu_B}{\mu_A^2 + \mu_B^2} \cdot \frac{2\sigma_A \sigma_B}{\sigma_A^2 + \sigma_B^2} \quad (6)$$

4 Results and Discussion

Figure 4a-b show the original Landsat-TM PAN and JERS-1 image with Gamma MP filtering added. Both of images has a same spatial resolution 12,5 m has after resampling that can be employed into fused image filter, see Figure 5.

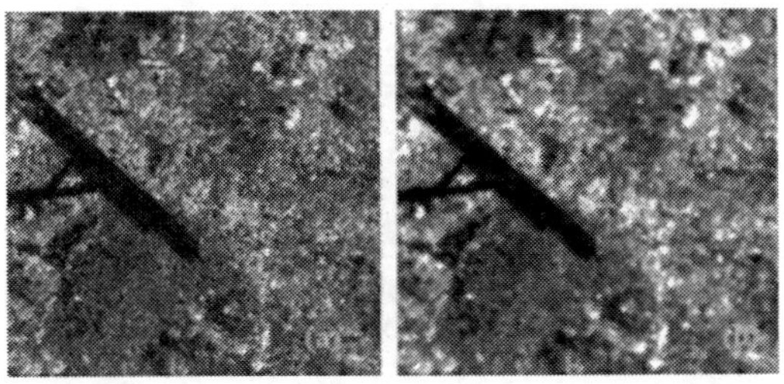

Fig. 4. Image filter before fused, (a) Original image, (b) Gamma MP

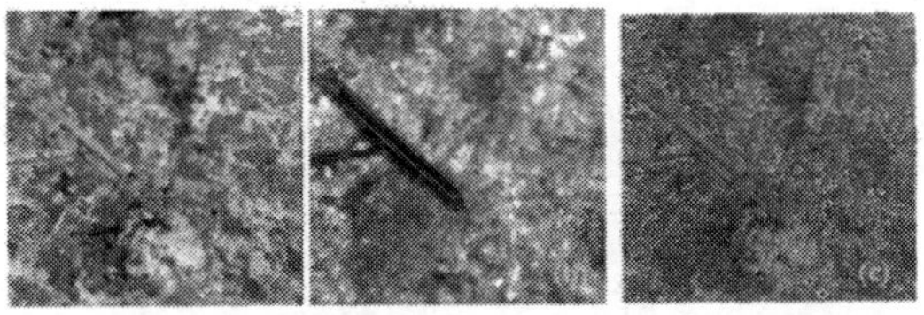

Fig. 5. Fused image filter, (a) Gamma MP-Wavelet IHS, (b) Gamma MP-Gram Schmidt, (c) Gamma MP-HPF

A thorough examination of spectral quality is made for filtering fused images using the following seven statistical parameters: mean, bias, STD, RMSE, Cov, and UIQI. The fused image that best preserves the original spectral information, and hence exhibits the highest spectral quality, can be characterized with the following conditions: (i) the mean and SDT values are closer to those of the original MS images, (ii) the smallest values for the error parameters (RMSE, Bias, UIQI). Tables III summarize the results of the present analysis. The highest value has been obtained in the GS-fused image since closer with original image and smaller bias. Thus, the GS method produces the result that has the least color distortion as a whole and the best preservation of spectral characteristics. In the universal index quality image (UIQI) is evaluated to study the similarity between the originally fused image and each of the filtering-added images. A UIQI index is considers the similarity of two images on the basis of three different factors, namely, loss of correlation, radiometric distortion, and contrast distortion. A Wavelet-HIS has a higher value.

Table 2. Inter Band Correlation of Filter Fused Images

Methods	Band 1 &2	Band 1 & 3	Band 2 & 3
Original MS	0.925	0.866	0.966
Wavelet-IHS	-0.079	0.529	-0.158
Gram Schmidt	0.920	0.858	0.965
HPF	0.352	0.743	0.373

As another test, we can examine the inter-band correlation that should be preserved in image fusion. Table 2 shows the comparison of the inter-band correlations (B1/B2, B1/B3, and B2/B3), among the original optical image and between the original and fused SAR images. The highest correlation around 0.920 and 0.965 were seen for the combination of Band 1/2 and Band 2/3, irrespective of the fusion method employed. The results in Table 3 show that both GS give values reasonably in agreement with those in the original MS images.

5 Conclusions

We have compared to combine Speckle Filter with Fusion methods to Integrating Optical & SAR image. Based on spectral quality assessment (Mean, STD & Cov) GS followed by PCA are for best, closet to original optical image value. The spectral analyses (Bias, DIV, RMSE) of the filter fused images indicate that the results generated with GS, Wavelet HIS, and HPF methods out performance preserve spectral and spatial information.

Acknowledgment

We would gratefully acknowledge like to thanks the anonymous reviewers for valuable comments and suggestions

References

1. Yuhendra, Joshapat T.S., Assessment of multi temporal image fusion for remote sensing application, International Journal on advance science engineering information technology, 7(3), 778-784, 2017
2. Zeng, Y., Zhang, J., Van Genderen, J.L., Zhang, Y., Image fusion for land cover change detection, Int. J. Image and Data Fusion, 1(2), 193-215. 2010
3. Chibani, Y., 2007, Integration of panchromatic and SAR features into multispectral SPOT images using the 'a trous' wavelet decomposition. Int. J. of Remote Sensing, 28, 2295–2307.
4. Zhu, L., Tateishi, R., 2006. Fusion of multi-sensor multi temporal satellite data for land cover mapping, Int. J. Remote Sensing, 27(5), 903-918.

5. Cao, G., Hou, P., Ya-Qiu, J., Xianqiang, M., 2009. Fusion of features in multi-temporal SAR imagery to detect changes I urban areas, Int. J. Remote Sensing, 30(20), 5989-6001
6. Ehler M, Klonus S, Astrand P.J, Rosso P. Multi-sensor for pansharpening in remote sensing, International Journal Image and Data Fusion.2010;1,1, 25-45
7. Molch, K., 2010. Multi-sensor and multi-temporal fusion of VHR satellite imagery based on KIM, IEEE Geoscience and Remote Sensing Letter, 7(1).
8. Kandrika, S., Ravinsankar, T., 2011. Multi-temporal satellite imagery and data fusion for improved land cover information ectraction, Int. J. Image and Data Fusion, 2,1, 61-73.
9. Wurm, M., Taubenbock, H., Schardt, M., 2011. Object-based image information fusion using multi sensor earth observation data over urban areas, Int. J. Image and Data Fusion, 2,2, 121-147.
10. Yuhendra, Alimuddin, I., Josaphat Tetuko, S.S., Kuze, H., 2012. Assessment of pan-sharpening methods applied to image fusion of remotely sensed multi-band data, Int. J. of Applied Earth Observation & Geoinformation, 18,165-175.
11. Otazu X, González M, Fors O, Núñez J. Introduction of Sensor Spectral Response Into Image Fusion Methods. Application to Wavelet-Based Methods, IEEE Transactions on Geoscience &Remote Sensing.2005;43(10), 2376-2385.
12. Chen, L., Lee, L., 1992. Progressive generation of control framework for image registration, Photogrammetric Engineering & Remote Sensing, 58(9):1321-1328.
13. Lee C, Bethel J, 2001. Georegistration of Airborne Hyperspectral Image Data. IEEE Trans. on Geoscience and Remote Sensing. 39(7): 1347-1351.
14. Choi M. A new intensity-hue-saturation fusion approach to image fusion with a tradeoff parameter, IEEE Trans. Geosciences Remote Sensing.2006;2 44, 1672-1682.
15. Karathanassi V, Kolokousi P, Ionnidou S. A comparison study on fusion methods using evaluation indicators, Int. J. Remote Sensing.2007; 28(10), 2309-2341.
16. Ling Y, Ehler M, Usery E.L, Madden M. FFT-enhanced IHS transform method for fusing high-resolution satellite images, ISPRS Journal of Photogrammetry & Remote Sensing. 2007; 61, 381–392
17. Kumar U, Mukhopadhyay C, Ramachandra T.V. Pixel based fusion using IKONOS imagery, Int. J. Recent Trend in Engineering. 2009; 1(1),173-175.
18. Bovolo F, Bruzzone L, Capobianco L, Garzelli A, Marchesi S. Analysis of effect of pan-sharpening in change detection, IEEE Geoscine. Remote Sensing Letter. 2010; 7(1)
19. Shah V. P, Younan N. H, and King R. L. An efficient pansharpening method via a combined adaptive PCA approach and contourlets. IEEE Trans. Geosciences Remote Sensing.2008; 4.
20. Kumar U, Mukhopadhyay C, Ramachandra T.V. Pixel based fusion using IKONOS imagery, International Journal Recent Trend in Engineering.2009;1(1),173-175.
21. Wang L, Cao X, Chen J. ISVR: an improve synthetic variable ratio method for image fusion, Geocarto International.2008; 23(2), 155-165.
22. Rahman M.M, Sri Sumantyo J.T, Sadek M.F. Microwave and optical image fusion for surface and sub-surface feature mapping in Eastern Sahara, International Journal Remote Sensing. 2010; 31(20), 5465-5480.

Table 3. Quality Index Fused images with Gamma map filtering

Methods	Index							
	Band	Mean	STD	Cov	Bias	DIV	RMS	UIQI
Original Image	R	68	9	14	-	-	-	-
	G	96	6	79	-	-	-	-
	B	83	8	46	-	-	-	-
Wavelet-IHS	R	68	10	53	0	-2.785	1	0.87
	G	89	24	-18	0.073	1.227	18.0	0.93
	B	82	9	91	0.012	-0.978	1	0.80
Gram Schmidt	R	68	11	27	0	-0.928	11	0.49
	G	96	16	78	0	0.012	16	0.44
	B	83	9	47	0	-0.021	9	0.46
HFP	R	68	9	61	0	-3.35	0	0.86
	G	86	33	101	0.104	-0.27	27	0.80
	B	83	8	75	0.180	-0.63	0.18	0.65

Comparison Analysis of Simple Additive Weighting (SAW) and Weigthed Product (WP) In Decision Support Systems

Dede Wira Trise Putra*, *Adrian* Agustian Punggara

Institut Teknologi Padang, Informatics Engineering Study Program, Padang, Indonesia

Abstract. Decision support system is a way to help decision maker to choose the best decision from several available alternatives. In the process of decision support system required criteria and weights to be used in the calculation process. Simple additive weighting (SAW) and Weigthed product (WP) are methods in decision support systems that have a search method taking into account the weights held by the criteria. comparison analysis is performed to look at between the WP and SAW methods, methods that have a higher level of accuracy and are in accordance with the conditions. The SAW method uses a weighted weaning system whereas the WP method uses multiplication in calculating the attribute rating. From the weight of each criteria there will be used in the calculation to produce several alternatives. The object of the case study in this study is the determination of people's business credit in the banking world using seven criteria. the criteria used are personal character, credit status, business condition, income, guarantee, guarantee condition and installment. Results of testing using SAW method and WP method, it can help compare the best alternative level results by using the same data and criteria, so both methods can be used as consideration in decision making. WP method gives clear cost and benefit value compared to SAW, but in SAW result gives more clear result because it is based on predetermined value and weight.

1 INTRODUCTION

1.1 Background Issues

Technological advances make the speed and accuracy in making decisions become a demand in the industrial world, one of which is the banking world. In the banking world the accuracy in decision-making by a decision maker will make a fast and effective data turnover such as on granting people's business loans to customers. In determining of eligibility is based on existing criteria. Effectiveness which is guided this time it is necessary to build a system that can help decision maker in making integration decision so that can help and simplify the bank in determining eligibility of accepted of People Business Credit so that execution can be faster [1].

Decision Support System (DSS) is one software product developed specifically to assist in decision making process. The purpose of this system is as "information source" or "second opinion" which can be used as consideration in decision making or certain policy. In the process of DSS of People's Business Credit will be done by comparing SAW method with WP method, both methods are chosen because both of these methods in the process to find the value finally must use a target value in the form of criteria and their weight, but in the process of using their own way. Compare of these two methods aims to determine the level of the best value using the same data and criteria [2, 3].

This SAW method requires the decision maker to determine the weight of each attribute. Total score for the attribute is obtained by summing all the resulted of the rated multiplication and the weight of each attribute. The rating of each attribute must be dimensionless in the sense that it has passed the process of normalizing the previous matrix. The advantages of SAW method of its ability to do the assessment more precisely because it is based on predetermined criteria and preference weights. While the WP method is a completion method by using multiplication to attribute attribute rating, where the rating must be raised first with the weight of the attribute in question. So that can know relevant method for giving credit by yielding Output order of priority the prospective customers who deserve to receive credit start from highest to lowest [4,6].

1.2 Research purposes

The purpose of this study is to compare the highest level results using the same data and criteria between SAW and WP.

2. Literature Review

2.1 Decision Support System

* Corresponding author: dedewtp339@yahoo.com

Decision Support System (DSS) is a computer-based information system that produces various decision alternatives to assist management in handling various structured or unstructured problems using data and models. The purpose of the DSS to support decision-making choose alternatived the results of information processing with decision-making models and to solve problems that are semi-structured and unstructured.

DSS is designed to assist decision-making in solving problems. DSS is designed in such a way that it can be used or operated easily by people who do not have basic high and alternative computer operating abilities, and DSS is designed with an emphasis on high adaptability aspects. [8].

2.2 Simple Additive Weighting (SAW)

The SAW method is often also known as the weighted summing method. The basic concept of the SAW method is to find the weighted sum of performance ratings on each alternative on all attributes. The SAW method requires the process of normalizing the decision matrix (X) to a scale comparable to all existing alternative ratings. [5]. The formula for normalization is as follows:

$$Rij = \begin{cases} \frac{X_{ij}}{Max\, X_{ij}} \\ \frac{Min\, X_{ij}}{X_{ij}} \end{cases} \quad (1)$$

Information:
Rij : Performance alized performance rating.
Maxij : The maximum value of each row and column.
Minij : The minimum value of each row and column.
Xij : Rows and columns of the matrix.
With Rij is the normalized performance rating of Ai alternatives

The preference value for each alternative (Vi) is given as:

$$Vi = \sum_{j=1}^{n} Wjr_{ij} \quad (2)$$

Information :
Vi : The final value of the alternative
Wj : The specified weight
Rij : Normalization of the matrix
A larger value of Vi indicates that Ai's alternatives are preferred.

The advantages of the simple additive weighting method compared with other decision-making models lie in its ability to perform judgments more precisely because it is based on pre-defined value and preference weight.

2.3 Weighted Product (WP)

The Weighted Product (WP) method uses multiplication to attribute attribute rating, where the rating of each attribute must be raised first with the corresponding attribute's weights. This process is similar to the normalization process. [9].

Preferences for alternative Ai are given as follows:

$$Si = \prod_{j=1}^{n} X_{ij}^{wj} \; ; i = 1, 2, \ldots, m \quad (3)$$

Information:
Si: Vector Value Si
Xij: Alternatived Value against criteria
Wj: The weighted rank is positive for the profit attribute and is negative for the cost attribute

For calculating the relative preference values of each alternative, the following equations are given:

$$Vi = \frac{\prod_{j=1}^{n} xij^{Wj}}{\prod_{j=1}^{n} (xj)^{Wj}} \; ; i = 1,2, \ldots m \quad (4)$$

Information:
Vi: The value of alternative preferences
Xij: Alternated attribute value
Wj: The value of the criterion weight

The advantages of this method can provide value and cost to the value of each Alternative.

Table 1. Personal Character Model

No.	Criteria	Value	Weight
1	Good	100	10%
2	Enough	80	
3	Less	50	

Table 2. Credit Status Model

No.	Criteria	Value	Weight
1	Good	100	10%
2	Middle	80	
3	Bad	20	

Table 3. Model of Business Conditions

No.	Criteria	Value	Weight
1	Good	100	25%
2	Enough	80	
3	Less	60	
4	Very less	40	

Table 4. Earnings Model

No.	Criteria	Value	Weight
1	> 5 million	100	20%
2	> 4 million – 5million	80	
3	> 3 million – 4 million	60	
4	> 2 million – 3 million	40	
5	0 - 2 million	20	

Table 5. Guarantee Model

No.	Criteria	Value	Weight
1	Car License	75	15%
2	Bike License	75	
3	Building Certificate	75	

Table 6. Condition of Warranty

No.	Criteria	Value	Weight
1	Good	100	15%
2	Enough	80	
3	Less	60	
4	Very less	40	

Table 7. Installment

No.	Criteria	Value	Weight
1	12 month	100	5%
2	24 month	80	
3	36 month	60	

3 Research

3.1 Simple Additive Weighting (SAW) Value Calculation

Step in calculation SAW :

(1) Assessment criteria:
C1: Private Character
C2: Credit Status
C3: Business Condition
C4: Earnings
C5: Warranty
C6: Warranty Condition
C7: Installment

(2) The weighting of each Criterion
C1: 10% C2: 10% C3: 25% C4: 20% C5: 15% C6: 15% C7: 5%

(3) Alternative Value Table

Table 8. Alternative Values

Alt	Criteria						
	C1	C2	C3	C4	C5	C6	C7
N1	80	100	80	100	75	100	80
N2	50	100	100	80	75	100	80
N3	100	80	80	60	75	60	60
N4	100	80	80	80	75	80	80

(4) Perform normalization on the table by the formula **(1)**

$$R11 = \frac{80}{\max(80:50:100:100)} = \frac{80}{100} = 0.8$$

$$R21 = \frac{50}{\max(80:50:100:100)} = \frac{50}{100} = 0.5$$

$$R12 = \frac{100}{\max(100:100:80:80)} = \frac{100}{100} = 1$$

Etc.

Normalized table results :

Table 9. Normalization Table

0.8	1	0.8	1	1	1	1
0.5	1	1	0.8	1	1	1
1	0.8	0.8	0.8	1	0.6	0.75
1	0.8	0.8	0.8	1	0.8	1

(5) The final result is obtained from ranking the sum of the matrix multiplication R by the weights using the formula **(2)**

$$V1 = (0.8)(0.1) + (1)(0.1) + (0.8)(0.25) + (1)(0.2) + (1)(0.15) + (1)(0.15) + (1)(0.05) = 0.93$$

$$V2 = (0.5)(0.1) + (1)(0.1) + (1)(0.25) + (0.8)(0.2) + (1)(0.15) + (1)(0.15) + (1)(0.05) = 0.91$$

$$V3 = (1)(0.1) + (0.8)(0.1) + (0.8)(0.25) + (0.8)(0.2) + (1)(0.15) + (0.6)(0.15) + (0.75)(0.05) = 0.82$$

$$V4 = (1)(0.1) + (0.8)(0.1) + (0.8)(0.25) + (0.8)(0.2) + (1)(0.15) + (0.8)(0.15) + (1)(0.05) = 0.86$$

From the calculation using the SAW method obtained the highest end result is V1 = 0.93 (N1) with the best alternative value.

3.2 Weighted Product (WP) Value Calculation

Step in calculation WP :

(1) Assessment criteria:

C1: Private Character
C2: Credit Status
C3: Business Condition
C4: Earnings
C5: Warranty
C6: Warranty Condition
C7: Installment

(2) Giving weighted of each Criteria

Table 10. Criteria Table

Value	Weight	Information	Criteria Weight
5	25%	Very Good	Highest
4	20%	Good	
3	15%	Enough	
2	10%	Less	
1	5%	Very Less	Lowest

then the weighting is W = {2,2,5,4,3,3,1} with

$$W1 = \frac{2}{2+2+5+4+3+3+1} = \frac{2}{20} = 0.1$$

$$W2 = \frac{2}{2+2+5+4+3+3+1} = \frac{2}{20} = 0.1$$

$$W3 = \frac{5}{2+2+5+4+3+3+1} = \frac{5}{20} = 0.25$$

$$W4 = \frac{4}{2+2+5+4+3+3+1} = \frac{4}{20} = 0.2$$

$$W5 = \frac{3}{2+2+5+4+3+3+1} = \frac{3}{20} = 0.15$$

$$W6 = \frac{3}{2+2+5+4+3+3+1} = \frac{3}{20} = 0.15$$

$$W7 = \frac{1}{2+2+5+4+3+3+1} = \frac{1}{20} = 0.05$$

(3) Alternative Value Table

Table 11. Alternative Values

Alt	Criteria						
	C1	**C2**	**C3**	**C4**	**C5**	**C6**	**C7**
N1	80	100	80	100	75	100	80
N2	50	100	100	80	75	100	80
N3	100	80	80	60	75	60	60
N4	100	80	80	80	75	80	80

(4) Preferences for alternative Ai are calculated by the formula **(3)** as follows:

$$S1 = (80^{0.1})(100^{0.1})(80^{0.25})(100^{0.2})(75^{0.15})(100^{0.15})(80^{0.5}) = 87.6$$

$$S2 = (50^{0.1})(100^{0.1})(100^{0.25})(80^{0.2})(75^{0.15})(100^{0.15})(80^{0.5}) = 84.5$$

$$S3 = (100^{0.1})(80^{0.1})(80^{0.25})(60^{0.2})(75^{0.15})(60^{0.15})(60^{0.5}) = 72.2$$

$$S4 = (100^{0.1})(80^{0.1})(80^{0.25})(80^{0.2})(75^{0.15})(80^{0.15})(80^{0.5}) = 81$$

(5) To obtain the final result using the formula preferences **(4)** :

$$V1 = \frac{87.6}{87.6 + 84.5 + 72.2 + 81} = \frac{87.6}{325.3} = 0.269$$

$$V2 = \frac{84.5}{87.6 + 84.5 + 72.2 + 81} = \frac{84.5}{325.3} = 0.259$$

$$V3 = \frac{72.2}{87.6 + 84.5 + 72.2 + 81} = \frac{72.2}{325.3} = 0.221$$

$$V4 = \frac{81}{87.6 + 84.5 + 72.2 + 81} = \frac{81}{325.3} = 0.249$$

From the calculation using Weighted Product method obtained the highest final result is V1 = 0.269 (N1) with the best alternative value.

4 Testing and Results

Tests using SAW and WP methods were conducted using 10 customer data applying for credit. The customer data used is taken randomly based on data owned by the bank. After the data to be used has been assigned a value on each criteria, then the next step is done as in the explanation in section 3 above.

Based on these tests then obtained the results as the following table 12.

Table 12. Comparison of SAW and WP results

No	Prospective Customer	SAW Score	WP Score
1	Cstr 1	0.785	0.0355
2	Cstr 2	0.7825	0.0347
3	Cstr 3	0.75	0.0343
4	Cstr 4	0.735	0.0346
5	Cstr 5	0.725	0.0343
6	Cstr 6	0.725	0.0343
7	Cstr 7	0.7225	0.0335
8	Cstr 8	0.7125	0.0333
9	Cstr 9	0.7125	0.0333
10	Cstr 10	0.7125	0.0333

The scores that are matches in the table above have been sorted from the highest to lowest values. From these results the highest value becomes the highest alternative for decision makers to be worthy or not prospective customers approved credit loan proposal.

In the table cstr 3 and cstr 4 have different scores. In cstr 3 score on SAW is higher when compared with score on WP. While in cstr 4 WP score higher when compared with SAW score.

This is due to the difference of the cost and benefit value of each method. In SAW the value of cost and benefit in the form of the value of Max for benefit, Min for cost on the whole data. While the weighting criteria given based on the value and weight preference that has been determined. In weighted product the cost and benefit value is given in the form of plus for benefit and minus for cost, on weighted product weight for given criterion based on weighted value rankings the highest.

At these results, when decision maker is done make a decision then the results taken as the final decision is the score of SAW method based on the criteria used in data processing. So for the end result simple additive weighting gives more clear results than the weighted product because it is based on the value and weight preference that has been determined.

5 Conclusions and Recommendations

Results of the research can be concluded as follows :

(1) Simple Additive Weighting and Weighted Product method that has been done the calculation shows

differences in ranking results on the alternative obtained based on the same criteria and data that aims to find the best alternative.

(2) Results of rankings produced by both methods are not always the same because of the differences in the cost and benefit value of each method, whereby the WP provides more clear cost and benefit value than SAW, but on the results SAW gives more result more clearly than WP because it is based on predetermined value and weight.

(3) Simple Additive Weighting method is more suitable for use in credit cases where the results given are more obvious because they are based on predetermined assessments and weights.

(4) SAW and WP methods can be compared with other DSS methods and can use more data samples.

References

1. D.W.T. Putra, M. Epiyanto. Sistem Pendukung Keputusan Pemilihan Sepeda Motor Jenis Sport 150cc Berbasis Web Menggunakan Metode Analytical Hierarcy Process (AHP). Journal Teknoif, 5 (2), 16-24. (2017)
2. F. Azwary, Sistem Pendukung Keputusan Pemberian Kredit Usaha Rakyat Pada Bank Syariah Mandiri Cabang Medan Menggunakan Metode AHP. Medan: Universitas Sumatera Utara. (2010)
3. F.L. Fadly, Sistem Pendukung Keputusan Pemberian Kredit Motor Menggunakan Metode Simple Additive Berbasis Web (Studi Kasus: PT. FIF Group Simpang Empat Pasaman Barat). Padang: Institut Teknologi Padang. (2015)
4. Fitira. Analytic Hierarchy Process Metode Pendukung Keputusan Pemberian Kredit Pada Koperasi Mandiri Utama. Bandar Lampung: Institut Informatika dan Bisnis Darmajaya. (2013)
5. Haswan, Febri. Decision Support System For Election Of Members Unit Patients Pamong Praja. (2017)
6. Kusrini. *Konsep dan Aplikasi Sistem Pendukung Keputusan*. Yogyakarta: Andi Offset. (2007).
7. E. Turban et al. *Decision Systems and Intelegent Systems (Sistem Pendukung Keputusan dan Sistem Cerdas) Edisi 7 Jilid 1*. Yogyakarta: Penerbit Andi. (2005)
8. S.K. Dewi, *Fuzzy Multi Attribute Decision Making (Fuzzy MADM)*. Yogyakarta: Graha Ilmu. (2006).
9. N. Aini et al. Penerapan Metode Weighted Product dan Analytic Hierarchy Process Untuk Pemilihan Koperasi Berprestasi. Samarinda: Universitas Mulawarman. (2017)

MATEC Web of Conferences **215**, 01004 (2018) https://doi.org/10.1051/matecconf/201821501004
ICTIS 2018

Comparison of Case-Based Reasoning and Dempster Shafer on Expert System of Cassava Disease Identification

Minarni[*], *Indra* Warman, *Yuhendra* and *Wenda* Handayani

Institut Teknologi Padang, Informatics Engineering Study Program, Padang, Indonesia

Abstract. This study aims to develop a web-based expert system that can identify cassava disease using Case-Based Reasoning Method and Shafer Dempster Method, and to know the performance comparison of both based on the accuracy of identification. Case-Based Reasoning (CBR) is a computer-generated system that uses old knowledge to solve new problems. CBR provides solutions to new cases by looking at the oldest cases that are closest to new cases. The identification process is done by entering new cases containing the symptoms to be identified into the system, then perform the process of calculating the value of similarity between the new case and the base case using the nearest neighbor method. Dempster Shafer based on two ideas is the idea of obtaining degrees of confidence of subjective possibilities and the rule of dempster safer itself to combine degrees of confidence based on the evidence obtained. This expert system is built using PHP programming language and MySQL data base. The output of the system is the percentage of identification result of both methods. Testing and analysis results show that Case-Based Reasoning provides better identification accuracy than Dempster Shafer.

1 Introduction

Cassava (Manihot Esculenta Crantz) is one of the plants that can be consumed tubers and leaves. Cassava can be used as basic material of food and processed raw materials of home industry. One of the utilizations of cassava as the main ingredient of typical food of West Sumatra. Therefore, there is an effort to make cassava productivity not decrease. Based on data from Food Security Agency (Badan Ketahanan Pangan) of West Sumatra, cassava has decreased production by 19.22%. One of the causes of declining Indonesian cassava production is pests and diseases such as leaf mites, fungi and bacteria. Pest and disease attacks are caused by the wrong cropping pattern and the lack of knowledge of the farmers will attack pests and diseases. The lack of knowledge of the farmers, especially in terms of identifying pests and diseases in cassava.

To identify pests and diseases of cassava plants can be known from the symptoms that appear. The characteristics of plants affected by disease with other diseases are so similar that it confuses people to identify them. Conversely there are also plants affected by diseases with different characteristics but still confusing in remembering the name and handling of the disease. Handling of pests and diseases is done by experts in this field commonly known as Agricultural Extension Field (PPL). Data from the Government Agency's Performance Accountability Report (LAKIP) of the Food Crops Office of West Sumatera Province in 2015 that the number of Agricultural Field Agricultural Extension (PPL) for food crops and horticulture is only 234 people, while the number of farmers is 644,610 people [1]. From the data, it appears that the number of extension workers with farmers is not comparable. In addition, trainers are constrained by time and place, so a system is needed that can help farmers to identify. pests and diseases of cassava plants.

The expert system has the ability to facilitate practical problems when the expert is absent. And one of the implementation of expert systems in agriculture is to identify plant diseases. Research on expert system of plant disease diagnosis has been done by many previous researchers, including: Abu-Naser (2008) developed an expert system using two methods of diagnosis of plant diseases, namely descriptive method and graphics. Descriptive method is based on the symptoms experienced by the plant. While on the graphical method based on the picture. The result obtained is that users tend to choose graphical methods than descriptive methods [2]. Anton (2009) develops an expert system application with forward and backward chaining methods that can be used to diagnose diseases of rice plants with ease of access for users [3]. Shafinah (2013) conducted a research on methodological trends used in the development of expert systems to manage plant pests and diseases. The results obtained are rule based expert systems more desirable compared to case-based systems (Case-based Reasoning) [4].

The Certainty Factor (CF) method is also used as an inference engine in an expert disease detection system. With this CF method then the detection of symptoms of plant disease will get certainty that the plant is experiencing the actual disease. In this study using

[*] Corresponding author: minarni1706@gmail.com

backward chaining [5]. The case-based reasoning (CBR) method can be used for reasoning in the rice disease identification expert system resulting in 100% sensitivity and an accuracy rate of 82.69% [6]. CBR method is also used in the identification of corn plants with an accuracy rate of 74.63% [7]. Research on expert system to detect plant pests and diseases Dendrobium orchid using Case Based Reasoning (CBR) method with algorithm Similaritas Probabilistic Symmetric. A weighted value of less than 60 percent of the system will not provide suggestions, but the system will store symptom data in the database for a given solution by an expert [8].

The Dempster-Shafer method is also used for the identification of plant pests and diseases that result in a suitability rate of 86.67% [9]. This method can also be combined with the fuzzy method [10].

This study aims to develop a web-based expert system that can identify cassava disease using the method of Case-Based Reasoning and Dempster Shafer Method, and know the comparison of the performance of both methods from the side of identification accuracy. Some theories used in this study are as follows:

1.1 Expert System

Expert systems are computer-based applications that are used to solve problems as the expert thinks. Experts are people who have special skills that can solve problems that can not be solved by the common people [11]. In the structure of the expert system there are two parts, namely the development environment (development environment) and the consultation environment (consultation environment). Development environments are used by expert system makers to build their components and introduce knowledge into the knowledge base. The consulting environment is used by the user to consult with an expert [12].

1.2 Case-Based Reasoning

Case-Based Reasoning (CBR) is a process of remembering a case in the past, then reusing it and adapting it in a new case [13] The CBR cycle is shown in Figure 1.

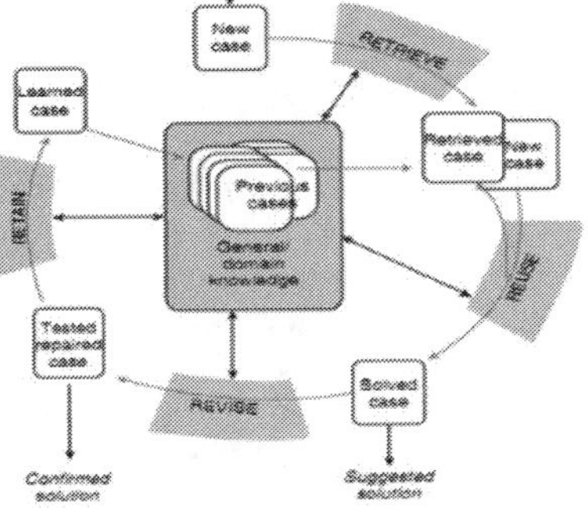

Fig.1. CBR Cycle [13]

The stages of CBR are as follows:

1. Retrieve
   Recover / recover the most similar / similar cases with the new case. This section refers to terms of identification, initial similarity, search and recovery and execution.
2. Reuse
   Reuse (use) information and knowledge of the case to solve the problem. The process of reuse of case solutions obtained in the new context is focused on two aspects: the difference between the previous and the current case, what part of the case has been obtained that can be transferred into a new case.
3. Revise
   Revise (review / refine) proposed solutions.
4. Retain
   Retain parts of the experience that may be useful for solving future problems

1.3 Nearest Neighbor Similarity

The Nearest Neighbor algorithm is one technique for finding the closest distance of each case (cases) in the database, and how similar the size (similarity) of each source case in the database with the target case. The similarity function in the case is formulated as follows [14]:

$$\mathrm{Sim}(T,Si) = \frac{\sum_{i=1}^{n} f(T,Si)*wi}{\sum_{i=1}^{n} wi} \quad (1)$$

Similarities usually is at a value of 0 to 1. A value of 0 means that the two cases are not similar absolute, contrary to the value of 1 case is similar to the absolute. Similarities usually is at a value of 0 to 1. A value of 0 means that the two cases are not similar absolute, contrary to the value of 1 case is similar to the absolute.

1.4 Dempster Shafer Inference

In general the theory of dempster shafer is written in an interval [15]:

a. Belief

$$[Belief, Plausibility] \quad (2)$$

Belief (Bel) is a measure of the strength of evidence (symptom) in support of a subset. Has a range between 0 (hence indicating that there is no evidence) until 1 indicates a certainty.

b. *Plausibility*
   (*Pl*) dinotasikan sebagai:

$$Pl(s) = 1 - Bel(\neg s) \quad (3)$$

Plausibility is also worth 0 to 1. If we are sure of $\neg$s, then it can be said that Bel ($\neg$s) = 1, and Pl ($\neg$s) = 0. Plausibility will reduce the level of confidence in the evidence. In the Dempster-Shafer theory we recognize

https://doi.org/10.1051/matecconf/201821501004

the frame of discernment denoted by θ (theta) and the mass function denoted by m. This frame is the universe of speech from a set of hypotheses so called environment. While the mass function (m) in Dempster Shafer's theory is the belief level of an evidence measure so it is denoted by (m). To overcome a number of evidences on Shafer's Dempster theory using a rule better known as Dempster's Rule of Combination

$$m3(Z) = \frac{\sum_{X \cap Y = Z} m_1(X).m_2(Y)}{1 - \sum_{X \cap Y = \emptyset} m_1(X).m_2(Y)} \tag{4}$$

1.5 Cassava Diseases

The classification of cassava disease in this study consists of 4 diseases and 2 pests where several diseases have the same symptoms [16].

2 Method

2.1 Context Diagram

The system is designed to identify pests and diseases of cassava plants based on data entered by the user. System users are divided into two groups: admin as user manager and expert (expert) as shown in figure 2, while user is a regular user (farmer). The user enters the symptom data encountered by the user. The system will process using case-based reasoning method and Dempster Shafer. The results of identification are then submitted to the user.

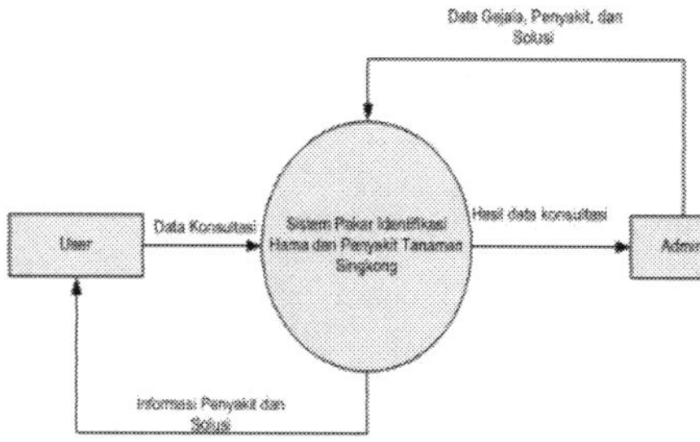

Fig.2. Context Diagram

Table 1. Case Representation

Hama dan penyakit	Gejala															
	G1	G2	G3	G4	G5	G6	G7	G8	G9	G10	G11	G12	G13	G14	G15	G16
H1	V	V														
H2			V	V												
P1					V	V									V	
P2							V	V	V							
P3										V	V	V				
P4													V	V		V

Table 2. Weight of Symptons

Kode Gejala	Nama Gejala	Bobot CBR	Bobot DS
G01	Akar Batang Rusak	5	0.9
G02	Umbi Rusak	5	0.9
G03	Daun menjadi kering	3	0.9
G04	Permukaan bawah daun menghisap cairan	3	0.9
G05	Daun Bercak Kebasahan	3	0.9
G06	Bentuk Daun Tidak Teratur	1	0.9
G07	Daun layu	5	0.9
G08	Akar Batang Membusuk	5	0.9
G09	Umbi Membusuk	5	0.9
G10	Bercak Coklat	5	0.9
G11	Lubang Bulat Kecil	1	0.9
G12	Jaringan daun mati	3	0.9
G13	Daun Kuning	3	0.9
G14	Daun Gugur	3	0.9
G15	Daun dikelilingi daerah hijau tua	1	0.9
G16	Pangkal batang terdapat benang putih	3	0.9
G17	Mati ujung	3	0.9

2.2 Case-Based Reasoning Inference

2.2.1 Retrieval Process

The retrieval process used in this study is to compare the symptoms of new cases with symptoms of cases that already exist in the base case, then the results of the comparison will be calculated the level of similarity. In this study, the calculation of similarity score using nearest neighbor. The symptom comparison uses the weight value set by the expert as shown in Table 2.

Sample Case:
The calculation of similarity value of new case (T) with old case (S) is presented in Table 3.

Table 3. Similarity Function New Case (K1) and Old Case (S1)

Kasus	Kasus Baru (T) (wi)	Kasus Lama (S1)	f(T, Si)
K1	Akar Batang Rusak (5)	Akar batang rusak (5)	1
	Daun bercak kebasahan (3)		0
	Bentuk daun tidak teratur (1)		0
	Umbi rusak (5)	Umbi rusak (5)	1

Calculation of similarity use equation (1)

$$Sim(T,Si) = \frac{(1x5) + (0x3) + (0x1) + (1x5)}{5+3+1+5} = \frac{10}{14} = 0{,}71$$

From the above similarity calculation results obtained value of 0.71 or 71%.

2.2.2 Reuse Process

In the reuse process the given identification solution is the solution that has the highest similarity value. For the above case, the highest similarity result is in S1 that is uret pest with similarity value equal to 0,71 or 71%, so the recommended solution is solution for pest uret.

2.2.3 Revise Process

Revisions are part of the system adaptation to cases that have not been identified. Revised case is done by the expert. Experts will revise case / weight based on the symptoms that exist in the base case of the system.

2.2.4 Retain Process

The retain process is the stage that plays a role to manage knowledge management on the system. This stage This stage stores the case into a knowledge base that will be used to solve new cases.

2.3 Dempster Shafer Inference

Calculations with the same case as above use the Dempster-Shafer method.
Then each of these symptoms will be tested based on the disease. For the above case tested with rule for Uret pest.

G1 (bel)=0.9; G1(θ)= 1-0.9 =0.1

G2 (bel)=0.9; G2(θ)= 1-0.9 =0.1
G3 (bel)=0.9; G3(θ)= 1-0.9 =0.1

G4 (bel)=0.9; G4(θ)= 1-0.9 =0.1

$$m3(Z) = \frac{0.9x0.9x0.9x0.9}{1-(0.1x0.1x0.1x0.1)} = \frac{0.651}{0.9999} = 0.65$$

3 Result and Discussion

Testing is done by the user directly with the system that has been designed. The test is carried out in two stages, the first stage of testing in accordance with the rule, while the second stage of testing performed using 34 test data. Table 4 shows the result on the first stage that the system using Case-Based Reasoning method was able to identify 100% true cassava plant disease. Whereas with Dempster Shafer method the system only able to identify equal to 75.66%. Recapitulation of the second stage test results is shown in Table 5.

Table 4. Test Result According to Rule

Case	The Type of Disease	Value	
		CBR	DS
1	Uret	100%	81%
2	Tungau Merah	100%	81%
3	Hawar Daun Bakteri	100%	73%
4	Layu Bakteri	100%	73%
5	Jamur Akar Putih	100%	73%
6	Bercak Daun Coklat	100%	73%
Average		**100%**	**75.66%**

Table 5. Recapitulation of Test Data Result

No.	The Type of Disease	Test Data	Identification of Correct	
			CBR	**DS**
1	Uret	13	9	4
2	Hawar Daun Bakteri	6	5	0
3	Tungau Merah	4	2	2
4	Layu Bakteri	6	2	4
5	Bercak Daun Coklat	2	2	1
6	Jamur Akar Putih	3	3	0
Total		**34**	**23**	**11**

Test results need to be evaluated to determine whether the system built feasible to be applied in identifying the disease of rice plants. Evaluation is done by calculating the sensitivity and accuracy using equations (5) and (6) [17].

$$Sensitivitas = \frac{T_P}{T_P+T_N} \quad (5)$$

$$Akurasi = \frac{T_P+T_N}{T_P+F_P+T_N+F_N} \quad (6)$$

The steps taken in testing the system by creating a confusion matrix based on each value of the test results system. Table 6 shows the confusion matrix from the results of the test Table 5.

Table 6. Confusion Matrix

Metho	Test Data	TP	TN	FP	FN
Case-Based Reasoning	34	23	0	11	0
Dempster Shafer	34	11	0	23	0

The calculation result of sensitivity value for Case-Based Reasoning and Dempster Shafer is 100% with the system accuracy value for Case-Based Reasoning 67.65% and 32.35% for Dempster Shafer. This shows that the expert system of cassava plant disease identification using Case-Based Reasoning inference can identify cassava plant disease well compared with Dempster Shafer.

4 Conclusion and Suggestion

This research produces expert system of cassava plant disease identification with Case-Based reasoning and Dempster-Shafer inference method. The calculation result of sensitivity value for Case-Based Reasoning and Dempster Shafer is 100% with the system accuracy value for Case-Based Reasoning value of 67.65% and 32.35% for Dempster Shafer. This shows that the expert system of cassava disease identification using Case-Based Reasoning inference can identify cassava plant disease well compared to Dempster Shafer. To get more accurate identification result, it is suggested that the weighting is done by some experts and taken on average to get better weighting.

Acknowledgement

The research was funded by the Directorate of Research and Community Service of the Ministry of Research, Technology and Higher Education (Kemristekdikti) for the funding of the National Strategic Research Institute (PSNI) research grant for 2018 under contract number: 324/27.O10.5/PN/ II / 2018

References

1. Tim Penyusun., Laporan akuntabilitas Kinerja Instansi Pemerintahan (LAKIP) 2015, (Dinas Pertanian Tanaman Pangan Sumatera Barat, Padang, 2015)
2. S.S. Abu-Naser, K.A. Kashkash and M. Fayyad., Journal of Artificial Intelligence, **1**, 2 (2008)
3. A. Setiawan, Jurnal Telkomnika, **7**, 3 (2009)
4. Shafinah, K., Sahari, N., Sulaiman, R., Yusoff, M. S. M., & Ikram, M. M., *Journal of Theoretical & Applied Information Technology*, **58**, 1 (2013)
5. M. Minarni, Anisah Fadhillah, Journal of Dynamics, **2**, 1 (2017)
6. M. Minarni, I. Warman, *Seminar Nasional Aplikasi Teknologi Informasi (SNATI)* (2017)
7. M. Minarni, I. Warman, Y. Yusuf, Jurnal Teknoif, **6**, 1 (2018)
8. P.A. Aconcagua, S. Wibisono, SINTAK, **1** (2017)
9. Y. Nurcahyo, N. Hidayat, R.S. Perdana, Jurnal Pengembangan Teknologi Informasi dan Ilmu Komputer, **2**, 3 (2018)
10. M. Muliadi, I. Budiman, M.A. Pratama, A. Sofyan, KLIK-Kumpulan Jurnal Ilmu Komputer, **4**, 2, (2017)
11. Kusrini, *Aplikasi Sistem Pakar*, (Andi Offset, Yogyakarta, 2008)
12. Sutojo, T, Edy Mulyanto, Vincent Suhartono. *Kecerdasan Buatan*, (Andi Offset, Yogyakarta, 2011)
13. Pal, S.K and Shiu, Simon C.K., *Foundation of Soft Case-Based Reasoning*, (John Wiley &Sons Inc Publication, USA, 2004)
14. Kusrini, Luthfi, E.T., *Algoritma Data Mining*, (Andi Offset, Yogyakarta, 2009)
15. Kusumadewi, S., *Artificial Intelligence (Teknik dan Aplikasinya)*, (Graha Ilmu, Yogyakarta, 2003)
16. Semangun, H., *Penyakit-penyakit Tanaman Pangan di Indonesia* (Gadjah Mada University Press, Yogyakarta, 2008)
17. Witten, I.H., Frank,E., Data Mining: Practical Machine Learning Tools and Techniques, 2 (Morgan Kaufmann, San Francisco, 2005)

QoS Analysis on OSPFv3 And RIPng Using GRE Tunneling on IPv6 Integrated Ipv4 Network

Indra Warman, *Alex* Franozal

Institut Teknologi Padang, Informatics Engineering Study Program, Padang, Indonesia

Abstract. Every year, the availability of public IPv4 addresses is running low. However, the IETF (Internet Engineering Task Force) has set a new addressing standard called IPv6 (Internet Protocol version 6). IPv6 implementations can not be immediately performed on all end-to-end lines, a transition phase is required, one of which is the GRE tunneling method. IPv6 has some differences with IPv4, then in line with the presence of IPv6 will required the protocol that compatible with IPv6, among which is the routing protocol. Some dynamic routing protocols are created to support and can run on IPv6 such as RIPng and OSPFv3. Aim of this study is examines OSPFv3 routing protocols and RIPng routing protocols in terms of Quality of Service (QoS). The test is done by using seven routers with three scenarios in each routing protocol, ie scenario with best path active condition, when the network changes in other words best path down, and the scenario with best path condition has changed and the network has returned to normal. Testing is done by testing QoS parameters (delay, packet loss, and throughput) when the client computer downloads files with the .iso extension from the server. Downloaded files have different sizes, from 100 Mega Byte to 1 Giga Byte. From the results obtained that OSPFv3 provides better QoS (delay, packet loss, and throughput) than RIPng on integrated IPv6 network using GRE tunnel and can be a reference when going to transition from IPv4 to IPv6 using GRE Tunnel.

1 Introduction

Based on data from LACNICLabs Opendata (opendata.labs.lacnic.net), from year to year the availability of public IPv4 addresses is descreasing, recorded on May 23, 2014 available 19,435,520 IPv4 for regional APNIC, but on May 24, 2017 the remaining 6,442,496 IPv4. However, the IETF (Internet Engineering Task Force) has set a new addressing standard called IPv6 (Internet Protocol version 6). There are some differences between IPv6 and IPv4 where IPv6 also required supporting protocols, one of them is routing protocol. Some dynamic routing protocols are created to support and can run on IPv6 such as RIPng and OSPFv3.

However, the outline of IPv6 implementation can not be immediately done in all end-to-end lines. The transition mechanism has been included in the IPv6 design, one of which is the tunneling method. Among the IPv6 over IPv4 tunneling methods that can be used are GRE (Generic Routing Encapsulation) tunneling. One of objectives of technology utilization is to produce services of good quality, as well as transition from IPv4 to IPv6. Proper application of routing protocols can help improve performance and provide good network service quality.

Researches related to this topic have been widely practiced. Performance testing of RIPng, OSPFv3 and EIGRP routing protocols in the IPv6 network using GNS3 based on throughput, jitter and packet loss parameters which then obtained various results in experiments for each routing protocol and combination of routing protocols. RIPng is better than OSPFv3 and EIGRP in terms of TCP throughput [1]. For UDP packets, the best jitter values are achieved by OSPFv3 and EIGRP, while RIPng-OSPFv3 obtains the highest jitter. RIPng is better in terms of packet loss, while OSPFv3 obtains the highest average packet loss.

Discuss various aspects of IPv4 and IPv6, IPv4 transition technology to IPv6, GRE (Generic Routing Encapsulation) and demonstrate how to configure IPv6 tunneling over IPv4 on routers using GNS3 and Wireshark. GRE tunnel runs well on the simulation and can complete IPv6 packet over IPv4 cloud [2]. Migration techniques from IPv4 network to IPv6 network using dual stack method and tunneling migration technique were simulated using GNS3.

Evaluate the performance of different routing protocols such as RIP and OSPF for IPv6 using the OPNET 14.5 simulator and obtain the result that Packet Delay variations in Video Conferencing, based on jitter parameters, end to end delay, received traffic, and traffic transmitted in voice and object response times and page response time in HTTP performs better in OSPFv3_RIPng (combination of RIPng and OSPFv3) than RIPng or OSPFv3. For real time applications, based on end to end delay parameters, received traffic and traffic sent in Video Conferencing, Response Time in

https://doi.org/10.1051/matecconf/201821501005

Query Database runs better in OSPFv3 than OSPFv3_RIPNG and RIPNG. In the case of the performance of each routing protocol, the overall performance of OSPFv3 is better than RIPng [3].

The transition from IPv4 to the IPv6, and how to reduce the risk of problems that will have a negative impact to the user and the service provider during the transition from IPv4 to the IPv6. Comparison of IPv6 transition mechanisms such as Dual Stack, Automatic Tunneling, and Manually Configured Tunneling in terms of security issues. The study offers a transitional model with Automatic Tunneling as well as Manually Configured Tunneling [4].

Saraj (2015) analyzes the most common tunneling protocols available for configuration in most network devices. The analysis of the research is based on math and deployment in testbed setup on LAN, CAN and MAN only. These activities include the behavior of tunneling protocols with applications that use TCP or UDP over the tunneling protocol. The tunneling protocols studied were ISATAP, GRE 6to4, and 6RD. The performance of the protocol is measured through throughput parameters, end-to-end delay, jitter, RTT and tunnel overhead in terms of TCP and UDP. The results obtained that ISATAP in most parameters have shown better performance than other tunneling protocols. In addition, 6to4 in most cases has shown comparative performance worst against the others. The final conclusion is that if the tunneling mechanism is configured on an end host, not on a network device such as a router, it can provide better performance than the other way around [5].

Juanda (2016) compares the distance vector routing protocol represented by RIPv2 with the protocol link state routing protocol represented by OSPF based on Quality of Service (QoS), the speed of the table update against the use of streaming video, testing when one link or down path to see the speed track displacement process, testing convergence time when the client is in a video stream when the best path suddenly down. The test was performed based on the standard configuration with changes in transmit parameters on the OSPF protocol path of 10 M. This research proved that the link state protocol represented by OSPF is better than the distance vector protocol represented by RIP based on jitter, packet loss, and faster parameters in terms of time required for convergence as well as for routing table updates [6].

This research combines the best tunneling method with the most widely used routing protocols obtained from the above research, so it can provide recommendations or references in the selection of the latest and best routing protocols on large-scale network conditions when transition from IPv4 to IPv6.

IP Address version 4 (IPv4) was published in 1981 as informed through RFC791. IPv4 has advantages in terms of ease of network planning and implementation. IPv4 has a 32 bit range. There are about 232 (4,294,467,295) IP addresses that can be used on IPv4. Of these 256 '/ 8' subnet blocks, there are approximately 35,078 blocks used for special needs (already reserved), 16 subnet blocks '/ 8' have been ordered for IP multicast, 16 subnet '/ 8' blocks are used for future use (future use), and several other subnet blocks are also used for special purposes (RFC5737). The IPv4 structure is shown in Fig.1

4	8	16		32 bit
Version	IHL	Type of *service*	Total Length	
Identification			Flags	Fragment offset
Time to Live		*Protocol*	*Header Checksum*	
Surce *Address*				
Destination Address				
Option + Padding				
Data				

Fig. 1. IPv4 Header

The Internet Engineering Task Force (IETF) initiated the development of IPv4 router protocols in the early 1990s. Here is an overview of major changes to IPv6 from IPv4: expanded address space; autocongiration; simplifying header format; enhanced support for option and extension.

bits 4	12	16	24	32
Ver	Traffic Class	Flow Label		
Payload Length		Next Header		Hop Limit
Source Address				
Destination Address				

Fig.2. IPv6 Header

IETF (Internet Engineering Task Force) has formed a team to overcome the interconnection process from IPv4 to IPv6 ie IETF IPNG Transition. The purpose of making this transition mechanism so that IPv6 packets can be passed on an existing IPv4 network or vice versa. During the interconnection process IPv4 and IPv6 networks must be able to communicate with each other IPv4 or IPv6 without reducing its reliability.

The dual stack transition method lies in the internet layer in the TCP / IP protocol that is responsible for the Internet Protocol (IP). Dual stack allows to have IPv4 and IPv6 address simultaneously in an interface.

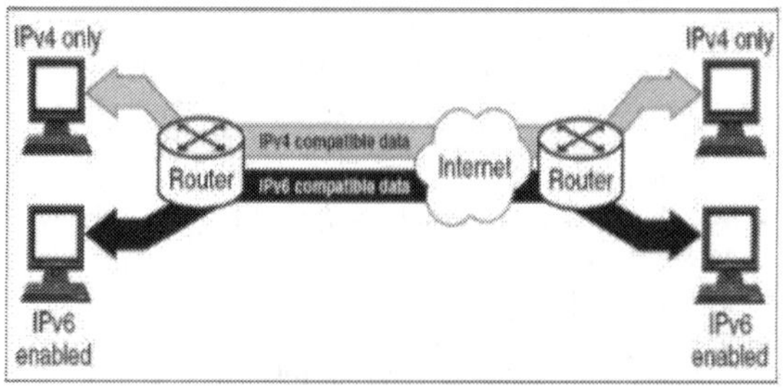

Fig. 3. Dual Stack [7]

Tunneling is a technique for passing IPv6 packets over an IPv4 network by encapsulating packets. Before being sent, the data packet has a slight alteration or modification, ie the addition of a header to the tunnel. When the data has passed through the tunnel and reached the destination or the end of the tunnel, the header of the data packet will be restored as before. Tunneling method that can be used generally divided into two, namely as follows: Static Point-to-Point IPv6 (Manual Tunnel and GRE Tunnel) and Dynamic Multipoint IPv6 (Automatic 6to4 and Intra-*Site* Auto *Tunneling Addres*sing *Protocol* (ISATAP))

GRE is a mechanism to encapsulate network layer protocols through other network layer protocols. The general specification was originally described in RFC1701, and IP packet encapsulation via IP is defined in RFC1702 as a specific implementation of GRE. The GRE specification has been formalized in RFC2784 and is commonly used to encapsulate IPv4 and IPv6 packets in IPv4 packets. RFC2890 extends RFC2784 with key edition (key) and sequence number. The IPv4 47 protocol is used when the GRE packet is encapsulated on IPv4. GRE can encapsulate multicast, broadcast, or other no-IP-type traffic.

Open Shortest Path First version 3 (OSPFv3) is a development routing protocol from OSPFv2 which is included in the interior of Gateway Protocol (IGP). In general the workings between OSPFv2 and OSPFv3 are the same. To achieve full convergence conditions, there are several stages to pass. Similar to OSPFv2, OSPFv3 also has 2 way state. OSPFv3 is capable of running on IPv4 and IPv6 based networks at once. OSPFv3 uses the Djikstra algorithm and uses cost as a metric. The path with the smallest cost value used as the main line. The cost value of OSPFv3 is obtained using the following formula.

$$Cost = \frac{Reference\ Bandwith\ (100\ MB)}{Interface\ Bandwith\ (MB)} \quad (1)$$

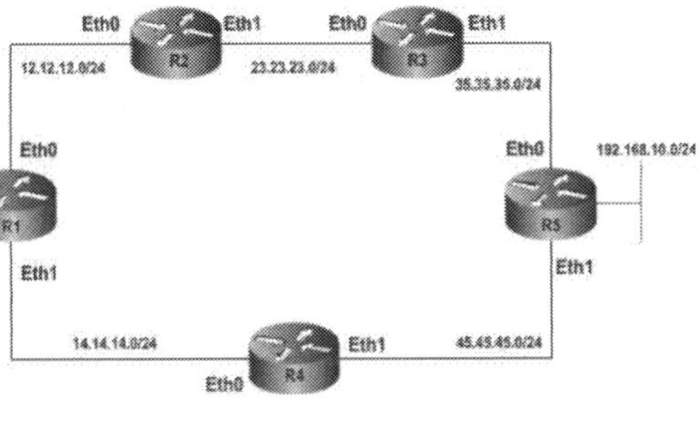

Fig. 4. Hop-Count Concept [8]

RIPng uses the UDP protocol on port 521 to transport, either in sending or receiving datagrams. RIPng is a development of RIPv2. Basically, the workings of RIPng are the same as RIPv2. But one of the fundamental differences is on IPv6 addressing support. RIPng is a distance-vector routing protocol known as the Bellman-Ford algorithm and entered in the Interior Gate Protocol class developed by IETF. Distance Vector Protocol is a dynamic routing technique that uses distance and direction as the main guide in routing. The distance is the number of routers passed, while the direction in question is the address of the router through. The use of the hop count can be explained as in Figure 4.

Quality of Service (QoS) defines the ability to provide services and defines the characteristics and characteristics of a service. Parameters of QoS is one benchmark indicator of the quality of service from the computer network itself. The QoS standard used refers to the International Telecommunication Union - Telecommunication (ITU-T) standard. ITU-T is part of ITU which is an international organization established to standardize, regulate and standardize international radio and international telecommunications. Quality of Service (QoS) has a flow of data packets that are used as measuring parameters of Service Internet Protocol Network: reliability; packet loss, bandwidth; and throughput.

2 Method

The topology used in this study is shown in Figure 5, on the topology there is one client laptop, one server, UTP cable, and six router units. The client and server laptops use IPv6 and are connected over IPv4 networks. The client and server laptops are connected by routers running dynamic routing protocol OSPFv3 or RIPng.

QoS testing on OSPFv3 and RIPng protocols is performed with three scenarios in each routing protocol, with the following details

1. OSPFv3 with best active path conditions
2. OSPFv3 when network changes
3. OSPFv3 with best path down comdition (Stable)
4. RIPng with the best active path conditions
5. RIPng when network changes
6. RIPng with best down condition (Stable)

Testing is done by testing the QoS parameters when the client computer downloads files with a 100 Mega Byte .iso extension for File1.iso, 300 Mega Bytes for File2.iso, 500 Mega Bytes for File3.iso, 700 Mega Bytes for File4.iso, and 1 Giga Byte for File5.iso from server. Variable QoS tested on each file consists of three parameters, namely the parameter delay, packet loss, and throughput. QoS testing is done by capturing the packet using wire shark tool, then calculation of the communication that occurs between the client and server to obtain the average value of delay and packet loss.

3 Result and Discussion

3.1. Testing of Topology

In QoS Analysis on OSPFv3 and RIPng Using GRE Tunnel Using Mikrotik Router is used 6 routers. In OSPFv3 topology, the six routers are divided into two separate backbone areas over the Internet using the IPv4 network. In the RIPng topology, the six routers are also divided into two sites, namely site A and site B. As for one area or site there is one client computer that will access the server located on another area or site. Topology testing is shown in figure 5.

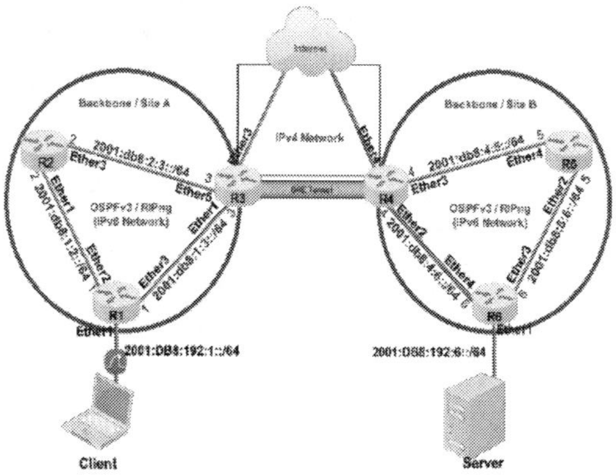

Fig.5. Topology Design

3.2. Average QoS Comparison

After obtaining the average results of three QoS tests on OSPFv3 and RIPng using GRE Tunnel, then the average table is displayed in the form of bar graph. The bar graph is displayed so that the QoS differences in each of the routing protocols are more clearly visible. Graphs are displayed in three views, ie. QoS charts on active best path conditions, QoS charts in the event of network changes due to the main down path, and QoS graphs in stable condition after the best path down.

Based on the figure 7, it appears that the average delay on OSPFv3 is better than RIPng for the best active path conditions.

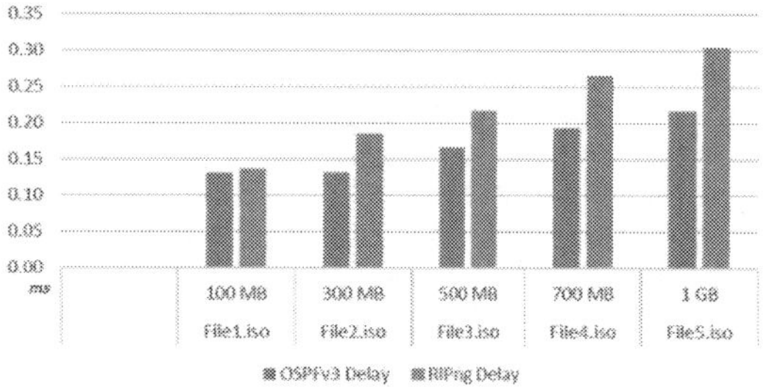

Fig.7. Chart of Comparison Delay Best Active Path Condition

In figure 8, OSPFv3 is better than RIPng based on the average packet loss on testing with the best active path conditions. In the packet loss parameter, it is found that the packet loss value in the initial frame of the download process is greater than the packet loss in the next frame, in other words the packet loss value continues to decrease in the next frame, thus the higher frame number will be the less number of packet loss produced. This applies to all test scenarios. While the number of frame number depends on the size of the file is transmitted. The larger the size of the file being transmitted, the more frames are transmitted, and the higher the frame number obtained. Figure 9 shows that the average throughput of OSPFv3 is better than RIPng on all tests.

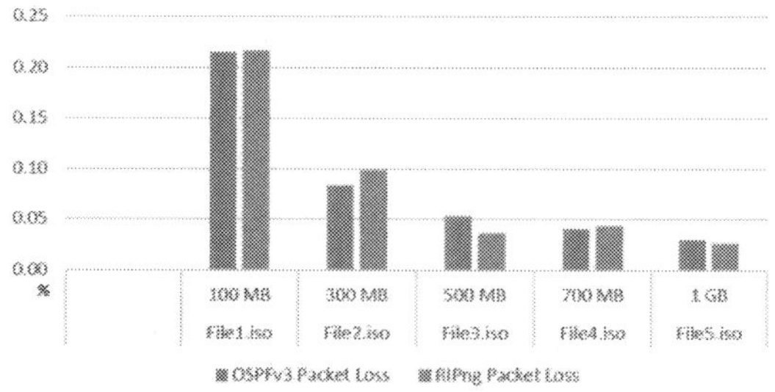

Fig. 8. Chart of Comparison Packet loss Best Active Path Conditon

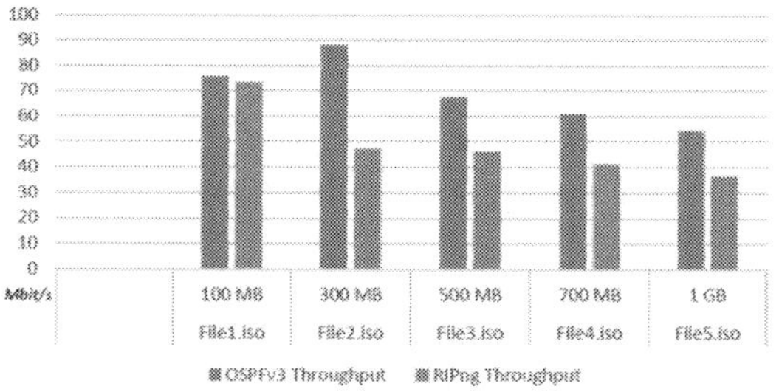

Fig.9. Chart of Comparison Throughput Best Active Path Condition

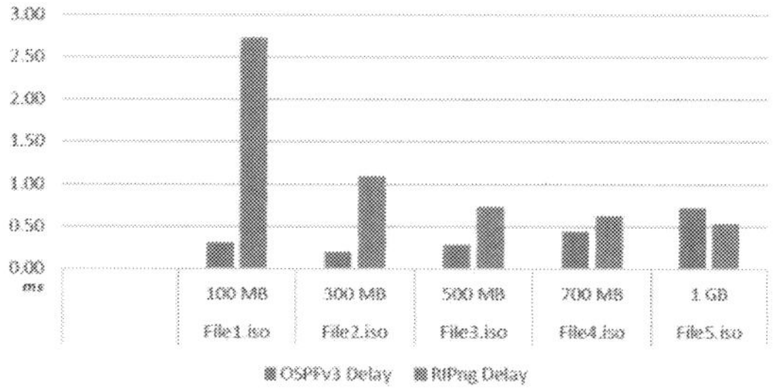

Fig.10. Chart of Comparison Delay Network Changes Condition

Figure 10 shows that overall delay in OSPFv3 is better than RIPng on network change conditions. The average delay in the RIPng routing protocol for network change scenarios is different from normal conditions, this is affected by the time it takes to update the routing table after the main path down until the file download process runs again and is influenced by the incremental number of frames from file1.iso to file5.iso. Where, the greater the load of transmitted files will be more and more frames are sent which is then calculated with the time required for the transmission of the file including the time required to update the routing table until the download process file runs back which then obtained the average value of delay. Figure 11 shows that the average packet loss in OSPFv3 is better than RIPng on all tests under network change conditions.

In Figure 12, it is seen that the mean throughput of OSPFv3 is better than RIPng based on the test sample on each test. The throughput in RIPng becomes different from the normal conditions, where the larger the load file size the larger the throughput will be. This is due to the effect of the time required to update the routing table after the best path down until the file download process runs again, and is affected by the incremental byte number from file1.iso to file5.iso, where the greater the load of files transmitted will be larger in size bytes which are then calculated with the time required for the transmission of the files to obtain throughput.

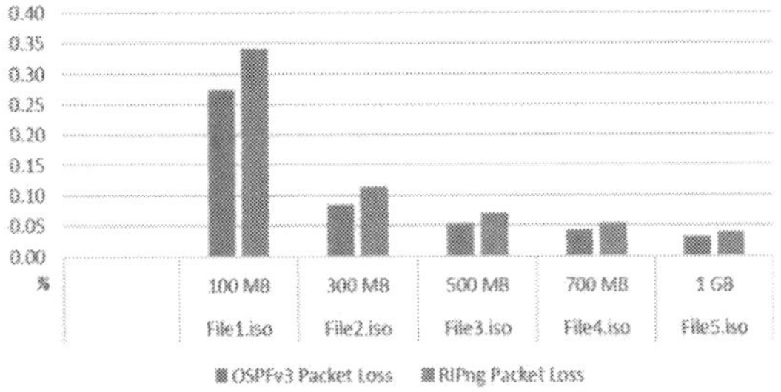

Fig.11. Chart of Comparison Packet loss Network Changes Condition

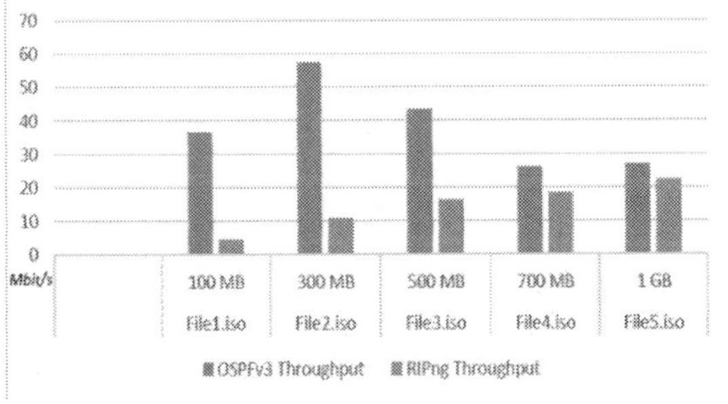

Fig.12. Chart of Comparison Throughput Network Changes Condition

Comparison of QoS in OSPFv3 and RIPng for stable network conditions after network changes so that the best paths are also displayed in the form of bar graphs. Based on the delay, packet loss, and throughput parameter are shown in figure 13, 14, and 15.

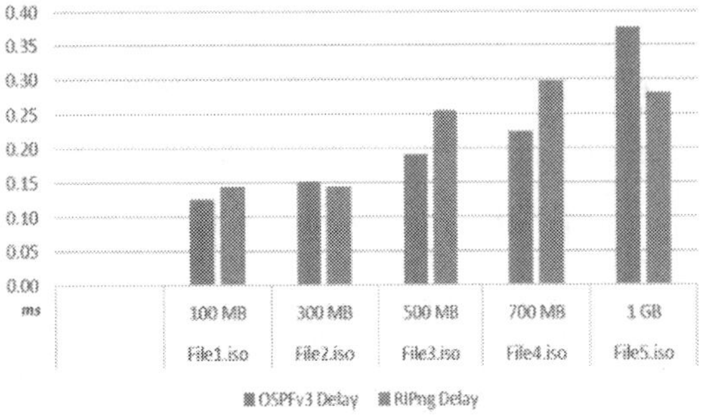

Fig.13. Chart of Comparison Delay Best Path Down Condition

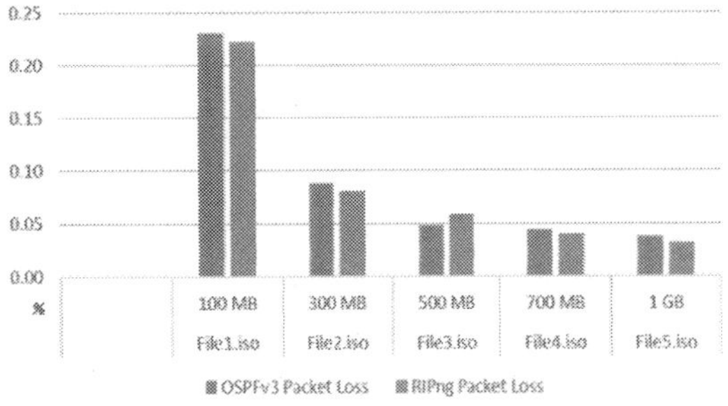

Fig. 14. Chart of Comparison Packet loss Best Path Down Condition

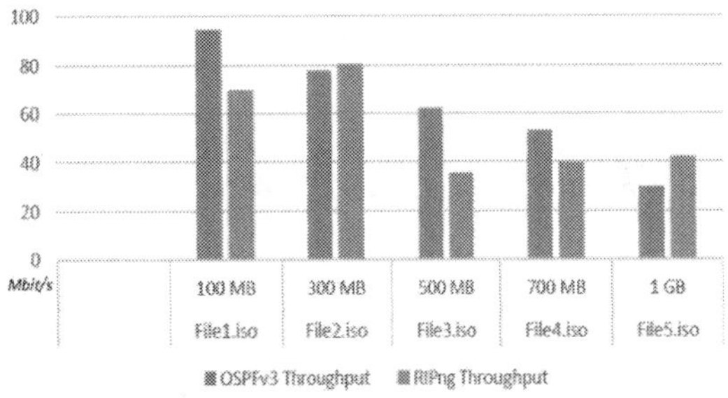

Fig.15. Chart of Comparison Throughput Best Path Down Condition

Based on the above test, the average value of delay, packet loss, and throughput of both routing protocols in all those scenarios are included in the good category based on ITU-T G.114 standard.

4 Conclusion and Recommendation

Based on QoS testing of OSPFv3 and RIPng protocol method using GRE tunnel, it is found that overall OSPFv3 is better than RIPng on delay, packet loss, and throughput parameters in all scenarios. In addition, the results obtained that the data load will affect the delay in other words the greater the size of the downloaded file, the greater the average delay obtained, except in the RIPng routing protocol for network change scenarios, this is because RIPng takes a longer time than OSPFv3 in updating the routing table until the download process runs again which is also the effect of the characteristics of each type of protocol, and also influenced by the number of incremental frames from file1.iso to file5.iso sent by the server to the client when the download process .

The characteristics of each protocol affect the results obtained, so for similar research it is advisable to analyze other routing protocols that are included in the Interior Gateway Protocol (IGP) and Enhanced Interior Gateway Routing Protocol (EIGRP) with RIPng for distance vector protocol, and OSPFv3 with Intermediate System to Intermediate System (IS-IS) on the type of link state protocol for IPv6 networks. It is also recommended to test the characteristics, QoS, and performance of each of these routing protocols against various other experimental scenarios.

References

1. Masruroh, Situ Ummi., Robby, Fadly., Hakiem, Nashrul., *Informatics and Computing (ICIC),* (2016)
2. Nixon, Dr. J Sebastian, Dr A Francis Saviour Devaraj., International Journal of Computer Science and Information Technology & Security (IJCSITS), **5**, 6, (2015)
3. Narula, Rajneesh., Aggarwal, Pallavi., International Journal of Technical Research and Applications, **2**, 6 (2014)
4. Hanumanthappa, International Journal of Computer Science and Information Security (IJCSIS), 3, 1 (2009)
5. Saraj, Tariq., Hanan, Abdul., Akbar, M. S., Yousaf, M., Qayyum, A., dan Tufail, M. (2015, December). *Information Assurance and Cyber Security (CIACS),* (2015)
6. Juanda, Dadan Hendra, *Analisa Perbandingan Metode Protokol Routing Distance Vector Dengan Protokol Routing Link State Terhadap Aplikasi Layanan Paket Data Real Time Menggunakan Router Mikrotik.* (Institut Teknologi Padang, Padang, 2016)
7. Reddy, M. P. R., Krishna, M. D. V., Madhavi, M. S. P., Reddy, M. B. R., dan Reddy, M. D. M. the future configuration version protocals of global and private ip-ipv6 securit featurs.Int. Journal of research Science & Management. (2014)
8. Komarudin, Ahmad Rosid., Pranozal, Alex., Feriansyah., dan Irpan, *Teori dan Konsep OSPF di Cisco dan MikroTik.* ID-Networkers, Jakarta, (2016)

Decision Support System Of Fruit Cultivation Using Technique For Other Reference Method By Similarity To Ideal Solution (TOPSIS)

Eva Yulianti*, *Rahmat Rizki* Nanda

Institut Teknologi Padang, Informatics Engineering Study Program, Padang, Indonesia

Abstract. Fruit cultivation is very promising for farmers. But there are problems faced by farmers, namely the lack of understanding of farmers with natural conditions that can affect crop yields. So with the selection of plants that are not appropriate, it does not get satisfactory results. Various types of fruit crops can be cultivated by farmers, such as oranges, guava, rambutan, watermelon, avocado, and so on. But it should be noted, that in the cultivation is expected to be cultivated plants in accordance with natural circumstances. This Designing created application to help determine the cultivation of fruit crops. In determining the cultivation of fruit crops in accordance with the criteria using the Technique Method for Others Reference by Similarity to Ideal Solution (TOPSIS) as a tool to facilitate decision-making process with several criteria of comparison, namely: temperature, sunlight, rainfall and humidity, height, harvest, selling power, susceptibility to disease, and care levels. This application is made based on the web by using PHP as a programming language and MySQL as the data storage. The use of decision support system application of the cultivation of these fruit crops can provide an output or alternative in accordance with the natural state of the area. And helps in making decisions to determine which fruits are suitable for cultivating for users based on selected criteria.

1 Introduction

The pattern of life by always eating fruits every day is a healthy lifestyle. This is because the fruits contain a variety of vitamins, minerals, and fiber that is needed by the body. For example, oranges. In the citrus fruit contained vitamin C is very good for maintaining endurance. So it is very good to be consumed every day.

Besides the purchase price of fruits that are affordable by consumers, cultivating fruits is also very promising for farmers. With proper cultivation and consideration of the natural state (temperature, sunlight, rainfall and humidity, altitude), harvesting, selling power, susceptibility to disease, and the level of care required, with appropriate action, it will most likely result in satisfying. But there are problems faced by farmers, namely the lack of understanding of farmers with natural conditions that can affect crop yields. So with the selection of plants that do not fit, then do not get optimal results.

Various types of fruit crops can be cultivated by farmers, such as oranges, guava, rambutan, watermelon, avocado, and so on. It should be noted, however, that in the cultivation it is expected that the crops will be cultivated in accordance with the natural conditions, such as temperature, sunlight, rainfall and humidity, and the altitude in West Pasaman Regency. And also need support criteria, such as easy maintenance, long harvest, high selling power, and free from disease.

With the use of computer technology, then this can help users / farmers in choosing plants in accordance with the above-mentioned considerations contained in the area. The term system is mentioned with Decision Support System (Decision Support System), which is a system that can assist users in making decisions on what plants are suitable cultivated. How to use the system is designed as easy as possible, ie after the user to register, then the next user can log into his account. Furthermore, the user simply select the name of the fruits that can be compared by the user to get the highest or the best value by using the Technique Method For Others Reference by Similarity to Ideal Solution (TOPSIS). The results of the assessment process are recommended to users based on the highest score. So by making the right decision through the utilization of the system, it is expected that farmers will get maximum and optimal cultivation results.

TOPSIS method is one of the methods used to solve the problem of Multi Attribute Decision Making (MADM). This method is based on the concept that the best chosen alternative not only has the shortest distance from the positive solution, but also has the longest distance from the ideal solution. The TOPSIS method has advantages, including simple and easy-tounderstand concepts, efficient computing that produces precise calculations with computers, and has the ability to measure the relative (non-fixed) performance of alternatives or multiple decision options in simple mathematical form.

2 Methodology

1.1 Decision Support system

Decision support systems are defined as a system intended to support managerial decision-makers in certain situations. Decision support systems are meant to be a tool for decision-makers to expand their capabilities, but not to replace their judgments.

Decision support system is an interactive computer-based system that helps decision makers utilize data and models to solve unstructured problems. There are several reasons for the use of Decision Support Systems, which are the unstable economic conditions, increased competition in the business world, the need for accurate new information, timely provision of information and efforts to reduce operating costs.

In addition, another reason in the development of Decision Support Systems is the change in end-user computing behavior, end-users are not programmers, so they need tools and procedures that are easy to use (Turban, 2005).

1.2 Technique For Others Reference by Similarity to Ideal Solution (TOPSIS) Method

The TOPSIS method is one of the methods used to solve MADM problems. The TOPSIS method is based on the concept that the best chosen alternative not only has the shortest distance from the ideal ideal solution, but also has the longest distance from the ideal solution. This concept is widely used in some MADM models to solve practical decision problems. This is because the concept is simple and easy to understand, computing efficient, and has the ability to measure the relative performance of decision alternatives in a simple mathematical form.

In general, TOPSIS procedure follows the following steps :

(1) Make a normalized decision matrix.
Topsis requires a rating on every criterion or subcriteria that is normalized. The normalized matrix is formed from the equation below :

$$r_{ij} = \frac{x_{ij}}{\sqrt{\sum_{i=1}^{m} x_{ij}^2}} \quad \text{.........} \quad (1)$$

Description :

rij is the normalized value of each alternative (i) to criterion (j) with i = 1,2, ..., m;
and j = 1,2, ..., n.
Xij is the value of an alternative (i) to criterion (j) with i = 1,2, .., m; and j = 1,2, ...n.

(2) Calculate a weighted normalized Matrix.
After calculating the normalized value, the next step is to calculate the weighted normalization value by multiplying the value in each alternative of the normalized matrix by the weights given by the decision maker. The equations in use are :

$$y_{ij} = w_i \, r_{ij} \quad \text{.........} \quad (2)$$

Description :

yij is a weighted normalized value
wi is the weight of each criterion
rij is the normalized value of each alternative where rij is the normalization value of each alternative (i) against criterion (j) with i = 1,2, ..., m; and j = 1,2, ..., n.

(3) Identify positive ideal solutions and ideal negative solutions.

Positive ideal solutions and negative ideal solutions can be calculated based on the weighted normalization values as follows:

$$A^{+} = (y1^{+}, y2^{+}, \ldots yn^{+}); \ldots\ldots\ldots\ldots\ldots\ldots \quad (3)$$

$$A^{-} = (y1^{-}-, y2^{-}, \ldots yn^{-}); \ldots\ldots\ldots\ldots\ldots \quad (4)$$

Where :

$$y_j^{-} = \begin{cases} \min y_{ij}; & \text{jika ij adalah atribut keuntungan(benefit)} \\ \max y_{ij}; & \text{jika ij adalah atribut biaya(cost)} \end{cases}$$

$$y_j^{+} = \begin{cases} \max y_{ij}; & \text{jika ij adalah atribut keuntungan(benefit)} \\ \min y_{ij}; & \text{jika ij adalah atribut biaya(cost)} \end{cases}$$

$j = 1,2, \ldots n$.

Symbol Description:

The positive Ideal solution (A^+) is obtained by finding the maximum value of the weighted normalization value (yij) if the attribute is a gain attribute and searching for the minimum value of the weighted normalization value (yij) if the attribute is the cost attribute.

The negative Ideal solution (A^-) is obtained by searching for the minimum value of the weighted normalization value (yij) if the attribute is the profit attribute and the maximum value of the weighted normalization value (yij) if the attribute is the cost attribute.

(4) Calculate the distance between the value of each alternative with the matrix of positive ideal solutions and the ideal negative solution matrix. The distance between alternative Ai with the ideal solution is formulated as follows:

$$D_i^+ = \sqrt{\sum_{j=1}^{n}(y_i^+ - y_{ij})^2}$$
.... (5)
i= 1,2,...,m.

The distance between alternative Ai with the ideal ideal solution is defined as:

$$D_i^- = \sqrt{\sum_{j=1}^{n}(y_{ij} - y_i^-)^2}$$
.... (6)
i= 1,2,...,m.

Symbol Description:

The distance between alternatives Ai with the positive ideal solution (yj^+) expressed in the Di^+ symbol is derived from the root value of the total value of each alternative obtained with the positive ideal solution (yi^+) minus the weighted normalization values for each latern (yij) then in the second.

The distance between alternatives Ai with the positive ideal solution (yj^-) expressed in symbol (Di^-) is derived from the root value of the sum of values of each alternative obtained with the weighted normalization value for each latern (yij) minus the positive ideal solution (yi^-) then in the second power.

(5) Determine the value of proximity of each alternative to the ideal solution (preference).

The value of Preferences for each alternative (Vi) as follows :

$$V_i = \frac{D_i^-}{D_i^- + D_i^+}$$
.... (7)

Symbol Description:

Vi (The value of preference for each alternative) is obtained from the value of the ideal ideal solution distance (Di^-) divided by the total value of the ideal solution solution negative (Di^-) plus the value of the ideal solution solution negative (Di^+).

1.3 *Context* Diagram

Context Diagram is a system design tool globally that shows the system in general and the parts of the sub system involved in the system as a whole, interconnection, and interaction between sub-systems.

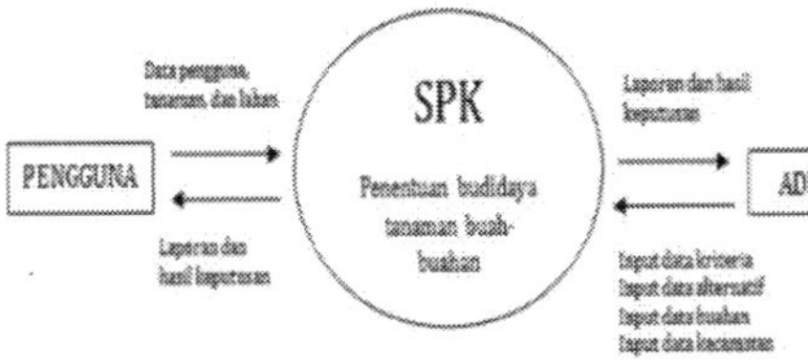

Figure 1: Context Diagram

1.4 *Entity Relationship Diagram* (ERD)

The relationship between some data in the database will be seen in the Entity Relational Diagram (ERD). ERD is a chart that describes for the means of database design, which consists of real objects.

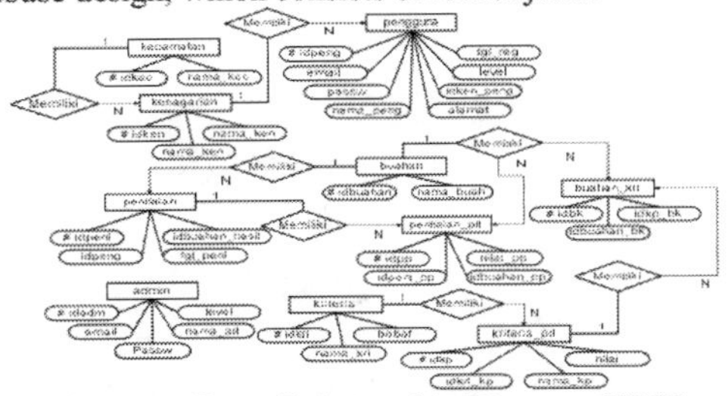

Figure 2 : *Entity Relationship Diagram* (ERD)

3 Discussion

1.5 Home Page

The home page is the first page that appears when users or visitors visit the website. On this page there are main menus, namely Home menu, About, List, and Login. This page view is shown in the following figure.

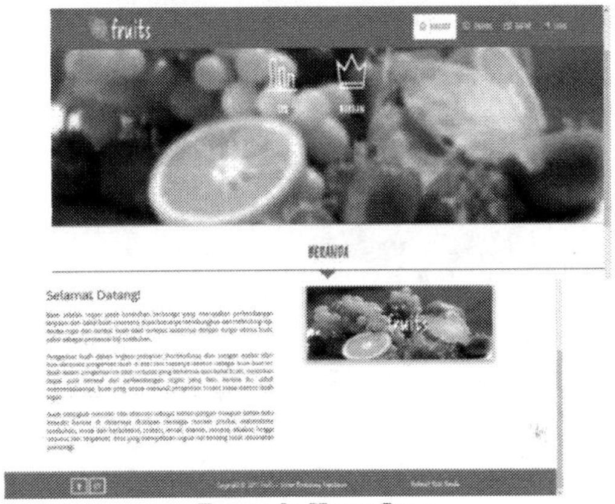

Figure 3: Home Page

1.6 Registration Page

The registration page is the page used by the end user to register. Thus, after successful registration then he can just make the determination of fruits in accordance with the conditions of land in the district. This page view is shown in the following figure.

Figure 4: Registration Page

1.7 Login Page

The login page is the page that is used as the entrance by the end user or the application manager.

https://doi.org/10.1051/matecconf/201821501006

Thus, only those who have been granted permission can enter next. This page view is shown in the following figure.

Figure 5: Login Page

1.8 Admin Page

The admin page is the page that displays the data of all the admin / managers who are granted permissions to manage the application. To access this page, it must be logged in as admin or operator. This page view is shown in the following figure.

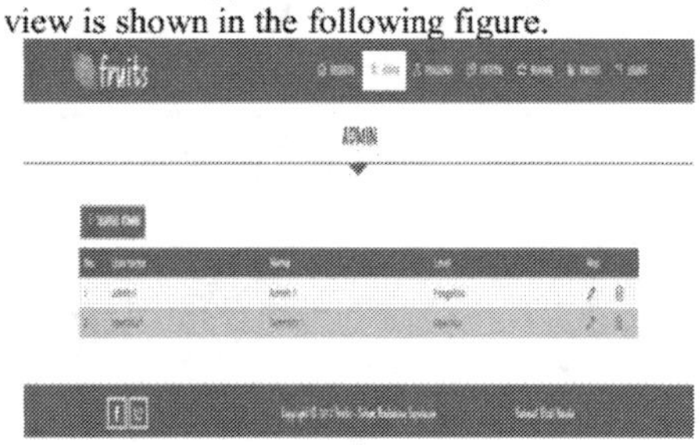

Figure 6: Admin Page

1.9 User Pages

The user page is the page that displays all user data that has been registered. There displayed username, name, address, and registration date. This page view is shown in the following figure.

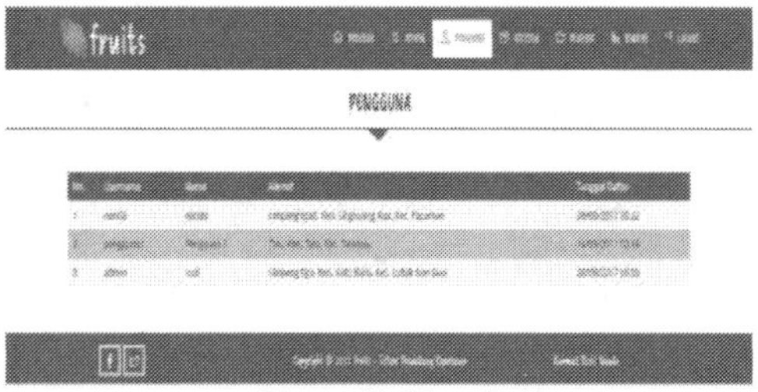

Figure 7: User Pages

1.10 Criteria Pages

Criteria page is a page that displays all the data criteria that are used as assessment for fruits. The data displayed are names, weights, and options. This page view is shown in the following figure.

Figure 8: Criteria Pages

1.11 Fruit Pages

The fruits page is a page that is used to display a selection of fruits that can later be compared by the user, thus displaying the best option for the user based on the state of the land in the district. This page view is shown in the following figure.

Figure 9: Fruit Pages

1.12 Assessment Page

An assessment page is a page that can be used by users who need advice / recommendations and as decision support in the determination of cultivation of fruit crops. Users simply choose the name of the fruits that are felt in accordance with his wishes. Then press the Process button, to start the judgment. This page view is shown in the following figure.

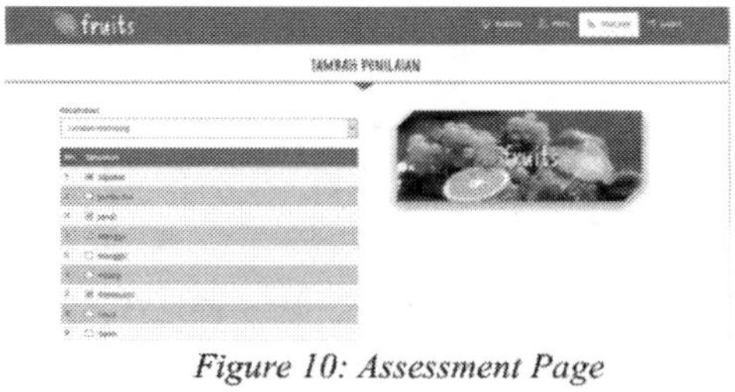

Figure 10: Assessment Page

The results of the assessment and suggestions for the best fruits are shown in the following figure.

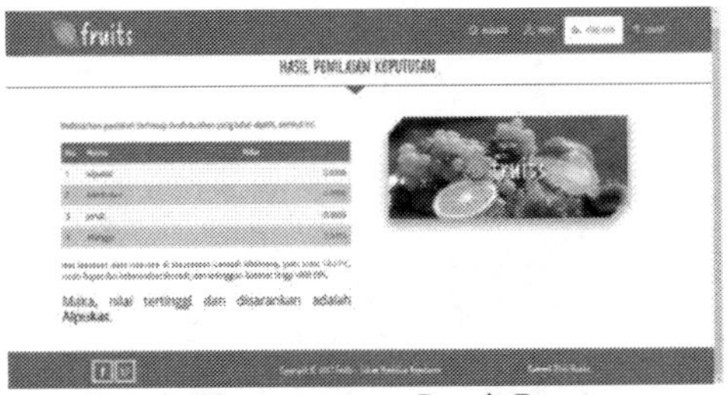

Figure 11: Assessment Result Page

1.13 History Page

A history page is a page that shows all the results of decision support processes or suggestions received by users based on the fruits they choose. This page view is shown in the following figure.

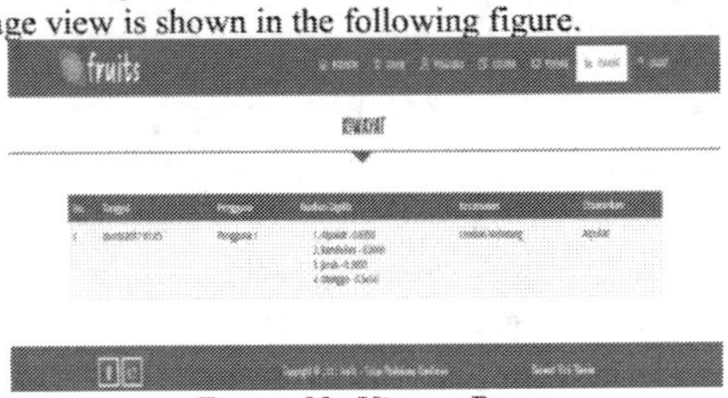

Figure 12: History Page

1.14 Calculation of TOPSIS Method

The following is an example of a case solved using the TOPSIS Method.

(1) A farmer in Pasaman wants to cultivate fruits that match the weather conditions in the area.

(2) Assessment

Table 1: Assessment of fruits

No.	Fruit	Criteria							
		1	2	3	4	5	6	7	8
1	Orange	2	3	2	3	3	3	3	3
2	Banana	3	2	3	1	3	3	3	1
3	Watermelon	3	3	3	3	1	1	2	2

Value Description :

Enough	= 1
Good	= 2
Very Good	= 3

(3) Give the weight of each criterion

Table 2: Criteria

No.	Criteria	Weight
1	Temperature	15%
2	Sunlight	15%
3	Rainfall and humidity	15%
4	Height	15%
5	Care	10%
6	Harvest Time	10%
7	Selling Power	10%
8	Disease	10%

(4) Calculating a normalized matrix

Table 3 : Roots result per rank

No	Fruit	Criteria							
		1	2	3	4	5	6	7	8
1	Orange	2	3	2	3	3	3	3	3
2	Banana	3	2	3	1	3	3	3	1
3	Watermelon	3	3	3	3	1	1	2	2
Number of rank results per criteria		58	58	58	55	55	55	58	32
Roots result per rank		7,62	7,62	7,62	7,42	7,42	7,42	7,62	5,66

To obtain a normalized matrix, it can use the following formula. For example, to obtain a normalized matrix value for Oranges in Criterion 1 (temperature).

$$r_{ij} = \frac{r_{ij}}{\sqrt{\sum_i^m = 1x_y^2}}$$

$$r_{ij} = \frac{2}{\sqrt{(2)^2 + (3)^{3+}(3)^3}}$$

$$r_{ij} = \frac{2}{\sqrt{4 + 27 + 27}}$$

$$r_{ij} = \frac{2}{\sqrt{58}}$$

$$r_{ij} = \frac{2}{7{,}615}$$

$$r_{ij} = 0{,}26$$

Thus, the normalized matrix values for Oranges in Criterion 1 (temperature) were 0.26 as shown in Table 4.

Table 4 : Normalized data

No.	Fruit	Criteria							
		1	2	3	4	5	6	7	8
Weight		**15 %**	**15 %**	**15 %**	**15 %**	**10 %**	**10 %**	**10 %**	**10 %**
1	Orange	0,26	0,39	0,26	0,40	0,40	0,40	0,39	0,53
2	Banana	0,39	0,26	0,39	0,13	0,40	0,40	0,39	0,18
3	Water melon	0,39	0,39	0,39	0,40	0,13	0,13	0,26	0,35

https://doi.org/10.1051/matecconf/201821501006

(5) Create a normalized weighted

To obtain a normalized weighted, it can use the following formula. For example, to obtain a weighted normalized value for Oranges in Criterion 1 (temperature) with a weight of 15%.

$$r_{ij} = w_i \times r_i$$
$$r_{ij} = 15\% \times 0{,}26$$
$$r_{ij} = 0{,}04$$

Thus, the weighted normalized values for Citrus in Criterion 1 (temperature) x with a weight of 15% are 0.04, as shown in Table 5.

Table 5: Normalized weighted table

No.	Fruit	Criteria							
		1	2	3	4	5	6	7	8
1	Orange	0,04	0,06	0,04	0,06	0,04	0,04	0,04	0,05
2	Banana	0,06	0,04	0,06	0,02	0,04	0,04	0,04	0,02
3	Water melon	0,06	0,06	0,06	0,06	0,01	0,01	0,03	0,04

(6) Looking for max and min values of normalized weights

Table 6: Max and min values

No.	Fruit	Criteria							
		1	2	3	4	5	6	7	8
1	Orange	0,04	0,06	0,04	0,06	0,04	0,04	0,04	0,05
2	Banana	0,06	0,04	0,06	0,02	0,04	0,04	0,04	0,02
3	Water melon	0,06	0,06	0,06	0,06	0,01	0,01	0,03	0,04
Max		0,06	0,06	0,06	0,06	0,04	0,04	0,04	0,05
Min		0,04	0,04	0,04	0,02	0,01	0,01	0,03	0,02

(7) Search for D^+ and D^- any alternatives

To obtain a positive ideal solution, then can use the following formula. For example, to get the value of Orange in Criterion 1 (temperature).

$$D_i^+ = \sqrt{\sum_{j=1}^{n} (y_i^+ - y_{ij})^2}$$

$$D_i^+ = \sqrt{\begin{aligned}&(0{,}04-0{,}06)^2+(0{,}06-0{,}06)^2+(0{,}04-0{,}06)^2+(0{,}06-0{,}06)^2+\\&(0{,}04-0{,}04)^2+(0{,}04-0{,}04)^2+(0{,}04-0{,}04)^2+(0{,}05-0{,}05)^2\end{aligned}}$$

$$D_i^+ = \sqrt{0{,}000775862}$$
$$D_i^+ = 0{,}027854301$$

Thus, the value of a positive ideal solution for Oranges in Criterion 1 (temperature) was 0.077032, as seen in Table 7.

Table 7: D^+ Value

No.	Fruit	Criteria							
		1	2	3	4	5	6	7	8
1	Orange	0,0003888	0	0,0003888	0	0	0	0	0
2	Banana	0	0,0003888	0	0,0016636	0	0	0	0,00125
3	Watermelon	0	0	0	0	0,0007727	0,0007727	0,0001722	0,0003133

Table 8 : D^- Value

No.	Fruit	Criteria							
		1	2	3	4	5	6	7	8
1	Orange	0	0,0003888	0	0,0016636	0,0007727	0,0007727	0,0001722	0,00125
2	Banana	0,0003888	0	0,0003888	0	0,0007727	0,0007727	0,0001722	0
3	Watermelon	0,0003888	0,0003888	0,0003888	0,0016636	0	0	0	0,0003133

Table 9 : D^+ and D^- values of each alternatif

No.	Fruit	D^+	D^-
1	Orange	0,027854	0,070009
2	Banana	0,057221	0,049019
3	Watermelon	0,044039	0,055791

(8) Search for V / results

To get a preference value, then can use the following formula. For example, to get the value of Orange

$$V_i = \frac{D_i^-}{D_i^- + D_i^+}$$

$$V_i = \frac{0{,}070008956}{0{,}070008956 + 0{,}027854301}$$

$$V_i = 0{,}715375293$$

Thus, the preference value for Orange is 0.715375293, as in Table 10.

Table 10 : Final Result

No.	Fruit	Vx
1	Orange	0,715375
2	Banana	0,461395
3	Watermelon	0,558859

From the value of Vx above, the highest value is 0.715375. Thus, it can be concluded that a very good alternative cultivated based on the available criteria are **Orange fruits**.

4 Conclusions and Recommendations

Based on the discussion done in this research, it can be concluded that Decision Support System Determination of Plant Cultivation Fruits can facilitate the farmers take decisions and can be useful for the general public as well. By building this application can support farmers in the determination of the cultivation of fruit crops with several criteria as a guide assessment in the determination of fruit crop cultivation.

The recomendation that can be submitted by writer to the next research is to develop this application with other method, such as linear regression method, B / C ratio, IRR and others. In order to compare the results which are more efficient and accurate.

References

[1] Arsyad, S.(1989). *Konservasi Tanah dan Air.* Bogor : Institut Pertanian Bogor.

[2] Aronoff, S.(1989). *Geografhic Information System : Management Perspective.* Canada : WDL publication Ottawa.

[3] Habibullah, A., & Winiarti, S. (2014). Sistem Pendukung Keputusan Penentuan Kesesuain Jenis Lahan Pertanian Untuk Budidaya Tanaman Buah-Buahan Menggunakan Metode Similarity Berbasis Web. *JSTIE (Jurnal Sarjana Teknik Informatika)(E-Journal)*, *2*(2), 336-344.

[4] Hasan. (2004). *Pokok-Pokok Materi Teori Pengambilan Keputusan.* Jakarta : Ghalia Indonesia.

[5] Kusrini. (2007). *Konsep dan Aplikasi Sistem Pendukung Keputusan.* Yogyakarta: Andi Offset.

[6] Kusumadewi, Sri. (2006). *Fuzzy Multi-Attribute Decision Making (Fuzzy MADM).* Yogyakarta: Graha Ilmu.

[7] Sulistyawati, T. (2015). *Sistem Pendukung Keputusan Untuk Penentuan Penerima Beasiswa Di Universitas Muhammadiyah Surakarta Berbasis Web Dengan Metode Topsis* (Doctoral dissertation, Universitas Muhammadiyah Surakarta).

[8] Turban, Efraim. (2005). *Decision Support Systems and Intelligent Systems (Sistem Pendukung Keputusan dan Sistem Cerdas) Edisi 7 Jilid 1.* Yogyakarta: Penerbit Andi

Design of Multicolour LED with Control and Monitoring System for Plant Growth

Ng Wei Choon[1], Nurul Amziah Md Yunus[1,2,*], Izhal Abdul Halin[1,2]

[1]Department of Electrical and Electronic Engineering, Faculty of Engineering, Universiti Putra Malaysia, 43400 Serdang UPM, Selangor. Malaysia.
[2]Advanced Material Synthesis and Fabrication Laboratory (AMSF), Faculty of Engineering, Universiti Putra Malaysia, 43400 Serdang UPM, Selangor. Malaysia.

Abstract. The aim of this work is to create an artificial environment LED based for plants where the goal is to control LED lighting and monitor plant growth. This will contribute on issue like food production. This work involves the use of a web development microcontroller kit, which will help to make online or IoT (Internet of Things) project and design easy. The microcontroller will come with an integrated Wi-Fi to collect and control variable parameter and also programming language to develop graphical user interface (GUI). It is expected that the plant growth environment can be monitored and controlled or set through cloud via Wi-Fi on the board. Multicolour light emitting diode (LED) lamps are used. This system will improve the performance of available plant growth area where it will become more flexible in term of providing artificial environment with a better supervision.

1 Introduction

There are some essential criteria for plant to grow well such as having a good surrounding temperature, soil moisture, surrounding humidity and light intensity. This is a design of plant growth multicolour LED based controller and monitoring system where an artificial environment includes parameters such as temperature, soil moisture, humidity and light intensity is prepared conducively for the plant growth. These parameters are under supervision through detail control by getting the information through designed graphical user interface (GUI) in PC or mobile application. The main component is the lighting source where its effect to the plant growth will be studied.

LED is used because it has low power consumption, generates less heat and has multiple colours [1]. Different colours of LEDs bring different effects to the plant growth. There are few types of visible light includes ultraviolet, violet, blue, green, yellow, red and far red. Some of the light might harm the growth of plant such as ultraviolet light. Exposure to ultraviolet light will retard the plant growth. For other band of visible light, violet light can enhances the colour, taste and aroma of plants. Blue, green, yellow, red and far red can improve the growth of plants in different aspect. These lights have different wavelength and energy level. Certain plants can yields more leaves and crops by combining red and blue light. Besides that, green light can enhance the chlorophyll production [2]. In most past researches, blue and red light shows the most significant improvement for the plant growth [3-5]. Hence, in this paper, multicolour LEDs focusing on the red and blue light colours are to be discussed for better plant growth.

As well known, plant growth is sunlight and weather dependent. Both sunlight and weather are intermittent. Crop production will be limited due to weather issue. For example, if there is natural disaster such as flood after few days raining, it will cause shortage of vegetables in the market and price rises because production cannot meet the demand. Moreover, plants need caring cares where there is need to make sure the plants gain sufficient water, nutrition and sunlight. For a large scale farm, these works are burden to farmers if only a few number of farmers are working. Furthermore, close distance monitoring is needed to make sure the plants grow well.

The main objective of this work is to create an artificial light environment with other controlling parameters for plant growth. Second, is to implement the plant monitoring and controlling system by using Raspberry Pi. Third, is to enable far distance real time monitoring.

2 System and Structure

The overview of entire system is shown in Figure 1. This system is divided into five parts: artificial light environment, main controller, sensors, actuators and user interface. Artificial light environment will be implemented by using common anode 4-pins LED strip. Common anode pin is connected to 12V supply and cathode pin of RGB will be connected to ground

* Corresponding author: amziah@upm.edu.my

in order to light them up. For example, to light up red LED, cathode of R is grounded.

For main controller, Raspberry Pi model B+ is used. Basically, the GPIO pins of the Raspberry Pi will be fully utilized in this system. The sensors and actuators will be connected to these GPIO pins to read or write the digital signal. Python will be used to program and interface the sensors part and actuators part so that the sensors and actuators are working together to maintain the environmental parameters at optimum level. Besides that, Raspberry Pi will also act as the web server where the data obtained from the sensors can be stored and transmitted to a website.

As for the sensors part, DHT11 isused to measure the surrounding temperature and humidity while soil moisture sensor is to detect the presence of water in the soil. Ultrasonic sensor and webcam are used to monitor the plant growth where ultrasonic sensor can detect the height of the plant whereas the webcam will capture the video of the plant. The water pump as one of the actuators is used for watering and producing the mist to increase the humidity. Fan is used to decrease the humidity while peltier is used to either warm up or chill down the surrounding temperature. For most of the actuators used, the required voltage is 12V but the voltage supply pins of the Raspberry Pi are only 3.3V and 5V. Therefore the relay is used to receive signal from Raspberry Pi and turn on or off the secondary circuit. The actuators will be connected to the external 12V voltage supply and to the output of relay. GPIO pin of the Raspberry Pi is connected to the input pin of the relay. Hence, GPIO pin can determine whether the relay to switch on or off the secondary circuit with actuators.

For the user interface, a website and mobile application are developed to ease the user to display the real time data from the plant. Besides that, the user can always notify the condition of the plant.

The growth of plant will then be monitored through the system. A sample from the type of vegetable plant, apple mint, is chosen and will be planted within this system. Apple mint is a perennial vegetable, herb plant that grows tall and is sometimes called the woolly mint. It is a member of the mint genus Mentha. This herb is generally grown as a culinary herb or ground cover. The mint leaves contains nutrients like iron, potassium, calcium, vitamin A and C, which replenish our body and alternative of antibiotics. The flowers can be used to make tea which if consumed promotes digestion, cures many ailments such as intestine problems, stomach pain and refreshes the mind [6].

The vegetative growth of the plants will be compared. The number of leaves, the height of the plants and the colour of the leaves will be compared. It is predicted that the vegetable can be harvested in shorter period by using this system and have better growth by using this system.

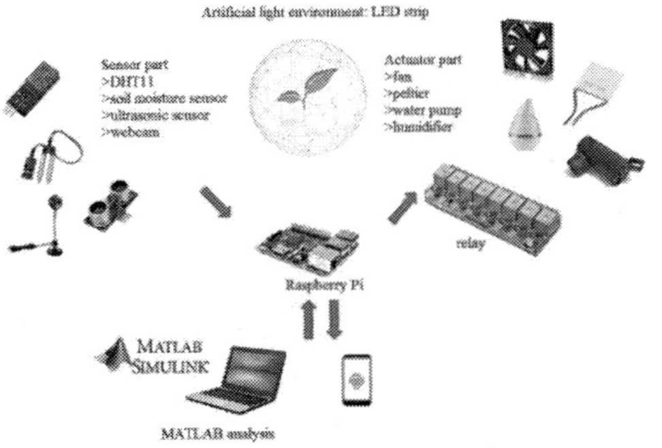

Fig. 1. Overview of the system.

3 Hardware Development

As mentioned earlier, Raspberry Pi B+a computer in sized of the credit card is used. The entire system designed is controlled by Raspberry Pi. Besides that, Raspberry Pi also acts as local web server for webcam and sensor data. The webcam video and sensor data can be viewed online in local network.

The artificial light source is common anode 4-pins LED strip and manipulating the input voltage to the 4-pins can change its colour. A desired colour can be set for the LED strip by always supply 12V to the common anode pin and ground the desired RGB cathode pin. Some colours require two or three RGB cathode pins to be grounded in order to have the desired colour of light-to-light up. For example, purple is combination of red and blue light. Both R and B cathode pins should be grounded in order to get the purple light from the LED strip.

Each sensor has its own way to be configured. For examples, there are four pins for ultrasonic sensor, which are ground, Vcc, trigger and echo. Ground pin is grounded and Vcc pin is connected to a 3.3V voltage source of Raspberry Pi as the power supply. Pulse signal will be generated at the GPIO pin of the Raspberry Pi using Python. Consequently, the ultrasonic sensor can emit an ultrasonic wave. When the wave meets an obstacle, it will reflect back and ultrasonic sensor can detect it and send signal to the Raspberry Pi through the echo pin. The time taken for the wave to get back/reflect to the ultrasonic sensor is used to multiply with the speed of wave and divided by 2 to determine the distance. All the hardware will be controlled by the Raspberry Pi, which acts as the main controller.

4 Software Development

Python is the main software part for entire system. Python is used to program all the sensors and actuators. By taking the ultrasonic sensor as example, the calculation is needed in order to show the distance. The calculation is programmed in Python and the distance will be shown. Besides that, the data obtained from the sensors will be stored to the MySQL database in the Raspberry Pi. Python can be used to store the data into the MySQL database. Moreover, *if else* statement is also written in Python for the actuators to be turned on or off to maintain the environmental parameters at optimum level which essential for plant growth.

A website is developed so that users can easily view the data of environmental parameters of the plant and the condition of the plant. The website will be developed in HTML and PHP. A login page will be made first to prompt the user to key in their id and password. The *id* and *password* are stored in the MySQL database where PHP script will compare the id and password. Only the authorized users can view the plant data. The website is created in local network where user can view the sensors data and live stream video of the plant in local network.

Blynk is used to enable sensor data online not only for local network. This mobile application will obtain the sensor data and display the data to the user when the smart phone is connected to internet.

Matlab and Simulink are used to analyze the data obtained. For example, Matlab function is used for colour segmentation for the artificial light environment. Mean RGB level and mean gray level of few artificial light environments are determined to identify the colour composition in the particular artificial light environment.

5 Results and Discussion

Two apple mints have been grown in the designed chamber with the proposed system (illumination of artificial light environment) and outdoor with illumination of sunlight. The duration taken for the experiment is 24 days.

For the artificial light environment, the composition of red and blue light is used where it is proven that red and blue light bring significant plant growth as also highlighted by other researchers [3-5, 7-8]. In order to verify the colours, Matlab was used to carry out colour segmentation to the created artificial light environment. Figure 2 shows the artificial light environment has high level of red and blue level (the top two lines, the most upper is red and just below is blue).

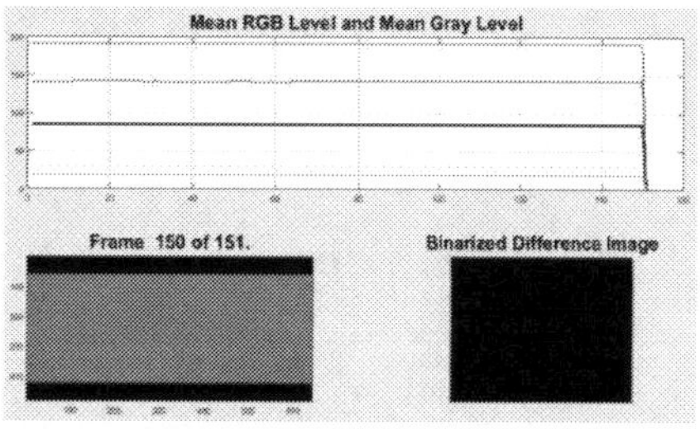

Fig. 2. Colour segmentation of the created artificial light environment.

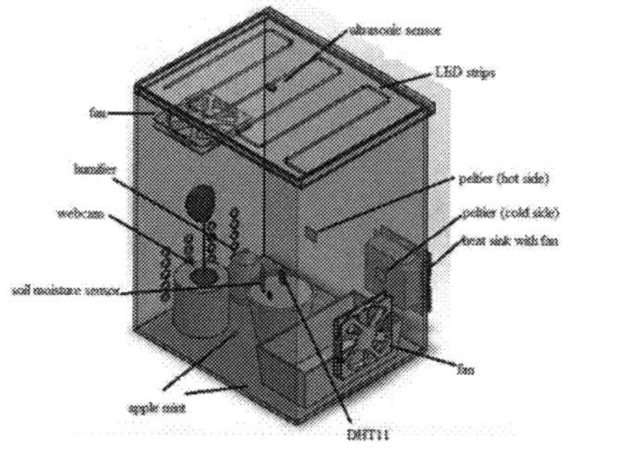

Fig. 3. Implementation of the system.

Figure 3 shows the designed plant growth chamber with the system. The fan on the top is to improve the air ventilation in the chamber where ventilation is an important criteria for plant growth according greenhouse design [9-10]. The surrounding temperature and humidity in this chamber have been detected by DHT11 and stored in MYSQL. The database will then be exported to the excel file and imported to Matlab for graphplot. Figure 4 shows the temperature in the system is within 30 to 35 degree Celsius; meanwhile the relative humidity is maintained at 75 to 90%.

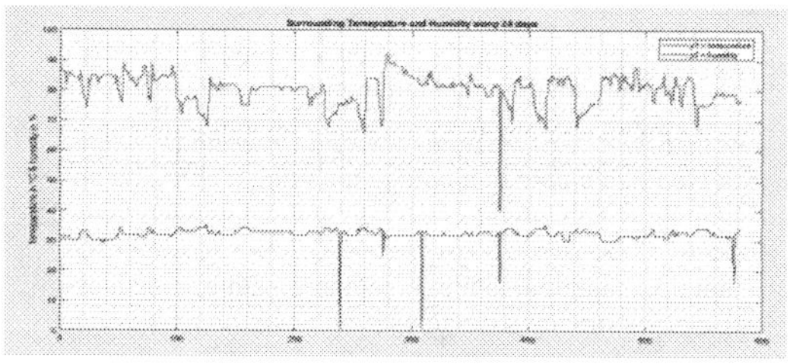

Fig. 4. Temperature and relative humidity in the chamber with the system, top graph is the temperature while bottom graph is the humidity.

Apple mints grown in the system with illumination of artificial light is compared with the one grown outside with illumination of sunlight. After 24 days, they are compared in four aspects, which are the height of the plant, number of leaves, area of the largest leaf of the plant and greenish of the leaves.

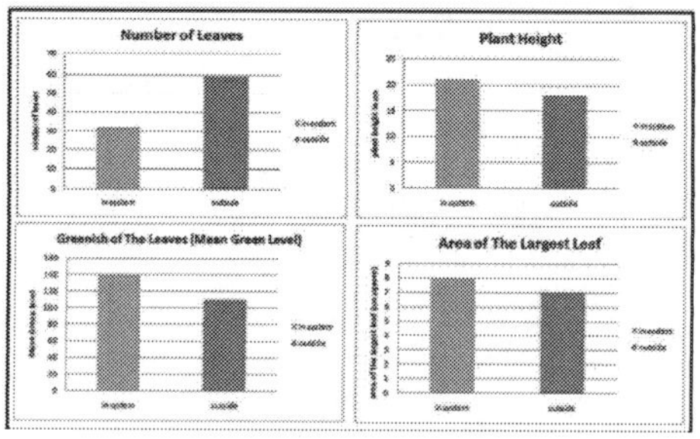

Fig. 5. Comparison of the apple mints in the system and outside the system.

Figure 5 shows apple mints grown in the chamber with illumination of purple (red+blue)colour, the artificial light is taller, consists of greener leaves and the largest size of leafisfound larger than the apple mints grown under the sunlight. Nevertheless, apple mint grown under the sunlight yield more leaves as compared to the apple mint in the system.

The sensors data such as temperature, humidity and plant height is continuously measured and saved into the database. A webpage created in the local network enables user to view the sensors data. The video of the plant is live streamed in the local network.

6 Conclusion

Multicolour LED, the artificial light system has been successfully developed. The Python programmed Raspberry Pi acts as the interface between the sensors, software and others hardware to detect and control the parameters for the better growth of plant. It is proven to be satisfactorily controllable as compared to the intermittent sunlight. Although the system may need further improvement for example consistency of LED intensity, water flow, soil moisture, temperature and humidity, the chosen plant, apple mints are found to grow better in the system. Besides that, far distance real time monitoring on plant is successfully enabled.

References

1. M.N. Khamis, LED Lighting with Remote Monitoring and Controlling System for Indoor Greenhouse. In: *2017 IEEE Asia Pacific Conference on Postgraduate Research in Microelectronics and Electronics*, Malaysia: 81-84. (2017)
2. R.J. Bula, 'Light-Emitting Diodes As A Radiation Source For Plants.' HortScience Journal, **26**(2): 203-205. (1991).
3. S.S.S. Yusof, Effect Of Artificial Lighting On Typhonium Flagelliforme For Indoor Vertical Farming. In *ProceedingsIEEE International Conference onAutomatic Control and Intelligent Systems (I2CACIS)*, Malaysia: 7–10. (2017)
4. J. Treder, The Effects Of LEDs On Growth And Morphogenesis Of Vegetable Seedlings Cultivated In *Growth Chambers.'In Proceedings2016 IEEE Lighting Conference of the Visegrad Countries (Lumen)* at Karpacz, Poland. (2016)
5. E. Danila, Efficient Lighting System For Greenhouses, In *Proc. 2016 International Conference and Exposition onElectrical and Power Engineering (EPE)*, Iasi, Romania: 439–444. (2016)
6. O.E. Hosam, Essential Oils of Mint between Benefits and Hazards, Journal of Essential Oil Bearing Plants. **16**(4), 429-438. (2013)
7. H. Wang, Effects Of Light Quality On CO_2Assimilation, Chlorophyll-Fluorescence Quenching Expression Of Calvin Cycle Genes And Carbohydrate Accumulation In Cucumis Sativus. Journal of Photochemistry and Photobiology B: Biology, **96** (1), 30–37. (2009)
8. Y. Li, Design Of Greenhouse Monitoring And Control System Based On LED Lighting. In *2015 12th China International Forum on Solid State Lighting (SSLCHINA)*, Shenzhen, China:123–126. (2015)
9. K.S. Kumar, Design And Technology For Greenhouse Cooling In Tropical And Subtropical Regions: A Review.'Energy and Buildings, 41(12), 1269–1275. (2009)
10. S. Kurpaska, Energy Effects During Using the Glass With Different Properties. Journal Technical Sciences / University of Warmia and Mazury in Olsztyn, 17(4), 351–360. (2014)

Motorcycle Parking Design with Simulation Approach Case Study: Rusunawa Penjaringan Sari 3, Surabaya

Yohanes R. Krisnanda[1], *Indri* Hapsari[1*], *Jerry* A. Arlianto[1], *Anton* J. Tjahjoanggoro[2], *Markus* Hartono[1], *Marselius* S. Tondok[2]

[1] Universitas Surabaya, Industrial Engineering, Raya Kalirungkut, Surabaya, Indonesia
[2] Universitas Surabaya, Faculty of Psychology, Raya Kalirungkut, Surabaya, Indonesia

Abstract. Rusunawa Penjaringan Sari 3 is flats owned by Surabaya City government with capacity 99 units. The current motorcycle parking lot has a total area 185.61 m^2 and the parking slot dimension is 2 m X 0.7 m. It can accommodate 100 until 145 motorcycles. This limitation space makes motorcycles must park randomly and irregularly, such as parking at the space for people walking and parking in parallel that can block a motorcycle that wants to go out. Improvements that we did for parking layout in this research is based on parking standard, published by Indonesia Directorate General of Land Transportation. Each motorcycle has parking alternative slot dimension 2 mx 0.85 m and the aisle width is 1.6 m and double way. Using simulation approach by ProModel, we developed 4 alternatives and compared them. The average time for residents to de-park until leave from parking space motorcycles decreased from 56.118 seconds to 17.342 seconds (alternative 1), 17.2273 seconds (alternative 2), 21.986 seconds (alternative 3), and 17.242 seconds (alternative 4).

1 Introduction

Rusunawa Penjaringan Sari 3 is a flat that established since 2010 and have aims to provide temporary shelter for residents as a victim of evictions. They can rent the unit and pay each month. This five floors building have capacity 99 units. Most of the occupants use motorcycle to support their mobility, and each unit may have more than one motorcycles. Total motorcycle residents recorded through observation and interview to each unit are 145 motorcycles and they are divided in two areas of parking. The first parking area is below the building with dimension20 m x 4.8 m and the capacity is 58 motorcycles, while another parking area is located outside the building with dimension of 15.45 m x 5.80 mand enough for 42 motorcycles. Due to the capacity of those parking area that only for 100 motorcycles, makes 45 motorcycles must park in parallel or in places that prohibited for parking. A good planning is needed to develop a new parking area that can accommodate the entire motorcycles and make the driver easier to park and de-park properly in available slots. When we observed at parking area, the aisle width in a narrow parking area is about 1 meter and the parking slot design is not complied with the standards of parking facilities. This is the root problem why the driver has trouble to park in parking area. The current parking slot dimensions is 2 m x 0.7 m, that is not fit with the standard.

In this research we developed alternatives for parking space with objectives to expand the capacity, faster park and de-park process, also offer the best alternative based on benefit cost ratio. We compared the result using simulation methods to see how our arrangement will work in certain conditions. Simulation is used because it can be solution for the problem. It is saving money, time and people because it is done by trial and error process. It can give capabilities and accuracy for the performance in complex system, it has strength as decision maker, give freedom to try different idea for result improvement, reduce the risk, time and destructive effect.

2 Literature review

Building parking lot for motorcycles requires variety of considerations and considers the standards that will guarantee sense of comfort and safety for the vehicle owner [1] namely:

1. Developers who build parking area should ensure the capacity and requirement based on Minnesota Asphalt Pavement Association. Some alternatives that can be used to maximize the parking area are:
   - Use rectangular shape
   - Use parallel long side
   - The second parking lane path should not interfere vehicle entrance and exit
   - The exit should not close to the current crowded streets
2. Angle parking that used to park vehicles. In general, the angle used is 60° to make it easier in enter and exit parking slot. Motorcycles that park in Penjaringan Sari 3 use 90° for more optimal utilization of parking space. However, this arrangement will make the

* Corresponding author: ihapsari@gmail.com

driver more difficult to park and de-park from the parking slot.

3. The dimensions of the parking area. Some dimensions that must be taken into account, such as:
   - The width and length of *slot* the parking vehicles must adapt the vehicle types. The motorcycle dimension parking slot that refers to the Directorate General of Land Transportation/ Direktorat Jenderal Perhubungan Darat [2] is 0.75 m x 2 m.
   - Pay attention to the angle of the parking slot to make easier for the rider to access the motorcycle.
   - The width to enter and exit along the parking area should be double way.
4. Signs/markers in the parking area. Providing sign/marker can give convenience to park and de-park every time. In general, marker of parking slot is line with the color white and yellow to give sign as a warning. Marker line must have 4-inch wide. For motorcycles in group could give a special color on the parking slot, for example blue for special needs or physical disability.
5. The security of the parking area [3]. Security is an important factor for the parking area which guarantee the safety to the vehicle owner. Some security alternatives for parking area are:
   - Lighting
   - Security cameras/CCTV.
   - Barrier gate to enter and exit from the parking area and it can only be accessed by occupants who has vehicle license.

To support the design of parking layout, this research needs simulation to run the model and compare the result. According to Kakiay [4] simulation modeling needs to consider three essential elements, namely: System*(system)*is a group of components or entities like human and machine that interact and act together to achieve the ultimate goal that is logical [5].

a. Entity*(entities)* is the items to be processed by the system (Arifin,2009). Entities are divided into several forms, including animate like customers or patients, lifeless like part or documents, and cannot be touched like technology advances that change physical letter to electronic mail(e-mail).

b. Attributes*(attributes)* is everything becomes the property of the entity.

In the process of simulation, model can deliver maximum results for the current state and for the future. The approach of real systems will be a conceptual model, but if it continues to simulation as experiment, it will get real data. Predictive approach comes from comparison result on real condition and new layout to find and analyze the differences [6]. For simulation steps in Figure 1 will start from step 1 which is define the object, set the limitations and requirements of the problem. Requirements needed to determine the resources, time, and costs to run the simulation project. Step 2 is to collect and analyze data from the real system. The results of this step is a conceptual model. In the step 3 create a simulation model for real system. Step 4 will validate the simulation model. The models will be checked and make sure that it describes the real system. Step 5 is conducting experiments by running simulations for each scenario of the model, then evaluates and analyzes the results. Last is step 6 to deliver the results. It will provide solutions or recommendations from the simulation results. Simulation will be used to evaluate parking space availability for existing layout and new layout design. By using simulation, the new design can accommodate more capacity [7].

Almost all the real condition from a problem can be modelled by simulation. Some requirements that must be fulfilled are the operational have implemented, the process easy to visualize and repeated, the activities are independent and various, the cost to decide and to invest is very big. System that is learn well will give a good model, so in simulation and real condition the model can give maximum result. Based on the concept in system, there are three simulation approach. Approach to real system will develop a conceptual model, but if it is learnt by experiment we will get real data. The other is simulation model approach by developing the model from real system and by simulating it. The prediction approach come from comparison real data and simulation data to see the difference between real condition and simulation model after the improvement.

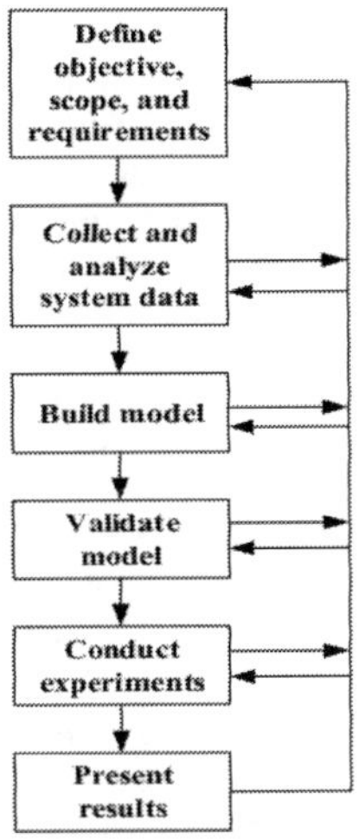

Fig. 1. Simulation Procedure [8]

Simulation model is visualization from real condition that will be analized to get the maximum result. In describing real system into the model, there is a possibility some mistakes were happened. The mistake is incompatibility between the simulation model and real condition, so the mocel cannot represent the condition. Verfiication and validation is important step to reduce or remove the errors [8]. The process can be seen in Figure 2.

Verification is a process to decide a simulation model has represented the conceptual model or not. The steps that can be done is review the model coding, check the logic output, check the animation and use tracing and debugging on software. Validation is the process to decide the conceptual has represent the real condition or not. To validate the model there are some steps like check the animation, compare with the real system, compare with other model, test with extreme condition, check the validation directly, test the historical data, sensitivity analysis, tracking and turing test.

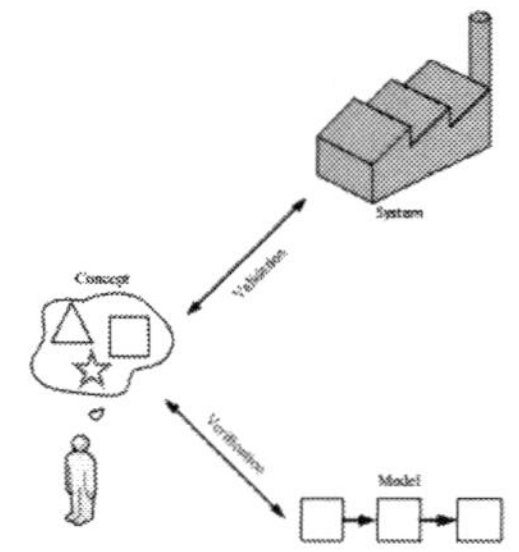

Fig 2. Verification and Validation [8]

3 Methodology

Motorcycles parking facilities in flat Penjaringan Sari 3 cannot accommodate all motorcycles owned by residents because of limited space and capacity. The existing parking area has no good arrangement so it is difficult for riders to park and de-park motorcycles. Another problem is there is no sign in parking area to manage all the motorcycles. Based on those problems, this research will design motorcycle parking area layout, parking slot, and motorcycles flow. The design will be run in simulation to prove how well this design if it is implemented.

There are primary data and secondary data collected in this research. Primary data come from observation to existing layout at the motorcycle parking area, layout of the flat surrounding, number and types of motorcycles owned by occupant, arrival time of the motorcycles, and time for motorcycle to enter and exit the parking area. For secondary data is reference about standard parking slot of motorcycles, comes from Planning and Operation Manual Parking Facilities that is issued by the Directorate General of Land Transportation [2].

4 Results and Discussion

By using software EasyFit Professional 5.2, we checked the data distribution. The data is time to enter and park the motorcycle and time between arrival. The distribution used in this study for initial layout is T (47 954, 60.07, 60.07), for new layout is (0.72545, 1.0371, 16:57, 18 367), and the time of arrival is (166.15).

Based on the observation, the dimension of motorcycle parking slot is 200 cm long and 75 cm wide, but it is also contained parking line that has width 10 cm. So, the total dimension of motorcycle parking slot as can be seen in Figure 3 is 200 cm long and 85 cm wide. The parking slot for every motorcycle will has dimension 175 cm long and 70 cm wide, with free space 5 cm at the front, 20 cm in the rear and 2.5 cm on right and left side.

There are two capacities that will be set for the new parking area. First is parking area consist of 145 motorcycles, this amount is based on the existing number of motorcycles that park in the flats parking area. Second is parking area that will be accommodate 297 motorcycles, because actually Surabaya City government as the operator allow maximum 3 motorcycles for each unit. Because there are 99 units in flats Penjaringan Sari 3, so there will be maximum 297 motorcycles.

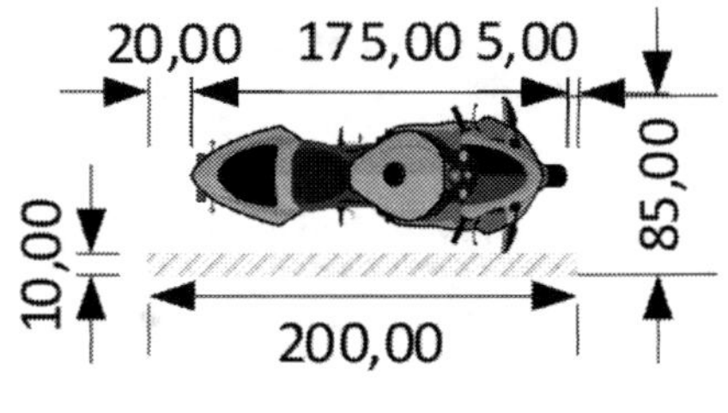

Fig 3. Satuan Ruang Parkir (SRP) for Motorcycle [2]

Another condition that must be set on parking area is exit and entrance must head to the 1st floor and 2nd floor because for now it is only one door with 2 meters wide. The aisle must be 1.6 meters for double way and 1 meter for one way. To make it clear, it needs sign like arrow to give direction for the riders. The new layout will use parking angle 90°to accommodate more motorcycles.

By considering buildings construction per level for parking area requires free space upwards of basic floor of at least 2.5 meters on each floor, construction of vehicles ramp to second floor 2.5 meters high and distance flatness is 5 meters, calculation of the building strength that has number and dimensions of the column to be used, we can summary the required space area as shown in Table 1.

Table 1. Summary of Alternative Capacity

	Alternati ve 1	Alternati ve 2	Alternati ve 3	Alternati ve 4
Size m^2	442.52	327.94	890.07	526.69
Capaci ty	159	189	300	317

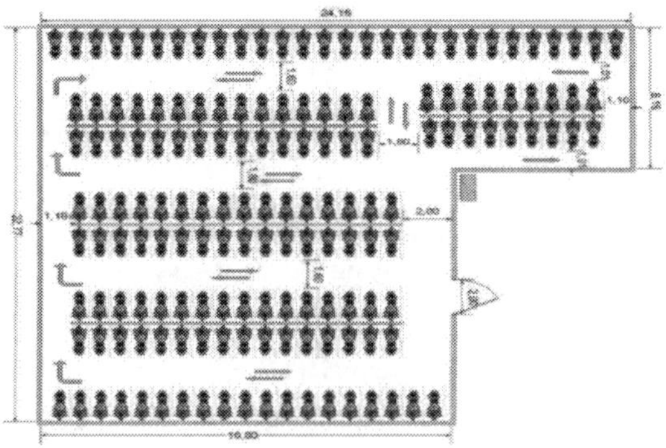

Fig 4. Layout and flow motorcycle for alternative 1

Alternative 1 in Figure 4 is an alternative construction of the parking building for existing number of motorcycles, allocated on the first floor. It will use the yard as the parking area as permission given by Kota Surabaya City government. With the new layout it can accommodate 159 motorcycles, more than existing number of motorcycles. In Figure 5, alternative 2 is the construction of a parking deck with a capacity of 189 motorcycles, allocated into two floors. The land use is less than alternative 1. We also made a regulation to separate female riders at first floor, and male riders at second floor. Alternative 3 in Figure 6is the construction of a parking deck with a capacity of maximum 300 motorcycles that is allocated in one floor. Alternative 3 requires a land area of 890.07 m^2 and located in two locations but still in flat's yard. Alternative 4 is the parking building with a highest capacity, 317 motorcycles, that is allocated into two floors. Alternative 4 in Figure 7 only require a land area of 526.69 m^2, less than alternative 3. The same regulation will be implemented in alternative 4.

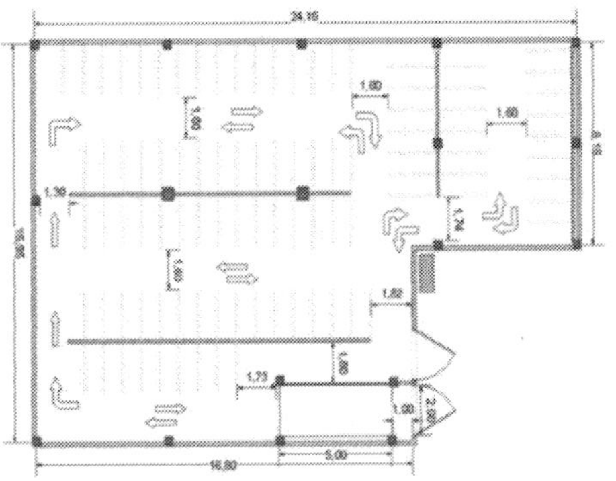

Fig 5. Layout and flow of motorcycles alternative 2

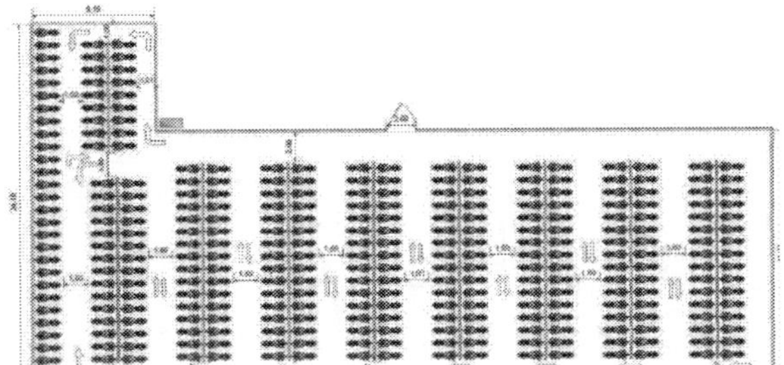

Fig. 6. Layout and flow motorcycle alternative 3

To create simulation model using ProModel Student Version 7, the components are location (entrance for the flats yard, entrance of flats, entrance of parking area), entities (motorcycle that goes to parking area, path networks from flats entrance to parking area and the surrounding), process, arrival (motorcycle that is came to entrance, and variable (parking slot capacity near to the exit door). The simulation has limitations and assumptions like the time taken for the ride of a motorcycle parking lot entrance to the second-floor parking area is 10 seconds and waiting time of the motorcycle for 8 hours.

For good simulation initial layout and the new layout each parking area is divided into 3 parts. The first is near or the closest location with the entrance. Usually it is become favorite for the riders because it is easier to park and de-park, and also it is needing less time to go out. But because of limited space, usually it only consists for few motorcycles. Second is medium location, not so far from the entrance and needs the bigger space. Third is far that has similar percentage with the near area but has the farthest location in parking area. The division is based on the assumptions based on observation that the favorite parking slot is within 5 meters in the parking area, then it continues to medium and far area. The division of the distance and the size of each location can be seen in Table 2.

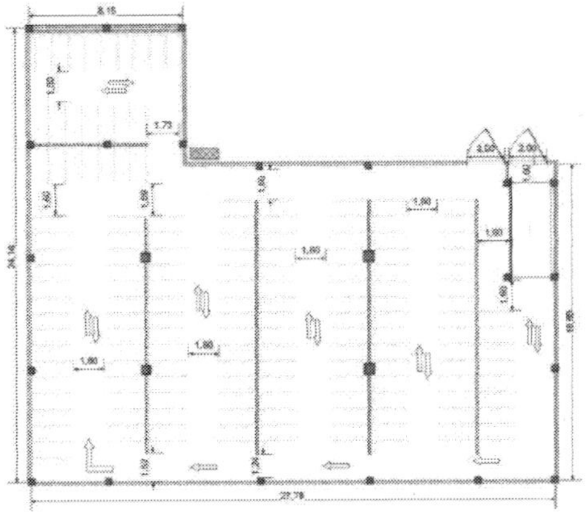

Fig. 7. Layout and flow motorcycle for alternative 4

Based on the simulation results showed that improvements of parking layout make a motorcycle out of the slot to be faster when compared to the initial state. At the beginning of the simulation results motorcycles time required to get out of his parking slot 56.118 seconds, while for each alternative as shown in Table 3.

The simulation is validated and verified using Minitab 17 with a significance level of testing (α) of 5%. The results of the validation stated that the model simulation with real conditions valid or H_0 is accepted. Testing to model alternatives give prove that model alternatives have shorter time for park and de-park from the parking area if it is compared with the initial model.

5 Conclusion

Limited parking space at Rusunawa Penjaringan Sari 3 Surabaya must be consider a serious problem for he residents.The existing number of motorcycles still cannot accommodate by the facility, moreover if the requirement is getting higher. To support the needs this research will proposed a new design of parking area that it used to be in area people walking. We designed four alternative of parking layout that consider the peak and non peak time, and also follow the rule by Indonesia Government. The result is very good, now riders can save the time until 75% effectively, and the capacity is getting bigger. Vallidation and verification have done and guarantee the simulation represent the real data. The model still has the assumptions like capacity distribution percentage or assumptions about favorite area. It is better to get the real data. However, this paper has offered some alternatives that can be used as motorcycle parking area.

Table 2. Capacity Distribution of Parking Area

	Under Building		Outside of the Building		
	Radius (m)	Capacity (units)	Radius (m)	Capacity (units)	
Near (30%)	6.1	16	4, 63	14	
Medium (45%)	15.3	28	11.58	20	
Far (25%)	20.4	14	15.45	8	
	Alternative 1		Alternative 2		
	Radius (m)	Capacity (units)	Radius (m)	Capacity Lt. 1	Capacity Lt. 2
Near (30%)	3.42	13	4.79	4	4
Medium (45%)	8.54	104	11.97	64	54
Far (25%)	11.39	42	15.95	27	36
	Alternative 3		Alternative 4		
	Radius (m)	Capacity (units)	Radius (m)	Capacity Lt. 1	Capacity Lt. 2
Near (30%)	7.11	22	8.33	15	30
Medium (45%)	17.78	142	20.84	101	74
Far (25%)	23.71	136	27.78	43	54

Table 3. Average Time Motorcycle Exit the Parking Slot

Alternative	Time (sec)
Alternative 1	17.342
Alternative 2	17.273
Alternative3	21.986
Alternative4	17.242

References

1. J. A. Stark, *Parking Lots: Where Motorists Become Pedestrians.* Albany University, (2012)
2. Direktorat Jenderal Perhubungan Darat, *Pedoman Perencanaan dan Pengoperasian Fasilitas Parkir,* Jakarta : Direktorat Jenderal Perhubungan Darat, (1998)
3. Menteri Perhubungan Republik Indonesia, *Peraturan Menteri Perhubungan Republik Indonesia Nomor PM 13 Tahun 2014,* Jakarta, (2014)
4. T. J. Kakiay, *Pengantar Sistem Simulasi,* Andi Publishing, Yogakarta, (2004)
5. A. Law, *Simulation Modeling & Analysis,* Boston : McGraw Hill, 2007. **Vol. IV**, (2007)
6. M. Arifin, *Simulasi Sistem Industri,* Yogyakarta : Graha Ilmu, (2009)
7. J. M. Harris, Y. Dessouky, A Simulation Approach for Analyzing Parking Space Availability at A Major University, *Proceedings of the Winter Simulation Conference,* (1997)
8. C. Harrell, K. G. Biman, B. O. Royce, *Simulation Using ProModel,* New York : McGraw-Hill, (2003)

MATEC Web of Conferences **215**, 01009 (2018) https://doi.org/10.1051/matecconf/201821501009
ICTIS 2018

Development and Designing Smart Traffic Light with Xbee Pro

Alfith Alfith *, Kartiria Kartiria

Institut Teknologi Padang, Department of Electrical Engineering, Indonesia

Abstract. The main function of the highway are used as a means to facilitate transportation, but today is often challenging due to all road users wanting more quickly reach its destination and precede each other. On the other hand, there is also a special car or entourage effect on traffic density, which in turn impact on congestion. To cope with this is actually the duty of the Traffic Police is not every day got in the way to manage traffic and will not be able to count the number of passing vehicles. To direct the traffic at any place such as a T-junction, an intersection, or intersection five solid pace of the traffic, the necessary traffic arrangements multifunctional tool called Smart Traffic Light. Called smart because the traffic light is deemed able to overcome three problems, such detect traffic density which affects the green light sensor uses the object infrared, able to detect the presence of specific signal from cars special like ambulance or fire engine or police or the like are automatically will change traffic lights red to green light using the XBee wireless module Pro and GPS, and seeks the traffic lights stay lit even though the supply of PLN extinguished using a spare battery. The system is capable of regulating the rate of traffic by arranging alternately road vehicle that passes a certain spot every day for nearly 24 hours a day and on these tools need to pair every day.

1 Introduction

The development of technology in this day and gerund very fast. Various kinds of works technology were created to facilitate humanity in running all kinds of daily activities. In Indonesia, especially users motor vehicles are increasing, consequently the number of vehicles goes up but the number of streets remains thus increasing the amount of traffic density which resulted in congestion. The jams such appear may be caused by some factors, one of which is the light regulator factor traffic [1]

Currently in Indonesia light-controlled technology traffic lights to continue to be developed in such a way, so the role of the traffic light is not just for avoiding congestion alone but also playing the improved role of traffic safety. Lights there at traffic that is currently applied is considered not yet optimal traffic congestion, not to mention there is a special car or an influential entourage on the traffic density that impacts on congestion. To tackle this fact is a police duty not every day are on the road to set up traffic and do not will be able to calculate the number of vehicles that passes. Therefore, a tool is required cross-multi functional. This tool is able to set the rate then crosses by arranging the vehicle's way taking turns that pass a certain place every day for almost 24 hours a day [2].

2 Research Methods

The method used in this research is with a field study of past the daily activities the real cross that will then be converted into miniature look like the real form of sample mocks follow actual shape. All traffic activity on the miniature will all be programmed through microcontroller using Code Vision software AVR. [3]

In addition to using the program, that method used in this study also simulated one part of the system block is a rectifier single full-wave phase. This simulation is done to get pure DC wave results after passing through filter C. The pure wave used for supply driver not to cause the ripple that can make output a less good circuit. Software that issued is Power Simulator (PSIM) foresees the results of a wave of input or output a circuit. [4]

Learn more from the system as a whole, can be seen in the block diagram shown in figure 1. Power of the transformer, in part used for the source of the rectifier, in part again used for charging accu source. In this project, used two microcontrollers for different needs. The first using ATMega 128, shocked port This microcontroller is used for display 7 segment, push button circuits, LCD, Xbee Pro(client), object sensors, and light to load. And the second microcontroller uses ATMega 162, ports in this microcontroller are used for GPS, Xbee Pro (server), and dipswitch. Second this microcontroller gets the source of the battery, so when the main supply goes out, work from both this microcontroller will keep running with getting backup of batteries, so system works plan still running. Wireless module in this research is used for data communication between Xbee obtained from GPS as a determinant of the existence of cars special that go, like the ambulance or fire fighters or police or the like [5-6].

*Corresponding author: alfith.st.tumangguang@gmail.com

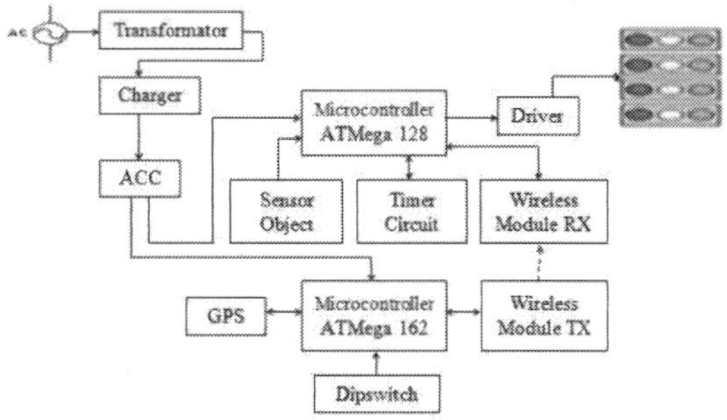

Fig. 1. System Blocks Diagram

3 Result and Discussion

The rectifier in this study is used to assure battery charger that works online to continue to supply the microcontroller in order lights up even if the primary source an off.

To design a rectifier circuit a full 1 phase wave is needed to calculate the value of the right components. Due to incorrect components values, it can cause voltage poor output results, such as the discharge of the ripple and the output voltage too big. To design this circuit, it is necessary defined several variables, namely:

- Input voltage : 12 V
- Capacitor : 4700 uF 50 V

From the data specified above, it can be calculated the values of components used, namely:

- **Value Vm**

$$Vs = \frac{Ns}{Np} x\ Vp \quad (1)$$

$$Vm = \sqrt{2}\ x\ Vs \quad (2)$$

$Vm = 16.97 Volt$

- **Output Voltage**

$$Vdc = Vm\left(1 - \frac{1}{4fR}\right) \quad (3)$$

$Vdc = 15.029 Volt$

- **Value of Ripple Factor**

$$RF = \frac{1}{4\sqrt{3}fRC} \quad (4)$$

$RF = 0.0976 Volt$

Battery Charger here functions to fill battery of constant current until it reaches specified voltage. When the voltage level is determined it has been reached, then the charging current will drop automatically to a safe level precisely pre-determined and withstanding the current charging up to be so slower the led indicator lights up indicating the battery has fully charged. The battery charging circuits used in this study is shown on figure 4 and battery charger test results shown in table 1. From the above component values, it can be simulated to wave rectifier with using PSIM as shown in figure 2 and figure 3.

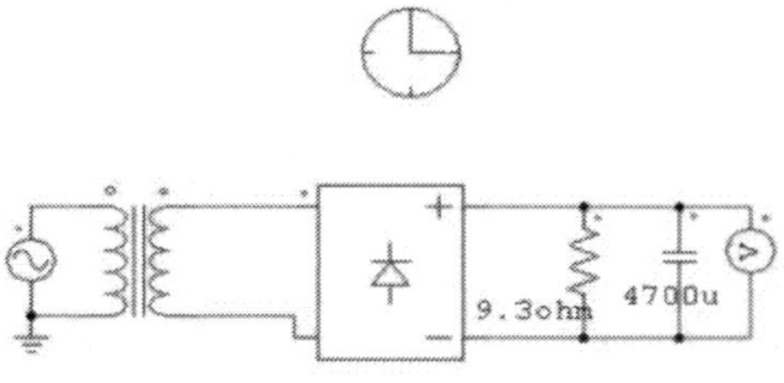

Fig. 2. Simulation Circuit of Single Phase Full-Wave Rectifier

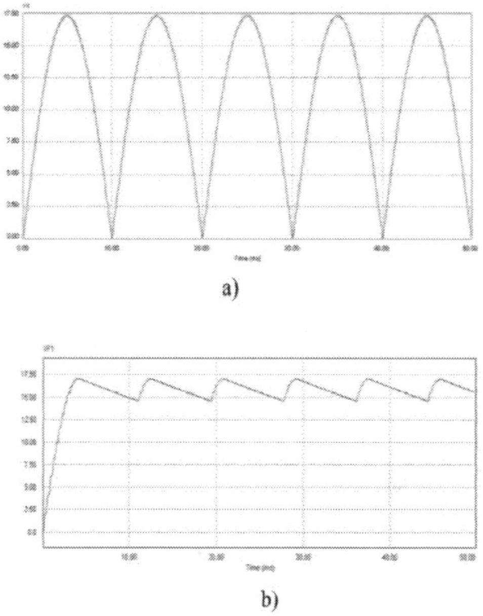

Fig. 3. Single wave full-wave rectifier wave output, a) without filter C; b) with filter C

Testing is done by using the battery 12 Volt 5 Ah with the result:

- Charging Voltage : 12.87 Volts
- Charging Flow : 1 Ampere
- Charging Duration (Ta) : 5 hours

$$Ta = \frac{Ah}{A} \quad (5)$$

Length of charging time of battery it is estimated that only 3 hours turns out in practice5 hours, because the input voltage is used still not great. However, in charging the battery, standard charging current ranges from 10% - 30% of Ah battery, the better use is the range 10% of Ah battery because it will not damage the battery. In practice this turns out the range used is:

$$1 = \frac{a}{5} x100\% \quad (6)$$

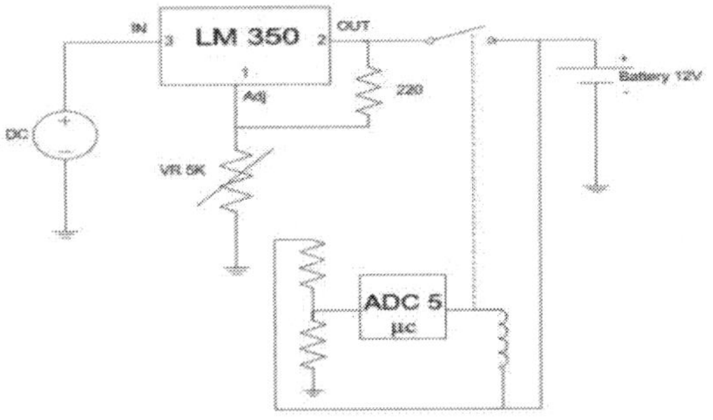

Fig. 4. Battery charger circuit

Table 1. Results of charging battery

No	Input Voltage (Volt)	Before connecting to battery Output Voltage (Volt)	Once connected to the battery Output Voltage
1	15	13.49	12.87
2	16	14.05	13.01
3	17	14.05	13.01
4	18	14.05	13.01
5	19	14.05	13.01
6	20	14.05	13.01
7	21	14.05	13.01

Table 2. Test data of relay work

NO	Reference Battery Voltage (Volt)	ADC readings (5)	Condition
1	13	255	Relay NO (Fully Charging)
2	12.8	231	Relay NC (Charging)

The circuit used is a circuit BCD to 7 segments to display seven segments of each side ith the intersection. Seven segments that used is common anode. Every seven segments of drive by 1 piece of IC 7447 so total overall for BCD to 7 segment series need 4 port microcontrollers. As for BCD to 7 segment circuits used on This study is shown in figure 5.

This d-latch circuit is used for minimizing the port used on microcontroller. If not using the circuit this, the port used for the seven segment its self-amounted to 4 ports. Due to the limited number of ports with the required ports, then this circuit is used so that only one-half ports are used. 1 full port for output and 4 bits for control of each IC. The IC used is DL-Latch IC type 74LS373N. The schematic of the driver circuit used can be seen in figure 6.

From the schematic of the circuit, it can be seen that the input comes from the seven-segment board itself that uses the BCD circuit of IC 7447. Each BCD input connected to input of each IC d-latch 74LS373N. All the output of the 74LS373N IC is paralleled on connector to enter into the microcontroller port need one full port, then VCC each IC coupled in with separate connector as the control is also included in the port microcontroller but only four bits are used.

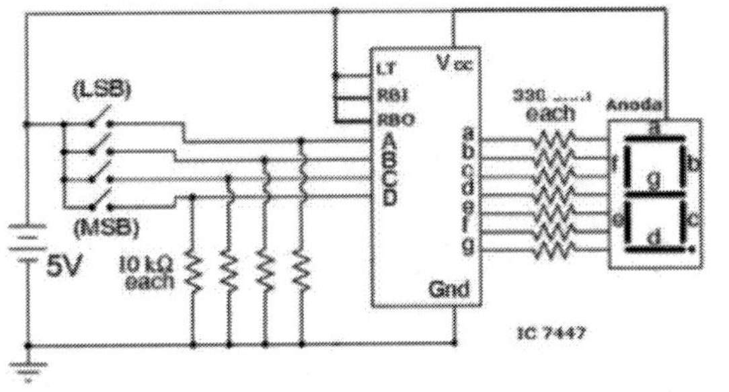

Fig. 5. BCD to 7 segment circuit

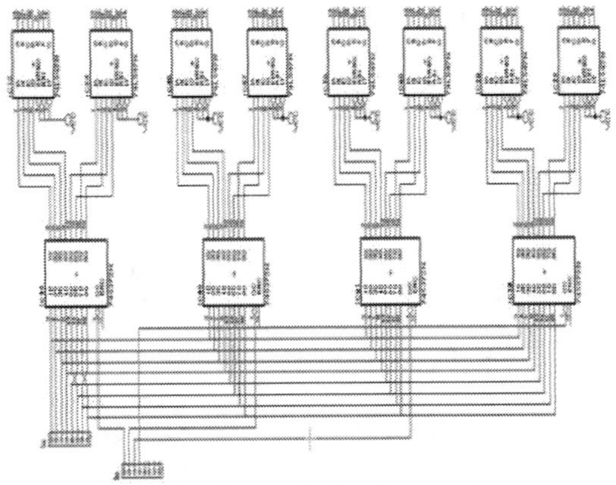

Fig. 6. Schematic of D-Latch circuit

In this case, X-bee pro wireless module used for communication between X-bee insides sending data onto GPS. Data that can be from GPS, received by Xbee transmitter (server) on microcontroller AT-Mega 162 and will be sent to second wireless module as Xbee receiver (client) on AT-Mega 128 microcontroller.

Communication happens to this module is communication between server-client Xbee without monitoring via PC but delivery results as well as data reception is displayed via LCD. The process of sending such data can be viewed through hyper terminals using serial cable.

Before using the Xbee ProModule, it is recommended to set baud rates module (figure 7) first and check whether the circuit is used is correct. Both steps can be done through X-CTU software. After baud rate set, can test circuits of "Test / query".

- Transmitter mode : Asynchronous
- Baud rate : 9,600 bps
- Data bit : 8 bits
- Stop bit : 1 bit
- Parity bit : none

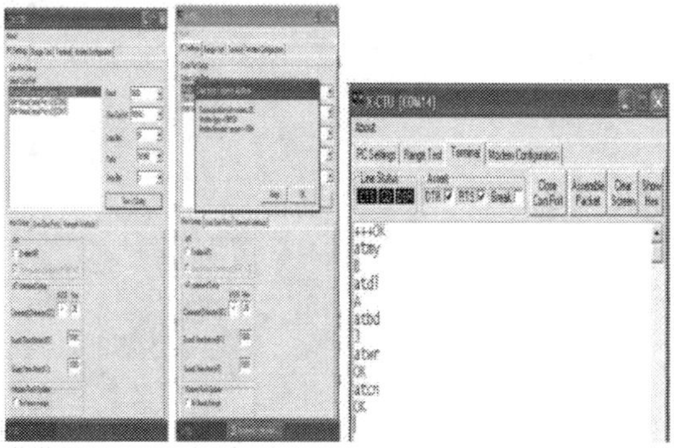

Fig. 7. Setting baud-rate module

When the comment states "OK" then the circuit that we design is correct. Next the process of addressing self-module, can already done using to comment instruction in the X-CTU form as well. After testing and self-addressing has been successful, communication tested to inter wireless module can be done. Results communication is displayed in hyper terminals.

GPS testing are done to retrieve data ontt the location or existence of that object shown in latitude and longitude coordinates on LCD screen (figure 8).

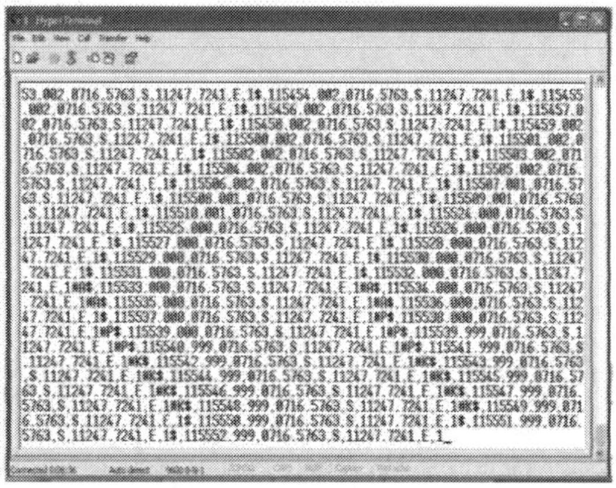

Fig. 8. GPS Testing

4 Conclusions and recommendations

After the planning process is done, manufacture and testing for tools as well as with comparing with supporting theories and from the data obtained then it can be taken conclusion:

1) The output voltage of the infrared sensor can work well in detecting objects, but in the dispersion between the receiver and the transmitter sensor the super-precise probe to obtain the appropriate output results.
2) Battery can back up the main supply work when it goes out with online battery system.
3) For data retrieval of GPS and Xbee pro, should be done in an open space, without barrier. Because of the sensitivity of GPS and Xbee pro used is limited. Moments Xbee pro tests, inter Xbee position must be straight and without any barrier, because can lead to chaotic output results. So also, with GPS, the antenna must be facing directly to the sky and without any obstruction. Latitude and longitude data obtained from GPS able to determine the location and from which direction comes an object.

References

1. Alfith, Alfith., Perancangan Smart Traffic Light Berbasis Microcontroller ATMega 16, Jurnal Momentum, **17** (1), 1-7, (2015).
2. Alfith, Alfith., Konfigurasi Battery Pada Pembangkit Renewable Energi, Journal of Teknik Elektro ITP, **4** (1), 46-50, (2015).
3. Syafaruddin, E. Karatepe, T. Hiyama, Artificial neural network-polar coordinated fuzzy controller based maximum power point tracking control under partially shaded conditions, *IET Renew. Power Gener.*, **3**(2), 239-253, (2009).
4. A. A. Hussein and I. Batarseh, A review of charging algorithms for nickel and lithium battery chargers. *IEEE Trans. Vehicular Technology*, **60** (3), 830-838, (2011).
5. B. Sahu, G. A. Rincón-Mora, Accurate, compact and power-efficient Li-Ion battery charger circuit, *IEEE Trans. Circuits Syst. II, Reg.* Papers, **53** (11), 1180-1184, (2006).
6. Y. C. Kuo, L. J. Liu, and H. C. Lee, Analog Controller IC Design for Single-Stage Photovoltaic Inverters, *International Conference on Fuzzy Systems and Knowledge Discovery*, pp. 2423-2426, (2011).

Design of Fuel Anti-theft Based on Micro-controllers using Short Message Service

Andi Syofian[1*], Yultrisna[2],

[1]Institut Teknologi Padang, Department of Electrical Engineering, 25143 Nanggalo, Padang, Indonesia
[2]Politeknik Negeri Padang, Department of Electrical Engineering, 25163 Limau Manih, Padang, Indonesia

Abstract. Theft of premium oil in Tank Trucks is very frequent done by irresponsible people. In general, the tank security system uses only the seal on the door of the faucet, therefore the seal can still be duplicated. To overcome this problem, its security system needs to be transferred to an electronic system with premium automatic delivery system control using HC-SR04 ultrasonic sensors and push-button. The system will send the fuel level information (premium) with SMS and display on the LCD when the charging or distribution is complete. There are 3 (three) premium levels that will be applied to the system. The first delivery condition of the tank is a 5 liter tank, the second condition from the tank to the gas station 1 3 liters and the third condition from the tank to the gas station 2 that is 2 liters. This system starts by activating the push button that functions as a motor drive switch and ultrasonic HC-SR04 sensor to detect premium level heights when premium sensitivity reaches heights will turn off the wiper motor driver. Premium volume will be informed to the user (the owner of the tank in the form of SMS using the SIM 900. The advantage of this tool is to detect premium theft in the premium tank by sending SMS ownership from the tank. This system can detect the theft of premium tanks via SMS, apply ultrasonic sensors (HC -SR04) to detect premium level heights the type of mass of the 0.76 kg premix affects the height at the volume of the tank. When the high volume of the 5 liter tank between the sensor and the premium is 7.63 cm, when the 2 liter volume high between the sensor and the premium is 13 , 63 cm, while at the time of empty tank (0 liters) the height of sensor with premium is 17,63 cm.

1 Introduction

Premium is a clear yellowish color distillate oil. Premium in Indonesia marketed by Pertamina with a relatively cheap price because it obtains a subsidy from APBN Premium is the premium for the most popular motor vehicles in Indonesia. Premium in Indonesia marketed by Pertamina has a relatively cheap price because it obtains a subsidy from the state budget. But recently the rampant premium scarcity is a problem that has an impact on society, especially for people who drive. The absence of the premium will cause the vehicle to not operate. This prompted many cases of premium theft in Indonesia. This theft mode is done by the driver or other party when the distribution on the truck tank often occurs theft with the term "urine arbitrary" or reduce the premium charge before getting to the gas station by irresponsible elements. Truck tank is a truck designed to transport a liquid or gas load. Until now for the security of premium shipping through Pertamina tank still handle it manually. So with the limited number of employees, all trucks can not be monitored optimally. On the system there is a push button to activate the wiper motor driver. The driver functions to control or disconnect and connect the current to the output to be used i.e. Motor Wiper. Wiper motor that will push it out and will stop when it is finished filling either to the truck tank or gas station 1 and gas station 2 with controlled by ultrasonic sensor that is HC-SR04. When the charging has finished LCD display will appear and sending SMS to the user about the remaining premium on the tank will be done in tandem [1-5].

2 Literature Review

Ultrasonic sensors are sensors that transmit sound waves and then monitor their reflections so that they can be used to determine the distance between sensors and objects that reflect back sound waves can be seen in Figure 1 below. One of the sensors that people often use in experimenting is HC-SR04. Handling distances range

*Corresponding author: andisyofian@itp.ac.id

from 2 cm to 400 cm, with a precision level of 0.3 cm. Detection angles that can be handled no more 15 °. The required current is not more than 2 mA and the required voltage is +5 V. The number of pins is 4, the details of each pin can be seen in Table 1 below.

Fig. 1. Sensor Ultrasonik HC-SR04

Table 1. Pin configuration on sensor HC-SR04
Distance = Speed * T / 2

Pin	Information
Pin1	Vcc (dihubungkan ke tegangan +5V
Pin2	Trig (to transmit sound waves)
Pin3	Echo (to receive the reflection of sound waves)
Pin4	Gnd (connected to ground)

SR04 The distance between the sensor and the object that reflects the sound waves is calculated using the following formula: Distance = Speed * T / 2.

Arduino Uno is a microcontroller board based on ATmega328. Arduino Uno has 14 digital input / output pins (of which 6 can be used as PWM output), 6 analog inputs, 16 MHz ceramic resonator, USB connection, power jack, ICSP header and reset button can be seen in Figure 2 below. built on what is needed to support the microcontroller, resources can use USB power (if connected to computer with USB cable) and also with adapter or battery. following Arduino Uno Atmega 328 can be seen in **Fig.2**.

Fig.2. Board arduino uno 328

GSM Shield or GPRS (General Packet Radio Service) Shield is a product for your wireless Arduino needs. SIM 900 GPRS Shield can be seen in **fig.3**. Operates on GSM / GPRS 850/900/1800 / 1900MHz frequencies for voice, SMS and data transfers with low data consumption.

Shield GPRS is controlled using AT commands (GSM 07.07, 07.05 and SIMCOM Enchanced AT Commands). Compatible with Arduino UNO, Duemilanove, Seeeduino, Mega, and other compatible Arduino board. [3].

IComSat v1.1 SIM 900 GSM / GPRS shield has the following features:

a. It has four levels of network frequency (Quad-band), which is 850/900/1800 / 1900MHz.
b. GPRS data packet class 10/8.
c. Controlled with AT commands (GSM 07.07, 07.05 and SIMCOM enhanced AT Commands).
d. Power ON / OFF and reset function are supported by Arduino.them.

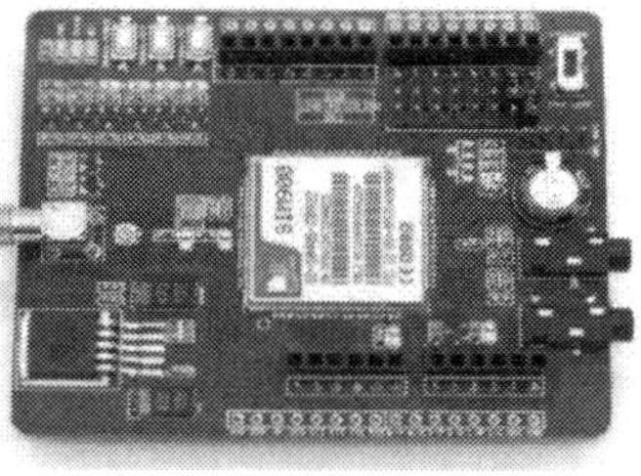

Fig.3. SIM 900 GSM shield

The data bus consists of 4 or 8 lines (depending on the mode of operation selected by the user). In 8 bit data mode, the path used is DB0-DB7, while for 4 bit data mode, the path used is DB4-DB7. Wiper motors are DC electric motors combined with natural magnets (ferrite magnets). As a stator and armature as its rotor. The following parts of the wiper motor can be seen in Fig.4.

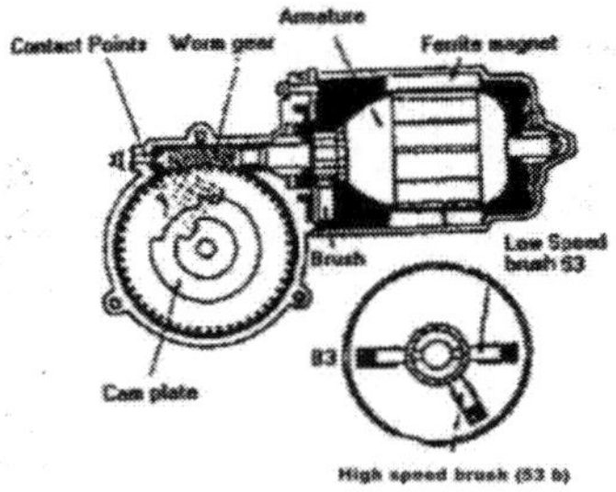

Fig.4. Parts of wiper motor

How it works Wiper motion is driven by a current flowed by the battery to the fuse and to the switch and onto the wiper motor so that the wiper motor can move properly. In Wiper, there are three movements that we often see that is slow (Low Speed), fast (High Speed) and slowly timed (Intermittent). Here is the movement of wiper motor seen in fig.5.

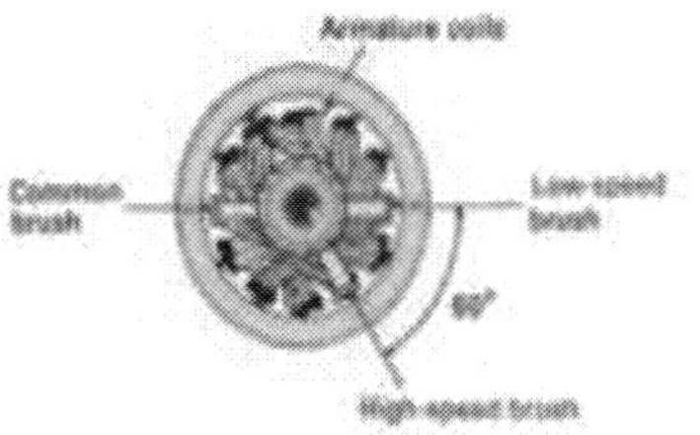

Fig.5. Movement of Wiper Motor

A relay is a device that operates on the basis of electromagnetics to drive a number of compacted contactors or an electronic switch which can be controlled from other electronic circuits by utilizing electric power as its energy source. The contactor will be closed (on) or open (die) due to the induced magnetic induction effect of the coil (inductor) when electrified.

Relay consists of 3 main parts, namely:

1. Common, is a part that is connected with Normally Close (under normal circumstances).
2. Coils (coils), are the main components of relays used to create magnetic fields.
3. Contact, which consists of Normally Close and Normally Open.

3 Experiment and Analysis

This test is done to find out the readability of sensors HC-SR04 and GSM shield, as shown in fig 6.

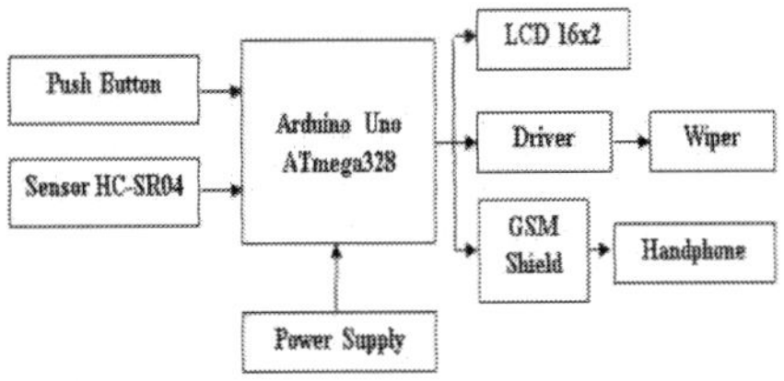

Fig.6. Block Diagram Prototype Premium Theft Detection on Microcontroller Based Truck Tank Using SMS Media (Short Message Service)

Tests performed at the measurement point (TP) can be seen in fig.7. Where measurements are made on the trigger pin and echo (sensor data) of the ultrasonic sensor.

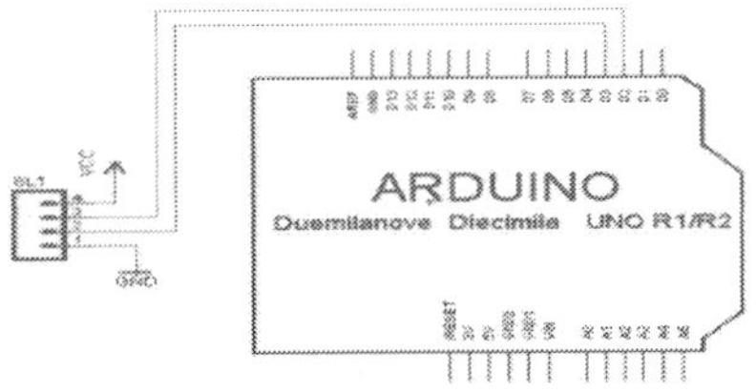

Fig.7. Trigger Voltage Measurement Circuit (TP1) and echo (TP2)

Table 2. Result of testing sensor distance

No	Actual distance (cm)	distance sensor (cm)	Eror %
1	10 cm	10.06	0.6 %
2	20 cm	21.00	5 %
3	30 cm	32.37	7.9 %
4	40 cm	43.65	9.02 %
5	50 cm	54.51	9.20 %
6	60 cm	65.56	10.90 %
7	70 cm	77.68	13.70 %
8	80 cm	90.96	13.20 %
9	90 cm	101.88	14.10 %
10	100 cm	114.19	13.70 %

From the results of Ultrasonic HC-SR04 sensor testing at the distance of the readable sensor with the distance measured manually (actual distance) there is a value difference (+) indicates that the tool made the measurement result is greater than the actual tool. In addition, measurement errors can also occur due to rounding of calculations at the time of making the program.

Using calculations below:

$$\rho = m/v$$

$$V = 1 \text{ liter} = 1 \ [\![dm]\!]^3 = 1/1000 \ m^3$$

Information:

ρ = density (premium = 760 kg / m ^ 3)

m = mass (kg)

v = volume (m ^ 3)

Here's a measurement table between the premium distance with the sensor:

Table 7. Ultrasonic sensor readings of HC-SR04 with Premium.

Volume	Sensor distance with premium oil
0 Liter	17.63 Cm
1 Liter	14.63 Cm
2 Liter	13.63 Cm
3 Liter	11.63 Cm
4 Liter	9.63 Cm
5 Liter	7.63 m

The overall test of the tool aims to know that the whole system functions as being cool both input and output. As for reference work tool.

Sensor Reader	SMS status	Condition of motor driver	LCD show
7.63	Accepted	Off	Shown Time Volume 5 Liter
13.63	Accepted	Off	Shown Time Volume 2 Liter
17.63	Accepted	Off	Shown Time Volume 0 Liter

4 Conclusion

Based on the above table it can be known, when the SMS will be received and at what distance the SMS will be received. The overall system test aims to know the course of the system, and to know the error that will occur on the system running so that the error can be anticipated and improved. In the table is known that the measured distance of the sensor will continue to increase along with the reduced premium detected.

References

1. Adi, Agung Nugroho mechatronics. Yogyakarta: PT. Graha Ilmu. (2010).
2. Kadir, Abdul, Practical Guide to Learn the Application of Microcontroller and Its Programming Using Arduino. Yoyakarta: CV. Andi Offset. (2012).
3. Kadir, Abdul. Arduino "Guide to Learn about Miscellaneous Microcontroller Based Projects". Yogyakarta: CV. Andi Offset. (2014)
4. Kadir, Abdul Smart Book of Arduino Programming.Yogyakarta: CV. Andi Offset. (2015).
5. Wekiardi, Hazni. Tugas Akhir. Short Message Service (SMS) Delivery Performation Analysis for prepaid subscribers on GSM network PT. Indosat Department Electrical engineering. Jakarta: Universitas Indonesia. (2008).

Identification Of Number Using Artificial Neural Network Backpropagation

Sitti Amalia

Institut Teknologi Padang, Electrical Enginering Department, Padang, West Sumatra, Indonesia

Abstract. This research proposed to design and implementation system of voice pattern recognition in the form of numbers with offline pronunciation. Artificial intelligent with backpropagation algorithm used on the simulation test. The test has been done to 100 voice files which got from 10 person voices for 10 different numbers. The words are consisting of number 0 to 9. The trial has been done with artificial neural network parameters such as tolerance value and the sum of a neuron. The best result is shown at tolerance value varied and a sum of the neuron is fixed. The percentage of this network training with optimal architecture and network parameter for each training data and new data are 82,2% and 53,3%. Therefore if tolerance value is fixed and a sum of neuron varied gave 82,2% for training data and 54,4% for new data

1 Introduction

Technology developed to create tools or facilities that can help and provide convenience for humans to perform activities in their life. Along with the development of technology, people always want to improve the quality and practicality of these tools. Therefore, there are machines that can interact with humans. This technology is called human machine technology. [1]

Human machine technology aims to create machines that have the ability to interpret information spoken by humans and act in accordance with the information submitted. In other words, create a machine with artificial intelligence so that it can interact with humans through sound. [2]

The human auditory system composed of the ear, nerves, and brain has the ability to distinguish one sound from another. This ability can be possessed by every human being if the human ever compares and senses the difference between one voice and another. The process of 'comparing and feeling' is part of the learning process in humans [2]. Sound processing techniques (speech processing) with sound recognition system (speaker recognition) developed based on the principles of this human hearing system. This system is used to recognize incoming sounds by comparing them with previously stored sounds on the system memory. This system makes it possible to use sound as a person's identification/proof [2] [3] [4].

The ability of a human hearing system to recognize sounds can be imitated to be implemented on machines, robots, security systems, etc. since its supporting components are available, ie microphone as an ear substitute, signal processing algorithms and Artificial Neural Networks ANN) that will perform the function as the brain.

Artificial Neural Networks are widely used in speech recognition because they can recognize well-tested sound patterns[4] [5] . This Artificial Neural Network is used because it has the ability to recognize patterns that are slightly changed from the original. This is similar to a human brain that is still able to recognize someone from a slightly changed voice over the phone. Artificial Neural Network is a model of computational system that works like a biological neural system, where Artificial Neural Network will serve as a substitute for the nerves and brain, which at the time will relate to the outside world, learning ability and generalization quickly and easily in recognition of a character pattern and easy to be implemented [5] . The artificial hearing system can be designed in such a way by mimicking some of the working principles of the human hearing system so that later the system can recognize sounds based on the sound waves it receives.

This network can recognize patterns of input from weights that are organized through a training. For this training process, the thing to note is to determine the right learning algorithm to get the weight.

Judging from the principle of backpropagation work (Backpropagation), it is seen that this algorithm can minimize errors may be close to or zero [4] [7] .So this study used Artificial Neural Network Backpropagation. Quite a lot of research and writing takes on topics related to speech recognition.

*Corresponding author: sitti@itp.ac.id

2 Literature Review

2.1. The Process Of Shaping The Human Voice Signals [7]

The process of spe`aking can occur if humans are able to issue an acoustic signal that we call also with sound. The human voice is produced by the interaction between the signaling organs.

The sound produced by the sound organs is generated due to the air pressure generated from the lungs which are then channeled to the windpipe. The air flowing through the windpipe will enter the larynx where there are vocal cords so that when air passes it vibrates so that it will produce air pulses. These air pulses will enter the vocal tract. In this section, resonance occurs air pulses which then form the sound patterns that produce voice signals. Sound signals generated from sound producing organs will be represented in the form of sound waves. Sound waves will form different types of patterns.

2.2 Definition of Artificial Neural Network[5]

Artificial neural networks are defined as information processing systems that have characteristics resembling human neural networks. Artificial neural networks are created as a generalization of the mathematical model of human understanding based on an assumption as follows:

1. Information processing that occurs in a simple element called a neuron.
2. The signal flows between nerve cells/neurons through a connecting link.
3. Each connecting connection has corresponding weights. This weight is used to multiply/multiply the signals sent through it.
4. Each nerve cell will apply an activation function to the weighted summation signal coming to it to determine its output signal.

Another definition of artificial neural networks is a biologically inspired computational model consisting of processing elements (called neurons) and their interconnected couples with the boundaries of coefficients (weights) to the connectors, which are neuronal structures, training, and recall algorithms which are put into structure [11].

Backpropagation network is one algorithm that is often used in solving complicated problems. This is possible because networks with these algorithms are trained using guided learning methods. In the network is given a pair of patterns consisting of the pattern of input and the desired pattern. When a pattern is given to the network, the weights are altered to minimize the difference in the pattern of output and the desired pattern. this exercise is done repeatedly so that all patterns issued by the network can meet the desired pattern.

The backpropagation neural network training algorithm consists of two steps: forward propagation and backward propagation is performed on the network for each pattern given during the training network.

2.2.1 Arsitektur *Backpropagation*

Backpropagation has several units in one or more hidden screens. Fig.1 is a backpropagation architecture with n input (plus a bias), a hidden screen consisting of p units (plus a bias), as well as m units of output units.

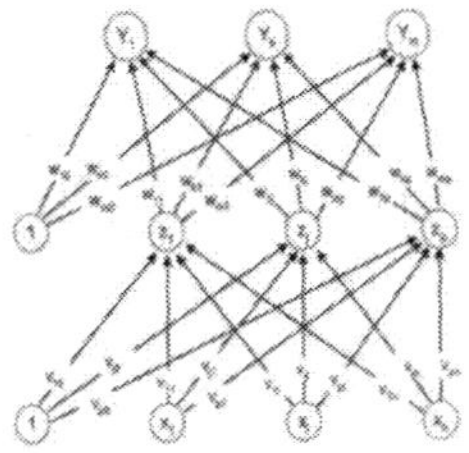

Fig. 1: Backpropagation Architecture

Vji is the line weight of the input unit xi to the hidden display unit Zj (Vj0 is the line weight that links the bias in the input unit to the hidden screen unit Zj).

Wkj is the weight of the hidden display unit Zj to the Yk output unit (Wk0 is the weight of the bias on the hidden screen to the Zk output unit).

2.2.2 Activation Function

In backpropagation, the activation function used must meet several conditions, namely: continuous, differentiated easily and is a function that does not go down. One function that meets these three requirements so often used is a binary sigmoid function that has a range (0.1).

$$f(x) = \frac{1}{1+e^{-x}}$$

with derivatives:

$$f'(x) = f(x)(1 - f(x))$$

Graph function is shown in Figure 2

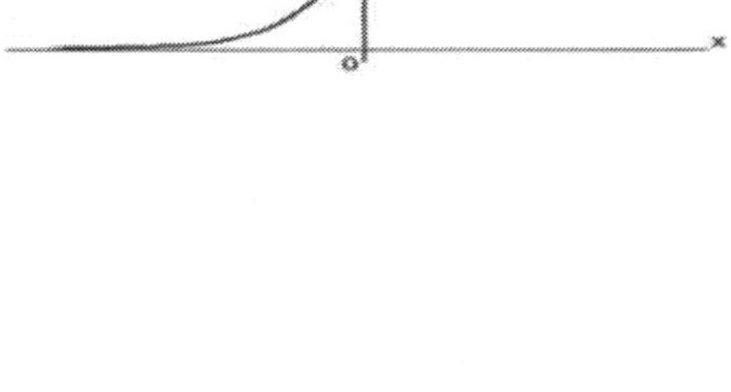

Fig. 2: Graphics sigmoid binary function

Another commonly used function is a bipolar sigmoid function that resembles a binary sigmoid function, but with a range of (-1,1).

$$f(x) = \frac{2}{1+e^{-x}} - 1 \qquad \text{pers(2.13)}$$

with derivatives:

$$f'(x) = \frac{(1+(f(x))(1-(f(x))}{2} \qquad \text{pers(2.14)}$$

Graph function is shown in Fig. 2

The sigmoid function has a maximum value of = 1. So for the target pattern 1, the input and output patterns must first be transformed so that all the patterns have the same range as the sigmoid function used.

Another alternative is to use the sigmoid activation function only on a screen that is not an output screen. In the output screen, the activation function used is the identity function:

$$f(x) = x$$

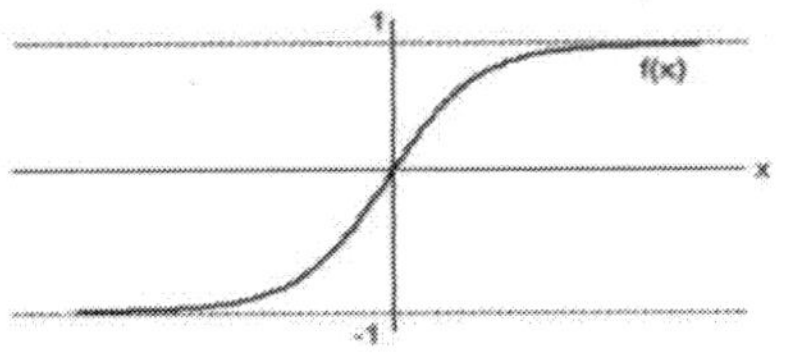

Fig. 3 : Graphics bipolar sigmoid function

2.3 The advantage of artificial intelligence [5]

Artificial neural networks have a large number of advantages compared with other calculation methods, namely:

a. The ability to acquire knowledge even under conditions of disturbance and uncertainty. This is because neural networks are capable of generalizing, abstraction, and extraction of statistical properties of data.

b. Ability to represent knowledge flexibly. Artificial neural networks can create their own representations through self-regulation or learning ability (self-organizing).

c. Ability to tolerate a distortion (error/fault), in which a small disturbance in the data can be regarded as mere noise.

d. The ability to process knowledge efficiently because it uses a parallel system, so the time required to operate it becomes shorter..

2.4 Training with and Without Supervision[5]

Based on how to modify the weight, there are 2 kinds of training that are known by the supervision (supervised) and without supervision (unsupervised). Training methods with supervision are used if the expected output is known previously. There are a number of existing data pairs (input-output targets) used to train the network until the desired weights are obtained. The data pair serves as a "teacher" to train the network to obtain the best possible form. "The teacher will provide clear information about how the system should change itself to improve its performance. In contrast, an unsupervised learning exercise does not require an output target or no "teacher" will direct the training process.

During the training process, the weighting value is arranged within a given range depending on the value of the given input. The purpose of this training is to group similar units within a particular area. Such training is usually very suitable for grouping (pattern classification).

2.5 Research Methodology.

In the first stage of data, retrieval is done by vocal recording 10 people, and each person pronouncing digit 0, 1, 2, 3, 4, 5, 6, 7, 8 and 9 are stored in one file with WAV format.

a. The second stage has extracted a feature of the recording data that has been stored in the file with WAV format. This feature extraction is performed digital screening of each speech data by using MFCC method. The result of the leaching obtained is spectral frequency, then it is domiciled so that the data form is a matrix.

b. The third stage is the process of building a neural network. The network model is a backpropagation network with guided learning system.

c. The fourth stage is a process of classification training on patterns of extraction of traits. Training is done by guided by correlating pattern of input with a goal (target). The training result is a weighted matrix that is stored to be called during the test process.

d. The fifth stage, namely testing of the ability of network systems that have been trained, in the testing process is used weights that have been obtained on the training results. As a network input used data that has been stored that has been characteristic extraction.

2.6 System Planning

Signal inputted to the computer via a sound card using a microphone. This sound signal was originally analog signals. These analog signals are then converted into digital form by using the ADC found on the sound card. The incoming sound signal is then processed to obtain the parameters. At first, the sound signal is clipped with a cuplik frequency that satisfies Nyquist criteria. Then the signal is blocked into frames. Signals that are still in the form of the frame are filtered by using a pre-emphasis which then carried out the windowing process. After that extraction parameter on MFCC to get cepstrum parameters. the resulting MFCC matrix will be the input on the artificial neural network. The process of this artificial neural network consists of two stages, namely the process of training and testing process.

In the training process will be obtained a result parameter. The results of this training will be stored as a reference model, where this pattern will be used in the testing process. After the training process is complete and each pattern has been obtained then the process will proceed with testing and decision making. The testing process is performed to test the ability of neural networks in recognizing each sound. This process is done by comparing the output of the sound being tested with the previously stored reference model. The system will correctly identify the sound when the sound is tested according to the trained person.

2.6.1 Training of Artificial Neural Network Backpropagation

The method used in this research is artificial neural network backpropagation. The structure of artificial neural networks used in the study are as follows:

a) Training using 100 training data.

b) There are 19 neurons in the input layer. This is matched to the number of matrix elements generated on the MFCC character extraction

c) There are 2 hidden layers with 35 neurons and 2 neurons.

d) A number of output neurons of 4 neurons, determined by the following considerations:

i. The words we will recognize are the numbers 0, 1, 2, 3, 4, 5, 6, 7, 8 and 9 as 10 character numbers.

ii. Each character will be converted into a bit encoding. The number of possible bits is 4 bits, which produces 24 different output variations.

2.6.1.a. Training

Since the artificial neural network used in this research is backpropagation, it first needs to build a network consisting of input layer, hidden layer, output layer, activation function at hidden layer and output layer, and training model used on backpropagation neural network using function :

```
net = newff (minmax (P), [35 2 4], {'logsig' 'logsig'
            'logsig'}, 'trainrp')
```

After finished building the network, the next step is to determine the parameters used during the training process, with the function:

```
net.trainParam.epochs    = 3000;
net.trainParam.goal      = 0.06;
net.trainParam.lr        = 0.1;
net.trainParam.mc        = 0.7;
net.trainParam.show      = 250;
```

After completion of forming the network and determining the parameters to be used in the training process, hereinafter is the training to be performed with the function:

```
net          = init (net)
[net, tr]  = train (net, P, T)
```

With:

Init =	function to initialize the weights and biases with new random values
Train =	function to train the network
P =	input data matrix
T =	target

Training will be carried out until the tolerance has been determined that is 0.006.

2.6.1.b. Testing

The test function used in backpropagation neural networks is:

```
A = sim (net, P)
```

At this stage of testing will be known to what extent the system can recognize the pattern of letters, against the pattern that has been trained.

2.7 Result and Analysis

2.7.1 Experiment Results

2.7.1.a. System Testing Trial with Number of Neurons in the First Hidden Layer 35 and Tolerance Value Vary from 0.05 to 0.07.

In this experiment aims to look at system capabilities when the parameters of the number of neurons in the hidden layer are constant at 35 and the tolerance values are varied from 0.05 to 0.07. The ability of this system is measured by the success rate in recognizing the entered word pattern. The results of this experiment can be seen in Appendix B and in Figure 5.1 below

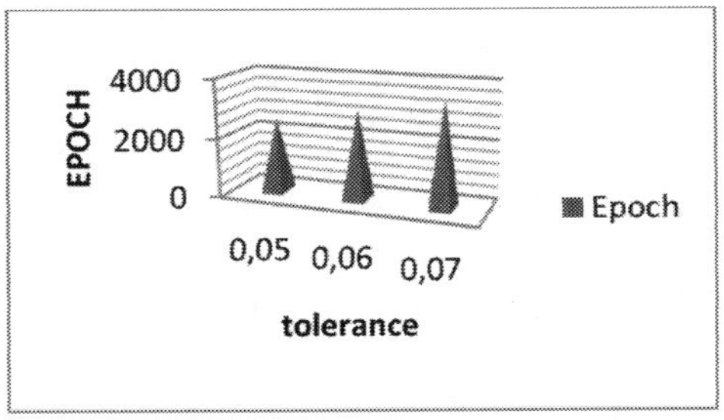

Fig. 4 : Graph of tolerance relationship to epoch

After the experiment, it is seen that the smallest tolerance of 0.05 is obtained at epoch 2500. When the tolerance value is enlarged then the number of an epoch is getting bigger, that is tolerance 0.06 epoch 3000, tolerance 0.07 epoch 3500. The graph of success rate can be seen in Figure 5.2.

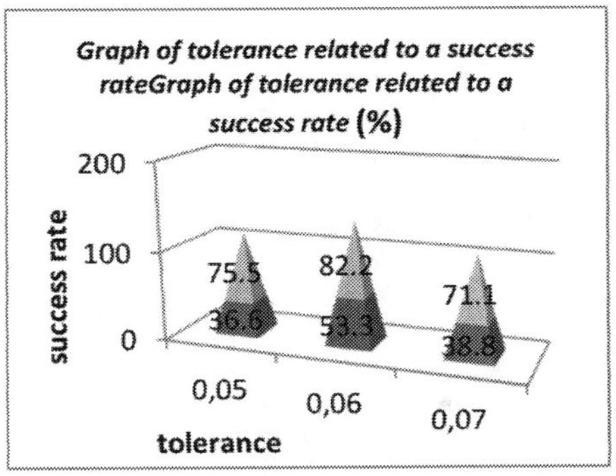

Fig. 5 : Graph of tolerance related to a success rate

Figure 5.2 above is a graph of tolerance related to the success rate of training data and new data (not trained). After the experiment, it was found that the greatest success rate of 82.2% for training data and 53.3% for new data was obtained at tolerance 0.06. When the tolerance value is magnified the smaller success rate is obtained, the tolerance 0.07 has a 71.1% success rate for training data and 38.8% for new data and tolerance 0.05 has 75.5% success rate for training data and 36.6% for new data.

2.7.1.b. System Testing Tests with Tolerance Value 0.06 and Number of Neurons in the First Hidden Layer Varies from 25 to 40.

In this experiment, it is aimed to see system capability when the parameter of constant tolerance value is 0.06 and the number of neurons in the hidden layer is varied from 30 to 40. The ability of this system is measured by the success rate in recognizing the entered word. The results of this experiment can be seen in Appendix B and in Figure 5.3.

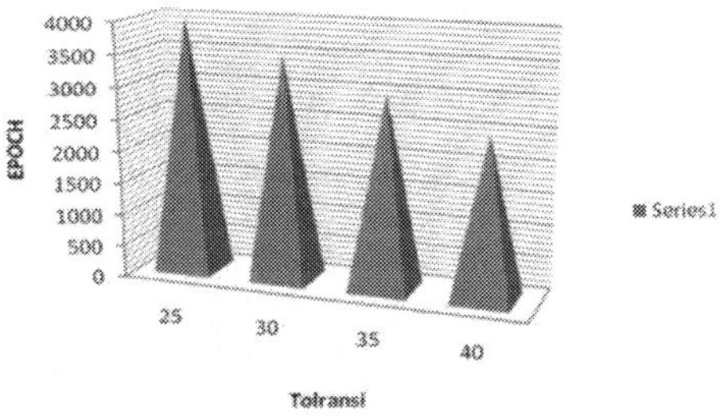

Fig. 6 : The graph of the number of neurons in relation to epoch

After the experiment, it was seen that to achieve a tolerance of 0.06 at the smallest number of neurons obtained at epoch 4000 and for the number of neurons obtained at epoch 3000, followed by the number of neurons 40 in epoch 2500

The graph of success rate can be seen in figure 7

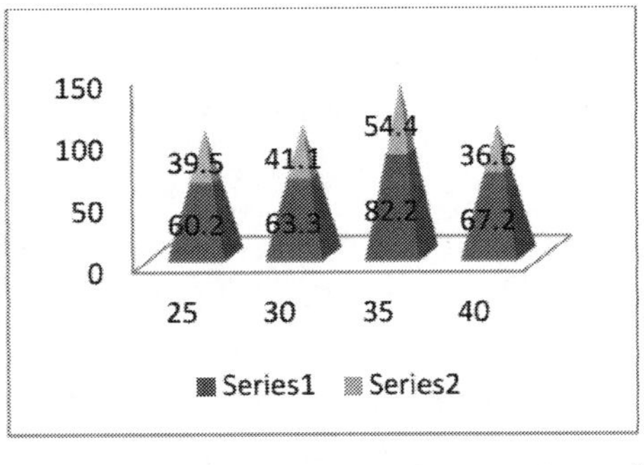

Fig. 7 : Graph of the relationship between the number of neurons to the success rate

After the experiment, it was shown that the greatest success rate of 82.2% for train data and 54.4% for new data was obtained on the number of layers 35. When the number of neurons was enlarged the smaller success rate was achieved, ie the number of neurons 40 had a success rate of 67.7% for training data and 36.5% for data. This tendency is also found when the number of neurons is reduced is the number of neurons 30 which has a success rate of 63.3.7% for the train data and 41.1% for the data neuron number 25 then obtained a low success rate of 60.2% for training data and 39.5% for new data.

2.8 Analysis

The rate of introduction of training data is higher than the rate of introduction of new data. Differences in recognition rates between train data and new data due to training data are have the same pattern structure as the data used during network training so as to produce a high level of recognition, while new data is data that has never been trained on the network although it has a similar pattern structure that produces a level of recognition that tends to be lower than the introduction rate of train data.

The amount of training conducted has an impact on the success rate of this system, the more training it has to do, the higher the success rate is also higher but it also depends on the tolerance value set.

The cause of this error is the ability of artificial neural networks that have begun to take on properties that are only specific to the training data (but not by the test data) so that they are trapped to local maximum conditions in the situation which the target the system is trying to reach are not found due to errors an increasing and unstable training that makes the system take decisions that are deemed to be closer to the desired target pattern.

3 Conclusions And Recommendations

Based on the analysis of the experimental results obtained, it can be taken several conclusions as follows:

1. Using artificial neural network introduction method got success rate of introduction to trainer data higher than with success rate of introduction to new data.
2. Simulation test result for tolerance values 0.05, 0.06, 0.07, and the number of hidden layer neurons obtained the success rate of training data of 75.5%, 82.2%, 71.1% and new data 36.6%, 53.3%, 38.8.3 %.
3. For the number of hidden layer neurons 25, 30, 35, 40 and tolerance values 0.06 obtained the success rate of training data of 60.2%, 63.3%, 82.2%, 67.7% and new data 39.5%, 41.1%, 54.4%, 36.6% .

After analyzing the system work and system output, for further research and development of this system, the authors suggest several things:

1. Simulation of different characteristic extraction algorithm method in the next research and development, such as the use of Linear Prediction Coefficients or combined Linear Prediction Coefficients with Mel-Frequency Cepstrum Coefficients (MFCC). So it is expected to give the extraction value more perfect traits
2., The expected increase the percentage of success in word recognition by using a combination of other artificial intelligence systems such as the combined Neural Network with HMM on further research

References

[1] Tolba, Hesham dan O'Shaughnessy, Douglas. *Speech Recognition by Intelligent Machines.* Sumber : Internet, file PDF

[2] Noel,Mike,*Principles of Speaker Recognition.* http://cslu.cse.ogi.edu/HLTsurvey/ch1node47.html

[3] Gu, Liang., *Perceptual Harmonic Cepstral Coefficients as the Front-End for Speech Recognition,* Signal Compression Laboratory Research Project. http://scl.ece.ucsb.edu/html/prpat_3.htm

[4] Liu, Wei, Huang, Xiaoling, Wang, Guan, Chai, Tianyou, *The Modeling and Application of Cost Prediction Based on Neural Network,* Research Center of Automation Northeastern University Shenyang, China.

[5] Jek Siang, Jong, 2005, *Jaringan Syaraf Tiruan & Pemogramannya Menggunakan MATLAB,* ANDI, Yogyakarta.

[6] Affan, Zaid, 2004, *Suatu Studi Sistem Identifikasi Sumber Suara Berdasarkan Koefisien Prediksi Linier dan Mel-Frequency Cepstrum Coefficient (MFCC) Dengan Menggunakan Jaringan Syaraf Tiruan Perceptron Lapis Jamak Perambatan Balik,* Tugas Akhir, Teknik Elektro Universitas Andalas, Padang.

[7] Lawrence R.Rabiner dan Biing-Hwang Juang. 1993. *Fundamentals of Speech Recognition.* Prentice Hall International, Inc

[8] Sanjit K.Mitra. 2001. *Digital Signal Processing : A Computer Based Approach.* Mc Graw Hill,Inc

[9] Hamza, Ade. 2006. *Pengenalan Identitas Sumber Suara Manusia dengan Menggunakan Metoda Fuzzy Neuro Network (FNN),* Padang, Universitas Andalas

[10] Hermawan,arief.2006. *Jaringan Saraf Tiruan, Teori dan Aplikasi,* ANDI, Yogyakarta

[11] Suyanto, 2005, *Algoritma Genetik dalam MATLAB,* ANDI, Yogyakarta.

[12] Silvana, Meza.2006 *.Optimasi Bobot jaringan Saraf Tiruan Menggunakan Algoritma Genetik dalam Identifikasi Suara.*Tugas Akhir, Padang, Teknik Elektro Universitas Andalas.

[13] Prihadi.2010. *Sistem Pengenalan Ucapan Jenis Digit Speech Recognition Menggunakan Logika Fuzzy.* Tugas Akhir.Padang: Teknik Elektro Universitas Andalas.

A Study of a CCD Camera for Vibration Measurement

Zulkifli Amin*, *Muhammad* Ikhsan

Universitas Andalas, Mechanical Engineering Department, Padang, Indonesia

Abstract. Vibration may occur in rotating equipment, for example on the transmission shaft of the gear. If the motor rotation is high enough, the load and torque could also be large enough. So that it can cause the shaft to vibrate and this vibration can damage the shaft. Therefore, the magnitude of vibration of the shaft need to be measured in order to monitor that the magnitude of the vibration is not high enough to damage the shaft. Usually for measuring the magnitude of this vibration is used a vibration meter. The weakness of the vibration meter is that the method of the measurement is by touching the measured object. So this measuring instrument is easily damaged by the vibration. An alternative to measure the vibration of a shaft is by applying an image processing method. Image processing is a method that performs processing of images digitally. The measurement of vibration by image processing method is tested on a vibrating shaft. The image of the vibrating shaft is captured by a CCD camera and then processed by a Matlab program to extract the value of vibration amplitude. From the tests performed, the measurement of vibration using the image processing method, the measurement can be done without touching the vibrating shaft. The obtained values of amplitude are deviate about 5.73% in average from the theoretical values. This method and tools can be used to measure the rotating shaft vibration amplitude provided the measurement instrument is calibrated prior being used by considering the value of deviation.

1 Introduction

Vibrations can occur in many components of machines for example on the transmission shaft gears. On the transmission shaft gears are mutually tangent for transmitting torque. This torque gives the load on the shaft radially. This load can cause the occurrence of deflection on transmission shaft rod. The deflection on the shaft causes the shaft not straight. This straightness deficiency causes the shaft to vibrate [1].

Rotating equipment produce vibration as a function of the dynamics of the machine such as un-straightness, misalignment and unbalance of the rotating parts. Measuring the amplitude of the vibration at certain frequencies can provide valuable information about straightness, alignment and balance of shafts, the bearing or gear condition, and the effects of the machine due to resonance from other structures Vibration caused by the rotating equipment such as motor, pump, and fan indicating the condition of the equipment. So, by conducting vibration analysis to check the characteristics of the vibrations, the condition of the equipment can be known [2].

Vibration measuring instrument commonly used is a vibration meter. This vibration meters are usually small and light. So, it is easy to carry. It generally consists of a probe and indicator to show the magnitude of the vibration. Vibration meter only gives information about the frequency of the vibration. This tool is generally used to determine mechanical condition and operation of an equipment. The weakness of the vibration meter is that the measurements is done only on a few specific points and the object to be measured need to be touched [3]. However, most machines in the industry, the vibration measurement point is located in a dangerous area. Sometimes, the vibration measurement point is difficult to reach when the machine is operating [4]. Therefore, to ease the vibration measurement and reduce the errors, it is proposed another method of vibration measurement. The method of vibration measurement by means of digital image capture on the objects, then the digital image is processed to be a numerical data which is used as the analysis vibration data. This method is usually called Digital Image Processing. A method of digital image processing is a method used to process or manipulate digital images which are stored in a two-dimensional scale [5].

The main components of the Machine Vision system consist of hardware and software. The hardware that will be used in machine vision are a camera and a computer. The camera is an optical tool that is used to record images captured by a sensor mounted on the camera. The camera will be in use is a digital type camera. A digital camera is a tool for creating images of objects for subsequent bias through the lens of CCD sensors and lately on BSI-CMOS sensors (Back Side Illuminated) more efficient power sensors for more sophisticated cameras whose results are then recorded in digital format to in digital save media [6]. An example

* Corresponding author: zulkifliamin@ft.unand.ac.id

of a software of a machine vision is Matlab. Matlab (Matrix Laboratory) is a program for numerical analysis and computation and is an advanced mathematical programming language formed on the premise of using matrix properties and forms. Matlab is a commercial product of the company Mathworks, Inc. which is developed using C++ and assembler languages [7].

2 Measurement Methods

This research was conducted to collect vibration data on the shaft that occurs by measuring the vibration indirectly with the camera aids. The camera is placed in front of the shaft with a distance of 30 cm. the camera will capture the pivot image directly on every second. The result will be processed later by Matlab. In the process there are three processes: Image Enhancement, image segmentation and image analysis. The purpose of the three processes is to determine the displacement position that occurs on the shaft when vibrating. The result of this process will be calculated by Matlab. The result of this calculation is the amplitude of vibration. The flow diagram of the measurement method can be seen in Figure 4.

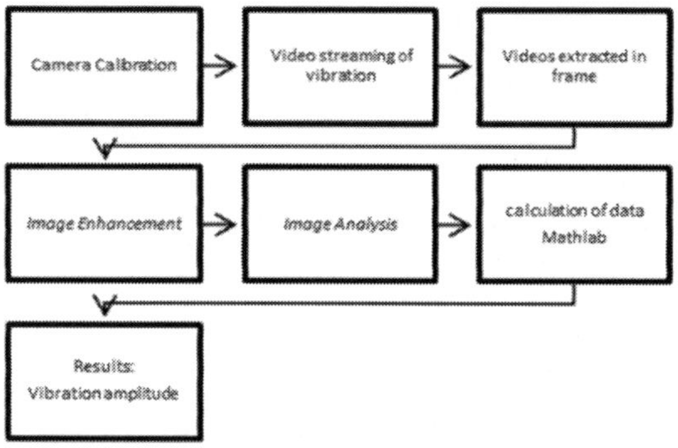

Fig. 4. Flowchart of the measurement method

As a constraint in designing a vibration measurement system on a cantilevered shaft with image processing method, the design specification is determined. The design of this test consists of two parts: vibration measuring instrument using image processing and model tested. The measurement test model can be seen in Figure 5.

Fig. 5.: Measurement test model

The vibration measuring device using image processing consists of a camera connected to a computer. The camera acts as a sensor of measurement and the computer as a transducer and a pointer or recorder during the measurement process. The model tested consisted of a shaft connected to a driving motor and loaded in the center of the shaft. The motor not only causes the axle to spin but also causes unwanted vibration effects. This vibration will be measured by a vibration measuring device using Image Processing.

3 Results and Discussion

The test results from three experiments of measuring the amplitude of vibration using the CCD camera are shown in Table 1. From data in the Table 1, there is a 5.73% difference between the results of the measurements made with this method of image processing compare to those of theoretical measurements. Although there is a difference of value of measurement, this still prove that the CCD camera can be used to measure the amplitude of vibration without touching the shaft. The accuracy of this vibration instrument can be improved by performing correlation and calibration to the CCD camera prior being used.

Table 1. Test results from three experiments of measuring the amplitude of vibration

n^{th} experiment	Measured amplitude (cm)	Theoretical amplitude (cm)	Error (cm)
1	0.117	0.376	0.178
2	0.343	0.376	0.339
3	0.361	0.376	0.359
		(Σe)	0.876
		(Σe^2)	0.276
			0.292

The standard error (SE):
Where: = average error of the *n*-th experiment
n = number of data

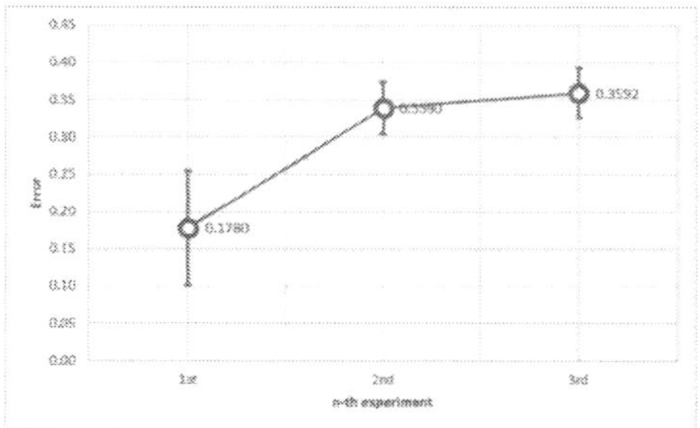

Fig. 6. Graph of vibration amplitude error from three experiments

The difference between the results of the measurements made with this method of image processing compare to those of theoretical measurements is due to lighting testing conditions that cause the camera difficult to focus on determining the light intensity released by the test model. In addition, the difference on test results is also due to that the speed of camera is not fast enough to capture the image frame. During period of measuring, the camera can only capture the shaft frame with a speed of 87 fps (frame per second) which is less fast. Speed of frame capture and lighting is very influential on program mapping. Mapping is done to determine the position coordinate of the vibrating shaft during frames capturing. In Figure 7 to Figure 9, it can be seen the script of the computer program as measurements software, image of the vibrating shaft captured by the CCD camera during measurements and the graph presenting the vibration measurements result respectively.

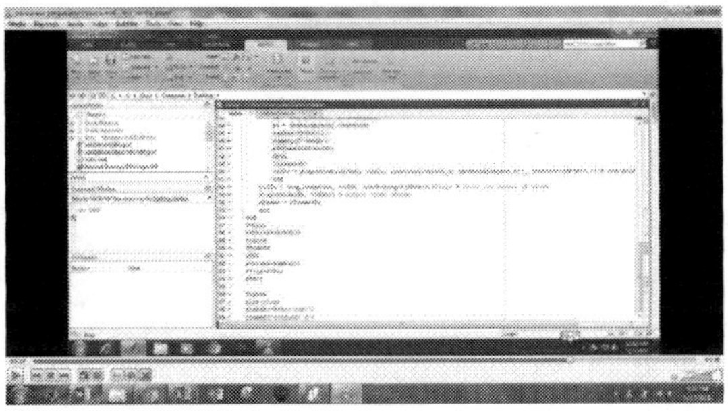

Fig. 7. Script of the computer program for taking measurements.

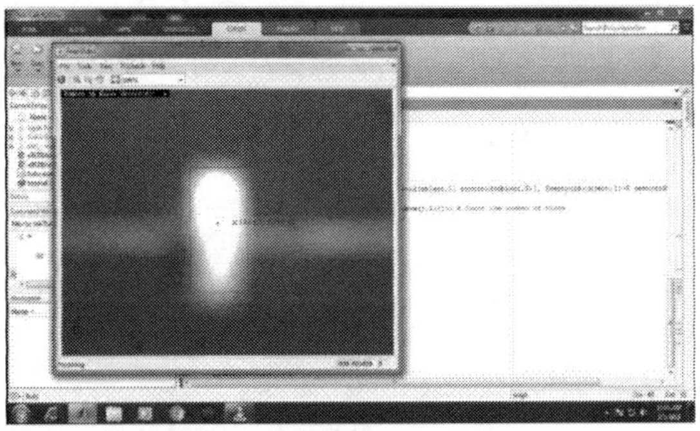

Fig. 8. Image of the vibrating shaft captured by the CCD camera during measurements.

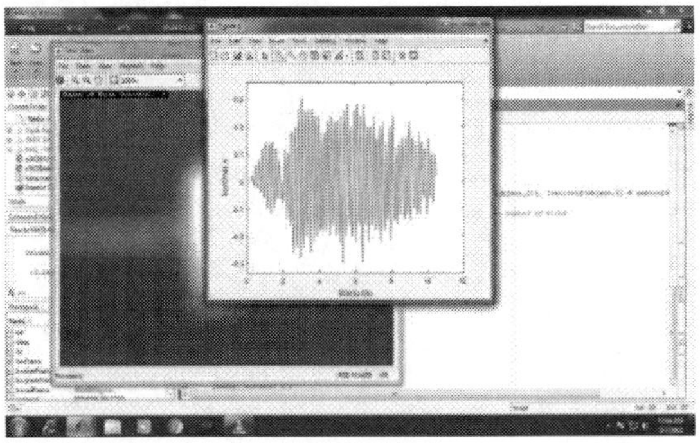

Fig. 9. Graph presenting the vibration measurements result.

This result shows that the average vibration amplitude that occurs for 10 seconds at the time of the test is 0.117 cm. The following graph of the test results can be seen in Figure 10.

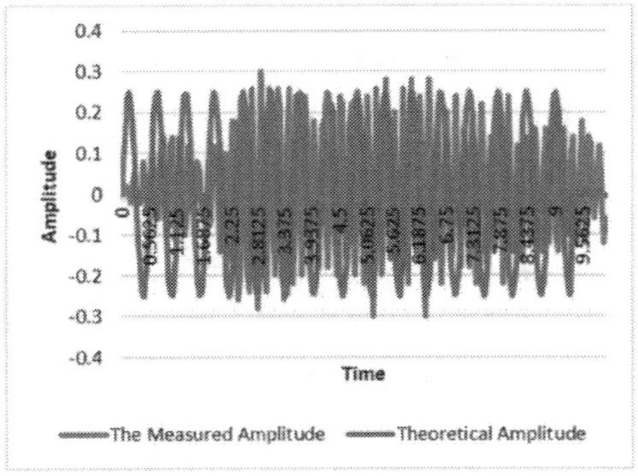

Fig. 10. Graph of measured and theoretical vibration amplitude

4 Conclusions and Recommendations

The conclusion of this research is (1) combining a CCD camera and an image processing method can be used to measure the amplitude of vibration without touching the vibrating component provided correlation and calibration have been done to the CCD camera prior being used. (2) the result of measurement of vibration measurement using image processing method shows the difference of measurement result of 5.73% from value of theoretical value. (3) the cause of the difference in the results of vibration with the method of image processing is due to the speed of camera frame capture and lighting intensity in the room.

The suggestion for this research is (1) to produce more precise measurements it is recommended to use a camera that has higher speed and resolution. (2) in the next research, the light intensity of the room should be properly adjusted so that the measurement more accurate.

References

1. Crowford, A. R. *The Simplified Handbook of Vibration Analysis*. Knoxville: SCI. (1992)
2. Harris Cyrill M., P. A. *eds. Harris' Shock and Vibration Handbook*. New York: McGraw Hill. (2002)
3. Mahmood, S. T. (kein Datum). *Use of Vibrations Analysis Technique in Condition Based Maintenance*. Stockholm: Royal Institute of Management.
4. Pain, H. J. *The Physics of Vibrations and Waves*. London: John Wiley (2000).
5. Rafael C Gonzalez, R. E. *Digital Image Processing*. Pearson Prentice Hall. (2013).
6. S Setiawan, A. A. *Pengantar Pengolahan Citra*. Jakarta: PT Elex Media Komputindo. (1992).
7. Vierck, R. K. *Analisis Getaran*. Bandung: Eresco. (1995).

The lifting force relationship of a BLDC motor rotor system to the blade rotation speed

Al Al*, *Arfita Yuana* Dewi[2] and *Taufal* Hidayat[3]

Institut Teknologi Padang, Electrical Engineering Department, Padang, Indonesia

Abstract In developing the knowledge and information about the Quadcopter aircraft, the parameters related to aircraft lift capability factors; fly long; flying high; type of motor; the type of propeller; including the sensors and control systems used. To find out of the BLDC motor voltage source to the rotor angle velocity (ω) relationship; rotor speed to wind velocity through rotor (v); rotor speed to rotor lift (Ft); wind speed to rotor lift; push the following rotor (Ct).Test and measurement results data show that; the lift force generated with rotational speed relationship is not proportional Nonlinearity occurs when the rotor is released from the self and starts pulling the strain gauge when the rotation speed reaches around 65 rps. Once the rotation speed of the rotor is able to reach up to 1.5 Newton lift then the thrust rising trend increasing sharply to the increasing the speed of rotation of the rotor. A special rotor that has BLDC motor specifications such as; 1200 KV, 12 Volt and 30 Ampere; blade with a radius of r 0.12 m; at a temperature of about 27 °C; in the condition there are no other wind currents then obtained thrust (Ct) of 1.732.

1 Introduction

Today, Quadcopter aircraft has become a trend of the world's people, whether used as a special purpose or as a hobby. The special use of Quadcopter aircraft such as military interests, the interests of mapping surveys and other purposes such as natural disaster relief (Al Al, 2017). The use of Quadcopter as a hobby has spawned a community of Quadcopter maniac societies, almost covering any country in the world as a Quadcopter. The existence of a Quadcopter will become more important to take a bigger role in various purposes, including for business support. They will be an integral part of everyday human life activities, from the simple things to the bigger interests, like defense and security of the region (Parhar 2016).

In the use of Quadcopter, both as a hobby or as a special need are still many obstacles or weaknesses such as; the plane easy to fall; the plane is easy to hit; the battery is not durable; vulnerable to weather conditions and others. In relation to that, Quadcopter's research and development is becoming more and more developed to cover the weaknesses of the existing Quadcopter aircraft as well as to improve aircraft facilities and capabilities (Magnussen, 2015). The vertical take-off landing (VTOL) Aircraft is a type of aircraft that can do take-off and landing perpendicular to the earth so it can be done in a narrow place. The UAV of this type is suitable for the survey location function in a narrow area such as urban residential areas or many shrubs areas (Al Al, 2016).

Pounds 2006 has been researching about Pilot, the quadrotor robot chassis and avionics using custom-built motor and battery off-the-shelf, into a highly reliable experimental platform. This vehicle uses the plant dynamics are tuned with mounted on board attitude control to stabilize flight. SISO linear controller is designed to regulate the conduct flyer.

The UAV has more dynamic stability than helicopters. Therefore, this aircraft does not require a special pilot to operate that. They are mostly used in different interests such as logistic purposes, agriculture, fire sensing, military exercises etc. Propeller and BLDC motors are integrated UAV rotor drive devices that generate a drive for takeoff. The process of rotor lift analysis is very complex and complicated. Analysis results this style is important, in choosing a motor for use on the UAV systems (Patel at. al 2017). Tao in 2016, examines the air traffic management system is unmanned. The purpose of this research is to: define the system; current system practices; how pilots use the system, and who has the authority; determine the physical architecture of what is needed in a system that handles a wide variety of aircraft.

In developing the knowledge and information about the Quadcopter aircraft, the data or parameters related to the lifting ability factor of the aircraft; long flight; high fly; type of motor used; the type of propeller used; including the sensors and control systems used. Accordingly, this study proposes to find a relationship between changes in BLDC motor voltage source to rotor angle velocity (ω); changes in rotor angle velocity to wind speed through the rotor (v); the change in the angular velocity of the rotor to the rotor lifts (***Ft***); changes in wind speed to rotor lift; rotor thrust coefficient (***Ct***).

* Corresponding author: al.mtdrs@gmail.com

2 Literature Review

The ability of aircraft to fly in the air is in principle based on; Newton's law; Archimedes; Pascal; Bernoulli, and the law of continuity. Newton's law describes the relationship between forces acting on an object and its motion. The law of Archimedes explains the upward pressure on an object when immersed in a liquid. Pascal's law states that the pressure given to the liquid is passed in all directions.

Bernoulli Law explains that the increase in fluid velocity causes a decrease in pressure on the flow. The Law of Continuity suggests the fact that the mass of the fluid moves will not change when the negative (Hydrodynamics 2006).

Newton's Law I states: every object will remain in perpendicular motion or remain in a static state if there is a resultant, force (F) works on that object:

$$\Sigma f = 0,\ a = 0, V = 0\ (konstan)$$

Newton's law II, states that the force is equal to the difference in momentum (mass multiplied by the speed) of each time change.

$$F = m . a$$

Newton's Law III states: that every action must have a reaction in the same direction and opposite direction ***(F_1 = F_1')***.

The law of Archimedes says that: If an object is immersed in a liquid thing, it will be pressured upward as large as the weight of a liquid dampened by it.

$$FA = \rho . g . v$$

Where: ***FA*** = Archimedes pressure (N/m^3)
ρ = Mass Type of liquid (Kg/m^3)
g = Gravitation (N/Kg)
V = Volume of Dyed Objects (m^3)

Pascal's law states that "the pressure given by liquids in a confined space is passed in all directions equally." The difference in pressure due to differences in the increase in the liquid is formulated as follows:

$$\Delta P = \rho . g . (\Delta H)$$

Where:
ΔP: hydrostatic pressure (Pa)
P: fluid speed (kg/m^3)
G: sea level rise against earth gravitation (m/s^2)
ΔH: altitude difference of fluid (m)

According to Bernoulli, an increase in the fluid velocity will cause a decrease in pressure on the flow. This principle is actually a simplification of the Bernoulli Equation, which states that the amount of energy at a point in a closed stream is equal to the amount of energy at another point on the same flow path. There are generally two forms of the Bernoulli equation; the first applies to incompressible flow, and the other is for compressible flow fluids.

Incompressible flow is a fluid flow characterized by an unchanged mass density (density) of the fluid along the stream. The form of the Bernoulli Equation for non-compressed streams is as follows:

$$p + \rho g h + \frac{1}{2}\rho v^2 = constant \quad (1)$$

where:
v = fluid speed
g = earth gravitation
h = altitude relative to a reference
p = fluid pressure
ρ = fluid density

The above equation applies to non-compressed streams with the following assumptions: that the flow is steady state and there is no inviscid friction. In another form, the Bernoulli Equation can be written as follows:

$$p_1 + \rho g h_1 + \frac{1}{2}\rho v_1^2 = p_2 + \rho g h_2 + \frac{1}{2}\rho v_2^2 \quad (2)$$

The compressible flow fluid is a fluid flow characterized by changing the mass density of the fluid along the stream. The Bernoulli equation for compressed streams is as follows:

$$\frac{v^2}{2} + \phi + \omega = constant \quad (3)$$

where:
ϕ = gravitational potential energy per unit mass; if gravity is constant then $\phi = gh$
ϕ w= enthalpy of fluid per mass unit.
ϕ

$$\omega = \varepsilon + \frac{p}{\rho} \quad (4)$$

where: ε is the thermodynamic energy per unit mass, also referred to as the specific internal energy.

The moving fluid mass does not change as it flows. This fact leads us to an important quantitative relation called the continuity equation.To clarify the details of this centre pay attention to Figure 1

Fig. 1. Mass Flow Rate

The volume of fluid flowing in the first part, V1, which passes through the area of A1 at rate v1 over the time range Δt is A1v1 Δt. By knowing the relationship of Volume and Mass type, the mass flow rate through the area A1 is

$$\frac{\Delta m}{\Delta t} = \frac{\rho_1 A_1 v_1 \Delta t}{\Delta t} = \rho_1 A_1 v_1 \quad (5)$$

The same situation occurs in the second part. The mass flow rate passing through A2 for the time span Δt is:

$$\rho_2 A_2 v_2$$

The volume of fluid flowing over the time span Δt in the area A1 will have an amount equal to the volume flowing in A2. Therefore:

$$\rho_1 A_1 v_1 = \rho_2 A_2 v_2$$

or ρ.A.V is constant.

Guido at. all 2016, investigates UAV Uses for capturing reliable GPS technology as a benchmark. Video processing algorithm for vehicle track acquisition based on OpenCV libraries. Assessment of the accuracy of video processing algorithms of an instrumentation vehicle is equipped with high precision GPS.

The video capture experiment was conducted in two case studies. The results of this experiment highlight the flexibility of UAV technology combined with video processing techniques in monitoring real-time traffic data. The Interests area is defined in which all points of the target vehicle trajectory collected through the GPS receiver are mapped.

Comparing this path monitored by the UAV with GPS traces used as a benchmark, the analysis shows that: Root Mean Square Equations Percentage in velocity evaluations equals 3.96% and 3.57%, for case studies 1 and 2 respectively.

While on the other hand, more deeply analyzes various error ranges such as: camera position; angle of incident; the position of the object or the fetch frame. The results are used for the measurement and eligibility of the obvjek position (Babinec 2016).

Research on lifts and drag force of a UAV by using Computational Fluid Dynamics (CFD) technique is proposed (K. S. Patel et al. 2014), because wind tunnel experiments are very difficult and additional cost more. This technique shows a close proximity to the real experiment.

In the principle, when the aircraft is on the air, there are four main forces acting on the plane, the thrust T, drag D, lift and weight of the plane (weight W). The four aerodynamic forces in flight are discussed by George Cayley, 2008.

Meanwhile, the quadcopter movements such as back and forth; Left and right; up and down, influenced by variations in direction, speed and acceleration of four rotors. for a quadcopter that has fixed blade parameters that can change is the speed and acceleration of the propeller angle [kranik 2011].

The propeller serves to transfer power by converting rotational motion into thrust to propel a vehicle like an aeroplane, through a mass of air, by rotating two or more twin blades from the main axle. A propeller acts as a rotating wing and produces a force that applies Bernoulli principles and Newton's laws of motion, resulting in a difference in pressure between the front and back or top-down or left-right surfaces.

The size of the blade used in quadcopter varies depending on the size of the quadcopter and the load to be lifted by the quadcopter. Therefore, to take into account how much the lifting power and the speed of a quadcopter it is important to know a relation between size, rotational speed with the lift of a propeller. The relationship between lift power size and speed such as equation 6 and 7 [Brandt, 2011].

$$T = (C_t . \pi . \rho . r^2 . v^2)/2 \qquad (6)$$

On the line, Coefficient thrust (***C_t***) can be expressed as equation 7.

$$C_t = 2.T/(\pi . \rho . r^2 . v^2) \qquad (7)$$

Where: $\boldsymbol{C_t}$ is thrust coefficient; ***T*** is rotor thrust; $\boldsymbol{\pi}$ is 3.14; $\boldsymbol{\rho}$ ***is*** density of air = 1.225***;*** ***r*** is radius of blade; ***v*** is air speed.

3 Methodology

In this study, empirical testing was done in the laboratory to find out the relationship amongst other things: changes in BLDC motor voltage source to rotor angle velocity (***ω***); changes in rotor angle velocity to wind speed through the rotor (***v***); the change in the angular velocity of the rotor to the rotor lifts (***Ft***); changes in wind speed to rotor lift; rotor thrust coefficient (***Ct***).

To obtain the results of these measurements than required materials and equipment as follows:

- 1200 Kv BLDC Motor
- 30 Amper Electronic speed controller (ESC)
- Voltage sensor
- 500 K Ohm Potentiometer
- Arduino Uno Microcontroller
- Mekanik stand up
- LCD display
- Blade propeller with radius (r) is 0.12 meter
- Digital Anemometer
- Digital Tachometer
- Digital Strain Gauge

Implementation of this rotor parameter measurement is done in accordance with the block diagram as in Figure 2.

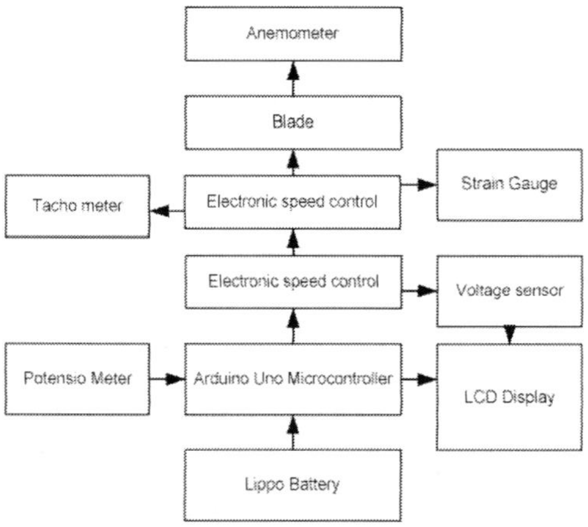

Fig. 2. Block diagram of measurement system

 https://doi.org/10.1051/matecconf/201821501013

The material and measurement equipment are shown as in Figure 3.

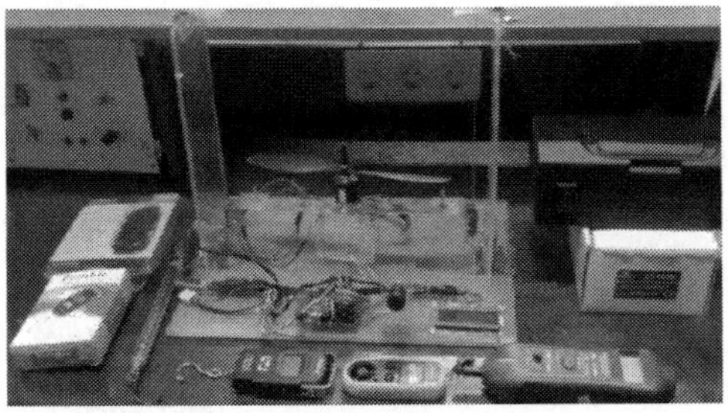

Fig. 3. The material and measurement equipmen

4 Result and discussion

For the first time, rotor parameters were measured only by self-loading weighing 165 grams. Overall the results are shown in Table 1.

Table 1. Self-Load

No.	Voltage source (Volt)	Rotor Speed (rpm)	Device condition	Airspeed km/h	Airspeed m/s
1	1	0	stag	0	0
2	1.5	0	stag	0	0
3	2	0	stag	0	0
4	2.26	964	stag	6.8	1.888889
5	2.5	2008	stag	13.7	3.805556
6	2.7	2633	stag	17.9	4.972222
7	2.85	2935	stag	19.3	5.361111
8	2.86	2972	cut in half	20.3	5.638889
9	2.96	3209	cut in half	21.4	5.944444
10	3	3339	cut in half	22.3	6.194444
11	3.1	3539	go up	23.5	6.527778
12	3.15	3627	go up	24.2	6.722222
13	3.25	3823	go up	25.1	6.972222
14	3.35	3957	go up	26	7.222222
15	3.5	4230	go up	28.3	7.861111
16	3.8	4643	go up	29.8	8.277778
17	4	4896	go up	32.3	8.972222
18	4.5	4967	go up	34.2	9.5
19	5	5285	go up	36.9	10.25

By observing Table 1 it can be seen that: providing a source ranging from 1 to 2 volts can not move propellers; by providing a source voltage between 2.26 to 2.85 volts the propeller has been able to spin but has not had the power to self-immerse; after being given between 2. 86 to 3-volt rotor conditions are now floating or starting to lift. At the moment the source voltage is given as much as 3.1-volt and the rotor has been lifted and higher. The start of the rotor lift is marked by the rotor rotation speed of 3539 rpm. While the highest angular spin speed reaches 5285 rpm when given 5 volts source voltage.

Next, the rotor parameters were tested with self-loads added with a load of 50 grams, bringing the total load to 215 grams and its content shown as in Table 2.

Table 2 Measurement With 215-Gram Load

NO	Voltage Source	Speed (rpm)	Device Condition
0	0	0	stagnan
1	1 Volt	0	stagnan
2	1,50 Volt	0	stagnan
3	2 Volt	0	stagnan
4	2,26 Volt	964	stagnan
5	2,50 Volt	2008	stagnan
6	2,70 Volt	2633	stagnan
7	2,85 Volt	2935	stagnan
8	2,86 Volt	2972	stagnan
9	2,96 Volt	3209	stagnan
10	3 Volt	3339	stagnan
11	3,10 Volt	3539	stagnan
12	3,14 Volt	3612	stagnan
13	3,15 Volt	3562	cutinhalf
14	3,25 Volt	3733	go-up
15	3,35Volt	3888	go-up
16	3,50 Volt	4034	go-up
17	3,80 Volt	4577	go-up
18	4 Volt	4708	go-up
19	4,50 Volt	4856	go-up
20	5 Volt	5185	go-up

With a load of 215 grams, it can be seen in table 2 that; between 1 to 3.14 volts source voltage, the rotor cannot be lifted. When given a 3.15-volt source voltage then the aircraft starts to float. Starting from the 3.25-volt source voltage and rushing up the rotor is already up and moving higher.

Furthermore, by providing a total weight of 315 grams, the result of the parameter measurement is shown as in Table 3. Table 3 shows that the rotor floats when the source voltage is given at 3.78 volts. Whereas, after the source voltage is given by 3.8 volts continues up to 5 volts, the rotor is raised and the higher.

Table 3 Measurement With 315-Gram Load

N0	Voltage source	Rotor Speed (rpm)	Device condition
	1 Volt	0	stag
2	1,50 Volt	0	stag
3	2 Volt	0	stag
4	2,26 Volt	964	stag
5	2,50 Volt	2008	stag
6	2,70 Volt	2633	stag
7	2,85 Volt	2935	stag
8	2,86 Volt	2972	stag
9	2,96 Volt	3209	stag
10	3 Volt	3339	stag
11	3,10 Volt	3539	stag
12	3,14 Volt	3612	stag
13	3,15 Volt	3562	stag
14	3,25 Volt	3716	stag
15	3,34Volt	3788	stag
16	3,35 Volt	3823	stag
17	3,50 Volt	3977	stag
18	3,77 Volt	4317	stag
19	3,78 Volt	4355	floating
20	3,80 Volt	4419	go-up
21	4 Volt	4581	go-up
22	4,50 Volt	4622	go-up
23	5 Volt	5079	go-up

Hereinafter, the measurement of rotor parameters with a total load of 365 grams, the results are shown in Table 4. The data in Table 4 shows that the source voltage between 1 to 3.8 volts has not been able to hold the rotor along with the load. The rotor begins to float at a given source voltage of 3.81 volts with a rotor rotation speed of 4355 rpm.

By providing a voltage source of 3.8 2volts to produce a rotor rotation speed of 4492-rpm rotor start moving upward, and so on the addition of source voltage up to 5 volts increase the speed of the rotor is marked with a peak rotation speed of 5079 rpm.

By examining the results of the test table 1 already with table 4, it is directly indicated that the increase in source voltage raises the increase to the speed of rotation of the rotor. The speed of rotation of the rotor makes the air velocity through it is proportional. The air velocity through the rotor is what will generate the rotor lift, according to the concept proposed by; Newton's law; Archimedes; Pascal; Bernoulli, and the law of continuity.

To know directly the relationship between; rotation speed of the rotor with a voltage source; speed of rotation of the rotor with wind speed and the rotation speed of the rotor to the resulting thrust, then continued simultaneous testing as a further explanation.

Table 4. Measurement With 365-Gram Load

N0	Voltage source	Rotor Speed (rpm)	Device condition
1	1 Volt	0	200
2	1,50 Volt	0	200
3	2 Volt	0	200
4	2,26 Volt	964	200
5	2,50 Volt	2008	200
6	2,70 Volt	2633	200
7	2,85 Volt	2935	200
8	2,86 Volt	2972	200
9	2,96 Volt	3209	200
10	3 Volt	3339	200
11	3,10 Volt	3539	200
12	3,14 Volt	3612	200
13	3,15 Volt	3562	200
14	3,25 Volt	3716	200
15	3,34Volt	3788	200
16	3,35 Volt	3823	200
17	3,50 Volt	3977	200
18	3,77 Volt	4317	200
19	3,78 Volt	4355	200
20	3,80 Volt	4419	200
21	3,81 Volt	4578	floating
22	3,82 Volt	4492	Go-up
23	4 Volt	4523	200
24	4,50 Volt	4611	200
25	5 Volt	4944	200

The rotor angular velocity and voltage source relationship test, the wind speed and the lift produced by the rotor are performed with stand up as Figure 4.

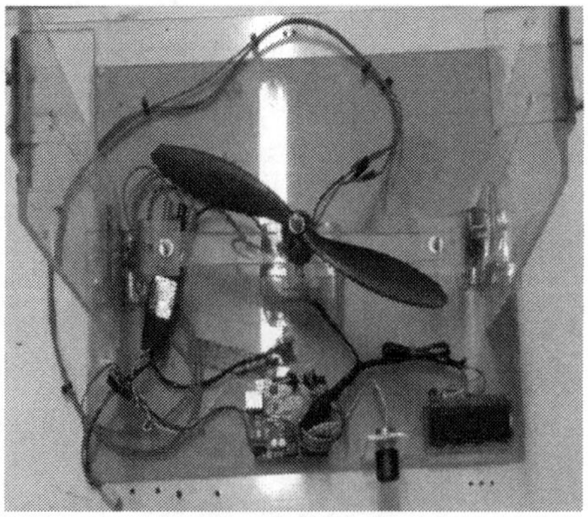

Fig. 4. Rotor under testing

The preparations and test instruments in FIG. 1 comprises blades with a radius of 0.0645 m; BLDC Motor 1200Kv; Electronic speed controller (ESC); Arduino microcontroller UNO; Lithium 30 A 5 V Battery; LCD display as an indicator of the voltage source; Anemometer; Digital Tachometer and Digital strain gauge.

While the test results between the rotor angular velocities to the voltage source obtained the results such as graphs in Figure 5.

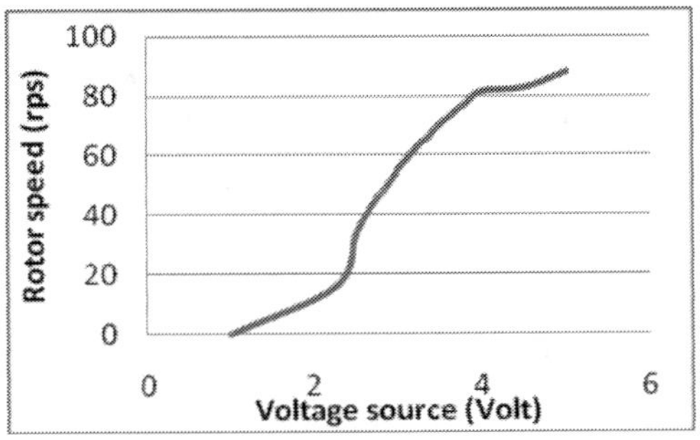

Fig. 5. Rotor speed vs Voltage source

The graphic of Figure 5 shows that the increase in voltage source raises the rotor speed but this increase is not liner as long as the increase in voltage source. Between 2.8 volts up to 4 volts, the rotor speed has a linear almost increase.

The results of the air velocity testing of the rotor speed are shown in the graph of figure 6. This graph illustrates that the increase in rotor speed produces air velocity proportional to the linear trend during the change.

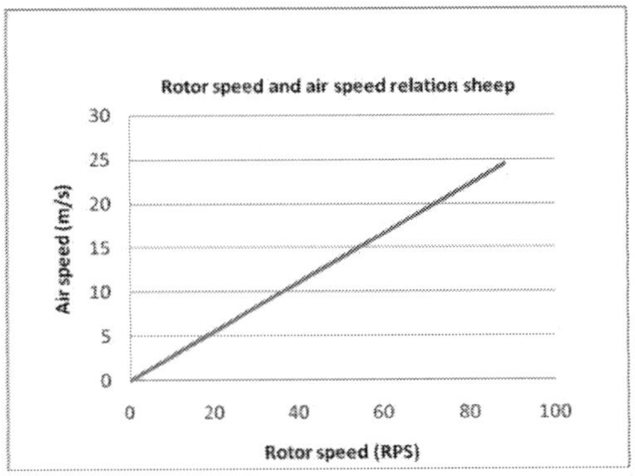

Fig. 6. Rotor and Air Speed Relationship

Measurement of the rotor lift to the change in rotation speed of the rotor angle is done by measuring instrument of the digital strain gauge and digital tachometer. The result is shown in the graph in figure 7. Figure 4 states that the increase in rotor speed causes an increase in the rotor thrust. the relationship of both parameters increase is not linear at all. On the graph shows that between zero to 60 rps starts with a linear trend, between 65 up to 75 rps trend occurs bend and after that greater than 75 rps obtained linear trend back. In a non-linear condition between 65 and 75 rps, a change of thrust state is used only to elevate itself until it begins to draw the strain gauge as a measure of the rotor's lift power.

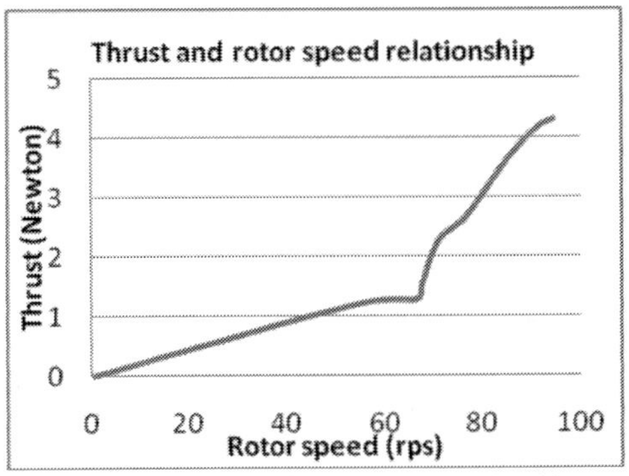

Fig. 7. A thrust and Rotor Speed Selationship

By using 1200 Kv / 5 Volt BLDC motor and blade which is has a radius r 0.12 m, and then according to equation $C_t = 2.T/(\pi.\rho.r^2.v^2)$ is obtained by the thrust coefficient (C_t) according to the wind speed as shown in the Table 5. Where: C_t is thrust coefficient; T is rotor thrust; π is 3.14; ρ ***is the*** density of air = 1.225***;*** r is the radius of the blade; v is airspeed.

Table 3 Average of *Ct* From Thrust and Air Speed *v*

Total thrust (Newto n	Airspee d (m/s)	π	ρ	radius r (m)	Coefficien t Thrust (Ct)
0	0	0	0	0	0
1.225	5.5	3.14	1.225	0.12	1.462219
1.225	5.9	3.14	1.225	0.12	1.270673
1.2838	6	3.14	1.225	0.12	1.287646
1.568	6.2	3.14	1.225	0.12	1.47287
2.254	6.5	3.14	1.225	0.12	1.926322
2.597	7	3.14	1.225	0.12	1.913717
2.842	7.5	3.14	1.225	0.12	1.82433
3.675	8	3.14	1.225	0.12	2.073381
4.165	8.5	3.14	1.225	0.12	2.081512
4.312	9	3.14	1.225	0.12	1.922186
				Total Ct	17.23486
				Average Ct	1.723486

After measuring more than 20 times, the average measurement value as shown in Table 5. Table 5 gives information that the conversion of wind speed generated by the rotor produces a comparable thrust.

Convertible results are influenced by many factors such as; the size and shape of the blade; earth gravitation; density of air; and constant changes. With blade conditions as described earlier and at an ambient temperature of 27° Celsius the coefficient of this rotor (Ct) of 1.723 is obtained.

5 Conclusion

After doing the measurement, testing and analysis of data then it can be concluded as follows. The increase in the rotation speed of the rotor is proportional to the increase of the source voltage applied to the motor bldc and the increase is not always linear as long as the voltage changes from 1 to 5 volts. The linear range occurs between 2.5 to 4 volts. The relationship between rotation speed and the resulting airspeed is proportional to the trend of linear.

The relationship between lift powers produced with rotational speed is not comparable. The nonlinearity occurs when the root is relieved of the weight of oneself and proceeds to start pulling the strain gauge when the rotation speed reaches around 65 rps. Once the rotation speed of the rotor is able to generate lift to reach 1.5 Newton then increase the endurance rotor has sharp increasingly.

Using a BLDC motor which is specifications as 1200 Kv, 12 Volt and 30 Ampere; blade with a radius of r 0.12 m; at a temperature of about 27 °C; in the condition is no other wind currents then obtained the thrust coefficient (*Ct*) of 1.732.

ACKNOWLEDGMENT

I would like to thank the Ministry of Research, Technology and Higher Education of Republic Indonesia and Institut Teknologi Padang in supporting this research.

References

1. A. Al, A.Y.D. Rachman, J.A. Saputro, Quadcopter capability development for additional low voltage distribution network location tracking, In International conference of applied science on engineering, business, linguistics and information technology, Padang-Indonesia, October 14th, (2017)
2. P. Parihar, P. Bhawsar, P. Hargod, Design & Development Analysis of Quadcopter, COMPUSOFT, An international journal of advanced computer technology, 5 (6), June (2016)
3. O. Magnussen, M. Ottestad, G. Hovland, Multicopter Design Optimization and Validation", Modeling, Identification and Control, Vol. 36, No. 2, pp. 67–79, ISSN 1890–1328. (2015)
4. A. Al, "*An Improved a Quadcopter Capability for Forestall Bump with The Ultrasonic HC SR04 Proximity Sensor Design,"* In International Conference on Technology, Innovation, and Society (ICTIS), (2016)
5. Pounds, P., Mahony, R., and Corke, P., "Modelling and Control of a Quad-Rotor Robot," In Proceedings of the Australasian Conference on Robotics and Automation, (2006)
6. Y. Patel, A. Gaurav, K. Srinivas, Y. Singh, A Review on Design and Analysis of the propeller used in UAV. In International Journal of Advanced Production and Industrial Engineering, IJAPIE-SI-IDCM 605, 20–23, (2017)
7. T. Jiang, J. Geller, Daiheng Ni, John Collura," *Unmanned Aircraft System traffic management: Concept of operation and system architecture,"* International Journal of Transportation Science and Technology 5 123–135. (2016)
8. G. Guido, V. Gallelli, D. Rogano, A. Vitale, Evaluating the accuracy of vehicle tracking data obtained from Unmanned Aerial Vehicles In International Journal of Transportation Science and Technology, 5 pp.136–151, (2016)
9. A. Babinec, J. Apeltauer, "On accuracy of position estimation from aerial imagery captured by low-flying UAVs", International Journal of Transportation Science and Technology, 5 pp. 152–166, (2016)
10. S.P. Karana, B.P. Saumil, CFD Analysis of an Aerofoil, In International Journal of Engineering Research, Volume No.3, Issue No.3, pp. 154-158, (2014)
11. T. Krajnık, V. Vonasek, D. Fiser, J. Faigl, AR-Drone as a Platform for Robotic Research, The Gerstner Laboratory for Intelligent Decision Making and Control Department of Cybernetics, Faculty of Electrical Engineering Czech Technical University, Prague, (2011)
12. J.B. Brandt, M.S. Selig, Propeller Performance Data at Low Reynolds Numbers, *49th AIAA Aerospace Sciences Meeting*, AIAA Paper 2011-1255, Orlando, FL, January (2011)

MATEC Web of Conferences **215**, 01014 (2018) https://doi.org/10.1051/matecconf/201821501014
ICTIS 2018

Data Logger Development to Evaluate Potential Area of Solar Energy

Asnal Effendi*, Arfita Yuana Dewi, Fauzan Ismail

Institut Teknologi Padang, Departement of Electrical Enginering, Padang, Indonesia

Abstract. The data logger was developed to evaluate potential area of solar panel. Current sensor and voltage sensor were integrated on data logger board to measure parameter that affected toward efficiency of PV system. The obtained Calculation power will be used for assessment and evaluation during collecting data. But, Maximum Power Point Tracking (MPPT) method will provide an efficient data of peak power. The benefit of using data logger is the ability to automatically collecting data on several period. The data can be plotted into V-I graph and P-V graph for analysis. The test bench result was recorded that the maximum power reaches 35W. This data logger with MPPT method can be used as portable recorder to compare the power in different area.

1. Introduction

Nowadays, solar energy contributed to support electric sources. It can reduce foreign energy dependence as well as energy-related environtmental impacts [1-2]. Another source like coal, hydro, nuclear, and gas are still used as a main source of energy. Solar radiation will be converted to sustainable-produced electricity by using photovoltaics (PV) technology. PV systems provided advantages to reduce gas emission was affected by green house, and reuse of marginal lands [2]. Installation of PV System utilize unused area, low productivity agricultural land, and special area such as roof top and wall. But, selected potential area to install PV System should be predicted to reach high efficiency.

Many literarures was introduced to predict solar power generation. Data mining method can be used to predict by recording interval, the number of training, and test datasets in review process. But, combination artificial neural network with data mining methods will provide an approach on predicted the area [3]. Fifty-two method implemented for solar power prediction were explained and the performance was compared.

This prediction method is important to determine a prospect of PV System investment. Climate, position (latitude and longitude), solar angel, radiation, and result power, become some of parameters which should be consireded before selects the area. So, the benefit and advantage of PV system will be shown clearly. The results of prediction will be obtained by recording a parameter during one-year duration or more. Then assessment and evaluation toward recording data shows value of prediction.

Periodically parameter recording for every hour should be logged automatically during one-year testing. The hardware of datalogger consist of sensor, controller, and memory. Data logger should be designed simple, lowcost, fast response, and large space memory. Althought many perameter are sugested to be logged in this case. But, recording current and voltage become a simple way to see the power output performance of PV System that could give description about results of average power in a years [4].

This paper presented data logger development to evaluate potential area of solar energy. Current and voltage is measured and calculate to produces power output. The Atmega328 is acted as a controller that connected with RTC clock and Memory chip. Recording parameter for every hour and real time gives an important result to be assessted. Then, an implementation of Maximum Power Point Tracking (MPPT) method provides result of data recording [5].

2. System Design

The data logger was developed to measure voltage and current from solar panel. Microcontroller ATmega328 is used to measure data from sensor and arrange recording data from sensor to memory. Then, the RTC modul also use as a timer to recording data from solar panel. The block diagram of data logger shows part of modul board which connected to ATmega328 is displayed on figure.1. Real time measurement of current and voltage for every hour against solar panel with varies load. Where the electrical specification of Solar panel is explained on Tabel.1.

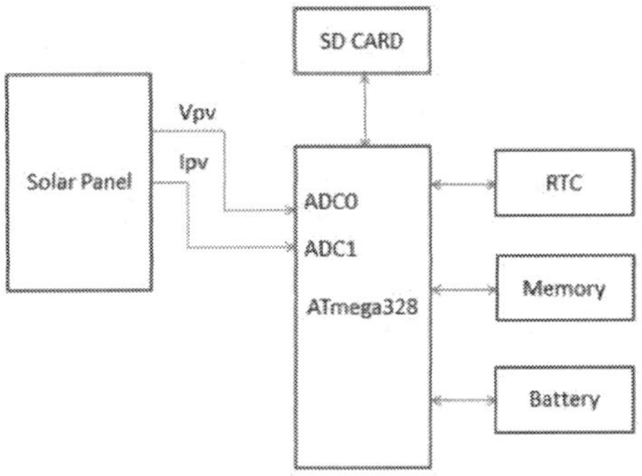

Fig.1. Block diagram of data logger system

* Corresponding author: asnal.effendi@gmail.com

Table.1 Solar Cell Module Specification

Modul Type	ASL –M50
Peak Power (Pmax)	50W
Open Circuit Voltage (Voc)	21 volt
Short Circuit Current (Isc)	1.45 A
Voltage at Max Power (Vmp)	16.8 volt
Nominal Voltage	12V
Tolerance	5%

The latest data will be displayed on LCD Module with 2x16 character that connected to Atmega328. ACS712-20A current sensor was measured real time current, and voltage divider circuit is used to sense the real time voltage from solar panel. Current, voltage and power calculation are saved in to memory internal of micro-controller. Then serial communication terminal can also be connected to computer to records all data saved on datalogger. As for component type of data logger module explained on Tabel.2.

Table.2. Component Specification of Data Logger System

No	Components
1.	2x16 LCD character
2.	Atmega328
3.	SD Card Module
4.	RTC module
5.	5V CMOS battery

An additional circuit is required for data retrieval. The test bench apply varies load during recording current, voltage, and power for every hour. Hence, the maximum power can be track by this method. Recording maximum power means the peak power can be accumulated to calculate cost and efficiency. The average value was produced by solar panel for every day becomes an important data to be saved. Where, the Maximum Power Point Tracking (MPPT) is a method to track a maximum power even though system on disturbance condition or variation on illumination.

Refer to figure.2 that maximum power of solar panel is required to determine the potential area for solar system. When the PV systems suffer a low conversion efficiency, so MPPT be an answered to track the maximum value when the irradiant changed. The method was summarized by [Soulmia and Chenni,2016]. The thin film solar photovoltaics array was developed for building or unflat area with apply MPPT Method.

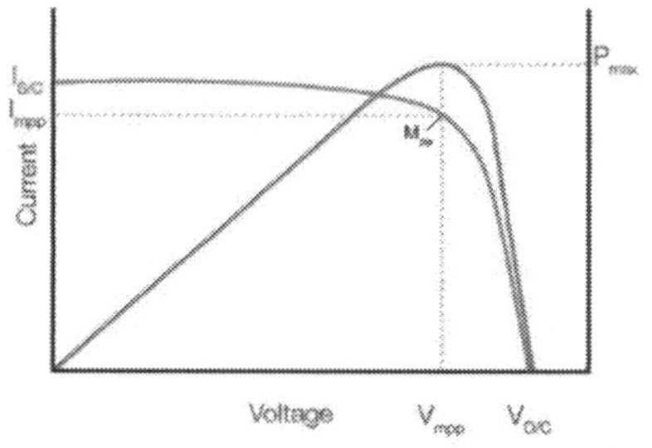

Fig.2. The normal I-V and P-V curve of solar panel.

3. Prototype Development

The data logger which integrated RTC circuit, curent and voltage sensor, 2x16 character LCD, SD Card Module to save data, and Atmega328 as a controller. This data logger board was install to 100Wp solar panel and connected to Solar Charging Circuit. Normally, this system will be charged battery and also loaded by steet light that displayed on Figure 3.

Fig. 3. Test Bench System of Photovoltaic

4. Testing and Result

The experiment has been done in front of Electrical Engineering Laboratory of Institut Technology Padang. The power measurement test was measured from 9 PM to 5PM with condition on sunny weather. The varies resistor was applied to search maximum power of solar panel.

Table.3 The first experiment on 15.00 PM

No	V	A	P	R
1	1.692	1.496	2.531232	1Ω
2	3.773	1.496	5.644408	2.8Ω
3	11.142	1.489	16.590438	7.5Ω
4	17.236	1.473	25.388628	17.5Ω
5	18.116	0.669	12.119604	27.5Ω
6	18.662	0.441	8.229942	47.5Ω
7	19.102	0.217	4.145134	94.5Ω
8	19.246	0.142	2.732932	141.5Ω
9	19.307	0.105	2.027235	188.5Ω

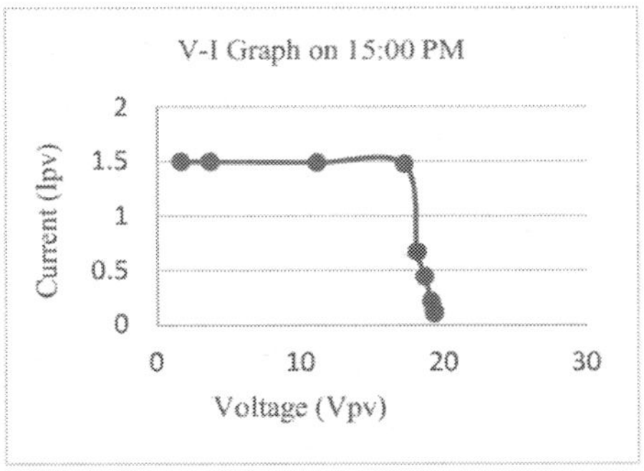

Fig. 4 The normal V-I Graph on experiment test 1

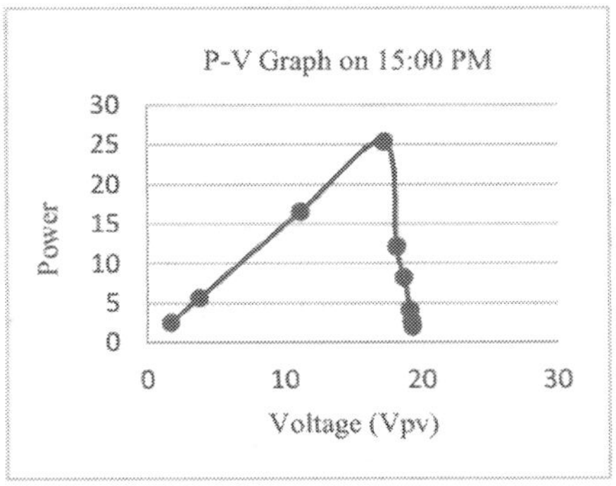

Fig. 5 The normal P-V Graph on experiment test 1

Table.4. The second experiment on 15.30 PM

No	V	A	P	R
1	2.92	2.818	8.22856	1Ω
2	7.8	2.728	21.2784	2.8Ω
3	16.43	2.133	35.04519	7.5Ω
4	18.52	1.063	19.68676	17.5Ω
5	19.04	0.7	13.328	27.5Ω
6	19.38	0.457	8.85666	42.5Ω
7	19.68	0.224	4.40832	82.5Ω
8	19.79	0.145	2.86955	136.5Ω
9	19.82	0.108	2.14056	183.5Ω

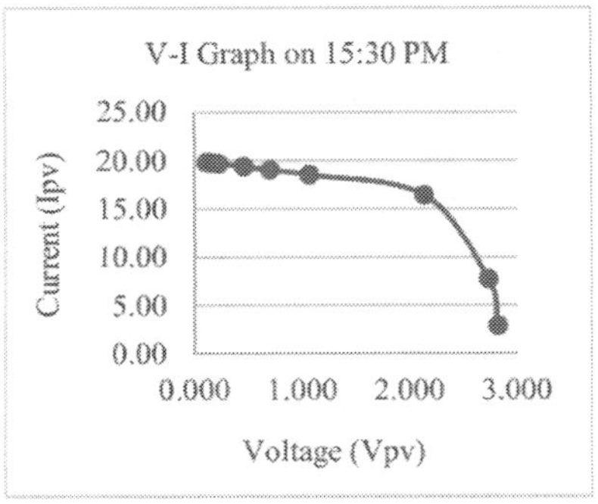

Fig..6. The normal V-I Graph on experiment test 2

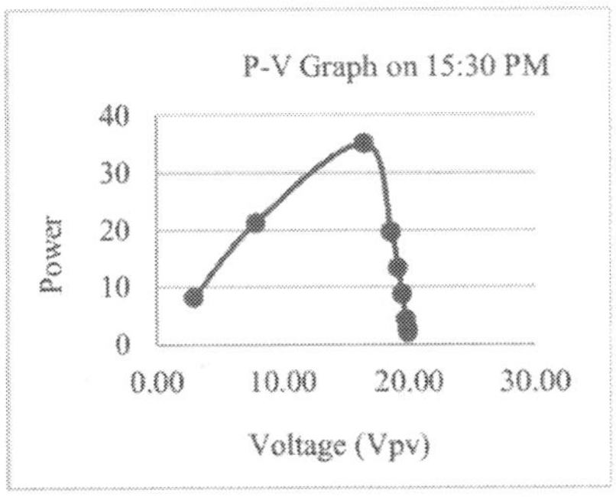

Fig.7. The normal P-V Graph on experiment test 2

Table.5 The third experiment on 16.00 PM

No	V	A	P	R
1	0.840	0.857	0.71988	1Ω
2	2.402	0.841	2.020082	2.8Ω
3	6.291	0.832	5.234112	7.5Ω
4	13.743	0.791	10.870713	17.5Ω
5	16.852	0.62	10.44824	27.5Ω
6	17.815	0.421	7.500115	42.5Ω
7	18.442	0.21	3.87282	82.5Ω
8	18.961	0.137	2.597657	136.5Ω
9	18.99	0.112	2.12688	183.5Ω

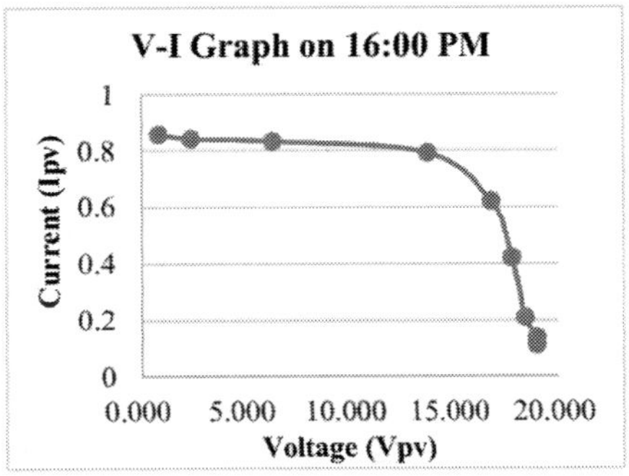

Fig.8. The normal V-I Graph on experiment test 3

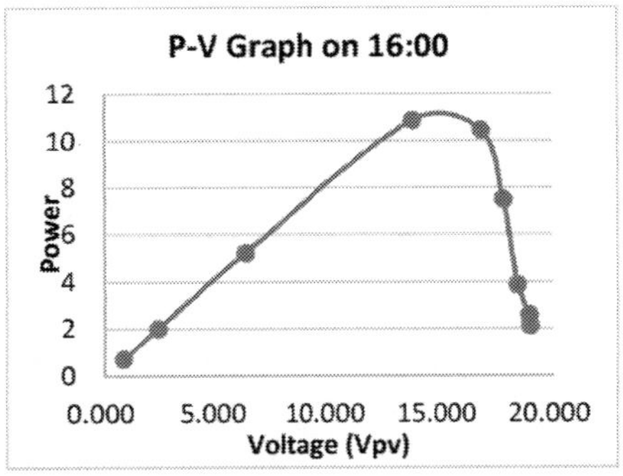

Fig.9 The normal P-V Graph on experiment test 3

Three experiment has been done to calculate maximum power of PV system for this place and condition.

35.045W of maximum power measurement was produced by this PV sistem. The experiment that collected by data logger couldn't give a good performance yet. So, the experiment should be done for another predicted place then verify.

5. Conclusions and recommendations

The experiment for this place and condition couldn't give a good performance yet. Do another test for selected place for brief conclusion. The data logger successes collected current, voltage and power from pv system. Then, the data saved on SD card provides an important data collecting from PV system.

References

1. Panwar, N. L., Kaushik, S.C., Kothari, S., Role of renewable energy sources in environmental protection: a review.' Renew.Sustain. EnergyRev.15, 1513–1524. (2011)
2. IPCC, 'Intergovernmental panel on climate change. IPCC Special report on renewable energy sources and climate change mitigation.' Summary for policy makers, Cambridge, United Kingdom and New York, USA. (2011)
3. Yesilbudak, M., Colak, M., Bayindir, R., A Review of Data mining and Solar Power Prediction.' International Conference on Renewable Energy Research and Application. 1117-1121. (2016)
4. Alami, M.E., Habibi.M., Bri, S., The Modeling of Maximum Power Point Tracking Controller for Increasing Efficiency of Solar Power System.' 3rd International Conference on Renewable and Sustainable Energy Conference (IRSEC). (2015)
5. Soualmia, A., Chenni, R., Survey of Maximum Peak Power Tracking Techniques used in Photovoltaic Power Systems.'Future Technologies Conference,430-443. (2016)

MATEC Web of Conferences **215**, 01015 (2018)
ICTIS 2018
https://doi.org/10.1051/matecconf/201821501015

A True Hybrid Solar Wind Turbine Electric Generator System for Smaller Hybrid Renewable Energy Power Plants

Mohammad Shafi Al-Ajmi[1], *Faizal* Mustapha[2], *Mohd. Khairol Anuar b.* Mohd Ariffin[2], *Nurul Amziah* Md. Yunus[3], *Izhal* Abdul Halin[3*]

[1]Ministry of Electricity and Water, Department of Electrical Distribution Networks (Jahra), Kuwait
[2]Universiti Putra Malaysia, Department of Aerospace Engineering, Selangor, Malaysia
[3]Universiti Putra Malaysia, Department of Electrical and Electronics Engineering, Selangor, Malaysia

Abstract Contemporary Hybrid Solar-Wind farms are implemented using separate solar Photovoltaic (PV) cell arrays and wind turbines, where electricity generated from both devices are combined. However, this solution requires a large amount of space to cater for the PV arrays and wind turbines of the system. This paper proposes a new type of renewable energy electric generator with a small power production footprint (PPF) that allows reduction in land usage. The technology introduced in this True Hybrid Wind-Solar (THWS) generator allows for the solar panels to rotate along with a VAWT wind turbine it is attached to through a specially designed electromechanical coupling mechanism. The working principal behind the connections described in this paper. The design of a hybrid circuit module that serves to combine current generated via the solar cells and wind generator and also automatically disconnects inactive wind or solar generators is also described. This is important in order to eliminate unwanted loads generated from the inactive generators from within the THWS itself.

1 Introduction

In the past decade, the world has seen an exponential increase in energy demand. Fig 1. shows the source of actual energy consumption from 1990-2015 and its projected path from 2016 to 2040 [1]. This ever increasing trend is due to population growth of the world.

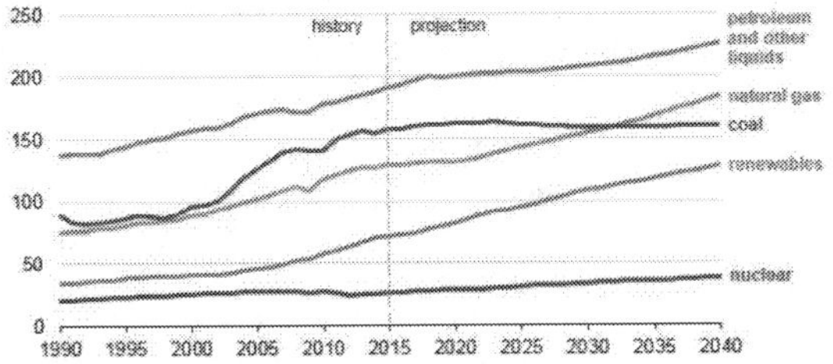

Fig. 1. Energy Demand Trends [1].

Simple analysis of Fig.1 shows that since 1990, the average energy demand from petroleum, natural gas and coal has risen by approximately 50 Quadrillion Btu at the end of 2017. Along with this unprecedented increase, a side effect of CO2 emission has also risen to levels of public concern [2] leading to Carbon taxation policies in the developing and developed nations[3].In contrast, it is observed that from 1990 to 2007, the demand for renewable energy is almost stagnant. However, from 2008, the rate has increased to approximately 2.63 Quadrillion Btu/year and is comparable to the rate of increase in the demand of petroleum and natural gas. This increase in the popularity of renewable energy sources during this period is due to its ability to mitigate CO2 emission problems as well as advancement in technology for producing renewable energy. For example, a study conducted in Thailand predicts that that the use of solar and wind as a means of electricity generation will in approximately 50 years lower CO2 emission by 69.66% [4].

The sources of renewable energy available today include solar, wind, biomass, ocean tides, geothermal, hydro power and etc [5]. Although all of these sources are able to produce electricity with zero or negligible CO2 emission, solar and wind generation methods are the most popular. For example, unlike ocean tide electric generators that must be built near the ocean, solar and wind farms can be implemented almost anywhere. Similarly, this is why solar and wind are preferred to when compared to geothermal and hydro power generation. However, the area required to produce solar or wind energy is extremely large. This will bring forth socio-economic issues such as lack of land for agriculture and housing.

* Corresponding author: izhal@upm.edu.my

This paper proposes a new renewable energy generating device that utilizes both solar and wind energy for the production of electricity in one embodiment. The main objective behind the design objective is to minimize the area required when an array of this new hybrid generator is used for large scale RE power generation.

2 Solar, Wind and Hybrid Wind-Solar Farms and Land Area Usage

Along with the rise in world demand for energy from renewable sources, a multitude of information is easily obtained concerning operators of large scale solar, wind and hybrid wind-solar energy for the public. These corporations have a public obligation to inform the public on the specifications of their plants. Table 1 shows five operational large scale solar power plants.

Table 1. Operational Large Scale Solar Power Plants.

Reference	Operation Start Year	Location	Number of Panels (million)	Output Capacity (MW)	Area (Hectar^2)
[6]	2016	Kamuthi, India	2.5	648	1000
[7]	2017	Qinghai, China	4	850	300
[8]	2017	Kurnool, India	4	900/1000*	2352
[9]	2016	Datong, China	NA	1000/3000*	NA
[10]	2016	Ningxia, China	NA	1500	4300

Note: * targeted capacity

It is clear that the area required is large to produce MW capacity plants. For example, the solar power facility in Kurnool with a targeted capacity of 1GWatt requires an area of 2,352 hectars^2. Once a piece of land has been commissioned to build a mega scale solar plant, it is rendered unusable for agriculture and settlement for at least a 20 year period which is as long as powers purchase agreement. This is one of the disadvantages of large scale solar energy generation.

Table 2. Operational Large Scale Wind Power Plants.

Reference	Operation Start Year	Location	Number of Wind Turbines	Output Capacity (MW)	Area (Hectar^2)
[11]	NA	Gansu, China	7,000	6,000/20,000*	NA
[12]	NA	California, USA	750	3,000	12,950
[13]	1986	Tamil Nadu, India	3,000	1,500	NA
[14]	2001	Rajathan, India	NA	1,064	NA
[15]	2012	Oregon, USA	NA	845	20,720

Table 2 shows five existing mega scale wind farms, their locations and output capacity. These farms are installed with large HAWT rated around the 1 MW capacity each. Again it is seen that thea rea requirements is extremely high. For example, 12,950 hectars^2 of land is required to produce 3GW from the facility in California [12]. This is mainly to adhere to safety regulations for placement distances between adjacent wind turbines.

Table 3. Operational Large Scale Hybrid Wind-Solar Power Plants.

Ref	Name/Location	Solar Cap. (MW)	Wind Cap. (MW)	Total Cap. (MW)	Area (Acres)
[16]	SECI-NREDCAP/India	120	40	160	1000
[17]	Arena Gullen/Australia	10	165.5	175.5	70
[18]	Fakken Wind Farm/Norway	20	54	74	NA
[19]	Hero Future Energies/India	28.8	50	78.8	NA

Recently, several hybrid wind-solar power plants have also been reported and are shown in Table 3. Information on its respective solar, wind and total output capacity is presented. These hybrid plants have dedicated land to house PV cell arrays and wind turbines to produce electricity. Similar to the solar and wind RE plants, the area required to produce hybrid RE power is also quite large. However, when compared to pure large scale solar or wind farms, the usage of land for the generation of hybrid RE power is much more efficient since only 0.16 acres to 2.5 acres of land is required to produce a capacity of 1MW [16,17].

The use of large amounts of land for generating green power is seen as a social-economic problem because once a piece of land is commissioned for a large scale solar, wind or hybrid wind-solar power plant, it cannot be used for agriculture or residential purposes for a period of at least 25 years or is based on the period of a power purchase agreement between the RE power producer and the government where the plant is erected. The land requirement for generating RE energy is large due to the dimensions of the devices used to produce electricity. For example, the most efficient and well-designed large scale solar or wind farms require on average 4 acres of land to generate 1MW of electricity at full capacity [6-15].

3 Available Hybrid Wind-Solar Generators

PV cells produce electricity by means of the photovoltaic effect while wind generators induce electrical current in a coil by cutting a moving magnetic flux through the rotation motion of the propellers of the wind turbine [20, 21]. Contemporary hybrid wind-solar farms are designed by connecting a solar farm with a wind farm, making them also a clean source of renewable energy [22]. As discussed in the previous section, although energy production is clean, socio-economic impact due to the use of large amounts of land for long periods of time is also an unwanted effect of hybrid wind-solar plants.

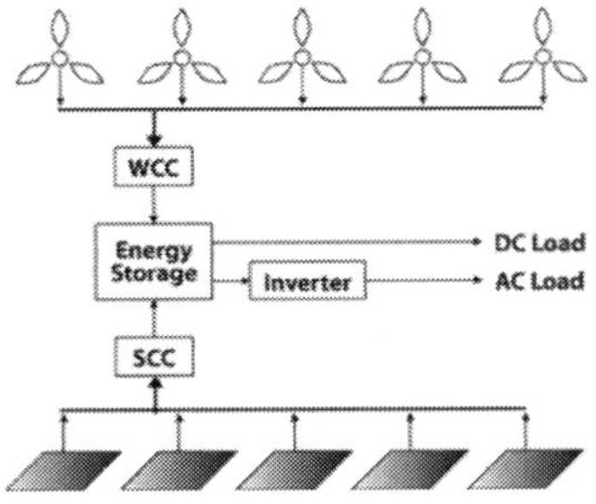

Fig. 2. Conventional Hybrid Wind-Solar Farm.

The simplified schematic of a conventional hybrid wind-solar farm is shown in Fig.2.When the wind blows, the turbines generate DC current that is fed directly to the wind charge controller (WCC) and when the Sun is shining, the solar panels also generate DC current that is fed to the solar charge controller (SCC). Both of the charge controller's charges the system's battery. The battery's DC output is then fed to an inverter which converts it to an AC power signal. The AC signal is then fed to a transformer and stepped up according to specifications of the host grid. It is concluded that the conventional type hybrid plant uses dedicated solar panels and wind turbines to generate hybrid renewable energy.

A hybrid wind-solar generator on the other hand is defined as renewable energy device capable of generating electricity from wind power and solar irradiation in one embodiment. These devices are a combinatioin of either a Horizontal Axis Wind Turbine (HAWT) or a Vertical Axis Wind Turbine (VAWT) system coupled with Photovoltaic Cells. Hybrid wind-solar genrators have a combined capacity of its wind generating components and solar generating components and are placed stratigically at areas of high wind density and high solar insolution. Although not yet reported, these new hybrid RE generators are promosing devices when it comes to implementing high capacity hybrid wind-solar farms that use up a small area. Such a device was first introduced commercially in 2008 by a company called Windstream Technologies situated in India.

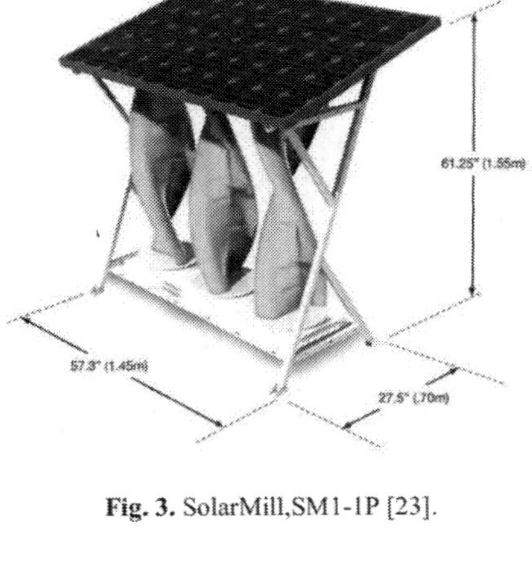

Fig. 3. SolarMill,SM1-1P [23].

As shown in Fig.3, the SM1-1P has a PV panel placed on top of a 3×1 array VAWT. It is noted that the PV panels are stationary. It generates at full capacity 740W where 500W comes from the VWAT system and the remaining 240W from its PV cells [23].

Fig. 4. TOYODA, TYD-WS4 [24].

Fig.4 shows another hybrid wind-solar generator from Tangsyan Toyoda Technology, China. Again, this device generates wind power using a VWAT system (300W). A 240W solar panel is mounted at the bottom of the wind turbine giving it a total capacity of 540W. It also houses a 100W street light [24].

Fig. 5. SkyWolf [25].

Another hybrid wind-solar generator known as the SkyWolf is shown in Fig.5. This system's capacity is 3.5kW. It uses a Diffused Augmented Wind Turbine (DAWT) system where the turbine is enclosed in several solar panels arranged in a conic configuration to maximize rotation speed via the wind tunnelling effect. The turbine's angle can be rotated by computer control to maximize for optimum wind and solar generation [25].

It is concluded that these commercially available hybrid wind-solar generators have fixed solar panels. Through the course of a day, the temperature of these panels will

https://doi.org/10.1051/matecconf/201821501015

rise causing its efficiency to drop. Moreover its capacity or footprint is too small, thus, a large area is required to arrange a large number of these devices to generate energy at a massive scale.

In this paper, we propose that rotating solar panels that move along with a wind turbines blade is to be used for the next generation of hybrid wind-solar generators. This will allow a much more compact device with high capacity. Moreover, the temperature of the PV panels are lower since the panels can rotate with the turbine's blade. In order to allow the solar panels to move in a circular motion with the blades.

4 Proposed True Hybrid Wind-Solar Electric Generator

The proposed True Hybrid Wind-Solar (THWS) Electric Generator is presented in Fig.6. Labels A, B and C are three different modules of the system are are called the Solar Blade Module (SBM), Moving Contact Module (MCM) and the Hybrid Output Module (HOM), respectively. This particular design is targetted for a total output capacity of 3.5kW.

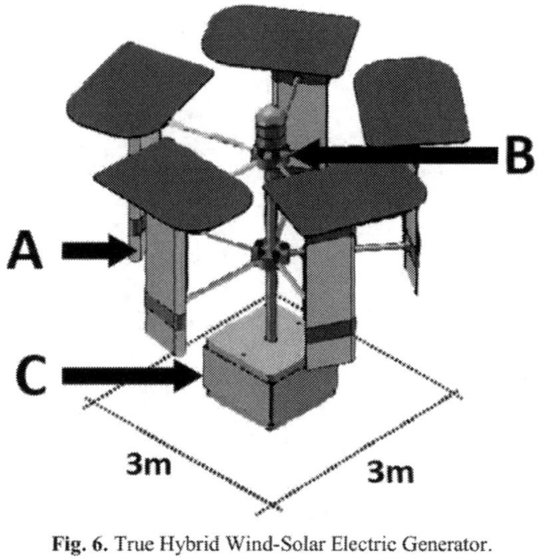

Fig. 6. True Hybrid Wind-Solar Electric Generator.

Each SBM is a modified Darrieus type blade where a 100W PV panel is attached to a plate fitted perpendicular to the Darries type blade. Since there are five SBMs, the expected capacity is 500W. The size of the blade and dimensions of the THWS generator is determined by the dimension of the PV cells used. In general, a 1m × 0.5m PV has a capacity of 100W, thus the THWS generator's footprint will 3m × 3m.

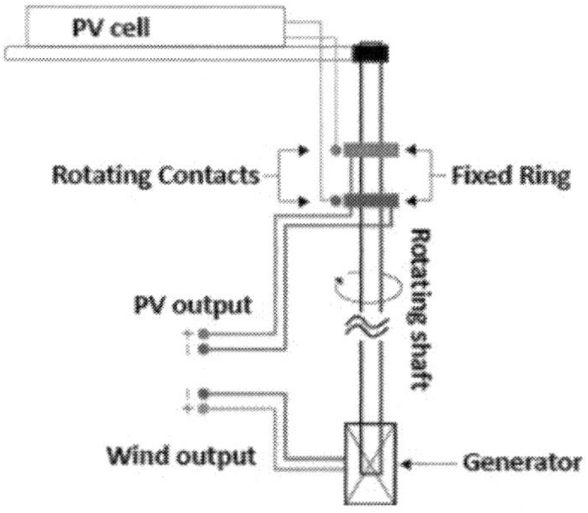

Fig. 7. True Hybrid Wind-Solar Modules Schematic.

Since all of the SBMs rotate, the problem of extracting the power signal produced by the PV cells is anticipated and the MCM is designed to tackel this problem. Fig. 7 shows the simplified circuit schematic of the TWHS generator. The MCM comprises of two fixed rings. The top fixed ring maintains connection from the PV cell's positive terminal to the PV cell output port of the THWS generator while the bottom ring does the similar for the negative terminal. The contacts of each respective PV output terminal orbits it's respective fixed ring as the SBM rotates in the wind. Electricity is tapped as the PV output terminal directly from the fixed ring with a voltage of 24V.

On the other hand, the HOM serves two purposes. The first is to generate electrical energy from the wind via the Generator shown in Fig.7. It is important to use a DC output generator for ease of combining solar and wind energy as the end product. A 3kW capacity output is expected from a VAWT with a footprint of 3m × 3m footprint of this design.

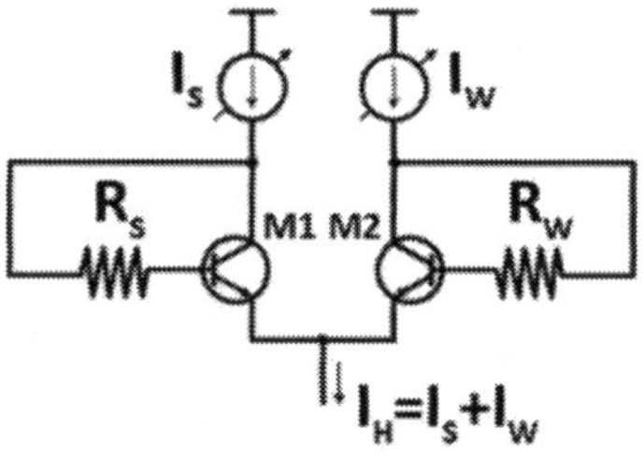

Fig. 8. Hybrid Power Selection Module.

The HOM's second purpose is to electrically isolate non-generating RE generators within the THWS generator. For example, on a windy night, the PV cells are dormant, thus the HOM will electrically isolate all of the SBM from the system. This also acts to prevent loading from the PV cell's juntion capacitance onto the system. Fig.8 shows the circuit contained in the HOM responsible for this task. Two power transistors, M1 and M2 capable of carrying 5A currents are used. I_S and I_W denotes the solar and wind currents, respectively. A base resistance, R_S and R_B are connected to M1 and M2 in order to induce a voltage drop when I_S and/or I_W are/is present. The generated voltage accross these resistances will turn on each respective transistor. When no voltage is induced, the transistor will turn off. In the case that the PV cells are not producing electricity, M1 turns off and I_H=I_W. When no wind is present, M2 turns off and I_H=I_S. However, when both PV cells and wind generator are producing current, both transistors are turned on, thus I_H=I_S + I_W.

5 Estimation of the THWS Electric Generator Power Production Footprint

The Power Production Footprint (PPF) is defined for the first time in this work as the area required by a plant to produce 1MW of electricity. PPF can be used to measure the land usage efficiency for RE plants for monitoring socio-economic effects or simply as data for the planning of a large scale RE plants. In this paper, it is used to compare between the efficiency of land usage for a plant composed of THWS Generators and a plant composed of PV cell arrays or wind turbine generators.

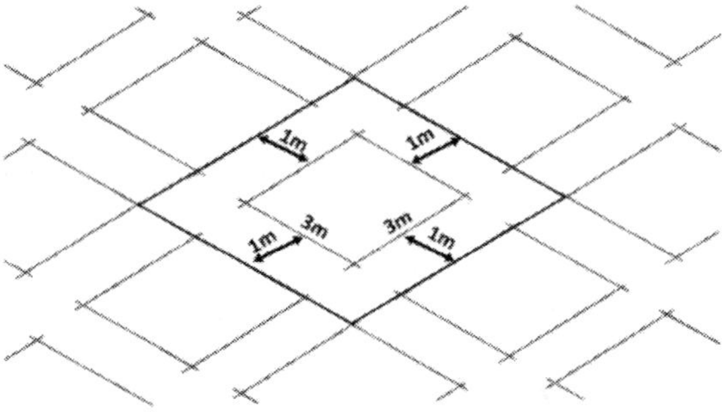

Fig. 9. THWS Generator Layout for Large Scale Power Plant.

Fig.9 is a depiction of the layout of several THWS generators arranged in a rectangular grid for the implementation of a large scale power plant. The raw footprint of one THWS is marked as 3m ×3m. To allow for safety and as a path for service and maintenance, it is suggested that the distance between two raw footprints is to be 1m. This results in a footprint of 3.5m^2 between two adjacent THWS generator units.

Since the capacity of one THWS generator is designed to be 3.5kW, 290 units are required to produce 1MW. With a footprint of 3.5m^2, the total area required using the arrangement in Fig.9 is 3552.5m^2 or equivalent to 0.88 acres of land. If a 20% more allowance is considered for other plant facilities such as transformers and inverters, the PPF of the THWS is approximately 1.06 acres/MW.

6 Conclusion

Analysis on area usage between large scale hybrid wind-solar power plants and their counterparts, either large scale pure solar or wind plants shows that the hybrid RE plants have a much smaller PPF, making them much more area efficient. For example, the hybrid facility in Australia has a PPF of only 0.16 acres/MW [17]. However, these RE power plants use the traditional hybrid wind-solar topology where dedicated PV cell arrays and wind turbines are used separately to produce hybrid renewable energy. Nontheless, it is noted that hybrid type farms are more area efficient and in the long term will lower the negative socio-economic impact such as shortage of land for agriculture and housing.

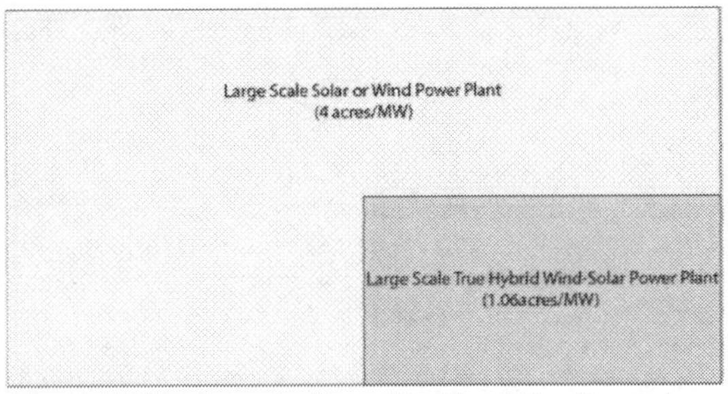

Fig. 10. THWS Generator Power Plant Land Size Comparison.

The recent emergence of hybrid wind-solar RE generators into the market have opened the opportunity for the development of large scale true hybrid wind-solar plants. However, either the generation capacity is too low or the PPF is too high in the existing models. Thus, the THWS electric generator is proposed in this paper. It is designed with a moving contact module that in the not so distant future will allow the blades of a wind turbine generator to be fabricated from PV material. In this work, placement of the PV cells in the porposed configuration not only allows a small PPF but also introduces a cooling effect to the PV panels which in turn boost the efficiency of the cells. The hybrid output is tapped out of the THWS generator via a dedicated HOM circuit. The THWS electric generator is designed for a 24V output with solar capacity of 500W and a wind capacity of 3kW giving a total output capacity of 3.5kW with a footprint of 3.5m^2. Arrangement of the THWS generator units in a rectangular grid will allow a PPF of only 1.06 acre/MW. As depicted in Fig.10, the PPF of a large scale THWS plant is approximately a quarter of the PPF of a conventional large scale solar or wind farm.

References

[1] British Petroleum (2016) BP Statistical Review of World Energy.London: Workbook (xlsx)

[2] Richard, S., Thomas, M.S. and Ruth, A.J., (2006) 'World Carbon Dioxide Emissions:1950-2050.' Review of Economics and Statistics, 80(1), 15-27

[3] Intergovernmental Panel on Climate Change (2012) Renewable Energy Sources and Climate Change Mitigation : Summary for Policymakers and Technical Summary.Africa: IPCC

[4] Tri, V. K., usumadewi,Pornphimol, W. andBundit, L., (2017) 'Long-term CO2 Emission Reduction from Renewable Energy in Power Sector: The case of Thailand in 2050.' Energy Procedia, 138, 961-966

[5] Antonia, V.H., Timothy, E.L., Jennifer, L.E. and Daniel, M.K., (2001) 'Renewable Energy: A Viable Choice' Environment, 3(10),8-20

[6] Business Insider (2017) India has built the world's largest solar power plant – and it can power 150,000 homes, URL:http://www.businessinsider.com/india-has-built-the-worlds-largest-solar-power-plant-2016-11/?IR=T (date accessed: 29November 2016)

[7] Alternative Energies (2017) Longyangxia Dam Solar Park in China is now the Biggest Solar Farm in the World, URL:https://www.alternative-energies.net/longyangxia-dam-solar-park-in-china-is-now-the-biggest-solar-farm-in-the-world/(date accessed: 19 January 2017)

[8] The Hindu (2017) With Kurnool solar park, State takes a giant leap, URL:http://www.thehindu.com/todays-paper/tp-national/tp-andhrapradesh/with-kurnool-solar-park-state-takes-a-giant-leap/article18289685.ece (date accessed: 29 Arpil 2017)

[9] Wikipedia (2017) List of photovoltaic power stations, URL:https://en.wikipedia.org/wiki/List_of_photovoltaic_power_stations (date accessed: 24April 2018)

[10] ESCN (2016) Ningxia builds the largest desert photovoltaic integrated area in the southern edge of the Tengger Deser, URL: http://www.escn.com.cn/news/show-310093.html (date accessed: 5 Arpil 2016)

[11] The New York Times (2018) It Can Power a Small Nation. But This Wind Farm in China is Mostly Idle, URL: https://www.nytimes.com/2017/01/15/world/asia/china-gansu-wind-farm.html (date accessed: 15 January 2017)

[12] Inside Climate News (2009) Alta Wind Farm, America's Largest Wind Power Project, Blows Closer, URL: https://insideclimatenews.org/news/20090727/alta-wind-farm-america%E2%80%99s-largest-wind-power-project-blows-closer (date accessed: 27 July 2009)

[13] Wikipedia (2018) Muppandal Wind Farm, URL:https://en.wikipedia.org/wiki/Muppandal_Wind_Farm (date accessed: 12April 2018)

[14] Industry About (2018) Jaisalmer Wind Farm, URL: available from https://www.industryabout.com/country-territories-3/962-india/wind-energy/45830-jaisalmer-wind-farm (date accessed: 3 February 2018)

[15] Power Technology (2018) Shepherds Flat Wind Farm, Oregon, URL:https://www.power-technology.com/projects/shepherds-flat-wind-farm-oregon/ (dateaccessed: 26 April 2018).

[16]SECI/NREDCAP/APTRANSCO – Solar-Wind Hybrid Power Plant 160 MW – Andhra Pradesh - Project Profile, December 2017.

[17] ARENA Wire, "Australia's first hybrid wind and solar farm", 2 February 2018, URL:https://arena.gov.au/blog/gullen/ (date accessed: 279 July 2018).

[18] Charlotte Tiller, "Case Study of a Large-Scale Solar and Wind Power HybridSystem at Fakken Wind Farm, Troms", Masters Thesis Dissertation, The Arctic University of Norway, June 2017.

[19] Vaselina Petrova, , "Hero Future Energies brings live India's 1st solar-wind hybrid", Renewables Now, 23 April 2018 (date accessed: 29 July 2018).

[20] Boyle, G. (2004) Renewable Energy: Power for a Sustainable Future. Oxford University Press.

[21] Hau, E. (2006) Wind Turbines, Fundamentals, Technologies, Applications and Economics, 2nd Ed. Berlin: Springer

[22] Yashwant, S., Gupta, S.C., Bohre, A.K. and Meng, W. (2016) 'PV-wind hybrid system: A review with case study' Cogent Engineering, 3(1), 1-31

[23] Windstream Technologies (2018) Windstream Technologies Economical Energy,URL: https://www.windstream-inc.com/products/solarmill [date accessed: 26April 2018]

[24] Tangshan TOYODA Technology, URL: http://www.wptyd.com/product/81.html (date accessed: 29 July 2018).

[25] SkyWolf Wind Turbine Corporation, URL: http://www.skywolfwindturbines.com/specifications/ (date accessed: 29 July 2018).

[26] Pierrick, I. (2016) 'Design and Test of a 3D-printed Horiontal Axis Wind Turbine', Universite Catholic de Louvain Master Thesis Dissertation, 53-54

Implementation of Maximum Power Point Tracking to Improving the Solar Cell Efficiency

Sepannur Bandri, Zulkarnaini Zulkarnaini, and Andi Sofian

Institut Teknologi Padang, Electrical Engineering Department, Padang, West Sumatra, Indonesia

Abstract. The sun is one of renewable energy sources. The use of sunlight using solar panels as a power plant began to be developed to reduce the use of fossil fuels. Solar panels have the advantage of being environmentally friendly because they do not have pollution-generating waste, are inexpensive and easy to apply. The power generated by solar panel is influenced by temperature and light intensity factor. The main problem of using solar panels is its efficiency is still low. This research presents an attempt to improve the energy conversion efficiency by solar panels by using Maximum Power Point Tracking method. The main principle of this method is adjusting the output voltage from the solar panel to obtain maximum power for different intensity of sunlight. The solar panel output voltage setting is performed using a buck boost converter controlled by MPPT system. The simulation results show that the use of this method of solar panel output power is higher by 64,78% - 87,06% than without MPPT.

1 Introduction

In the current energy crisis conditions, scientists are competing to find and examine the use of alternative energy sources to ensure the sustainability and availability of these energy sources. fossil energy as a major energy source is very limited and is subject to a threat of scarcity due to the use of such energy on a large and continuous scale. In addition, pollution rates resulting from fuel energy generation is very large. Therefore, there needs to be an alternative renewable energy source for the purpose of fossil energy sources. The solar energy is an environmentally friendly and clean energy source and is available to him in an infinite number of environments [4]. Solar power plants (photovoltaic arrays) are a new energy source and. Which is very promising to be developed in order to meet energy needs. This power plant utilizes sunlight as a source of energy to generate power that continues to use its use both in small scale and large scale [1].

This new modified alternative energy sources have been put forward by previous researchers like Tri et al. (2011) and Radhityo (2012), but to realize its large-scale utilization in our country Indonesia is experiencing delays, because it is related to development policy, as well as politics and understanding of society. In this study deliberately taken from the side that is relatively easy to realize, that is for use in the household scale. It is time to target only on the household scale but mention the big number of each household conscious to utilize this system, certainly not the least will provide convenience to the needs of power [1][3].

Photovoltaic has an optimum operating point called power point tracking (MPPT), where the optimum point varies According to irradiance and photovoltaic temperature. When the PV array is connected directly to the battery then the PV array disk to operate on battery, so that the PV array does not work at the point of maximum power (tracking the maximum power point). MPPT will calculate the address where the photovoltaic circuit will work optimally. With MPPT will make the photovoltaic array will work at its maximum voltage so as to produce maximum power. If a 24 Volt battery is installed in the output portion of the photovoltaic array using a boost converter and a 100% circuit efficiency using MPPT the charging current of the battery becomes 3.15A, the power extracted in accordance with the photovoltaic power rating of the array. Electricity emitted by the photovoltaic array is conditioned by the regulator's voltage using the technique of tracking the maximum power point for a proper charging of the battery. By extracting the power from the photovoltaic array, it is expected that the storage of electricity in the battery is maximum and lasts continuously [5]

2 Proposed Topology

Maximum Power Point Tracking (MPPT) is an electronic system that runs Photovoltaic (PV) modules in order to optimize the power available on the solar array. MPPT is not a mechanical system that can drive solar arrays to the point where the sun is most powerful. MPPT is an electronic system that alters the parameters generated by solar arrays so that solar arrays can transfer power to the

* Corresponding author: sepannur@itp.ac.id

maximum. MPPT can be used with a multilevel mechanical system and direct the solar array to the most powerful sunlight, but it needs a very different system [5].

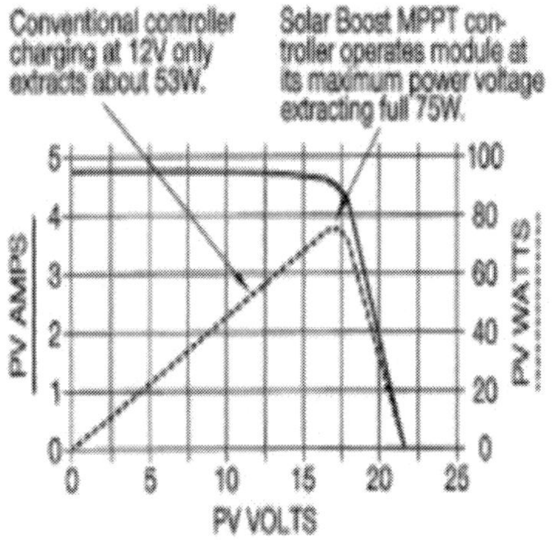

Fig. 1 MPPT characteristic

The conventional solar array controllers are forced to operate with battery voltage, so the solar array does not work at the maximum power point tracking. For example, see figure 1. If we force the solar array to work on a 12 V battery voltage when the power produced by the solar array is 75W, then the extractable power is only about 53 W only. Compared with determining the operating voltage directly, MPPT calculates the voltage at which the PV array can work maximally. For example, the maximum voltage on the PV array is 17 V, MPPT system will make the solar array work at its maximum voltage so that maximum power will be obtained. For example, in the solar array output section we install a 24 V battery then when used boost converter and 100% circuit efficiency, using MPPT current that charge the battery will be. So the power that is successfully extracted into 24 x 3.15 = 75 W. In practice this efficiency will be slightly lower, this is due to the loss of power caused by the MPPT circuit [6].

The model of circuit for MPPT is shown below: The two most important things in designing MPP tracker are the topology of the switch mode and the control mechanism. There are several switch mode topologies that can be used: boost, buck, buck-boost. In this study used the converter boost topology, with consideration boost converter can easily track MPPT because the output voltage on the boost converter is greater than the input voltage [4].

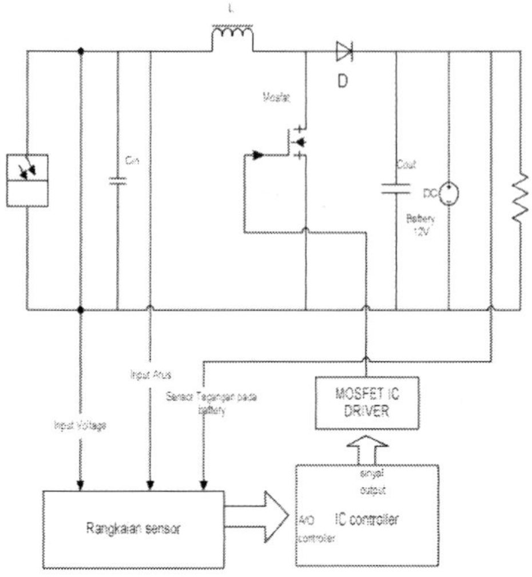

Fig. 2 Control mechanism of MPPT

The control mechanisms applied in this study are shown in Figure 2. MPPT power is detected by using signals from voltage and current input. Analog signals are converted by A/D converters into digital signals and processed inside the controller [5] [7]. The PWM output on the controller gives the MOSFET driver the input to drive the MOSFET according to the specified duty cycle, when the full battery feedback sensor gives the signal so that the controller will stop charging the battery [1].

3 Design of MPPT Circuit

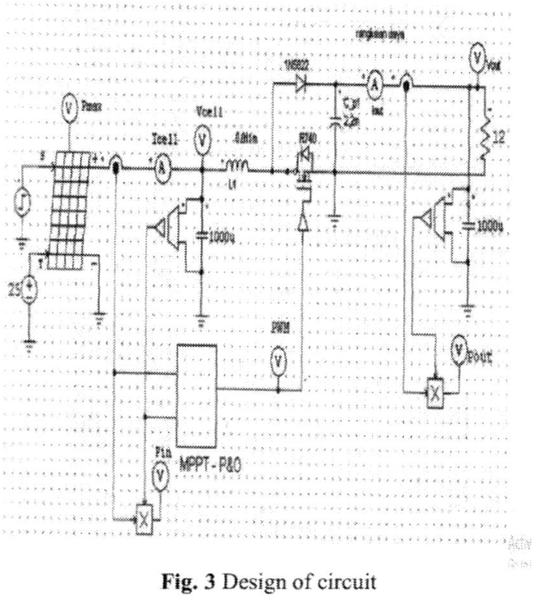

Fig. 3 Design of circuit

 https://doi.org/10.1051/matecconf/201821501016

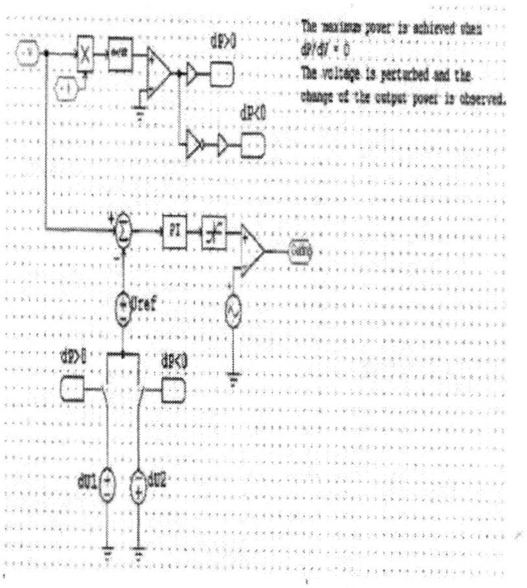

Fig. 4 MPPT circuit design

3.1 MPPT algorithm

MPPT algorithm used in programming Digital signal processing is the Perturbation and Observation (P & O) algorithm chosen because of its simplicity, both theoretically and in its writing. To write the MPPT algorithm on DSP microcontroller used C language which then compiled using Code Composer Studio (CCS). The P & O algorithm used is as follows:

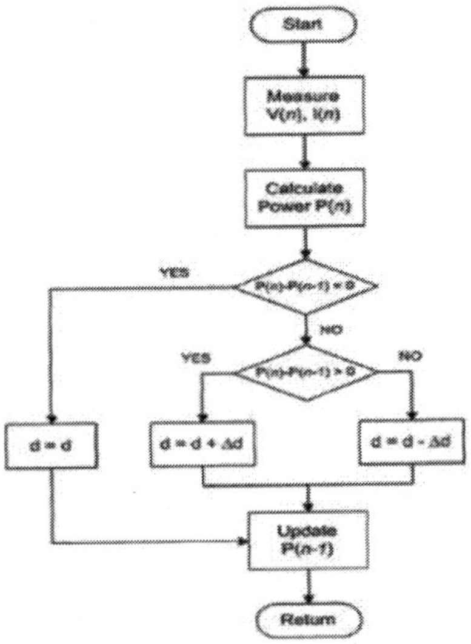

Fig. 5. MPPT Algorithm

There are two observable conditions of the above algorithm which can be described in the P-V curve of the solar panel as follows:

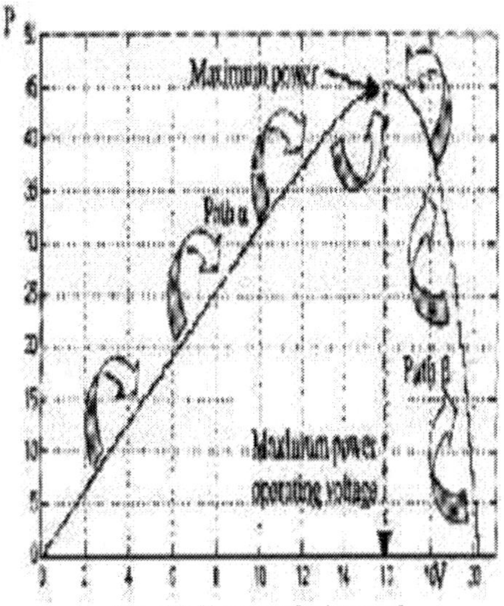

Fig. 6 P-V curve of solar panel

The first condition is when Pn> Pn-1. This condition can be described as α path in figure 6 above. From this situation it can be seen that the PV power will increase with increasing PV operating voltage. Therefore, small voltage perturb are done by increasing the duty cycle, it is necessary to reach the MPPT point. 2. The first condition is when Pn> Pn-1. This condition can be described as α path in figure 6 above. From this situation it can be seen that the PV power will increase with increasing PV operating voltage. 3. The first condition is when Pn> Pn-1. This condition can be described as α path in figure 6 above. From this situation it can be seen that the PV power will increase with increasing PV operating voltage. Therefore, small voltage peculators (V) are done by increasing the duty cycle, necessary to reach the point of MPPT.

3 Simulation Results

The power generated by solar panels is dependent on the exposure of the irradiance, the decrease of power is precisely at the time of decreased irradiation. at the time of the simulation of the dome irradiation from 1000 w / m2 to 900 w / m2 at t = 0 seconds, resulting in a decrease in the maximum output power of the solar cell. for voltage and current graph can be seen in the following curve.

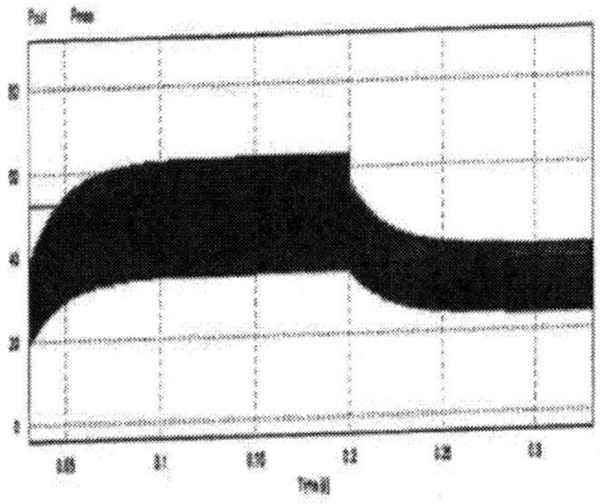

Fig. 7. Curve of power output

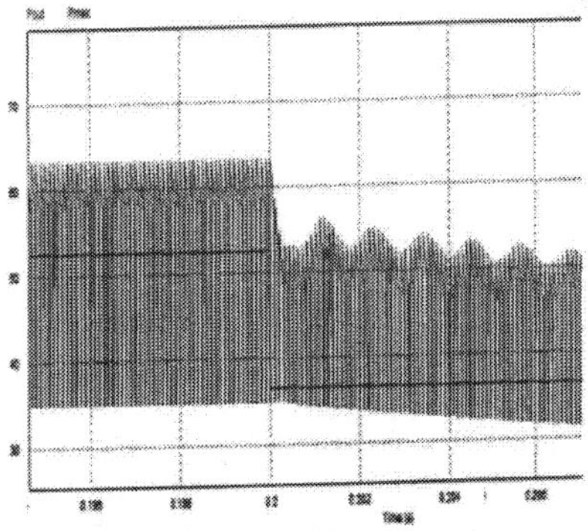

Fig. 8. perturbation of power output

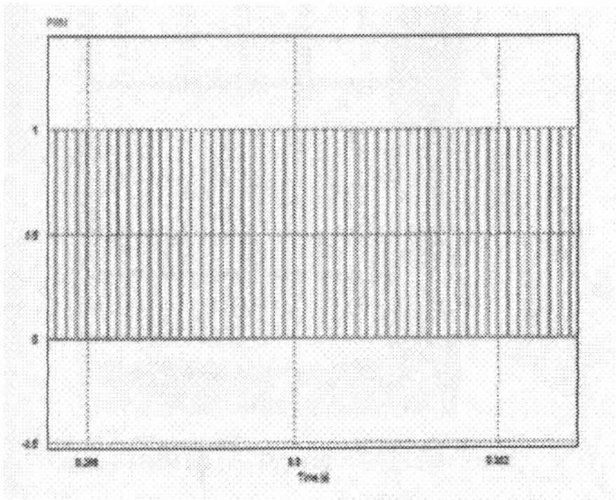

Fig. 9. PWM signal of controller

on the curve above, the input voltage is shown in red, the output voltage is blue, the MPPT input current is green and the MPPT output current is pink. in the voltage chart it is seen that the boost converter serves to increase the voltage, where the MPPT output voltage is greater than the input voltage. while on the current curve, the output current from MPPT undergoes oscillation, this indicates the perturbation process runs as it reaches the point of MPPT. MPPT output power cycles around maximum power, so the power generated using MPPT is approximately the maximum power value that solar panels can generate at each irradiance level. this indicates that the MPPT design has worked well. the implementation of the MPPT design can be seen in the picture below.

3 Conclusion

Topology boost converter design has been increased of efficiency of power 85% and the average increase of power 32.7% with the ideal PWM switching frequency to control Boost converter is 50 KHz. The working frequency limit of the duty cycle of boost converter is 10%-60%. The selection of working frequency is influenced by the efficiency of the converter

Acknowledgement

We would like to thank very much to the team of the laboratory of electrical engineering of the Institut Teknologi Padang whose helped us in research in the laboratory. We would also like to thank for Ministry of Research, Technology and Higher Education' Republic of Indonesia whose helped fund this research in accordance with the research contract number **325 / 27.O10.5 / PN /II/ 2018**

References

1. Tohid Nouri,et.all., *Generalized Transformerless Ultra Step-Up DC-DC Converter with Reduced Voltage Stress on Semiconducto*r, IET Power Electronics, **vol.7**, issue 11, pp.2791-2805, (2014)
2. Po-Wa Lee,et.all., *Steady-State Analysis of An Interleaved Boost Converter with Coupled Inductor*, IEEE Transaction On Industrial Electronics, **vol 47**.No.4, pp 787-795, (2000)
3. Wang, P. et al., *Input-parallel Output-series DC-DC Boost Converter with a Wide Input Voltage Range*, for Fuel Cell Vehicles. , 9545(c), (2017)
4. Vazquez, A. et al., *Different Modular Techniques Applied in a Synchronous Boost Converter with SiC MOSFETs to Obtain High Efficiency at Light Load and Low Current Ripple*. IEEE Transactions on Industrial Electronics, 0046(c), pp.1–1, (2017)
5. Cadirci, I. et al., *Unity power factor boost converter with phase shifted parallel IGBT operation for medium power applications*. Electric Power Applications, IEEE Proceedings ,149(x), pp.237–244, 2002.
6. Corcau, J.I. et al., *Multisim implementation and analysis of a DC to DC boost converter with two parallel stages*. International Conference on Electrical Drives and Power Electronics, Proceedings, pp.88–93, (2015)
7. Sen, G. et al, *Comparison of current balancing configurations for Primary Parallel Isolated Boost Converter. International Aegean Conference on Electrical Machines and Power Electronics*, ACEMP 2011 and Electromotion 2011 Joint Conference, (September), pp.449–454, (2013)A. Mecke, I. Lee, J.R. Baker jr., M.M. Banaszak Holl, B.G. Orr, Eur. Phys. J. E **14**, 7 (2004)

MATEC Web of Conferences **215**, 01017 (2018) https://doi.org/10.1051/matecconf/201821501017
ICTIS 2018

Experimental Study to Performance Improvement of Vapor Compression Cooling System Integrated Direct Evaporative Cooler and Condenser

Arfidian Rachman[1] and *Lisa* Nesti[2]

[1] Institute of Technology Padang, Mechanical Engineering Department, 25143 Padang-West Sumatra, Indonesia

[2] Polytechnic ATI-Padang, Logistic Management Industry Department, 25143 Padang-West Sumatra, Indonesia

Abstract. For areas with very hot and humid weather condition increased latent and sensible load are a major problem in cooling systems that will increase compressor work so that electricity consumption will also increase. Combined condenser with direct evaporate cooling will increase the heat removal process by using an evaporative cooler effect that will increase the efficiency of energy use. This paper presents the study of the use of evaporator cooling and condenser. This paper mainly calculated energy consumption in steam compression cooling systems and related problems. From the results of this study, the use of condensers with evaporative cooling, power consumption can be reduced to 46% and performance coefficient (COP) can be increased by about 12%, with 1,2 kW cooling capacity.

1 Introduction

Energy is a very important factor in encouraging strong economic development for growth in any country. With the rising prices of fossil fuels [1]. The savings and reductions in energy consumption, help reduce global warming.

The increase in living standards and demand for human comfort has led to an increase in energy consumption. The amount of energy consumed by air conditioners, refrigerators, and water heaters is increasing rapidly, and occupies about 30% of total power consumption [3]. Electricity consumption for air conditioning systems has been estimated at about 45% for residential and commercial buildings [4]. Due to the rapid growth in world population and economy, total world energy consumption is projected to increase by about 71% from 2003 to 2030 [5]. Therefore, any attempt to reduce the overall cooling system energy consumption will contribute to large-scale energy savings at the international level. Reduced cooling unit energy consumption can be achieved by improving performance. This can be done by lowering the compressor power consumption, increasing the heat dissipation capacity of the condenser, or reducing the difference between condenser and evaporator pressure.

Higher condensation temperatures lead to an increase in pressure ratio across the compressor, thereby increasing the compressor's work and thereby reducing compressor life and coefficient of performance (COP). High outdoor temperatures above 35°C in summer are one of the reasons, leading to a decrease in the coefficient of performance (COP) of most air-cooled units to the range of 2.2 to 2.4 [6]. In addition, if this temperature stays above 45°C for long periods of time, the AC will be over trip due to excessive condenser working pressure. Chow and Cengel [7,8] mentioned that the air conditioning performance coefficient decreased by about 2-4% for every 1°C increase in condenser temperature.

In Middle Eastern countries, atmospheric temperatures during summer are approaching 40-45°C sometimes higher. During this condition, the AC compressor works continuously and consumes more electrical power and COP decreases [9]. Therefore, it is necessary to lower the ambient air temperature before passing through the condenser coil, to lower the temperature and pressure of the condenser. This can be achieved by using evaporative cooling, which lowers the condensation temperature from the dry ball temperature outdoors to near wet ball temperatures [10]. The efficiency of evaporative cooling is essentially unaffected by high environmental temperatures in dry climates. The most significant evaporative coolant benefits during peak periods of utility when the difference between the largest dry and wet ball temperature [11]. This can result in significant overall energy and demand savings because any small reduction in electricity consumption in the housing sector can save significant amounts of energy [12,13].

2 Methodology

2.1 Experimental

The new air conditioning systems with independent condenser and cooling evaporative cooling are shown schematically in Figure 1. It mainly consists of

https://doi.org/10.1051/matecconf/201821501017

evaporative cooling and steam compression cooling systems, measuring instruments and control devices.

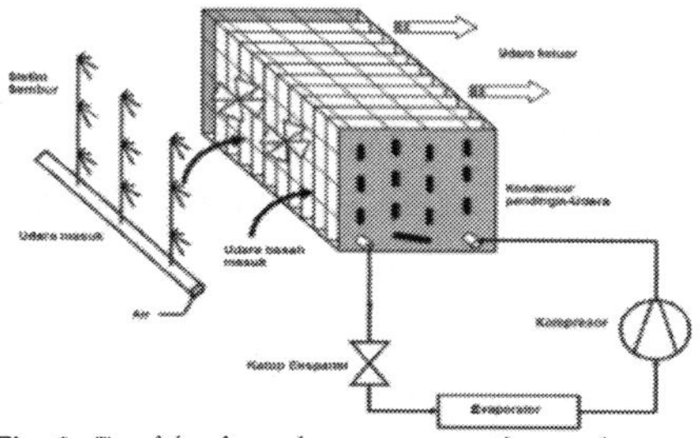

Fig. 1. Combined condenser evaporative cooler

2.2 Measurement

The water flow rate of the shell and tube evaporative coolers is measured using a volume flow meter with an accuracy of ± 0.5%, the total airflow rate of the evaporative fan is controlled by the frequency converter. Anemometer is used to measure air flow rate (maximum 4.8 m/s). Relative humidity was measured using a psychrometer with an accuracy of 1%. Thermo-gun is used to measure various temperatures, and the data collected is analyzed.

2.3 Theoretical Analysis

The cooling system components comprising one compressor, evaporative cooling water pump, and a single phase power fan are measured separately. The cooling capacity can be calculated by applying the equilibrium energy equations as follow:

$$Q_c = \dot{m}_w C_{pw} (\dot{T}_{in} - T_{out}) \quad (1)$$

The cooling capacity can be calculated by the equation

$$Q_c = \dot{m}_r (h_1 - h_3) \quad (2)$$

Furthermore, the compressor input power and heating capacity are also calculated in Equation 3 and Equation (4):

$$W_C = \dot{m}_r (h_2 - h_1) \quad (3)$$

$$Q_h = \dot{m}_r (h_2 - h_3) \quad (4)$$

The overall performance of the air conditioning system is evaluated by the performance coefficient (COP), which can be obtained by the equation

$$COP_c = \frac{Q_c}{W_C + W_{pump,e} + W_{pump,c} + W_{fan,c}} \quad (5)$$

As for the condensing coil on the condenser, the heat exchange from the condenser is affected by the heat transfer coefficient (K_o), which can be calculated as follows:

$$K_o = \frac{1}{\frac{1}{\alpha_k}\frac{F_o}{F_i} + \frac{1}{\alpha_{wa}}} \quad (6)$$

According to the Cooling Principles and Tools (Zhang 1987), the heat transfer coefficient (k) of the refrigerant in the condensation coil is calculated in Eq. (7).

$$\alpha_k = 0.683 r_s^{1/4} C_m (t_k - t_w)^{-1/4} d_i^{-1/4} \quad (7)$$

The values of $r_s^{1/4}$ and C_m with the temperature difference can be seen in table 1 (Zhang, 1987).

Table 1. Value of $r_s^{1/4}$ dan C_m

T (°C)	0	10	20	30	40	50
$r_s^{1/4}$	21.26	21.039	20.792	20.513	20.192	19.811
C_m	86.68	83.30	79.65	75.81	71.65	66.84

The coefficient of heat transfer for water (α_w) out of the condenser coil can be calculated in equation (8) by reference (Parker and Treybal, 1962).

$$\alpha_w = [982 + 15.58 t_w](\frac{\Gamma}{d_o})^{\frac{1}{3}} \quad (8)$$

The coefficient of heat transfer for air (α_{wa}) out of the condenser coil is calculated in equation (9) according to the reference (Zhang, 1987).

$$\alpha_{wa} = 0.88 \frac{C \lambda_{wa} Re_{wa}^{m} Pr_{wa}^{0.36}}{d_o} \quad (9)$$

The values of the parameters *C* and *m* in the temperature difference are shown in table 2.

Table 2. Values of parameters *C* and *m*

Re	Array of inline tubes		Arrangement of multilevel tubes		S1/S2
	C	*m*	*C*	*m*	
<200~10^3	0.52	0.50	0.6	0.5	-
=10^3~$2x10^5$	0.27	0.63	0.35 $(S_1/S_2)^{0.2}$	0.6	<2
>$2x10^5$	0.02	0.84	0.021	0.84	-

3 Results and Discussion

3.1 Effect of dry air inlet temperature

To improve the cooling performance of air conditioning systems with evaporative cooling, many factors influence it. Meanwhile, to limit the number of tests, only four key parameters have been tested: the water temperature in the evaporative cooler, the dry air ball temperature, the air velocity and the rate of water spray. Therefore, experimental testing is conducted under different conditions. Based on the experimental results, the thermodynamic properties of the refrigerant at different points of the cooling cycle are obtained (figure1) and parameters such as mass flow rate, cooling capacity, compressor input power and COP of the system are also calculated.

For dry temperature conditions 30°C to 32°C, with relative humidity of 80%, evaporative cooler with variation of 0.03kg/ms to 0.05 kg/ms, air velocity 4m/s to 4.8m/s, and under the 50Hz compressor frequency condition the variation of the cooling capacity with the inlet water temperature of the evaporator is plotted in fig. 2 and 3.

https://doi.org/10.1051/matecconf/201821501017

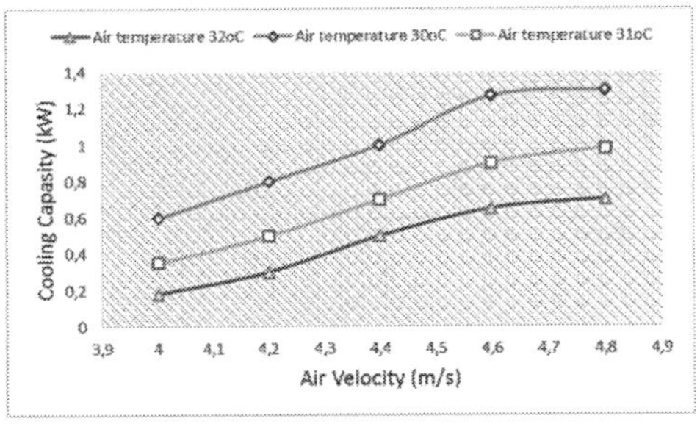

Fig.2. Variation of cooling capacity with dry ball temperature and air velocity

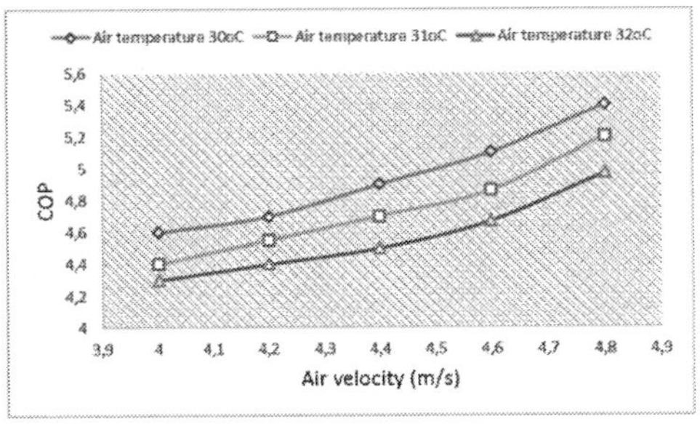

Fig. 3. COP variation with dry air temperature and air velocity

It can be seen that the cooling capacity and COP of air cooling system with evaporative cooler will increase as air speed increases from 4 m/s up to 4.8 m/s, but the cooling capacity and COP of the evaporative cooling system decreases when the dry-ball temperature increases from 30°C to 32°C This is due to the fact that the temperature and condensation pressure increase with increasing dry ball temperature, so the specific cooling capacity decreases and the specific compressor power increases.

3.2 Effect of air velocity and spray water rate

Under the 70Hz compressor frequency condition, 80% relative humidity, temperature of dry air 32°C and water inlet temperature evaporative 27°C. Variations of cooling capacity and COP with water spray rate and air velocity are plotted in Figures 4 and 5.

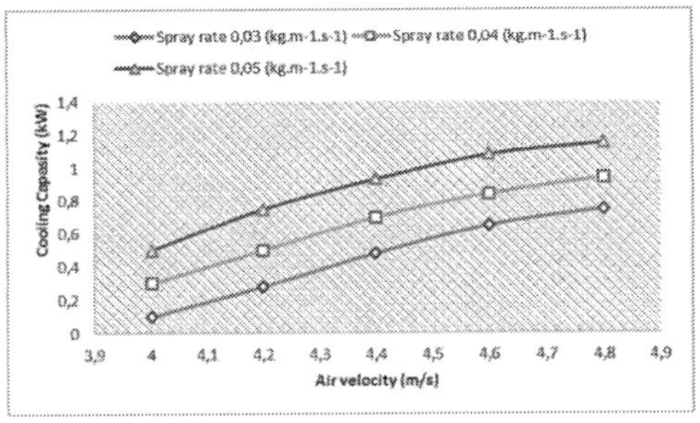

Fig. 4. Variation of cooling capacity with spray water rate and air velocity

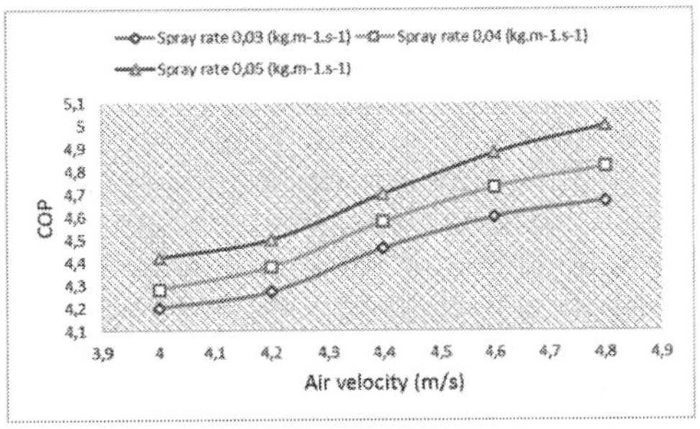

Fig. 5. Variation of cooling capacity with spray water rate and air velocity

As shown in Fig. 4 and 5, when air velocity of 4.0 m / s and spray water rate increased from 0.03 to 0.05 kg/m-s, cooling capacity and COP increased from 0.4 to 1.2 kW and 4.4 to 4.9, respectively. The main reason is that the cooling water soaks the condensation roll better as the spray water rate increases from 0.03 to 0.05 kg/m-s, and the moisture vapor also increases. Therefore, the higher heat transfer coefficient and mass transfer will increase due to higher rate of bursts. Furthermore, the temperature difference between cooling water and refrigerant decreases with increasing spray water rate, and condensation temperature also decreases. Thus, cooling capacity and COP increase with increasing water spray.
On the other hand, the cooling capacity and COP of the air conditioning system with the evaporative cooler condenser increases with the air velocity rising from 4 m/s to 4.8 m/s. With a water spray condition of 0.04kg/m-s, the cooling capacity and COP increased from 0.23 to 0.8 kW and 4.2 to 4.8 respectively. This is mainly because the higher air velocity increases the heat exchanger coefficient, and the condensation temperature and lowers the pressure.

4 Conclusions

From the research has been done, the improvement of air conditioning system performance with evaporative cooling condenser combined, and the variation between influenced factors, such as evaporator air temperature, dry temperature, air velocity and water spray rate, cooling capacity, COP has been analyzed. The main conclusions are as follows.

1) The experimental tests show that the cooling capacity and COP of the air conditioning system with the combined evaporative cooling-condenser increased significantly with increasing inlet temperature of evaporator, air velocity and water spray rate. COP increased by 12% with air velocity increasing from 4.0 to 4.8 m / s and with spray rate increasing from 0.03 to 0.05 kg / m-s.

2) It was also found that an increase in dry air ball temperature would decrease COP.

References

1. B.Choudhury, P.K. Chatterjee and J.P. Sarkar. Review paper on solar-powered air conditioning through adsorption route. Renew Sustain Energy Rev; 14:2189–95. (2010).
2. M.M. Rahman and H.Y.Rahman. Performance of newly developed integrated space conditioning and domestic water heating device. J Energy Environ; 5:23–7. (2011).
3. K.A. Jahangeer, A.O Andrew, M.d Raisul. Numerical investigation of transfer coefficients of an evaporatively cooled condenser. ApplThermEng; 31:1655 16. (2011)
4. N. Kalkan, E.A Young and A. Celestas. Solar thermal air conditioning technology reducing the footprint of solar thermal air conditioning. Renew Sustain Energy Rev; 16:6352–63. (2012)
5. P.Wimolsiri. Solar cooling and sustainable refrigeration,http://www.egi.kth.se/proj/courses/4A1623/files/ARHPTSustainRefrig 2005.pdf.
6. J.C. Lam. Residential sector air-conditioning loads and electricity use in HongKong. Energy Convers Manag; 41:1757–68. (2000).
7. T.T. Chow and X.Y. Yang. Placement of condensing units of split-type air conditioners at low-rise residences. Appl. ThermEng; 22:143 14. (2002)
8. Y.A. Cengel, M.A. Boles. Thermodynamics: an engineering approach. 3rd edition.
9. S. Nikhil. Study and optimization of performance parameters of air-conditioner by using waste water of water-cooler. Int J EmergTechnol Adv Eng 2014; 4:2250 24. Boston: McGraw-Hill; (1998).
10. R.J. Dossat. Principal of refrigeration. New Jersey: Prentice Hall; (1991).
11. B.Christine Evaporative condenser lab and field-test results; (2012).
12. H.M. Ettouney, E.l Dessouky, W.Bouhamra, A.l. Azmi. Performance of evaporative condensers.Heat TransfEng; 22:41–55. (2001)
13. H. Hajidavalloo. Application of evaporative cooling on the condenser of window-air-conditioner.ApplThermEng; 27:1937 19. (2007)
14. L. Huanwei, Z. Qiushu and L.Yuling. Experimental study on cooling performance of air conditioning system with dual independent evaporative condenser. International Journal of Refrigeration (2014).
15. W.K. Brown. Fundamental concepts integrating evaporative techniques in HVAC systems. ASHRAE Trans, 96(Part1):1227–35. (1990)
16. K. Harby, R. Doaa Gebaly. Performance improvement of vapor compression cooling systems using evaporative condenser: An overview. Renewable and Sustainable Energy Reviews 58 347-360, (2016)

Methods of calculation of energy losses of the refrigerator when opening its doors

S.P. Petrosov[1], M.A. Lemeshko[1*], A.V. Kozhemyachenko[1], S.E. Bashnjak[2]

[1]Institute of Service and Businesses (branch) DSTU "Don State Technical University", in Shakhty, Rostov region, 346500
[2]Don State Agrarian University, Persianovsky settlement, Rostov region, 346600

Abstract. The problem of energy supply and the problem of energy efficiency of energy consumers are global problems. In the modern world, scientists pay much attention to the tasks of creating new and improving traditional sources of electricity. The tasks of increasing the energy efficiency of electricity consumers remain relevant in the global economy. One of the relatively capacious energy consumers is the Park of refrigerators, household and commercial purposes, which are also being improved in order to increase their energy efficiency. Modernization and improvement of household and commercial refrigerators include the task of designing and using more efficient refrigerators. Energy consumption of compression refrigerators, along with other operational factors, depends on the processes of heat exchange and mass transfer of air from internal chambers to the ambient air. When the doors of the refrigerator chambers are opened, the cooled air in the chambers is replaced with the warmer air of the environment. This process causes the cost of operation of the refrigeration machine and characterizes its energy consumption. In order to minimize this power consumption, knowledge of the process of cool air outflow of their open refrigerator chambers is required. Currently, this process is poorly understood. The article presents an approach to the description of the process of motion of the cooled air from the refrigerator chamber, the main assumptions necessary for the construction of a mathematical model of this process are given, and a method for calculating the heat in the refrigerator chambers associated with the replacement of the cooled air with the ambient air inside the chambers is proposed. The method is based on the laws of gas dynamics, supplemented by some experimental studies. In particular, the well — known Navier-Stokes equation is used as the initial basis. This equation supplemented by the continuity equation of the air flow and other functional dependencies. As a result of mathematical transformations and arguments about the physics of the mass transfer process, finite equations are obtained, which allow describing both the performance of the cooled air flow and the amount of heat introduced into the chambers by external warm air. Mathematical dependences are developed for calculation of parameters of motion of a stream of the cooled air and heat inflows, thus the temperature of ambient air and temperature in chambers of the refrigerator are considered. The results of the research will be useful in the design of new refrigerating machines with reduced energy consumption.

1 Introduction

Household and commercial compression refrigerators are widely used in everyday life, in medicine, in trade, in public catering establishments, in hotel and restaurant business. The European standard EN 16001: 2009, adopted in most European countries, as well as the national standards of a number of states, regulates the requirements for reducing energy consumption of the used equipment, including the requirements for reducing energy consumption in household and commercial refrigerators. At the same time, it is important to solve the problems of reducing operating losses caused by opening the doors of refrigerating and freezing chambers.

The method of calculating heat inflows into the refrigerator chambers at opening doors is necessary for solving the problems of reducing energy consumption in this class of refrigerating machines [2].

* Corresponding author: lem-mikhail@yandex.ru

Relatively warm environment air out of the refrigerator has lower density than the density of cooled air in the freezing or refrigerating compartments, causes the outflow of the cooled air from the refrigerating compartment. Essentially, it is the replacement of cooled air with warmer air [5].

Having determined the value and nature of changing cooled air outflow rates in the current moment when the door is opened, it is possible to determine the volume of replaced air and, consequently, energy costs necessary for restoring the temperature in the cooled compartment. For this purpose, the problem of calculating the air movement velocity when opening the refrigerator chambers [6] doors has been solved, and the technique for calculating heat inflow into the chambers has been developed [7,8]. Let us consider some general prerequisites and solutions of the pointed problem, considered by means of a physical model, partially described in the work [3].

2 Development of a method

Solving the tasks of regulating cooled air out flow from the refrigerator chambers is possible by means of using the laws of gas dynamics. To use these laws, some assumptions are adopted

- viscous gas motion is equal to the air motion is the main object of the present research.

-Gas is perfect, i.e., pressure p, density and absolute temperature

T satisfy the state of the equation of Mendeleev-Clapeyron law

$$p=\frac{\rho\cdot R_0\cdot T}{m}, \quad (1)$$

where: R_0 – is the universal gas constant;

m – is molecular weight of the gas.

- The coefficient of specific heat "c" does not depend on the absolute temperature of the gas and is a physical constant of the gas.

- When the gas moves, only the viscosity of the first kind is taken into account (the resistance of the surrounding warm air to the cold air flow).

- The coefficient of thermal conductivity of the gas « λ » is proportional to the coefficient of dynamic viscosity μ, i.e, Prandtl criterion is satisfied

$$\frac{\mu\cdot c}{\lambda}=\sigma=const. \quad (2)$$

- The gas is "Newtonian" environment, subordinated to the well-known Newton generalized law about the linear connection between the stress tensor and the strain rate tensor.

- External forces do not affect the air flow inside of the refrigerator. For this model, one can consider the assumption

$$F_x=0; F_y=0; F_z=-mg, \quad (3)$$

where g – is acceleration of gravity.

As there is the basic equation describing the motion of any viscous gas, the well-known Navier-Stokes equation describing the dynamics of a viscous gas per unit mass is used.

$$\begin{cases}\rho\frac{du}{dt}=\rho F_x-\frac{\partial p}{\partial x}+\mu\left(\frac{\partial^2 u}{\partial x^2}+\frac{\partial^2 u}{\partial y^2}+\frac{\partial^2 u}{\partial z^2}\right)+\mu\frac{\partial}{\partial x}\left(div\bar{V}\right)-\frac{2}{3}\frac{\partial}{\partial x}\left(\mu\cdot div\bar{V}\right);\\ \rho\frac{dv}{dt}=\rho F_y-\frac{\partial p}{\partial y}+\mu\left(\frac{\partial^2 v}{\partial x^2}+\frac{\partial^2 v}{\partial y^2}+\frac{\partial^2 v}{\partial z^2}\right)+\mu\frac{\partial}{\partial y}\left(div\bar{V}\right)-\frac{2}{3}\frac{\partial}{\partial y}\left(\mu\cdot div\bar{V}\right);\\ \rho\frac{dw}{dt}=\rho F_z-\frac{\partial p}{\partial z}+\mu\left(\frac{\partial^2 w}{\partial x^2}+\frac{\partial^2 w}{\partial y^2}+\frac{\partial^2 w}{\partial z^2}\right)+\mu\frac{\partial}{\partial z}\left(div\bar{V}\right)-\frac{2}{3}\frac{\partial}{\partial z}\left(\mu\cdot div\bar{V}\right);\end{cases}$$

(4)

where: u, v, w – are the projection of the velocity vector $\bar{V}$ on the axis OX, OY, OZ;

$\bar{F}=\left(F_x;F_y;F_z\right)$ – is the vector of external volume forces acting on the gas at each point of space;

μ – is the coefficient of dynamic viscosity;

$$div\bar{V}=\frac{\partial u}{\partial x}+\frac{\partial v}{\partial y}+\frac{\partial w}{\partial z}.$$

where:

$$\frac{du}{dt}=\frac{\partial u}{\partial t}+\frac{\partial u}{\partial x}u+\frac{\partial u}{\partial y}v+\frac{\partial u}{\partial z}w;$$
$$\frac{dv}{dt}=\frac{\partial v}{\partial t}+\frac{\partial v}{\partial x}u+\frac{\partial v}{\partial y}v+\frac{\partial v}{\partial z}w; \quad (5)$$
$$\frac{dw}{dt}=\frac{\partial w}{\partial t}+\frac{\partial w}{\partial x}u+\frac{\partial w}{\partial y}v+\frac{\partial w}{\partial z}w.$$

To the equations described above, the equation of the continuity of the air flow is added [4]:

$$\frac{\partial\rho}{\partial t}+\frac{\partial(\rho u)}{\partial x}+\frac{\partial(\rho v)}{\partial y}+\frac{\partial(\rho w)}{\partial z}=0.$$

(6)

Under the above assumptions, the system of equations describing the air outflow from the refrigerating chambers contains seven unknown functions: u, v, w, ρ, p, T, μ. In the above formulated problem six equations are proposed, as to the seventh equation which is essential for system closure, a diffusion equation or the heat balance equation can be proposed.

Let us state the boundary conditions of the problem. Initial elementary values are to be taken as an example of real calculations.

1) Equality of zero velocity is situated on a fixed rigid boundary inside of the refrigerator cabinet
2) The initial cold air flow velocity from the cabinet is zero at each point of the rectangular section at the exit of the cabinet.
3) The set air temperature inside of the cabinet at the initial moment of cold air outflow from the cabinet is equal to $T_{хол} = 5^0 C$.
4) At the initial time, the temperature outside of the refrigerating cabinet is constant and equal to $T_{комн} = 25^0 C$.
5) The air velocities outside the refrigeration unit at the initial moment of opening the door at each point of space are zero..

At the first stage, to simplify the task of cold air outflow from the refrigerating cabinet, it is additionally supposed that the process is isothermal, i.e, the temperature of freely air outflow is constant at each point of the air outflow. In fact, such condition means that the diffusion process of mixing cold (freely outflow) air and warm (room) is excluded. It is also assumed that the cold air outflow is the incompressible (non-expanding) environment.

Under such assumptions, the following equalities are evident

$$T = const_1,\ p = const_2,\ \mu = const_3. \quad (7)$$

Since the airflow is assumed to be incompressible, so

$$div\bar{V} = \frac{\partial u}{\partial x} + \frac{\partial v}{\partial y} + \frac{\partial w}{\partial z} \equiv 0. \quad (8)$$

Under the assumptions made, the continuity equation is satisfied.

By the condition (8) the last two terms in each equation of the system (4) are equal to zero by means of using formulas (1), (4) and assumptions(6), (7), system (5) can be transformed to a simpler form:

$$\begin{cases} \rho\left(\frac{\partial u}{\partial t}+\frac{\partial u}{\partial x}u+\frac{\partial u}{\partial y}v+\frac{\partial u}{\partial z}w\right)=\mu\left(\frac{\partial^2 u}{\partial x^2}+\frac{\partial^2 u}{\partial y^2}+\frac{\partial^2 u}{\partial z^2}\right); \\ \rho\left(\frac{\partial v}{\partial t}+\frac{\partial v}{\partial x}u+\frac{\partial v}{\partial y}v+\frac{\partial v}{\partial z}w\right)=\mu\left(\frac{\partial^2 v}{\partial x^2}+\frac{\partial^2 v}{\partial y^2}+\frac{\partial^2 v}{\partial z^2}\right); \\ \rho\left(\frac{\partial w}{\partial t}+\frac{\partial w}{\partial x}u+\frac{\partial w}{\partial y}v+\frac{\partial w}{\partial z}w\right)=-\rho mg+\mu\left(\frac{\partial^2 w}{\partial x^2}+\frac{\partial^2 w}{\partial y^2}+\frac{\partial^2 w}{\partial z^2}\right); \end{cases} \quad (9)$$

After the above assumptions, the system (9) is a system of three equations relative to three unknown functions u, v, w, i.e., the system (9) is closed.

It is also assumed that the cold air outflow from the cabinet occurs without changes in the horizontal transverse direction i.e. that the ordinates of the trajectories of the air flow motion are constant and the change in the geometry of the flow occurs only in the plane XOZ (Figure 1).

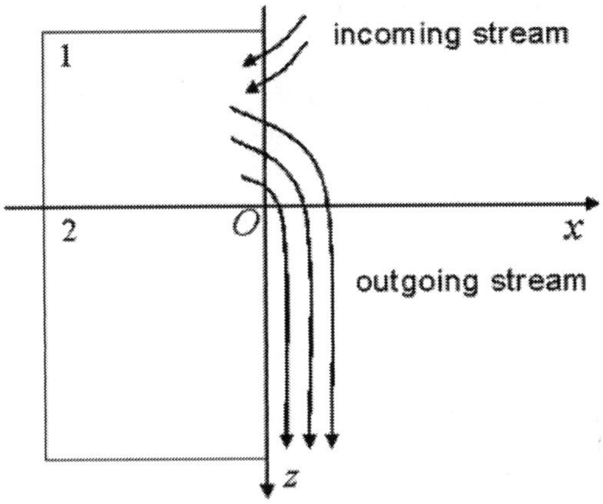

1 –cooling chamber;
2 –freezer.

Fig. 1. The air flows motion with the open door of the fridge in the plane XOZ

The assumption of the geometry invariability of the flow in the direction of the axis OY implies that the values of the function vanish $v = v(x, y, z) \equiv 0$ and functions are $u = u(x,z); w = w(x,z)$, i.e. they do not depend on the variable « y ». Thus, the real three-dimensional flow is replaced by the two-dimensional model

Under these conditions, the system (9) is simplified

$$\begin{cases} \rho\left(\frac{\partial u}{\partial t}+\frac{\partial u}{\partial x}u+\frac{\partial u}{\partial z}w\right)=\mu\left(\frac{\partial^2 u}{\partial x^2}+\frac{\partial^2 u}{\partial z^2}\right); \\ \rho\left(\frac{\partial w}{\partial t}+\frac{\partial w}{\partial x}u+\frac{\partial w}{\partial z}w\right)=\rho mg+\mu\left(\frac{\partial^2 w}{\partial x^2}+\frac{\partial^2 w}{\partial z^2}\right). \end{cases}$$

(10)

in addition the process of the air outflow is supposed to be stationary in time, then

$$\frac{\partial u}{\partial t} \equiv 0, \frac{\partial w}{\partial t} \equiv 0 \quad (11)$$

and the system (10) becomes simpler in the form

$$\begin{cases} \left(\frac{\partial u}{\partial x}u+\frac{\partial u}{\partial z}w\right)=\frac{\mu}{\rho}\left(\frac{\partial^2 u}{\partial x^2}+\frac{\partial^2 u}{\partial z^2}\right); \\ \left(\frac{\partial w}{\partial x}u+\frac{\partial w}{\partial z}w\right)=mg+\frac{\mu}{\rho}\left(\frac{\partial^2 w}{\partial x^2}+\frac{\partial^2 w}{\partial z^2}\right). \end{cases} \quad (12)$$

Since the system (12) contains two equations and two unknown functions, it is closed.

The system (12) can be classified as a system of two nonlinear partial differential equations of the second order. At the present time methods of solving such problems are unknown in technical literature. In this paper, the system (12) is proposed to be solved by means of approximate analytical methods.

The expressions, in both equations of the system (12) determine the forces of aerodynamic resistance of the air environment of the room, which delays the cold air flow, flowing out of the refrigerating chamber.

The system of equations (12) will be transformed proceeding from the fact that in technical aerodynamics the resistance force of the air environment is approximately determined by the formulas (in the so-called zone of quadratic resistance) [9].

$$\frac{\mu}{\rho}\left(\frac{\partial^2 u}{\partial x^2}+\frac{\partial^2 u}{\partial z^2}\right),\ \frac{\mu}{\rho}\left(\frac{\partial^2 w}{\partial x^2}+\frac{\partial^2 w}{\partial z^2}\right) \quad (13)$$

$$\frac{\mu}{\rho}\left(\frac{\partial^2 u}{\partial x^2}+\frac{\partial^2 u}{\partial z^2}\right)\approx-\frac{\mu k}{\rho}u^2;$$

$$\frac{\mu}{\rho}\left(\frac{\partial^2 w}{\partial x^2}+\frac{\partial^2 w}{\partial z^2}\right)\approx-\frac{\mu k}{\rho}w^2,$$

here k — is the coefficient determined experimentally.

Since the coefficient of dynamic viscosity μ has units of measure kg $\frac{кг}{м \cdot с}$, then from equations (13)we get that, k is measured in - $\frac{с}{м^3}$.

The minus in the right-hand side of equalities (13) indicates that the second partial derivatives of the projections of the velocity vector are negative because of the inhibitory effect of the viscous environment.

Using formulas (13) the system (12) is transformed in the form

$$\begin{cases} \left(\frac{\partial u}{\partial x}u+\frac{\partial u}{\partial z}w\right)=-\frac{\mu k}{\rho}u^2; \\ \left(\frac{\partial w}{\partial x}u+\frac{\partial w}{\partial z}w\right)=mg-\frac{\mu k}{\rho}w^2. \end{cases} \quad (14)$$

The system (14) is basic for determining air flow velocities when it flows freely out of the refrigerating chamber in a stationary mode.

Let us consider that the free air flow from the refrigerator cabinet depends on the time of outflow. First, let us investigate the behavior of the free air flow inside of the refrigerating chamber. Since the bottom of the refrigerating chamber is horizontal, the airflow inside of the chamber is supposed to be one-dimensional i.e. the only horizontal component of the velocity vector will be affected $u=u(x;t)$, and the values of the vertical component will be neglected, which means

$$w=w(x;t)=0\,. \quad (15)$$

Gravity forces acting on the horizontal projection of the velocity vector for the air flow inside of the refrigerating chamber will not be taken into account.

In the basic system of equations of the air flow motion under the condition (15) the second equation is identically satisfied, taking into account (15) the system of equations (10), describing the non stationary motion of cooled air, transformed into one equation relative to the unknown function $u=u(x;t)$

$$\frac{\partial u}{\partial t}+\frac{\partial u}{\partial x}u=\frac{\mu}{\rho}\frac{\partial^2 u}{\partial x^2}. \quad (16)$$

If we apply the same transformation to the equation (16) as for the system (12), the equation (16) will be transformed proceeding from the fact that in technical aerodynamics the resistance force of the air environment is approximately determined by the formula (in the zone of quadratic resistance)

$$\frac{\mu}{\rho}\frac{\partial^2 u}{\partial x^2}\approx-\frac{k\mu}{\rho}u^2. \quad (17)$$

Paying attention to the formula (17) the equation (16) after transferring all expressions of the equation to the left-hand side, it takes the form

$$\frac{\partial u}{\partial t}+\frac{\partial u}{\partial x}u+\frac{k\mu}{\rho}u^2=0. \quad (18)$$

Approximate solutions of the equation (18) will be found in the form

$$u(x;t)=b_0(t)+b_1(t)e^{-x}, \quad (19)$$

where $b_0(t), b_1(t)-$ are new unknown functions from a variable «t».

To find the solution of equation (18), let substitute it into the function $u=u(x;t)$ in the form (19), after simplifying we obtain the following:

$$\frac{db_0(t)}{dt}+\frac{\mu k}{\rho}b_0^2(t)+\left(\frac{db_1(t)}{dt}+\left(2\frac{\mu k}{\rho}-1\right)b_0(t)b_1(t)\right)e^{-x}+ \tag{20}$$
$$+\left(\frac{\mu k}{\rho}-1\right)b_1^2(t)e^{-2x}=0.$$

Equating the "free term" of equation to zero (20 73) paying attention to the degrees of the function, e^{-x}, we obtain

$$\frac{db_0(t)}{dt}+\frac{\mu k}{\rho}b_0^2(t)=0. \tag{21}$$

The equation (21) is an ordinary differential equation with separating variables, the general solution has the form

$$b_0(t)=\frac{1}{\frac{\mu k}{\rho}t+C_1}, \tag{22}$$

where C_1 – is an arbitrary constant.

to find the function $b_1(t)$ the expression for the function e^{-x} is equated to zero in the equation (20-73)

$$\frac{db_1(t)}{dt}+\left(2\frac{\mu k}{\rho}-1\right)b_0(t)b_1(t)=0 \tag{23}$$

In the equation (23), instead of the function $b_0(t)$, we substitute the function (22), which is a solution of equation (21)

$$\frac{db_1(t)}{dt}+\left(2\frac{\mu k}{\rho}-1\right)\frac{b_1(t)}{\frac{\mu k}{\rho}t+C_1}=0. \tag{24}$$

The equation (24) is also an equation with separable variables with general solution

$$b_1(t)=C_2\left(\frac{\mu k}{\rho}t+C_1\right)^{-2+\frac{\rho}{\mu k}}, \tag{25}$$

C_2 – is arbitrary constant

Thus, an approximate solution of equation (18) is obtained in the form (19) up to terms of order e^{-2x}, where the functions $b_0(t)$ and $b_1(t)$ are determined by formulas (22), (25)

The values of the constants C1 and C2 can be found according to the initial conditions by the well known method. As a result of the calculations, it is obtained:

$$\begin{cases} C_1=\dfrac{\mu k-\rho}{U_0(2\mu k-\rho)}; \\ C_2=-\dfrac{\mu k\cdot U_0\left(\dfrac{\mu k-\rho}{U_0(2\mu k-\rho)}\right)^{2-\frac{\rho}{\mu k}}}{\mu k-\rho}. \end{cases} \tag{26}$$

Thus, in the form (19) an approximate solution of the task is obtained for determining the airflow rates inside of the refrigerating chambers where the functions $b_0(t)$, $b_1(t)$, are determined by formulas (22), (25), but arbitrary constants C_1, C_2 – are according to the formulas (26).

It was found experimentally that the quantity is $\mu k-\rho>0,$ therefore inequalities are

$$C_1>0, C_2<0.$$

We define the sign of the function as $u(x;t)$. For this we do substitutes in the expression (19) functions $b_0(t)$, $b_1(t)$ from (22), (25) and the values of the constants C_1, C_2 in accordance to (26), so after simplifications, we get

$$u(x;t)=\frac{1}{\frac{\mu k}{\rho}t+\frac{\mu k-\rho}{U_0(2\mu k-\rho)}}-\frac{\left(\frac{\mu k-\rho}{U_0(2\mu k-\rho)}\right)^{2-\frac{\rho}{\mu k}}}{(U_0)^{-1}\left(1-\frac{\rho}{\mu k}\right)e^{x}}\left(\frac{\mu k}{\rho}t+\frac{\mu k-\rho}{U_0(2\mu k-\rho)}\right)^{-2+\frac{\rho}{\mu k}}. \tag{27}$$

Let us transform the function (27) to a convenient form for calculations

$$u(x;t)=\frac{U_0\left(2-\frac{\rho}{\mu k}\right)}{\left(\frac{\mu kU_0(2\mu k-\rho)}{\rho(\mu k-\rho)}t+1\right)\left(1-\frac{\rho}{\mu k}\right)}-\frac{U_0e^{-x}}{\left(1-\frac{\rho}{\mu k}\right)}\left(\frac{\mu kU_0(2\mu k-\rho)}{\rho(\mu k-\rho)}t+1\right)^{-2+\frac{\rho}{\mu k}}. \tag{28}$$

In the expression (28) we change the variable

$$\frac{\mu kU_0(2\mu k-\rho)}{\rho(\mu k-\rho)}t=\xi. \tag{29}$$

After the substitution (29), the function $u(x;t)$ will take the form

$$u(x;\xi)=\frac{U_0}{\left(1-\frac{\rho}{\mu k}\right)}\left(\left(2-\frac{\rho}{\mu k}\right)(\xi+1)^{-1}-(\xi+1)^{-2+\frac{\rho}{\mu k}}e^{-x}\right). \tag{30}$$

We represent the function (30) in the form:

$$u(x;\xi)=\frac{U_0}{\left(1-\frac{\rho}{\mu k}\right)}\left(\left(1-\frac{\rho}{\mu k}\right)(\xi+1)^{-1}+(\xi+1)^{-1}\left(1-(\xi+1)^{-2+\frac{\rho}{\mu k}}e^{-x}\right)\right). \quad (31)$$

As $\mu k-\rho>0,$ so $1-\frac{\rho}{\mu k}>0$. From the substitution (28) it is easy to see that $\xi>0$, then expression $(\xi+1)^{-2+\frac{\rho}{\mu k}}e^{-x}<1$ and function (31) are positive for all « x » and $\xi>0$, the function $u(x;t)$ is positive for all « x » and $t>0$.

Let us clarify the sign of the derivative of the function $u(x;t)$. We differentiate the function $u(x;\xi)$ relative to the variable « ξ »

$$\frac{\partial u(x;\xi)}{\partial\xi}=\frac{U_0}{\left(1-\frac{\rho}{\mu k}\right)}\left(-\left(2-\frac{\rho}{\mu k}\right)(\xi+1)^{-2}-\left(-2+\frac{\rho}{\mu k}\right)(\xi+1)^{-3+\frac{\rho}{\mu k}}e^{-x}\right),$$

or

$$\frac{\partial u(x;\xi)}{\partial\xi}=-\frac{U_0\left(2-\frac{\rho}{\mu k}\right)}{\left(1-\frac{\rho}{\mu k}\right)(\xi+1)^2}\left(1-(\xi+1)^{-1+\frac{\rho}{\mu k}}e^{-x}\right). \quad (32)$$

From the received representation (32), it is easy to see that each factor on the right-hand side of the equation is positive, i.e.. $\frac{\partial u(x;\xi)}{\partial\xi}<0$ for all« x » и $\xi>0$. It follows from the linearity of the substitution (28) that expressed as $\frac{\partial u(x;t)}{\partial t}<0$ for all « x » are $t>0$.

Thus the function $u(x;t)$ is positive for all« x » и $t>0$,as it monotonically decreases in time, i.e, the velocity of air outflow decreases with time. As a result of experimental studies it was obtained that the height of the air outflow from the chambers at the exit is changed with time by the law

$$h(0;t)=\frac{H_1}{3}e^{-\alpha t}. \quad (33)$$

The value of the parameter α was determined experimentally, it turned out to be equal to $\alpha=0,21$. value $h(0;t)=\frac{H_1}{3}e^{-\alpha t}$.

Let us determine the flow rate of chilled air freely flowing out of the chamber. According to [8], the flow rate of the investigated air flow at the exit of the chamber is determined by the formula

$$\Pi=h(0;t)\cdot u(0;t)\cdot b, \quad (34)$$

where b – is refrigerating chamber width.

In the experiment, the value is $b=0,5м$.

Using the formula (28) we obtain

$$u(0;t)=\frac{U_0}{\left(1-\frac{\rho}{\mu k}\right)}\left(\frac{\left(2-\frac{\rho}{\mu k}\right)}{(\beta t+1)}-(\beta t+1)^{-2+\frac{\rho}{\mu k}}\right). \quad (35)$$

where $\beta=\frac{\mu k U_0(2\mu k-\rho)}{\rho(\mu k-\rho)}$.

Thus, the flow consumption (rate) is determined by formula (34), where the functions $h(0;t)$ and $u(0;t)$ are determined by formulas (33), (35). Heat loss in the free air outflow from the refrigerating chamber is determined by the formula [1]:

$$Q=c\cdot\Pi\cdot\rho\cdot(T_x-T_П) \quad (36)$$

where c – is specific air heat

Using the formulas (33) we get

$$Q=c\cdot\rho\cdot h(0;t)\cdot u(0;t)\cdot b\cdot(T_x-T_П) \quad (37)$$

Thus, according to the formula (37), the heat loss for the cold chamber is determined.

3 Conclusions and recommendations

1. The basis of the method to determine heat inflows into the chambers of the refrigerator, after opening the doors, is the Navier-Stokes equation, which is added by the equation of motion continuity.
2. To solve the problem, well-founded assumptions are made, to obtain a closed system of equations.
3. In order to carry out practical calculations, a three-dimensional model describing the air motion is transferred into an adequate two-dimensional model.
4. The obtained mathematical expressions allow us to calculate the outflow of cooled air from the refrigerator compartment and the amount of heat (heat loss) with free air outflow from the refrigerating compartment when the refrigerator doors are opened.

References

1. A. P. Baskakov, B. V. Berg, O. K. Vitt – M.: Energoatomizdat, (1991)
2. R.O. Dating. Refrigerants: Service Pointers. – Refrigeration Service and Contracting. 39. (1971)
3. Y.G. Fomin, et al. Mathematical model of heat leakage in Camera of Refrigerator 1 (361) News of higher educational institutions. Technology of textile industry. S. Ivanovo, 158-161. (2016)
4. L.G. Loitsyansky. Mechanics of liquids and gases (Nauka. Moscow, 1978)
5. M.A. Lemeshko, Z.V. Gornostaeva, E.V. Duvanskaya, I.N. Danileko. Determination of the projections of the velocity Vector of the cooled Air from the Refrigerating Compartment with the door open. ARPN Journal of Engineering and Applied Sciences. **10**(2), 954-958. (2015)
6. M.A. Lemeshko, E.V. Duvanskaya, S.P. Petrosov, V.N. Kohanenko. Mathematical Model of Refrigerated Air from the Fridge Speed Calculation. World Applied Sciences Journal, **30**(9):1145-1151 (2004)
7. M.A. Lemeshko, V.V. Laletin M.F. Mizik. Determination of the speeds of the movement of cooled air when opening the doors of the cabinet of a domestic refrigeration appliance [Electronic resource] // "Engineering Bulletin", № 4. (2011). – available from: http://www.ivdon.ru/magazine/archive/n4y2011
8. M.A. Lemeshko, M.F. Mizik, Mathematical model of free flow of cooled air from the chamber of a domestic refrigeration device. / Izvestiya of higher educational institutions. North-Caucasian region. Series: Engineering. **4** (173) 16-18. (2013)
9. S.A. Chaplygin, Izbrannye trudy. Mekhanika zhidkosti i gaza, matematika, obshchaya mekhanika (Selected Works. Mechanics of Fluids and Gas, Mathematics, General Mechanics), (Nauka: Moscow, 1976)

MATEC Web of Conferences **215**, 01019 (2018) https://doi.org/10.1051/matecconf/201821501019
ICTIS 2018

Partial Discharge Analysis on Isolator of Transformer

Bachtiar Antonov, *Thomas* Thomas

Institut Teknologi Padang, Electrical Engineering Department, Padang, West Sumatra, Indonesia

Abstract. Transformer has an important role in the world of electricity, especially high voltage. The selection of transformer isolation and routine maintenance should be in the same direction to maintain the reliability of transformer performance and work safety. Partial discharge is caused by many factors, both from the transformer itself, breakdown voltage and the use of an old transformer. The external factor is the temperature around the transformer which results in a decrease in the reliability of the insulator. Both must be based on a standard. As technology advances, in the field of electrical, electronics, computerization has a standard called IEEE Std C57.104 ™ -2008 which is a revision of IEEE Std C57.104-1991. It is designed for science and technology guidance concerning all provisions concerning the security of the worker itself. Which later, by applying the standard is expected transformer service users can suppress loss of production and work accidents. Indication of occurrence of Partial discharge (PD) occurs in transformer at MCC CLO2 (transformer 1) where TDCG 25975 ppm and transformer EN-2M also occur Partial Discharge (transformer 2) with TDCG 5920.6 ppm, while at transformer VE-12 (transformer 3) is still in normal condition where the TDCG value is only 630 ppm. If the Partial Discharge is fatal and damaging the transformer, replacement of the transformer should be done immediately. But the condition of the field not be done directly because of many stages to be done, which directly affect the production process and costs.

1 Introduction

The use of high voltage is one effort to reduce the loss of energy in the system of transmission and distribution of electrical power from a power generator which is located far from each other. Because by raising the voltage then the current flowing into small so that the energy loss due to the current and the resistance of the carrier becomes small. In a good transmission and distribution system the quality of insulation is absolutely necessary to ensure the reliability and quality of electric power supply.

Transformer plays an important role in the work process in the industrial world. Transformers should be given special attention, both in monitoring and maintenance. The performance of the transformer is influenced by many factors, both from the transformer itself and from external factors. With the choice of solid and liquid solid isolation will reduce the risk of Partial Discharge. Partial Discharge is a partial discharge on the transformer, ie damage to certain parts of the transformer. PD is not only caused by the transformer itself, but also surrounded by the outside of the transformer or the environment. Short-term caused by PD not directly visible on the operation, but the PD will be fatal if left constantly. Problem formulation From the background then the authors formulate, whether Partial discharge and how to overcome it (1-5).

Partial Discharge on the transformer has a wide scope. For that researchers will limit the problem, namely:

1. Not to discuss the effect of the gas dissolved transformer gases but only to measure the amount of gas that occurs and compare with IEEE Std C57.104 ™ -2008 standard.
2. The measurement under study is the occurrence of Partial Discharge on, transformer, especially transformer in PT. Indah Kiat Pulp and Paper, Perawang.

Partial discharge (PD) is the event of electrical spark loss locally in an isolation section in both the inner and surface cavities due to potential differences in the isolation. This phenomenon arise caused by many factors such as quality of dielectric material, gap / cavity in dielectric material, or any damage or imperfection in work post (6).

The load imbalance in a system of electric power distribution is always the case and the cause of the imbalance is the one-phase loads on low voltage network subscribers. Due to the imbalance of the load, the current flows through the neutral of the transformer. The current flowing in the neutral of the transformer causes losses, ie losses due to neutral currents in neutral carriers and losses due to neutral currents flowing to the ground (7-8).
The cause of the occurrence of partial discharge can be done by conducting tests and measurements on the isolation by using the detector of the occurrence of partial discharge. PD tests and measurements relate to quality and quantity values. Quality values can be obtained from the characteristics when testing on certain materials.

While the value of quantity is the nominal value of the PD that has dimensions pico Coloumb (pC). Both of these values must meet the standard on the test, so the quality of the new equipment can be assessed (9).

Based on the magnitude of Partial discharges, there are several forms of failure that can occur, namely:

1. 10-15 pC has not happened insulation isolation
2. <300 - 500 pC early deterioration of quality of insulation
3. 1000 - 3000 pC the development of failure, on paper isolation has been a complete failure.
4. 10.000 - 100.000 pC damage oil insulation resistance occurs. (10)

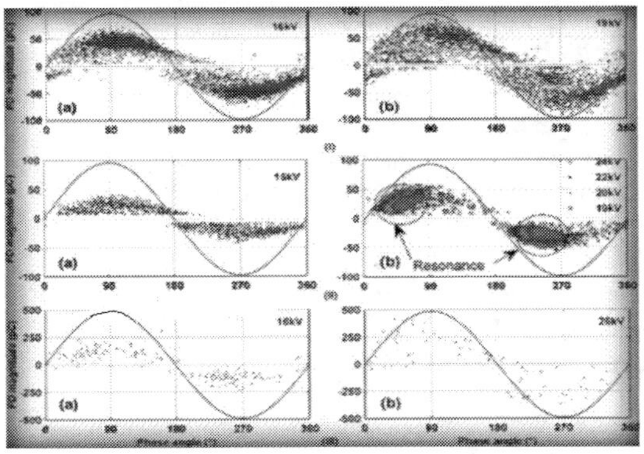

Fig. 1. Partial discharge Grafic

Internal discharge is a Partial discharge that occurs due to a cavity, usually containing air, in isolation. The presence of a cavity inside the insulation makes the dissemination of the electric field in uneven insulation. The electric field in and around the cavity becomes larger than the average electric field in the isolation as shown in fig 2 (11).

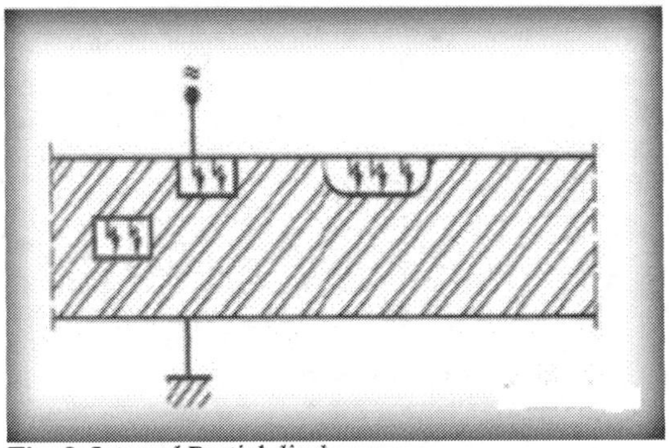

Fig. 2. Internal Partial discharge

Surface discharge is a Partial discharge that occurs on the outside of the insulation or the surface of the insulation. Surface discharge occurs in components where the external discharge touches the surface of the insulation (12).

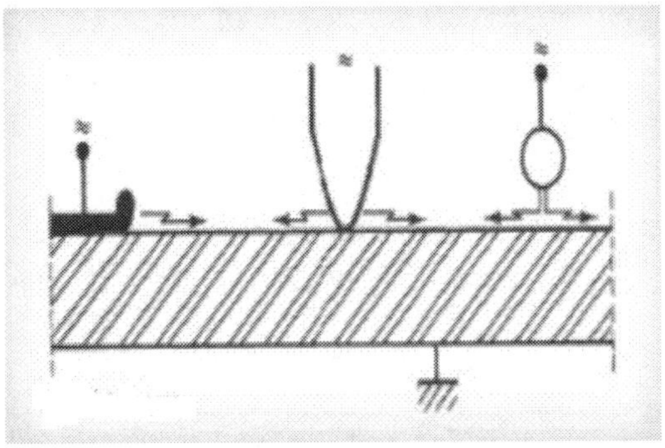

Fig. 3. Surface Partial discharge

In the fig 3 shows some source of surface discharge. At the right and center of the image, the surface discharge occurs due to the presence of an electric field strong enough to cause discharge on the surface of the insulation. The insulating material is a tool used to separate the parts that are on hold or the active parts. The insulating material is an apparatus used as a barrier and safety on electrical equipment having sufficient electric power to ensure the safety system required when the electrical equipment is operating or not operating. The insulating materials used in high voltage engineering are differentiated into: solid insulating materials, liquid insulation materials and gas insulation materials (13)

Failure of isolation is related to Partial Discharge. Partial discharge is the event of loose electrical sparks locally on an isolation section of both the inner and surface cavities due to the potential difference in the isolation. Electromechanical failure is a failure caused by the difference in polarity between the electrodes flanking the solid insulating material resulting in electrical pressure on the material. Electrical pressure that occurs cause mechanical pressure that causes the pull of attraction between the two electrodes. At a voltage of 106 volts / cm causes mechanical pressure 2 to 6 kg / cm2. This mechanical pull or pull This mechanical pull or pull is a force acting on solids associated with Young Modulus (14):

$$Y = \frac{F/_A}{\Delta L/_L} \quad (1)$$

$$\varepsilon_0 \varepsilon_Y = \frac{V^2}{2d^2} = yLn\frac{d_0}{d} \quad (2)$$

$$R = \frac{(S_T - S_0)xVx10^{-6}}{T} \quad (3)$$

Determining the amount of gas dissolved in transformer oil This method is used for comparison between gas space analysis results with the result of gas analysis dissolved in oil. Determine the space of gas and gas dissolved in oil. It should be noted that the equivalent

 https://doi.org/10.1051/matecconf/201821501019

value calculated from the TCG, and the experiments measured by probability are often different. This condition is rare, but this equation is needed for the determination of TCG concentration limiting values (15).

$$TDCG_g = \sum_{C_1}^{C_n}\left[\frac{\frac{F_c}{B_c}}{\sum_{G_1}^{G_n}\frac{F_G}{B_g}}\right]x100 \qquad (4)$$

Observation of insulation damage in use by the amount of dissolved gas.This method is very appropriate to be used to monitor the condition of damage to transformer insulation material with the calculation of the number of changes in the amount of gas. The amount of gas change is changed, because of the age of the oil itself caused by PD. Because the damage is easily seen when the amount of gas is plotted against time. It can be shown by the equation:

$$\text{TDCG}_V = \frac{FG(V)}{1000000} \qquad (5)$$

Transformer is an electrical equipment that serves to raise and lower the voltage. Step-up transformer serves to raise the voltage, while the step-down transformer serves to lower the voltage. In principle, the transformer consists of two coils (winding), namely primary coil and secondary coil. When the primary coil flows through the current will cause magnetic flux (magnetic field) around it. The strength of the magnetic field is influenced by the magnitude of the flow of electrical current. After the primary coil is flowed by the current and there is GGL (electromotive force) the secondary coil gets the current from the primary coil (15).

In the heating transformer may arise due to energy losses in winding and iron core. The heating process in this transformer will take place continuously during its operation and will cause a rise in temperature on winding and iron core. If this heating process is not balanced with the cooling process, there will be overheating which may result in damage to the transformer. The presence of oil as a filler liquid in the transformer can help the cooling process of winding and core. One of the advantages of oil that can fill the gap or space that will be isolated and simultaneously through the process of energy conversion can channel as well as reduce heat arising from energy loss (16-17)

2 Research Methods

This research is very useful to extend the life of the transformer and reduce the number of work accidents. Monitoring of transformer performance with 2 methods, first using Dissolved Gas Analysis (DGA) method and second using Power Partial Discharge (Power PD) Acoustic method. In this study the author took 3 samples of transformers. Using this method, the type information and the amount of gas contained in the transformer oil will be clearly visible. Steps of sampling the transformer oil using DGA method are as follows: 1. Stage of preparation 1. Prepare a bucket to accommodate transformer oil. 2. Install the oil flushing unit on the drain valve main tank transformer. 2. Implementation stage 1. Open drain valve main tank transformer. 2. Perform the process of cleaning / flusing first (remove the oil from the main tank transformer by opening the faucet stop). 3. Close the faucet stop. 4. Place the needle on the syringe. 5. Open the valve on the syringe and inject the syringe on the silicon hose. 6. Suck oil from the hose. 7. Make sure there is no air (air bubbles) that enter into the syringe. 8. Close the valve back on the syringe. 9. Transfer the oil from the syringe to the bottle / vial by injecting the oil into the bottle / vial without removing the lid. 10. Take ± 50 ml of oil sample for DGA test 11. Wait for the test results from the DGA tool. Performance of measurements with the Acoustic Emission Method, various tools are needed to assist the measurement and analysis of the results obtained as follows: 1. Device PD-TP-500A PD TP-500A is a portable diagnostic system, which periodically monitors Partial Discharges on equipment such as Transformers. PD TP-500A will detect, analyze, and locate the signal source. 2.Sensor In TP-500A PD device there are 2 sensors to check that is: 1. AE (Acoustic Emission) Sensor Is an elastic wave in the material, which is caused by the rapid release of local voltage energy. The source of the event is the phenomenon releasing the elastic energy into the material, which then propagates as an elastic wave. Acoustic emissions can be detected in the frequency range up to 100 MHz, but most of the released energy is in the range of 1 kHz to 1 MHz. A rapid stress release event produces a stress spectrum that starts at 0 Hz, and typically falls off several MHz. 2. HFCT Sensor (High Frequency Current Transformer) Wideband sensor range, High Frequency Current Transformer (HFCT) HVPD is used to measure partial discharge on the power cord and on the connected HV cable remotely. 3. Cables and Connectors 4. PC / Laptop to display results from checking. 5. Software support to analyze data from measurement or checking results, here I use PowerPD TP500A software. Steps in testing: 1. Attach the AE sensor to the transformer tank wall. 2. Install the HFCT sensor on the grounding. 3. At the time of measurement the result will be displayed on the laptop, the results will display the wave patterns (expected testers are required to have experience to recognize the wave pattern captured by the sensor).

3 Results and Discussion

From all analyzes that have been done, the comparison of 3 pieces of the transformer as shown in fig: 4. The graph shows the dissolved gas content in the three transformers being tested. MCC CLO2 transformer occurs Partial Discharge, where the Hydrogen content has reached 24329 and the calculation of TDCG reached 25975 ppm. In the EN-2M transformer, Partial Discharge occurs, where the Hydrogen content has reached 4150 and the calculation of TDCG reaches 5920 ppm. No VE-12 transformer occurs, Partial Discharge, where Ethanenya 41.9 content and TDCG calculation results only 630 ppm.

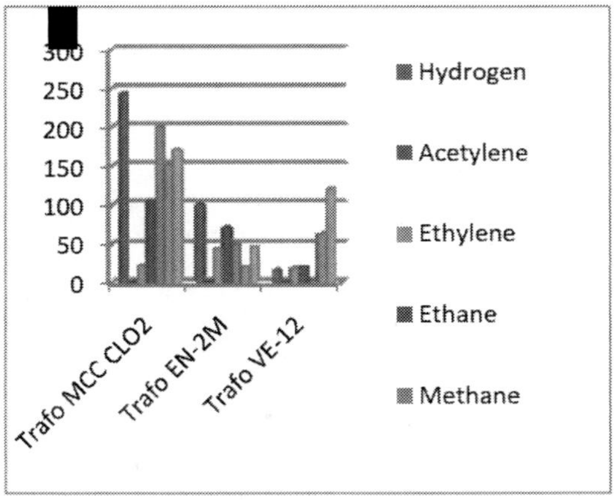

Fig.4. Partial discharge value on the transformer being tested

References

1. Antonov Bachtiar, Doni Aprinaldo (2015), *Optimalisasi Penyeimbang Beban Pada Trafo Distribusi Terhadap Susut Energi (Aplikasi Feeder Sikakap).*
2. Antonov Bachtiar, Bayu Dirgantara (2017), *Optimalisasi Penyeimbangan Beban Transformator Dengan Metode Seimbang Beban Seharian (SBS) Pada Gardu Depan Kantor Rayon PT. PLN (persero) Rayon Kayu Aro.*
3. Nasrul Harun (2016), *Rekondisi Transformator Untuk Mengatasi Menurunnya Kemampuan Isolasi Pada Trasformator Daya 20 Kv.*
4. Aria (2015), *IEEE-Std.-C57.104-2008-IEEE-Guide-for-the-Interpretation-of-Gases Generated-in-Oil-Immersed-Transformers*, http://www.ns-aria.com.
5. Djukarna (2013), *Transformator,* https:// www.djukarna.wordpress.com.
6. Tobing, Bonggas L (2012), *Dasar-Dasar Teknik Pengujian Tegangan Tinggi,* Erlangga, Jakarta.
7. Abduh, Syamsir (2001), *Teknik Tegangan Tinggi, Dasar Pembangkit dan Pengukuan, Salemba* Teknika, Jakarta.
8. Bastian (2009), *Tugas Akhir, Transformator.* 3.2, Institut Teknologi Bandung. Bandung
9. Demmassabu, A.R, Petras, L.S dan Lisi,F (2014), *Analisa Kegagalan Transformator Daya Berdasarkan Hasil Uji DGA dengan Motode TDCG, Key Gas, Roger'S Ratio, Duval'S Triangle Pada Gardu Induk, Junal Teknik Elektro*, ISSN, 2301-8402, Manado.
10. Nafiar rizky (2015), *Prinsip kerja transformator*, https://www. insinyoer. com/prinsip-kerja-transformator/.
11. Pramananda (2011), *Analisa Partial Discharge Pada Minyak Isolasi Dengan Menggunakan Metode Deteksi Sinyal Akustik*, Jurnal Ilmiah, Jakata.
12. Adrian firman (2009), *Isolation transformer*, https://www. *elektronicaution*. wordpress.com.
13. Arora, Rohit Kumar (2013), *Different DGA Techniques for Monitoring of Transformers, International Journal of Electronics and Electrical Engineering*, Mumbai.
14. Laniya, H and Prof, K.K, Dudani (2015), *Partial Discharge Detection and Localization in High Voltage Transformers Using an Acoustic Emission Technique, International Journal,* ISSN(O) : 2348-4470, ISSN(P) : 2348-6406, India.
15. Soebagio (2012), *Transformator*, ITS Press, Surabaya.
16. Yulistya Negara (2013), *Teknik Tegangan Tinggi, Prinsip dan Aplikasi Praktis*, Graha Ilmu, Yogyakarta. PT. PLN (Persero) : Buku *Pedoman Pemeliharaan Transformator Tenaga,* Jakarta.
17. Tadjuddin (1998), *Partial Discharge dan* Kegagalan *Bahan Isolasi,* (online), http://www.elektro indonesia.com /elektro /ener13a.html, 2016.

STABILITY ANALYSIS 0f 20 kVSYSTEMat PT PLN (PERSERO) RAYON MUARALABUH BEFORE and AFTER INTERCONECTION by IPP (PLTMH PT. SKE)

Arfita Yuana Dewi, Asnal Effendi, Ridwan
InstitutTeknologi Padang. Electrical Engineering department, Padang, West Sumatra, Indonesia

Abstract. In the rapid development of the world as it is today, the electricity has a very important role in supporting people activities. PT PLN (Persero), which in this case as Government State Owned Company that directly manage the provision of electrical energy is required to be ready to face the development of electricity demand in Indonesia. In distribution system of electricity, problems often occure because of the length of line distribution system which cause voltage drop, technical losses, power losses, etc. One of them happened to PT PLN (Persero) Rayon Muaralabuh. Where the distance between the main substation (GI Solok) with the first connecting substation is ±110 KMS. This distance cause 9.62 % voltage drop during peak load. This nominal of voltage drop happens for just the first connecting substation that will be the source of division for all working areas of PT PLN (Persero) Rayon Muaralabuh. This factor encourages PT PLN (Persero) West Sumatra Area Solok to agree if Independent Power Plant (IPP) takes part in generating electricity, which will be distribute to PT. PLN (Persero) West Sumatera Area Solok Rayon Muaralabuh through interconnection system. The simulation of power flow using Etap 12.6.0 is used to analyze the stability of 20 kV system voltage at PT PLN (Persero) Rayon Muaralabuh before and after interconnection. Based on the result of simulation and Etap calculation, the highest voltage drop before interconnection by IPP is on Feeder express LubukGadang which is 13,71 %. After the interconnection by IPP, the voltage drop on that feeder becomes 4,326%, and the highest voltage drop is 4,855 %. Therefore, the voltage drop after the interconnection by the IPP already meets the standards allowed by SPLN No. 72 of 1987 which is maximum 5 % voltage drop. The precentage of technical losses in PT PLN (Persero) Rayon Muaralabuh before interconnection is 13,074 %, and after interconnection is decreased to 8,306 %.

INTRODUCTION

In the rapid development of the world as it is today, electricity has a very important role in supporting people activities. People needs electricity can be seen in daily life, such as : lighting, electronic devices, industries, communications, and etc.PT PLN (Persero), which in this case as Government State Owned Company that directly manage the provision of electricity is required to be ready to face the development of electricity demand in Indonesia.

Provision of electricity by PT PLN (Persero) to consumer through several stages. Beginning with power generation, the electricitywhich has been generated will be raised into High Voltage (HV) then transmitted through the transmission line. After that the voltage of this electricity will be reduced into medium voltage, then it will be distributted to the substation. To fulfill low voltage consumers demands electricity from medium voltage will be distributted to distribution transformator in order to reduce the voltage into low voltage.

In the distribution system of electricity, problems often occur due to the length of the distribution line resulting some impacts, including; drop voltage, technical losses, power losses, etc.These impacts encourages PT PLN (Persero) West Sumatra Area Solok to agree if Independent Power Plant (IPP) takes part in generating electricity, which will be distribute to PT. PLN (Persero) West Sumatera Area Solok Rayon Muaralabuh through interconnection system. Where the distance between the main substation (GI Solok) to first connecting substation is ±110 KMS.

Thelong-distance of distribution from GI Solok to PT PLN (Persero) Rayon Muaralabuhcauses voltage drop that receivedby PT PLN (Persero) Rayon Muaralabuh. Where, Outside Peak Load Time (LWBP) the send voltage of GI Solokis 20.4 kV and received in PT PLN (Persero) Rayon Muaralabuh only 18.7 kV, which means voltage drop reaches 8.33%. Peak load time (WBP) of send voltage from GI Solokis 20.8 kV and received in PT PLN (Persero) Rayon Muaralabuh only 18.8 kV, which means voltage drop reaches 9.62%. The voltage received in PT PLN (Persero) Rayon Muaralabuhis just incoming voltagefor GH Balun which is the source of distribution for all working areas in PT PLN (Persero) Rayon Muaralabuh.

IPP (Independent Power Producer) which in this case is PT SeloKencana Energy (SKE), is a private company which works in Micro Hydro Power Plant (PLTMH). This power plant began operation in 2013. The operation pattern of this power plant is parallel to the 20 kV system of PT PLN (Persero) Rayon Muaralabuh also called interconnection system. With the existence of Micro

 https://doi.org/10.1051/matecconf/201821501020

Hydro Power Plant (PLTMH) owned by PT SeloKencana Energy which is interconnected with PLN's 20 kV system, it is very helpful for PT PLN (Persero) Rayon Muaralabuh to fulfill electricity demand in Solok Selatan District which reaches 7.8 MW during peak load. The power plant owned by PT SeloKencana Energy with 2 X 4 MW capacity, has participated together with PT PLN (Persero) Rayon Muaralabuhto reduce voltage drop, technical losses for South Solok Regency and surrounding areas.

Before the interconnection with private power plants PT. SKE, medium voltage distribution system of PT PLN (Persero) Rayon Muaralabuh is assisted by PLTD Balun with 2 X 1 MW operating capacity. PLTD Balun is a privately-owned machine with lease status at PT PLN (Persero). The existence of 2 units of operation and 1 unit of standby of PLTD machine is not enough to help PT PLN (Persero) Rayon Muaralabuh system to fulfill consumer needs.As evidenced is the "rotating blackout" system at PT PLN (Persero) Rayon Muaralabuh.

With the interconnection on 20 kV system with IPP (Independent Power Producer) is very helpful for PT PLN (Persero) Rayon Muaralabuh to fulfill electricity needs in South Solok district which is increasing from time to time, with service voltage that meets the standard.

This study aims to analyze the stability of 20 kV System Voltage at PT PLN (Persero) Rayon MuaralabuhBefore And After Interconnection With IPP (PT SKE).

II. BASIC THEORY

The distribution system is the whole component of a power system that connects directly between large power sources (such as transmission substations) with electricity consumers (Figure 2.1) shows a series of power distribution systems.

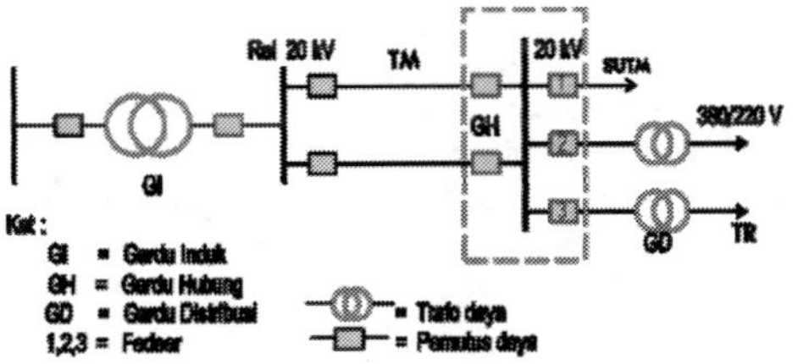

Fig.1One-Line Diagram of Electrical Power Distribution System

The distribution network generally consists of two parts, namely as follows:

1. Primary Distribution System

Namely power system that distributes electricity from the sub transmission substation (GI) to the distribution substation (GH). This system is a medium voltage (JTM) or primary voltage system.

2. Secondary Distribution System

Namely the power system that distributes electricity from the distribution substation (GH) to the consumer. This system is often called the low voltage system (JTR).

2.1 Primary Distribution System Types

In this service the primary distribution system has several variations of form, where each form of system has several advantages and disadvantages. In general there are four basic forms of primary distribution network system which are :

1) Radial primary distribution system
2) loop / ringprimary distribution system
3) Primary ring distribution system
4) Primary grid (network)distribution system
5) Spindle and clusterdistribution system.

2.1.1 Radial Primary Distribution System

This radial primer network is the most common and commonly used form, mainly used in load areas with low load density. This system has one power line to the load, then all the load on the channel will lose power when a channel is interrupted.

The main advantage of this radial system is its simple shape and low cost. The weaknesses of the system is the continuity of service is bad, low reliability, and high voltage drop, especially for the at the end of the distribution line. The large current density of this type of radial is found in the line between the power source and the substation and the smallest happens at the end of the line. In accordance with the level of current density, the cross-sectional area may vary. The primary radial type distribution network is represented by (Fig. 2).

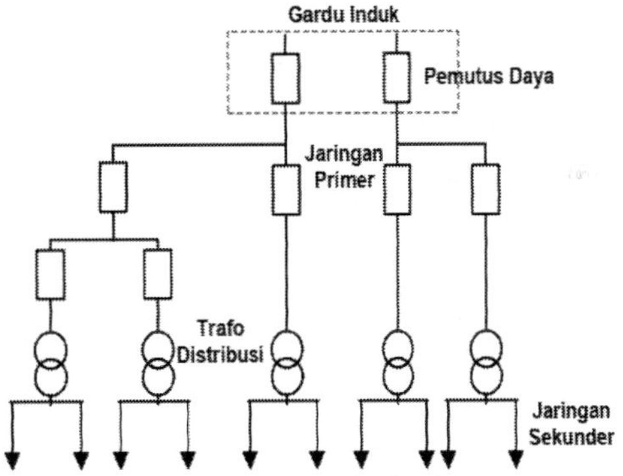

Fig. 2 Radial Primary Distribution System

2.1.2 Loop Primary Distribution System

Loop primary distribution system is typically used to serve loads that require good service continuity such as: Commercial buildings or factories with medium and large loads. In principle, the primary distribution line of the loop type is a line that starts from a point or rail to the load zone, then returns to the source point of the rail or the original power. In Medium Voltage Network (JTM) loop structure, enabling an alternative power supply for distribution substations, so that the system reliability is better.

In case of power disturbance with one of the feeders, the

load breaker in the GI will open and this will cause blackout in all distribution systems. Faced with these conditions, the action to be taken is to ensure and localize the power disturbance areas. Furthermore, areas that are not involved in power disturbance can be supplied from other feeders. Loop distribution linealso needs attention in short circuit current which is big .

Medium Voltage Line Configuration (JTM) loop structure, of course very desirable by all units of PLN. Because loop distribution linehas more advantages when compared with radial systems, the loop system can also promote to customers of PLN, especially large-capacity customers to be proposed to become a premium customer. Where one of the absolute conditions for premium customers is supported from 2 (two) different sources. The loop-type distribution network is shown by (Fig. 3).

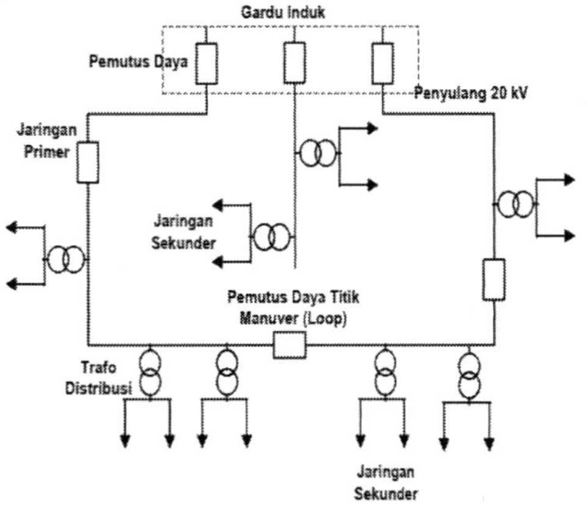

Fig. 3. Loop Primary Distribution System

2.1.3 Ring Primary Distribution System

Ringprimary distribution system is generally similar to loop type distribution line, the difference is only the number of resources more than one. In other words, The primary ring type distribution line is a loop type whose distribution substations can receive more power than a single source point. The primary line type distribution lineoften develops into a grid shape. The following is The primary line type distribution line (Fig. 4).

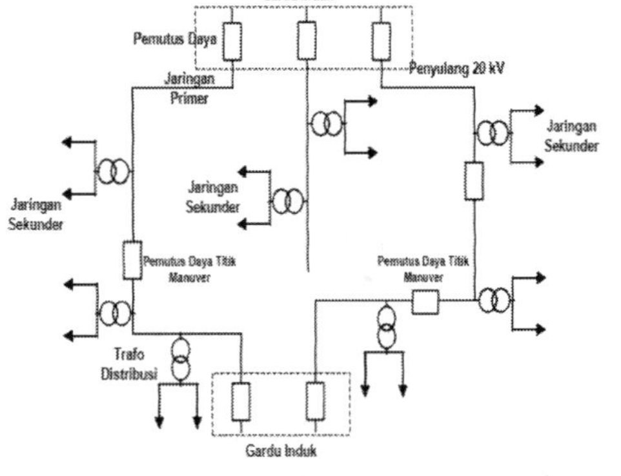

Fig.4. Ring Primary Distribution System

2.1.4 Grid Primary Distribution System

This system is an interconnection between some substations (GI) so that the load will receive power from various directions. Reliability of this system if there is power disturbance on one feeder, the consumer will still be supplied from other feeder so that the customer still served. Development of this type of distribution network would require large cost, because there are many substations needed. Primary grid type distribution line as in (Fig. 5).

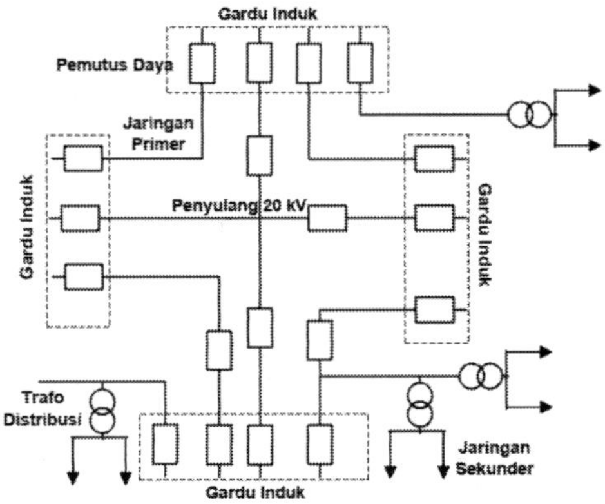

Fig.5. Grid Primary Distribution System

2.1.5 Spindle and Cluster Primary Distribution System

In this system is often used in big cities, this system is the development of radial system. Power will be supplied from power plants or substations through some feeder or distribution substations and ends in switching substation. The specialty of this system is the presence of a free line that is not burdened by any load which will be the immediate reserve lineto reflection substation with the shortest path. For normal conditions on this system all switches on the reflection will be in open condition and if a system is not using a reflection substation, but the feeder state is primarily connected to the backup line then this is called the cluster type. While the spindle type system uses a substation reflection as it should. The primary spindle distribution line is found in (Fig. 6) and the cluster type distribution line as seen in (Fig. 7).

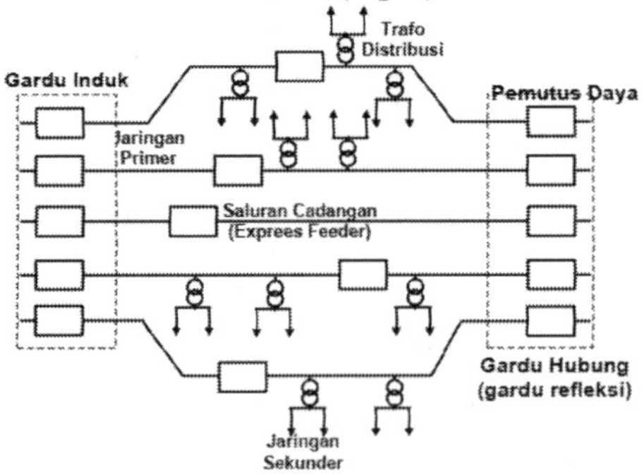

Fig.6. Spindle Primary Distribution System

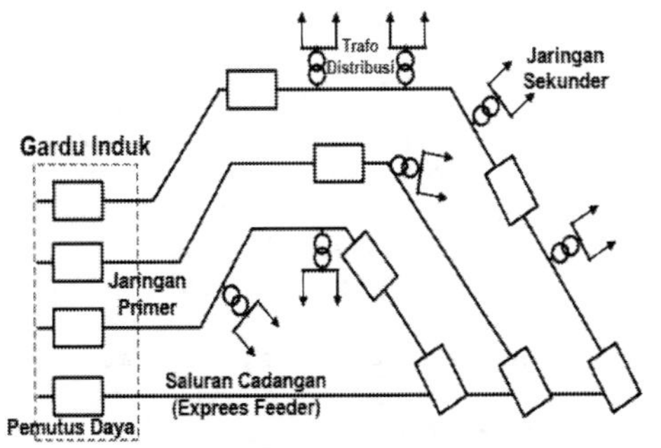

Fig.7. Cluster Primary Distribution System

2.2 Voltage Drop

The voltage drop is the voltage loss between the send/source voltage and the receive voltage. The voltage drop is caused by the resistance and current on the alternating line, the magnitude dependson the impedance and the power factor at the load. Power lines generally serve loads that have lagging power factor. The factors that caused the difference of voltage distribution system are:

1. Consumers have equipment that requires a certain voltage.
2. Location of the consumer spread, so the distance of each customer with the point of service is not the same.
3. The occurrence of voltage drop.

Voltage drop in distribution line can also be said to be a loss of power during power delivery. The magnitude of the voltage drop depends on the amount of load current flowing on the distribution line, the length of the distribution line and the type of wire to deliver the load.

The voltage drops allowed under SPLN No. 72 of 1987 are as follows:

1) SUTM = 5% from voltage line in radial system
2) SKTM = 2% from voltage line inspindle and gugus system
3) Distribution Transformator = 3% from volatge line
4) SUTR = 4% from volatge line
5) SambunganRumah = 1% from minimum voltage line

Drop Voltage formula :

$$\text{Vdrop} = \text{I x (R Cos}\varphi + \text{X Sin}\,\varphi) \text{ x } \ell$$
$$= (\text{I} . \text{Z}) \text{ x } \ell$$
$$= (\text{Vs} - \text{VR})$$
$$\text{Vs} = \text{VR} + (\text{I} . \text{Z})$$
$$\text{Vs} = \text{VR} + \text{Vdrop}$$

Percentage Drop Voltage Formula ::

$$(\text{Vdrop})\% = \frac{\text{Vdrop}}{\text{Vs}} x\ 100\ \%$$

Where :

Vs = Voltage Source
VR = Voltage Receive
(Vdrop)% = Precentage Voltage Drop (%)
I = Load current (A)
Z = Impedance
ℓ = Length of the channel (m)
V = Voltage (V)
R = Conductive Resistance (Ω)
X = Conductor Inductive Reactance (Ω)
Cosφ= Power factor
Sin φ= Sinus angle of load
φ= phase angle of load

1. Conductor
2. Length of the channel
3. Wire Size
4. current carrying capacity

2.3 Power Losses

Power loss is the amount of electricity lost during the delivery of electricity in a certain time (usually in the watthour). This loss is influenced by the amount of difference between the received power and the power sent. The magnitude of 3 phase power can be seen from the following formula:

$$P\ 3\phi = \sqrt{3}.\ (V\ (L-L)x\ I).Cos\varphi$$
$$= \sqrt{3}.\ (\sqrt{3}\ .\ V\ (L-N)\ x\ I).Cos\varphi$$
$$= 3\ .V(L-L)\ x\ I\ xCos\varphi$$

Where :

P 3ϕ = 3 phase power (Watt)
V L-L = voltage phase-phase
V L-N = Voltage Phase-Neutral
I = Load Current (Ampere)
Cos φ =Power Factor

Factors that caused power losses are :

1. Power losses in distribution system

Three phase Power losses with load at the end of the line:

$$\text{P Losses} = (\text{Ps} - \text{PR})$$
$$= (\text{I}^2 \text{ x Z Total})$$
$$= \text{I}^2 . (\text{R.Cos}\varphi + \text{jX.Sin}\varphi) .\ell$$

So the Energy Losses is :

$$\text{E} = (\text{P Losses x t})$$

Where :

P Losses = Power losses (Watt)
Ps = Power sent (Watt)
PR = Power received (Watt)
I = Current (Ampere)
Z = Impedance (Ω)
R = Conductive Resistance (Ω)
X = Conductor Inductive Reactance (Ω)
Cos φ = Power factor
Sin φ= Sinus angle of load
φ = phase angle of load
ℓ = length of the channel (km)
t = time (jam/killo Watt)

2. Unbalanced Load.
3. Error in kWh meter.
4. Loss contact.
5. Ireegular use of electricity.

2.4 Electric Transient and Analysis Program (ETAP) 12.6.0

ETAP 12.6.0 is a comprehensive analysis software to design and simulate a power supply system. The analysis offered by ETAP used by the authors is the voltage drop, and the network losses. ETAP also provideS a warning to undervoltage and overvoltage bus so can be known which bus is not in optimal operation.In order to analyze a series of circuitneeds complete and accurate circuit data so the calculation from ETAP can be answered.

III. ANALYSIS

To complete the data needed in the analysis and calculation required data in accordance with the purpose of the study. The data is taken in accordance with the research which from data distribution system PLN Rayon Muaralabuh. The data are as follows:

1. Data of all feeders at Rayon Muaralabuh and MuaralabuhExpress Feeder GH AlahanPanjang.
2. Table impedance JTM type AAAC
3. Transformer data of all related feeders
4. The peak load data of each related feeder.

4.1 Distribution Operation Pattern

Condition before interconnection with IPP (PLTMH PT SKE).The condition of 20 kV system at PT PLN (Persero) Rayon Muaralabuhbefore interconnection with IPP of Hydro Micro Power Plant (PLTMH) owned by PT SeloKencana Energy, Rayon Muaralabuh system assisted by two units of PLTD owned by PT. SINARINDO, as shown in Fig. 9.

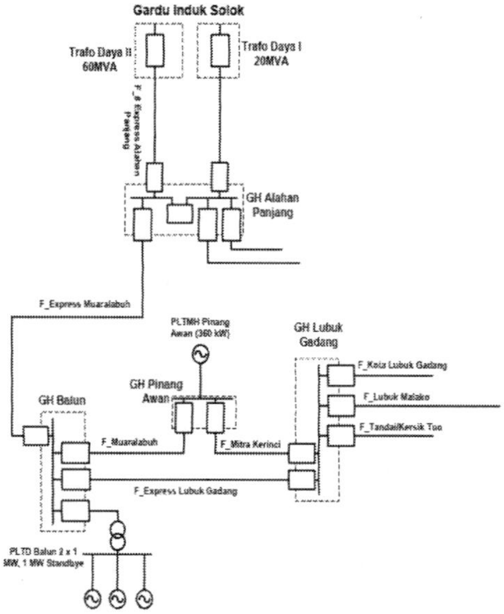

Fig. 9. Single Line Diagram Muaralabuh before interconnection

As shown in Figure 4.1, the distribution system of 20 kV PT PLN (Persero) Rayon Muaralabuh is supplied by one unit of substation (GI) that is GI Solok. In GI Solok there are two units of power transformer that serves to lowered the high voltage 150 kV transmission into medium voltage distribution 20 kV. Power Transformator I with a capacity of 20 MVA while PowerTransformator II with a capacity of 60 MVA. For distribution system 20 kV PT PLN (Persero) Rayon Muaralabuh, suported by power transformator II (Bus II) through feeder 8 express AlahanPanjang to the Alahan Panjang Substation. Furthermore, from AlahanPanjangSubstationuntil working area of PT PLN (Persero) Rayon Muaralabuh distributed through feeder express AlahanPanjang.

At GH Alahan Panjang other than incoming feeder 8 express Alahan Panjang, there is also incoming from feeder 4 MuaraPanas which is sourced from bus I GI Solok, this become supply for two outgoing feeder at GH AlahanPanjang. Two outgoing feeder is working area PT PLN (Persero) Rayon KayuArowhich are: FeederTalangBabungo and FeederSungaiNanam. These Feeders allow to manuver the 20 kV supply system at PT PLN (Persero) Rayon Muaralabuh, if there is any power disturbance to feeder 8 Express GI Solok until GH Alahan Panjang.

Sistem distribusi 20 kV pada PT PLN (Persero) Rayon Muaralabuh ini masih menggunakan sistem radial.Hal ini disebabkan karena sistem 20 kV PT PLN (Persero) Rayon Muaralabuh hanya disupplay oleh satu unit gardu induk.Oleh karena itu tingkat kehandalannya rendah.

The conductor that is used in Feeder 8 Alahan Panjangfrom GI Solok until GH Alahan Panjang is AAAC 240 mm². The conductor that is used in Feeder 8 Alahan Panjangfrom GH Alahan Panjang until GH Balun is AAAC 150 mm² on the main line, while in the branch use AAAC 70 mm² AAAC 35 mm². This causes the voltage drop in the substation receiver at PT PLN (Persero) Rayon Muaralabuh large enough.

A. Kondisisesudahinterkoneksidengan IPP (PLTMH PT. SKE)

The condition of 20 kV system at PT PLN (Persero) Rayon Muaralabuh after the interconnection with IPP which in this case is Hydro Micro Power Plant (PLTMH) owned by PT SeloKencana Energy, as shown in Fig. 10.

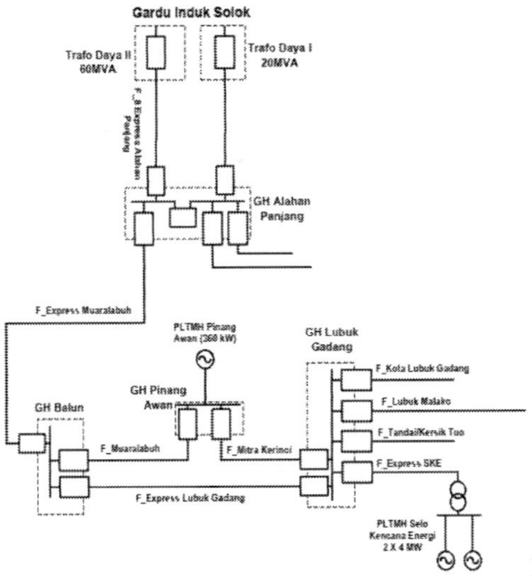

Fig. 10. Single Line Diagram Muaralabuh after interconnection

4.2 Calculation Using Etap 12.6.0 Simulation

Calculation with etap simulation adjusted for research purposes, that is as follows:

1. Calculate the percentage of voltage drop on 20 kV system PT PLN (Persero) Rayon Muaralabuh (using Etap12.6.0 simulation)
2. Calculate technical losses on the 20 kV system of PT PLN (Persero) Rayon Muaralabuh (using Etap12.6.0 simulation)
3. Calculate the stability of 20 kV system voltage at PT PLN (Persero) Rayon Muaralabuh before and after interconnection with IPP (PLTMH PT SKE) (using equation and Etap simulation 12.6.0).

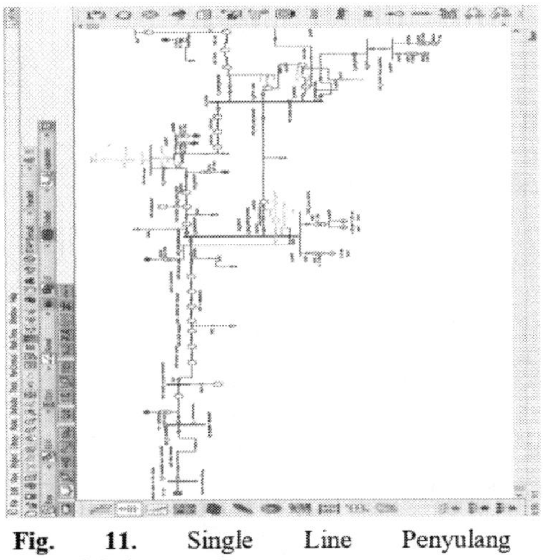

Fig. 11. Single Line Penyulang Rayon MuaralabuhDenganEtap

After creating a single line diagram distribution system of Rayon Muaralabuh in Etap, proceed with input value; load capacity on distribution transformers, source voltage, channel length and the type of conductor used. After that simulation of power flow on 20 kV system of PT PLN (Persero) Rayon Muaralabuh by clicking the load flow analysis toolbar. Here is the result of power flow simulation on 20 kV distribution system PT PLN (Persero) Rayon Muaralabuh using Etap 12.6.0.

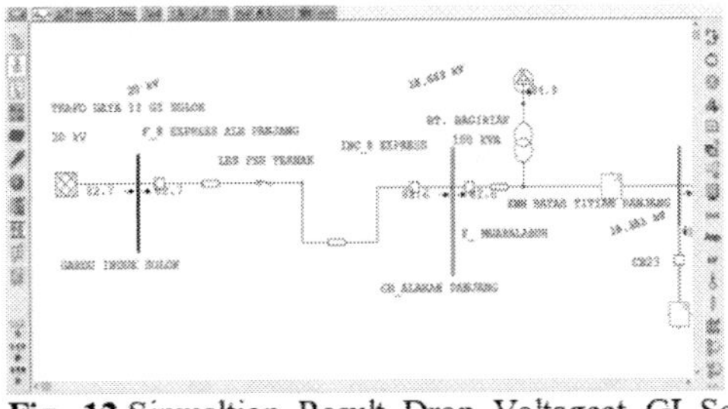

Fig. 12. Simualtion Result Drop Voltageat GI Solokdan GH AlahanPanjang

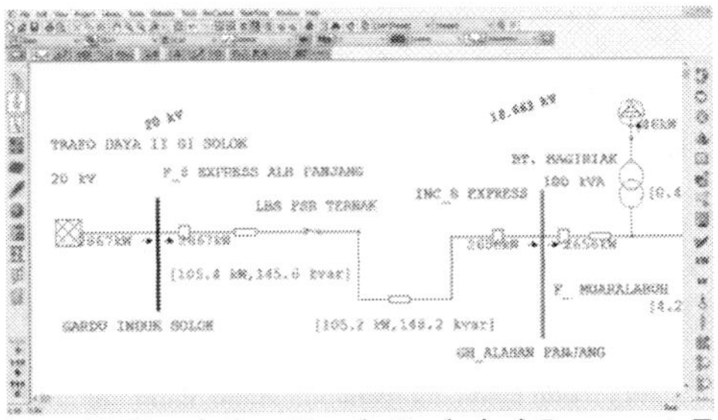

Fig. 13. Simulation Result Technical Losses at Feeder 8 Express AlahanPanjang

From simulation and calculation results with Etap 12.6.0, so can be made data table comparison measurement and calculation of voltage drop, technical losses and 20 kV system voltage stability at PT PLN (Persero) Rayon Muaralabuh before and after interconnection with IPP (PLTMH PT SKE) as follows:

Based on the comparison table between the calculation usingetap with validation formula above, it can be shown that the difference between the two calculations does not exceed 1% (one percent). So it can be stated that the result of calculation of voltage stability with Etap 12.6.0 simulation, can be a benchmark for performing voltage stability analysis.

4.3 Saving Power

Saving Power is the amount of loss (measured by the value of power) that can be saved or reduced as a result of a program or activity, which if the activity is not executed will condition.

From the calculation of technical losses before and after interconnection with IPP (PLTMH PT SKE), it can be calculated saving power in one month (number of days

30) regardless of point of transaction with power plant, as follows:

E1 = 857.808 kWh/month
E2 = 573.840 kWh/month
Esaving = E1 – E2
= 857.808 - 573.840
= 283.968 kWh/month.

4.4 Saving Cost

Saving cost is defined as a loss (measured by monetary value) that can be saved or deducted as a result of a program or activity, which if the activity is not executed will cause harm or remain the same as the previous state. In this discussion, saving cost is calculated based on sent energy that can be saved (which has been lost) and multiplied by the average price of energy per kWh at PT PLN (Persero) Rayon Muaralabuh in that period.

With the change of operation pattern of distribution system of 20 kV at PT PLN (Persero) Rayon Muaralabuh which interconnect with IPP (PLTMH PT SKE) hence 283,968 kWh / month reducement of technical losses. If this amount multiplied by the average price of energy per kWh at PT PLN (Persero) Rayon MuaralabuhRp 926, - then get a saving cost of Rp 262.954.368, - per month.

IV. CONCLUSION

1. The highest voltage drop of distribution system 20 kV at PT PLN (Persero) Rayon Muaralabuh before interconnection with IPP (PLTMH PT SKE) based on the result of simulation Etap 12.6.0 is 13.71%, while after interconnection down to 4.855%. The condition after this interconnection, in accordance with the standard voltage drop on SPLN No. 72 of 1987 is a maximum of 5%

2. Technical losses of 20 kV distribution system at PT PLN (Persero) Rayon Muaralabuh before interconnection with IPP (PLTMH PT SKE) based on simulation result of Etap 12.6.0 ignoring transaction point 13.074% while after interconnection down to 8,306 %. This number explains that the decreasement of 20 kV losses in PT PLN (Persero) Rayon Muaralabuh after interconnection with IPP (PLTMH PT SKE) is 4,768%.

3. Percentage of 20 kV system voltage stability at PT PLN (Persero) Rayon Muaralabuh after interconnection with IPP (PLTMH PT SKE) based on result of simulation Etap 12.6.0 is equal to 10,576% better.

4. Saving energybecause of the interconnection system (ignoring the point of transaction based on the result of Etap 12.6.0 calculation) in one month is 283,968 kWh. This number explains that saving cost or rupiah saved at PT PLN (Persero) Rayon Muaralabuh after interconnection with IPP (PLTMH PT SKE) in one month (reference to rupiah average per kWh at PT PLN (Persero) Rayon MuaralabuhRp926), - is Rp 262,954,368, -.

REFERENCES

1. Basri, Hasan (1997): *Power System Distribution.* Jakarta: ISTN.
2. Hasyim'ari, Jatmikodan Ivan BachtiarRivai (2003): *Drop Voltage Reapair for Consumer.* Surakarta: MuhammadiyahUniversity
3. Malik, Muh. Nasir (2009): *Losses Analysis Primary Distribution in Adhyaksa Makassar Feeder.* Makassar: MakassarUniversity.
4. Utomo, HendroWahyu (2010): *Analysis of Power Losses and Voltage Profilein APJ Surakarta.* Surakarta: MuhammadiyahUniversity
5. Pitoy, RanggaSenando (2016): *Analysis of Energy Losses in Distribution Network.* Manado: PoliteknikNegeri.
6. Rahman, Fadli (2017): *Analysis of express feeder building to Load Flow in Sungai Dareh Feeder at PT PLN (Persero) Rayon Sitiung. Padang: InstitutTeknologiofPadang.*
7. S, Alfredo Donald andEdyErvianto (2016): *Analysis Study of Power Losses : Load Curve Approachin PT. PLN (Persero) Area Pekanbaru.* Pekanbaru: RiauUniversity
8. Sampeallo, Agusthinus S., Wellem F. GalladanRendi A. Oematan (2013): Analysis of Voltage Drop *20 kV System Based on Load Change (Study Case Penfuiand Oebobofeeder PT PLN (Persero) Rayon Kupang).* Kupang: Nusa Cendana University.
9. SPLN (1985) No. 64: *Instructions for Selectionand Use of Fuser In Medium Voltage Distribution System* : PT PLN (Persero) Jakarta
10. SPLN (1987) No. 72*: Design Specification For Medium Voltage Network (JTM) And Low Voltage Network Jakarta: PT PLN (Persero) Jakarta.*
11. Waluyo, Soenarjo dan Andi Ali Akbar (2007): *Calculation of Power Shuts On Medium Voltage Distribution System of Air and Cable Channels*
12. Bandung: ITENAS.
13. Winardi, Bambang, Agung Warsito dan Meigy Restanaswari Kartika (2015): *Technical Shock Improvement Analysis and Suspense Voltage on Repeater KLS 06 in GisKalisari Using Etap Software 7.5.0.*Semarang: DiponegoroUniversity.

MATEC Web of Conferences **215**, 01021 (2018) https://doi.org/10.1051/matecconf/201821501021
ICTIS 2018

Study of Coordination on Protection Relay in High Voltage Transmission 150 kV (Payakumbuh – Koto Padang, West Sumatra)

Zulkarnaini Zulkarnaini[1], *Muhammad* Rizki[2]

[1]Lecturer of Electrical Engineering Department, Padang Institute of Technology, 91944 Nanggalo Padang, Indonesia
[2]Student of Electrical Engineering Department, Padang Institute of Technology, 91944 Nanggalo Padang, Indonesia

Abstract. The disturbance of the high voltage transmission can be caused by a short circuit, overload, lightning surge, and other natural disturbances. That disturbance can lead to disruption of the distribution of electricity and damage to the electric power system installation equipment. A reliable protection system that can identify the disturbance quickly and also can securing affected parts of the system from other parts that can still operate normally are needed. Protection system operation may fail due to various factors; therefore, in addition to primary protection required backup protection that can work as primary protection fails to work. Distance relays can be used as primary protection as well as remote backup protection on high-voltage transmission. While overcurrent relay (OCR) and ground fault relay (GFR) is used as a local backup if distance relay failed to work. This research conducted a study of protection relays coordination for primary protection or backup protection on the high-voltage transmission that connects to Payakumbuh substation and Koto Panjang substation. Coordination is done by calculating the distance relay settings that use as primary protection as well as remote backup protection relay settings and calculating the overcurrent and ground fault relay that used as local backup protection. From the calculation, we get setting time to coordinate distance relay, overcurrent relay, and ground fault relay. Setting time was conducted to the first zone of the distance relay within 0 sec, and the second zone within 0.4 sec and third zone within 1.2 sec. For overcurrent relay and ground fault relay use time delay 1 second where the value is above the value that used in the second zone of distance relay. Distance relay can be coordinated with the auto-reclose relay to close the circuit breaker automatically sometime after a temporary disturbance. Setting that use to auto reclose relay is dead time 1 second and reclaim time 40 second. The coordination between the distance relay with auto-reclose relay can improve the quality of distribution of electrical energy.

1 Introduction

Electrical energy is a primary requirement for everyone. It uses to distribute electricity from generating centers to the consumers using transmission systems. High Voltage Transmission is one of electric power transmission that plays a very important role in maintaining the quality and reliability of power systems, which is often disturbed. Disturbance can be a form of short circuit, overload, lightning surge, typhoon, bad weather, and others. Such disturbance may result in disruption of continuity of operation and damage to the electrical system [Arismunandar, A. Susumu Kuwahara. 2004]. Electrical protection systems can be failed by operation due to various factors. To anticipate the failure, it is needed the backup protection.

High-Voltage air passages use distance relays as primary protection and have local backup protection as well as remote backup protection. Local backup protection systems use Over Current Relay (OCR) and Grund Fault Relay (GFR), while remote backup protection uses distance relay second zones from other substations. In order to work selectively, the primary protection and backup protection must be coordinated primarily on the backbone [Mardensyah, Adrial. 2008]. Along with the increasing load and also the age of equipment that is getting old, then setting protection can be less accurate. To be able to ensure the setting of protection relay is required calculation in accordance with the conditions of equipment installed and the current load. Therefore the research is done.

1.1 High Voltage Transmission Protection

The power network was divided into the power plant, transmission line, and distribution networks, as shown in Figure 1.

https://doi.org/10.1051/matecconf/201821501021

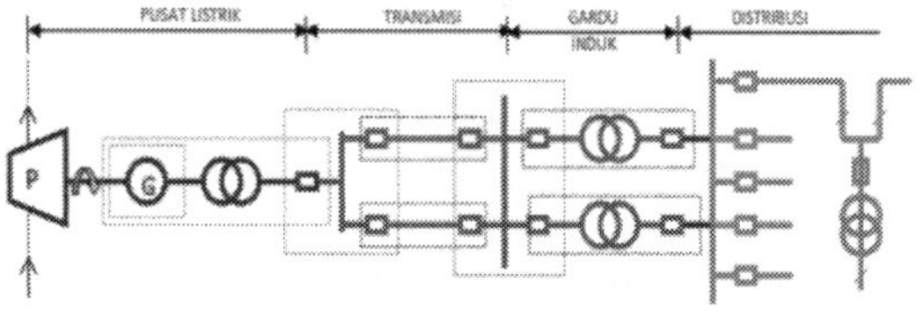

Fig. 1. Power system Network (PT PLN, 2014).

To improve the reliability of the supply of electrical energy, the needed for adequate protection systems is inevitable. Furthermore, a protection system must be able to work optimally. Protection System Transmission consists of primary protection and backup protection as follows [Priyono, Sugeng, 2011]:
- Relay for main protection
• Distance Relay (Basics or Step, PUTT, POTT, Blocking)
• Differential Relay (Pilot, Current, Phase)
• Directional Comparison Relay (Impedance, Current, Super Imposed)
- Backup protection is as follows:
• Local reserve protection system: OCR & GFR
• Remote backup protection system: Zone 2.

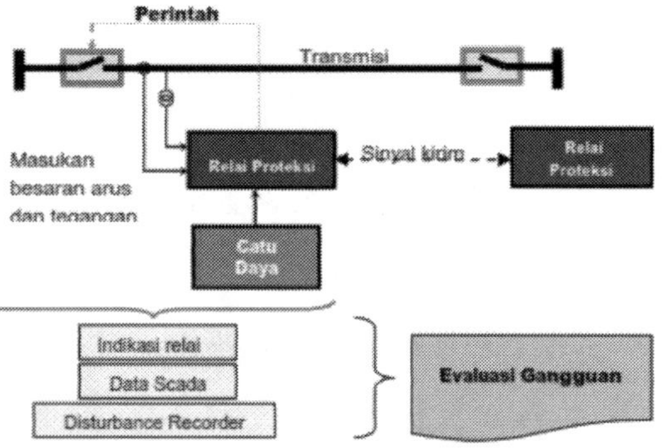

Fig. 2. Block Diagram Protection Transmission (PT PLN, 2014).

1.2 Power Protection System Components

Electrical power protection systems generally consist of several components designed to identify the condition of the electrical power system and work-based information obtained from the system such as current, voltage, and phase angle. Information obtained from the electrical power system will be used to compare the magnitude of the threshold setting on the protection equipment. If the amount obtained from the system exceeds the threshold setting of the protection equipment, then the protection system will work.
Equipment protection generally consists of several elements designed to observe the condition of the system. [Stanley H. Horowitz and Arun G. Phadke 2014]

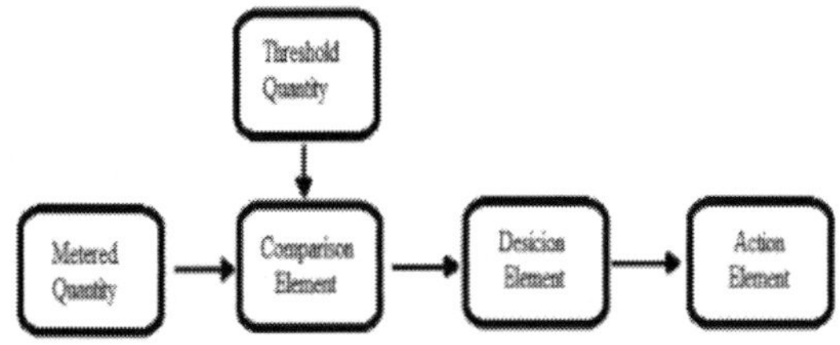

Fig. 3. Electrical Power System Protection Element (PT PLN, 2014).

1.3 Characteristics of Distance Relay

Distance relays can be classified by impedance characteristics (R-X) in polar coordinates, the number of input relay, and the methods used to compare those inputs. Generally, the method used is to compare two inputs to determine whether the disturbance that occurs is inside or outside the work area relay. Distance relay has several work characteristics, including [Antonius dan Fikriansyah. 2014]:

1.3.1 Characteristics of Mho

In the R-X impedance diagram is a circle with the diameter of the circle intersects the center point of the coordinate system; the magnitude of the diameter represents the range and phase angle settings of the mho characteristic. After the range and phase angle set the same as the impedance of the protected transmission line. This distance relay will work if the measured impedance is inside the circle.

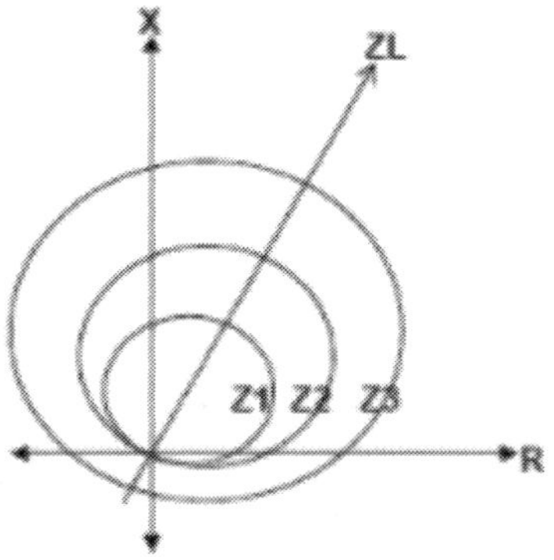

Fig. 4. The working of Mho Characteristics

1.3.2 Characteristics of quadrilateral

The characteristics of quadrilateral work can be established by determining the forward reach and resistive reach settings that can be set independently. Figure 4 shows the four sets of limits or range of quadrilateral working characteristics. Four release boundary setting i.e. the upper limit shows the range of reactance range, then the left and right borders are positive resistance settings and the negative resistance as well as the lower border shows the directional element.

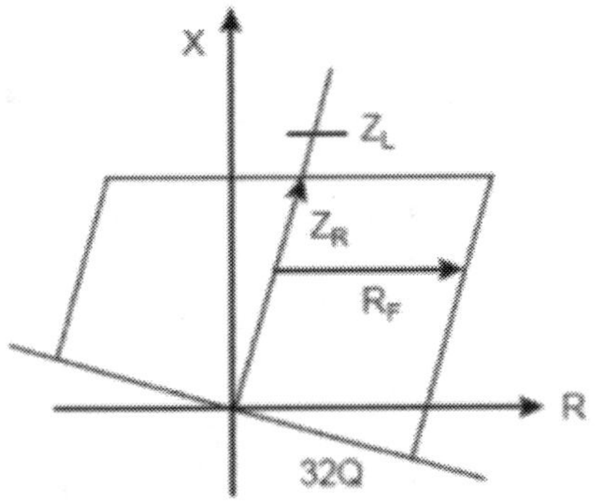

Fig. 5. Characteristics of Quadrilateral

1.3.3 Security pattern teleprotection distance relay

In order to improve the coordination of the protection system's time on the high-voltage transmission, a device that can send and receive signals from one or more releases in Station to relay in other Station is required. Protective release equipment is an equipment that can send and receive signals from one release to another. If the distance between one Station with another Station is far enough then needed a communication medium that can be used to send a signal. The communication channel used can be an optical fiber, Power Line Communication (PLC) or through the microwave.[Sunil S. Rao].

The security patterns used in the distance relay include:

- Direct Underreach Transfer Trip (DUTT)

For the DUTT pattern logic, the circuit scheme can be shown in Figure 5.

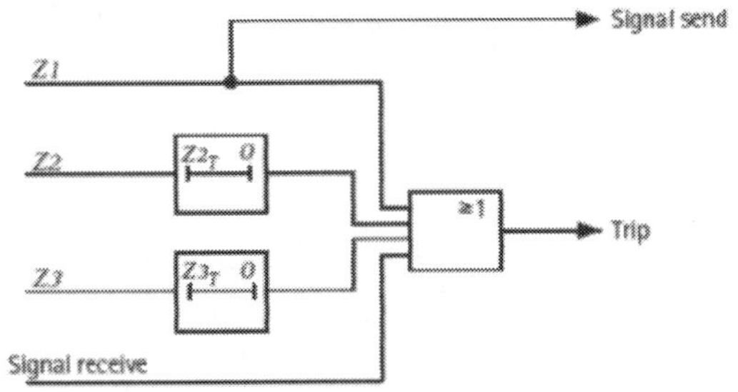

Fig. 6. Logic circuits direct underreach transfer trip

- Permissive Underreach Transfer Trip (PUTT)

The working principle of the PUTT pattern is: if the disturbance felt at the one release distance zone, the relay will send a trip signal to CB. At the same time, it sends a signal to the relay at the other terminal.

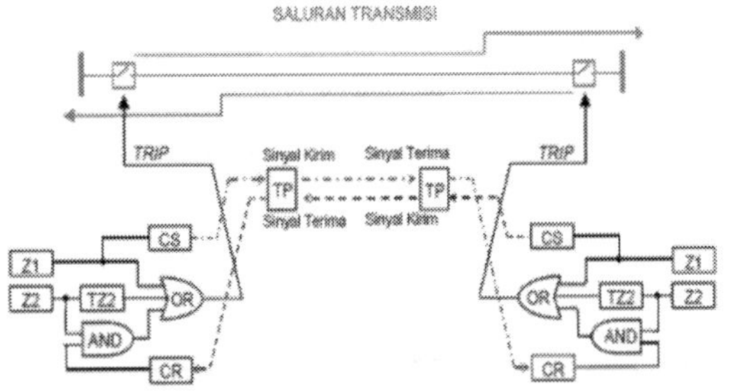

Fig. 7. Logic circuits PUTT scheme

- Permissive Overreach Transfer Trip (POTT)

The working principle of the POTT pattern is that if there is a disturbance felt by the two-distance relay zone, the relay will send the signal to the other end terminals and the other ends of the terminals will only work if the interference is also felt by the two relay. The logic drawing circuit is shown in Figure 7.

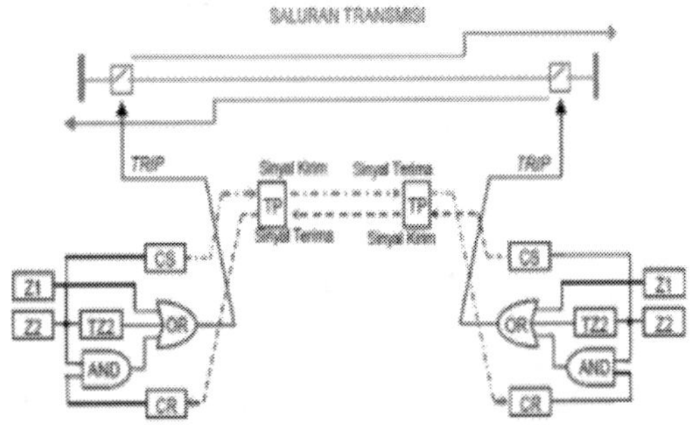

Fig. 8. Permissive overreach transfer trip

- Blocking scheme

In this pattern, tele-protection equipment will send a signal to the TP equipment on the substation in front of it if the distance relay detects the disturbance at the back. Then the relay will give an instantaneous trip command, the rule shown in Figure 9.

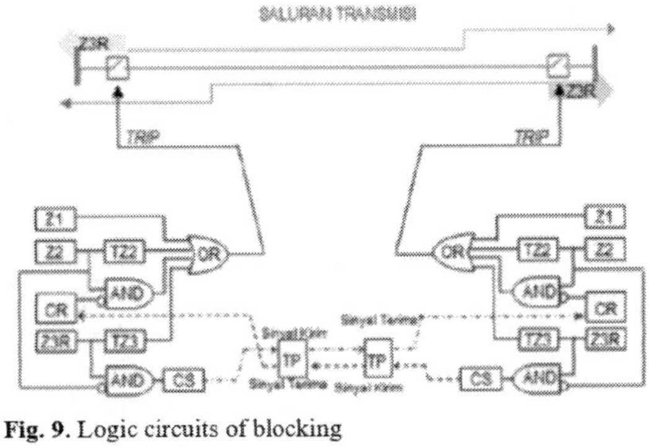

Fig. 9. Logic circuits of blocking

1.4 Over Current Relay (OCR)

Protection systems in high-voltage transmission use more OCR and GFR as a local back up protection. OCR is a relay that works when the current exceeds the predetermined setting thresholds. OCR has some working characteristics [PT. PLN (Persero). 2010. SPLN T5.002-1/2010].

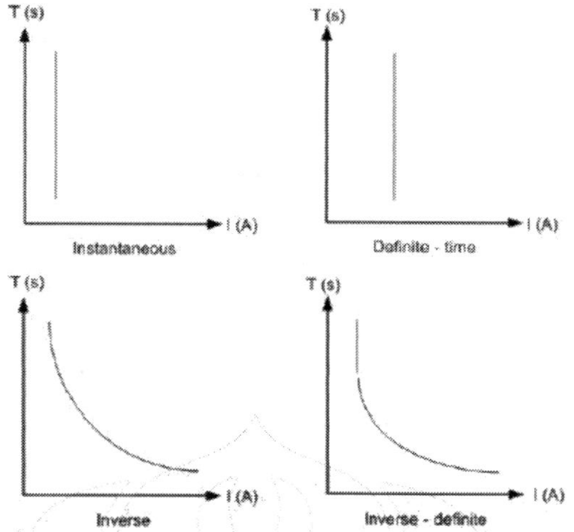

Fig. 10. Characteristics of OCR

$$T_{OCR} = 1\ sec \quad (1)$$

$$TMS = \left[\left(\frac{I_{3sc}}{I_{set}}\right)^{0.02} - 1\right]\frac{T}{0.14}$$

$$TMS = \left[\left(\frac{19939}{817}\right)^{0.02} - 1\right]\frac{T}{0.14}$$

$$TMS = 0.47 \quad (2)$$

1.5 Ground Fault Relay (GFR)

The fault of the ground is one of the most common disturbances in transmission lines; this is because the transmission is used using air insulation, so it is very susceptible to soil disturbance. To detect any current flowing from the system to the ground or also called the residual current.

IR = IA + IB + IC ; IR= Residual current

GFR is a working relay based on the amount of residual current flowing from the system. The following figure 11 shows the measurement of the residual current from the three-phase system [Haskarya, Henry, 2016].

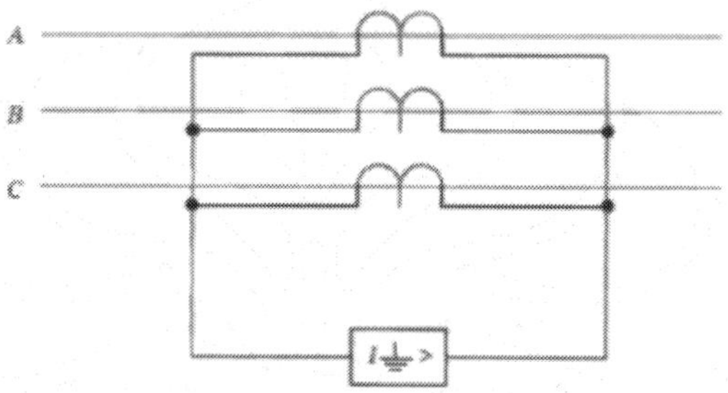

Fig. 11. Residue current measurement scheme

2 Method

The type of research is a case study which aims to coordination study of protective releases for high-voltage transmission Substation of Payakumbuh - Koto Panjang. Network Transmission 150 kV Koto Panjang - Payakumbuh consists of 248 towers, two transmission lines, and two ground wires with a total length of 84.844 km (169,688 kms) [PT PLN (Persero), 2014, KEPDIR 0520-3].

1. Equipment data
   a. Specifications of protection relay
   b. Ratio CT and PT
   c. Impedance, ratio, and capacity of power transformer
   d. Impedance or transmission line impedance
2. Power system configuration

The configuration of the electric power system used to coordinate the protective relay protection settings on high-voltage Transmission is a 150 kV system configuration of the Sumbagteng System as of April 2017.

3. Short circuit current

The short circuit current calculation for the coordination of the settings OCR and the GFR on the transmission line is done using the help of the software application DigSillent Power Factory version 15.1 assuming the configuration of the system conditions under normal operating conditions by 2017.

2.1 Data Required

Method of calculation/ data analysis is done with the steps as follows:

1. Calculate the value of channel impedance 150 kV Transmission Station Payakumbuh-Koto Panjang
2. Calculate the value of setting relays, OCR, and GFR for the 150 kV Transmission Payakumbuh-Koto Panjang

Calculation distance relay coordination, OCR, and GFR for 150 kV Transmission Payakumbuh - Koto Panjang.

2.2 Trasmission Impedance Data 150 kV

The data of high-voltage transmission impedance and channel length was used for calculation of distance relays protection settings based on the data obtained from P3B Sumatera.

Table 1. Data of impedance transmission 150kV.

SUTT 150 kV	Type of Conductor	Electric Current	Channel Length	Channel Impedance (/km)
Pyk – Koto Pjg	ACSR HAWK 1x330 mm^2	790 Amp	85.11 km	0.09805 + j0.41606 Ω
Pyk – Batu sangkar	ACSR HAWK 1x340 mm^2	790 Amp	26.19 km	0.09356 + j0.41790 Ω
Pyk – Pdg Luar	ACSR 1x240 mm^2	645 Amp	32.18 km	0.12745 + j0.42397 Ω
Koto Pjg -	ACSR 1x435 mm^2	940 Amp	17.91 km	0.07260 + j0.39117 Ω

Bangkinang				
Koto Pjg – Garuda Sakti	ACSR 1x435 mm^2	940 Amp	64.01 km	0.07260 + j0.39117 Ω

In doing the analysis and calculation used formulas given on the theoretical basis and as a validation calculation used software DigSILLENT Power Factory version 15.1.

3 Results and Discussion

The simulation was used to see the maximum short circuit current using the Calculation Short Circuit menu. The maximum short-circuited current is a short-circuit current which is the number of incoming/ sync generating units with the maximum Sumbagteng system. The assumptions used in assisting these calculations are:

a. The impedance used is 0.1 Ohm for resistance and 0 Ohm for reactance.
b. Short circuit duration:
   1. Breaker Time: 60 milliseconds
   2. Fault Clearing Time: 120 milliseconds according to SPLN No. 52-1 Year 1984
c. Short circuit interruption simulated on high voltage Transmission connecting Station Payakumbuh - Koto Panjang.

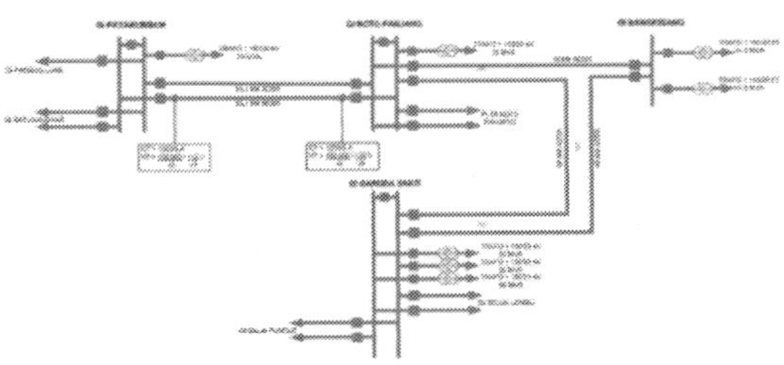

Fig. 12. The diagram one line on Payakumbuh – Koto Panjang Station (PT PLN, 2014).

3.1 Setting Relay Protection Transmission 150 kV Payakumbuh – Koto Panjang Station

3.3.1 Calculation of OCR

The calculation of relay protection settings was done by manually calculate based on the completeness of the data obtained.

Table 2. Calculation of OCR 150 kV Transmission Payakumbuh – Koto Panjang.

Basic Calculation	I_{set}	TMS
Current Setting	900 Amp	0.325
Using CCC	948 Amp	0.45
Using CT_{primer}	1500 Amp	0.38
Highest Load	817 Amp	0.47

Based on the simulation of a three-phase short circuit in DigSILLENT Power Factory version 15.1 application obtained OCR setting characteristics as follows:

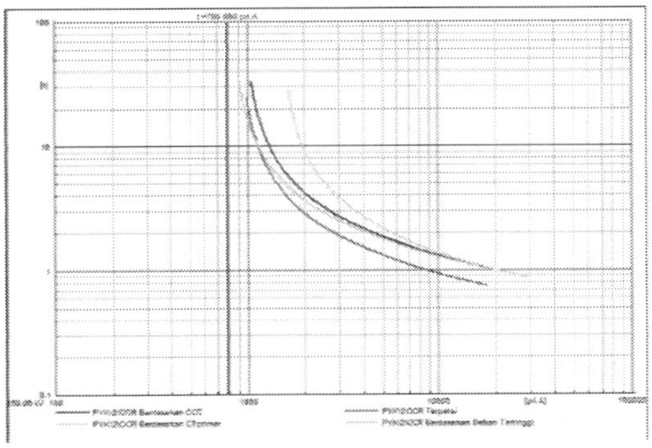

Fig. 13. Characteristics of OCR calculation transmission 150 kV Payakumbuh – Koto Panjang.

Figure 13 shows the characteristics of OCR setting calculation Transmission 150 kV Payakumbuh - Koto Panjang. The current setting is sufficiently low so that the possibility of conducting trips due to more load will be easy to happen, as well as setting if we use the highest load data ever achieved; this causes the carrier capability to be lower than the ability to deliver the maximum current he has. However, if the setting used based on the primary CT was used, this value is too high. So it can damage the equipment; especially it can cause the conductor to overheat which is very risky if it left. So the most optimal setting is the setting using the lowest equipment capabilities. In this case, delivery capability or known as CCC (Current Carrying Capacity). This setting is not too low or not too high and safe for all equipment.

3.3.2 Calculation of GFR

Merk Relay : Siemens Reyrolle
Type : 7SR11
Conductor : ACSR HAWK 1x330 mm2CCC=790
Characteristic : *Standard Inverse – IEC*
Setting of GFR installed:
Setting : 0.10* In Amp td / t : 0.550 (*SI-IEC*)
Inst. : *Block* * In Amp
td / t : *Block* (*Definite*)
Ratio CT = 1250/5
Ampere, In = 5 *Ampere*
Based on DigSILLENT simulation result for a single phase short circuit to ground at 150 kV Station Payakumbuh to Koto Panjang, it obtained maximum short circuit current: Is = 3493 A.

Table 3. Calculation of GFR 150 kV Transmission Payakumbuh – Koto Panjang.

Basic Calculation	I_{set}	TMS
Current Setting	125 Amp	0.55
Using CCC	158 Amp	0.46
Using CT_{primer}	250 Amp	0.39
Highest Load	136 Amp	0.48

Based on the simulation of short circuit 1 phase to the ground in DigSILLENT Power Factory application version 15.1, it got characteristic of GFR release setting as follows:

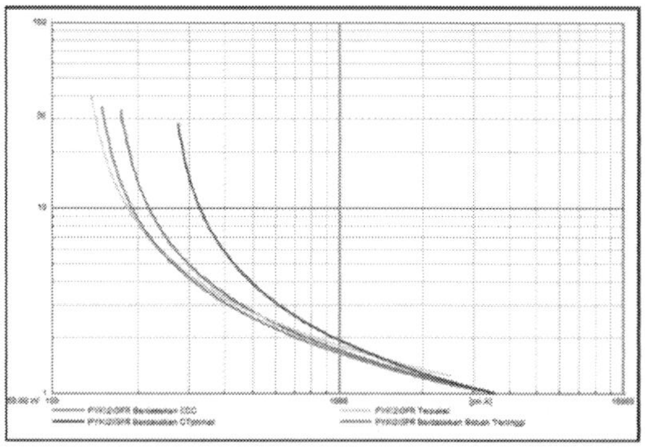

Fig. 14. Characteristics of GFR calculation transmission 150 kV Payakumbuh – Koto Panjang.

Figure 14 shows the characteristics of GFR Transmission 150 kV Payakumbuh - Koto Panjang. The current setting is quite low; this is a bit risky because there is a possibility of trip GFR in the transformer or a malfunctioning relay, as well as calculations based on the highest load setting, is also quite low. But, if we use the setting based on the primary CT, the setting is too high, so the releases are inaccurate in detecting interference. Then the most optimal setting is the setting using the lowest equipment capabilities, in this case, the delivery capability or known as CCC (Current Carrying Capacity). This setting is considered quite optimal and can maintain the security and lifetime of all equipment.

3.2 Setting Distance Relay of Payakumbuh – Koto Panjang Station

Time Delay : T1 = 0.00 sec
T2 = 0.40 sec
T3 = 1.20 sec

Table 4. Data distance relay.

Mode	Value
Program Mode	Standard Scheme
Standard Mode	PUP Z2
Fault Type	Both Enabled
Trip Mode	1P, Z1 Z2 & CR
tReserval Guard	46.00 ms
Unblocking Logic	None
SOTF/TOR Mode*	00000100010 000
SOTF Delay	10 s
ZIExt Fail	Disabled

Based on recalculation of distance relay setting for high voltage air transmission line at 150 kV carrier from Station Payakumbuh to Koto Panjang, the characteristics of distance releasing work as seen in the picture below (based on DigSILLENT Power Factory simulation):

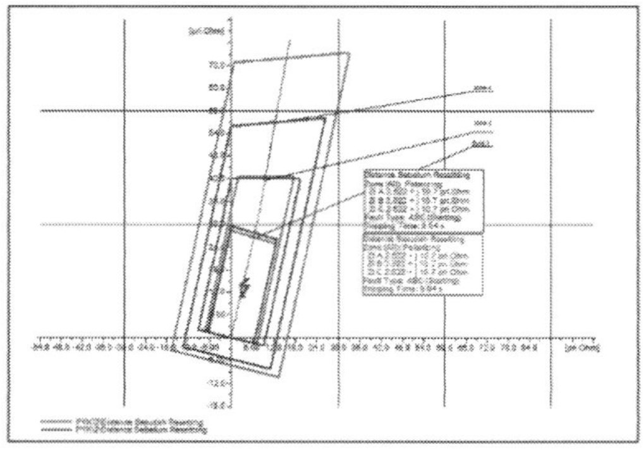

Fig. 15. The work characteristics of distance relay transmission 150 kV Payakumbuh – Koto Panjang.

4 Conclusion and recommandations

1. To anticipate the failure of the relay release operation, it uses more relay current and ground disturbance as protection of local reserve at high voltage air channel with delay time set more than delay zone two releases. Based on the calculation and analysis of relay settings OCR, GFR and Distance it can be concluded as follows:
Here is the coordination of more OCR and GFR:
OCR TMS = 0.45 (T = 1 sec)
GFR TMS = 0.63 (T = 1 sec)

2. By calculating the error factor on the distance release protection as the main safeguard as well as the remote

backup guard for the high-voltage 150 kV Transmission of Payakumbuh - Koto Panjang channel which has a channel length of 85.11 km, the coordinate of the settings obtained is:
Phase Fault
Zona 1= 68.08 *kM* (T=0.0 sec),
Zona 2 = 101.02 *kM* (T=0.4 sec),
Zona 3 = 173.68 *kM* (T=1.2 sec),
Ground Fault
Zona 1 = 2.57 + j 5.18 Ω (T=0.0 sec),
Zona 2 = 4.00 + j 7.77 Ω (T=0.4 sec),
Zona 3 = 5.48 + j 13.27 Ω (T=1.2 sec).

3. For temporary disturbances, the distances relay can be coordinated auto reclosing which works to close the breaker automatically. The auto reclosing relay coordination setting used is: Dead Time = 1 sec and Reclaim Time = 40 sec.

References

1. A. Arismunandar, S. Kuwahara, *Electric power engineering* **3**, (Pradnya Paramita, Jakarta, 2004)
2. M. Adrial, *Coordination study of relay protected relocation at high voltage of substation Gambir Lama – Pulomas*, (Indonesia University, 2008)
3. Nugroho, A. Setyo, *Distance relay coordination, over current relay and ground foult relay against resistive short circuit interruption* (Diponogoro University, 2011)
4. Priyono, Sugeng, *Koordinasi sistem proteksi trafo 30 MVA di Gardu Induk 150kV Krapyak* (2011)
5. PT PLN (Persero), *KEPDIR 0520-3 guidance of maintenance of protection and delivery control* (Jakarta, 2014)
6. E. Supriyadi, *Electrical protection system* (Adicipta Karya Nusa Jakarta, 2005)
7. S. S. Rao, *Switchgear and protection*, 10th Edition, KHANNA Publishers, (Delhi, 1994)
8. A.M.A.E. Aleem, *Design and Implementation of AProgrammable Simulation for the Estimation of the Over currentProtection Relays Immunity Against Decaying DC offset*, M.Sc. Dissertation (Office of Graduate Studies of Cairo University, 2007)
9. S. H. Horowitz, A. G. Phadke, *Power system relaying*, 4th Edition John Wiley & Sons, Ltd. (2014)
10. K. Kasinathan, *Power system fault detection and classification using wavelet transforms and adaptive resonance theory neural networks*, M. Sc. Dissertation (Office of Graduate Studies of Kentucky University, 2006)
11. S.H. Horowitz, A.G. Phadke, *Power system relaying, 3rd Edition*, Research Studies Press Limited (England, 2008)
12. B.R. Bhalja, R.P. Maheshwari, *High-resistance faults on two terminal parallel transmission line: analysis, simulation studies, and an adaptive distance relaying scheme*, IEEE transactions on power delivery **22** (2) (2007)
13. Anharul, Eddy, Coordinate relay on transmission network 150kV, J. JomFTEKNIK **3** (2) (Riau, 2016)
14. Antonius, Fikriansyah, Analysis and rearranging of distance relays on high voltage transmission line 150 kV Keramasan - Bukit Asam, Mikrotiga **1** (3) (Palembang, 2014)
15. H. Henry, Coordination of SUTT protection in GIM liwang-tuban consequences addition of power plant steering Tanjung Awar-Awar. J. Teknik ITS **5** 2 (Surabaya, 2016)
16. PT. PLN (Persero), Pattern *of transmission line protection section 1 height voltage 66 kV dan 150 kV* (2010)
17. Sugiyantoro, Bambang, *Effect of arc resistance on relay performance distance on transmission150 kV*, CITEE (Jogjakarta, 2017)

Tower-Footing Resistance and Lightning Trip-outs of 150 kV Transmission Lines in West Sumatra in Indonesia

Yusreni Warmi [1,*], and *Koji* Michishita [2]

[1]Padang Institute of Technology, Padang, West Sumatra, Indonesia
[2]Graduate School of Science and Technology, Shizuoka University, Hamamatsu, 4328561, Japan

Abstract. The trip-out rates calculated by taking account of the reduction in the tower-footing resistance due to the ionizing effect agree well with the observed ones. This indicates the importance of the impulse resistance in the analysis of the lightning performance of the line. The trip-out rate at the lower arm is high for the cases of the average grounding resistance of 33.3 ohms, and the rates at the upper arm are high for the cases of the average grounding resistance of 5.6 ohms. Such à trend can be simulated by the IEEE method using the impulse resistance. The trend for the trip-out ratio to become high with the increase in the span length is significant after improvement of the tower-footing resistance. However, the trend is weak before improvement of the tower-footing resistance. This is because in the case of the high tower-footing resistance the flashover occurs before the arrival of the wave reflected from the adjacent towers due to the high potential rise of the tower. Therefore, the degree of the influence of the span length on the trip-out ratio is dependent on the tower-footing resistance. The local lightning activity significantly affects the trip-out rate.

1 Introduction

An electric power transmission system in Indonesia more commonly uses an overhead line than an underground cable. An overhead transmission line is quite susceptible to lightning strokes due to high construction. There is a 150 kV transmission line from Payakumbuh to Koto Panjang in West Sumatra, passing the area whose average number of thunderstorm days per year (IKL: Isokeraunic levels) reached up to 165, and the frequency of direct lightning strokes to the transmission line was high. This line is the trunk line between West Sumatra sub-system (Padang UPT) and Riau sub-system (Riau UPT). The intensity of a lightning stroke is very high, due to the layout of the transmission line that is surrounded by mountain, hill and near the sea [1-2]. Thus, they had a threat of lightning from the sea, and the lines that cross the mountain and hill are structures that appear on the surface of the ground and become an easy target for lightning stroke. Therefore, it must have à high degree of immunity against lightning strokes.

According to the data from the Distribution and Load Control Centre Sumatra (Sumatra P3B), the main cause of the trip-outs is lightning, amounting to 66% of all trip-outs [3-5]. In addition to causing blackouts, lightning overvoltage also causes the trip-out of the transmission line.

An example of these incidents is the Payakumbuh–Koto Panjang blackout that lasted as long as 10 minutes in 2010. In 2011, the blackout is also caused by the outage of Circuit 1 and 2 for 39 and 57 minutes, respectively [3-5].

Lightning performance of a transmission line has been studied for a long time. According to [6-8], the high ratio of trip-outs of 110 kV to 138 kV lines in China, Mexico, and Malaysia for five years were 62%, 50%, and 79%, respectively. In Japan, the high ratio of lightning trip-outs of 110 – 154 kV lines was 75% [9].

Lightning trip-outs mean the operation of a circuit breaker at the substation due to flashover caused by lightning [10]. Furthermore, it is shown that the tower-footing resistance has a significant influence on the back-flashover protection performance: the lower the tower-footing impedance, the less the back-flashover rate [10-18] In this paper, lightning performance of the 150 kV transmission line in West Sumatra is studied. To the best of our knowledge, this is the first time that the lightning performance of the transmission line in West Sumatra high lightning activity area and the high lightning trip-out area is studied. In fact, the overhead line located in hilly areas will be much closer to the clouds, thus having more frequency of lightning strokes. West Sumatra is located in a tropical area. Therefore, the air has a humidity, which explains the high-intensity lightning, namely 20 to 40 flashes/100 km-year [19] for the high isokeraunic level area. According to [20] the lightning trip-out rate of 110 kV to 154 kV line from 1980 to 2000 was 1.7 to 2.8 trip-out/100 km-year. There is a 150 kV transmission line from Payakumbuh to Koto Panjang in West Sumatra, passing an area whose average number of thunderstorm days per year (IKL: Isokeraunic levels) reached 165, and the possibility of direct lightning strokes to the transmission line, including the strokes to the transmission tower, is high [3-5].

* Correspondence to: Yusreni Warmi. E-mail: yusreni@itp.ac.id
* Padang Institute of Technology, Padang, West Sumatra, Indonesia.

2 Transmission Line under Study

2.1 Line configuration

The location of the transmission line under study in West Sumatra is shown in Figure 1. as the blue line. Among 248 towers, 156 towers (63 %) are located on hills, 51 towers (20.5 %) in rice fields, and 41 towers (16.5 %) in the forest [1,21]. In figure 1 shows a plan of a 150-kV overhead transmission line between Payakumbuh - Koto Panjang under study, shown in the middle, with the total length of 86 km. The studied line is a double-circuit, balanced-insulation, and transposed transmission line. The IKL was as many as 165 days/ year in the area where the line segment between No. 1 to No. 140 towers, 47 km in length, locates, while the IKL was 22 days/ year in the area where the line segment from No. 141 to No. 248 towers locates. The thunderstorm in this area often moves from the northeast to the southwest.

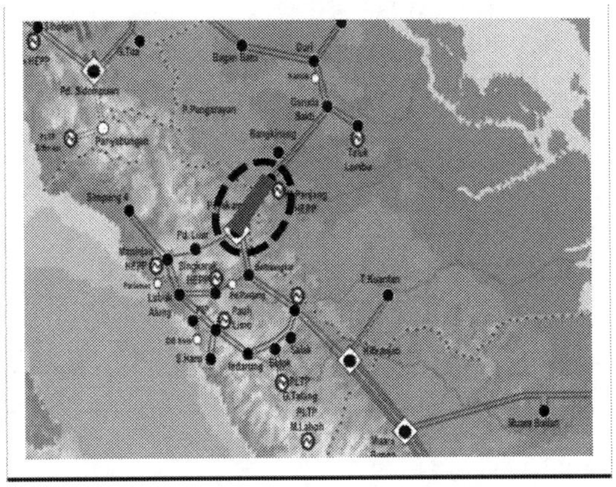

Fig. 1. Location of Transmission line under study.

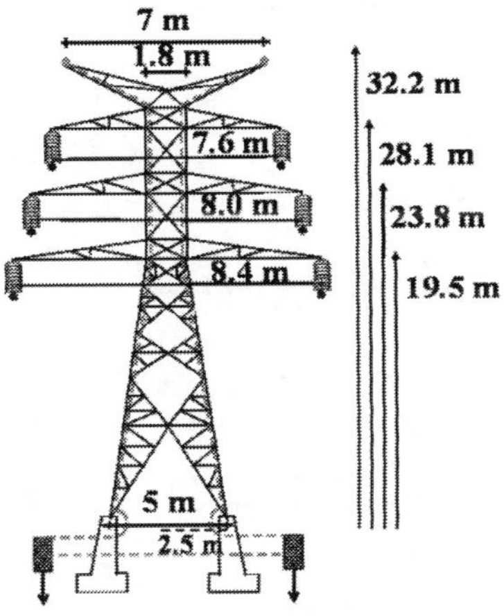

Fig. 2. Configuration of representative tower.

Fig. 2 shows the configuration of one of four types of towers with almost the same dimensions [22]. The types of towers might be chosen dependent on the easiness of the construction. The range of the span length was from 147 m to 434 m with an average of 333 m.

Table 1. Shows the dimension, the component ratio and the frequency ratio of the lightning trip-outs dependent on tower types. The four types of towers had almost the same dimensions [19,22,23]. The types of towers might be chosen dependent on the easiness of the construction. The range of the span length was from 147 m to 434 m with an average of 333 m.

Table 1. Shows the dimension, the component ratio and the frequency ratio of the lightning trip-outs dependent on tower types. The four types of towers had almost the same dimensions [19,22,23]. The types of towers might be chosen dependent on the easiness of the construction. The range of the span length was from 147 m to 434 m with an average of 333 m.

Table 1. Line condition.

	Tower Types			
	A	B	C	D
d_{OHGW}	7.0	6.8	6.8	7.0
d_{Upper}	7.6	7.0	7.0	7.6
d_{Middle}	8.0	7.4	7.4	7.6
d_{Lower}	8.45	7.8	7.8	7.6
d_{Tower}	5.0	5.4	5.4	5.6
h_{OHGW}	32.2	31.7	31.7	31.7
h_{Upper}	28.1	27.7	27.7	27.7
h_{Middle}	23.8	23.6	23.6	23.6
h_{Lower}	19.5	19.5	19.5	19.5
Crossing angle of line	0° - 3°	0° - 20°	20° - 40°	40° - 60°
Component ratio (%)	53.6	28.6	10.7	7.1
Frequency ratio of tripout (%)	60.5	30.2	8.1	1.2

Figure 3. Shows the distribution of the length of an arcing horn gap installed at each tower [22,23]. The arcing horn gap is arranged 75% to 85% of the length of the insulator string, 1.2 m to 1.6 m. At the towers with frequent insulator damages, the length of an arcing horn gap is shortened to 0.9 – 1.0 m, and as a result, more than half of the horns had the length from 0.9 m to 1.0 m. The 4 to 6 pieces of the TLAs were installed at 10 towers among No.1 to No.140 towers dependent on the frequency of the flashovers [22,23]. The arcing horn gap is arranged 75% to 85% of the length of the insulator string, 1.2 m to 1.6 m. At the towers with frequent insulator damages, the length of an arcing horn gap is shortened to 0.9 – 1.0 m, and as a result, more than half of the horns had the length from 0.9 m to 1.0 m. The 4 to 6 pieces of the TLAs were installed at 10 towers among

No.1 to No.140 towers dependent on the frequency of the flashovers [22,23].

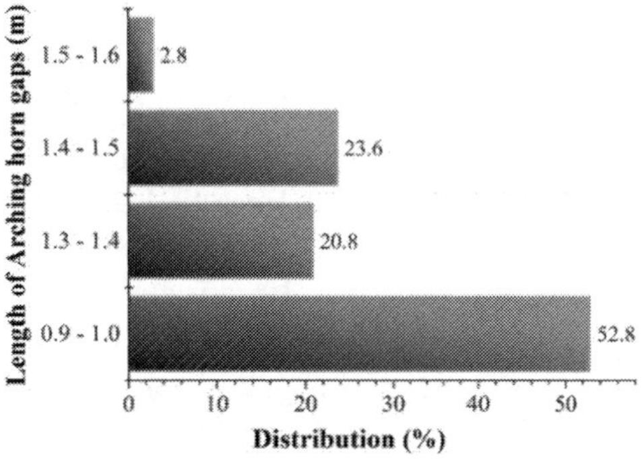

Fig. 3. Distribution of the length of an arcing horn gap from No. 1 to No. 140 towers [22]

2.2 Tower-footing résistance

Figure 4. Shows the average tower-footing resistance as a function of the tower-number group before and after the improvement of the tower-footing resistance, carried out from 2010 to 2014.

The average tower-footing resistance for the tower-number group before and after the improvement was in the ranges from 24 to 50 Ω and from 4 to 6 Ω, respectively. The average periods before and after the improvement were 3.3 and 1.8 years, respectively.

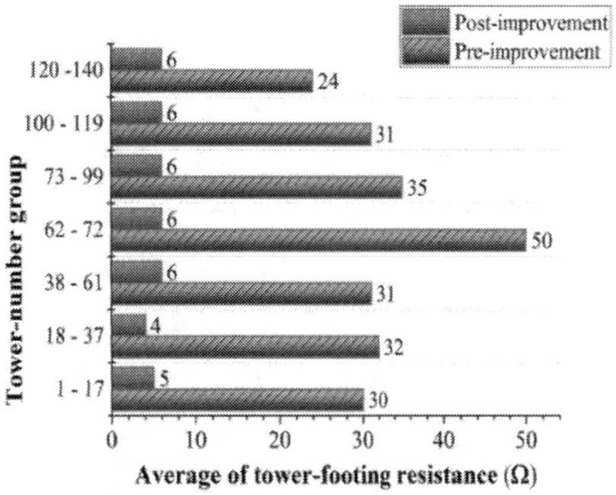

Fig. 4. Measurement data of average value of tower-footing resistance at No. 1 to No 140 towers.

3. Factor Influencing Lightning Trip-outs

3.1 Lightning activity

Figure 5. Shows the trip-out rate as a function of the line segment expressed by the tower-number group. The rate decreases with the increase of the tower number with which the location of towers first directs toward the east and then to the south. In the area of the line, the lightning activity is high in the north and weakens in the south as is indicated by the decrease of the IKL from 165 to 22 days/ year. The lightning activity might be the cause of the decrease of the rate of the line segment with the increase of the tower number.

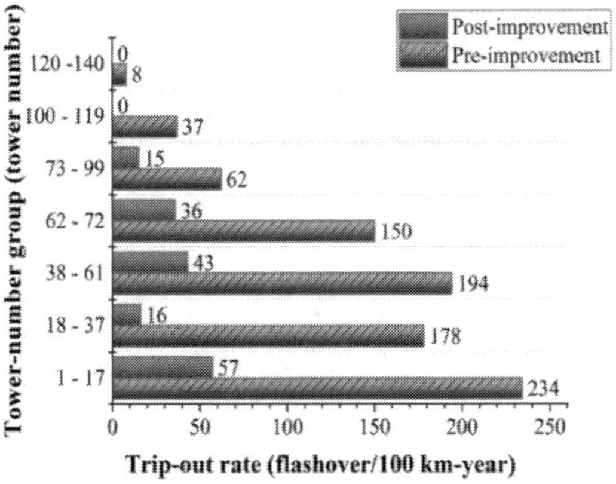

Fig. 5. Trip-outs rate as a function of the tower-number group.

Since the trip-out rates of the line segment between No. 73 – No. 140 towers are relatively low probably due to the low lightning flash density, the following analysis will be made for the line from No. 1 to No. 72 towers to clarify the degree of influence of some factors.

3.2 Tower-footing résistance

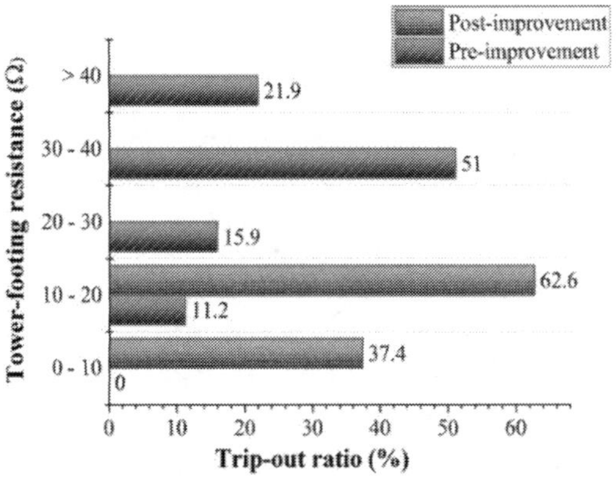

Fig. 6. Trip-out rate as a function of tower-footing

Figure 6. Shows the trip-out ratio of the number of trip-outs for a tower for a year as a function of the tower-footing resistance. The number of towers in the tower-footing resistance segment was from 10 (10 – 20 Ω) to 32 (20 – 30 Ω) before the improvement, and that was 5 (10 – 20 Ω) and 67 (0 – 10 Ω) after the improvement. The trip-out ratio increases with the increase of the grounding resistance excluding the trip-out ratio of the segment for 30 – 40 Ω before the improvement of tower-footing resistance. Table 2. shows the parameters of towers with frequent lightning trip-outs and the grounding resistance of 8 towers out of 10 is in the range of 30 - 40 Ω. This is the reason for the high trip-out rate in the resistance segment of 30 - 40 Ω.

Before the improvement of tower-footing resistance, the highest number of flashover was found at No. 16 tower with the tower-footing resistance of 35 Ω and the average tower-footing resistance at the towers experiencing flashover was 48 Ω. After the improvement of the tower-footing resistance, the highest number 2 times, was found at 7 towers (No. 10, 16, 19, 46, 50 and 61 towers with the tower-footing resistance of 10 Ω and No. 47 tower with the tower-footing resistance of 15 Ω) and the average tower-footing resistance of the towers with flashover was 11 Ω.

Table 1. Parameters of towers with frequent trip-outs before improvement of tower footing resistance

Tower No.	Grounding resistance (Ω)	Span length (m)	Altitude (m)	Tower top height difference (m)	Number of trip-outs
10	38	308	269	8.95	11
16	35	416	158	24.70	18
17	35	385	154	22.45	12
19	38	422	201	20.75	6
43	36	389	110	7.90	6
46	31	286	151	3.25	6
48	45	321	166	4.55	10
50	25	278	166	8.70	8
61	31	402	266	179	6
67	33	222	307	12.65	8

3.3 Span Length

Figure 7. Shows the lightning trip-out ratio of the number of flashover for a tower for a year as a function of the span length.

The number of towers in the span length range was from 10 (150 – 250 m) to 32 (351 –450 m). It is reported that the trip-out ratio is high for towers with long span length because of the increase of the lightning flashes to the line [4-8]. The trend that the trip-out ratio becomes high with the increase of the span length is significant after the improvement of the tower-footing resistance. However, the trend is weak before the improvement of the tower-footing resistance. This is because in the case of the high tower-footing resistance the flashover occurs before the arrival of the wave reflected from the adjacent towers due to the high potential rise of the tower. Therefore, the degree of the influence of the span length on the trip-out ratio is dependent on the tower-footing resistance.

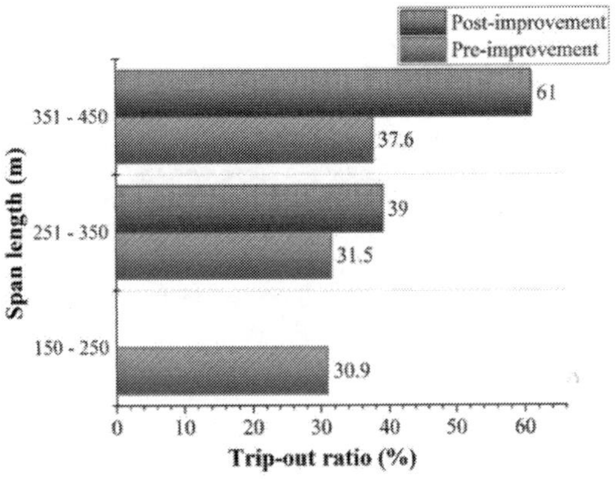

Fig. 7. Trip-outs rate as a function of the span length.

3.4 Altitude of towers

Figure 8 shows the trip-out ratio as a function of the altitude of the towers. The number of towers in the altitude range was from 6 (301 –400 m) to 43 (100 – 200 m). It is reported that with the increase of the altitude, the trip-out ratio increases [20]. However, such a trend can't be seen in Fig. 8 because the altitude of 6 towers out of 10 in Table 3 is in the range of 100 - 200 m. The degree of the influence of the altitude of the tower is not significant on the transmission line under study.

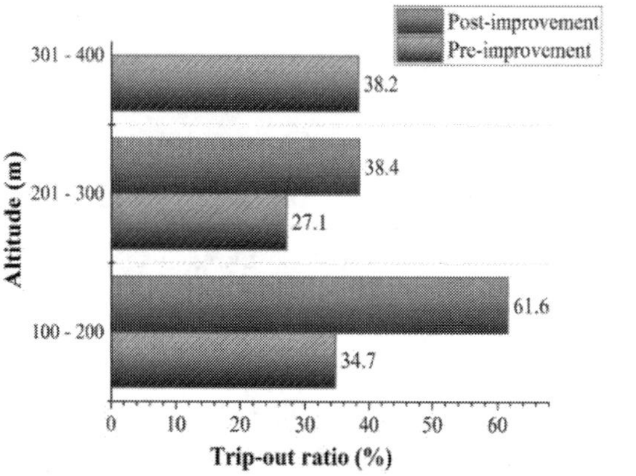

Fig. 8. Trip-outs rate before and after improvement as a function of the altitude.

3.5 Height difference of tower tops

Figure 9. Shows the trip-out ratio as a function of the height difference of the tower top. The height difference of tower tops is calculated as the average difference between the absolute value of the tower top from two adjacent towers. The number of towers in the tower top difference range was from 13 (21 – 50 m) to 44 (0 – 20 m). It is reported that the larger the difference of the tower-top height, the higher the trip-out ratio [20]. However, in our dataset, there seems almost no relation because the difference of the 44 towers out of 72 is in the range of less than 20 m with 83 trip-outs out of 143. The result of the investigation shows that the difference of the tower top is not a dominant factor on the transmission line under study.

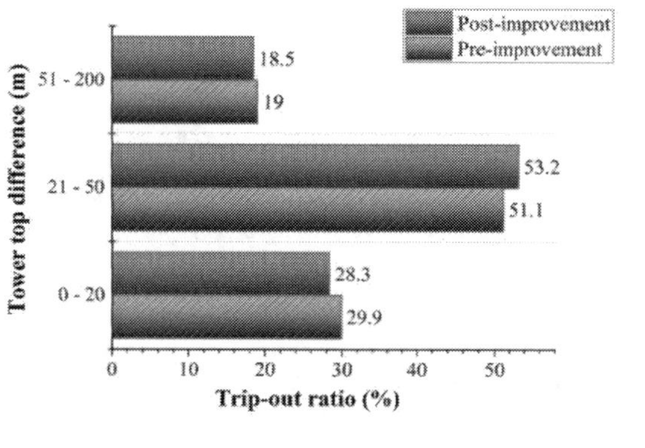

Fig. 9 Effect of tower-height difference on the trip-out ratio.

4. Location of Flashover

Figure 10. Shows the trip-out rate in circuits I and II of the line between No. 1 and No. 140 towers. The high rate of lightning trip-outs before and after the improvement of the tower-footing resistance is seen in circuit I. This is due to the placement of circuit I on the north side from No. 1 to 37 towers, and on the east side from No. 38 to No. 140 towers. In this area, the thunderstorm often approaches the line from the northeast and the towers often located on the ridge of the mountain. Therefore, the insulator voltage on the circuit I is high due to the topology.

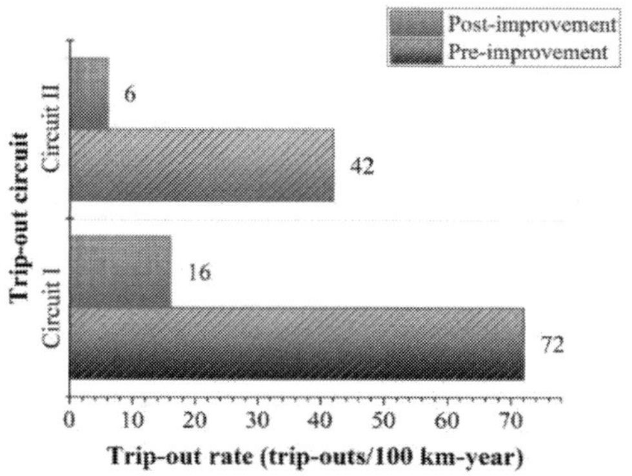

Fig. 10 Rate of trip-outs for circuits I and II.

5. Analysis

5.1 Method of analysis

The critical current resulting in the flashover is evaluated at two times, namely two μs and 6μs, as in the case of the IEEE FLASH program by assuming the front duration of the lightning current two μs. Such a simplified method is used because the objective of this thesis is to Improve the lightning protection design of the transmission line. In the process, the insulator voltage is calculated by the difference between the phase voltage and the arm voltage as in [1]. The voltage and current are calculated by the distributed constant circuit theory by taking account of the coupling between the OHGW and the phase conductors, the reflection at two adjacent towers and the reflection at the interface of the struck tower and the ground.

The corona-coupling model is incorporated through the approximate diameter of the corona sheath [1]. The ionizing effect of the ground is taken into account [2,7] through a straightforward method (four parallel), and the power-frequency voltage is also taken into account.

The critical flashover voltage (CFO) is calculated based on the time to flashover by (4.2) [1,2,3,4,8,9].

https://doi.org/10.1051/matecconf/201821501022

$$\mathrm{CFO} = \left(400 + \frac{710}{t^{0.75}}\right) \mathrm{D} \qquad (1)$$

where CFO is critical flashover voltage, t is time to flashover and D is the gap or insulator length (m)

5.2 Line model and lightning incidence to transmission line

A 47 km–long double-circuit line with the span length of 333 m, simulating the range from No. 1 to No. 140 towers, was selected to estimate the lightning performance of the transmission line under study. As the most of the flashovers occur at the length of an arcing horn gap of 0.9 m, the length of an arcing horn gap is assumed to be 0.9 m.

The ground flash density is calculated by (2.2) [1-5] by assuming the thunderstorm day is equal to the IKL of 165 days-year. In this way, the ground flash density is calculated to be 23.65 flashes/.

Lightning incidence to overhead lines was calculated to be 548.4 flashes/100 km-year through (2.3) [1-2].

The cumulative frequency distribution of the lightning current is assumed to be given by (2.4) [1-2].

The back-flashover rate, BFR, is given as the product of this probability and the number of strokes that terminate on the towers. For simplicity, the number of strokes to the towers is assumed to be 60% of all strokes to the line as in (6) [1-2].

$$\mathrm{BFR} = 0.6\, \mathrm{N_S}\, \mathrm{P(I_C)} \qquad (2)$$

where I_C is the critical current resulting in back-flashover.

6. Results and Discussion

6.1 Trip-out Rates

Figures 11 (a) and (b) shows the comparison of observed trip-out rates with the analysis by the IEEE FLASH program version 1.81. The IEEE Flash program recommends using tower-footing resistance measured at low frequency because this value can be estimated easily [1]. In the analysis, the average tower-footing resistance with the flashover (47.7 or 10.7 Ω) and the average tower footing resistance at towers No. 1–140 (33.3 Ω or 5.6 Ω) are used, respectively. The average impulse resistance of towers, the reduced resistance of the towers due to the ionizing effect before and after the improvement is set 23.8 Ω and 5.4 Ω, respectively, by assuming the impulse resistance is about 50% of the low-current value [2,3,4]. The impulse resistance is also used in the analysis. The trip-out rates by the IEEE Flash program are in good agreement with the observation result before and after the improvement of the tower-footing resistance when the impulse resistance of the tower is used in the analysis. Meanwhile, the observation result is lower than the trip-out rates by the IEEE Flash in another case.

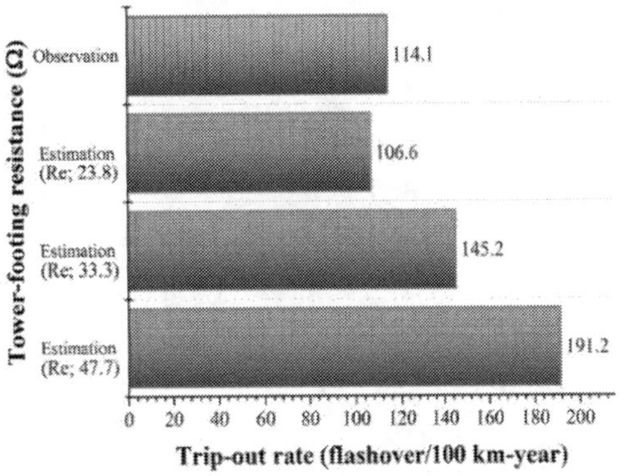

(a). Trip-out rates before improvement of tower-footing resistance.

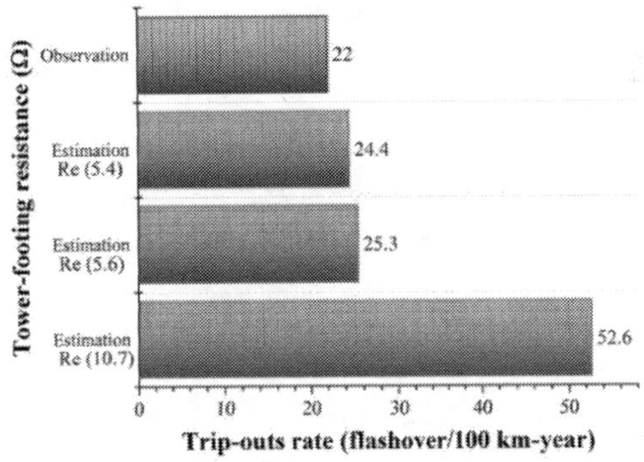

(b). Trip-out rates after improvement of tower-footing resistance.
Fig. 11. Trip-out rates by the IEEE FLASH program with lightning trip-outs observation before (a) and after (b) improvement of tower-footing resistance (Re).

Figures 12 (a) and (b) Shows the dependence of trip-out rates on arm location. The calculated results agree reasonably well with the observation of lightning trip-out rate. From these results, it is shown that the IEEE Flash program and the IEEE method provides reasonable estimates of the trip-out rates for the line under study by taking into consideration the ionizing effect.

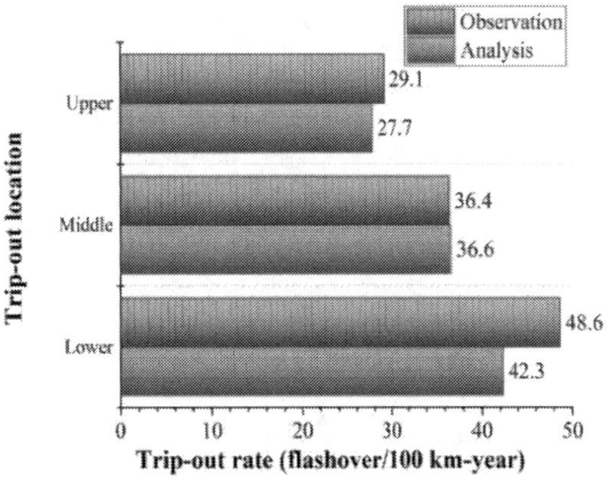

(a). Trip-out rates before improvement of tower-footing resistance.

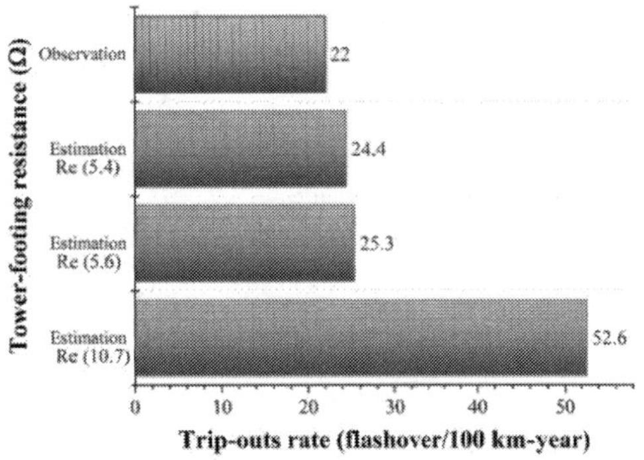

(b). Trip-out rates after improvement of tower-footing resistance.

Fig. 12. Dependence of trip-out rates on arm location

7. Conclusion

The results of the lightning trip-out in West Sumatra in Indonesia are presented. It is shown that the main cause of the trip-outs is lightning, which causes 66% of all trip-outs. The main conclusions are as follows:

1. The lightning trip-out rates of the studied line are significantly affected by the tower-footing resistance and the length of an arcing horn gap for the transmission lines under study.

2. The trip-out rates calculated by taking into account of the reduction of the tower-footing resistance due to the ionizing effect agree well with the observed ones. This indicates the importance of the impulse resistance in the analysis of the lightning performance of the line.

3. The trip-out rate at the lower arm is high for the cases of the average grounding resistance of 33.3 ohms, and the rates at the lower arm are high for the cases of the average grounding resistance of 5.6 ohms. This trend can be simulated by the IEEE method using the impulse resistance.

4. The trend that the trip-out ratio becomes high with an increase in the span length is significant after the improvement of the tower-footing resistance. However, the trend is weak before the improvement of the tower-footing resistance. This is because, in the case of the high tower-footing resistance, the flashover occurs before the arrival of the wave reflected from the adjacent towers due to the high potential rise of the tower. Therefore, the degree of the influence of the span length on the trip-out ratio is dependent on the tower-footing resistance.

5. Local lightning activity significantly affects by the trip-out rate. The high rate of lightning trip-out before and after the improvement of the tower-footing resistance is seen in circuit I. This is due to the placement of circuit I on the north side of towers No. 1 to 37 towers and on the east side of towers No. 38 to No. 140. In the next area, the thunderstorms often approach the line and the towers from the northeast.

6. The trip-out rate of the line under study can be reduced to less than half of the present rate, 22 flashovers/100 km–year if the tower-footing resistance of all the towers is set to less than 10 Ω and the length of the arcing horn gap is set to more than 1.2 m.

References

[1] Joint CIRED/CIGRE Working Group 05, "Protection of MV and LV Networks Againts Lightning Prt I: Basic Information", IEE Conf. Publ. No. 438, vol. 1, 1997.
[2] Evgeni Volpov and Evgeni Katz, "Characterization of Local Environmental Data and Lightning Caused Outages in the IECO Transmission Line Network," *IEEE Trans. On Delivery*, vol. 31, Issue. 2, pp. 640–647, April, 2016.
[3] Meteorological and Geophysical of Padang Panjang, "Annual report," BMKG Padang Panjang, Indonesia, Dec. 2010.
[4] Y. Warmi and K. Michishita, "Investigation of Lightning Performance on 150 kV Transmission Line in West Sumatra", 9th Asia-Pacific International Conference on Lightning (APL 2015), 23 - 27 June 2015, Nagoya, Japan.
[5] Y. Warmi and K. Michishita, "A Study on Lightning Outages on 150 kV Transmission Line of Payakumbuh-Koto Panjang in West Sumatra in Indonesia", 19th International Symposium on High Voltage Engineering (ISH 2015), 23 – 28 August 2015, Pilsen, Czech Republic.
[6] J. He, X. Wang, Z. Yu, and R. Zeng, "Statistical Analysis of Lightning Performance of

Transmission Lines in Several Regions of China," *IEEE Trans. Power Deliv.*, vol. 30, no. 3, pp. 1543–1551, 2014. https://ieeexplore.ieee.org/document/6924796/.

[7] R. de la Rosa, G. Enriquez, and J. L. Bonilla, "Contributions to lightning research for transmission line compaction," *IEEE Trans. Power Deliv.*, vol. 3, no.2, pp.716–723,Apr.1988. https://ieeexplore.ieee.org/document/4310/.

[8] I. M. Rawi and M. Z. A. A. Kadir, "Investigation on the 132kV overhead lines lightning- related flashovers in Malaysia," *in Proc. VIII International Symposium on Lightning Protection (SIPDA)*, Balneario Comboriu, Brazil, Oct 2015, pp. 239 – 243. https://ieeexplore.ieee.org/document/7339293/.

[9] M. Miyazaki, K. Nishiyama and M. Miki, T. Miki, "Overview of Statistical Data on Lightning Outages of Transmission Line in Japan," *CIGRE*, C4-, 202, Japan, 2016.

[10] IEEE Guide for Improving the Lightning Performance of Transmission Lines, IEEE Standards board 1243-1997.

[11] Subcommittee for transmission lines, study committee a lightning risk, "Application Guide for Transmission Line Surge Arrester," CRIEPI Report H-07 2012 (in Japanese).

[12] Transmission and distribution committee, "A simplified Method for Estimating Lightning Performance of Tranmission Lines, " *IEEE Trans.Power Apparatus and System,* vol. PAS-104, no. 4, pp 918 – 932, July, 1985.

[13] F. M. Gatta, A. Geri, S. Lauria, M. Maccioni, and F. Palone, "Tower Grounding Improvement vs. Line Surge Arresters: Comparison of Remedial Measures for High-BFOR Subtransmission Lines," *IEEE Trans. Ind. Apl.*, vol. 51, no. 6, pp. 4952 – 4960, June 2015. https://ieeexplore.ieee.org/document/7131509/.

[14] S. Wu and W. Sun, "Back flashover protection performance analysis of 220kV double circuit transmission line," *in Proc. Asia-Pacific Conference Power and Energy Engineering, (APPEEC)*, Wuhan, Cina, March 2011, pp. 1– 4. https://ieeexplore.ieee.org/document/5749070/.

[15] A. Ametani and T. Kawamura, "A method of a lightning surge analysis recommended in Japan using EMTP," *IEEE Trans. Power Deliv.*, vol. 20, no. 2, pp. 867–875, Apr. 2005. https://ieeexplore.ieee.org/document/1413327/.

[16] J. Sardi and M. Z. A. Ab Kadir, "Investigation on the effects of line parameters to the lightning performance of 132 kV Kuala Krai-Gua Musang transmission line," *in Proc. 7th International Symposium on Power Engineering and Optimization, (PEOCO)*, Langkawi, Malaysia, June 2013, pp. 594 – 599. https://ieeexplore.ieee.org/document/6564617/?denied.

[17] E. F. Koncel, "Potential of a Transmission-Line Tower Top When Struck by Lightning," *Trans. Am. Inst. Electr. Eng.*, vol. 75, no. 3, pp. 457 – 462, Jan. 1956. https://ieeexplore.ieee.org/document/4499327/.

[18] A. Holdyk and B. Gustavsen, "Inclusion of Field Solver-Based Tower Footing Grounding Models in Electromagnetic Transients Programs," *IEEE Trans. Ind. Apl.*, vol. 51, no. 6, pp. 5101 – 5106, 2015. https://ieeexplore.ieee.org/document/7056439/.

[19] Meteorological and Geophysical of Padang Panjang, "Annual report," BMKG Padang Panjang, Indonesia, Dec. 2014.

[20] Subcommittee for transmission lines, Lightning protection design committee, "Guide to Lightning Protection Design for Transmission Line, "CRIEPI Report T-72 2002 (in Japanese).

[21] The Distribution and Load Control Center Sumatra (Sumatra P3B), the monthly report, Sumatra P3B, Padang UPT, Indonesia, 2013.

[22] Y. Warmi and K. Michishita, "Horn Length Estimation for Decrease of Trip-out Rates on 150 kV Transmission Line in West Sumatra in Indonesia," Joint Conference of The thenth International Workshop on High Voltage Engineering (IWHV 2016) and 2016 Japan-Koroea Joint Symposium on Electrical Discharge and High Voltage Engineering (JK 2016 on ED & HVE), ED–16–127, SP–16–056, HV–16–112, Miyazaki, Japan (2016.11.4). https://ci.nii.ac.jp/naid/40021027830/.

[23] Y. Warmi and K. Michishita. "Tower-footing Resistance and Lightning Trip-outs of 150 KV Transmission Lines in West Sumatra in Indonesia. " International Review of Electrical Engineering (IREE). Vol 12. No 3. ISSN 1827 – 6660. https://doi.org/10.15866/iree.v12i3.12233.

MATEC Web of Conferences **215**, 01023 (2018) https://doi.org/10.1051/matecconf/201821501023
ICTIS 2018

Windings Design for Single-phase Induction Motors Base on 4-phase Induction Motor (Case study: identical windings design)

Zuriman Anthony [1]*, *Erhaneli Erhaneli* [1], *Zulkarnaini Zulkarnaini* [1]

[1]Electrical Engineering Department, Institut Teknologi Padang, Indonesia

Abstract. A 1-phase induction motor usually has a complicated windings design which compares to polyphase induction motor. In addition, a large capacitor start is required to operate the motor. It is an expensive way to operate the motor if it compare to polyphase induction motor. So, a new innovation method is required to make the motor more simple and cheaper. This research is purposed to study a new winding design for a single-phase capacitor motor. Winding design of the motor was conducted to a simple winding design like a 4-phase induction motor that has four identical windings. The comparator motor that use in this study was a Three-phase induction motor with data 1400 RPM, 1.5 HP, 50Hz, 380/220V, Y/Δ, 2.74/4.7A, 4 poles, that had the same current rating which the proposed method. The result showed that the motor design on this proposed method could be operated at 88.18 % power rating with power factor close to unity.

1 Introduction

The Induction motors usually used in many sectors, especially in industrial and home application, because this motor is simple and robust construction. At present, there are two types induction motor in application, three-phase and single-phase motor. The three-phase motor is usually supplied by a 3-phase system, whereas a single-phase motor with a 1-phase system [1].

The 3-phase motors usually operate on a three-phase system. The motors are usually produced in high power ratings. They operate normally by using Three-phase power supply. The motors have 3 identical windings separated by 120 degrees electricity. The number of turns of each winding is equal, so that the motor can operate with a balanced current on each winding when the 3-phase balanced source is used in the motor [1-2]. In the development of operating system, the 3-phase motor had been operated on 1-phase power system [3-9]. The motor was operated on 1-phase power supply by installing some capacitors to the windings of the motor [3-8]. The modification technique was developed by adopting 2 windings principle of single-phase capacitor motor. Some evaluation methods had been developed by some research to find a simple method for analyzing the characteristics of the motor [3,10].

Single-phase induction motor is a motor that usually produced at low power rating. The motor is operated on a single-phase supply and usually used in some home applications, such as fans, etc. The motor usually has 2 windings, auxiliary and main windings [1]. The motor will operate with better performance when capacitors are installed on the motor. These capacitors serve to produce the phase difference between the two windings (auxiliary and main windings) of the motor which aims to produce a large torque to the motor [1-2]. This method is called conventional method because the motor only has 2 windings. Although the performances the motor had been developed [11-14], the construction design of the winding of the motor still has the same with the conventional methods.

This paper is focused to study a new technique and construction of the winding of a single-phase capacitor motor. The motor has four windings that we called U, V, W and X windings. All of the windings are identical windings that have the same cross section area.

2 Winding Design of Induction Motor

2.1 Three Phases Winding Design

Three-phase induction motor has three identical windings that are separated from each other by 120 degrees. The design of the motor windings can be modeled as shown in Fig. 1.

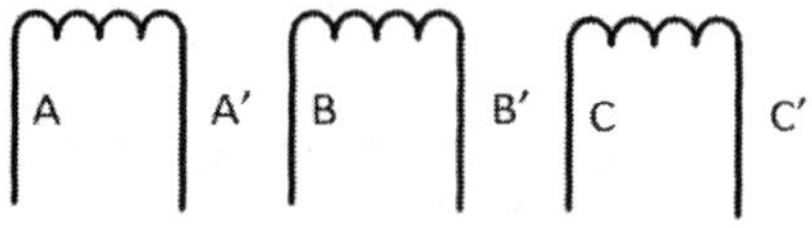

Fig. 1. Three phases windings design of a three-phase motor

The windings of a three-phase motor can be connected in two variation standards, Wye (Y) and delta (Δ) as shown in Fig. 2 and Fig. 3 respectively.

* Corresponding author: antoslah@gmail.com

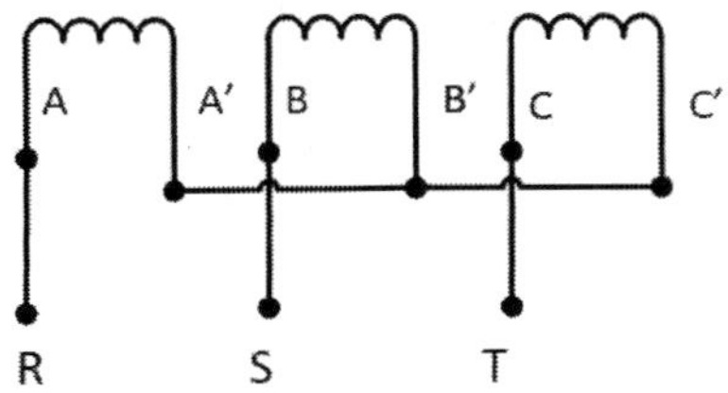

Fig. 2. Wye winding connection of a three-phase motor

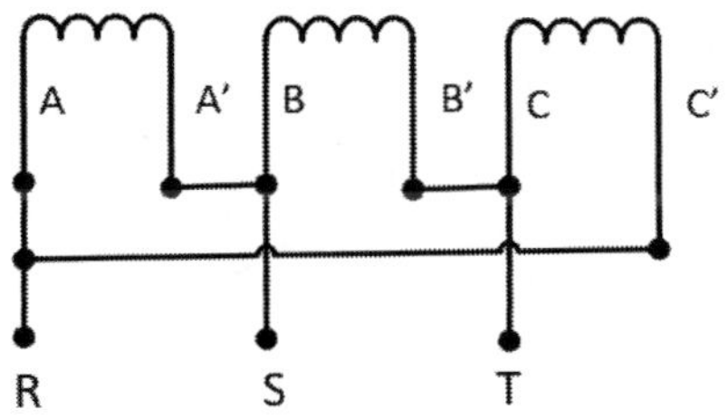

Fig. 3. Delta winding connection of a three-phase motor

Figs. 1, 2 and 3 show that the 3-phase motor has three identical windings, A (A to A'), B (B to B') and C (C to C'). The letters R, S and T in Figs. 2 and 3 are the spots for which a three-phase source is connected to supply the motor.

2.2 Conventional 1-phase Capacitor Motor

Single-phase capacitor motor usually has 2 windings. The windings are called main and auxiliary windings respectively. Both windings are usually used for starting. A 1-phase capacitor motor usually used capacitors that installed in series with one of the windings as shown in Fig. 4. Fig. 5 shows the windings design of a conventional 1-phase capacitor start capacitor run induction moto.

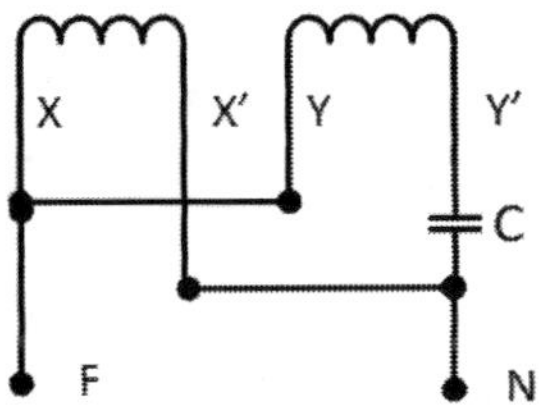

Fig. 4. Windings of a 1-phase capacitor motor

From the data shown in Fig. 4 and Fig. 5 can be explained that the letter X to X' is main winding and Y to Y' is auxiliary winding. C is capacitor installed at auxiliary winding in Fig. 4. Cs and Cr in Fig. 5 are the start capacitor and the run capacitor respectively. Letter 'F' and 'N' in Fig. 4 and Fig. 5 are line power and Neutral of the single-phase supply system respectively.

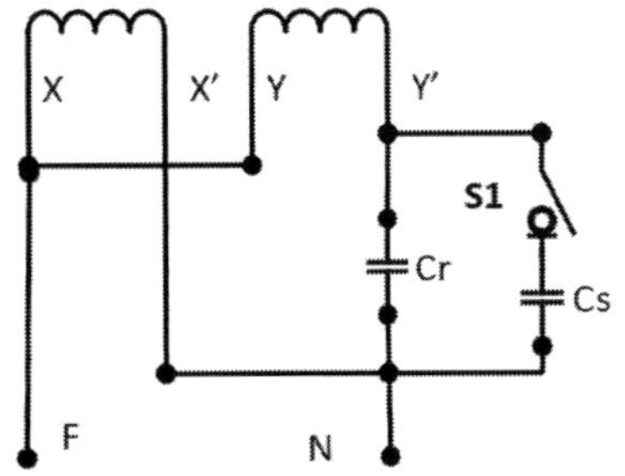

Fig. 5. Two windings of a conventional single-phase capacitor motor

2.3 Four Phases Windings design

Four phases windings design of the motor has four identical windings that are separated from each other by 90 degrees. The model of the windings design is shown in Fig. 6.

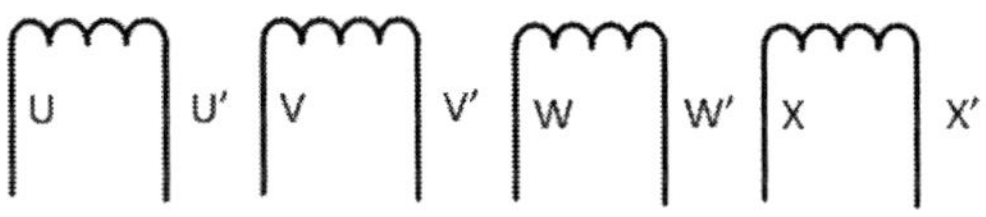

Fig. 6. Four phases windings design of the motor

3 Research Method

This study is proposed to show a new windings construction of a single-phase capacitor motor by using 4 phases windings design. The induction motor used as comparator for this study was a three-phase induction motor with data 1400 RPM, 1.5 HP, 50Hz, 380/220V, Y/Δ, 2.74/4.7A, 4 poles. The motor had 3 identical winding of 0.65 mm^2 in size. The proposed method had 4 windings constructed in the stator that we mark as U, V, W and X as shown in Fig. 7. The 3 windings (U, V, W) are connected together and we call the auxiliary windings and the 'X' windings is called the main winding. The windings of the proposed method were made the same size of 0,65 mm^2 like an identical four-phase induction motor.

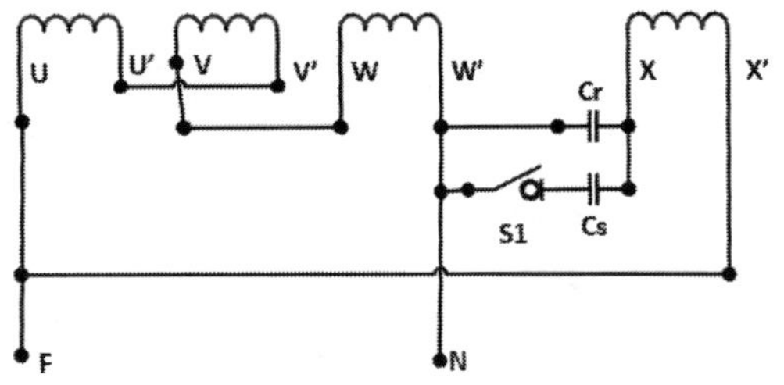

Fig. 7. Windings design on proposed motor

'S1' in Fig. 7 is a centrifugal switch that use to disconnect the start capacitor after the motor reach the running condition.

Total capacitance of the capacitor (Cst) as shown in Fig. 7 can be calculated by using the formula published by Anthony [4] as follows.

$$Cst = \frac{(0{,}1757).I_N}{(f).V_{LN}}(Farad) \quad (1)$$

The capacitance of the run capacitor (Cr) can be calculated as follows.

$$Cr = \frac{I_{ph}}{(\omega).(A_Z.V_{LN})} = \frac{I_{ph}}{(A_Z).(2.\pi.f).(V_{LN})}(Farad) \quad (2)$$

Where:

$$A_Z = \frac{N_U + N_V + N_W}{N_X} \quad (3)$$

I_{ph} = rating current of the motor winding (A)
V_{LN} = Line to neutral voltage (V)
f = Frequency of the source power system (Hz)
A_Z = Constanta of Zuriman Anthony
N_U = total slots used by 'U' windings
N_V = total slots used by 'V' windings
N_W = total slots used by 'W' windings
N_X = total slots used by 'X' windings

Further, the capacitance of the start capacitor (Cs) in the Fig. 7, can be calculated as follows.

$$Cs = Cst - Cr(Farad) \quad (4)$$

The voltage 'Vc' on the run capacitor and the reactive power donated by the run capacitor (VARc) can be calculated respectively as follows.

$$Vc = A_Z.V_{LN} \quad (5)$$

$$VARc = \omega.Cr.(V_C)^2 = (A_Z)^2.\omega.Cr.(V_{LN})^2 \quad (6)$$

The apparent power (S) and the line current (I_L) of the motor can be calculated by the following formula.

$$S = VARc \quad (7)$$

The line current (I_L) enters into the motor can be calculated as follows.

$$I_L = \frac{S}{V_{LN}} \quad (8)$$

When the motor is operated with a nominal winding current, the motor will operate with a power factor close to unity. Therefore, the power factor (*PF*) and power input (*Pin*) of the motor can be defined as follows.

$$PF = Cos(\varphi) = 0{,}98 \quad (9)$$

$$Pin = S.Cos(\varphi) \quad (10)$$

4 Results and Discussion

The 1-phase proposed motor was tested in the laboratory. The characteristics of the motor then compared to the characteristics of the comparator motor. The result of this study can be explained as follows.

(1) Output Characteristic

The output power characteristic of the motors is shown in Fig. 8.

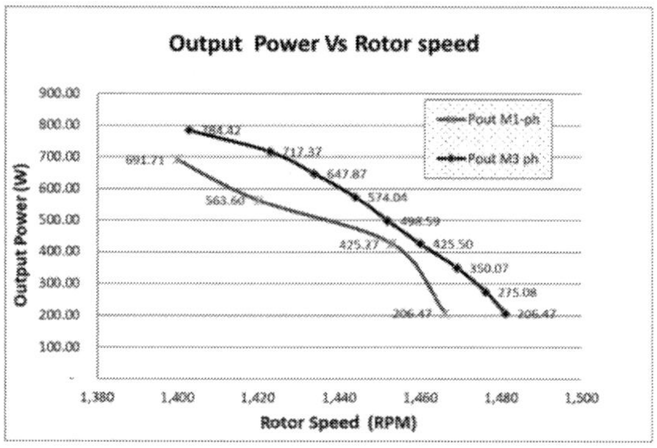

Fig. 8. Output power characteristic of the motors

From the Fig. 8 can be explained that the Output Power of the proposed motor (Pout M1-ph) is 691.71W that is 88.18% Output Power of the comparator motor (Pout M3 ph). So, the proposed motor could operate almost close to the rating power of the comparator motor.

(2) Power Factor Characteristic

The power factor characteristics of the motors are shown in Fig. 9.

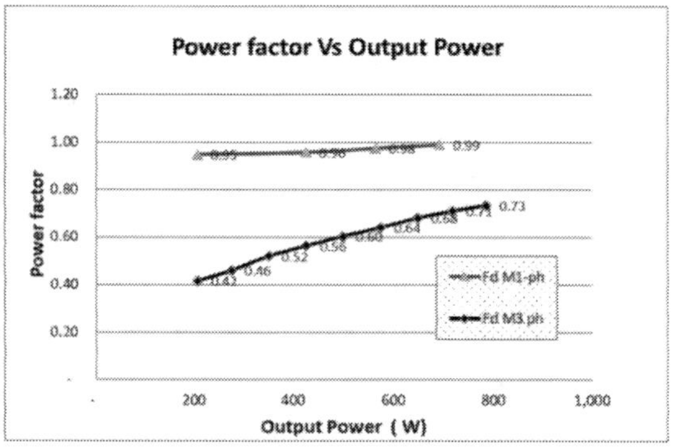

Fig. 9. Power factor characteristics of the motors

From the data in Fig. 9 can be seen that the power factor of the proposed method (Fd M1-ph) always between 0.95 and 0.99 that was better than the three-phase induction motor. (Fd M3 ph). That is because the capacitor used in equation (2) is set to improve power factor to become close to unity.

(3) Efficiency Characteristic

The efficiency characteristics of the motors are shown in Fig. 10

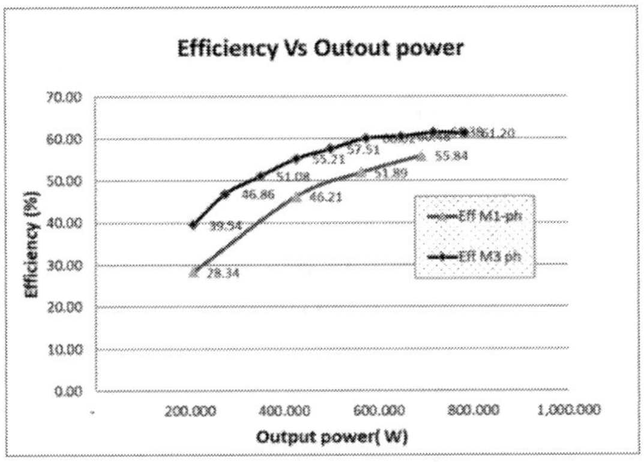

Fig. 10. Efficiency characteristics of the motors

From the data shown in Fig. 10 can be explained that the efficiency of the 3-phase motor (Eff M3 ph) is better than the proposed motor (Eff M1-ph). That is because the proposed motor uses the same size of the winding (0.65 mm^2) both the main and the auxiliary windings. Of course, the current of both the main and the auxiliary is limited not to higher than the current rating of the windings. So, the proposed motor did not work optimally. So, for better performances of the motor, the auxiliary windings of the proposed motor should be bigger than the main windings.

5 Conclusions and recommendations

This study is proposed to show a new winding design for a single-phase capacitor motor by using 4 phases winding design. The proposed motor could be operated at 88.18 % Output Power of the comparator motor, on power factor close to unity. But, the efficiency of the proposed motor lower than the comparator motor because all windings of the proposed motor is the same in size. So, for better performances of the motor, the auxiliary windings of the proposed motor should be bigger than the main windings. It will be discussed in the next topic of papers.

Acknowledgements

We would like to thank very much to the team of the laboratory of electrical engineering of the 'Institute of Technology Padang (Institut Teknologi Padang)' that helped us in research in the laboratory. We would also like to thank for 'Kopertis Wilayah X' and 'Directorate for Research and Community Service, Directorate General for Research and Development at the Ministry of Research, Technology and Higher Education' Republic of Indonesia whose helped fund this research in accordance with the research contract number 320/27.O10.5/PN/II/2018.

References

1. P. C. Sen, *Principles of Electrical Machines and Power Electronics*. (John Wiley & Sons, 1996).
2. S. J. Chapman, *Elecrical Machinery Fundamentals*. (McGraw-Hill, 2005).
3. Z. Anthony, Equivalent Circuits for the M31D-ZA Motor " s Method (Case Studies : Currents and Power Factor of the motor). *IJETT* **25**, 49–52 (2015).
4. Z. Anthony, A Simple Method For Operating The Three-Phase Induction Motor On Single Phase Supply (For Wye Connection Standard). *IJETT* **5**, 13–16 (2013).
5. Z. Anthony, A Simple Method for Operating the Delta Connection Standard of the 3-phase Induction Motor on Single Phase Supply. *IJETT* **15**, 444–447 (2014).
6. Z. Anthony, Analyzing Characteristics of the Sheda " s Method for Operating the 3-phase induction Motor on Single Phase Supply (Case studies : output power and efficiency of the motor). *IJETT* **33**, 175–179 (2016).
7. Y. A. Al-turki, H. Al-umari, Application of the reference frame theory to the dynamic analysis of a three-phase induction motor fed from a single-phase supply. *Elsevier* **53**, 149–156 (2000).
8. N. A. Ahmed, Three-phase induction motor operating from single-phase supply with an electronically controlled capacitor. *Electr. Power Syst. Res.* **73**, 121–128 (2005).
9. A. K. Adapa, V. John, Active Phase-Converter for Operation of Three-Phase Induction Motors on Single-Phase Grid. (2016).
10. Z. Anthony, E. Erhaneli, B. Busran, A new equivalent circuit of the three-phase induction motor (case studies: Current and power factor of the motor). *ARPN J. Eng. Appl. Sci.* **12**, (2017).
11. T. H. Liu, Maximum torque control with a controlled capacitor for a single-phase induction motor. *IEEE Trans. Ind. Electron.* **42**, 17–24 (1995).
12. T. Liu, M. Lin, H. A. Wu, Single phase induction motor drive with improved performance. **47**, 29–38 (1998).
13. K. Makowski, Determination of performance characteristics of a single-phase shaded pole induction motor by circuit-field method. *Electr. Eng.* **84**, 281–286 (2002).
14. E. Muljadi, Y. Zhao, Y., T. A. Lipo, T. H. Liu, Adjustable ac capacitor for a single-phase induction motor. *IEEE Trans. Ind. Appl.* **29**, 479–485 (1993).

A Discussion of Magnetoelectric Composite Design by Bonding the Ferromagnetic Material Graded Layers in Induction Motor

Zuriman Anthony [1,2*], *Hairul* Abral [3], *Refdinal* Nazir [4]

[1] Program Doctoral Student of Andalas University, Indonesia, Mechanical Engineering Department
[2] Institute of Technology Padang (Institut Teknologi Padang), Indonesia, Electrical Engineering Department
[3] Andalas University, Indonesia, Mechanical Engineering Department
[4] Andalas University, Indonesia, Electrical Engineering Department

Abstract. Induction motors are the most electric motors widely used in the community, both in the industrial and in the household applications. The power and efficiency of the motors are determined by the type of ferromagnetic material used in the core of the motor. If a very good ferromagnetic material with high permeability is applied to the core of the induction motor, then both the energy conversion and the efficiency of the motor will increase. But, if the ferromagnetic material is not good with low permeability is used in the induction motor, of course, the conversion of energy generated by the motor will be low so that the motor efficiency becomes decreased. In other cases, when ferromagnetic materials with high permeability are used, these ferromagnetic materials will become more fragile than using ferromagnetic materials with lower permeability. Therefore, a good strategy is needed in designing the core material of the induction motor. This study was intended to provide an overview of the potential use of a composite material of Fe and ferromagnetic material that was made in the Graded Magnetostrictive Layers. This research was conducted using several studies of the results of research on the composite material of the magnet. The results of the study show that a composite material of Fe and ferromagnetic materials provided a great potential in applying to induction motors to increase power and efficiency of the motor.

1 Introduction

Induction motors are electric motors of alternating current which are widely used both in the industrial sector and in the household sector [1]. The efficiency of the motors are strongly influenced by the type of ferromagnetic material used in the motors, the air gap distance between the stator and the rotor, the shape of the rotor, and the type of material and number of coil windings used on the motor [1-4]. Some methods had been developed to improve performance of the motor by operating the motor on single-phase supply. The methods can improve power factor, starting torque and efficiency of the motor [5,6]. Some research had developed to analyze the motor by using equivalent circuit to improve performance of the motor [7-9].

Ferromagnetic material is the main material in the induction motor which is very useful in strengthening the magnetic field of the motor resulting great torque and efficiency in the motor [1]. The performance of these ferromagnetic materials is strongly influenced by the permeability, currents, and the internal and external influences of materials [1,10]. One of the external influences affecting the ferromagnetic materials is the heat that arises in the process of cutting ferromagnetic material either by mechanically or laser, and the effect of welding materials that can decrease the properties of ferromagnetic material [11,12]. In addition, the decrease of the ferromagnetic material properties may also be caused by the influence of heat originating from within the stator core as a result of the magnetization of the stator and from the influence of the surrounding heat as a result of rotor heat induction to the stator [1,3,10,13]. The heat that occurs in this motor (both from the stator and the rotor) can increase the power loss and decrease the performance and efficiency of the motor [1,2].

To analyze the characteristic of ferromagnetic materials, several studies have been undertaken by previous researchers by developing modeling and use approach formulas for analyzing the properties of ferromagnetic materials. Such as those used to predict thermal transient behavior due to heating process [3], the effect of cutting materials [12], the magnetic field and iron core losses on the rotor [14], and to find out the magnetic properties of the material that can be used in the practical evaluation of simpler hysteresis effects [15]. From the results of analyzes that have been done through these studies, it turns out the heat that occurs in this ferromagnetic material can reduce the magnetic properties or the quality of ferromagnetic materials.

* Corresponding author: antoslah@gmail.com

To minimize the effect of heat on ferromagnetic material of the induction motor can be done by choosing more precise ferromagnetic cutting technique [11,12], to design optimally the shape of the rotor slot [16] and the use of copper material on the rotor winding rather than the aluminum [3]. However, the use of copper materials would require a more expensive cost than the aluminum material.

Improvements in the properties of ferromagnetic materials can also be done by coating (laminated composite) ferromagnetic materials that are less good but strong physically with excellent ferromagnetic materials so that this excellent material that has a dominant effect [17] or by the use of magnetic fluids based on heat-synthesized synthesized nanoparticles [13] which has been used for electronic devices. Improved motor efficiency by improving the properties of this ferromagnetic material can also be done by using an amorphous laminate material at the core of the stator [18], soft magnetic composites (SMC) on the stator [2], and the use of magnetic wedge in the stator coil slot to reduce air passage flux distortion, magnetization currents, start current and temperature rise [19,20].

Besides that, the magnetic properties of demagnetization can be overcome by increasing the number of pole magnetic of stator and the use of a permanent magnetic ferrite material on the rotor surface, as has been applied to permanent magnetic synchronous motors [21]. However, increasing the number of pole magnetic stator is not possible to be applied to the induction motor because will decrease the speed of the motor. Therefore, we need a new method that is simple and cheaper to be applied to the induction motor in an effort to improve motor performance.

2 Research Method

This paper describes the results of a review of several journals that become reverence with the topic of study leads to an effort in improving the performance of induction motors in focusing on ferromagnetic materials on the motor. A simple method is offered to improve motor performancey.
motor

3 Results and Discussion

With reference to the results of research conducted by several studies of before, it can be described some of the following studies.

From the result of [22], there were 4 resins used to obtain the materials composites of the stator. They are HRJ-10236 (RA), SBP-128 (RB), SP6600 (RC) and SP6601 (RD) with mass proportions of 0.5%, 1.0%, 1.5%, 2.0%, 2.5% and 3.0%. The specifications and the magnetic properties of the composites are shown in table 1 and table 2 respectively.

Table 1. Resin Specifications [22]

Specifications	HRJ-10236	SBP-128	SP6600	SP6601
Curing at 154 °C	50-90 s	30-65 s	15-30 s	15-30 s
Density (g/cm^3)	0.350	0.355	0.352	0.334
Hexamine content (%)	7.5-8.5	8.5-9.5	6.9-7.9	6.5-8.5
Granulometry (M# 200)	min. 97%	min. 97%	min. 97%	min. 99.9%

Table 2. Specifications of magnetic properties for the composites [22].

Composite	B_{max} [T]	B_r [T]	H_c [A/m]
Fe-RA0.5	0.64	0.10	272
Fe-RA3.0	0.45	0.04	223
Fe-RB0.5	0.61	0.10	261
Fe-RB3.0	0.45	0.04	255
Fe-RC0.5	0.63	0.11	280
Fe-RC3.0	0.43	0.05	271
Fe-RD0.5	0.58	0.11	260
Fe-RD3.0	0.42	0.04	243

Table 2 shows that the less resin content (Fe-RA0,5) or in other words, the higher the Fe percentage in the composite, the maximum magnetic flux density (Bmax) will be greater. This means that the higher Fe content will strengthen the maximum magnetic flux density of soft magnetic composite material.

From the result of [23], also show the same characteristic with [22], although in deference case. This paper [23] had researched used three kinds different average particle size of iron powders (140, 107 and 75 μm). They are shown in Fig. 1, Fig. 2 and Fig. 3.

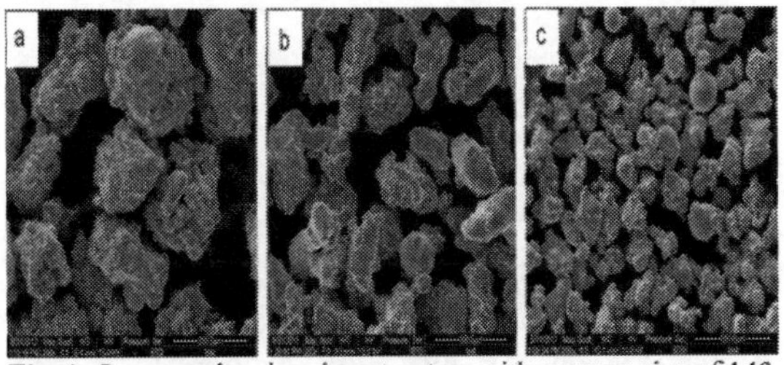

Fig. 1. Iron powders in microstructure with average size of 140 μm (a), 107 μm (b) and 75 μm (c) respectively [23].

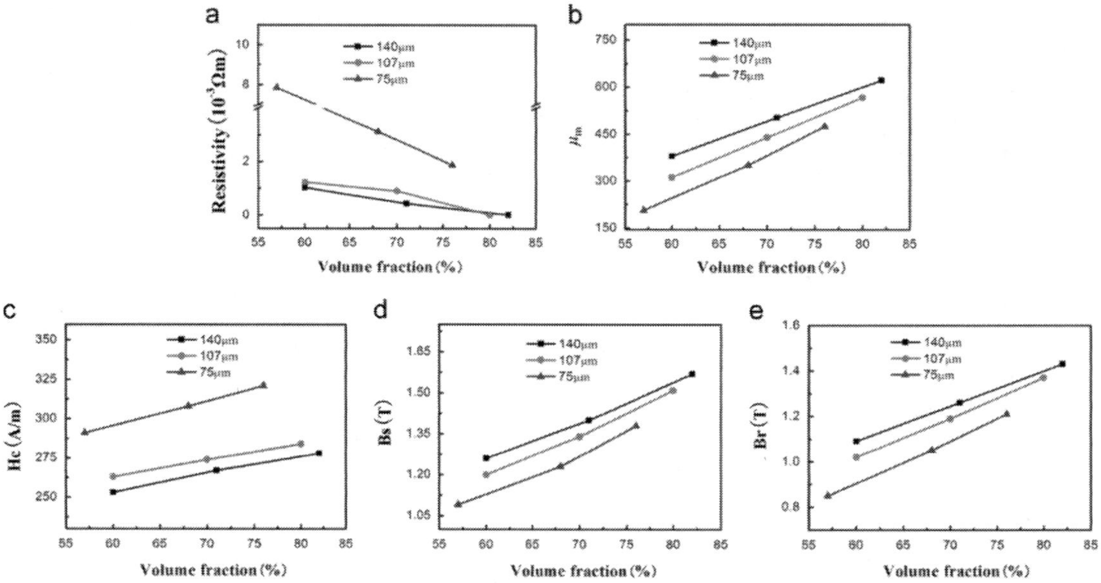

Fig. 2. Relationship of resistivity (a), maximum relative permeability (b), coercivity (c), saturation magnetic flux density (d) and residual magnetic flux density (e) of Fe/silicate glass composites with iron particle volume fraction respectively [23].

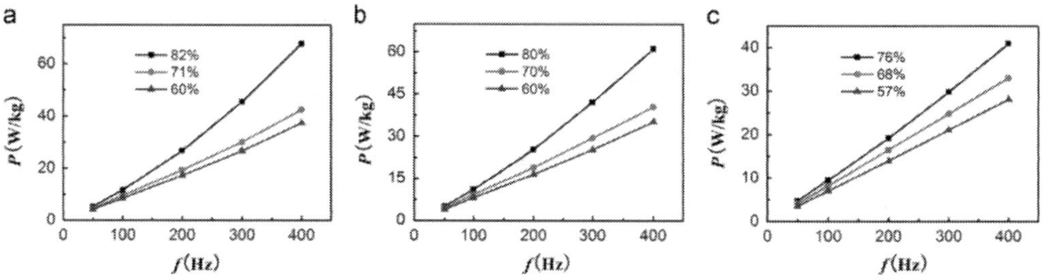

Fig. 3. Relationship of core loss (W) versus frequency (f) of some Fe/silicate glass composites with average size of 140 μm (a), 107 μm (b) and 75 μm (c) respectively at the induction level of 1 T [23].

From Fig. 2 it is seen that the magnetic flux density (Bs and Br) will increase when the Fe content in the compound material is to increase as shown in Figures (2d) and (2e). On the contrary, as more silicate mixture will reduce the core loss as shown in Fig. 3.

From both results above it can be seen that increasing the Fe content in the compound material will enlarge magnetic flux density (Bs and Br). With the greater the magnetic flux density (Bs and Br) the greater the energy that can be transferred from the stator to the rotor that effect for improving the capability of the motor. On the other hand, adding a mixture of insulating / silicate to the material will minimize losses in the core. Therefore, the stator core design of the induction motor is recommended by using a multilayered core material such as a transformer core, by means of a core layer made of a fine ferromagnetic layer and combined with an iron (Fe) layer so that the core construction of the material is expected to be cheaper with better energy conversion. Research with this method is in the process of further action as a study.

4 Conclusions and Recommendations

From the results of the above-described study it is concluded that it is possible to construct an induction motor with the stator by using a multilayered core material such as a transformer core, by means of a core layer made of a fine ferromagnetic layer and combined with an iron (Fe) layer so that the core construction of the material is expected to be cheaper with better energy conversion. Research with this method is in the process of further action as a study.

References

1. P. C. Sen, *Principles of Electrical Machines and Power Electronics*. (John Wiley & Sons, 1996).
2. A. Krings, *et al.* Characteristics comparison and selection guide for magnetic materials used in

electrical machines. *2015 IEEE Int. Electr. Mach. Drives Conf.* 1152–1157 (2015). doi:10.1109/IEMDC.2015.7409206

3. F. Ahmed, E. Ghosh, N. C. Kar, Transient Thermal Analysis of a Copper Rotor Induction Motor using a Lumped Parameter Temperature Network Model. *IEEE* (2016).
4. I. Boldea, Electric Generators and Motors: An Overview. *CES Trans. Electr. Mach. Syst. IEEE* **1**, 12 (2017).
5. Z. Anthony, A Simple Method for Operating the Delta Connection Standard of the 3-phase Induction Motor on Single Phase Supply. *IJETT* **15**, 444–447 (2014).
6. Z. Anthony, A Simple Method For Operating The Three-Phase Induction Motor On Single Phase Supply (For Wye Connection Standard). *IJETT* **5**, 13–16 (2013).
7. Z. Anthony, Equivalent Circuits for the M31D-ZA Motor " s Method (Case Studies : Currents and Power Factor of the motor). *IJETT* **25**, 49–52 (2015).
8. Z. Anthony, E. Erhaneli, B. Busran, A NEW EQUIVALENT CIRCUIT OF THE THREE-PHASE INDUCTION MOTOR (CASE STUDIES : CURRENT AND POWER FACTOR OF THE MOTOR). **12**, 6967–6974 (2017).
9. Z. Anthony, E. Erhaneli, B. Busran, A New Method for Analyzing the Characteristics of The 3-Phase Induction Motor. in *International Conference on Technology, Innovation, and Society (ICTIS) 2017* 145–151 (ITP Press, 2016). doi:10.21063/ICTIS.2016.121
10. H. S. Ju, *et al.*, Efficient Deperming Protocols Based on the Magnetic Properties in Demagnetization Process. *IEEE Trans. Magn.* **51**, (2015).
11. P. Rasilo, U. Aydin, T. P. Holopainen, A. Arkkio, Analysis of iron losses on the cutting edges of induction motor core laminations. *Proc. - 2016 22nd Int. Conf. Electr. Mach. ICEM 2016* 1312–1317 (2016). doi:10.1109/ICELMACH.2016.7732694
12. K. Bourchas, *et al.*, Influence of cutting and welding on magnetic properties of electrical steels. *2016 XXII Int. Conf. Electr. Mach.* 1815–1821 (2016). doi:10.1109/ICELMACH.2016.7732770
13. Y. Shlapa, S. Solopan, A. Belous, Effect of Mechano-Chemical Processing in the Synthesis of Weakly Agglomerated Ferromagnetic La 1-x Sr x MnO 3 Nanoparticles on their Properties. *IEEE* 282–286 (2015).
14. Z. Haisen, Z. Dongdong, W. Yilong, Z. Yang, X. Guorui, Piecewise Variable Parameter Loss Model of Laminated Steel and its Application in Fine Analysis of Iron loss of Inverter-Fed Induction Motors. *IEEE* 1–8 (2016).
15. D. Herceg, D. Herceg, M. Prsa, Using Padé Approximation in Takács Hysteresis Model. *IEEE Trans. Magn.* **51**, 1–5 (2015).
16. S. Sobhani, H. Yaghobi, M. Samakoosh, Optimize efficiency and torque in the single-phase induction motor by adjusting the design parameters. *12th Int. Conf. Environ. Electr. Eng. EEEIC 2013* 237–241 (2013). doi:10.1109/EEEIC.2013.6549623
17. C. Yang, *et al.*, Large Converse Magnetoelectric Properties Without Bias in Composite of Rosen-Type Piezoelectric Transformer and Magnetization-Graded Ferromagnetic Material. *IEEE Trans. Magn.* **51**, 8–11 (2015).
18. M. Dems, K. Komeza, Performance Characteristics of a High-Speed Energy-Saving Induction Motor with an Amorphous Stator Core. *IEEE Trans. Ind. Electron.* **61**, 3046–3055 (2014).
19. T. R. Gaerke, D. C. Hernandez, The temperature impact of magnetic wedges on TEFC induction motors. *IEEE Trans. Ind. Appl.* **49**, 1228–1233 (2013).
20. M. Lavanya, P. Selvakumar, D. S.Vijayshangkar, D. C. Easwarlal, Performance analysis of three phase induction motor using different magnetic slot wedges. *IEEE* 164–167 (2014).
21. I. Petrov, M. Niemela, P. Ponomarev, J. Pyrhonen, Rotor Surface Ferrite Permanent Magnets in Electrical Machines: Advantages and Limitations. *IEEE Trans. Ind. Electron.* **64**, 5314–5322 (2017).
22. M. M. Dias, *et al.*, Influence of resin type and content on electrical and magnetic properties of soft magnetic composites (SMCs). *Powder Technol.* **237**, 213–220 (2013).
23. W. Ding, *et al.*, Effect of iron particle size and volume fraction on the magnetic properties of Fe/silicate glass soft magnetic composites. *J. Magn. Magn. Mater.* **378**, 232–238 (2015).

Optimization of compaction pressure on brick

Ade Indra[1*], *Edison* Edison[1], *Hendri* Nofrianto[2]

[1]Institut Teknologi Padang, Mechanical Engineering Department, Padang, Indonesia
[2]Institut Teknologi Padang, Civil Engineering Department, Padang, Indonesia

Abstract. Bricks are one of the building materials that serves as a wall or anchoring the load. Therefore, it must be made according to the standards. In our previous observations, many found bricks were traditionally not quality, because the process of making bricks that are not right. Bricks are a class of ceramic materials that must be hard and should not be crushed when immersed in water. The method in this study focuses on optimizing compaction pressures, with printed pressures that are varied in MPa units. The results obtained as follows, in terms of mechanical properties of Compressive Strength increases with the addition of compaction pressure, an increase of 36% (brick becomes strong). In terms of physical properties of Density increased (porosity becomes smaller). For Suction rate down, this shows less water absorption. The results obtained in accordance with national and international quality standards.

1 Introduction

West Sumatera is located on the west coast of the island of Sumatera, which in recent years have often shaken by earthquakes with a high scale. The earthquake that occurred in 2005, 2007 and the last on 30 September 2009 with 7.9 on the Richter scale, many homes, offices, and other buildings damaged. Damage caused to the building is on the wall, made of clay brick. In building construction, clay bricks are used as a buffer to the existing load on it, such as the construction of houses and foundations. If the strength of the clay brick used is not the same with SNI and other standards, it will be very dangerous for the safety of people living in the building [1].

This should be our common concern, how to create and process quality clay brick accordance with SNI. From our observations on the clay brick home industry in the Payakumbuh West Sumatera, there are three weaknesses in the making, namely: 1) Material and composition used has not been qualified. 2) The compaction pressure of a clay brick process. 3) Firing temperature of the fuel of rice husk is very low (600°C), should be 1000°C [1]. To resolve this problem, further research is needed, so that the clay brick produced meets quality standards.

This research is a continuation of our earlier research team, focused on reviewing the compaction pressure, which is also a requirement to get the results of quality bricks.

2 Materials and Methods

Clay brick is one of the building materials, made of clay with or without impurities, is burned at high temperatures, and not destroyed soaked in water [2]. Composite bricks reinforced with fly ash is in the maximum addition of 50% fly ash. For the addition of over 50%, the compressive strength of the bricks fell. While the physical characteristics of the bricks using fly ash is lighter, smaller water absorption, and more solid [3].

The clay consists of microscopic particles and sub-microscopic shaped flat plate and mica particles, clay minerals, and other minerals are very fine with a size of 0.002 mm. The use of clay for brick making, should note a few things: (a) meet the plasticity and cohesive, so it can be easily formed. Clay has a value of plastic, can cause the bricks to crack or break when burned, (b) clay must have the ability to dry high and shrinkage dry low (maximum 10%), (c) not contain grains of chalk and gravel larger than 5 mm, (d) sandy clay will produce brick better when compared with the use of pure clay.

Water is used to process the binding reaction material in the manufacture of bricks. Clay brick is made of clay with or without a mixture of other materials through the combustion process. Clay bricks baked at high temperatures, do not disintegrate when immersed in water, and has a small hole cross-sectional area of 15% of the area of the flat pieces.

The effect of firing time and temperature on compressive strength, water absorption, bending strength, weight loss, firing shrinkage and densities of clay brick were determined. For a given clay and method of manufacture, higher compressive and bending strengths, higher density and lower absorption are associated with higher firing temperatures. Increasing firing time only slightly altered the

*Corresponding author: adeindra@itp.ac.id

mechanical and physical properties of clay brick. However, firing temperature significantly affected the physical properties. The results suggested that firing temperature was the key factor to modulate the physical properties of bricks. However, the effect of firing time was not significant. The results obtained in this study can only be compared to the properties of bricks produced under similar conditions with similar raw materials [4].

Research bricks have been done to determine of compaction pressure, variation is 30; 60; 90; 120; 150; 180; 210; 240; and 270 kPa. The results obtained as follows, the mechanical properties: Compression Strength increases as the addition of compaction pressure of 35.75 kg/cm^2 become 45.80 kg/cm^2, an increase of 28% (brick becomes stronger). Judging from the physical properties: density increased from 2.06 g/cm3 became 2.24 g/cm3, an increase of 8.9% (porosity becomes smaller). For Suction rate dropped from 16.17 g/dm^2/min to 14.82 g/dm^2/min, this indicates the water absorption becomes smaller [5]. Class of divisions brick based on compressive strength [6].

Table 1. Compressive strength and coefficient of variation for solid brick for wall pair (SNI 15-2094-2000)

Class	Minimum average compressive strength of brick Kg/cm^2 (MPa)	Variation coefficient of the average compressive strength of the tested (%)
50	50 (5)	22
100	100 (10)	15
150	150 (15)	15

The size and tolerance of bricks for the wall pair [6], can be seen in Table 2.

Table 2. Size of brick (SNI 15-2094-2000)
Unit in mm

Module	High	Wide	Long
M-5a	65 ± 2	90 ± 2	190 ± 4
M-5b	65 ± 2	100 ± 2	190 ± 4
M-6a	52 ± 3	110 ± 2	230 ± 5
M-6b	55 ± 3	110 ± 2	230 ± 5
M-6c	70 ± 3	110 ± 2	230 ± 5
M-6d	80 ± 3	110 ± 2	230 ± 5

One of the properties of brick that affect to construction work is water absorption. Water absorption should be controlled, to prevent the loss of water from the mortar. The maximum water absorption for bricks is 20 g/dm^2/min, when the suction rate of brick value greater than 20 g/dm^2/min, then the bricks need to be soaked in water before paired to the wall [7].

Theoretical density of the single phase can be determined from the literature, while the actual density of single phase or composites tested using Archimedes theory [8]. Methods and stages of research as follows:

The process of getting Samples

Intake sample material to make brick is home industry Koto Panjang, Lamposi Tigo Nagori, Payakumbuh. The material consists of clay mixed with white sand with a composition of 2:1 (as matrix), while for reinforcing materials used silica RHA, which is the result of burning rice husk waste.

Manufacture of test samples

The Molding process of brick with size samples test of 5x5x5cm with variation compaction pressure: 0.5; 0.7; 0.9; 1.1; 1.3; and 1.5 MPa. Further drying is done without direct sunlight. The combustion process carried out test samples with methods that have been developed in previous studies, with rice husk fuel. The process of making the test sample as shown in Figure 1.

Fig 1. the manufacturing process of the test sample: a) mold, b) green body, c) the burning process, d) sample test

3 Results and Discussion

From the research that includes making samples, burn, making of the specimen, and the test can be described as follows.

3.1 Firing Process

Firing processes refer to our previous study, using a furnace with a temperature setting of approximately 930 ° C, as shown in the Table 3 and Figure 2.

Extra air in the burning process, the temperature is increased significantly when compared with no addition of air. Rising temperatures expected because more complete combustion, which is a proper balance between fuel with air. This occurs in speed of air blown of 0.25 m/s; 0.5 m/s and 0.75 m/s (burning temperature qualify for clay materials)

https://doi.org/10.1051/matecconf/201821501025

Table 3. Burning Temperature

Speed of air blown (m/s)	Max temperature (^{0}C)
0	498,3
0,25	934,7
0,50	964,3
0,75	1.035
1,00	824,0

← Temperatures used

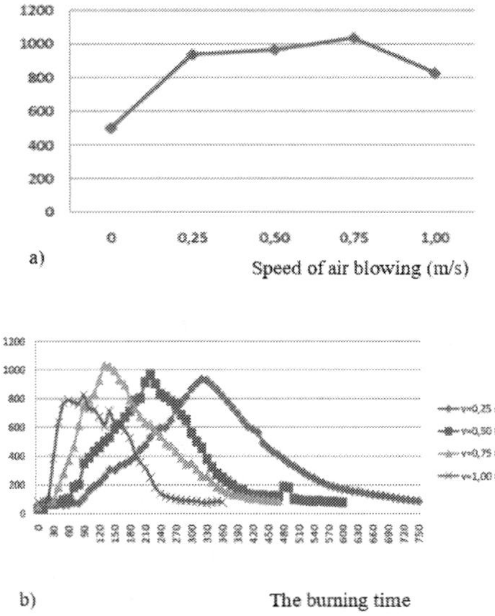

Fig 2. a) Variation of burning temperature with speed of air blown. b) Variation of firing temperature with burning time

3.2 Density

The density test is shown in the following scheme in figure 3.

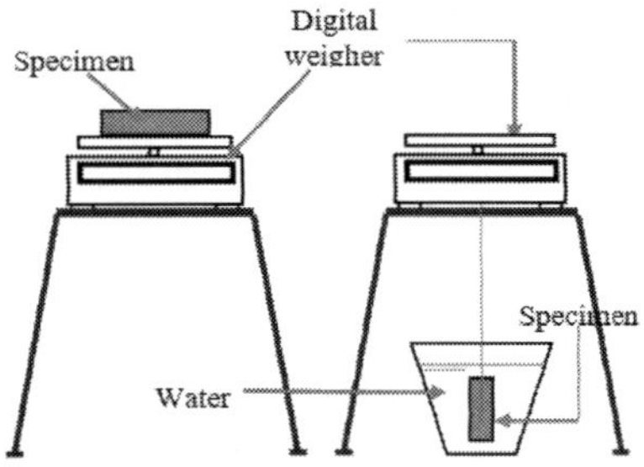

Fig. 3. scheme of density test

The test results density as shown in Table 4 and Figure 4. higher compaction pressure, the higher the density. but has not increased significantly to the increase in relative density, the highest value is 90.49%. It also relates to the value of water absorption remains high (see Table 6). it is quite common for ceramic products with pores large enough

Table 4. density test results

Compaction pressure (MPa)	Density (gr/cm3)	Relative Density (%)
0.5	2.29	88.68
0.7	2.30	88.98
0.9	2.30	89.11
1.1	2.30	89.22
1.3	2.31	89.63
1.5	2.33	90.49

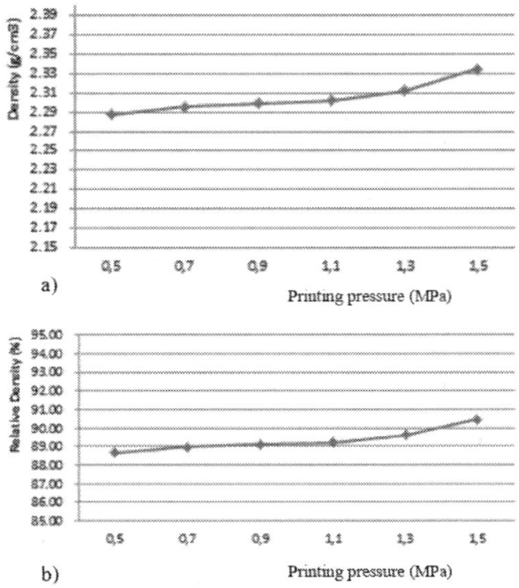

Fig 4. a) Variation of density with compaction pressure, b) Variation of relative density with compaction pressure

3.3 Suction Rate and Water Absorption

The suction rate test is shown in the following scheme in figure 5

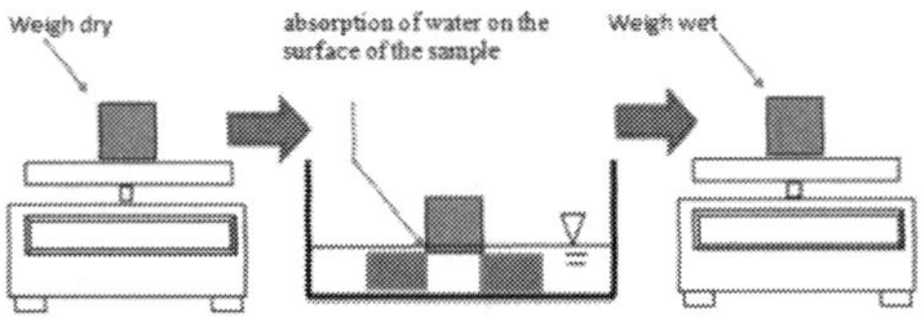

Fig 5. Scheme of suction rate test

From the test data suction rate, the suction rate on average has been under 20 g/dm^2/min, the soaking time 3 and 4 minutes as a data table 5, meaning that the brick before use should be soaked in water approximately 3 minutes, this also supported by water absorption test data (Figure 7) where most of the test samples had a water absorption above the specified limit of 20%.

From figure 6 it can be seen that there is a significant relationship between suction rate by compaction pressure, the higher the compaction pressure then lower the suction rate, it is suspected that the density of the composite material when molded, so that the occurrence of contact tangentially between the granular material after molded process [8]. Water absorption as shown in Table 6 Figure 7, that there is no significant relationship between the water absorption by the compaction pressure variation, is suspected to be the micro cracks in the test specimen which is probably caused by the quality of the composite material.

Table 5. Suction rate test results

Compaction pressure (MPa)	Average Suction Rate ($g/dm^2/min$)	
	3 min	4 min
0.5	21.98	13.23
0.7	15.01	16.98
0.9	13.30	7.73
1.1	10.56	8.85
1.3	12.34	14.06
1.5	11.26	11.63

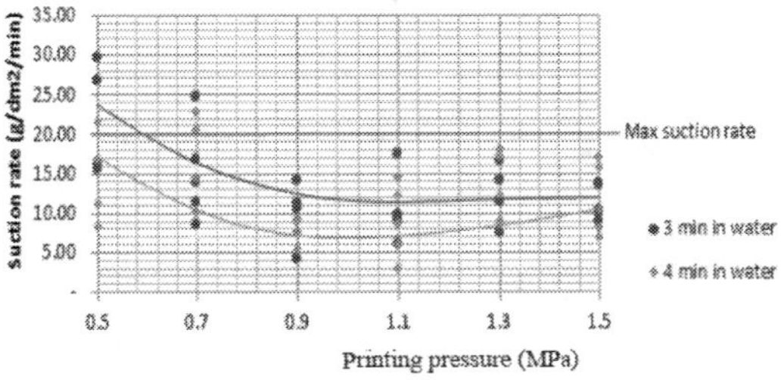

Fig 6. The variation of Suction rate with compaction pressure

Table 6. Water absorption test results

Compaction pressure (Mpa)	Average Water Absorption (%)
0.5	23.59
0.7	23.90
0.9	23.90
1.1	23.51
1.3	23.60
1.5	23.17

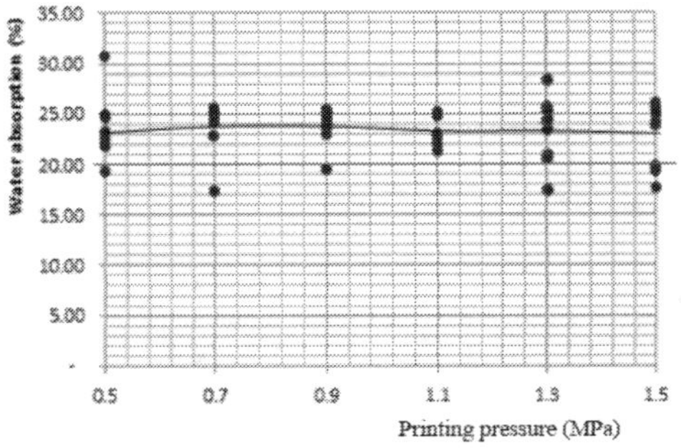

Fig 7. Variation of water absorption with compaction pressure

In the use and specification of clay bricks water absorption porosity is often taken as a guide for the prediction of frost resistance, in that bricks of high strength and low porosity have generally proved to be frost resistant in practice. However, it has been shown that frost damage is a result of complex patterns of freezing of pore water, and porosity alone is not the determining parameter of frost resistance. Thus several types of relatively porous clay bricks (notably some hand-made bricks) [9].

The capillary suction properties of masonry materials are relevant in respect of both construction practice and weathering performance. During construction wet trade practices rely upon the suction of masonry materials to encourage bonding between mortar or plaster and brickwork or block work. In brick or block laying excessive suction causes rapid removal of water from the soft mortar and can, in principle, result in incomplete hydration and a weak or porous hardened mortar. Similar considerations apply in the application of the renders or plasters to brick or block substrates [9].

3.4 Compressive Strength

The compressive strength test is shown in the following scheme in figure 8.

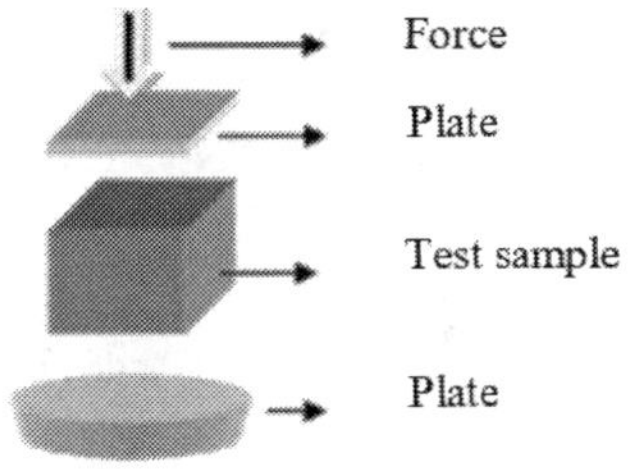

Fig. 8. Scheme of compressive strength test

Compressive strength is one of the parameters used to determine the strength and ability of a material to accept the load until the material is cracked and broken. The compressive strength test is performed using Universal Testing Machine. The cross-sectional area of the tested sample is the plane in direct contact with the load. The test process can be seen in figure 9, test results can be seen in table 7 and Figure 10

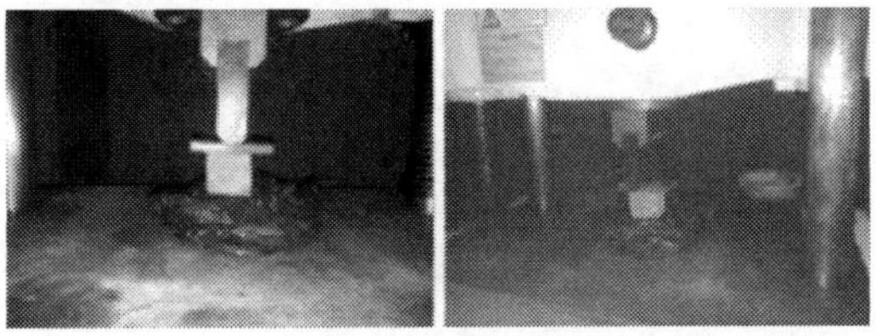

Fig. 9. Process of compressive strength test

Table 7. Compressive strength test results

No	Compaction pressure (Mpa)	Compressive Strength (kg/cm2)
1	0.5	47.07
2	0.7	46.20
3	0.9	64.24
4	1.1	63.02
5	1.3	61.43
6	1.5	59.48

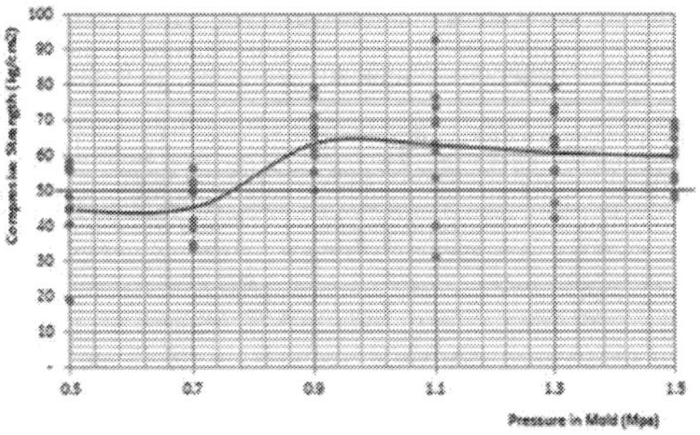

Fig. 10. Variation of compressive strength with compaction pressure

From the test results data in Table 7 and Figure 10, the average value of compressive strength test increases with the addition of pressure during printing. Seen from the garfic, the print pressure of 0.5 and 0.7 of the compressive strength value is still below the minimum standard of SNI 15-2094-2000, indicated by a red horizontal line. At print pressures of 0.9 to 1.5, indicating a good compressive strength and above the minimum standard required by SNI 15-2094-2000 (as shown in the Table 1). The results concluded that 0.9 or 1.0 MPa print pressure yielded an optimum compressive strength value of 64.24 kg / cm2.

4 Conclusions

From the results of discussion, the optimum compaction pressure is between 0.9 to 1 MPa. The average suction rate has been below 20 g/dm^2/min, it is recommended that the bricks should be immersed in water for 3 minutes before use in construction.

Acknowledgments

Given to:

- Directorate General of Higher Education, the Ministry of Ristek and Dikti, the Republic of Indonesia, which has funded research in Hibah Bersaing scheme, budget year 2016
- Kopertis Region X, which has helped the administration in this research
- LP2M, Instiut Teknologi Padang, which has helped the administration in this research
- Mechanical Engineering Laboratory, Institut Teknologi Padang, which has helped the facility and equipment in this research

References

1. A. Indra, N. Nurzal, H. Nofrianto. Improvement of Mechanical Properties of Composites Clay / Silica RHA for Quality Red Brick Applications, *Proceeding of national conference mechanical engineering XIII*, Universitas Indonesia (2014).
2. Y. Romadhona,, Effect of increase Incinerator Ash on brick quality with clay from Temanggung district, Civil Engineering UNS
3. Muhardi, Characteristics of Clay Bricks improvement with addition of fly ash, Journal of Civil Engineering, **7**(2), 165-179 (2007)
4. S. Karaman, S. Ersahin, H. Gunal, Firing temperature and firing time influence on mechanical end physical properties of clay bricks. Journal of scientific and industrial research. Vol. **65**. 153-159 (2006)
5. A. Indra, N. Nurzal, H. Nofrianto, Optimizing compaction pressure on the composite clay/silica RHA for application bricks SNI quality, *Proceeding of National Conference SPI-ITP* (2014)
6. SNI 15-2094-2000. Solid brick for wall couple. ICS 91.100.20 (2000)
7. PEDC. Material Engineering, Bandung. (1983)
8. M. Barsoum, Fundamental of ceramics, (The Mc Graw Hill Companies Inc, US, (1997)
9. M.A. Wilson, M.A. Carter, W.D. Hoff. British Standart and RILEM water absorbtion test, Journal of Material and structures, **32**, 571-578, (1999)

Crystal structure, thermal expansion and long-term behaviors of $SmBaCoO_{5+\delta}$ as cathode for intermediate-temperature solid oxide fuel cells

Adi Subardi[1*], *Yen-Pei* Fu[2]

[1] Department of Mechanical Engineering, Sekolah Tinggi Teknologi Nasional (STTNAS), Yogyakarta 55281, Indonesia
[2]Department of Materials Science & Engineering, National Dong Hwa University, Shou-Feng, Hualien 97401, Taiwan

Abstract. $SmBaCo_2O_{5+\delta}$ (SBC) was studied as cathode material for intermediate-temperature solid oxide fuel cells (IT-SOFCs). The crystal structure, thermal expansion behavior, and electrochemical performance with long-term operation of SBC were characterized. An orthorhombic layered perovskite structure was observed in SBC cathode by a GSAS program for refinement. The average thermal expansion coefficient (TEC) is 21.6 x $10^{-6}K^{-1}$ in the temperature range of 100°C-800°C. For long-term testing, the polarization resistance of SBC cathode increases gradually from 25.77 Ω cm^2 for 2 h to 38.77 Ω cm^2 for 96 h at 600°C, and an increasing-rate for polarization resistance is around 13,8% h^{-1}. Based on the electrochemical properties, SBC cathode with mixed ionic and electronic conductor (MIEC) behavior is a potential cathode for intermediate temperature solid oxide fuel cells based on a SDC electrolyte.

1 Introduction

Fuel cell is an electrochemical device that converts chemical energy into electrical energy with high efficiency and low pollutant emissions [1, 2]. Intermediate-temperature (600-800°C) solid oxide fuel cells (IT-SOFCs) have been intensively investigated for both centralized and distributed power generations in the past decades [3-6]. Unfortunately, high performance and reliable for IT-SOFCs still remain a big challenge, mainly due to the sluggish oxygen surface kinetics at the electrolyte surface and reluctant oxygen reduction reaction (ORR) activity in the cathode [6].

The electrochemical activity of the cathode dramatically decreases with decreasing temperature. The cathode becomes the limiting factor in determining the overall single cell performance. Therefore, the development of new cathodes with high-electrocatalytic activity for the oxygen-reduction reaction is critical for intermediate-temperature solid oxide fuel cells (IT-SOFCs) [4, 5].

The commercialization of SOFC-technology has shown delayed progress due to the prohibitive cost per unit power and unverified long-term durability [4,7]. To achieve a guarantee of reliability, the examination of degradation mechanisms of SOFCs during long-term operation is necessary. Reactions between components are one of the main degradation mechanisms, and it' the cause of the fast degradation of SOFC performance because of resistive reaction-layers [8].

Co-based Perovskite oxides are promising cathodes, because they show higher oxide-ion conductivities at intermediate temperature (600-800°C). Numerous materials related to cobalt-based oxides have been reported such as $PrBaCo_2O_{5+\delta}$ [9], $NdBaCo_{2-x}Ni_{x}O_{5+\delta}$ [10], $Ba_{0.5}Sr_{0.5}Co_{0.8}Fe_{0.2}O_{3-\delta}$ [11], $Sm_xSr_{1-x}CoO_{3-\delta}$ [12], $GdBaCo_2O_{5+\delta}$ [13], and so on.

In this paper, the double-perovskite structure oxide of $SmBaCoO_{5+\delta}$ (SBC) was prepared and characterized. The electrochemical properties with long-term testing of an SBC cathode on SDC electrolyte were analyzed over the intermediate temperature (600-800°C).

2 Experimental

2.1 Cathode and electrolyte materials preparation

$SmBaCoO_{5+\delta}$ (SBC) oxide was synthesized by the solid state reaction process as reported previously [14]. Stoichiometric amounts of Sm_2O_3, $BaCo_3$ and CoO powders were used as starting materials. These powders were mixed under ethanol using zirconia balls for 12 h. The ball-milled mixture was dried and ground into a powder with mortar and pestle, and then calcined in air at 1100°C for 4 h.

The $Ce_{0.8}Sm_{0.2}O_{1.9}$ (SDC) powder was synthesized by co-precipitation using $Ce(NO_3)_3.6H_2O$ and Sm_2O_3 as the starting materials. These starting materials were dissolved in distilled water in stoichiometric ratio amounts and then added to an ammonia solution. The

* Corresponding author: subardi@sttnas.ac.id

detailed preparation procedure of SDC is described in reference 14.

2.2 Material characterization

The structure of the sintered cathode powder was characterized by X-ray powder diffractometer (XRD; Rigaku D/MAX-2500V), with a scanning rate of 4°/min and scanning range of 20-80°, using a Cu K_{α}(1.5418 Å) radiation source. The powder XRD pattern and lattice parameter was analyzed by Rietveld refinement using the GSAS program.

2.3 Thermal expansion coefficients (TECs) measurement

The pellet for determining the thermal expansion coefficient of the SBC was pressed into cylindrical form with diameter of 5 mm by uniaxial pressure. The SBC green body was sintered at 1200°C in air for 2 h. The thermal expansion coefficient (TEC) of the sample was investigated by a thermal mechanical analyzer (TMA) from room temperature to 800°C with heating rate of 10°C/min.

2.4 Symmetrical cell fabrication

Preparation of sample for symmetrical cell has been reported previously [14, 15], it can be described in detail as follows. The cathode paste consists of cathode powder, solvent, binder, and plasticizer. The cathode paste was applied by screen-printing on both sides of SDC electrolyte disk. On one side, the cathode paste was painted as the working electrode (WE) with surface area of 0.385 cm^2. The Ag reference electrode (RE) was placed away from the WE by about 0.3-0.4 cm. Such a distance was chosen to avoid measurement errors due to the misalignment of the working and counter electrodes [15-17]. The cathode counter electrode (CE) was placed on the other side of the SDC disk then heated at 800°C for 2 h in air.

2.5 Long-term testing of electrochemical property

The symmetrical cell measurement for long-term testing was carried out under air ($p(O_2)$ = 0.21 atm) at temperatures of 600°C from 2 to 96 h at intervals of 4 h. The AC impedance measurement was performed using the VoltaLab PGZ301 potentionistat with frequency applied range from 100 kHz to 0.1 Hz with 10 mV AC signal amplitude. Under the cathodic polarized condition, the EIS was conducted as a function of the applied cathodic voltage (E). The EIS fitting analysis was performed with the Zview software. Linear sweep voltammetry was measured between -0.3 and 0.1 V with sweep rate 0.5 mV/s versus the RE.

3 Result and Discussion

3.1 SBC cathode characterization

Figure 1 shows the refinement of SBC patterns including the measured XRD data, the calculated profile and the difference between them. There are no peaks due to impurities in the structure of SBC, where the powder calcined at 1100°C, suggesting that the SBC is successful synthesis.

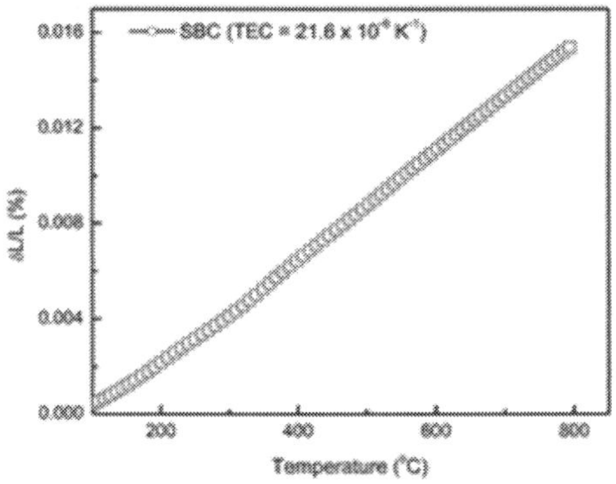

Fig.1. Observed (crosses) and calculated (solid line) XRD profiles and the difference (bottom line) for SBC cathode

Cell parameters regarding SBC obtained from the Rietveld refinement is listed in Table 1. The experimental data is highly agree with the calculated profiles, suggesting that cations are well ordered in the perovskite lattice [18,19].

Table 1. Crystallographic information for SBC measured at room temperature, cell parameters obtained by the Rietveld refinement*

Atom	Wyckoff position	x	y	z	Uiso	Occ.
SM1	2p (½ y ½)	1/2	0.23981	1/2	0.0174	1.0000
BA2	2o (½ y 0)	1/2	0.24946	0	0.0120	1.0000
CO3	2r (0 ½ z)	0	1/2	0.24619	0.0091	1.0000
CO4	2q (0 0 z)	0	0	0.24703	0.0058	1.0000
O5	1a (0 0 0)	0	0	0	0.0770	1.3871
O6	1e (0 ½ 0)	0	1/2	0	0.0021	0.8262
O7	1g (0 ½ ½)	0	1/2	1/2	0.2256	0.8367
O8	1c (0 0 ½)	0	0	1/2	0.0074	1.1426
O9	2s (½ 0 z)	1/2	0	0.19535	0.0753	1.1285
O10	2t (½ ½ z)	1/2	1/2	0.23585	0.1557	1.1552
O11	4u (0 y z)	0	0.25902	0.21623	0.0240	1.1849

*R_p = 0.20, R_{wp}= 0.23, R_{exp} = 0.23, orthorhombic (Space group:Pmmm), a = 3.8901 Å,
b = 7.8099 Å, c =7.5797 Å, v = 230.28 $Å^3$

3.2 Thermal expansion coefficients of SBC

The thermal compatibility between cathode material and other components is the main factor related to the working stability of SOFCs. Since a large difference of the thermal expansion coefficients (TECs) between these components will introduce interfacial stress during thermal cycling and resulted in cracks and cell degradation [20]. The pellet used for determining the thermal expansion of SBC was sintered at 1200°C for 2 h in air. The TECs of the sample was measured by a thermomechanical analyzer from 1room temperature to 800°C and the result as shown in Figure 2. The average TEC of SBC is 21.6 x 10^{-6} K^{-1} and TECs at various temperature range are listed in Table 2. The SBC specimen shows a linear expansion in the low temperature region (100-300°C) and a slight increase in slope at higher temperatures region (300-800°C). At higher temperature, a part of the smaller Co^{4+} were reduced to larger Co^{3+} or Co^{2+} with a loss of oxygen, C^{3+} ions are easy to transit from low-spin to high-spin state [14,21-23].

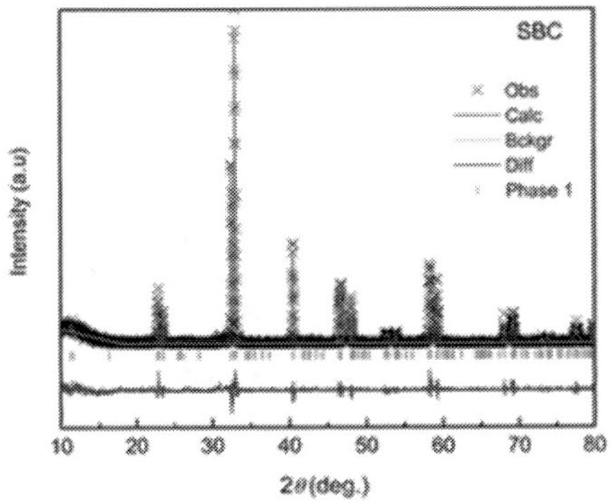

Fig.2. Thermal expansion behavior from 100°C to 800°C

Table 2. TECs for SBC at various temperature range

Sample	TEC x 10^{-6} (K^{-1})		
	100-800°C	100-300°C	300-800°C
SBC	21.6	18.8	22.8

3.3 Long term testing of SBC

To evaluate the stability the SBC for a long-time operation, the performance of a SBC|SDC|SBC symmetrical cell was tested, and polarization resistance (R_p) values were recorded dependence of time under stationary air at 600°C as shown in Figure 3.

The R_p values increased gradually with time from 25.77 Ω cm^2 for the initial 2 h to 38.77 Ω cm^2 for 96 h long-term testing. A slight increase in cathodic polarization resistance is observed that an increasing-rate is around 13.8%h^{-1} from the initial 2 h to 96 h. Cathode delamination from electrolyte may be one possible cause of increasing in polarization resistance at initial fast degradation [24]. The delamination between layers causes the decline of reaction site for ORR, leading to increase polarization resistance. The TEC difference between SBC and SDC is approximately 5.3 x $10^{-6}K^{-1}$.

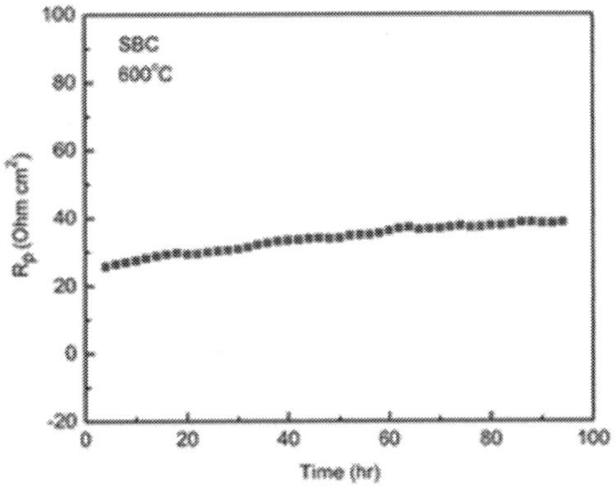

Fig. 3. Polarization resistance (R_p) of under static air at 600°C for long-term testing.

The interface may be easily detached during a 96h operation at 600°C due to the large TEC difference. With increasing the testing time, the following slow degradation in the MIEC-cathode performance may be several possible mechanisms such as (1) the grain size of SBC may coarsen [25], and (2) inter-diffusion may occur between SBC and SDC interface [26].

3.4 SEM images

The cathode microstructure is closely related to the electron and oxygen transportation, the reaction kinetics, charge transport, and mass transport preprocess. These properties influence the performance of solid oxide fuel cell [27,28].

Fig.4. SEM image of cross-section view for SBC|SDC half-cell.

The microstructure of a cross-section of SBC|SDC half-cell as shown in Figure 4 revealed the adhesion between the cathode and electrolyte is quite good. The SBC particles distributed uniformly, and the particle size ranged from 1 to 2 μm.

4 Conclusions

This study mainly investigated the long-term performance of $SmBaCo_2O_{5+\delta}$ (SBC) as potential cathode material for IT-SOFC. For long-term testing, the polarization resistance of SBC increases gradually form 25.77 Ω cm^2 for 2 h to 38.77 Ω cm^2 for 96 h at 600°C and an increasing-rate for polarization resistance is around 13.8% h^{-1}. The average thermal expansion coefficient (TEC) value of SBC is 21.6 x 10^{-6} K^{-1}. At higher temperature, a part of the smaller Co^{4+} were reduced to larger Co^{3+} or Co^{2+} with a loss of oxygen, Co^{3+} ions are easy to transit from low-spin to high-spin state.

Acknowledgement

The authors would like to thank Ministry of Science and Technology of Taiwan for financially supporting this research under contract number: MOST 104-2119-M-259-003 and MOST 104-2113-M-259-005.

References

1. E.P. Murray, T. Tsai, and S.A. Barnett, A Direct-Methane Fuel Cell with a Ceria-Based Anode. Nature, **400**, 649-651. (1999)
2. S.H. Cui, J.H. Li X.W. Zhou, G.Y. Wang, J.L. Luo, K.T. Chuang, Y. Bai, and L.J. Qiao, Cobalt Doped $LaSrTiO_{3-\delta}$ as an Anode Catalyst: Effect of Co Nanoparticle Precipitation on SOFCs Operating on H_2S-Containing Hydrogen. J. Mater. Chem., **1**, 9689-9696. (2013)
3. B.C.H. Steele and A. Heinzel, Materials for Fuel Cell Technologies. Nature, **414**, 345-352. (2011)
4. E.D. Wachsman, and K.T. Lee, Lowering the Temperature of Solid Oxide Fuel Cells Science. **334**, 935-939. (2011)
5. D.J.L. Brett, A. Atkinson, N.P. Brandon, and S.J. Skinner, Intermediate Temperature Solid Oxide Fuel Cell. Chem. Soc. Rev., **37**, 1568-1578. (2008)
6. X. Zhang, L. Liu, Z. Zhao, B. Tu, D. Ou, D. Cui, X. Wei, X. Chen, and M. Cheng, Enhanced Oxygen Reduction Activity and Solid Oxide Fuel Cell Performance with a Nanoparticles-Loaded Cathode. Nano Lett., **15**,1703-1709. (2015)
7. T.H. Lee, K.Y. Park, N.I., Kim, S.J. Song, D. Ahn, K.A. Abul, J. Hwang, K.H. Hong, S. Bhattacharjee, S.C. Lee, H.T. Lim, and J.Y. Park. Robust $NdBa_{0.5}Sr_{0.5}Co_{1.5}Fe_{0.5}O_{5+\delta}$ Cathode Material and its Degradation Prevention Operating Logic for Intermediate Temperature Solid Oxide Fuel Cells. J. Power Sources, **331**, 495-506. (2016)
8. K. Park, S. Yu, J. Bae, H. Kim, and Y. Ko, Fast Performance Degradation of SOFC Caused by Cathode Delamination in Long-Term Testing.' Int. J. Hydrogen Energy, **35**, 8670-8677. (2010)
9. D.J. Chen, Ran, R., K. Zhang, J. Wang, and Z.P. Shao, Intermediate Temperature Electrochemical Performance of a Polycrystalline $PrBaCoO_{5+\delta}$ Cathode on Samarium-Doped Ceria Electrolyte.' J. Power Sources, **188**, 96-105. (2009)
10. Q. Zhou, F. Wang, Y. Shen, and T. He, Performance of $LnBaCo_2O_{5+\delta}$-$Ce_{0.8}Sm_{0.2})_{1.9}$ Composite Cathodes for Intermediate-Temperaure Solid Oxide Fuel Cells. J. Power Sources, (195), 2174-2181. (2010)
11. J.H. Kim, M. Cassidy, J.T.S. Irvine, and J. Bae, Electrochemical Investigation of Composite Cathodes with $SmBa_{0.5}Sr_{0.5}Co_2O_{5+\delta}$ Cathodes for Intermediate Temperature Solid Oxide Fuel Cell. Chem Mater., **22**, 883-892. (2010)
12. G.R. Zhang, X.L. Dong, Z.K. Liu, W. Zhou, Z.P. Shao, and W.Q. Jin, Cobalt-Site Cerium Doped $Sm_xSr_{1-x}CoO_{3-\delta}$ Oxides as Potential Cathode Materials for Solid Oxide Fuel Cells. J. Power Sources, **195**, 3386-3393. (2010)
13. B. Wei, Z. Lu, and T. Wei, Nanosized $Ce_{0.8}Sm_{0.2}O_{1.9}$ Infiltrated $GdBaCo_2O_{5-\delta}$ Cathodes for Intermediate-Temperature Solid Oxide Fuel Cells. Int. J. Hydrogen Energy, **36**, 6151-6159. (2011)
14. A. Subardi, M.H. Cheng, and Y.P. Fu, Chemical Bulk Diffusion and Electrochemical Properties of $SmBa_{0.6}Sr_{0.4}Co_2O_{5+\delta}$ Cathode for Intermediate Solid Oxide Fuel Cells. Int. J. Hydrogen Energy, **39**, 20783-20790. (2014)
15. D. Chen, and Z. Shao, Surface Exchange and Bulk Diffusion Properties of $Ba_{0.5}Sr_{0.5}Co_{0.8}Fe_{0.2}O_{3-\delta}$ Mixed Conductor. Int. J. Hydrogen Energy, **36**, 6948-6956. (2011)
16. S.B. Adler, B.T. Henderson, M.A. Wilson, D.M. Taylor, and R.E. Richards, Reference Electrode Placement and Seals in Electrochemical Oxygen Generators. Solid State Ionics, **134**, 35-42. (2000)
17. J. Winkler, P.V. Hendriksen, N. Bonanos, and M. Mongensen, Geometric Requirements of Solid Electrolyte Cells with a Reference Electrode. J. Electrochem. Soc., **145**, 1184-1192. (1998)
18. H. Ding, X. Xue, and X. Liu, High Performance Layered $SmBa_{0.5}Sr_{0.5}Co_2O_{5+\delta}$ Cathode for Intermediate-Temperature Solid Oxide Fuel Cells. J. Power Sources, **194**, 815-817. (2009)
19. A. Jun, J. Kim, and J. Shin, 'Optimization of Sr Content in Layered $SmBa_{1-x}Sr_xCo_2O_{5+\delta}$ Perovskite Cathodes for Intermediate-Temperature Solid Oxide Fuel Cells. Int. J. Hydrogen Energy, **37**, 18381-18388. (2012)
20. T. Chen, S. Pang, X. Shen, X. Jiang, and W. Wang, Evaluation of Ba-Deficient $PrBa_{01-x}Fe_2O_{5+\delta}$ Oxide as Cathode Materials for Intermediate-Temperature Solid Oxide Fuel Cells. *RSC Adv.*, **6**, 13829-13836. (2016)
21. K. Huang, H.Y. Lee, J.B. Goodenough, Sr- and Ni-Doped $LaCoO_3$ and $LaFeO_3$ Perovskites: New Cathode Materials for Solid Oxide Fuel Cells. J. Electrochem. Soc., **145**, 3220-3227. (1998)
22. M.A.S. Rodriguez, and J.B. Goodenough,

$LaCoO_3$ Revisited. J. Solid State Chem., (116), 224-231. (1995)
23. A. Subardi, C.C. Chen, and Y.P. Fu, Electrical, Thermal and Electrochemical Properties of $SmBa_{1-x}Sr_xCo_2O_{5+\delta}$ Cathode Materials for Intermediate-Temperature Solid Oxide Fuel Cells. Electrochi. Acta, **204**, 118-127. (2016)
24. A. Subardi K.Y. Liao, and Y.P. Fu, Oxygen Transport, Thermal and Electrochemical Properties of $NdBa_{0.5}Sr_{0.5}Co_2O_{5+\delta}$ Cathode for SOFCs. J European Ceramic Society, (2018)
25. K. Chen, and S.P. Jiang, Review-Materials Degradation of Solid Electrolysis Cells, J. Electrochem. Soc., **163**, 3070-3083. (2016)
26. W.C. Jung, and H.L. Tuller, Investigation of Surface Sr Segregation in Model Thin Film Solid Oxide Fuel Cell Perovskite Electrodes. Energy Environ. Sci., **5**, 5370-5378. (2012)
27. J.H. Nam, and D.H. Jeon, A Comprehensive Microscale Model for Transport and Reaction in Intermediate Temperature Solid Oxide Fuel Cell. Electrochi. Acta, **51**, 3446-3460. (2006)
28. M. Anderson, J. Yuan, and B. Sunden, Review on Modeling Development for Multiscale Chemical Reaction Coupled Transport Phenomena in Solid Oxide Fuel Cell. Appl. Energy, **87**, 1461-1476. (2010)

Solid-State Fermentation of Banana Peels Potential Study for Feed Additive

Akbarningrum Fatmawati*, *Tuani* Lidiawati, *Stephen* Hadinata, *Mikhael* Adiarto

University of Surabaya, Chemical Engineering Department, Jl. Raya Kalirungkut Surabaya, Indonesia

Abstract. Agricultural solid wastes present abundantly on earth as crops harvesting as well as processing are countinuesly run. Banana peels are one of agricultural solid wastes produced anywhere the banana processing presents. The peels present abundantly in tropical countries such as Indonesia. The carbohydrate content of banana peels make it useful for the production of many chemicals, including feed. Meanwhile the large need in feed in farming including fish farming could prevent farmer to obtain substantial profit. This research studied the possibility of banana peel as one of abundant Indonesian agricultural solid waste to be utilized as fish feed which is known requiring certain level of protein content. This was done by fermenting the peels in fixed bed reaction mode using surface aeration and non-aeration. The fermentation was conducted using yeast *Saccharomyces cerevisiae* Y1536 and *Rhizopus Oryzae* FNCC 6157. The reaction time was varied for 1, 3, and 5 days. The important parameters studied were protein contents, and amylase activity of the fermented banana peels. Despite aeration indicated more operational cost, it showed significant impact on the fermentation of banana peels. The best condition for fermentation using *Saccharomyces cerevisiae* Y1536 were 5 day fermentation with surface aeration which result in the increase of protein content up to 4.05%, the decrease of fiber content up to 1.08%, and amylase activity of 9.99 DP. Whilst the fermentation using *Rhizopus Oryzae* FNCC 6157 obtained its best result at 1 day fermentation with aeration, which are protein content increase up to 4.04% and fiber content decrease up to 0.69%. However, the fermentation using this mold showed its best amylase activity result of 12.75 DP at 5 day surface aerated fermentation.

1 Introduction

Waste produced from domestic, agriculture, and industrial activity has found causing many environemtal and health problems. Agricultural activities produces several waste including solid wastes, which in spite of causing environmental and health problems, they store economical potential to be transformed either chemically or non chemically into more beneficial products. Agricultural wastes which can be liquid, slurries or solids, are byproducts of growing and first processing of raw agricultural products such as fruit and vegetables, crops, meat and poultry as well as dairy products. Manures, fertilizers, and residues from slaughterhouse are also included as agricultural solid wastes [1]. Currently, many researches have attempted to utilise agicultural solid wastes to produce more valuable products and improve economy such as fired clay materials for building manufacturing, green desiccants in desiccant-cooling systems, biofuels, bio-oil and char, and animal feed [2-6]. Generally agricultural wastes still contain useful nutrition components which are good for animal consumption. The potential of agricultural solid waste for animal feed should be encouraged because of its benefit for both environment and the farmers.

In fish farming activities, the productivity of fish farmers is usually constrained by production cost where the feed cost can cover up to 50-80% of the total operational cost [7-9]. Protein is the main ingredient of the commercial diet of fish which constitutes 40-56% of the diets [10-11]. Many kinds of fermented fiber-rich agricultural waste had been used for fish or shrimp feed additives such as papaya processing waste, corncob, rice husk and apple pomace [9, 12-14]. This carbohydrate-rich and low protein content agriculture wastes can be low cost fish energy source. However, carbohydrate amylolytic activity in carnivorous fish is lower than herbivorous fish [15]. Therefore, adding amylase activities on the carbohydrate feed will be advantageous.

Nutrient enrichment had been attempted by fermentation process which can increase protein content, required metabolic enzymes, and pathogenic bacteria inhibitory substance. Several fungi had shown to have either amylolytic or cellulolytic activities and therefore can be used to ferment carbohydrate-rich wastes while

* Corresponding author: akbarningrum@staff.ubaya.ac.id

after fermentation they can provide protein sources needed for feed component. Some fungi such as *Saccharomyces cerevisiae*, *Candida utilis*, *Aspergillus niger*, and *Rhizopus oligosporus* have been known to be able to increase the protein content of biomass through fermentation [9]. Fermented corn-cob by mold consortium consisting of *Trichoderma viridae, Trichoderma reesei, Aspergillus oryzae*, and *Rhizopus oligosporus* had been used in feed formulation of Java barb fish and had been shown to increase the growth of Java barb [13]. Yeast protein is easily digestible and widely used for fish and shrimp feed supplement which in spite of providing protein source, it can enhance immune system and stimulating bacterial disease resistance [12]. When used as feed additive, the increased protein content of apple pomace after fermentation using *G. butleri* had been able to increase 44% in body mass of fish [16].

This research attempted to investigate the effect of solid-state fermentation of abundantly available waste banana peels by fungi *Saccharomyces cerevisiae* and *Rhizopus oryzae* on the protein and fiber content as well as the amylase activity of the peels in order to see its potential for fish feed additive. Solid-state fermentation itself has many applications including production of a large number of enzymes used in feed industry [17] The expected results were the increase of protein content of the banana peels and the availability of amylolitic activities of fermented banana peels.

2 Materials and Methods

2.1 Materials and Preparation Stage

The banana peels used in this research is from the species of *Musa acuminate* or *Musa balbisiana* or in Indonesian name, Pisang Kepok. The peels were collected locally from market and banana processing food seller. Immediately after collection, the peels were washed and cut into small size (1x 0.2 cm). The protein and fiber content of the peels were analyzed before fermentation.

There were two types of fermentation microorganism used in this research. The first type is yeast *Saccharomyces cerevisiae* Y1536 obtained from Institute Pertanian Bogor culture collection (IPBCC) while the second type is mold *Rhizopus oryzae* FNCC 6157 obtained from Food and Nutrition Development and Research Center (FANDARC), Gadjah Mada University (UGM). The fungi cultures were cultivated using potato dextrose agar (PDA).

2.2 Fermentation Stage

Prior to fermentation, the fungi cultures being used in the fermentation stage were transfered into 25 mL potato dextrose broth (PDB). The broths were shaken for 24 hours at speed of 150 rpm using incubator shaker.

The fermentations were conducted using tray solid-state bioreactors set up from Erlenmeyer flask in which the banana peels were stacked. As much as 225 grams of banana peel was firstly steamed for 30 minutes inside Erlenmeyer flask. It is then cooled and inoculated with 24 hour broth innoculum in biological safety cabinet to prevent contamination. The fermentation system set up is shown on Fig 1. This fermentation was conducted with and without aeration. To prevent contamination from outside air, membrane filters were mounted on the top of the Erlenmeyer flasks. The reaction time was varied 1, 3, and 5 days. At the end of fermentation, the peels were analyzed for the protein and fiber content as well as amylase activity.

Fig. 1. Solid-state fermentation set up

2.3 Chemical and Biological Analysis

The protein contents of the fermented banana peels were analyzed using total nitrogen (Kjelhdal method). The fiber contents were analyzed using fiber anaylisis by SNI 01-2891-1992. The amylase activities of the fermented banana peels were assayed using method by Fuwa (1954) [18]. The method was colorimeterically and the activity was expressed as dextrinising power (DP). Principally the substrate for dextrinising power determination used was commercial cassava amylose which was prepared according to Fuwa method. The values of DP were measured by the change of blue values of amylose-iodine complexes. Amylase unit (1 DP) was defined as the amount of amylase which would produce 10 percent fall in blue colour intensity of amylase-iodine complexes.

3 Results and Discussions

The locally collected banana peels were analysed for the total carbohydrate, fiber, lipid, protein, water, and ash contents. The result showed that the banana peels studied contained 79.59-85.66 % water. By dry basis, the peels also contained 55.05-58% total carbohydrate, 6.5-8.18% fiber, 7.36-12.23% lipid, 2.08-3.18% protein, and 13.97-20.24% ash. The result showed that the peels were rich in carbohydrate and were very suitable for energy sources. However, in order to be used as fish feed additives, effort must be done to improve their protein content as well to decrease the fiber contents. These can be achieved through fermentation. The process of fermentation by amylase producing fungi can also produce amylase enzyme which may be needed for increasing feed digestion rate of fish.

 https://doi.org/10.1051/matecconf/201821501027

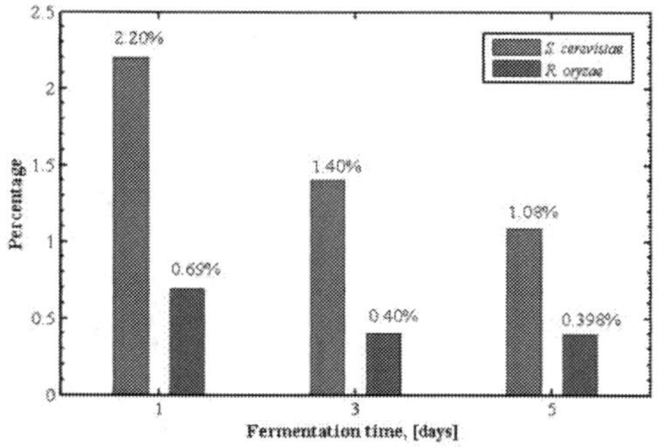

Fig. 2. Fiber content with aeration

The fiber contents resulted after fermentation is shown on Fig. 2 for aerated fermentation and Fig. 4 for non-aerated fermentation. While the protein content after fermentation is shown on Fig. 3 for aerated fermentation and Fig. 5 for non-aerated fermentation. From Fig.2, it is shown that the *Rhizopus oryzae* FNCC 6157 can decrease fiber faster and higher than *Saccharomyces cerevisiae* Y1536. It is understood that mould produces hydrolytic enzymes very well and better than yeast. By comparing Fig. 2 and Fig. 4, it can be said that aeration affected fiber decrease in the fermentation of banana peels by *Saccharomyces cerevisiae* and *Rhizopus oryzae*. This aeration increased the growth rate of those fungi and therefore increased the production of cellulase, fiber hydrolyzing enzyme.

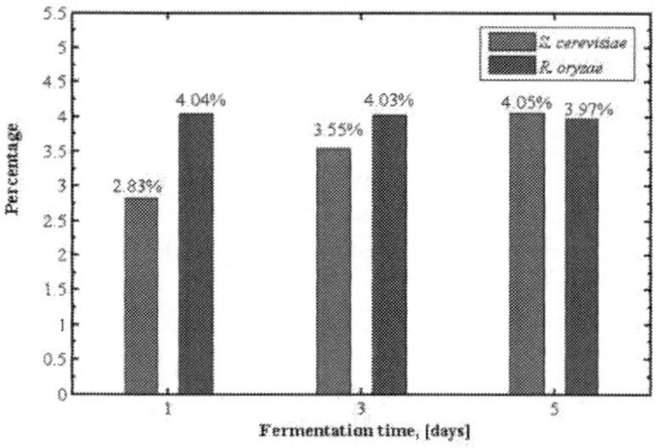

Fig. 3. Protein content with aeration

Fig.3 and Fig. 5 presents the protein content of the banana peels after fermentation with aeration, and without aeration, respectively. The protein content increases with fermentation time. The figures also show that *Rhizopus oryzae* fermentation caused protein increase higher than *Saccharomyces cerevisiae*. This protein content increased because the fungi grew and used the banana peels as substrate, broke down the complex carbohydrate of the peels and synthesized protein as the component of fungi cell. The increase of protein content of banana peels made them potential to be used as animal feed additive, including fish feed additive.

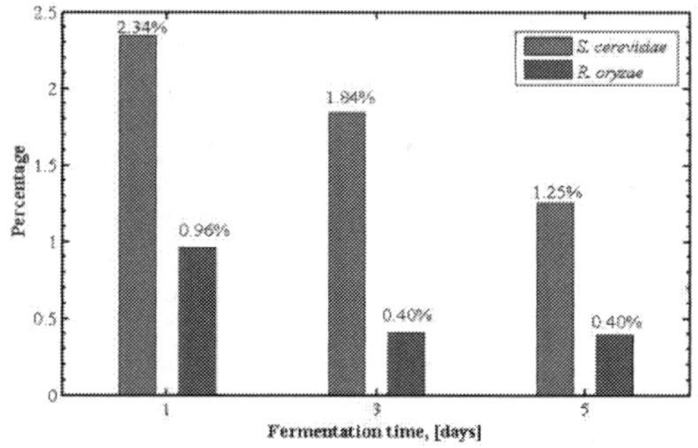

Fig. 4. Fiber content without aeration

The protein content increase was higher in fermentation with aeration compared to without aeration for each of the fungi because aeration favored the fungi growth. In the result of this research, it also can be seen that the highest protein content can be achieved up to 4% for 3 day aerated fermentation by *R. oryzae*. Higher protein content improvement can be achieved by lengthening the fementation time by *S. cereviae*.

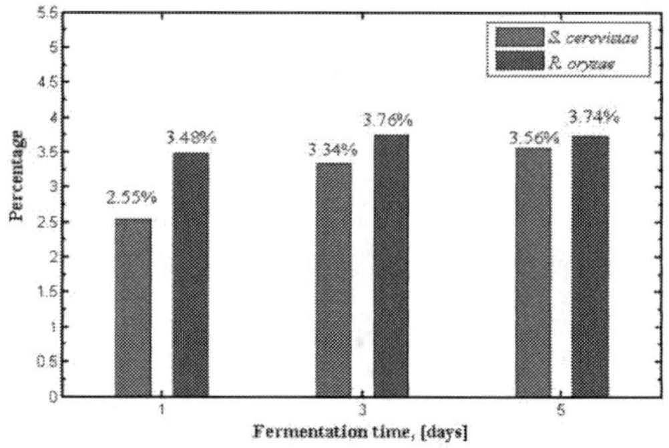

Fig. 5. Protein content without aeration

The amylase activity profiles after fermentation with and without aeration are shown in Fig. 6 and Fig. 7. The activity increased with fermentation time for each of the fungi because this enzyme was needed for their growth on banana peels which are composed mostly by starch.

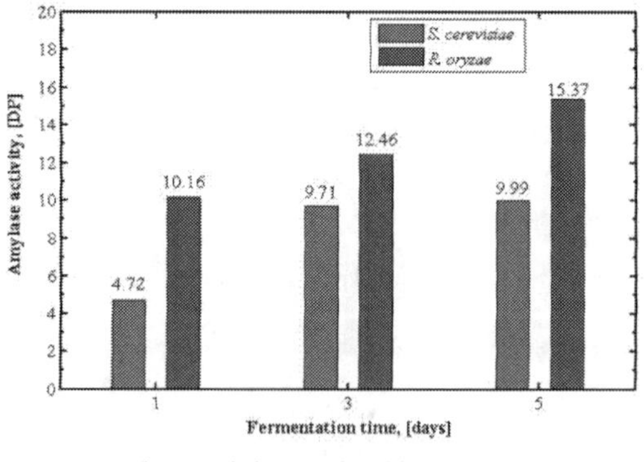

Fig. 6. Amylase activity result with aeration

The amylase activity produced by *Rhizopus oryzae* was higher than that produced by *Saccharomyces cerevisiae*. That is the reason for the higher growth rate of *R. oryzae* which cause the higher protein content and the lower fiber content resulted from *Rhizopus* banana peel fermentation as depicted from previous figures. The highest amylase activity was achieved by 5 day aerated fermentation by *Rhizopus oryzae* which resulted as high as 15.37 DP. As Comparison, 1 mL Taka amylase resulted in 6.5 DP [18].

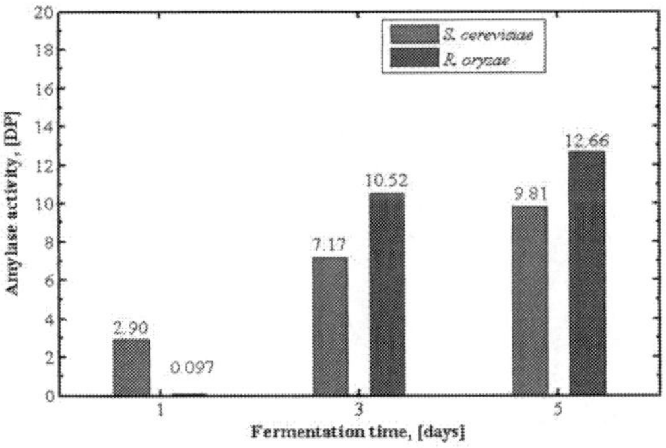

Fig. 7. Amylase activity result without aeration

The results has shown the potential usage of fermented banana peel as fish feed additive according to the increasing protein content, decreasing fiber content amylolitic enzyme to increase feed digestion. Previous publications have also shown that mixture of fungi such as *T. viridae*, *T. reseei*, *A. oryzae*, and *Rhizopus oligosporus* can ferment corn-cob to produce organic acid (citric, pantoteni, acetic and lactic), fatty acids, glucose, vitamin, mineral and various enzymes (lipase, protease and cellulase) [13]. Living cultures of Zygomycetes including *Rhizopus oryzae* have been used as probiotic organism to prevent fish infectious disease [19]. In spite of that, *Saccharomyces cerevisiae* is included as authorized probiotic in feeding stuffs under Council Directive 70/524/EEC [20]. Higher protein content from banana peel fermentation than obtained in this research could be achieved combining with other molds or with *S. cerevisiae* and other probiotic microorganisms in the future.

4 Conclusions and Recommendations

Banana peels fermentations by *Saccharomyces cerevisiae* Y1536 and *Rhizopus oryzae* FNCC 6157 had shown their potential as fish feed additive because of the increasing protein content and decreasing fiber content after fermentation. The fermentation also showed the presence of amylase activity needed for fish feed digestion. Banana peels fermentation by *Rhizopus oryzae* FNCC 6157 resulted in better protein increase, fiber decrease as well as amylase activity.

References

1. A.D. King Jr., A.D. Hocking, and J.I. Pitt, Dichloran-Rose-Bengal Medium for Enumeration of moulds from Foods. Applied and Environmental Microbiology, **37**(5), 959-964, (1979)
2. O. Kizinievič, V. Kizinievič, I. Pundiene, D. Molotokas, Eco-friendly fired clay brick manufactured with agricultural solid waste. Civil and Mechanical Engineering, **18** (4), 1156-1165. (2018)
3. N. Asim, Z. Emdadi, M. Mohammad, M.A. Yarmo, K. Sopian, ReviewAgricultural solid wastes for green desiccant applications: an overview of research achievements, opportunities and perspectives. Journal of Cleaner Production, **91**, 26-35, (2015)
4. P.K. Swain, Utilisation of Agriculture Waste Products for Production of Bio-Fuels: A Novel Study. Materials today: Proceedings, **4** (11) (part 3), 11959-11967, (2017)
5. I. Hawash, J.Y. Farah, G. El-Diwani, Pyrolysis of agriculture wastes for bio-oil and char productions. Journal of Analytical and Applied Pyrolysis, **124**, 369–372 (2017)
6. O.O. Oduguwa, M.O. Edema, A.O. Ayeni, Physico-chemical and microbiological analyses of fermented corn cob, rice bran and cowpea husk for use in composite rabbit feed. Bioresource Technology **99**, 1816–1820. (2008)
7. A.F.M. El-Sayed, Alternative Dietary protein sources for farmaed tilapia, Oreachromis spp. Aquaculture, 149-168, (2002)
8. F.A. Masoodi, B. Sharma G.S. Chauhan, Use of Apple Pomace as Source of Dietary Fiber in Cakes. Plant Foods for Human Nutrition, **57**, 121-128, (2002)
9. G.S. Dhillon, S. Kaur, K.S. Brar, Perspective of Apple Processing Wastes as Low-Cost Substrates for Bioproduction of High Value Products: A Review. Renewable and Sustainable Energy Reviews, **27**, 789-805, (2013)
10. V.T. Namulawa, C.D. Kato, J. Rutaisire, P.J. Britz, N. Beukes, B.I. Pletschke, C. Whiteley, Enzyme Activity in The Nile perch Gut: Implications to Nile perch Culture. International Journal of Fisheries and Aquaculture, **5**(9), 221-228. (2013)
11. S. Mukherjee, D. Parial, N. Khatoo, A. Chaudhuri, S. Senroy, S. Homechaudhuri, and R. Pal, 'Effect of formulated algal diet on growth performance of *Labeo rohita* Hamilton.' J. Algal Biomass Utln., **2**(4), 1–9, (2011)
12. H.Y. Kang, P.Y. Yang, W.G., Dominy, C.S. Lee, Bioprocessing papaya processing waste for potential aquaculture feed supplement – Economic and nutrient analysis with shrimp feeding trial. Bioresource Technology, **101**, 7973–7979, (2010)
13. R. Rostika, R. Safitri, Influnce of Feed Containing Corn Cob was Fermented by Trichoderma sp, Aspergillus sp. And oligosporus to Rate of

Growth of Java Barb (Puntius gonionitus). APCBEE Procedia, **2**, 148 – 152. (2012)
14. A.A. Zaid, O.G. Taiwo, Comparative Utilisation of Biodegraded Rice Husk ini Diet of Clarias gariepinus. Journal of Fisheries and aquatic science, **3**(5), 312-319, (2008)
15. M.C. Hidalgo, E. Urea and A. Sanz, Comapartive study of digestive enzymes in fish with different nutritional habits. Proteolytic and amylase activities. Aquaculture, **170**, 267-283, (1999)
16. F. Vendruscolo, R.C. da Silva, E. Esposito, and J.L. Nienow, Protein Enrichment of Apple Pomace and Use in Feed for Nile Tilapia. Applied Biochemistry and Biotechnology, **152**, 74-87, (2009)
17. L. Thomas, C. Larroche, and A. Pandey, Current Developments in Solid-State Fermentation. Biochemical Engineering Journal, **81**, 146-161, (2013)
18. H. Fuwa, A New Method for Microdetermination Of Amylase Activity By The Use Of Amylose As The Subtrate. The Journal of Biochemistry, **41**(5), 583-603, (1954)
19. L.B. Edebo, Zygomycetes for Fish Feed. US Patent No. 2009/0136617 A1
20. P. Pandiyan, D. Balaraman, R. Thirunavukkarasu, E. G. J. George, K. Subaramaniyah, S. Manikkam, B. Sadayappan, Probiotics in aquaculture, Drug Invention Today. **5**(1), 55-59, (2013)

Effect of pH on the stability of W1/O/W2 double emulsion stabilized by combination of biosilica and Tween-20

Lanny Sapei[1*], *Tokok* Adiarto[2], *Roi* Handomo[1], *Sonny Hutomo* Chandra[1]

[1]Universitas Surabaya, Department of Chemical Engineering, Indonesia
[2]Universitas Airlangga, Department of Chemistry, Indonesia

Abstract. Indonesia is amongst agricultural countries whose majority of the population consume rice as their staple food. Rice rice production tends to increase year by year followed by the increasing of their byproducts such as rice husks. The majority of rice husk waste has been generally thrown away by burning on site which cause pollution and may negatively impact on the environmental sustainability. In fact, rice husk waste contains of about 20% silica which potentially be used as emulsion stabilizers. Biosilica could stabilize the interface between water and oil due to their hydrophilicity and hydrophobicity characteristics in nature. However, their wettability was greatly influenced by pH. In this experiment, the effect of pH of the outer continuous phase (W_2) was investigated. The primary emulsion (W_1/O) was prepared by mixing a 40% water phase containing gelatin 3% w/w relative to the aqueous phase and Tween-20 of 1.1% w/w relative to the primary emulsion with the remaining oil phase for 5 minutes. The primary emulsions were then dispersed into the aqueous phase (W_2) of various pH (2; 3; and 5.7) by using a mixture of Tween-20 and biosilica as emulsifiers. The result showed that the most stable double emulsion was obtained upon the acidic pH of 2. There was no differences between the stability of double emulsion prepared at pH 2 and that of pH 3 after 7 days. However those prepared without pH adjustment (5.7) tended to be instable in the long-term. This implied that acidic pH would increase the packing density of biosilica in the interfaces thus enhancing the barrier properties of the droplets against coalescences. A stable food grade double emulsion would be very beneficial to develop low-fat emulsion products in various food applications. Furthermore, the inner aqueous phase could be used as a vehicle to encapsulate bio-active agents such as nutrients or antioxidants for the advancement of developments of functional food products.

1 Introduction

Indonesia is amongst one of the biggest agricultural countries with the majority of population consume rice as their staple foods. Paddy production in 2015 was 75.36 million tons which was increased of about 6.37% compared to the production in 2014 with the paddy field increase of 0.32 million ha according to Statistics Indonesia [1]. Paddy milling produce wastes. One of its wastes is rice husk which is usually burnt and still underutilized. In fact, rice husk is rich in silica which could be used as a substitute of synthetic emulsifier for food emulsions stabilization. Emulsion stabilized by particles was found by Pickering in 1907 so that the resulting emulsion has been known as pickering emulsion [2]. Silica has been used as food additives (E551) besides it has been considered as essential nutrition since it imparts health benefits such as strengthening bones and improving immune response, as well as neutronal and connective tissue health [3]. Pichot, *et. al.* (2010) studied on the effect of types and concentration of surfactants and colloidal particles on the emulsions stability. Tween-60 and *Sodium Caseinate* were used as emulsifiers for O/W while lecithin and colloidal silica particles were used as emulsifiers for W/O emulsion. Emulsion stabilized by mixed surfactants and silica particles had smaller droplets compared to the emulsion stabilized by either surfactant or silica particle. Furthermore, the droplets were getting bigger with the increase of surfactant concentrations and silica particles were gradually detached from the interfaces. These effects were hardly seen in W/O emulsions [4]. Pichot, *et. al.* (2012) investigated the influence of pH on the stability of O/W emulsions stabilized with the combination of silica particles, Tween-60, and sodium caseinate and W/O emulsions stabilized with silica particles and lecithin. Surfactants were dispersed in aqueous phase followed by silica particles (0.2 – 2%) with the variation of pH of 2-10 of the aqueous phase. Vegetable oil was added to the aqueous phase and mixed with a high shear mixer. Emulsion formed at pH 2 showed the highest stability due to the smaller contact angle of silica particle in the O/W interfaces thus increasing its emulsifying properties [5]. There have been increasing applications of W/O or O/W emulsions in food

* Corresponding author: lanny.sapei@staff.ubaya.ac.id

industries. Nowadays, along with the increasing demands of healthy foods, W/O/W emulsions have been of interest to create food emulsions with lower fats. Cofrades, *et. al.* (2013) prepared W/O/W emulsions in meat systems.The primary W/O emulsion with 80% oil fraction was prepared using 6% PgPr as emulsifier. Olive oil was used for the oil phase. The emulsification was conducted at 3250 rpm for 5.5 minutes at 50°C. Furthermore, 6% whey protein, 0.5% sodium caseinate, and 0.6% NaClwas added into the outer aqueous phase. The 40% primary emulsion was then dispersed within the outer aqueous phase using a Thermomix blender at the mixing speed of 700 rpm for 5.5 minutes at a room temperature. The fat content was reduced from 11% to 7% [6]. L. Sapei, *et. al.* (2012) developed W/O/W emulsion for food applications. The inner aqueous phase was added with varying concentration of gelatin (0%, 3%, and 10% w/w) and NaCl (0 - 8% w/w). PgPr of 6% as emulsifier was added into the canola oil phase. The inner aqueous phase was then emulsified into the oil phase with the fraction of 40% using a rotor-stator homogenizer (Polytron PT 10/35, kinematik, CH-6010, Swiss) at 27,000 rpm for 3 menit at 65°C. The resulting primary emulsion of 20% was then dispersed into the outer aqueous phase containing 1% w/w polysorbate 80 at 10,000 rpm for 2 minutes. The most stable W/O/W was obtained with gelatin concentration of 3%. The synergistic effect on the overall W/O/W stability due to the addition of gelatin and NaCl was observed [7]. The use of particles in stabilizing food-grade emulsions seems promising. Particles have to be combined with the polymeric emulsifiers in order to obtain emulsion with high level of stability [4, 8]. There have been few investigations of using biosilica as emulsifiers. The objective of this research was exploring the use of rice husk biosilica combined with Tween-20 in developing food-grade W/O/W double emulsions. These emulsions contained lower amount of fat with lower amount of polymeric emulsifier which were quite promising to be furthermore developed and incorporated into healthy and nutritious foods.

2 Materials and Methods

Materials

Rice husk wastes were obtained from Mojokerto, East Java, Indonesia; Tween-20 (Merck, Germany); Gelatin (SAP Chemicals, Indonesia); HCl 37% (Mallinckrodt, USA); palm oil consisting of about 40% of saturated oil and 60% of unsaturated oil (Sunco, PT. Milkie Olco Nabati Industri, Bekasi, Indonesia); demineralized water.

Biosilica preparation

Rice husk wastes were cleaned, washed with water, and dried at 105°C for 2 hours in an oven (Memmert, Germany) prior to leaching process. Process leaching was conducted in a vessel equipped with a condenser and an impeller. The solvent used was 5% citric acid. After leaching, the filtered rice husks were rinsed with demineralized water for several times and then dried at 105°C for 2 hours in an oven (Memmert, Germany). The dried leached rice husks were subsequently thermally treated in a furnace (Ney VULCAN D-550, Denstply Ceramco, USA) at 750°C for 5 hours. The resulted white ashes were pure biosilica which were screened using 200 mesh screening prior to use.

Primary emulsion preparation

The primary emulsion was water in oil emulsion whereby 40% of aqueous phase (W_1) was dispersed in oil phase. Gelatin of 3% and Tween-20 of 2.8% was added to the aqueous phase in a 100 ml beaker glass. The mixture was mixed using a magnetic stirrer and slowly heated until 68°C for 30 minutes on a hotplate (Cimarec, Malaysia). The oil phase consisted of only oil was also preheated to 68°C for 30 minutes. The aqueous phase was dispersed into the oil phase by premixing using a magnetic bar at 68°C for 30 minutes followed by mixing using a rotor-stator homogenizer (IKA T25 digital ULTRA TURRAX, Germany) at 24,000 rpm for 5 minutes. The temperatures were well monitored using an alcohol thermometer. The beaker glasses were covered with aluminum foils in order to prevent the evaporation of liquids. The minor losses of liquid were compensated by adding several drops of liquid prior to emulsification.

Double emulsion preparation

Double emulsion ($W_1/O/W_2$) was prepared by dispersing the primary emulsion (W_1/O) into the outer aqueous phase (W_2). The outer aqueous phase was prepared by adding combination of biosilica of 0.5% and Tween-20 of 1% as mixed emulsifiers while the pH was brought into acidic environment at 2 and 3 by the addition of several drops of HCl 37% solution. The pH of outer aqueous phase prepared without pH adjustment was about 5.7. The outer aqueous phase was stirred using a magnetic bar while being slowly heated to 68°C. The primary emulsion (W_1/O) with a fraction of 20% w/w was dispersed into the W_2 phase using the rotor-stator homogenizer (IKA T25 digital ULTRA TURRAX, Germany) at 10,000 rpm for 2 minutes. The resulting double emulsions were then characterized macroscopically and microscopically for their stability. The stability was monitored for the first 2 hours and after 7 day storage.

Determination of double emulsion stability

The stability of double emulsion ($W_1/O/W_2$) was simply determined macroscopically by comparing the height of emulsion at final condition with that of initial condition. Double emulsion ($W_1/O/W_2$) was poured into a flat-bottomed 40 ml glass vial (ID = 25 mm and height= 95 mm) until ¾ part of the glass. The height of initial emulsion was measured as well as the height of emulsion after a certain time. Emulsion was distinguished from the cream or oil layer based on their milky appearance. The double emulsion stability was calculated according to the equation (1).

$$\%S = \frac{h_o - h_t}{h_o} \times 100\%$$

whereas h_o= initial height of emulsion, h_t= height of emulsion after a certain time, the emulsion height was monitored every 1 minute for the first ten minutes followed by every 5 minutes for the first one hour and every 10 minutes for the subsequent one hour. Afterwards, the emulsion height was monitored every 24 hours up to 7 days. Additionally, the stability of double emulsion ($W_1/O/W_2$) was investigated microscopically using an optical microscope (Olympus, Japan) equipped by a camera (Optilab, Indonesia). A drop of $W_1/O/W_2$ emulsion was put into an objective glass and covered by a cover glass. The droplet size of primary emulsion and inner aqueous droplet could be observed. The occurrence of double emulsion could also be further confirmed.

3 Results and Discussion

Food grade double emulsions stabilized by rice husk biosilica were developed. Biosilica were combined with Tween-20 as the emulsifier mixtures in the outer aqueous phase. The double emulsion was obtained from 2 stages emulsifications. The first stage was the emulsification in order to obtain W_1/O emulsion which was stabilized by Tween-20 and gelatin. The second stage was the emulsification of W_1/O into outer aqueous phase (W_2). The concentration of mixed emulsifier of Tween-20 and biosilica significantly influenced the overall stability of the resulting double emulsion as could be seen in Table 1. The double emulsions stabilized by Tween-20 or biosilica only were amongst the least stable emulsions with stabilities attainment of 60-70% after 7 days. The most stable double emulsion with the highest stability of ~93% after 7 days was obtained when 1% Tween-20 was combined with 0.5% biosilica. When biosilica concentration was decreased or increased, the long-term double emulsion stability after 7 day storage was getting lowered. There was a synergistic action between biosilica and Tween-20 when being combined together. Tween-20 was easily adsorbed into the interfaces followed by the attachment of biosilica particles on the interfaces protecting the oil droplets against flocculations or coalescences. When only polymeric emulsifier was used, it would be easily detached from the interfaces causing emulsion destabilisation in the long-term. On the other hand, when only particles were used, the attachment of the particles in the interfaces was quite difficult and leaving the emulsion unstabilised [4]. Furthermore, there was hardly creaming seen in the double emulsion stabilised by 1% Tween-20 and 0.5% biosilica as depicted in Figure 1 in contrast with those emulsions stabilised with Tween-20 or biosilica only which demonstrated creaming and even oil separation, respectively. The addition of Tween-20 as surfactant could decrease the interfacial tension thus facilitating the phase dispersion into another phase without the occurrence of flocculations [9]. Based on these results, the mixture of 1% Tween-20 and 0.5% biosilica was selected to formulate double emulsions with varying pH of the outer aqueous phase in order to investigate of the effects of pH on the overall double emulsion stability.

Table 1. Stability of double emulsion $W_1/O/W_2$ stabilized by mixture of biosilica and Tween-20 on the outer aqueous phase

Mixed emulsifiers	Stability (%)	
	after 2 hours	after 7 days
1% Tween-20 only	88	70
0.5% biosilica only	78	60
1% Tween-20 + 0.25% biosilica	100%	76.92%
1% Tween-20 + 0.5% biosilica	100%	92.98%
1% Tween-20 + 0.75% biosilica	73.84%	73.84%
1% Tween-20 + 1% biosilica	84.48%	77.58%
1% Tween-20 + 1.25% biosilica	84.48%	77.58%

Fig. 1. Observation of double emulsions $W_1/O/W_2$ stabilities after 7 day storage stabilized by different emulsifiers on the outer aqueous phase (W_2), (a) Tween-20 1% only; (b) Biosilica 0.5% only; (c) Tween-20 1% and biosilica 0.5%

The double emulsion $W_1/O/W_2$ developed as depicted in Table 1 were prepared without pH adjustment and the outer aqueous phase had the pH of ~5.7. The acidic pH of outer aqueous phase was adjusted by the addition of HCl solution into pH of 2 and 3. The stability profiles of the resulting double emulsions at several pH adjustments with storage time could be seen in Figure 2. It was obvious that the acidic pH seemed beneficial since there were increase of stability of double emulsions prepared at both pH 2 and 3 compared to that prepared without pH adjustment after 7 day storage. The appearances of double emulsions after 2 hours were shown in Figure 3. Theys all seemed similar and quite stable. There were no significant differences in their appearance after 7 day storage. Furthermore, the double emulsions microstructures prepared at pH 2 and pH 5.7 after 2 hours and 7 days were demonstrated in Figure 4. In general, the double emulsion formations prepared at different pH of outer aqueous phase seemed similar up to 7 days.

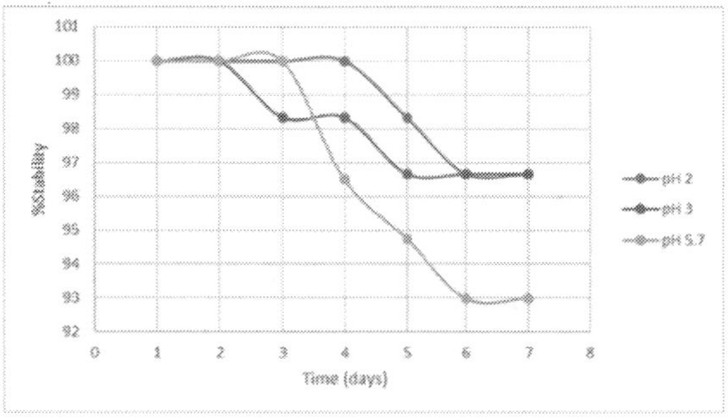

Fig. 2. The effect of pH of the outer aqueous phase on the stability of double emulsions $W_1/O/W_2$

Fig. 3. Observation of double emulsions $W_1/O/W_2$ stabilities after 2 hours with adjusted outer aqueous pH, (a) 2; (b) 3; (c) 5.7

Emulsions stabilized by biosilica were more stable against coalescence when the pH of the system was shifted to acidic pH. As system pH approach acidic environment (pH < 4), biosilica particles tended to have no charge thus enabled the particles to form aggregates covering the oil-water interface. In turn, the aggregates could form a closely packed layer acting as a rigid barrier against droplets coalescences. At a higher pH (pH > 4), biosilica particles tended to dissociate to form SiO^- which had a negative charge. The negatively charged silica particle would be more hydrophilic [10] and tended to be withdrawn into the aqueous phase rather than staying on the oil-water interfaces. Additionally, the negatively charged silica particles did not form closely packed aggregates since they repelled each other thus lowering their properties as barriers against flocculations and coalescences in the long-term. The proposed mechanisms of biosilica particle stabilization at low (pH < 4) and higher pH (pH > 4) were depicted in Figure 5.

4 Conclusions and recommendations

Rice husk biosilica enhanced the stability of double emulsion $W_1/O/W_2$ with the combination of polymeric emulsifier such as Tween-20. Furthermore, the action of stabilizing silica particles on the oil/ water interfaces was favored by the acidic environment (pH < 4) of the outer aqueous phase. The silica particles tended to form a closely packed layer due to the biosilica particles aggregations thus increasing the barrier properties against flocculation and coalescence. Consequently, the resulting double emulsions had higher stabilities after 7 day storage. This implied the promising application of biosilica particles in stabilizing low fat food grade based emulsions for producing healthier and highly nutritious processed foods. However, the long-term stability of the double emulsion would still have to be investigated and improved either by the optimization of the formulation or by the modulation of operating conditions of the process.

Acknowledgements

We wish to thank Ms. Dyah Ayu Ambarsari for the technical assistance during the experiments conducted at Polymer and Membrane Laboratory, University of Surabaya, Surabaya, East Java, Indonesia.

References

1. Badan Pusat Statistik (BPS), *Statistics Indonesia*, Rice production in Indonesia in 2015, (2015).
2. N.G. Eskandar, S. Simovic, C.A. Prestidge, Interaction of Hydrophilic Silica Nanoparticles and Classical Surfactants at Non-Polar Oil-Water Interface, Journal of Colloid and Interface Science, **358**, 217-225, (2011).
3. M.A. Farooq, K.J. Dietz, Silicon as versatile player in plant and human biology: overlooked and poorly understood. Frontiers in plant science, **6**, 994 (2015).
4. R. Pichot, Stability and Characterisation of Emulsions in The Presence of Colloidal Particles and Surfactants, University of Birmingham: Birmingham, (2010).
5. R. Pichot, F. Spyropoulos, I.T. Norton, Competitive Adsorption of Surfactants and Hydrophilic Silica Particles at The Oil–Water Interface: Interfacial Tension and Contact Angle Studies, Journal of Colloid and Interface Science, **377**, 396–405, (2012).
6. S. Cofrades, I. Antoniou, M.T. Solas, A.M. Herrero, F. Jimenez, Preparation and Impact of Multiple (Water in Oil in Water) Emulsions in Meat Systems. Journal of Food Chemistry, **141**, 338-346, (2013).
7. L. Sapei, M.A. Naqvi, D. Rousseau, Stability and Release Properties of Double Emulsions for Food Applications, Journal of Food Hydrocolloids, **27**, 315-323, (2012).

8. J. Frelichowska, M.A. Bolzinger, Y. Chevalier, Y., Pickering Emulsion with Bare Silica. Colloids and Surface A: Physiochemical and Engineering Aspects, **343**, 70-74, (2010).
9. T.F. Tadros, Emulsion Formation and Stability, Wiley-VCH Verlag GmBH & Co.KGaA, Weinheim, Germany, ISBN: 9783527647941, (2013).
10. A. Dyah, Destabilisation of Pickering Emulsion Using pH", Colloids and Surfaces A: Physicochem. Eng. Aspects **402**, 2–12, (2012).

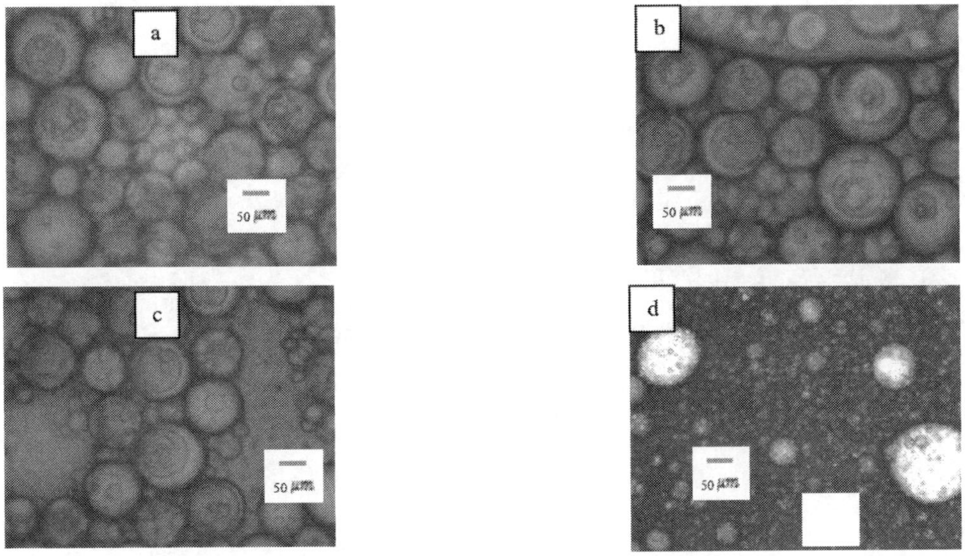

Fig. 4. The microstructures of double emulsions $W_1/O/W_2$ prepared at different pH after a certain time of storage, (a) pH 2, t = 0; (b) pH 2, t = 7 days; (c) pH 5.7, t = 0; (d) pH 5.7, t = 7 days

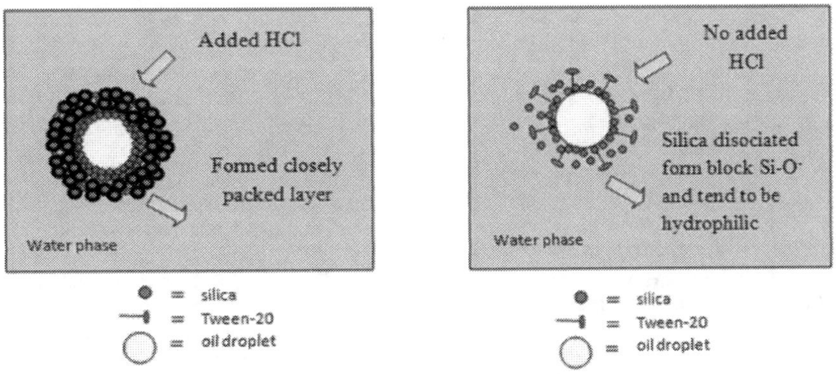

Fig. 5. Proposed models of pickering emulsion stabilized by biosilica under the influence of pH a) low pH (pH < 4) and b) higher pH (pH > 4).

The Effect of Fly Ash Composition and Drying Time Concrete Brick in Density Test

Nurzal, Mastaryanto Perdana, Heru Pratama Putera

Institut Teknologi Padang, Mechanical Engineering Department, Padang, West Sumatra, Indonesia

Abstract. This study uses the fly ash (FA) from coal combustion power plant Sijantang Sawahlunto. By utilizing fly ash in concrete brick can reduce the negative impact on the environment, composition of fly ash in concrete brick at 0, 5, 10, and 15 wt.% FA concrete brick added material (sand, cement and water as a binder). Influence of drying time 7, 14, 21, 28, and 35 days. Test specimen based on SNI 03-0349-1989, with size of 34 x 12 x 9 cm. The results showed that the composition of 5 wt.% fly ash with 28 days drying time was found to be the highest density with 2,230 gr/cm3, while the lowest density in the composition test was 15 wt.% fly ash with 35 days drying time with the density 1,946 gr/cm3. In this study, the density of normal concrete brick density with density 2,208-2,230 gr/cm3 and light concrete brick density of 2,000-1,946 gr/cm3, and also found a normal and light concrete brick category that is 2,022-2,053 gr/cm3.

1 Introduction

Housing and building development are increasing every year, along with population growth. One of the most common component of construction material used is concrete brick which is applied to wall in housing, building and fence. concrete brick is a concrete brick mold consisting of a mixture of cement, sand and water. concrete brick consists of two types of hollow concrete brick and solid concrete brick. concrete brick is one of the alternative substitutes of red concrete brick with the aim of reducing the cost of red concrete brick but has a quality that is not less good in red concrete brick. The use of concrete brick is considered more practical, economical and much in production with a relatively cheaper price variant [1]. *Fly ash* comes from coal combustion in steam power plants and an industrial waste that can cause negative impacts on the environment. Utilizing *fly ash* as raw material for a mix of concrete brick making is one solution to overcome it. Superior properties are owned by *fy ash*, such as: hardness, high strength and able to work well, so commonly applied in the field of construction, mechanical and chemical industry [2]. The purpose of this research is to know the composition of *fly ash* and the drying Time to density on concrete brick manufacturing and to determine the grouping based on the weight of the concrete brick.

2 Teoritis and Methods

Concrete brick is a material formed from a mixture of sand mixed with aggregate, cement and water to react perfectly. According to its shape, the concrete brick can be divided into two types, namely, hollow concrete brick and solid concrete brick. 28-day-old concrete brick has a physical weight of 12.128 kg, density of 2.118 gr / cm^{3,} water absorption of 12.876% and compressive strength of 1.97 MPa [3]. The effect of the use of *fly ash* on compressive strength and water absorption in mortar, obtained: the addition of *fly ash* with a certain percentage of the weight of the cement turned out to increase the compressive strength of mortar. The increase of compressive strength occurred at percentage of *fly ash* by 10% with compressive strength at age 56 days at 100,72 gr/cm^2 and projection of characteristic compressive strength at age 28 day equal to 66,69 gr/cm^2, at percentage *fly ash* of 20 % with a compressive strength at age 56 days of 93.96 gr/cm^2 and a projection of a characteristic compressive strength at age 28 days of 62.16 gr/cm^2, at a percentage of *fly ash* by 30% with compressive strength at age 56 days of 83 , 41 gr/cm^2 and projection of characteristic compressive strength at age 28 day was 55,17 gr/cm^2 and at percentage of *fly ash* 40% with compressive strength at age 56 day 70,12 gr/cm^2 and projection of compressive strength characteristic at 28 days age of 46.42 gr/cm^2. While on mortar withcontent, the *fly ash* 0%compressive strength of the age of 56 days was 59.89 gr/cm^2 and the projection of compressive strength was 28 days at 42,34 gr/cm^2 [4]. The mechanical properties of the concrete brick mixed with fly ash show the addition 5% *fly ash* resulting in a compressive strength of 20.76 MPa, 10% *fly ash the* result of compression strength 26.00 MPa, 15% *fly ash* obtained compression strength 22.40 MPa, while the normal concrete brick is without *fly ash* obtained the compressive strength 16.46

* Corresponding author: nurzall@gmail.com

 https://doi.org/10.1051/matecconf/201821501029

MPa [5]. Factors affecting the quality of concrete brick: a good concrete brick has a flat surface and perpendicular to each other and has a high compressive strength. Factors affecting the quality of the concrete brick are dependent on water cement factor, age, density, shape and rock structure and aggregate size on the concrete brick. Concrete brick is classified into 2 groups namely normal concrete brick and lightweight concrete brick. The normal concrete brick is classified as a concrete brick which has density of about 2.200 – 2.400 gr/cm^3, while for light concrete is a concrete brick that has density < 2.000 gr/cm^3 or lower and supported with maximum absorption 25% according to SNI 03-0349-1989 with a maximum compressive strength of 0.3 - 40 MPa [6].

Table 1. Concrete brick Quality [7]

NO.	Quality Requirement	Unit	Solid concrete brick Quality			
			I	II	III	IV
1	Bruto compressive strength and minimum average	Kg/cm^2	100	70	40	25
2	Bruto compressive strength of each specimen is minimum	Kg/cm^2	90	65	35	21
3	Maximum water absorption	%	25	35	-	-

Table 2. Terms of Standard Size and Concrete Brick Size Tolerance [7]

FA Composition (wt.%)	Cement (kg)	Sand (Fine Sand + Aggregate) (kg)	Fly Ash (kg)	Water (Liter)
0	30	463	0	30
5	30	439,85	23,49	45
10	30	416,7	44,67	54
15	30	393,55	63,53	63

Concrete brick has the following advantages

1. Concrete brick has a larger dimension of red brick so that the installation time is faster without having to be soaked before installation and installation cost is cheaper.
2. Making it easier without requiring burning process.
3. No need to be plastered if the workmanship is neat.
4. Can be made perforated for air ventilation and the possibility of water seepage is very small because it is watertight.

Disadvantages:

1. Easy to crack the hair on the wall.
2. Easy to be perforated and easily broken because there are holes on the inner side.
3. Less good for heat and sound insulation.

Composition Concrete brick

The composition for the manufacture of concrete brick work is as follows:

Table 3. Concrete brick composition for 70 spesimens

No	Type	dimensions (mm)			Minimum wall thickness (mm)	
		Length	Width	Height	outside	inside
1	Solid	390 ± 5	90 ± 2	100 ± 2	-	-
2	Hollow : Small	390 ± 5	190 ± 5	100 ± 2	20	15
	Large	390 ± 5	190 ± 5	200 ± 3	25	20

The production of a concrete brick wth composition 0 wt.% fly ash needed 0.42 kg of cement and 6.61 kg sand. For 5 wt.% fly ash used 0.004 kg cement, 6.23 kg sand and 0.38 kg fly ash.

Fig.1: Material used: (a) Fly ash, (b) Cement, (c) sand, and (d) Mineral Water

Shape and Size Specimens

Based on SNI SNI 03-0349-1989, Specimens were produced in the form of rectangular bar (length, L = 34 cm, width, B = 12 cm, thickness, W = 9 cm).

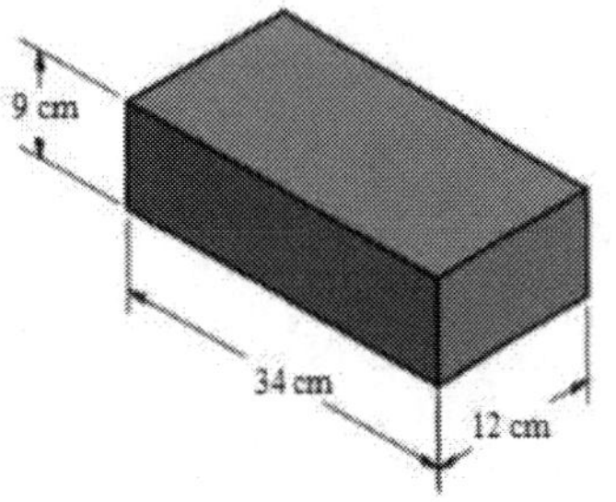

Fig.2: Shape and size of Concrete brick

Compaction Process

Base on the Composition of Materials concrete brick (Table3). The materials are manually mixing to homogeneous and flush with mineral water until it forms a paste after that into a mold concrete brick. The concrete brick compaction is done manually, then concrete brick was placed above the board and let it harden for 1 night and not exposed to direct sunlight to avoid cracking, after that concrete brick is dried in for 7, 14, 21, 28, and 35 days.

Density Test

Measureing density is used Archimedes method:

$$\text{Density} = \frac{W_u}{W_u - W_f} \cdot \rho_{air}$$

Where:

ρ_{water} = density of water = 1 g/cm^3
W_u = weight in air (g/cm^3)
W_f = weight in water (g/cm^3)

3 Results and Discussion

The 0 wt.% *fly ash, the* longer the drying time, the density increases, due to the chemical reaction between cement and water (hydration) which causes the brick to become hard after some time (water absorption increases, and compressive strength drops).

Tabel 4. Average Density

Fly Ash Composition (wt.%)	Average Density (gr/cm^3)				
	7 Days	14 Days	21 Days	28 Days	35 Days
0	1.962	1.970	1.983	1.993	2.000
5	1.978	2.208	2.220	2.230	1.953
10	1.985	1.986	2.053	2.001	1.948
15	1.992	1.984	1.975	1.967	1.946

Drying time of 7, 14, 21 days increased density value and reached maximum density value in 28 days drying time of 2,230 gr/cm^3, this happened at composition 5 wt.% *fly ash* and density value of brick decreased until 1,953 gr/cm^3 at drying 35 days. This result is similar to the research done by Tjokrodimulyo, 1995: on the addition of *fly ash* as much as 5 wt.% *fly ash* and the duration of drying of 28 days cement will have hardness reaching the maximum value can be known also from the bright cement color than before and also proven also from research [8].

The density increased from 1.985 to 2.053 gr/cm^3 on the drying time of 7, 14 and 21 days after that decreased density composition 10 wt.% fly ash. All densities in this composition are light brick categories.

The composition of 15 wt.% *fly ash* increased density value at 7 days drying time, which is the same because the water content is still high so the density value increases. In the old variation of drying 14 days with the variation of the composition there is an increase in density value at 5 wt.% composition and there is a decrease in density value in the composition of 10 and 15 wt.% *fly ash* This is caused by the hydration of cement and *fly ash* which causes heat so that bubbles arise produce gas to produce pores that make concrete brick progressively lighter. In the long variation of drying of 21 days, 28 days and 35 days the same increase of density value in 5 wt.% *fly ash* and degradation of 10 and 15 wt.% *fly ash value.* This is due to the decreasing density due to the grain factor of the sample, the pore, and the composition of the material itself. Aggregate items may be less strong because of two things that are composed of weak materials or composed of strong but not good particles in the binder [9].

The pores on the concrete brick are caused by fly ash particle size smaller than the size of the cement particles will cover the pores that cause the lighter concrete brick. In the chart obtained density value 1.946-2.230 gr/cm^3. The density values of 1.946-2.000 gr/cm^3 include the light concrete brick category and the density value of 2.200-2.230 gr/cm^3 the normal concrete brick category while the density value 2.001-2.053 gr/cm^3 was in the category between light concrete brick and concrete brick normal.

4 Conclusion

The results of the research can be concluded as follows:

1. the composition of 5 wt.% fly ash with 28 days drying time was found to be the highest density with 2,230 gr/cm^3, while the lowest density in the composition test was 15 wt.% fly ash with 35 days drying time with the density 1,946 gr/cm^3.
2. The density of normal concrete brick density with density 2,208-2,230 gr/cm^3 and light concrete brick density of 2,000-1,946 gr/cm^3, and also found a normal and light concrete brick category that is 2,022-2,053 gr/cm^3.

References

1. Sagel, Ing R et al (1994). Guidelines for Concrete Work. Erlangga Publishers, Jakarta.
2. Boccacini, AK, (1995) Glass-Ceramics from Filter Dust from Waste Incinerators. Cramics International Journal, 21, 231-235.
3. Darmono (2009) Penerapan Teknologi Produksi Bahan Bangunan Berbahan Pasir Bagi Korban Gempa Di Kulonprogo Serta Analisis Mutu Dan Ekonominya. Fakultas Teknik Universitas Negeri Yogyakarta
4. Andoyo (2006). The Influence of Fly Ash's Uses of Pressure and Water Absorption on Mortar. Unpublished Undergraduade Thesis, Semarang State University.
5. Siagian, Henok and Dermawan Agus (2011) Tests of Concrete brick Mixed Mechanics of Fly Ashes
6. Neville, A.M and Broks, JJ (1987) 'Concrete Technology.' Longman Scientific & Technical, London
7. Indonesian National Standard (SNI) 03-0349-1989 Concrete Concrete brick for Couple Wall.
8. Tjokrodimuljo, Kardiyono (1995) 'Concrete Technology. Yogyakarta
9. Mulyono, T., (2008) Concrete Technology, Andi Publisher, Yogyakarta. Indonesian Concrete Regulation (PBI, 1971) About Aggregates

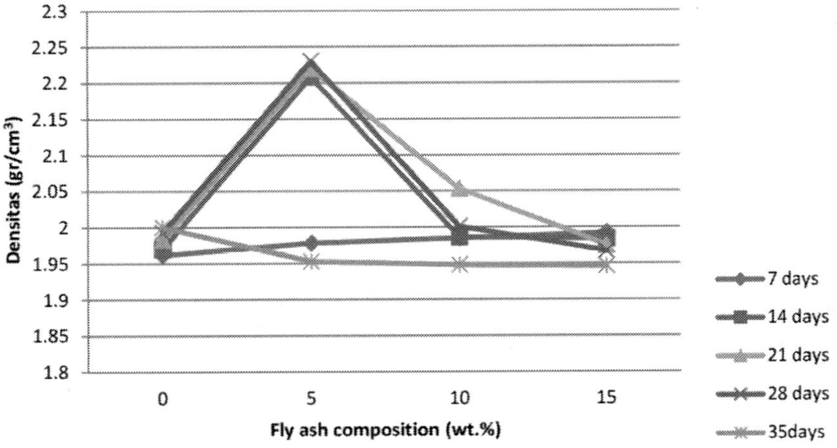

Fig. 3: Relationship fly ash composition with density

MATEC Web of Conferences **215**, 01030 (2018) https://doi.org/10.1051/matecconf/201821501030
ICTIS 2018

Experimental Tests and Analytical Studies of Bearing-Type Axial Steel Connection

Yosafat Aji Pranata*, Noek Sulandari, Roi Milyardi

Department of Civil Engineering, Universitas Kristen Maranatha, Indonesia

Abstract. The capacity of the bolted connection on steel tensile rods can be determined through capacity analysis and connection failure. In term of capacity analysis and failure of steel tensile connection, the specified tensile connection capacity is generated based on several parameters such as cross-section of rod, grade of steel, thickness and grade of the steel plate, and grade and diameter of bolts. The capacity of steel tensile connections as a result of capacity analysis and connection failure often has a lower value than the connection capacity in real conditions. In this research, the comparison of 30x30x3mm angle cross-section connections with BJ37 grade quality was connected with 2 mm steel plate (also BJ37 grade) using 8 mm bolt connectors (A307 grade), through capacity analysis, failure study, and experimental study with type of failure is bolt bearing failure. In the capacity analysis study and the failure of steel tensile connections obtained a nominal capacity is 14.21 kN with the type of failure is shear failure. In the experimental study was tested 3 specimens, the average value of ultimate capacity was 18.67 kN and the failure for all of the three specimens are shear failures. The conclusion that can be drawn from this research is both the result of analytical calculations and experimental testing in the laboratory showed a good agreement and have the same trend. The test specimens were designed on the basis of analytical calculations for bolt bearing failure, experimental test results for all of three specimens all showed a failure pattern of bolt shear. The nominal strength from the results of the analytical study with the ultimate load of the experimental study results has a difference of 31.4% with higher experimental results. Through this research is expected to be a learning-media to know one type of failure on the steel connections that is bolt shear failure, obtain a comparison between analytical calculation results referring to applicable design standards, and the results of experimental testing in the laboratory.

Introduction

Steel is widely used in the bridge structure, which is specifically a bridge with a type of truss structure as shown in Figure 1. The truss structure transmits axial forces acting like tensile and compressive forces through their components. The rod components that make up the truss are interconnected to each join with the pin type (not holding the moment or shear). The connection between components can be connected using a steel plate (side) and a mechanical connector such as bolt. The axial joint system of the tensile rods of steel comprises several types of failure probabilities, which are tensile, shear (bolt failure), bearing, and block shear types [1,4,6]. The type of tensile failure is failure occurs in the drag rod, the type of shear failure is a failure occurs on the bolt, the type of failure of the bearing is a failure occurs due to the bolt effect on the hole connection, as long as the combination of block shear type is a failure occurs in the block shear. The tensile strength of the steel tensile joints can be determined through capacity analysis and connection failure, inter alia referring to the regulations of SNI 1729: 2015 [4] or AISC 360-16 [1]. The connectivity capacity is determined based on several structural parameters such as the cross-section type and the grade of steel, the thickness and grade of the connecting plate, and the diameter and grade of the connection bolts. The capacity of steel tensile joint connections resulting from capacity analysis and connection failure often has a lower value than the connection capacity in real conditions.

Figure 1 Truss Steel bridge [5].

* Corresponding author: yosafat.ap@eng.maranatha.edu

The objective of the study is to study the strength capacity of axial joint of steel tensile connection by analytical method and experimental testing in the laboratory. The scope of the research is the test object that is observed is the axial connection of the pull rod, the loading method is uniaxial tensile, the number of specimens are three specimens, the test using Universal Testing Machine, in analytical calculation used assumption of 240 MPa for yield strength and 370 MPa of ultimate strength, the failure to be observed is the bolt failure on the bolt hole, the cross-section of the steel is the angle L30.30.3, the bolt used is 8 mm diameter and A307 grade.

2 Basic Theory

The analysis of the strength of steel tensile joints using bolts is based on SNI 1729:2015 [4]. The equations that must be met according to the LRFD (Load Resistance Factor Design) or in Indonesian called DFBK (Desain Faktor Beban Ketahanan) method. The strength according to the melting limit of the gross cross section in accordance with SNI 1729: 2015 Chapter D2 (a) (Equation 1).

$$\phi R_n = \phi \times F_y \times A_g \qquad (1)$$

Which are:

ϕ = resistance factor for tensile yield limit, 0,90
F_y = yield strength of steel
A_g = gross cross-section of steel rod

The strength of the pull rod according to the limit of collapse on the net section in accordance with SNI 1729: 2015 Chapter D2 (b) is shown by Equation 2.

$$\phi R_n = \phi \times F_u \times A_e \qquad (2)$$

Which are:

ϕ = resistance factor for tensile ultimate limit, 0,75
F_u = ultimate strength of steel
A_e = net cross-section of steel rod

The effective net width (A_e) is calculated following the provisions of SNI 1729: 2015 Chapter D3, as in Equation (3) and Equation (4).

$$A_e = U \times A_n$$

$$U = 1 - x / l$$

Which are:

U = shear lag factor
x = excentricity of connection
l = length of connection

The net width of the trunk section cross section (A_n) is calculated following the provisions of SNI 1729: 2015 Chapter B4.3, which can be written as Eq. (5).

$$A_n = A_g - n \times d \times t$$

Which are:

n = number of bolt in the line of tensile failure
d = hole diameter for net cross-section of tensile rod
t = thickness of plate

The strength of the bolt shear at the pivot type connection, according to SNI 1729:2015 Chapter J3.6 is shown by Equation 6.

$$\phi R_n = \phi \times F_{nv} \times A_b$$

Which are:

ϕ = resistance factor for shear of bolt 0.75
F_{nv} = nominal shear stress of bolt
A_b = nominal cross-section of bolt

The strength of the bolt hole (ϕR_n), according to SNI 1729:2015 Chapter J3.10 (a) is shown by Equation 7.

$$R_n = 1.2 \times l_c \times t \times F_u \leq 2{,}4 \times d_b \times t \times F_u$$

Which are:

ϕ = resistance factor in term of bearing strength 0.75
l_c = clear distance hole to hole
d_b = bolt diameter

The shear strength of the block (ϕR_n) on the steel rod joints, in accordance with SNI 1729:2015 Chapter J4.3 is shown by Equation 8.

$$R_n = 0.6 \times F_u \times A_{nv} + U_{bs} \times F_u \times A_{nt} \leq 0.6 \times F_y \times A_{gv} + U_{bs} \times F_u \times A_{nt}$$

Which are:

ϕ = resistance factor in term of block shear 0,75
A_{nt} = tensile net area
R_n = nominal strength
A_{nv} = shear net area
A_{gv} = gross area
U_{bs} = reduction coefficient for block shear failure

Experimental tests of tensile strength of tensile bars are based on ASTM E8 / E8M - 16a Standard Test Methods for Tension Testing of Metallic Materials (ASTM, 2016) with a crosshead test rate of 0.015 mm/mm/min. Figure 2 shows the Universal Testing Machine (UTM) used for experimental testing.

Fig. 2. Universal Testing Machine for tensile testing of steel joints.

3 Case Study

In this study, the steel tensile beam test of the elbow profile is equal to the quality foot BJ-37 size 30x30x3mm spliced with BJ-37 thickness steel plate 3 mm using A307 diameter bolt 8 mm diameter which has the connection configuration as shown in Figure 3. With the configuration of steel tie rod connections such as shown in Figure 2, two models of study were studied: an analytical study of the strength of steel tapered joints using bolts according to the DFBK method determined by SNI 1729:2015 and experimental studies of steel tensile joints testing using bolts in the laboratory.

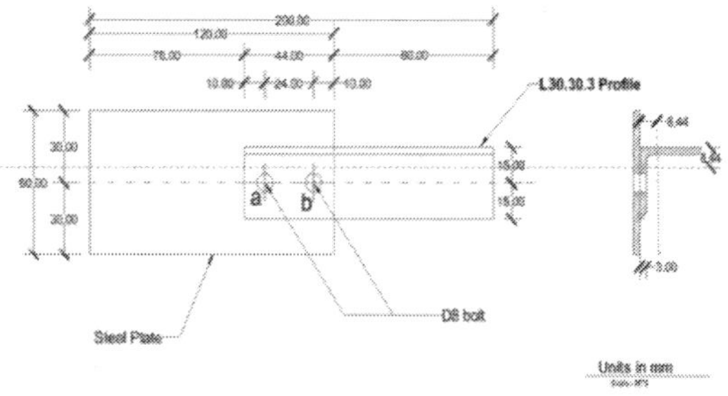

Fig. 3. Configuration of axial tensile steel connection

3.1 Analytical Study

The strength of the angle (L) rod according to the yield and the ultimate limits calculated according to Equation 1 to Eq. 5, the following results are obtained: Strength of the stem according to the melting limit conditions:

ϕ $R_n = 0.90 \text{ x } F_y \text{ x } A_g = 37303$ N

The strength of the stem according to the boundary condition of pull collapse:

ϕ $R_n = 0.75 \text{ x } F_u \text{ x } A_e = 24594$ N

The strength of the bolt shear at the base-type connection is calculated according to Equation 6, with the following results: Sliding strength of connection using 2 pieces of bolts:

ϕ $R_n = 0.75 \text{ x } n_{baut} \text{ x } F_{nv} \text{ x } A_b = 18900$ N

The strength of the bolt hole base is calculated according to Equation 7. For this calculation it is necessary to determine the net distance (lc) between the edges of the bolt a to the edge of the tied rod and the edge of the bolt a and bolt b as shown in Figure 3.

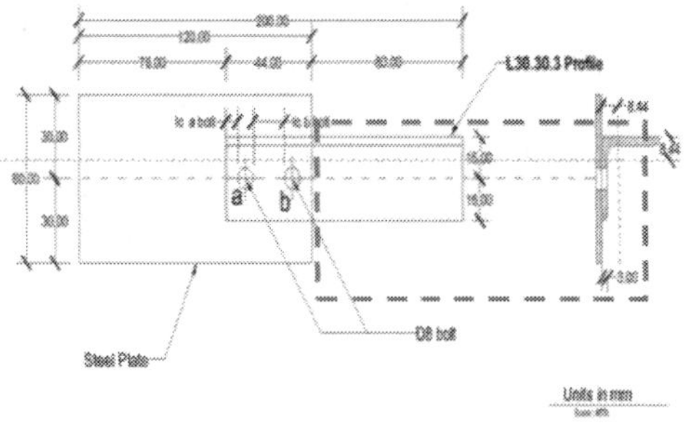

Fig. 4. Determine the clear distance (l_c) hole to hole of bolts

The strength of the bolt hole:

$R_n = 1.2 \text{ x } l_c \text{ x t x } F_u \leq 2.4 \text{ x } d_b \text{ x } t \text{ x } F_u$

bolt a:	3552	≤	1420 8	→	R_{na} =	3553	N
boltt b:	1065 6	≤	1420 8	→	R_{nb} =	1065 6	N

so:	R_n =	R_{na} + R_{nb}					
	R_n =	14208	N N	and		ϕ R_n = 10656	

The shear strength of the steel tank trunk connection joints is calculated according to Equation 8. The determination of the sliding block area is shown in Figure 4.

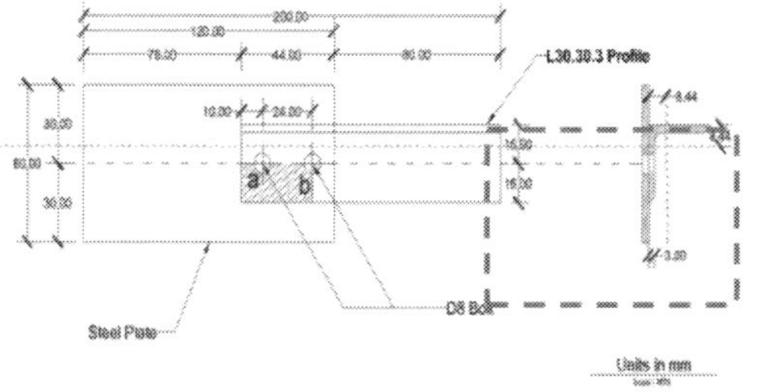

Fig. 5. Determining the block shear

Block shear strength:

$R_n = 0.6 \text{ x } F_u \text{ x } A_{nv} + U_{bs} \text{ x } F_u \text{ x } A_{nt} \leq 0.6 \text{ x } F_y \text{ x } A_{gv} + U_{bs} \text{ x } F_u \text{ x } A_{nt}$

Fracture:	$0.6 \text{ x } F_u \text{ x } A_{nv} + U_{bs} \text{ x } F_u \text{ x } A_{nt}$	=	20646	N
Yield:	$0.6 \text{ x } F_y \text{ x } A_{gv} + U_{bs} \text{ x } F_u \text{ x } A_{nt}$	=	24678	N

The smallest value that determines, so R_n = 20646 N and ϕ R_n = 15485 N.

Table 1. Strength/Capacity of Steel Axial Connection

Analysis	ϕ R_n (kN)	R_n (kN)	Summary
Yield Tensile Strength	37.30	41.45	-
Ultimate Tensile Strength	24.59	32.79	-
Bolt Shear Strength	18.90	25.20	-
Bearing Strength	10.66	14.21	Critical
Block Shear Strength	15.49	20.65	-

The summary of the tensile steel tie connection capacity is shown in Table 1, which is based on the analytical calculation of the capacity of the melting yield limit, the ultimate strength, the bolt strength, the bolt hole or bearing strength, and the block shear strength. From the analytical study, the configuration of the joints in this study as shown in Figure 1 has a limit of 14.21 kN (without ϕ).

3.2 Experimental Study

In the experimental study testing of steel tensile joints were prepared 3 specimens according to the configuration of Figure 1. Tensile tests were performed using Universal Testing Machine (UTM). On specimens welded a special clamp of stainless-steel material to ensure the steel connection receives an axial force optimally as shown in Figure 6. Before tensile testing begins, the three test objects are erect on the bolts so that all trimmed steel rod joint elements can work optimally to load. The initial conditions of the three test pieces of steel tug joints are shown in Figure 6. Tensile testing is performed on each connection with axial force axial force of 5mm/min until each specimen fails due to the axial force of attraction received. The tensile test results are shown in Figure 7.

In Figure 8, the three specimens experience a failure on the plate according to the predicted of the analytical study. Tensile test result, obtained load curve to deformation (P-D curve). From the P-D curve we get the proportional limit load value (P_y) and the ultimate load value (P_u) of the steel tensile bearing test specimen shown in Figure 9 and Table 2.

Fig. 6. Setup of specimen on Universal Testing Machine (UTM)

(a) Specimen 1 (b) Specimen 2 (c) Specimen 3

Figure 7 All of 3 (three) specimens.

(a) Specimen 1 (b) Specimen 2 (c) Specimen 3

Fig. 8. Failure of 3 (three) specimens

From Table 2 we get the average value of the three test pieces of steel tug joints. For a proportional limit load (P_y) of 12872.33 N and for ultimate load (P_u) of 18669.33 N. Design limit (R_n) of analytical study results of 14.21 kN or 14208 N (without ϕ). When compared with the ultimate load value of the experimental (P_u) experimental results on average of 3 (three) specimens is 18669.33 N means that the experimental study results have 31.40% greater value.

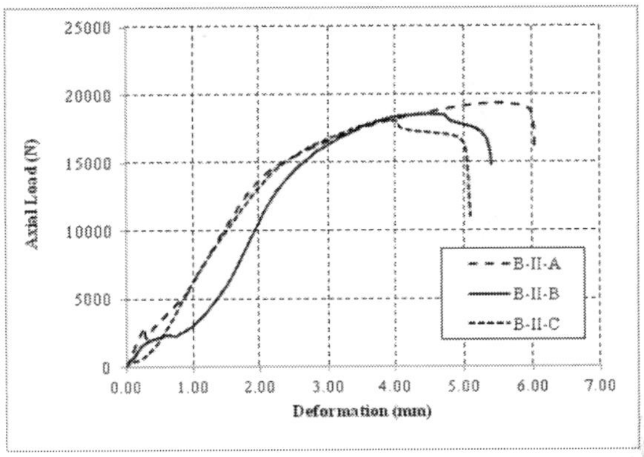

Fig. 9. P-D curves of Steel Axial Connection Specimen

Table 2 Results of Proportional (P_y) and Ultimate (P_u) Loads

Specimen	P_y (N)	D_y (mm)	P_u (N)	D_u (mm)
B-II-A	11565.42	1.65	19376.36	5.47
B-II-B	15231.94	2.70	18581.79	4.48
B-II-C	11819.64	1.77	18049.83	3.86
Average	12872.33	2.04	18669.33	4.60

4 Conclusion

The conclusions that can be obtained from this research are both the result of analytical calculations and experimental testing in the laboratory showed a good agreement and the same trend. The test specimen was designed on the basis of analytical calculations for bolt bearing failure, experimental test results for 3 (three) test specimens all showed a failure pattern of bolt shear. The nominal strength of the analytical study with the ultimate load of the experimental study results has a difference of 31.4% with higher experimental results. Through this research is expected to be a learning-media to know one type of failure on the steel connections that is bolt shear failure, obtain a comparison of analytical calculation results referring to applicable planning standards and the results of experimental testing in the laboratory.

References

1. American Institute of Steel Construction, ANSI/AISC 360-16, Specification for Structural Steel Buildings, American Institute of Steel Construction, (2016).
2. American Society for Testing and Material, ASTM E8/E8M–16a Standard Test Methods for Tension Testing of Metallic Materials, American Society for Testing and Material, (2016).
3. W. Dewobroto, Struktur Baja Perilaku, Analisis dan Desain - AISC 2010 Edisi ke-2, Penerbit Jurusan Teknik Sipil UPH, Tangerang (*in Indonesian*), (2016).
4. Badan Standardisasi Nasional, SNI 1729:2015 Spesifikasi Untuk Bangunan Gedung Baja Struktural, Badan Standardisasi Nasional, Jakarta (*in Indonesian*), (2015).
5. W.T. Segui, Steel Design, 6th Edition, (Cengage Learning, 2018).
6. N. Sulandari, R. Milyardi, Y.A. Pranata, Studi Eksperimental dan Analitis Kapasitas Sambungan Baja Batang Tarik dengan Tipe Kegagalan Geser Baut, Jurnal Teknik Sipil, Volume **13** Nomor 1 (*in Indonesian*), (2017).URL: http://www.dijkstaal.nl/en/projects/steel-bridges/modular-steel-truss-bridges.

https://doi.org/10.1051/matecconf/201821501031

Procurement management/ material supply on construction projects

Maksum Tanubrata[1*], *Ika* Gunawan[2]

[1] Maranatha Christian University, Faculty of Engineering, Department of Civil Engineering, Bandung, Indonesia,
[2] Maranatha Christian University, Faculty of Economics, Department of Management, Bandung, Indonesia

Abstract. Material inventory management is one part of the logistics system devoted to project implementation on material procurement as per the needs plan procurement management is a very important material function, since the material inventory for a construction project involves a considerable investment cost. In general, every construction project involves complex activities, which involves the sharing of activities and operations. Material acquisition activities require good planning and control considering the large percentage of material costs to the total cost of the project. So if less effective material handling will result in loss of time, cost and quality. then this should receive high attention from contractors for the smooth and performance to be achieved in the implementation of construction projects.

1 Introduction

Material management is intended to support in order to ensure the smooth and efficient implementation of construction projects. The material management objectives include first, buy at a cheap price. Material management aims to buy materials at good and cheap prices. Material management aims to buy materials at a good price. A good price is not always a cheap price in the market. The price is the price that includes discounts and transportation to the project site. Secondly, Product material. Material dating at the right time with the amount and quality that fit with the minimum cost plan. Thirdly, Success delivery Concerning work activities related directly to time and cost. Activities related to those objectives are binding the vendor's efforts to implement on an agreed schedule. Fourthly, Relationships with vendors, good relationships with vendors will provide improved service to contractors. Fifthly, Material storage is an activity to manage inventory of material in a storage area. Material acceptance must conform to the specified order specifications. Sixthly, material use basically the material usage required can be fulfilled in accordance with the time required. Seventhly, material and material quality much happens at the time of delivery of materials by vendors, incompatible with specified specifications and material damage. Then the task of material management to be able to determine the quality of the vendor. Lastly, administration system providing effective and efficient administration logistic services [1, 2].

A material management organization on a construction project, completed by a section of the organization that can perform its work according to the required functions in an integrated manner. The shape of the material management organization structure is like the picture below. The duties and responsibilities of each part of the organization are as follows [1]:

1. Practical analysis of material needs (make material requirements analysis) and determine the amount of material inventory.
2. Material ordering section (control the ordering of materials as needed and booking according to frequency based on the number of needs in each period).
3. Material Control and Control Section (report the material state on the purchasing department, prepare the schedule and delivery of materials from the source on the project, supervise the delivery of materials, supervise material compilation and supervise the distribution of materials).
4. The material budget section (record the cost of material expenditure, payment to vendor, and provide a report on the logistics section).
5. Parts of materials warehouse (material acceptance and material distribution)

2 Procurement Material

Material inventory is a process of activity where a number of materials are placed in stock to anticipate material needs and market conditions for a certain period so as to ensure the continuity of completion of work activities. A construction project will not run smoothly if it does not use inventory systems and controlled materials to meet the needs. But if the inventory is too large will be detrimental, otherwise if the material inventory is too small also not profitable contractor.

2.1 Factors affecting material procurement

* Corresponding author: maksum.tanubrata150@gmail.com

The main factor factors that influence and materials for a construction project there are several kinds that will be inter-related in the process. The factor is [2-4]:

1. Estimated usage, Prior to material purchases the planning is carried out including the estimated material used including storage as well as ordering in the construction project implementation according to the timetable and the applicable type of work.
2. Determination of expenditure, the amount of material inventory depends on the determination of the amount of expenditure specified in the schedule of material inventory.
3. Lead Time / waiting time, charging time is the time required between material ordering with the arrival of material in order to minimize the cost opportunity loss.
4. The actual material use, information on the characteristics of the results of similar material use from the period may be one of the factors that need attention.
5. Market situation, the condition of a material on the market needs to be considered in the supply of materials, because the completeness of the material in the market is not always appropriate material inventory, because the completeness of the material in the market does not always match the applicable inventory. This situation must be implemented by purchasing materials in large enough quantities but optimum for the project.
6. Economic situation and condition, situations and economic conditions that may affect the targets in the planning that do not specify the needs and disadvantages for the project.
7. Warehousing conditions, wide access and warehouse conditions need to be planned so that it is easy to make acceptance, storage, distribution and administration of material management effective.

2.2 Procurement arrangements of materials

Procurement arrangements include:

1. Material selection. Factor factors to consider: (a) Material must not be ordered at a particular vendor without the permission of the consultant planner. (b) All materials must meet the technical requirements of the implementation of work and other technical regulations such as construction regulations, building materials regulations as a reference for planning. (c) The shape, size, placement and installation should be in accordance with the planning and the previous measurement.
2. Material handling Activities include: (a) Material storage. Storage of materials must meet the conditions free of any kind of a damage caused by the accumulation, transportation, demolition of work activities, traffic and security disturbances. (b) Material protection, materials shall be protected from any kind of damage, contamination, staining, discoloration or shape from the time of transportation, lifting, storage, workmanship and installation. (c) Material acceptance, any arrival of material on the field shall be notified to the supervisory consultant, to be subject to prompt review and quality requirements as well as any material must be guaranteed or guaranteed by holding a guarantee or guarantee.
3. Material distribution. The material distribution activity involves moving material from storage to the required material work location with several processes: (a) administration process, (b) information delivery process, (c) expense process, and (d) transportation process

2.3 Material Cost Control Process

Material controls meet the accuracy, identification of timeliness and control of all materials required, from design to receipt of materials in the field. Good material control is consistent, comprehensive, and supportive at the time of procurement and during construction. In material management control there are several things to note:

1. Material demand. The material request begins with applying to the purchasing department in case in the owner is required to procure the necessary materials. Reservations must clearly state what is needed to ensure the right materials. Orders must include all information required by the bidder to calculate material costs, such information as: the need for delivery schedules, packing, delivery to the location, transportation used.
2. Check the truth of material acceptance. The material ordered to the supplier, concerning the quantity, variety and quality of the material must be verified. If not suitable or less, then the buyer can return the goods, and the lack of material can be disordered again.
3. Stock control. The function of a stock control is to provide the required goods in quantity of quality in accordance with the time specified by the cost and the most economical way.
4. Storage and material safeguards. Storage control is required to make an estimate of the need the future, where additional stock material information about the state of the material deposited onto the field is entrusted to the shift agent. To reduce high storage costs, materials such as reinforcement are stored outside the warehouse. Material losses can be minimized by setting up sufficient materials of light, the presence of guards or security guards, the location of parkers far enough away from the warehouse. Vehicles and people should not have easy access to the warehouse. Employed employees are employees with good records.

2.4 Schedule of the preparation

Schedules is an important factor in construction activity, as it provides an overview of the time-related work required to complete the project. The fault of project schedule creation can make project completion longer which impacts the budget spike like overhead cost. There are several things that need to be considered:

1. Schedule covers the entire work. When scheduling, it should first describe the type of work to be done with consideration of the interrelationship between the work of one to another, so it can describe the relationship between the activities and the time required on each work item.
2. Schedule must be an activity and cost. Each project activity to do the work requires a fee, including labor costs, equipment rental fees, and overhead costs.
3. The schedule should be easy to understand and easy to use. Includes plans, drawings or specifications that should be read by more than one person and considered as a prefix for communicating information in a language that is easy to understand. In this case the networking method is used.

2.5 Networking

Complete system in preparing network as follows: (1) Identify the project environment and a describe it as component of the activity component. (2) Component activities in the order of dependence logic into network work. (3) Provide the period of each activity. (4) Identify critical path, float, and projects completion period. (5) Improving the usability and utilization of resources.

Networking benefits: (1) Estimate the most economical project schedule. (2) Seek minimal fluctuations in resource use. (3) Complete the sequence of project activities that have a large number of components with complex dependencies. (4) Can find out the length of time estimation of projects completion period

2.6 Preparation of materials

A list of materials was created to make it easier for the planner to see the details of the type of material to be used during the construction project. Details consist of:

1. Time or when the material will be used. A description of the time of material use is required so that the executor can estimate when ordering or purchasing a material should be done. It is intended that ordering or purchasing materials is not done too quickly which eventually cause the material buried in the project location because it is not the time to be used or used.
2. The amount of material required for each material. The amount of each material needs is very useful. By knowing the amount of material used, the implementer can estimate the amount of cost required for material procurement.
3. The relevance of the material to the material. The main purpose of this linkage is to enable the executor to know what kind of material to order and what material does not need to be ordered.

3 Discussion

3.1 Material history Requirement Planning (MRP)

MRP began to be used widely in production management activities since the early 1970s in line with the growing computer and growing with the discovery of various other new concept concepts. This concept first appeared in the manufacturing industry with the characteristics of each period of activity is a process of repetition (representative). Material Requirement Planning (MRP) is a method used to plan the material thoroughly according to the data needs that are influenced by the level of inventory at hand and the acceptance schedule based on the time stages when the material is needed. Data required for Materials Requirement Planning (MRP) method are:

1. Master Schedule (planning a schedule)
2. Bill of material (type, quantity and material specification)
3. Lead time
4. Terms of demand for goods
5. The amount of inventory that still exists.
6. The number of mini8mum items specified.

3.2 Definition of Material Requirement Planning (MRP)

According to M. Syamsul Ma'arif et al, in production, MRP is regarded as a life view in manufacturing business management [5]. Besides that, MRP is a system of planning and scheduling of material needs for production that require several stages of the process or in other words production plans for a number of finished products that translated into raw materials needed by using leisure time (lead time) so that can be determined when and how many are ordered for each component of a product made.

The lot for lot a method (LFL) is an approach using the concept on the basis of a discrete ordering with consideration of minimization of the shipping cost, the ordered quantity equals the required amount.

The fixed period requirement (FPR) method is an approach using the concept of a lot of size with a fixed period, where reservations are made a based on a certain period of time. Gross requirement is the requirement of iron material obtained from bill of quantity. The net requirement is the need for gross material reduced by the stock of existing materials.

3.3 Ability of MRP System

There are four capabilities that become the main feature of MRP's system:

1. Be able to determine the needs at the right time. The point is to determine precisely, when, a job is

completed or when material should be available on a planned schedule.

2. Establish minimum requirements on each item. Knowing the need for finished products, material requirement planning (MRP) can precisely determine the scheduling system (based on priority) to meet all minimum requirements of each component item.
3. Determine the implementation of the booking plan. The point is to give an indication of when the booking or cancellation of the booking must be made, either ordering outside or made by yourself.
4. Determine the rescheduling or preparing of a planned schedule.

4 Conclusion

Procurement management is urgently needed on a construction project implementation and need for further explanation about procurement / supply of goods by MRP (Material Requirement Planning)

References

1. A. Sofyan. Production and Operations Management, Rev. edition. (LPFE-UI, Jakarta, 1999)
2. M. Lubis, Development of Prototype Electronic Procurement System (E-procurement) for construction project, master's thesis, Yogyakarta: Islamic University of Bandung. (2006)
3. R, Freddy. Manajemen inventory application in the field of business, management, (PT King Grafindo Persada, Jakarta, 1995).
4. R. Barry, J. Heizer, Principles of operations management. (PT Salemba Emban Patria, Jakarta, 2001)
5. M.S. Ma'arif, H. Tanjung, Manajemen Operasi, (Grasindo, Indonesia, 2003)

Design of Structural Damage Identification Applications Web-Based

Anisya Anisya[1], *Fajar* Nugroho[2]

[1]Institut Teknologi Padang, Department of Informatics Engineering, Padang, Indonesia
[2]Institut Teknologi Padang, Department of Civil Engineering, Padang, Indonesia

Abstract. The current building construction and maintenance Note well, certainly will be utilized as desired. If a building is experiencing interference, then all activities will be obstructed so that the building requires maintenance activities. Building maintenance activities include the maintenance of the structure, architectural, mechanical, electrical, and outer space. On systems that are running now the surveyor directly monitor to location which requires a fee and take a long time. Technology websites that are built can be used for building maintenance activities in the form of a data string entered by the Manager of the building and the response of the Contracting Party. With this technology produces a system that can help in the process of monitoring a building that suffered damage and need repair.

1 Introduction

Buildings have a very important function for human life, especially to perform daily activities so that buildings need to be done in order for the building's maintenance are able to stand up well in a long period. As stated in the regulation of the Minister of public works number: 24/PRT/M/2008 about the guidelines of building maintenance and upkeep of buildings in Indonesia then any required maintenance. As for the aspect to note in maintenance of the building is aspects of architecture, structures, mechanicals, electricals, and outers space [1].

Building maintenance management is often related to the innovative strategy and future sustainability. Various working methods are introduced to the performance of building maintenance management [2]. Maintenance is often defined as the series of activities undertaken either care of the building structure and services to ensure the intended functions and optimal performance of a building's life cycle [3].

Maintenance of the building serves to maintain the physical buildings as well as the age of the building in accordance with plans. Construction of new buildings is generally not accompanied by an increase in maintenance activities. Usually one cause is less planning of a maintenance system and good supervision [4]. Maintenance is a way to safeguard the condition of buildings in order to be always in good shape fit function [5]. Building maintenance activities that cause an inadequate building suffered damage over time [6]. In fact less maintenance activities observed by the owner of the building. According to Labombang in Thohir [7] maintenance activities less observed because of several factors, including: maintenance activities seen not urgent compared with development activities, organizational structure maintenance is not always there [8], and the Facility Manager assumes that the maintenance building is just a technical issue that is not related to the purpose of the function of the building as you wish.

In each building, surely the presence of the Manager of the building. With this, the building manager also has full responsibility will be building maintenance. Because if there's anything the incident or event digedung, the first party which asked for responsibility is the Manager of the building. Over time, many changes in both physically on a building that is already so. A Building manager when performing maintenance activities, A building manager should report to the construction workers about the damage parts of what happened to the building manager. Every building manager has a complaint of damage to the building as evidence of logging reports of damage to buildings of a building manager. On the current state of each building are using telephone communication Manager to report any damage to the building contractors. With the condition that occurs when this causes reporting history missing for granted so that the recording and reporting of damage to the building could not be controlled, because of the lack of a history or record of the inspection history of the building.

From the explanation above, the authors conducted a study to design applications Web-based reporting of damage to buildings that only focuses on the structure of the building.

* Corresponding author: nisa.anisya@gmail.com

2 Building Maintenance

In each building, surely the presence of the Manager of the building. With this, a building manager also has full responsibility will be building maintenance. Because if there's anything the incident or event in building, the first party which asked for responsibility is the Manager of the building. Over time, many changes in both physically on a building that is already so. A building manager when performing maintenance activities, a building manager should report to the construction workers about the damage parts of what happened to the building manager. Every building manager has a complaint of damage to the building as evidence of logging reports of damage to buildings of the building manager. On the current state of each building using telephone communication Manager to report any damage to the building contractors. With the condition that occurs when this causes reporting history missing for granted so that the recording and reporting of damage to the building could not be controlled, because of the lack of a history or record of the inspection history of the building.

From the explanation above, the authors conducted a study to design applications Web-based reporting of damage to buildings that only focuses on the structure of the building.

Several theories related to this research are:

a. Building

Building is the physical manifestation of human work Copyright its main function is as a place of human activity at once limiting or a patron of the influence of the outside environment. According to the law – the Republic of Indonesia number 28 in 2002 about the Building. The building is defined as a form of physical work of construction that blends in with its position, as a place of human conduct its activities, for the residence, religious activities, business activities, social and cultural activities, and special events [8].

b. Purpose of the maintenance

Generally, the main objective of the maintenance process is: [6]

- To extend the age of buildings
- To ensure the availability of equipment and also benefit from the investment of a maximum
- To ensure the safety of humans who use the building.
- To ensure readiness of the Operational of any equipment or supplies in the face of emergency situations such as fire

c. Component maintenance building

The scope of the care and maintenance of the building, among others, are: [4]

- Architectural
- Structural
- Mechanical (Manage of Water, Sanitation, Plambing and Transportation)
- Electrical (power supply, Lighting, telephone, communication and Alarm)
- Maid (housekeeping).

d. The categories of building damage

According to John OE in Malitha [9], there are 5 (five) different kinds of categories damage to the structure of a building that is as follows:

- Light damage to a building non-structure
  A building zoned non-structure suffered damage when things happen as follows:
  1. Cracks smooth (the width of the gap is smaller than 0.075 cm)
  2. On the stucco plastering tumbling Flakes
  3. Include a limited breadth

  The action that needs to be done is repair (repair) in architecture without emptying the building.

- Damage to Light the structure of a building zoned
  Light level structure suffered damage when things happen as follows:
  a. small Crack (the width of the gap between 0.075 to 0.60) at Plaster wall
  b. loose and tumbling
  c. Includes spacious great
  d. damage to those parts of non-like structures on the chimney, lipstank, etc
  e. ability to shoulder the load of the structure not much diminished.
  f. be eligible function
  The action that needs to be done is repair (repair) is the architecture so that the endurance
  the buildings remain preserved. Repair with mild damage on the structure can be done without emptying the building.

- Damage to the structure of the medium level
  Medium Level Structure Damage happen when things as follows:
  1. large Crack (the width of the gap is greater than 0.60 cm) on the wall
  2. Cracks in many places, such as the load carrier walls, columns, chimneys, tilt and collapse.
  3. the ability of the structure to bear the burden of already reduced most
  4. be eligible function

  Actions you need to do is:
  1. Recovery of parts of structures in retaining (strengthening) to withstand earthquake loads
  2. Repair (repair) in architecture
  3. Buildings emptied and can be inhabited again after the restoration process is finished

- Damage to the structure of the level weight

  A building zoned heavy levels of structure damage if things happen as the following:
  1. Wall bearers load split and collapse
  2. separate buildings due to the failure of the elements of a binding element.
  3. approximately 50% of the main elements of damage
  4. Not be eligible function

  The action that needs to be done is to destroy the building or done restoration and thoroughly before retaining the building habitable again. In conditions of damage such as this, the building became very dangerous, so it must be emptied.

- The Total Damage

  A building classified as damaged total/fallen if things happen as follows:
  1. fallen Buildings entirely (>65%)
  2. most of the major components of the structure of the damaged
  3. does not qualify function

  The action that needs to be done is to destroy the buildings, clean up the site, and set up the new building.

c. Theory Website

This website may also be interpreted as a collection of pages that display text data information, still or moving image data, data, animation, sound, video and or a combination of both, be it static and dynamic. On the website page there is a hyperlink.

d. Database

According to Yuswanto in [9], Database is a collection of data/information regularly based on specific criteria that are related. In the world of computer, database can be categorized is very special because it has always been the main thing in designing computer systems. Surely there is some reason why the database becomes its own priorities in performance such as:

a. The database contains not only the data but also contains a plan or capital data.
b. Database can be the primary source being used simultaneously by different users in accordance with their needs.

3 Overview

3.1 Explanation System

The system is designed to be used by two groups of users, i.e. contractors and the building manager, which will start its input from the contractor who insert data of building damage which they build.

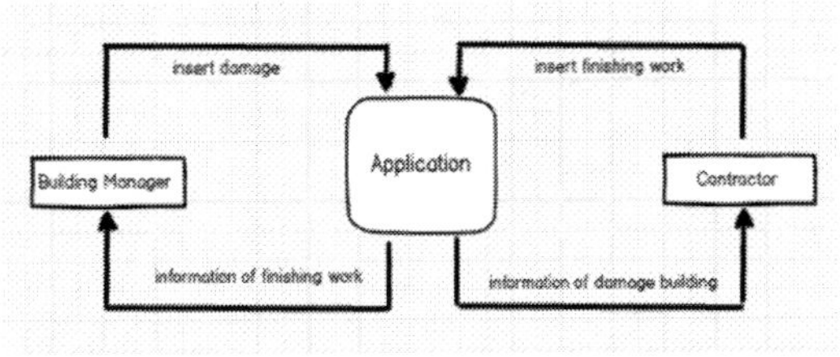

Fig. 1. Context Diagram

3.2 Question from System

The system is run by started with a few questions. Questions can be seen from the following table 1. If question 1 is correct then it will go to question 1.1. otherwise the question number 2 will appear.

Table 1. Questions in the system

No	Categories	Information
1.	Non-Structured Light Damage	Smooth cracks (more gaps smaller than 0.075 cm) in stucco
1.1		Plastering spills fall
1.2		Covers limited area
2.	Structured Light Damage	Small cracks (gap widths between 0.075 and 0.60) on the wall
2.1		Plastering is loose and collapsed
2.2		Covers a large area
2.3		Damage to non-structural parts such as flue, lipstank, etc
2.4		Worthy function
3.	Damage Structure medium level	Big cracks (gap more than 0.60 cm) on the wall
3.1		cracks are widespread in many places, likes load bear wall, columns, sloping chimneys and collapsed
3.2		The ability of the structure to carry the load has been partially reduced
3.3		Worthy function
4.	Damage Structure weight level	The load-bearing wall is split and collapses
4.1		Buildings are separated by the failure of binder elements
4.2		Approximately 50% of the main elements damaged
4.3		Not functional
5.	Total Damage	Building full-collapsed (> 65%)
5.1		Most of structure main component are damaged.
5.2		Not functional

Case examples with questions answered as follows:

1. In which part of the crash:
   a. structures (Columns, beams, walls, etc) ➔ True
   b. Non-structures (chimneys, lipstank, etc)
2. Does the fallen buildings > 65%?
   a. Yes
   b. Not ➔ True
3. How to measure crack?
   a. Cracking smooth (width slit < 0.075 cm) on the stucco 1
   b. Small Cracks (the width of the gap between 0.075 to 0.60) on the wall
   c. Large Crack width slit > 0.60 cm on the wall

4. What is the area of crack?
   a. Includes extensive limited ➔ True
   b. Cracked in many places
5. Do stucco off and tumbling?
   a. Yes ➔ True
   b. Not
6. Be what stucco that fell:
   a. Flake ➔ True
   b. a piece
7. What is the condition of the bearers of the load:
   a. the ability to shoulder the burden of already reduced ➔ True
   b. Wall to shoulder the burden of already split and collapse
8. How about the ceiling cracked area of experience:
   a. Cracking smooth (width slit < 0.075 cm) ➔ True
   b. Small Cracks (the width of the gap between 0.075 to 0.60)
   c. large Crack (width slit > 0.60 cm)
9. Whether the ceiling is exposed to seepage water so as to make the ceiling is black:
   a. Yes
   b. Not ➔ True
10. Is there a section apart from the outskirts of ceiling?
    a. Yes
    b. Not ➔ True
11. The condition of the floor:
    a. Cracking smooth (width slit < 0.075 cm) ➔ True
    b. small Cracks (the width of the gap between 0.075 to 0.60)
    c. large Crack (width slit > 0.60 cm)

If the person managing the building inputs by answering such cases means the type of damage is minor damage. This result is obtained from the criteria on the type of damage. The above question will appear on a system that will be answered by the person who manages the building on a choice answers provided.

4 Conclusions and Recommendations

Based on the results of the analysis of the system then it can be inferred: (a) this research aims to design applications for the reported building damage in particular building structures from the Manager of the building to a Contracting Party with the web-based. (b) from the results of analysis conducted is obtained the draft database consisting of 8 tables. (c) information appearing on the system in the form of location information, time reporting the damage, part what happen damage and type of damage.

In this study only analyzed to design reporting application damage on buildings only for building structures, it is also recommended for maintenance aspects of buildings more like architecture, electrical, mechanical, and outer space.

Acknowledgement

Thanks, was delivered to research institutions and community services (LP2M) Institut Teknologi Padang (ITP) for funding research grants for the year 2018.

Reference

1. W. Hartono, Sugiyarto, and L. Kurniawan, Sistem pemeliharaan aset berbasis android untuk bangunan gedung (studi kasus evaluasi gedung iv fakultas teknik universitas sebelas maret surakarta), vol. **23**, no. 39870423, pp. 390–400, 2016.
2. I. Puķīte and I. Geipele, Different Approaches to Building Management and Maintenance Meaning Explanation, *Procedia Eng.*, vol. **172**, pp. 905–912, 2017.
3. P. O. Akadiri, E. A. Chinyio, and P. O. Olomolaiye, Design of A Sustainable Building: A Conceptual Framework for Implementing Sustainability in the Building Sector, *Buildings*, vol. **2**, no. 4, pp. 126–152, 2012.
4. T. H. Setiawan and S. D. Pusphita, Manajemen Pemeliharaan Pusat Belanja Dengan Studi Kasus Cihampelas Walk Bandung, vol. **8**, pp. 76–90, 2012.
5. N. Mohd-Noor, M. Y. Hamid, A. A. Abdul-Ghani, and S. N. Haron, Building maintenance budget determination: An exploration study in the Malaysia government practice, *Procedia Eng.*, vol. **20**, no. November 2015, pp. 435–444, 2011.
6. Y. Supriyatna, Estimasi Biaya Pemeliharaan Bangunan Gedung, vol. **9**, no. 2, pp. 147–154, 2007.
7. M. A. Thohir, Prioritas Pemeliharaan Dan Rehabilitasi Gedung Sekolah Dengan Metode Dynamic Programming (Studi Kasus: SMP Negeri 4 Salatiga), 2018.
8. E. Mawardi *et al.*, Kajian konsep operasional pemeliharaan gedung sma bina generasi bangsa meulaboh aceh barat 1), vol. 1, pp. 811–822, 2018.
9. Anisya and E. Allazi, Rekayasa Perangkat Lunak Penjadwalan dan Pemesanan Iklan Radio (Studi Kasus : Radio Classy FM), *J. CoreIT, Vol.3, No.2, Desember 2017*, vol. 3, no. 2, pp. 82–88, 2017.

 https://doi.org/10.1051/matecconf/201821501033

The Risk Analysis of Andalas University Hospital Construction Project

Zaidir[1*], Melani Novia Putri[2], Alizar Hasan[2]

[1] Andalas University, Department of Civil Engineering, Padang 25163, Indonesia.
[2] Andalas University, Department of Industrial Engineering, Padang 25163, Indonesia

Abstract. Construction project activities have various risks during their implementation. Every work item on the project has different levels of risk and can affect the project so that it will have an impact on increasing cost and time of project completion. PT. Adhi Karya Tbk is carrying out the project of Andalas University Hospital, where in its implementation there will be many possibilities of risks that will occur. Therefore, it is necessary to identify and analyze the variables of risks that may occur as well as proposing appropriate risk mitigation measures for minimize the potential risks. Risk identification and risk analysis were done using Risk Breakdown Structure (RBS) and Analytic Hierarchy Process (AHP) method respectively. Based on data compilation, variables of risk are grouped in 4 types, namely risk of engineering consist of 8 variables, risk of production consist of 5 variables, risk of construction consist of 9 variables and risk of financial consist of 2 variable, with total of risk are 24 variables. Risk analysis with AHP method is obtained 5 (five) risk priority based on the highest value on each risk type. The five priority risks were a risks of increasing of material prices (extreme), a risk of increasing of procurement costs (high), workplace accidents risk in the project area (medium), mistaken translating the DED to shop drawing (medium) and a quality of goods and services produced by vendors not meet the specifications in contract (medium). To reduce the possibility and impact the risks posed mitigation measures for the risk priority highest were proposed.

1 Introduction

The construction project activities have a risk in their implementation. Each item of work has a different level of risk, depending on its activity. Risk is defined the possibility that something bad or unpleasant will happen. The risks in the construction project however could not be eliminated, but could be reduced or transferred from one party to another. When the risk occurs, it will impact on the disruption of overall project performance so it can cause additional costs, time, and quality of work.

Research of Sandyafitri and Kurniawan [1-2], concluded that implementation of risk management on a project will be able to: 1). reduce delays time of execution of work and increase of project cost, 2). known risk with low, medium and high levels so that the parties involved in the project can anticipate and mitigate to reduce the impact that will caused by such risks, 3). determined risk category with high risk level and medium risk, so that risk can be anticipated by top management with how to prevent the source of the risk.

The research purposes are: a). to identify possible risks on the implementation of Andalas University Hospital construction project with Risk Breakdown Structure (RBS) approach, b). to determine a risk weightof each risk variable with Analytic Hierarchy Process (AHP) approach, c). to determine a risk category for each priority risk based on risk assessment matrix and d). to formulate mitigation actions to risk priorities in order the risks are not recurring and the rate of occurrence of risk is reduced.

2 Literature Reviews

Project construction is a series of activities to build a civil construction such as buildings, bridges or other infrastructures. There are various activities within the construction project where the project activity is a temporary within a limited period of time with the allocation certain funding to achieve a target has been decided. With so many activities and parties involved in the implementation of construction projects, can cause many problems of a nature complex [3]. Figure 1 shows the parties involved in construction projects [4].

* Corresponding author: zaidir@eng.unand.ac.id

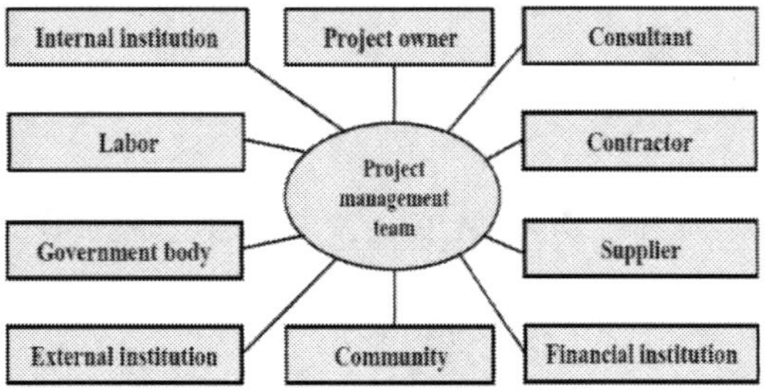

Fig. 1. Parties involved in construction projects

2.1 Risks in Construction Projects

Risks in a construction project are defined as an explanation of unfavorable consequences, both financially and physically as a result of decisions taken or due to environmental conditions at the site of an activity. The risks in a construction project area something that can't be eliminated, but can be minimized their impact.Risk can have an indirect impact on project implementation schedule. The risk categories in construction projects can be grouped in external risks and site conditions, economic and financial risks, technical and contractual risks and managerial risk [5], as shown in Table 1.

Table 1. The risk categories in construction projects

Level 1 **The importance of each risk factor**	*Level 2* **Major risks**	*Level 3* **Risk factors**
Relative importance of each risk factor	External and site condition risks	Unforeseen site ground condition
		Weather condition
		Difficult in obtaining permits and ordinances
		Changes in government actions
	Economic and financial risks	High inflation/increase price
		Delayed payments on contract
		High interest rate
		Poor cost control
	Technical and contractual risks	Defective design
		Design change by owner
		Inadequately compensated variation order
		Delay in providing detail drawing
	Managerial risks	Defective construction work
		Low labor and equipment productivity
		Inadequate project program
		Problems with availability of labor, material and equipment

2.2 Risk Breakdown Structure Method

The Risk Breakdown Structure (RBS) method is mainly used to do categories each risk. RBS is a grouping of risks in a composition hierarchical organizational risk that is logical, systematic, and structured according to the structure organization or project. The goal of RBS implementation is the clarity of risk stakeholders and increased understanding of organizational or project risks within the context of that framework logical and systematic [6].

2.3 Analytic Hierarchy Process (AHP)

Analytic Hierarchy Process (AHP) is one of the deep methods to support decision making developed by Thomas L. Saaty [7]. This decision support model describes multifactor problem or complex multicriteria becomes a hierarchy. The hierarchy is defined as a representation of a complex problem in a multilevel structure. With a hierarchy, a complex problem can be brakedown into groups which is then organized into a hierarchical form so that the problem will appear more structured and systematic [5]. The steps of the AHP method are as follows:

(1) Arrange a hierarchy of problems. Problems to be solved are described into its elements, such as criteria and alternatives which are then compiled into a hierarchical structure.
(2) Assessment criteria and alternatives. The criteria and alternatives assessment is done by pairing comparisons with an assessment of the importance of two elements at a certain level in relation to the above level.
(3) Combine the opinions of respondents. Combining the opinions of respondents is done for each matrix of comparison of each respondent so that obtained matrix of comparison of new pairs which is combined of answer all respondents.
(4) Determination of priority matrix. The paired comparison assessment result that has been done then presented in the form of comparison matrix.
(5) Consistency test. Consistency test is used to determine the level of consistency of the risk weighted value obtained. Results of evaluation are received if the consistency ratio (CR) $\leq$ 0.1.

3 Results and Discussions

3.1 Risk Variable Identification

The identification of risk variables is obtained from the discussion and deep interview with PT. Adhi Karya Tbk Project Production Manager (PPM). Identification of risk variables were also obtained from literature such as journals, prior research, text books and so on. Identification of risk variables is performed for possible risks occurred on the implementation of the construction project of Andalas University Hospital. With the development stages of Risk Breakdown Structure (RBS) through bottom up approach, the result of identifying the risk variable in the project construction of Andalas University Hospital were shown in Table 2.

Table 2. Identified Risk Variables on the Andalas University Hospital Project

Risk type	Risk Code	Risk Variables	Source
Engineering	R01	Permits process take time	PT.Adhi Karya Tbk
	R02	Access to location is not smooth	PT.Adhi Karya Tbk
	R03	Project location is not yet free	PT.Adhi Karya Tbk
	R04	Field conditions are not in accordance with the DED data	PT.Adhi Karya Tbk
	R05	Calculation of production capacity not in accordance with the planned	PT.Adhi Karya Tbk
	R06	Mistaken translating DED to shop drawing	PT.Adhi Karya Tbk
	R07	Price estimates (wages, material and equipments) do not match the field conditions	PT.Adhi Karya Tbk
	R08	Design changes by owner	Ratnaningsih et.al. (2014)
Production	R09	Quality of goods and services produced by vendors not meet the specifications	PT.Adhi Karya Tbk
	R10	Materials used less than required	Ismael and Junaidi (2014)
	R11	The accumulation of material	Ismael and Junaidi (2014)
	R12	Inaccurate time of ordering of materials	Ismael and Junaidi (2014)
	R13	Shortage of construction materials	Ismael and Junaidi (2014)
Construction	R14	Delay of construction activity	PT.Adhi Karya Tbk
	R15	Mistaken in job execution	PT.Adhi Karya Tbk
	R16	Accident in the project area	PT.Adhi Karya Tbk
	R17	Mistaken determines the job stages	PT.Adhi Karya Tbk
	R18	Mistaken in construction method	PT.Adhi Karya Tbk
	R19	Mistaken in determine equipment and supporting materials	PT.Adhi Karya Tbk
	R20	Weather disturbances that cause project delays	Ismael (2013)
	R21	Shortage of labor	PT.Adhi Karya Tbk
	R22	Project management is less competent	Ismael and Junaidi (2014)
Financial	R23	Additional procurement costs	PT.Adhi Karya Tbk
	R24	Increase in building materials prices	Ismael and Junaidi (2014)

From the Table 2, it have 24 (twenty four) risk variables identified on the implementation of the University Andalas hospital project. Each identified risk variables are grouped by type. There are 4 (four) types or risk, namely engineering, production, construction, and financial risks. Risk analysis is done by using Analytic Hierarchy Process approach (AHP). The AHP approach was used to perform inter-pair comparisons risk variables in each type of risk. Through paired comparison analysis, we found the most influential risk weight to the project. Assessment was conducted by 3 (three) experts by filling out the questionnaire.

3.2 Risk Analysis

Risk analysis is performed using AHP approach. AHP approach is used to perform pair-wise comparisons between risk variables in each type of risk. By paired comparison analysis it will get the most influential risk weight. After obtained pair-wise comparison matrix, then done normalization result of matrix of pair-wise comparison to get weight value at each variable of risk. Recapitulation of risk weight values for each risk variables are shown in Table 3, 4, 5 and Table 6.

Based on the normalization of comparison matrix on each risk variable, the highest weight was obtained for each risk variable. In the engineering risk variables, the risk that has a highest weight value is the risk of mistaken translating DED to shop drawing (R06) with a weight value of 0.26. In the production risk variables, a highest value of weight is a quality of goods and services produced by vendors not meet the specifications (R09) with weight value of 0.45. For construction risk variables, a highest value is an accident in the project area (R16) with weight value of 0.19, while for the financial risks a both risk of additional procurement costs (R23) and increase in building material prices (R24) have a same weight value of 0.50.

Table 3. Weight Assessment of Engineering Risk Variables

No.	Risk Code	Potential Risk Priority	Weight value
1	R01	Permits process take time	0.04
2	R02	Access to location is not smooth	0.06
3	R03	Project location is not yet free	0.18
4	R04	Field conditions are not in accordance with the DED data	0.17
5	R05	Calculation of production capacity not in accordance with the planned	0.11
6	R06	Mistaken translating DED to shop drawing	0.26
7	R07	Price estimates (wages, material and equipments) do not match the field conditions	0.14
8	R08	Design changes by owner	0.04

Table 4. Weight Assessment of Production Risk Variables

No.	Risk Code	Potential Risk Priority	Weight value
1	R09	Quality of goods and services produced by vendors not meet the specifications	0.45
2	R10	Materials used less than required	0.18
3	R11	The accumulation of material	0.08
4	R12	Inaccurate time of ordering of materials	0.14
5	R13	Shortage of construction materials	0.16

Table 5. Weight Assessment of Construction Risk Variables

No.	Risk Code	Potential Risk Priority	Weight value
1	R14	Delay of construction activity	0.04
2	R15	Mistaken in job execution	0.13
3	R16	Accident in the project area	0.19
4	R17	Mistaken determines the job stages	0.13
5	R18	Mistaken in construction method	0.14
6	R19	Mistaken in determine equipment and supporting materials	0.11
7	R20	Weather disturbances that cause project delays	0.07
8	R21	Shortage of labor	0.05
9	R22	Project management is less competent	0.13

Table 6. Weight Assessment of Financial Risk Variables

No.	Risk Code	Potential Risk Priority	Weight value
1	R23	Additional procurement costs	0.50
2	R24	Increase in building materials prices	0.50

3.3 Risk Assessment and Category

Based on the value of the consistency ratio obtained in each risk variable, then a weight of each risk variable is acceptable because it has a ratio value consistency ≤ 0.1. The final results of risk that has priority weight the highest in each type of risk can be seen in Table 7. Once obtained potential risk priority, then performed the risk assessment of the potential risk matrix that priority has been obtained.

The value of priority risk level is calculated by multiplying the value of the possibility of risk with the impacts. The average values and risk level of the expert judgments on the potential risk variables can be seen in Table 8. The highest risk level is the rise in the price of building materials (R24) with a risk level of 20.

Based on the risk level assessment of the potential risk priority, the risk can be categorized into the risk matrix shown in Table 9. After the risk assessment matrix is obtained, the risk is then grouped into risk category based on the value of the risk level obtained. Recapitulation of risk assessment matrix results can be seen in Table 10. Based on the risk assessment matrix obtained, there is an area level for the five identified risk priorities.

Table 7. Potential Risk Priority and Weight Value

No.	Risk Type	Risk Code	Potential Risk Priority	Weight value
1	Engineering	R06	Mistaken translating DED to shop drawing	0,26
2	Production	R09	Quality of goods and services produced by vendors not meet the specifications	0,45
3	Construction	R16	Accident in the project area	0,19
4	Financial	R23	Additional procurement costs	0,50
5	Financial	R24	Increase in building materials prices	0,50

Table 8. Potential Risk and Risk Levels

No.	Risk Code	Potential Risk Priority	Average experts opinion		Risk levels
			Possibility	Impacts	
1	R06	Mistaken translating DED to shop drawing	4,00	2,00	8,00
2	R09	Quality of goods and services produced by vendors not meet the specifications	3,00	2,00	6,00
3	R16	Accident in the project area	3,00	3,00	9,00
4	R23	Additional procurement costs	4,00	3,00	12,00
5	R24	Increase in building materials prices	5,00	4,00	20,00

There is one risk variable in the extreme and high category which are the increase of building material price (R24) and the additional procurement costs (R23), and three risk variables that are in the medium category namely the mistaken translating DED to shop drawing (R06), the quality of goods and services produced by vendors not meet the specifications (R09), and an accident in the project area (R16).

Table 9. Risk Assessment Matrix

Possibility	Impacts				
	1	2	3	4	5
5				R24	
4		R06	R23		
3		R09	R16		
2					
1					

Table 10. Risk Assessment Matrix Recapitulation

Color code	Risk category	Risk code
TR ≥ 20	Extreme	R24
10 ≤ TR < 20	High	R23
5 ≤ TR < 10	Medium	R06, R09, R16
0 ≤ TR < 5	Low	-

Table 11. Causes and Impacts of Risk Priorities

Risk Code	**Potential risk priority**	**Causes**	**Impacts**
R06	Mistaken translating DED to shop drawing	Drawing engineer is less skilled.	Reworks
R09	Quality of goods and services produced by vendors not meet the specifications	- Vendors pay no attention to material specifications. - Vendor cheating	Job delays
R16	Accident in the project area	- Workers are not careful - Workers do not care about safety. - Contractors do not care about the Personal Protective Equipment (PPE/APD)	- Decrease of company performance -The insurance costs to an accident workers.
R23	Additional procurement costs	Less careful in market surveys during the procurement process.	Increase of project costs
R24	Increase in building materials prices	- Inflation - Lack of materials stock	Increase of project costs

3.3. Evaluation and Treatment of Risks

Risk evaluation is the process of determining the risk treatment according to the level risks that have been obtained. This risk evaluation can be used in help decision making based on risk analysis. Risk evaluation is used for strengthens the results of expert judgment on identified risks.Based on risk analysis conducted, there are 5 (five) potential risk priorities. From these five priority risks have causes and impacts. The causes and impacts of these five risk priorities can be seen in Table 11. Based on the known causes and impacts of the risk, mitigation measures can be taken on each of these risk priorities. Risk treatment is conducted to reduce the possibility of risk occurrence and risk impact. Each risk variable has different risk treatment depending on the level of risk. Figure 2 illustrates the risk treatment map of each risk priority.

Table 12. Mitigation Measures at Potential Risk Priority

Risk Code	**Risk Variable**	**Risk Category**	**Mitigation**
R06	Mistaken translating DED to shop drawing	Medium	- Make corrections to drawings design Beforetranslating them to shop drawings. - Selecting an expert drawing engineer
R09	Quality of goods and services produced by vendors not meet the specifications	Medium	- Goods and services are returned to the vendor. - Selecting a competent and qualified vendor.
R16	Accident in the project area	Medium	- Detect as early as possible potential risks in the project. - Use a personal protective equipment (APD/PPE). - Conducting socialization and safety instruction before thework begins to workers
R23	Additional procurement costs	High	- Performing efficiency - Transferring risk to the insurance company
R24	Increase in building materials prices	Extreme	- Price adjustments based on the articles contained in thecontract and price negotiations with owner. -Purchasing of material at the beginning via bank payment

Table 12 shows mitigation measures which could be done for risk priority which have been found and figure 2 shows the risk is spread in two risk treatment areas, namely detect and monitor and prevent at source. The risks in the detect and monitor area consist of the risk of mistaken translating DED to shop drawing (R06) and the risk of quality of goods and services produced by the vendor does not meet the specifications agreed upon in the contract (R09).

4 Summary

From the risk analysis which have been done on Andalas University Hospital project, the follows could be summarized :

1. There are four types of risks identified in accordance with the project organization structure of PT. Adhi Karya Tbk were engineering, production, construction and financial risks with total risk variable are 24 items.
2. It was obtained 5 (five) priority of risk variables with highest weight for each risk type, there is: (a) mistaken translating DED to shop drawing. (b) quality of goods and services produced byvendors not meet the specifications. (c) accident in the project area (d) additional procurement costs. (e) increase in building materials prices.
3. The most influential risk categories are as follows: (a) extreme, which is the risk of increase in building material prices with risk level value is 20. (b) high, namely the risk of additional procurement costswith risk level value is 12. (c) medium, are the risk of accident in the project area, mistaken translating DED to shop drawing, and the quality of the goods and services produced by the vendor does meet the specifications.

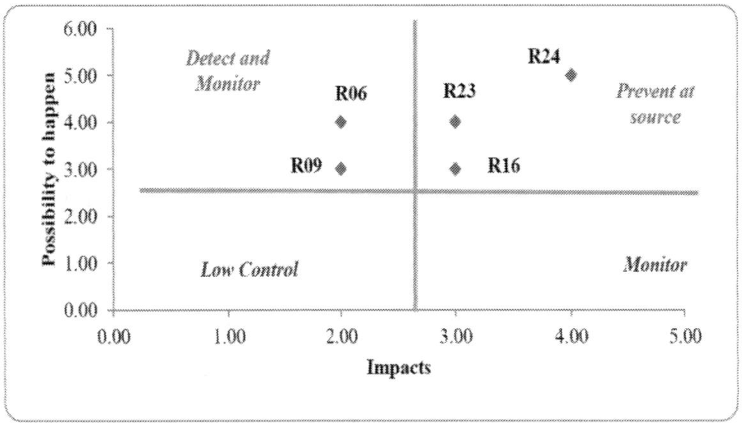

Fig. 2. Risk treatment map of each risk priority

References

1. A. Sandyavitri, Risk Management in Construction Project, Media Komunikasi Teknik Sipil, Jurusan Teknik Sipil Fakultas Teknik Universitas Riau. (in Bahasa) (2009)
2. T. Kurniawan, Enviromental Risk Assessment using Analytical Hierarchy Process Approach and Risk Management ISO 31000 (Case study : Waste water Treatment Installation of RSUP Dr. Djamil Padang), Final Project, Industrial Engineering Department, Engineering Faculty Andalas University, Padang. (in Bahasa) (2013)
3. I. Ismael, Building Project Delay, Cause and Its mitigation, Jurnal Momentum. **1** (14), 47-48. (2013)
4. I.W. Ervianto, Construction Project Management, (Andi Offset, Yogyakarta,, 2005)
5. Efrizon, Risk Management Study using Risk Breakdown Structure Approach and Analytical Hierarchy Process (Case Study : Jalan Manggopoh-Padang Sawah Simpang Empat Project). Thesis, Teknik Manajemen Konstruksi Universitas Bung Hatta. Padang. (in Bahasa), (2014)
6. L.J. Susilo, V.R. Kaho, Risk Management based on ISO 31000 for Non-bank industrial, (PPM Manajemen, Jakarta, 2011)
7. T.L. Saaty, The Analytic Hierarchy Process for Decisions in a Complex World, New York. Pittsburgh, University of Pittsburgh, (2012)

An evaluation of mechanical properties of clay brick for masonry wall in Indonesia

Muhammad Ridwan[1]*, *Ruddy Kurniawan*[2], *Agus*[1]

[1] Institut Teknologi Padang, Civil Engineering
[2] Universitas Andalas, Civil Engineering

Abstract. In principle, the main construction of the non-engineered building in Indonesia is the wooden structure. It can be seen from traditional houses in Indonesia. However, In the last two centuries, the use of brick masonry as wall component has been becoming the primary material. Another side, some places in Indonesia are the seismic areas and earthquake-prone areas. Learning from the earthquake that has happened in the last ten years, the building that used clay brick for masonry wall mostly suffered damage and destruction when subjected to a relatively high intensity of the earthquake. This paper used data from several places and some references. There have significant differences in the mechanical properties of the bricks. Generally, Indonesian bricks masonry have limited capability and substantial differences in the mechanical properties when compared to another country bricks. By the considering, the Indonesian bricks masonry that has low mechanical properties, so that it is proposed to use brick masonry to non-seismic only. It should be considered to use clay brick as the main component of the wall for a particular region in Indonesia. Next, the zoning of allowed masonry structure in Indonesia is proposed.

Keywords: mechanical properties, brick, masonry wall.

1 Introduction

The brick masonry structure has become a favorite choice for society building in developing countries, notably in Indonesia as a base material for build the society buildings. Here, the resource of the main elements for the brick is straightforward to obtain, so it has become a source of small industries that grow like the mushroom in every region. In Another side, the emergence of trend uses of the brick masonry into a prestige for the community. It would be a pride to have a house that is mostly using the material from a brick and is called a permanent home. Likewise, the brick masonry wall is low price and influenced the Europa style. The house of in Indonesian people is from wood. It was seen from the existence of traditional houses from across the archipelago, and all the houses are from wood. The general Indonesia people had known that buildings made from wood are resisted to the effect of seismic loading. In fact, in every region of Indonesia, almost 80% use bricks as the primary material of masonry [**1**]. In some developing countries, traditional clay bricks are produced locally without following any technical inspection or standard and the quality varies from region to region. These bricks are used for houses and simple buildings, not only in village areas but also in the urban region. In general, masonry structures are very good in resisting gravity loads, but do not perform well when subjected to lateral in-plane and out-of-plane loading, such as seismic loads caused by an earthquake. As countries locate in a high risk seismic region, many masonry houses experienced severe damage during past earthquakes that caused many injuries and deaths. The houses collapsed gradually in brittle failure without ductility.

Ridwan *et al.* [**2**] in his research to verify and validate the calculation method proposed in obtaining the ability of out-of-plane from masonry is very low

Based on the findings mentioned above, the mechanical characteristics of brick quality of masonry structure need to be evaluated.

2 Active seismic zone in the world

Indonesia and some developing countries locates in active seismic zone in the world. There are have five active tectonic plates, earthquakes occurred daily in the region, with a magnitude of 5 in Richter scale or larger. **Fig. 1** shows the epicenters of recorded earthquakes during the period of 2017. A total of 11,594 earthquakes are plotted. This seismic has the potential to produce an earthquake with magnitude greater than 8.7. As example, the subduction zone in Sumatra is known for producing mega-thrust earthquakes such as the moment magnitude Mw 8.8-9.2 in 1833, the Mw 8.3-8.5 in 1861, the Mw 9.0-9.3 in December 2004, the Mw 8.7 in March 2005 and the Mw 8.4 in September 2007 [**3**]. Based on the recent seismic activity, Aydan O. et al. [**4**] identified a segment of the subduction zone facing Padang City that has not ruptured in the last 213 years. This seismic gap has the potential to produce an earthquake with

* Corresponding author: mhd.rid.wan.itp@gmail.com

magnitude greater than 8.7. The seismic gap is located in between the 1833 and 1861 fault ruptures, and it is estimated to have an approximate recurrence interval of 230 years [**5**]. As a result, the potential earthquake rupture length in the Sumatra fault is not likely to exceed 100 km, so the maximum magnitude expected from such an event is estimated as Mw 7.5 [**6,7**].

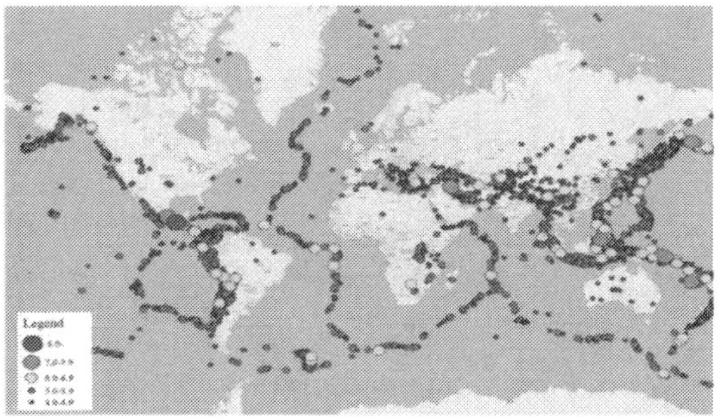

Figure 1. World earthquakes during the period of 2017 [**28**]

From previous seismic events, it has been seen that brick masonry often presents an inadequate behavior to seismic actions, showing extensive cracking and disintegration due to combined in-plane and out-of-plane loadings. This behavior is due to the low quality of materials,

3. Conditions of non-engineered construction in developing countries

Most of the buildings in Nepal, Pakistan, Indonesia, India, Peru, Turkey and Egypt utilize fired clay bricks as wall material, with one brick thickness (see **Fig. 2** and **Fig. 3**). In terms of wall height to thickness ratio, the highest ratio is found in Indonesia (19.83), while the smallest is found in Egypt (9.00) [**8**]

Most of non-engineered constructions provide beams and few of them provide columns. This depends on the structural system adopted in the surveyed country. In Indonesia, most of the surveyed sites exhibit confined masonry, so both columns and beams are available. On the other hand, in Pakistan, Egypt, and India, where most of the selected sites are unconfined masonry, the buildings are only provided with beam/lintel. From all of the selected countries, it was found that most of non-engineered construction had poor detailing on the connection of the structural elements [8].

Most of countries have building regulation/codes and/or guideline on non-engineered construction at the national level, such as India, Indonesia, Pakistan, Peru and Nepal. Unfortunately, the building regulation/codes or guidelines on non-engineered structure are mostly not implemented by the countries, excepting for a few big cities. It was also found that some countries have problems on disseminating these regulations to the workers. In Turkey and Egypt, the non-engineered building code at the national level is not available. However, both countries have local offices in charge of building administration in the surveyed cities. In Turkey, the national building code is only for engineered structure [**8**].

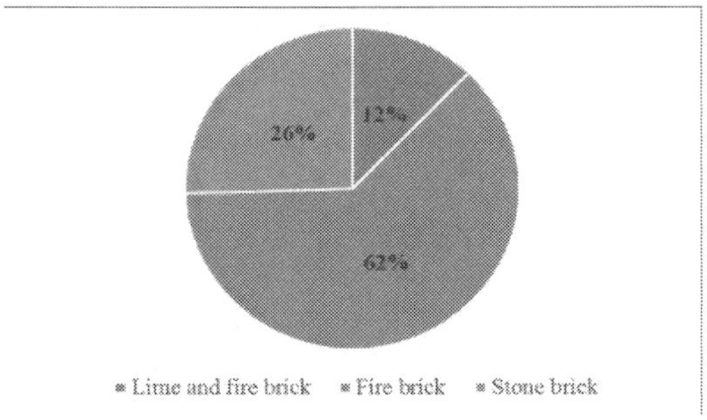

Figure Error! No text of specified style in document. Percentage of wall materials used in developing countries

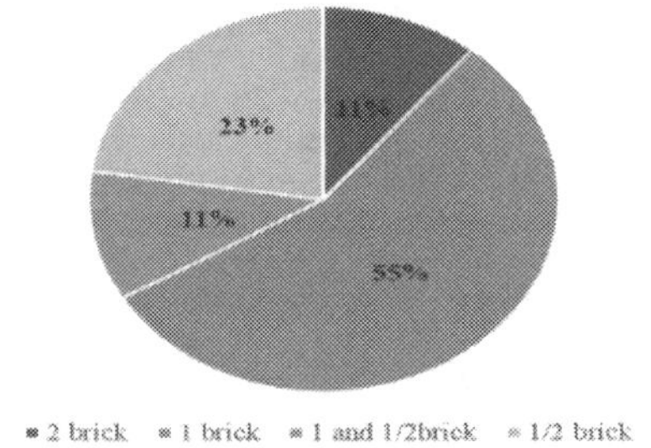

Figure 3 Percentage of wall thickness used in developing countries

Some mistakes are often found in many masonry houses or simple structures. In **Fig. 4**, fence wall built on not properly connected to the column and supporting beam. This wall was constructed without any column or tie beam. Such brick wall will collapse during earthquake because there is no lateral in plane stiffener in wall structures.

Figure 4 Buildings in Padang, Indonesia after earthquake September 30, 2009 (7.6 on Richter scale). Damages to an unconfined single story school building [29]

A masonry house (shown in **Fig. 5**) is considered to be a semi engineered structure, since the structural column and tie beam were not properly installed.

Figure 5 Confined masonry: formwork present after construction of walls; note lack of columns on right side. [30]

There is no closed tie beam constructed at the upper part of the wall to confine the whole structure. It can be expected that some partial damages will occur during earthquake.

In **Fig. 6**, a simple reinforced concrete frame is placed at the corner of masonry house. The beam, which is retaining part of the wall structure, is not correctly connected with anchorage to end support. There are also no closed tie beam and column found in this structure. This type of house is classified as a non-engineered structure and will experience damage during an earthquake, especially at the corner of wall opening.

Figure 6 Typical earthquake damage: a house without vertical tie-columns and without top bond-beams in Attics (1988 Bovec earthquake) [31]

4. Investigation of the quality of bricks masonry

Brick masonry (BM) is a building construction method in which a two-phase composite material is formed of regularly distributed brick and mortar [**9**]. Normally, bricks (clay bricks) contain the following ingredients: silica (sand) around 50% to 60% by weight, alumina (clay) around 20% to 30% by weight, lime around 2 to 5% by weight, iron oxide $\leq$ 7% by weight and Magnesia less than 1% by weight [**10**]. Usually, the bricks show higher values for compressive strength and stiffness than the mortar. However, the opposite is true in some of the developing countries. For example, the mechanical properties of bricks in some areas of Indonesia show significantly lower values than those of mortar because construction materials are sometimes manufactured in family-run industries [**11**]. This is due to culture, economics, source and material of the bricks. In spite of the use of low-quality bricks, the design code for masonry structures in Indonesia (SNI-2094-2000) is based on the design code of other countries, namely, the DIN 105 standard of Germany and the ASTM C 67-94 standard of the USA.

Hence, most investigations are focused on bricks showing higher strength and when compared to the mortar used in masonry structures. However, as mentioned above, this is not always the case [**12**] in some developing countries. It was reported in [Indra et al. 2013] that bricks in Payakumbuh, located in the West Sumatera Province of Indonesia had a significantly low compressive strength of 2.9 MPa on an average. Similarly, Putri [**13**] reported a brick strength of 2.5 MPa in Padang city. Elhusna *et al.* [**14**] observed that the compressive strength of bricks in Bengkulu Province was within the range of 2.4–6.7 MPa. Wisnumurti et al. [**15**] investigated the strength of bricks from four different areas in East Java. According to their investigations, the compressive strength was within the range of 0.55–0.9 MPa, and the modulus of elasticity of the low-quality bricks was within the range of 279–571 MPa. In addition, Basoenondo [**16**] reported that the compressive strength and the modulus of elasticity of bricks in the West Java Province were 0.5–2.87 MPa and 220–540 MPa, respectively. It is noteworthy that the test was based on the American standard ASTM E-111 owing to the lack of an Indonesian standard for the evaluation of the elastic modulus of bricks.

Most of the non-engineered constructions at countries use baked clay or stone masonry for the wall materials. Brick sizes in Turkey, Nepal, Indonesia, Peru and Pakistan are relatively similar, meanwhile in India and Egypt bricks have different sizes compared to the others. Peru has the highest brick compressive strength, while Turkey has the smallest brick compressive strength compared to the other countries. Test results from sites in each country showed that some do not have adequate strength for the brick (see **Fig. 7**). [**8**]

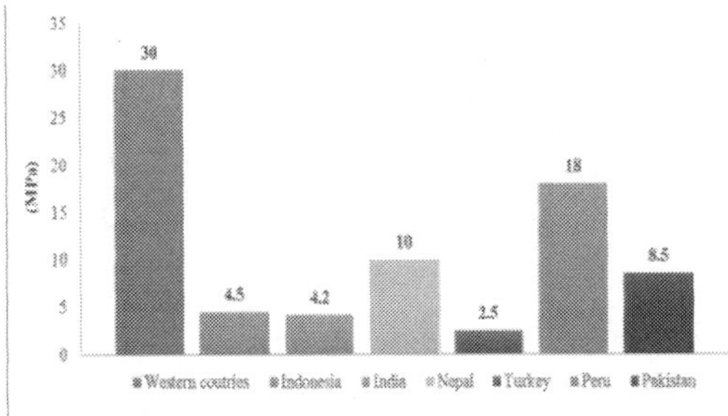

Figure 7 Average bricks compressive strength

General-purpose bricks in western countries have higher strength and stiffness than mortar, as discussed by Gumaste *et al.* [**12**]. They reported that bricks in India have a relatively lower strength (3–20 MPa) and elastic modulus (300–15000 MPa). Similarly, Indonesian bricks have lower strength and stiffness [**16**].

The general theory is based on the assumption that mechanical properties of brick elements are higher than those of mortar [**17**]. In most cases, the ideal elasticity used in the design refers to formulas specified in overseas regulations. These assumptions may result in inappropriate design for the construction of masonry structures using Indonesian bricks.

Most of the countries use ordinary Portland cement as plaster and mortar cementing agent. Pakistan found to have the highest mortar strength, even though the mix is similar with other countries. On the other hand, Peru has different mortar mix compared to the other countries, but it produces the same compressive strength. The mortar thickness in Egypt is found to be the thickest (25 mm), while Turkey and Pakistan have the thinnest mortar layer (10-20 mm and 11.5mm respectively) (see Fiq. 8). The common plaster mix is either 1:6 or 1:4 (PC;sand) , except in Peru where the mix is 1:1. Turkey has the thickest plaster (20-30 mm), while Nepal has the thinnest plaster (10 mm) (see **Fig. 9**). [**8**]

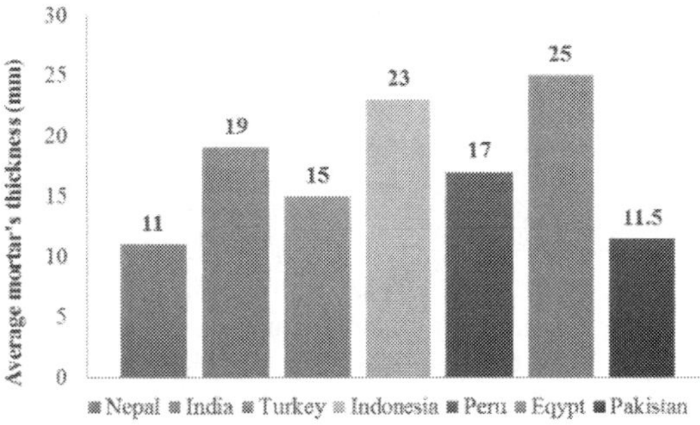

Figure 8 Average mortar's thickness

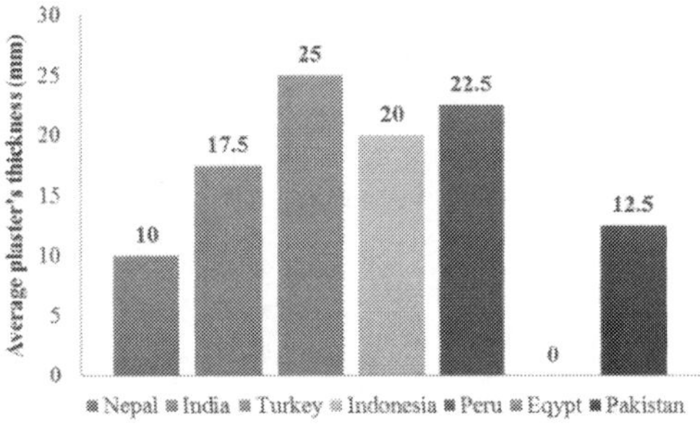

Figure 9 Average plaster's thickness

Ridwan *et al* [**1**] was observed that typical mortar has a lower elasticity than bricks in the homogenization process (Table 1). His proposed analytical approach can significantly contribute to a safer analysis and design of masonry structural systems built with low-quality bricks in various developing countries, such as Indonesia.

Table 1 Moduli of elasticity for homogenization

Author (s)	Ebrick (MPa)	Emortar (MPa)
[18]	6740	1700
[19]	12500	1200
[20]	1000	Emor/Eb <1
[21]	20000	1<Eb/Emor<1000
[22]	10000	0.49
[23]	11000	Eb/Emor = 1.1-11
[24]	11000	2200
[25]	22000	7400
[26]	13000	4000
[27]	20000	2000

5. Discussion.

The above investigations that need several considerations and to be observed because Indonesia's position is in the seismic area while the quality of the bricks is lower than some another developing countries. Brick masonry walls are assumed to be nonstructural while that is used as building structural part. Based on previous researches data (**Table 1**) that the concept of a composite of masonry is the compressive strength of the brick is greater than mortar. This condition will be opposite when using the material of brick from Indonesia Mechanical properties of bricks used in western countries for making the regulation are higher brick quality than mortar while In Indonesia the quality of brick is low and mortar quality can be higher.

The production of brick in Indonesia is a majority made by family industry, so it is one causes of difficulty to be improved the quality of brick. By given that Indonesia consists of various areas that have the level of disaster risk due to earthquakes then the use of brick needs to be proposed by divide the area of the Indonesia territory in usage brick for example in the three regions. In this paper, we propose three areas according to the disaster map released by BNPB on **Fig. 10** [**32**]. The division are;

1. Green color zone is safe zone to use masonry.
2. Yellow color zone that is allowed to use masonry with strict rules such as reinforced masonry, using an anchor and confined masonry.
3. Red color zone that are not intended to use masonry.

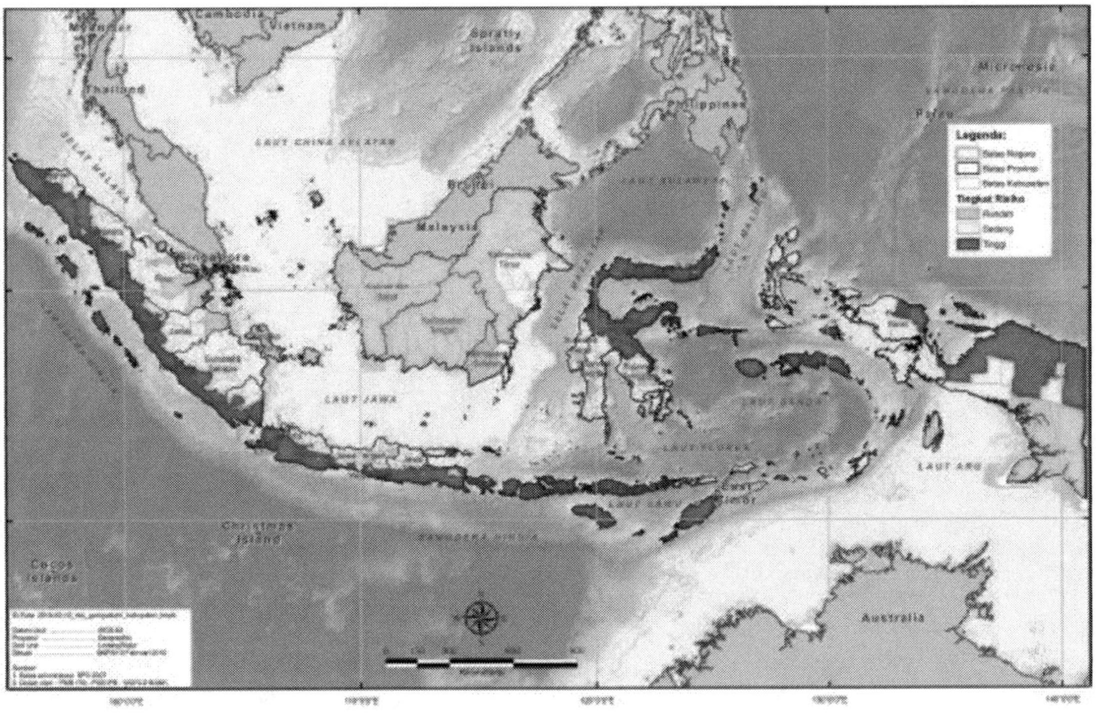

Figure 10. Earthquake risk index in Indonesia

Conclusion

The brick has become a favorite masonry material for society houses including use as building partitions in Indonesia. However, Indonesian bricks is low quality and some places in Indonesia are the seismic zones. The developed countries that are in the earthquake zone have left the brick as the primary material of the wall. This condition need of policy and rule on the use of bricks following the condition of Indonesia brick, as well to improve the quality of bricks. Next, the map zone that have three level from low to high-level disaster for masonry structure is proposed. For the high level of disaster should be no used the bricks anymore for structural of construction and switch to other types of materials. For the middle level of the disaster zone should pay attention to the procedures and specifications of bricks following the regulations to avoid failure. Considering the existence of an existing brick home industry existed then the use of brick is highly recommended for areas that are not prone to earthquake disaster.

References.

1. M. Ridwan, I. Yoshitake, A. Y. Nassif, Proposal of Adv. Civ. Eng. 2017 (2017)
2. M. Ridwan, I. Yoshitake, A. Y. Nassif, Constr. Build. Mater. 152 (2017),
3. M. Irsyam et al., Journal of Earth System Science. 117, 865–878 (2008).
4. Ö. Aydan, F. Imamura, T. Suzuki, I. Febrin, A. Hakam, M. Mera and P. Rina D., Japan Society of Civil Engineers (JSCE)-Japan Association for Earthquake Engineering (JAEE), Japan. (2007)
5. J. Zachariasen, K. Sieh, F. W. Taylor, R. L. Edwards, W. S. Hantoro, Journal of Geophysical Research. 104, 895–919 (1999).
6. D. Natawidjaja, H., California Institute of Technology, USA. (2002)
7. R. McCaffrey, The Annual Review of Earth and Planetary Science, 37, pp.345–66. (2009),
8. T. S. Okazaki, Kenji; Pribadi, S. Krishna, Kusumastuti, Dyah; Saito, 15th World Conference on Earthquake Engineering (15WCEE) (2012).
9. G. Ma, H. Hao, and Y. Lu, J. Eng. Mech., 127(5), pp.421-431. (2001),
10. B. Punmia, K Jain, A. & K. Jain, A. Basic civil engineering, Firewall Media. (2003).
11. A. Indra, , S. Elfina, Nurzal and H. Nofrianto, H., National Strategic Research, Indonesia. (2013)
12. K. Gumaste, , R. Nanjunda, K., B. Venkatarama Reddy, B. and Jagadish, K. (2006), Mater Struct, 40(2), pp.241-253.
13. P. Putri, Procedia Eng., 95, pp.510-517. (2014)
14. Elhusna, A. Wahyuni, and A. Gunawan, A. Procedia Eng., 95, pp.504-509. (2014),

* Corresponding author: mhd.rid.wan.itp@gmail.com

15. Wisnumurti, S. Dewi, and Soehardjono, A. Procedia Eng., 95, pp.172-177. (2014)
16. E. Basoenondo, , Build Environment: Disertasi. (2008)
17. T. Paulay, and M. J. N. Priestley, , John Wiley and Sons, New York. (1992)
18. I. Stefanou, K. Sab, and Heck, J. Int. J. Solids and Struct, 54, pp.258-270. (2015)
19. F.Cluni, and V.Gusella, Int. J. of Solids and Struct., 41(7), pp.1911-1923. (2004),
20. A.Cecchi and R. Di Marco, J. Eng. Mech., 128(6),688-697. (2002)
21. A. Zucchini, and P. Lourenco, B., Int. J. Solids and Struct., 39(12), pp.3233-3255. (2002)
22. A. Rekik, , Allaoui, S., Gasser, A., Euro. J. Mech. - A/Solids, 49, pp.67-81.(2015)
23. G. Pande N., Liang J. X. and Middleton J., Computers and Geotechnics, pp.243-265. (1989)
24. A. Anthoine, , Int. J. Solids and Struct., 32(2), pp.137-163. (1995)
25. J. Lee, Pande, G., Middleton, J. and Kralj, B. Computers and Structures, 61(4), pp.735-745. (1996).
26. Gabor, A., Bennani, A., Jacquelin, E. and Lebon, F. Comp. Str., 74(3), pp.277-288. (2006)
27. P.Lourenço B., Delft University Press, Stevinweg 1, 2628 CN Delft, The Netherlands. (1996)
28. https://en.wikipedia.org/wiki/List_of_earthquakes_in_2017#/media/File:Map_of_earthquakes_in_2017.svg
29. *https://www.researchgate.net/profile/I_Gede_Adi_Susila/publication/318085641/figure/fig2/AS:511433301557248@1498946609570/Figure-6-Buildings-in-Padang-Indonesia-after-earthqauke-September-30-2009-76-on.png*
30. *http://eqclearinghouse.org/co/20100112-haiti/wp-content/uploads/2010/03/3-Residential.jpg*
31. *http://db.world-housing.net/pdf_view/88/*
32. *http://geospasial.bnpb.go.id/2010/02/19/peta-indeks-risiko-bencana-gempabumi-di-indonesia/*

https://doi.org/10.1051/matecconf/201821501035

Seismic Performance of Existing R/C Building with Irregular Floor Plan Shape

Agus*, Muhammad Ridwan, Febriyan Ramadhana

Institut Teknologi Padang, Civil Engineering Department, Padang, West Sumatra, Indonesia

Abstract. Building with irregular floor plan has the eccentricity of force to the centre of building isappears to be more susceptible to deformation and damage when subjected to earthquake movements than with regular floor plan. This study aims to determine the seismic performance of buildings with the irregular floor plan in displacement and drift by service and ultimate performance limit. The object of research is Padang Pariaman public works office building. The evaluation method used non-linear static analysis (Pushover) which is one method to evaluate the seismic performance of the building. Push-over analysis performed by providing a static load in the lateral direction gradually to achieve a specific displacement target. This research is based on SNI-1726-2012, ATC-40 and FEMA 356. The results of the analysis show that the maximum lateral force of 10909.9 kN occurs in step-6 pushover analysis with a displacement of 0.165 m, maximum drift = 0.0705 m and maximum in-elastic drift = 0.025 m. This means the building is included in the IO (Immediate Occupancy) performance level. Although there is damage from small to medium level, still has a big threshold against the collapse, which means the building is safe against the earthquake.

1 Introduction

Earthquake disasters basically happen because of damage to buildings not because the earth shakes. Based on the experience of a major earthquake that occurred in West Sumatra-Indonesia on 30 September 2009, many caused the collapse of the building structure. The collapse of reinforced concrete buildings is generally caused by failure of the column structure [1]. On the other hand, the irregular shape of the floor plan has a profound effect on the movement of the building. Ahmed Abdelraheem Farghaly (2010), who conducted a study on the Influence of Irregular Floor Plan on the seismic response of the building, showed that the base shear induced in a perpendicular direction ranged between 40% and 80% of the base shear in the direction of the earthquake motion. In addition, the top displacements for T and L models increased up to 1.9 times the top displacement in the I-model [2].

To investigate the vulnerability of existing buildings due to the earthquake, nonlinear static pushover analysis was performed to evaluate the apparent strength of existing buildings. A study by Sameh A. El-Betar (2017) found that the existing building vulnerability occurred at the ground accelerations (*ag*) greater than 0.125 g on Egyptian seismic map, while the EC-94 buildings designed behaved elastically up to (*ag*) equal to 0.2 g and if exceeded a slight damage may occur [3]. On the other hand, studies of the effect of floor characteristics on seismic performance of Soft Storey RC Frames with Pushover Analysis by B. Shiva Kumaraswami (2015) show that structural ductility decreases when structures are irregular and higher, as are the stages of structural collapse. The seismic performance evaluation of Bethesda Hospital Yogyakarta building structure by Edi Purwanto (2016) has proved that in performance-based design, the performance level for hospital building is Immediate occupation (OI) fulfilled in actual with pushover analysis [4-5].

The following research aims to determine the seismic performance of buildings with the irregular floor plan in displacement and drift by service and ultimate performance limit. The object of research is Padang Pariaman- Indonesia public works office building is a two-story reinforced concrete building with a distinctive architectural form. Built in areas of strong earthquake risk, the seismic performance evaluation of this building is interesting and important and for that reason, non-linear static analysis (Pushover analysis) is used as one of the methods.

2 Literature Review

Many countries always set and update their seismic standards. Several standards that determine the performance level of seismic buildings include SNI 1726-2012, ATC-40 1996 and FEMA 365. This performance level shows the description of the damage experienced by the building after the earthquake. For the estimation of building performance characteristics, different failure criteria are incorporated in a

* Corresponding author: agus@itp.ac.id

methodology established to predict the failure mode of the buildings [6].

SNI 1726-2012

The ultimit limit performance of the buildings structure are determined by the maximum deflection and the maximum drift due to the Earthquake Plan in the condition of the structure of the building on the verge of collapse, namely to limit the possibility of collapse of building structures that can cause human casualties and to prevent collisions. The maximum drift according to SNI 1726 - 2012 section 8 is as follows [7]:

- Must not exceed R 0.03 times height of the building level or 30 mm, depending on which is the smallest value.
- Must not exceed 0.02 times the relevant of height of the building level

ATC – 40 1996

Building performance levels based on ATC-40, 1996 are divided into the following five stages [8]:

- *Immediate Occupancy* (IO)
  Conditions that explain vertical and lateral load-bearing systems are almost identical to those prior to the earthquake, and the risk of loss of life due to structural collapse is negligible.
- *Damage Control*
  Where after the earthquake, the damage occurred within the range between IO and LS
- *Life Safety* (LS)
  Where after the earthquake, significant damage to the structure occurs. The main components of the structure are not dislocated and collapsed, so the risk of loss of life to structural damage is very low.
- *Limited Safety*
  Conditions that explain that after the earthquake, the damage occurred in the range between LS and CP
- *Structural Stability / Collapse Prevention* (CP)
  The condition of the structure after the earthquake was so severe that the building could have either partially or totally destroyed the structure and the possibility of casualties caused by large structural damage

FEMA 365

In the displacement coefficient method (FEMA 356), the calculations were performed by modifying the linear elastic response of the SDOF system structure equivalent to the modification factors *C0, C1, C2* and *C3* so as to calculate the switching target by specifying the effective vibration time (*Te*) to calculate the inelastic condition of the structure building [9].

$$\delta_t = C_0.C_1.C_2.C_3.S_a.\left(\frac{T_e}{2.\pi}\right)^2.g \qquad \ldots\ldots\ldots 1$$

Where :

δ_t transition targets

Te effective natural vibration time.

C_0 modification factors to convert *spectral displacement* structure of SDOF equivalent becomes *roof displacement* structure of MDOF system.

C_1 modification factor to relate the maximum inelastic switching with the switching of linear elastic response. C_1= 1,0 for $Te \geq Ts$ and

$$C_1 = \left[\frac{1+(R-1).\frac{T_s}{T_e}}{R}\right] \text{ for } T_e < T_s \qquad \ldots\ldots\ldots 2$$

Where :

C_2 modification factors to show *pinched hysteresis shape,* degradation of stiffness and decreased strength in the maximum switching response, accordingly FEMA 356 table 3-3.

C_3 modification factor to show the transitional rise due to the p-delta effect. For buildings with positive post-melting stiffness behavior then C_3= 1,0. As for the building with post-melting negative stiffness behavior,

$$C_3 = 1{,}0 + \frac{|\alpha|(R-1)^{\frac{3}{2}}}{T_e} \qquad \ldots\ldots\ldots 3$$

R :is *strength ratio*, can be calculated by the equation:

$$R = \frac{S_a}{V_y/W}.C_m \qquad \ldots\ldots\ldots 4$$

Where :

Sa is the acceleration of the response spectrum at the effective fundamental natural vibration time and the damping ratio in the direction under consideration.

Vy is the base shear at the yield point

W is the effective weight of seismic.

Cm effective mass factor, table 3-1 FEMA 356.

a is the stiffness ratio of the post-yield to the effective elastic stiffness, in which the nonlinear transitional relationship is idealized as a bilinier curve.

Ts the characteristic vibration time of the spectrum response.

g acceleration of gravity 9,81 m/det^2.

3. Performance Evaluation of Reinforced Concrete Seismic Performance

Description of the building

The object of research is Padang Pariaman- Indonesia public works office building is a two-story reinforced concrete building. The following are the specifications and drawings of the Building structure plan. Total building height 11.36 m, building length 46,000 m, building width 46,000 m, compressive strength of concrete is 25 MPa , and tensile strength of steel reinforcement is 390 MPa.

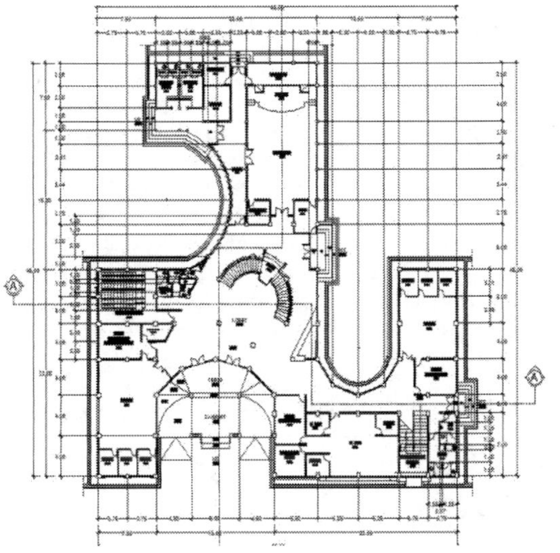

Fig. 1. Building plan

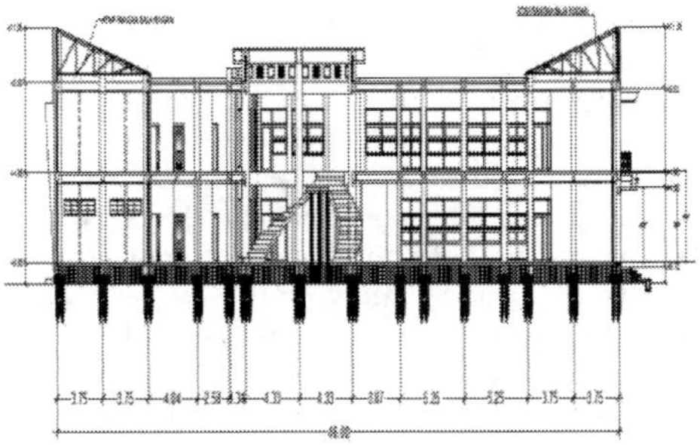

Fig. 2. Cross section A-A

Structural Modeling
The structure modeling is made in 3-dimensional drawing using SAP 2000 V 14 program with reference to drawing plan.

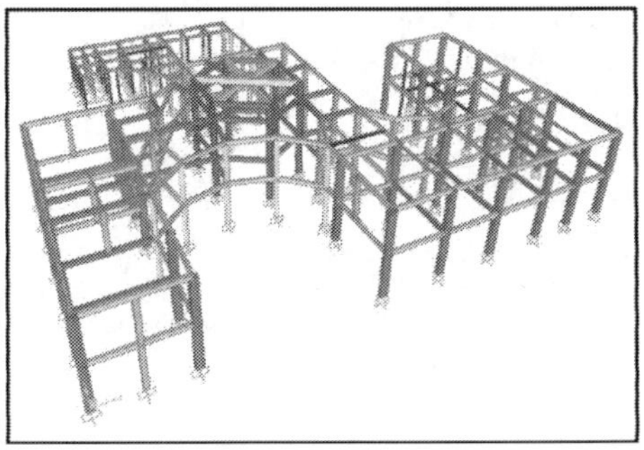

Fig. 3. 3D Structured Modeling

The load analysis on Padang Pariaman- Indonesia public works office building covers dead load (DL), additional dead load (SDL), live load (LL), earthquake lateral load (EL). There are some lateral loading provided for pushover analysis. Each load is defined as a different load case and will be preceded by a gravity loading that is adjusted to the mass of the building (during an earthquake). As previously defined, building masses include 30% live load, 100% dead load, and 100% additional dead load. The value of spectrum response in accordance with the latest Indonesian regulation is SNI 1726-2012.

4 Analysis Results

The result of pushover analysis shows that at the loading of stage 6 there are 8 points of the beam structure that has been at the maximum limit of shear force that can be retained so that the beam almost collapse. There has been a displacement of 16.46 cm with a shear force of 10909.9 kN. This means there is damage from mild to moderate, where some of the beams have collapsed.

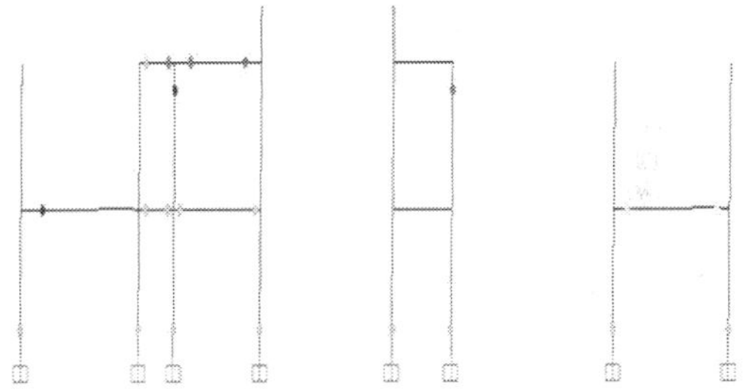

Fig. 4. Portal As 17 Distribution of Plastic Joint Stage 6

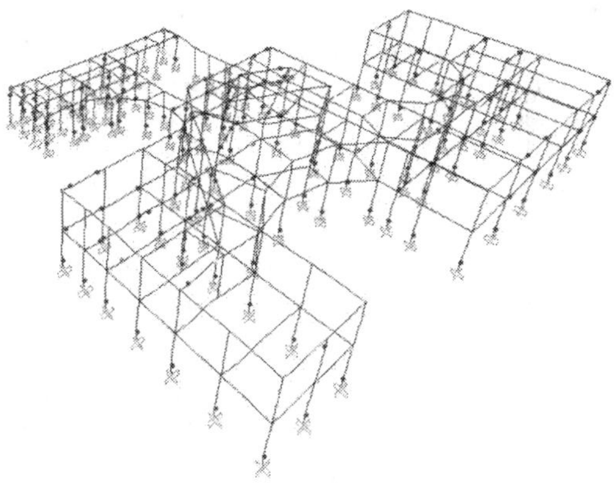

Fig. 5. Plastic Jointing Mechanism (loading of stage 6)

The result of a pushover analysis in the form of a capacity curve shows a comparison of shear forces to the displacement. Here are the output output curves of *ATC-40*, and *FEMA 356*.

 https://doi.org/10.1051/matecconf/201821501035

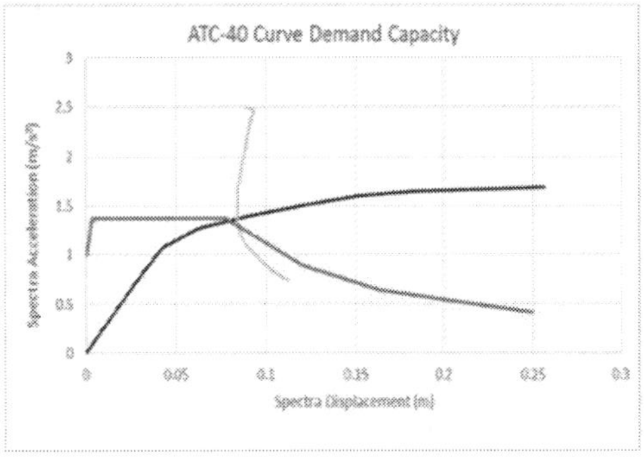

Fig. 6. *Atc-40 Curve Demand Capacity*

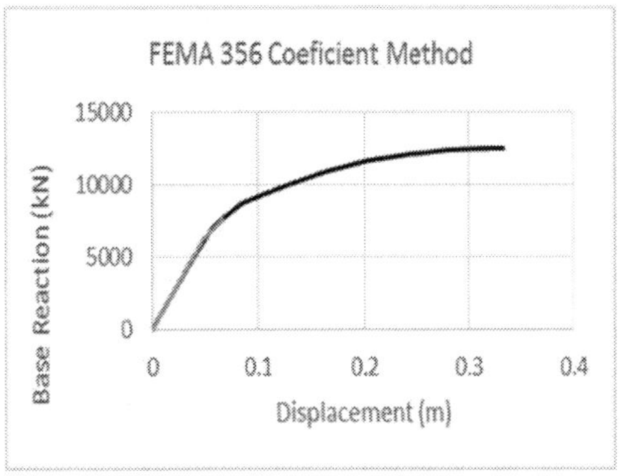

Fig. 7.*FEMA 356 Coefficient Method.*

Output for the capacity curve of the ATC-40 Capacity Spectrum (figure 6) shows the Spectra Acceleration comparison of Spectra Displacement. The point of performance point is in the cross-cutting curve of capacity (black) with the damping variable line (yellow). While the red line is a damping line with a ratio of 0.2. From figure 6 obtained performance point value of 9642.845 kN with displacement of 0.114 m.

Building performance based on displacement target the ATC-40 Coefficient Method is:

- *Maximum Drift* = Dt / Htot
  = 0.067 / 9,5 m
  = 0.00705 m = 7,05 cm
- *Maximum in-elastic drift* = Dt – D1 / Htot
  = 0,067 – 0,043 / 9,,5 m
  = 0,0025 m = 2,5 cm

So based on the above table, it can be concluded that the structure has an Immediate Occupancy (IO) performance level because the value of Maximum Drift = 0.0705 m <Maximum total drift = 0.01 m and Maximum in-elastic drift = 0,025 m <Maximum in-elastic drift = 0.005 m.

For the capacity curve of FEMA 356 Coefficient Method only displays the comparison between displacement and displacement. Performance point is in intersection between the curve line capacity (black) with bilinear curve curve (red) that is equal to 7694.966 kN with the movement of 0.067 m.

In SNI 1726 - 2012, the limit of drift (Δ), ie shall not exceed the drift permission level (Δ <0.02 x hsx) where (hsx) is the height of the level calculated from the base of the building, ie 9.5 m = 950 cm. When compared to the maximum displacement occurring (= 16.46 cm) is still within the threshold specified by SNI 1726 - 2012.

Based on the results obtained from the pushover analysis using the *ATC-40* method, *FEMA 356* obtained the performance level of the building is on *Immediate Occupancy (IO)* which means the building is safe against earthquake.

Table 1. Building Performance Level

Parameter	*Performance Level*			
	Immediate Occupancy	*Damage Control*	*Life Safety*	*Struktur Stability*
Maksimum Total Drift	0.01	0.01 s.d 0.02	0.02	$0.33\ h\frac{Vi}{Pi}$
Maksimum Total In-elastic Drift	0.005	0.05 s.d 0.015	*No limit*	*No limit*

5 Conclusions

After analyzing and evaluating seismic performance of existing R/C Padang Pariaman- Indonesia public works office building with irregular floor plan shape, the following conclusions can be drawn:

1. The maximum lateral force of 10909.9 kN occurs at step-6 *pushover analysis* with *displacement of 0.165 m, maximum drift = 0.0705 m* and *maximum in-elastic drift = 0.025 m.*
2. The building belongs to the IO performance level category (Immediate Occupancy). Although there is damage from small to medium level, but still has a big threshold against the collapse, which means the building is safe against the earthquake.
3. The design concept of strong Column Weak Beam has been fulfilled in the planning of this building because the beam collapsed first. This is shown the formation of plastic joints starting from the beam element.

References

1. Maidiawati and Sanada, Y., 2008. Investigation and Analysis of Buildings Damaged during the September 2007 Sumatra, Indonesia Earthquakes, Journal of Asian Architecture and Building Engineering, Vol. 7, No. 2, pp.371-378.
2. Ahmed Abdelraheem Farghaly. 2010. Influence of Structural Irregularity in Plan Floor Shape on Seismic Response of Buildings. Journal of Engineering Sciences, Assiut University, Vol. 38, No. 4, pp. 911-928.
3. Sameh A. El-Betar .2017. Seismic Performance of existing R.C. Framed Buildings. HBRC Journal. Vol. 13. Pp. 171 - 180
4. B. Shiva Kumaraswami .2015. Study on Indfluence of Floor Characteristics on the Seismic Performance of

Soft Storey RC Frames from Pushover Analysis. International Journal of Engeneering Research and Technology (IJERT), Vol. 4, Issue 05, pp. 616 – 622.
5. Edi Purwanto .2016. Structural Performance Evaluation with Pushover Analysis Case Study: The Integrated Central Surgery Building, Bethesda Hospital in Yogyakarta. Applied Mechanics and Materials , Vol 845, pp. 265-273
6. Constantinos Repapis, Elizabeth Vintzileou and Christoszeris. 2006. Evaluation of Seismic Performance of Existing RC Buildings : I. Suggested Methodology, Journal of Earthquake Engeneering, Vol. 10, Issue 2.
7. Badan Standardisasi Nasional. 2012. Tata Cara Perencanaan Ketahanan Gempa Untuk Struktur Bangunan Gedung dan Non Gedung- SNI 03-1726-2012, Bandung: Kementrian Pekerjaan Umum.
8. Applied Technical Council (ATC 40 : 1996), Seismic Evaluation and retrofit of Concrete Building. California Seismic Safety Commission, Redwood City, California.
9. Federal Emergency Management Agency (FEMA 365 : 2000), Prestandard and Commentary for The Seismic Rehabilitation of Buildings, Washington D.C.

Effects of Single and Multi Openings in Brick Infills on the Seismic Response of Infilled RC Frames

Maidiawati[1]*, Jafril Tanjung[2], Hamdeni Medriosa[1] and Yulia Hayati[3]

[1] Padang Institute of Technology, Civil Engineering Department
[2] Andalas University, Civil Engineering Department
[3] Syiah Kuala University, Civil Engineering Department

Abstract. Many researchers have performed a lot of studies of the seismic behavior reinforced concrete (RC) frame with masonry infill. They found that masonry infill affects the lateral strength, stiffness and ductility performance of the RC frame structures. However, when openings appeared in the panel infill for door and windows, the responses of the overall structure are entirely changed. The primary purpose of this study is to experimentally investigate the behavior of brick infilled RC frames possessing single opening and two openings. Four specimens of 1/4-scale single bay RC frames with brick infills were made that were one bare frame, one frame with full infill and two frames with infills having a central opening and two openings with the opening ratio of 25%. The specimens were tested under lateral reversed cyclic loads. Consequently, different responses of failure mechanism, lateral strength, stiffness and energy dissipated were observed among the specimens. The brick full infill failed in shear with propagation cracks in central part of the panel, but in the case of the infills with single and two openings, the cracks were dominated at the corners of the openings. The in-plane strength, stiffness and dissipated energy of infilled frames decreased when openings appeared in the panel. However, the seismic performance of brick infilled frame with the opening of 25% of panel area is better than those of bare frame. The brick infilled frames with a central opening and two openings are similar in lateral strength and dissipated energy. It seems that area and position of the openings control the seismic response to the overall infilled frame structure of the openings

1 Introduction

Brick masonry walls are very commonly used as partition in reinforced concrete (RC) buildings around the world, including in Indonesia as one of the high seismicity regions. Mostly, the brick-masonry wall is assumed as a non-structural element and ignored in seismic design calculations.

Large numbers of studies related to evaluating the brick masonry wall contribution on seismic performance of RC frames have been carried out (Choi et al., 2017; Maidiawati et al., 2011; Tanjung and Maidiawati, 2017; Zovkic et al., 2012; Dautaj et al., 2018). They mainly studied seismic behavior and performance of frames with solid masonry infill. The authors experimentally tested the RC frame infilled with brick infill for investigating its seismic behavior by comparing to those of bare frame (Maidiawati et al., 2011; Tanjung et al., 2017). Besides, an analytical model of infilled frame was developed and applied to calculate the seismic performance of RC building by considering the brick masonry infill as clearly stated in Reference (Maidiawati and Sanada, 2017). Nevertheless, these studies neglected the brick infills with openings by assuming that the infills with openings did not contribute to the seismic performance of frame structure (Choi et al., 2005). However, several references explained that infills with opening still contribute to the lateral strength of frame structure depended to type and size of the opening (Maidiawati et al., 2017; Mohammadi and Nikfar, 2013; Mondal and Jain, 2008). The authors tested brick masonry infilled frames with door and window openings in infills by applying monotonic lateral loading (Maidiawati et al., 2017). It was found that openings in infill changed the failure mechanism of structure and decreased the seismic resistance and stiffness of overall infilled frame structures.

The current study experimentally investigated the seismic behavior RC frame installed with brick infill having single and multi-window openings under cyclic lateral loading. The structure responses of failure modes, lateral strength, stiffness, and energy dissipation are discussed in this paper.

2 Experimental specimens

Four of 1/4-scaled single story and single bay RC frame specimens were prepared to experimentally clarify the effects of single and multi-openings in unreinforced brick infill on seismic response of RC frame structuregle bay RC frame specimens. They consisted of an RC bare frame (BF), an RC frame infilled with solid clay brick-masonry (IFSW) and one of brick masonry infilled RC frame with a central opening (IFOW-1) and one of infilled frame with two openings

(IFOW-2). The dimension and detailed structure of all specimens were all the same to RC frame elements. Figure 1(a) shows the detailed drawing of the RC frame elements. The columns clear height was 750 mm with their cross-sectional dimension of 125x125 mm, 4D10 longitudinal rebars and ϕ4-50 transverse hoops. The cross-sectional dimension of the upper beam was 200x200 mm with 4D13 longitudinal reinforcements and a hoop of ϕ8-50. The cross-sectional dimension of the footing beam was 700x200 mm with 16D13 for the longitudinal reinforcements and ϕ8-50 for the hoop.

The infill element used 1/4 scale clay bricks of dimensions of 60 mm in length, 30 mm in width and 13 mm in height. The scaled brick units were arranged with mortar beds in the interior clear height of frames. The ratio of cement:water for mortar was 1:0.5. Finishing mortar with 5.0 mm thickness used for plastering both wall surfaces. The average compressive strength of brick is 10.9 N/mm2. No shear connectors were used between infill and boundary columns. Figures 1(b), 1(b), and 1(c) show the RC frame with solid brick infill, RC frame with brick infill having a central opening, and RC frame with brick infill having two openings, respectively.

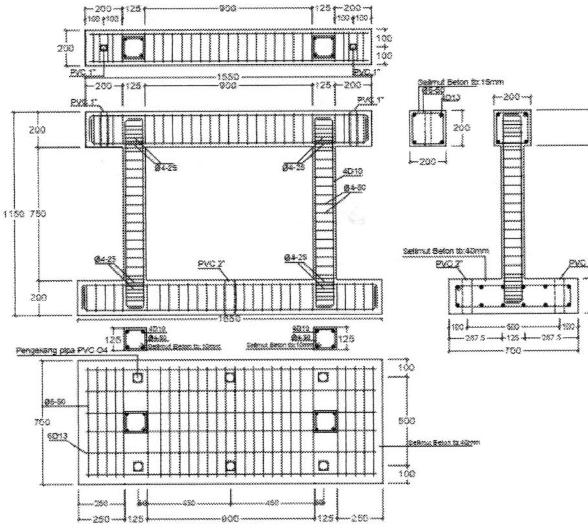

(a) Detailed drawing of the RC frame element

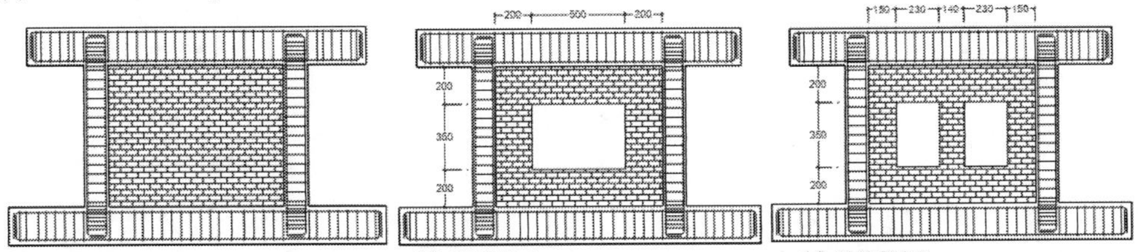

(b) IFSW (c) IFOW-1 (d) IFOW-2

Fig. 1: Detailed drawing of specimens.

3 Material properties

Table 1 shows the compressive strength of concrete (fc'), the compressive strength of brick masonry prism (fm'), yield strength (fy) and tensile strength (fu) of reinforcements as the material properties of specimens.

Table 1. Material properties of specimens

Specimen	f_c' (N/mm2)	f_m' (N/mm2)	f_y (N/mm2)	f_u (N/mm2)
BF	49.9	-	390.2 (for Ø4)	598.3 (for Ø4)
IFSW	49.9	13.0	346.8 (for Ø6)	448.6 (for Ø6)
IFOW-1	49.9	13.0	462.0 (for D10)	619.7 (for D10)
IFOW-2	49.9	13.0	421,1 (for D13)	582.4 (for D13)

4 Test method

4.1 Loading system

The test models were constructed and tested at the testing facility in Structural and Construction Material Laboratory of Civil Engineering Department, Syiah Kuala University. The specimens subjected by reversed cyclic lateral loads using a horizontal hydraulic jack with a capacity of 500 kN without axial load. Figure 2 demonstrates the schematic representation of the test setup and loading system.

The lateral reversed cyclic loading applied to the specimens referred to FEMA 461 standard (FEMA 461, 2007). The loading history of cyclic loading applied to specimens is shown in Figure 3. The lateral load with initial cycle to R=1/800 was applied to specimen and then followed by two cycles to R=1/400, 1/200, 1/100, 1/50, 1/25, 1/12.5, and 1/10, however, the loading stopped when the specimens failed. The drift angle R; ratio of lateral displacement to column height, is used for controlling incremental loading.

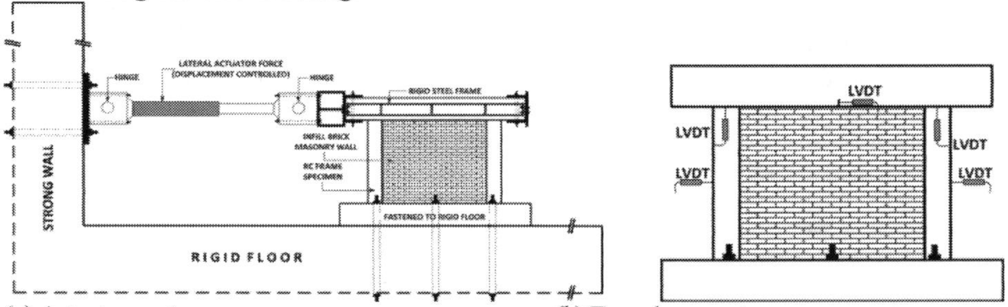

(a) Actuators set-up (b) Transducers set up

Fig. 2: Schematic representation of test setup

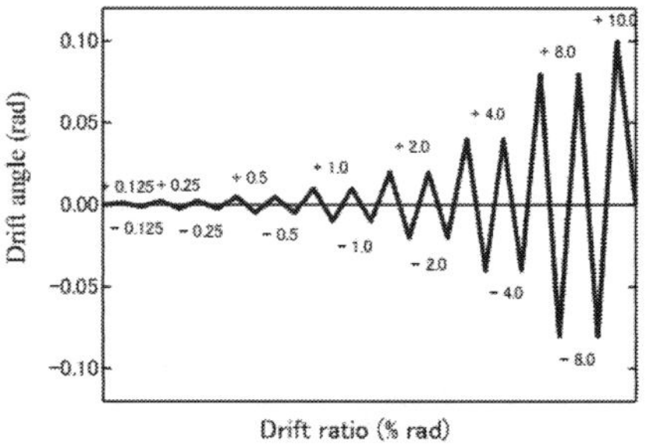

Fig. 3: Loading history

4.2 Measurement

Several measurement devices of LVDT were placed on the columns of specimen to quantify the horizontal and vertical displacements of both columns, as shown in Figure 2(b). During the test, the incremental applied cyclic lateral loads, as well as displacements, were recorded. Initiated cracks and crack propagation were marked in the columns and the infills at the peak and residual drifts to identify the failure process of specimens. Failure mode and the final cracking pattern of the specimen were noticed.

Test results and discussion

5.1 Failure process

Table 2 summarizes the failure process of all specimens. Comparison of crack patterns of specimens at the final condition after testing are exhibited in Figure 4.

Table 2. Failure process of specimens

cycles	BF Specimen	IFSW specimen
1/800	No crack in this cycles	Separation cracks between column and wall at a drift ratio of 0.05.
1/400	Initial flexural crack at the top of the tensile column at 0.16 drift ratio.	Initial flexural crack at the tensile column at drift ratio 0.17. Initial shear crack at the tensile column at the drift ratio of 0.21.
1/200	Initial shear crack at the bottom of the compressive column at a drift ratio of 0.5.	Initial shear crack at the center of panel wall at a drift ratio 0.45.
1/100	Propagations of flexural cracks at the ends of both columns.	Propagation of shear cracks at the ends of both columns and peeling off of the wall plaster.

1/50	Development of flexural cracks to flexural-shear cracks.	Development of shear crack width at the ends of columns and spalling of wall plaster.
1/25	Propagation of shear crack at the ends of columns.	Shear failure of the brick wall in the in plane direction and then degradation of lateral strength.
1/25.5	Shear failure at the bottom of the compressive column at a drift ratio 7.85.	Failure of the wall in out of plane direction. Shear failure at the bottom of the compressive column.
1/10	Shear failure in both columns. Degradation of lateral strength	Shear failure of both columns.
cycles	IFOW-1 Specimen	IFOW-2 Specimen
1/800	Initial shear crack at the left top corner and at the right bottom corner of opening at the drift ratio 0.06.	Initial shear crack at the left top corner of the opening at the drift ratio 0.04. Initial flexural crack in the wall between two openings at drift ratio 0.06. Separation cracks between column and wall at a drift ratio of -0.06.
1/400	Separation cracks between columns and wall. Initial flexural crack at the tensile column at the drift ratio 0.25.	Initial flexural crack at the top of the tensile column at a drift ratio of 0.26.
1/200	Initial shear crack at the tensile column at a drift ratio 0.47. Propagation of flexural cracks at the middle height of both columns.	Initial shear crack at the top of the tensile column at a drift ratio of 0.51
1/100	Development of shear cracks at the corners of the opening. Propagation of shear cracks at the ends of both columns. And propagation of flexural cracks along both column height.	Development of shear cracks at the corners of the opening. Propagation of shear cracks at the ends of both columns. And propagation of flexural cracks along both column height.
1/50	Initial peeling off the plaster at the corner of the opening.	Development of shear cracks at the corners of the opening. Peeling off the plaster at the corner of the opening.
1/25	Spalling of plaster of the wall. further shear failure of the wall at the corner of the opening. Propagation of shear cracks at the top of the column. And then degradation of lateral strength	Spalling of plaster of the wall. Initial failure of the wall in out of plane direction. Degradation of lateral strength
1/12.5	Shear failure of the tensile column. Initial failure of the wall in out of plane direction	Shear failure of the tensile column. Initial failure of the wall in out of plane direction
1/10	Totally collapsed of the wall in out of plane direction	Totally collapsed of the wall in out of plane direction

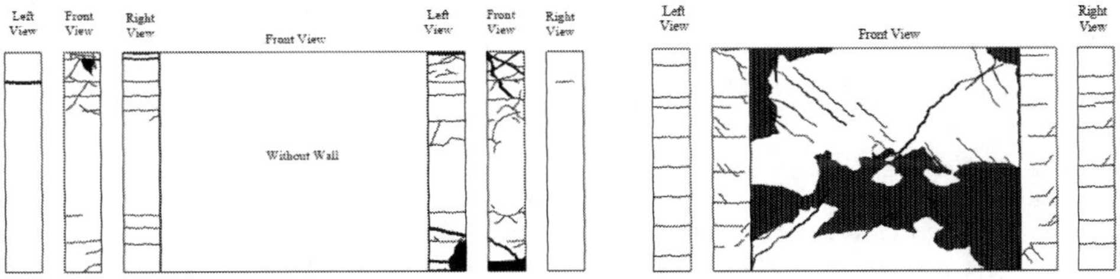

(a) BF (b) IFSW

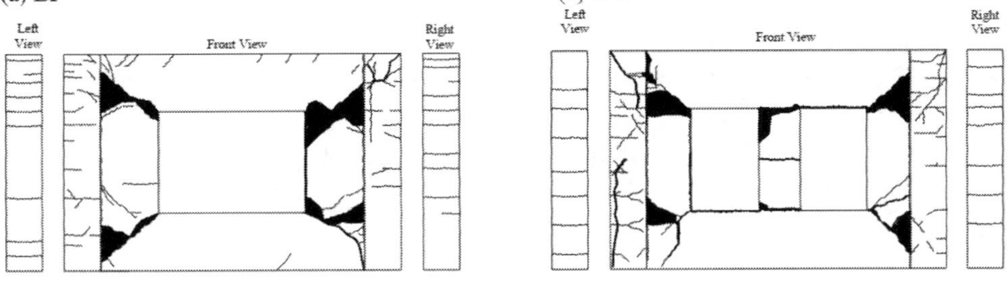

(c) IFOW-1 (d) IFOW-2

Fig. 4: Crack pattern of specimens

5.2 Lateral strength vs. lateral displacement

The relationship between lateral strength vs. Lateral displacement is shown in Figure 9 which indicates the seismic performance of specimens. The maximum lateral strength of 51.3 kN achieved at 57.8 mm lateral displacement. In the cases of the IFSW, IFOW-1 and IFOW-2 specimens attained to the maximum lateral strengths of 127.7 kN, 74.7 kN and 74.3 kN at the drift ratios of 0.93%, 1.86%, and 0.98%, respectively. These results revealed that the IFOW-1 and IFOW-2 specimens with the opening ratio of 25% are similar in lateral strength. It seems that reduction of lateral strength of infilled frame structure is influenced by the ratio of opening to panel area, even though the infill has single or multi openings. The deformation capacity was evaluated as the lateral strength degraded to 80% after the peak of lateral strength that it was obtained at drift ratios of 8.4% for BF, 1.9% for IFSW, 7.7% for IFOW-1 and 6.8% for IFOW-2. It indicates that the ductility performance of infilled frame with a single opening is higher than those of RC frames with solid infill and infill with two openings. The single and two openings with a ratio of 25% of panel decreased the lateral of infilled frame to 58%. The stiffness of infilled frame decreased to 30% and 60% as single and two openings appeared in infill, respectively. However, the seismic performance of infilled frames with single and two openings were better than those of bare frame.

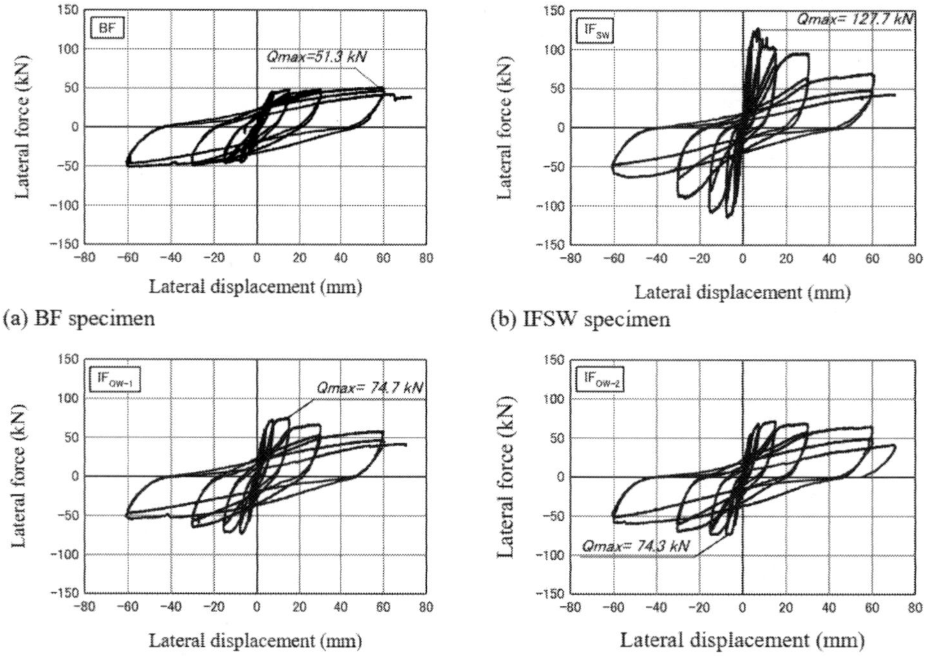

(a) BF specimen (b) IFSW specimen

(c) IFOW-1 specimen (d) IFOW-2 specimen

Fig. 5: Lateral force-Lateral displacement relationship

5.3 Dissipated energy

For elements of RC structure designed to resist seismic load which accommodate damage without collapse, the energy produced by the seismic event can be dissipated by hysteretic response of RC elements without a significant reduction in strength (Rodrigues et al., 2012). Therefore the amount of energy dissipated of structures may be evaluated by calculating the area enclosed by hysteresis loops curves indicated in Figure 5. Consequently, the dissipated energy in each loading cycle and the cumulative energy dissipation are presented in Figure 6. The energy dissipation of RC frame with solid infill is higher 1.6 times than those of the bare frame, 1.4 times than that of RC frame with a central opening and 1.3 times than those of RC frame with two openings infill. It indicates that energy dissipation of infilled frame was reduced as opening existed in infill. In the case of RC frames with infill with a central opening and infill with two openings, they were similar in energy dissipation. Significant reduction of energy dissipation in the second cycle was observed on the RC frame with solid infill. It reduced to 50% of the first cycle energy dissipation as shown in Figure 6(a). In the cases of bare frame (BF) and infilled frame with openings (IFOW-1 and IFOW-2), significant degradation of energy dissipation in the second cycle occurred at drift angels R=1/400 to R=1/100 that was about 70% of the first cycle energy dissipation, but reduction was only about 20% at drift angles R=1/50 to R=1/12.5.

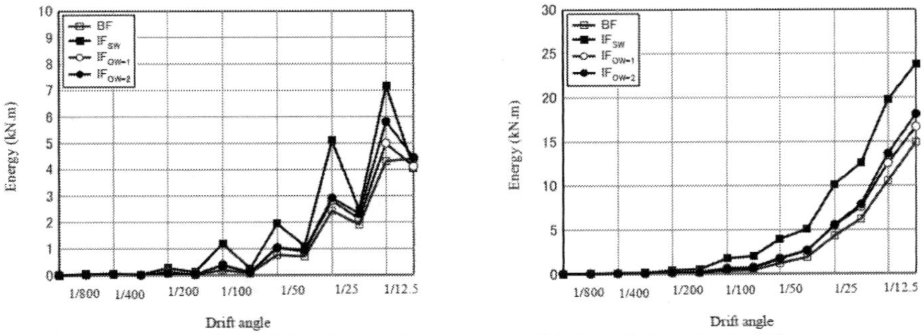

(a) Dissipated energy in each loading cycle (b) Cumulative dissipated energy
Fig. 6: Dissipated energy of specimens

6 Conclusions

This paper reported the seismic responses of RC frames with a central opening infill and RC frame with two openings infill under the cyclic lateral loading tests which were compared to seismic responses of the solid infilled frame and the RC bare frame. The ratio of opening size to panel area was 25% for infill with central opening and infill with two openings. The following are the major findings:
Brick infilled frames with a central opening and two openings were similar in lateral strength and dissipated energy but they were little different in lateral stiffness.
The brick infill with a central opening and two openings of 25% of panel area decreased the lateral strength of the solid infilled frame to 58%. However, their lateral strengths were higher about 1.4 times than those of bare frame.
The stiffness of infilled frame structure dropped to 30% due to a central opening and 60% due to two openings appeared in infill.
The dissipated energy of the solid infilled frame was higher about 1.6 times than that of the bare frame. But, it decreased to 70% as openings of 25% appeared in infill.

Acknowledgment

This paper reports the results of research developed under financially supported by the Ministry of Research, Technology, (DIKTI) Indonesia, with the reference 529/27.O10.4.2/PN/2017. The authors sincerely acknowledge to Prof. Katsuki Takiguchi Lab., Departement of Mechanical and Environmental Informatics, Tokyo Institute of Technology, Japan; Dr. Abdullah, Civil Engineering Dept., Syiah Kuala University, head and staffs of Structure and Construction Material Lab., for supporting and providing the structural testing facilities.

References

1. Choi, H., Nakano, Y., and Sanada, Y. (2005) 'Seismic Performance and Crack Pattern of Concrete Block Infilled Frames.'In Bulletin of ERS, 38
2. Choi, H., Sanada, Y., and Nakano, Y. (2017) 'Diagonal Strut Mechanism of URM Wall Infilled RC Frame for Multi Bays.' In Procedia Engineering Proceedings of the 6th International Workshop on Performance, Protection & Strengthening of Structures under Extreme Loading, Held December 11-12 2017 at Guangzhou (Canton), China.
3. Dautaj, A. D., Kadiri, Q., and Kabashi, N. (2018) 'Experimental study on the contribution of masonry infilling the behavior of RC frame under seismic loading.' Engineering Structures, 165, 27-37.
4. Maidiawati, Sanada, Y., Konishi, D., and Tanjung, J. (2011) 'Seismic Performance of Nonstructural Brick Walls Used in Indonesian R/C Buildings.' Journal of Asian Architecture and Building Engineering, 10 (1), 203-210.
5. Maidiawati and Sanada, Y. (2017) 'R/C Frame-Infill Interaction Model and Its Application to Indonesian Buildings.' Earthquake Engineering and Structural Dynamics, 46 (2), 221-241. DOI: 10.1002/eqe.2787
6. Maidiawati, Tanjung, J., and Medriosa, H. (2017) 'Experimental Study on the Influence of the Opening in Brick-masonry Wall to Seismic Performance of Reinforced Concrete Frame Structures.' In: AIP Proceeding of the International Conference of Global Network for Innovative Technology and AWAM International Conference in Civil Engineering, Held August 8-10 2017 at Penang Malaysia.
7. Mohammadi, M., and Nikfar, F. (2013) 'Strength and Stiffness of Masonry-Infilled Frames with Central Openings Based on Experimental Results.' Journal of Structural Engineering, 139, 974-984
8. Mondal, G., and Jain, S., K. (2008) 'Lateral Stiffness of Masonry Infilled Reinforced Concrete (RC) Frames with Central Opening.' Earthquake Spectr Earthquake Engineering Research Institute (EERI), 24 (3), 701-723. DOI: 10.1193/1.2942.376

9. Rodrigues, H., Varum., H., Arede, A., and Costa, A. (2012) 'A Comparative Analysis of Energy Dissipation and Equivalent Viscous Damping of RC Columns Subjected to Uniaxial and Biaxial Loading.' Journal of Engineering Structures, 35, 149-164.
10. Tanjung, J., and Maidiawati (2017) 'The Experimental Investigation on Beneficial Effects of The Local Brick Masonry Infills to Seismic Performance of R/C Frame Structures in West Sumatera.' International Journal of Civil Engineering and Technology, 2 (10), 687-697.
11. Zovkic, J., Sigmund, V., Guljas, I. (2012) 'Cyclic testing of a single bay reinforced concrete frames with various types of masonry infill.' Earthquake Engineering and Structural Dynamics, 42 (8), 1131-1149. DOI: 10.1002/eqe.2263

Development of a Relative Vulnerability Index (RVI) for Estimation of Building Vulnerability towards Tsunami Hazard

Leli Honesti[1*], Muhd Zaimi Abd Majid[2], Nazwar Djali[3], Meli Muchlian[1], Syofyan Z[1]

[1] Department of Civil Enginering, Faculty of Civil Enginering and Design, Institut Teknologi Padang, Indonesia
[2] Department of Structure and Material, Faculty of Civil Engineering, Universiti Teknologi Malaysia, Malaysia
[3] Department of Civil Enginering, Faculty of Civil Enginering and Design, Bung Hatta University, Indonesia

Abstract. Tsunami hazard is an adverse event, which causes damage to properties and loss of life. The study on the effects of tsunami hazard on building vulnerability can help establish and improve the resilience of the building. The problem in assessing the building vulnerability towards tsunami hazard is significant whereby available models for assessing the risk are not applicable for buildings in Padang, Indonesia. The study developed a new Relative Vulnerability Index (RVI) model to estimate building vulnerability for assessment the risk. Literature review was carried out with regards to model development. The model was grouped in two categories of vulnerability, namely the Water Inundation (WI) and the Building Vulnerability (BV). The water inundation comprises tsunami inundation factor. Then, the building bulnerability consists of both internal and external factors. Contribution of each factor is 1/3 or 33.33% of the overall weighting of the new RVI scores. The new RVI model has applied a formula of 1/3 water (tsunami) inundation factor + 1/3 internal factor + 1/3 external factor. The total value of all weights put together should be equal to 100. To use the model, it is necessary to investigate two internal and external factors based on the characteristics of a building and specific geographichal feature of an area. In conclusion, this study has successfully developed a new RVI model for building vulnerability towards tsunamis. In comparison to other approaches, the model offers an adaptable methodology for the characteristics of the buildings and spesific geographical features of the area.

1 Introduction

Indonesia is a big country which is highly exposed to tsunami risk. In the last two centuries, there were four major earthquakes that occurred in the Sumatra subduction zone, which include in 1833 with a magnitude of 8.8 to 9.2 Richter scale [1](McCloskey et al., 2008), and in 1797 with a magnitude of 8.5 to 8.7 Richter scale [2](McCloskey et al., 2010). On the 26th of December, 2004 with a magnitude of 9.0 to 9.3 Richter scale, the region of Aceh was shaken by a tsunami. The tsunami ruptured major fault zones ocean – Australia along the 1300 km [3](Suppasri et al., 2010). The impacts of this tsunami have caused serious damaged on infrastructure and buildings along the coast with 300,000 reported casualties. On the 28th of March, 2005, the Sumatran megathrust subduction zone collapsed in the magnitude of 8.7 Richter scale earthquake in Nias, where more than 200 buildings were destroyed [4](Briggs et al., 2006).

Hazard assessment, vulnerability and risk contribute substantially to identify and establish tsunami risk zones for buildings along coastal areas. Tsunami simulation can be considered as water vulnerability [5](Honesti et al., 2014). Mardiatno (2008) classified the height of run up into three categories; namely low, medium and high levels and classified tsunami inundation risk into five categories; namely very low 1 (>0 – 0.25 m), low 2 (>0.25 – 0. 5 m), moderate 3 (>0.5 – 1 m), high 4 (>1 – 2 m) and very high 5 (>2 m) [6]. Muchlian and Honesti (2017) has been modelled tsunami simulations from Pagai and Sipora block sources in Air Tawar sub-district, Padang. The tsunami wave height from the Pagai block is greater than the tsunami wave from the Sipora block. The inundation area from Pagai source is approximately 47 nested grids, and more than two-thirds of area are safe from tsunami, while the inundation area from Sipora source is approximately 19 nested grids and more than three quarters of area are safe from tsunami [7].

The problem in assessing the building vulnerability towards tsunami hazard arises as previous models for assessing the risk are not suitable to be applied in the area. Example, many buildings in Ulak Karang sub-district, Padang, especially along the river, are made of traditional brick [8](Honesti et al., 2015). This is mainly due to the fact that there are uncertainties in the models for the building as well as the physical area characteristics of West Sumatra, Indonesia.

In the PTVA-3 model, the factors of vulnerability consist of structural vulnerability and water vulnerability. The structural vulnerability is determined by building vulnerability factors (BV) and protection factors (Prot). The building vulnerability factors (BV)

* Corresponding author: leli.honesti@itp.ac.id

include: 1) number of stories; 2) building material; 3) ground floor; 4) foundation; 5) shape and orientation of building; 6) movable object as well as 7) preservation condition. The protection factors on the other hand include: 1) building row; 2) natural barrier; 3) sea wall height and shape; as well as 4) brick wall around building. The formula of the PTVA-3 model is as follow:

$$RVI = (2/3) \times (\text{"SV\_1\_5"}) + (1/3) \times (\text{"WV\_1\_5"}) \quad (1)$$

Where "SV_1_5" is the structural vulnerability and "WV_1_5" is water vulnerability. "SV" is the standarized score for the structural vulnerability (Dall' Osso et al., 2009) [9].

The problem in complex and one of challenges faced is in the calculation of the RVI model for assessing the building vulnerability, particularly within the coastal region of Indonesia. For solution of this problem, it is important to develop the RVI model for the building vulnerability to tsunami hazard. The model especially for areas of Indonesia and the same characteristic areas. The main purpose of this research is to develop a new model to assess building vulnerability caused by tsunamis. The study developed a model in the form of a new Relative Vulnerability Index (RVI) model.

2 Method

This study focuses on establishing building vulnerability model, particularly for areas in Indonesia as well as those areas with the same characteristics. Here, a new RVI model was developed according to the adoption of some model about building vulnerability. The model is more accurate and more adaptable towards the variation of tsunami inundation factor and building vulnerability factors. The building vulnerability assessment was undertaken through a detailed survey in the fields. Then, the new RVI score for each inundated building was calculated using the new RVI model developed. In this case, a building vulnerability is influenced from the conditions inside of the building, known as the internal factors, and from the conditions outside of the building, with the exception of tsunami inundation, known as the external factors. The internal and external factors were established by analyzing the factors influencing building vulnerability towards tsunami inundation.

The concept of two group factors offers a useful framework for understanding the causes and effects of building vulnerability. In this context the two groups of factors indicating the levels of vulnerability can be identified on the basis of a function. The factors were developed from the RVI-3 model as well as a number of literatures by experts in the field. For example, a geophysics expert stated that existence of barrier islands, distance from the river, gap between buildings and distance from the shoreline affect building vulnerability towards the worst effects of a tsunami.

3 Results and Discussion

The building vulnerability to tsunami hazard is generally determined by internal and external factors of a building. These factors in this study are based on the tabulation data by finding the factors most often used by researchers in previous studies. Hajar (2006); Jelínek et al. (2009); Dall'Osso et al. (2009(a),(b)); Sumaryono (2010); Atillah et al. (2011); Barros et al. (2015) and Sivakumar and Sivagamasundari (2015) have taken the factors associated with building vulnerability [9-16].

Through this study, the internal and external building vulnerability factors have been established. There are construction material; 2) number of stories; 3) foundations; 4) preservation condition; 5) building age; 6) ground floor hydrodynamics; 7) shape and orientation of the building as internal factors and 1) movable objects; 2) building row; 3) height of concrete fence; 4) natural barrier; 5) the presence of a seawall; 6) distance from the shoreline; 7) distance from the river; 8) obstacle islands and 9) gap between buildings as external factors. Then, compared to the building vulnerability in other researchers, every researcher used the factors that are different compared with the others. Here, with the result that the writers combined several factors by selecting the factors that contribute greatly to the building vulnerability due to tsunami hazard. Based on the result of tabulation and the selection of internal and external factors in this research, there are some differences of factors used by every researcher in the previous researches. This is due to the fact that many factors used have significant influence of these factors on the determination of building vulnerability, but several factors did not chose because the factors do not influence significantly to the building vulnerability.

This study discusses on the process of developing an RVI model for building vulnerability developed. In developing the new RVI model, it was found that in some studies the RVI is based on vulnerability level. In PTVA-3, the RVI scores for every building were determined using a weighted attribute. The new model was developed to estimate the vulnerability pattern within predicted factors which is based on a subjective procedure that relies heavily on the expert judgement of the authors developed.

The new RVI score model was developed to provide the first order assessments of building vulnerability to tsunami hazard. The output of this model is "a New Relative Vulnerability Index" (new RVI) model for every building. In this model, the new RVI model was grouped in two categories of vulnerability, namely the Water Inundation (WI) and the Building Vulnerability (BV). The Building Vulnerability (BV) consists of both the internal and the external factors.

Reinaldi (2002) have used two scenarios to assess building vulnerability affected by an earthquake in Semarang. Here, the classification of vulnerability is presented in an RVI map of building vulnerability towards earthquake hazard. Furthermore, building vulnerability is a combination of social, disaster and physical building factors [17]. Based on the simplest model in pair wise comparison matrix of Syabri (1997)

[18], the assessment scenarios of building vulnerability can be written in the following forms (2 and 3) in scenario 1 and 2.

$$VL = 33.33\%\ TDF + 33.33\%\ TSF + 33.33\%\ TPF \quad (2)$$

$$VL = 60\%\ TDF + 20\%\ TSF + 20\%\ TPF \quad (3)$$

where, VL is vulnerability level, the TDF and the TSF are the total disaster factors and the total social factors respectively. Then, the TPF is the total physical factors. These two scenarios are usually used by alchemists (Syabri, 1997). Using the pair wise comparison matrix, the levels of vulnerability can be classified into four categories: Very Low ($V < 1.50$); Low ($1.50 \leq V \leq 2.00$); Medium ($2.00 < V \leq 2.5$); High ($2.50 < V \leq 3.00$) and Very High ($V > 3.00$).

Afatia et al. (2012) have analysed the risk of a pyroclastic flow of the Semeru volcano by using the pair wise comparison matrix. The pair wise comparison matrix is a tool to rank a set of decision-making criteria and rate the criteria on a relative scale of importance. Making decisions requires comparing alternatives with respect to a particular set of criteria. If there are more than two criteria, determining which criteria is more important can it self be a serious problem. One would like to be able to rank the criteria in order of importance, and to assign to the criteria some relative ranking indicating the degree of importance of each criterion with respect to the other criteria. Every criterion is ranked based on rising interest rates, then the value of each weight is multiplied to get the weighting of each criteria [19].

The ranking of hazard, vulnerability and capacity are of the same importance if a pair wise comparison matrix for decision making of a risk analysis for scenario 1. The pair comparison of scenario 1 is presented in Table 1. Here, the weight of each criterion is 0.333, with the total of all the weights must be 100%. Table 2 (scenario 2) demonstrates that the pair wise comparison matrix of hazard criteria is of utmost importance. Having said that, the vulnerability is five times more important than the capacity. Thus, the last criteria introduced here is the capacity (most unimportant).

Based on the scenario 1, the new RVI can be determined as follows:

$$(RVI) = (1/3) \times (WI) + (1/3) \times (IF) + (1/3) \times (EF) \quad (4)$$

where: WI is water inundation and this relation gives as a result a value of WI ranging between 0 to 100. IF is the internal factor for building vulnerability. The minimum total weight is 0 and maximum total weight is 100. EF is the external factor for building vulnerability and the maximum total weight is also 100.

4 Conclusion

There are three main factors that need to be considered in calculating building vulnerability to tsunami hazard in the study area, namely the tsunami inundation factor, the internal, and the external vulnerability factors. In the context of this RVI, it can be determined in equation (4). A new RVI model was developed according to adoption from some model about building vulnerability. The model is more adaptable towards the variation of tsunami inundation factor and building vulnerability factors. The building vulnerability assessment is undertaken through a detailed survey in the fields. Findings from this study have established the new RVI model based on several factors including water inundation factor, internal and external factors for assessing building vulnerability towards tsunami hazard based on the building and coastal characteristics.

References

1. J. McCloskey, A. Antonioli, A. Piatanesi, K. Sieh, S. Steacy, S. Nalbant, M. Cocco, C. Giunchi, J.D. Huang, and P. Dunlop, Tsunami threat in the Indian Ocean from a future megathrust earthquake west of Sumatra. Earth and Planetary Science Letters. **265** (1-2). 61-8, (2008)
2. J. McCloskey, D. Lange, F. Tilmann, S.S. Nalbant, A.F. Bell, D.H. Natawidjaja, and A. Rietbrock, The September 2009 Padang Earthquake. Nature Geoscience. **3**. 70–71. (2010)
3. A. Suppasri, F. Imamura, and S. Koshimura, Effect of the rupture velocity of fault motion, ocean current and initial sea level on the transoceanic propagation of tsunami. Coastal Engineering Journal. **52**(2). 107-132, (2010)
4. R.W. Briggs, K. Sieh, A.J. Meltzner, D.H. Natawidjaja, J. Galetzka, B. Suwargadi, Y. Hsu, M. Simons, N. Hananto, I. Suprihanto, D. Prayudi, J.P. Avouac, L. Prawirodirdjo, and Y. Bock, Deformation and slip along the Sunda megathrust in the great 2005 Nias–Simeulue earthquake. Science. **311**(5769). 1897–1901, (2006)
5. L. Honesti, M.Z.A. Majid, M. Muchlian, and N. Djali., Assesing Building Vulnerability to Tsunami Hazard in Padang. Jurnal Teknologi (Sciences & Engineering). **69** (6), 5–9, (2014)
6. D. Mardinatno, *Tsunami Risk Assessment Using Scenario-Based Approach, Geomorphological Analysis and Geographic Information System: A Case Study in South Coastal Areas of Java Island-Indonesia*. (University of Innsbruck, Germany, 2008)
7. M. Muchlian, and L. Honesti, *Pemodelan Numerik Gelombang Tsunami untuk Menentukan Luas Area Inundasi (Studi Kasus Daerah Air Tawar Padang)*. in Prosiding Seminar Nasional Fisika Universitas Andalas (SNFUA). Padang: Physics Department: 95-102, (2017)
8. L. Honesti, M.Z.A. Majid, N. Djali, and M. Muchlian, Modeling the Potential Risk of Building Vulnerability toward Tsunami Hazard in Ulak Karang and Pasir Jambak Sub-District, Padang. Jurnal Teknologi (Sciences & Engineering). **72**(4). 41–47, (2015)
9. F. Dall'osso, M. Gonella, G. Gabbianelli, G, Withycombe, and D. Dominey-Howes, Assessing the vulnerability of buildings to tsunami in Sydney.

Natural Hazards Earth System Sciences. **9**. 2015–2026, (2009)

10. F. Dall'Osso, M. Gonella, G. Gabbianelli, G. Withycombe, and D. Dominey-Howes, A revised (PTVA) model for assessing the vulnerability of buildings to tsunami damage'. Natural Hazards Earth System Sciences. **9**. 1557–1565, (2009)
11. M. Hajar, *Pemetaan Tingkat Kerawanan Bencana Tsunami Menggunakan Data Pengindraan Jauh dan Sistem Informasi Geografi (SIG) Studi Kasus: Kota Padang*. (Bogor: Marine Science and Technology Department, Bogor Agricultural University, 2006)
12. R. Jelinek, S. Eckert, G. Zeug, and E. Krausmann, *Tsunami Vulnerability and Risk Analysis Applied to the City of Alexandria, Egypt*. (Italy: European Commission, 2009)
13. Sumaryono. *Assessing Building Vulnerability to Tsunami Hazard Using Integrative Remote Sensing and GIS Approaches*. (München: Ludwig-Maximilians-Universität, 2010)
14. A. Atillah, D.E. Hadani, H. Moudni, O. Lesne, C. Renou, A. Mangin, and F. Rouffi, Tsunami vulnerability and damage assessment in the coastal area of Rabat and Sal´e, Morocco. Natural Hazards Earth System Sciences. **11**, 3397–3414, (2011)
15. J.L. Barros, A. Emídio, A. Santos, and A.O. Tavares, Composite methodology for tsunami vulnerability assessment based on the numerical simulation of 1755 Lisbon tsunami—application on two Portuguese coastal areas. 'In: Safety and Reliability: Methodology and Applications. ed. by Nowakowski, T. et al. London: Taylor & Francis Group: 1581, (2015)
16. I. Sivakumar, and R. Sivagamasundari, A Statistical Model for Assessing Building Vulnerability to Tsunami In Coastal Region'. Asian Journal of Civil Engineering (BHRC). **16** (4). 547–555, (2015)
17. Reinaldi. *Mikrozonasi Gempa Maksimum dan Tingkat Kerentanan Terhadap Bahaya Gempa Di Kodya Semarang*. (Maranatha University, Bandung, 2002)
18. I. Syabri, *Kajian Resiko Kegempaan di Kotamadya Bandung*. (ITB Department, Bandung, 1997)
19. N.N. Afatia, A. Deliar, R. Virtriana, Matrices scenario of pairwise comparison in risk analysis of pyroclastic flows of Semeru Volcano, East Java'. Jurnal Lingkungan dan Bencana Geologi, **3**(3), 211 – 227, (2012)

Table 1. Scenario 1: Pair wise comparison matrix and the criteria scores of hazard, vulnerability and capacity [19]

Criteria	Hazard	Vulnerability	Capacity	Weight
Hazard	1/1	1/1	1/1	0,3333
Vulnerability	1/1	1/1	1/1	0,3333
Capacity	1/1	1/1	1/1	0,3333

Table 2. Scenario 2: Pair wise comparison matrix and the criteria scores of hazard, vulnerability and capacity [19]

Criteria	Hazard	Vulnerability	Capacity	Weight
Hazard	1/1	5/1	9/1	0,7231
Vulnerability	1/5	1/1	5/1	0,2157
Capacity	1/9	1/5	1/1	0,0612

MATEC Web of Conferences **215**, 01038 (2018) https://doi.org/10.1051/matecconf/201821501038
ICTIS 2018

Feasibility Analysis of Surface Rail in The Revitalization of The Railway Road

Wilton Wahab

Institut Teknologi Padang, Department of Civil Engineering, Padang, Indonesia

Abstract. *The railway lines are an integral construction made of steel, concrete or other construction are located on the surface, below and above ground or dangling along with devices that direct the course of the train. Reflecting on the success of the revitalization of the railway line Padang-Pariaman, PT. Railway DIVRE II West Sumatra recently returned to the revitalization of the railway line Lubuk Alung–Kayu Tanam. In this final project feasibility analysis back to the road construction railroad Lubuk Alung-Kayu Tanam considering this path has not been used and an increase in the construction of the railroad on the route. The methodology used is the collection of data from related parties subsequently perform the calculation and analysis of railroad construction that has been revitalized. Data obtained from the calculation of the voltage rails on existing condition of 1380.34 kg/cm² and the voltage rails after revitalized by 840.601 kg/cm² while rail voltage maximum allowed is 1325 kg/cm², the rail existing deserves to be revitalized. Iron bearing on the condition of the existing able to withstand a load of 6761.69 kg, while the load caused by railbus is 8568.986 kg so that the iron bearing existing not worth traversed railbus axle 18 ton and made improvement to the concrete pads. After upgrading, held their concrete pads capable of 23241.678 kg load and expenses incurred as a result of railbus axle 18 tons of concrete pads amounted to 6986.276. Concrete pads so deserve to be passed railbus axle 18 tons. The results of this thesis states that the construction of a rail road Lubuk Alung-Kayu Tanam deserves to be revitalized because of the condition of the existing construction rails and bearings are not able to withstand the stresses and loads that occur due railbus 18 tons passing through.*

1 Preliminary

Transport has now grown into one of the most basic human needs. Starting from the smallest scope of human life, medium scope up to the widest scope. A country with different characteristics of its activities, its culture, and its physical, is definitely in contact with transportation. The effects of the need for movement/movement of people and goods will cause a demand for the provision of infrastructure and means of action to create a movement that goes with the condition of safe, convenient and smooth, and economical in terms of time and cost. In the end, the need for transportation is not only a natural need just, but it is necessary to have a good system so that the objectives of the above movements can be achieved [1]. The current evolving transportation system has embodied a form of ministry through various means of mechanistic movement that almost extends to all networks of territory on earth. Thus, today through modern transportation systems it is not difficult to reach the center of human activity from different angles of movement. The development of transportation technology in the future will be directed to the ability to overcome the demands of freight limitations, mileage, the speed of movement, comfort, safety, and cost reduction. In addition to the fulfillment of transportation limitations above, the dimension of transportation technology system will also be based on improving the quality of human life and the goals of fulfilling the needs of globalization. One example of the success of Indonesian transportation technology is the improvement of railway performance to reduce congestion due to the increase of private vehicles such as monorail and MRT (Mass Rapid Transit) in Jakarta [2].

West Sumatra as one of the developing provinces in Indonesia is also currently being incessant to develop railway transportation mode. As we know that the railway in West Sumatra had experienced suspended animation until in 2007 the Padang-Pariaman railway line was reactivated. The success of revitalization system and technology of transportation mode of railway transportation of Padang -Pariaman line need to be fully supported by good infrastructure. Not only the Padang - Pariaman railway course, beginning in November 2016 and DIVRE II WEST SUMATERA also reactivated the Lubuk Alung - Sicincin - Kayu Tanam railway line called the Pioneer Train. The difference is that if the Padang-Pariaman railway line is still crossed by BB locomotives, the Lubuk Alung-Kayu Tanam line is crossed by a railbus type train with an axle load of 18 tons, where the load is larger than the locomotive that usually crosses this line is 11 tons. In the revitalization of the railway that was once vacuumed

* Corresponding author: wahab.wilton@yahoo.com

at the beginning of 2000, DIVRE II SUMATERA BARAT has been rebuilding or repairing infrastructure in the form of emplacement, road equipment, security and telecommunication, lighting, water supply and others that support the smooth revitalization of railway Lubuk Alung - Kayu Tanam [3-7].

2 Study of Literature

According to Ministerial Regulation No. 60 of 2012 on the technical requirements of the railway line, the speed is divided into speed of plan, maximum speed, operation speed and commercial speed.

Axle pressure is the load received by the rail of an axle. For all classes, the maximum axle load is 18 tones. To calculate the maximum axle pressure, it can use the formula.

$$\bar{P} = \frac{0{,}4}{1+C} x \frac{G}{a} \quad \ldots\ldots(1)$$

To be able to determine the strength of a rail in holding the load through it can be confused using some of the following formulas:

a. Load Calculation on Boogie (Pb)

$$Pb = \frac{\text{W locomotive}}{2} \quad \ldots\ldots(2)$$

b. Load Charge

$$Pg = \frac{\text{Heavy Style On Boogie}}{2} \quad \ldots\ldots(3)$$

c. Static Load Calculation (Ps)

$$Ps = \frac{\text{Style On Gandar}}{2} \quad \ldots\ldots(4)$$

d. Dynamic Load Calculation (Pd)

$$Pd = Ps\left(1 + 0{,}01\left(\frac{V_{maks}}{1{,}609}\right) - 5\right) \ldots\ldots(5)$$

e. Calculation of Reduction Factor / Damping (damping Factor, λ)

$$\lambda = \sqrt[4]{\frac{K}{4EI_x}} \ldots\ldots(6)$$

Where:
K = Modulus of Elasticity of Rail Road
E = Modulus of Elasticity of Steel Constructor of Railway
Ix = Moment of Inertia Rail

f. Maximum Moment Calculation (Mm)

$$M_m = \frac{Pd}{4\lambda} \ldots\ldots(7)$$

Where:
Pd = Dynamic Load
λ = Rail Reduction Factor

g. Voltage Calculation Happened (δ)

$$\sigma = \frac{M_1 x Y}{I_x} \ldots\ldots(8)$$

Where:
M1 = The moment due to the superposition of some axles (0.85 x Mm)
Y = Distance of bottom edge of rail to neutral line

The value of the voltage that occurs on the rail shall not exceed the rail permit voltage according to JNR in Regulation No. 10, 1986 presented in the following table 1:

Table 1. Regulation No. 10, 1986

Class	Rail	Voltage (kg/cm2)	Permit Voltage (kg/cm2) According to JNR
I	R 60 R 54	1042 1195	1325
II	R 54 R 50	1146 1236	1325
III	R 54 R 50 R 42	1097 1183 1474	1663
IV	R 54 R 50 R 42	1048 1130 1409	1843
V	R 42	1343	1843

Steps to calculate the imposition according to Regulation No. 10 of 1986 are as follows:

a. Calculation of Train Charge Distribution to Bearing (Q)

$$Q = 2\,x\,F\,x\,S \ldots\ldots(9)$$

Where:

$$Y_{max} = 0{,}393\,x\,\frac{Pd}{K.X_1} \ldots\ldots(11)$$

$$X_1 = \frac{\pi}{4\lambda} \ldots\ldots(12)$$

b. Calculation of Bearing Reduction Factor (Dumping Factor, λ pads)

$$\lambda = \sqrt[4]{\frac{K}{4EI_x}}$$

c. Calculation of Moments at Points C and D (Right at the Bottom of the Rails)

$$M_{c/d} = \frac{Q_1}{4\lambda} x \frac{1}{\sin\lambda L + \sinh\lambda L} x \begin{bmatrix} 2\cosh^2\lambda a(\cos 2\lambda c + \cosh\lambda L) - \\ 2\cos^2\lambda a\,(\cosh 2\lambda c + \cos\lambda L) - \\ \sinh 2\lambda a\,(\sin 2\lambda c + \sinh\lambda L) - \\ \sin 2\lambda a\,(\sinh 2\lambda c + \sin\lambda L) \end{bmatrix} \ldots\ldots(13)$$

d. Calculation of Moment in Middle Bearing

$$M_0 = -\frac{Q_1}{2\lambda} x \frac{1}{\sin\lambda L + \sinh\lambda L} x \begin{bmatrix} \{\sinh\lambda c\,(\sin\lambda c + \sin\lambda(L-c))\} + \\ \{\sin\lambda c\,(\sinh\lambda c + \sinh\lambda\,(L-c)\} + \\ \{\cosh\lambda c\,x\cos(L-c)\} - \\ \{\cos\lambda c\,x\cosh\lambda(L-c)\} \end{bmatrix} \ldots\ldots(14)$$

e. Calculation of the moment that can hold the bearing

$$Assumption\ M_s = M_{bearing}$$

$$M_{bearing} = \left(\frac{5}{6}\tau_1\right) x\,W \ldots\ldots(15)$$

Where:
τ = Bearing permit voltage by type Bearing Load Calculation (Q1)

$$Q_1 = \frac{M_{Bearing}}{M_{c/d}} \qquad (16)$$

f. Bearing Analysis
The bearing load analysis shall qualify that the load capacity of being retained by the binate shall be higher than the load incurred.

$$(Q_1 > Q) \qquad (17)$$

4 Discussion

The preparation stage is the stage of activity before beginning data collection and processing. To analyze the construction of the railway road Lubuk Alung - Wood Planting required data related to the objectives to draw the right conclusions, therefore conducted data inventory through agency surveys, interviews with related parties whose policies have influence and relationship to the perfection of construction. At this stage, the data processing for the calculation of the construction of railbus 18 tons and the maximum speed of 60 km/hour is calculated; (1). Existing rail construction analysis (R33), (2) Analysis of existing bearing construction, (3) Analysis of rail construction after revitalization (R54), (4) Analysis of bearing construction after revitalized (concrete). To facilitate the calculation of the calculation of the rails and pads can be seen in the following table 2:

Table 2. Comparison of Voltage Occurring and Rail Permit Tension

Rail Type	Occurred voltage < Permit voltage		Explanation
	Occurred voltage (Kg/cm²)	Rail Permit Voltage (Kg/cm²)	
R33	1380,34	1325	Unsatisfactory
R54	840,601		Satisfying

Table 3. Comparison of expenses that can be bearing and the distribution load from rail to bearing

Bearing Type	$(Q_1) < (Q)$		Explanation
	Resistibl e loads (Q_1)	Distribution load from rail to bearing (Q)	
Steel	6761,39 Kg	Unsatisfactor y	Unsatisfactor y
Concret e	840,601 Kg	Satisfying	Satisfying

From the table 3, we can see that on the existing condition of railway line Lubuk Alung - Kayu Tanam using rail type R33, the voltage that occurs on the rail if traversed by railbus with axle 18 tons is 1380.34 kg / cm², this value is greater than the voltage permitted under Regulation No. 10 of 1986 is 1325 kg / cm2, this means that the R33 rail is not feasible to be traversed by the railbus and must be replaced with larger rail dimensions.

The load distribution occurring on the pads due to a railbus axle pressure of 18 tones is 8568,898 kg, and greater than the load capacity of being retained by iron bearings 6761,39 kg, therefore the iron bearings are not feasible to pass by a railbus rail type 18 train ton. Increasing the dimension of rail type R33 to rail type R54 produce rail voltage of 840,601 kg / cm2. The resulting voltage which is smaller than the maximum voltage permitted by JNR in Regulation No. 10 of 1986 amounted to 1325 kg / cm2. Then the R54 type rail is safely traversed by a railbus railway type of 18 tons. Substitution of the type of iron-bearing into concrete pads produces a bearable load of bearings of 23,241,678 kg, and this is greater than the distributed load that occurs on the bearing that is 6986,277 kg. Thus the concrete bearing is able to withstand the burden of railbus with axle 18 tons.

Physically, the existing condition of Lubuk Alung - Kayu Tanam railway line that was built during the Dutch colonial period was designed to be traversed by the locomotive of BB type with 11 tons. The existence of train development in the world is very influential on the development of railways in Indonesia. Due to the demands of technological development and transportation efficiency required Up-Grade and revitalization so that the long railway is not operated adjusted to a load of locomotives through it, especially the railway line Lubuk Alung - Kayu Tanam. Currently, the railway track class of Lubuk Alung - Kayu Tanam has been upgraded from class II level I to class I road.

Based on the Regulation of the Department (PD) No. 10 of 1986 that the first class rail tracks using rail type R54 and R60 (see table), so DIVRE II West Sumatra to increase dimensions of crossroads Lubuk Alung - Kayu Tanam from R33 to R54 by considering several factors other than the permit rail and bearing stress factors that have been analyzed beforehand although the volume of traffic on this line has not been as many as other class I lanes.

The first-class road in the revitalization of the Lubuk Alung-Kayu Tanam railway line is not the only reason for the writer to choose R54 instead of R33. Medium-term and long-term development plans are also taken into account in the selection of rail dimensions, namely the Trans Sumatra railway which is planned to be operational for several years. If this revitalization activity starts from the increase of rails R33 to R42 which is the smallest dimension according to PD 10 the year 1986 with the rail age ranged between 35-40 years then in terms of economic aspects are less profitable and will happen waste. When the Trans Sumatra route has activated the rail and bearing construction must also be adjusted to traffic volume, type of locomotive, train type and axle load through it. That is the reason why R54 as one of the best dimensions at this time according to Regulation of Service (PD) 10 the year 1986 was chosen as replacement dimension of R33 in the revitalization of railway line of Lubuk Alung - Kayu Tanam

Although the railway class at the crossroad of Lubuk Alung - Kayu Tanam has increased to become the first class railway with a maximum speed of 120 km / h (Regulation of Service (PD.10) 1986), but the relatively hilly West Sumatera geographical condition causes the limited geometric improvement of railroads such as arch and bend so that PT. Kereta Api Indonesia provides specific rules that the maximum speed for the railroad in West Sumatra is only 60 km / h, and it is not possible to meet the maximum speed required.

5 Conclusion

1. The voltage occurring at the rail in the existing condition is 1380.34 kg / cm2 and greater than the permitted voltage acceptable by the rail 1325 kg / cm2, it is necessary to increase the rail dimensions.
2. The load distribution from a train to bearing in existing conditions is 8568,986 kg, while the load capable of being retained by R33 iron bearing is only 6761,59 kg, the value is not eligible so that the iron-bearing must be replaced.
3. After increasing the dimension of the railway line, Lubuk Alung-Kayu Tanam can be seen that the voltage that occurs on the rail is equal to 840,601 kg / cm2, the voltage that occurs on the rail is smaller than the permitted voltage that can be held by rail of 1325 kg / cm2.
4. The replacement of the iron-bearing to the concrete pads in the revitalization of the railway line of Lubuk Alung-Kayu Tanam following the required standard of bearings capable of holding 23241,678 kg bearings greater than the load that occurs on the bearing 6986,276 kg.
5. Overall, it can be concluded that the improvement of rail and bearing construction in the revitalization of the Lubuk Alung - Kayu Tanam railway line is feasible.

Referensi

1. Darmawan, Teknologi Jalan Rel, PT Kereta Api Indonesia: Bandung. (2001)
2. Surakim, H., Konstruksi Jalan Rel dan Keselamatan Perjalanan Kereta Api, Nuansa Cendikia: Bandung. (2014).
3. Sunggonokh, Teknik Sipil,: Bandung. (1995)
4. Perumka, Peraturan Dinas (PD) No 10, Tahun 1986 PT. Kereta Api Indonesia (Persero): Bandung, (1986)
5. Peraturan Menteri Perhubungan Republik Indonesia No.60 Tahun 2012 tentang Persyaratan Teknis Jalur Kereta Api, Jakarta.
6. Peraturan Pemerintah No.56 Tahun 2009 tentang Penyelenggaraan Perkeretaapian: Jakarta
7. Undang-Undang No.23 Tahun 2007 tentang Perkeretaapian: Jakarta

Difference in Press Angle to the Quality of Briquettes

Nofriady Handra*, *Hafni* Hafni and *Hendriwan* Fahmi

Institut Teknologi Padang, Mechanical Engineering Department, Padang, West Sumatra Indonesia

Abstract. The development of biomass has been an important issue for the past several decades and would remain to be attractive in the future due to its clean, renewable, and carbon–neutral properties. The use of Empty Fruit Bunch (EFB) has been the condition of fibre and conditions of EFB is still fresh. The fiber used has been cut to size between ± 0.5 mm to 5 mm. The purpose of this research is to determine the effect of difference press angle to the quality of briquette. Effect of the angle of the mold on the duration of combustion shows the difference in the time value that is not significant between the angles 65°, 55° and 45°. The rotation of the screw shaft slows down at an angle of 45° with a round of 84.5 rpm, while the rotation of the shaft has increased in rotation at 65° angle with rotation of 90.6 rpm. Differences in the cone angle affect the value of the burning time of the specimen and the rotation of the screw shaft so that it affects the engine performance.

1. Introduction

Biomass energy has attracted as one of the potential alternatives as it is an ideal renewable energy source with several advantages like lower sulfur, CO neutral emission, and abundant availability generally in the form of waste from agriculture as well as other 2 sources. Bio-energy derived from biomass is a promising, inexhaustible, sustainable source and can help in minimizing the rising environmental, economic, and technological issues related to depleting fossil fuels.

Increasing environmental and energy dependency concerns have been the motivation for the increased use of bio-energy as a substitute for fossil energy. The development of biomass has been an important issue for the past several decades and would remain to be attractive in the future due to its clean, renewable, and carbon–neutral properties [1].

Energy and fuels are the important links in the civilization and human development. The issues associated with the use of the fossil fuel, demand and supply gap, ever increasing prices, global warming and other environmental issues made the world to think for alternate sources of energy like solar, wind, ocean and biomass which are the only indigenous renewable energy sources capable of replacing large amount of solid, liquid and gaseous fossil fuel [2]

Palm oil is one of the commodities traded agricultural products, both for domestic and export industries. Following the processing of palm oil, eventually leaving palm Empty Fruit Bunch (EFB), which generally are not processed again by the oil industry in the processing of palm oil. Remaining empty bunches this poses a problem for venues and transportation disposal resulting in additional production costs for the processor. EFB in exile usually burned, it also creates problems for the environmental damage that air pollution and odor [3].

One of the optimistic technologies for alleviating these problems is briquetting, which has been studied by many researchers. The technology may be defined as a densification process for improving the handling characteristics of raw material and enhancing the volumetric calorific value of the biomass. Considerable amount of research on briquetting technology has been conducted [4].

Based on several problems in background discussions and see the potential of environmentalists, EFB waste must be managed wisely in order to demand the use of renewable alternative energy biomass, biomass utilization technology and produce environmentally friendly heat energy. The development of agricultural wastes for solid fuels is also triggered by the current condition, where fossil fuels which have been a mainstay for households or industries have increased prices [5]. Given the fact, the waste is very potential to be a solid fuel that is relatively cheaper and is expected to minimize environmental problems during the resulting waste handling. Utilization of EFB as a source of energy in the form of briquettes, in addition to providing financial benefits, also helps in environmental conservation. EFB can be made charcoal with a relatively simple process. For purposes of utilization as charcoal, EFB needs to be further processed into charcoal briquettes to increase their density and provide a regular shape by applying appropriate pressure to the briquette mold angle [5][6].

One of alternative solution is to treat the agricultural waste into briquettes, a solid alternative fuel, cheap and meet the technical specifications, namely by

* Corresponding author: nof.hand11@gmail.com

the pressure on the mold. The purpose of this study is to determine the effect of different press briquette angle, so as to produce optimal briquette output in terms of physical properties.

2. Materials and Methods

2.1 Material

The results of the study will produce bio-briquette from EFB waste. EFB wastes are obtained from the oil palm industry located in TAL Ltd – Riau Province. Waste obtained is after going through the process of enumeration with the engine so that the palm fiber are obtained that are rougher and still fresh. EFB used first to be smoothing up to ± 5 mm, draining to moisture content ± 0.8 %. The EFB waste as shown in Fig.1

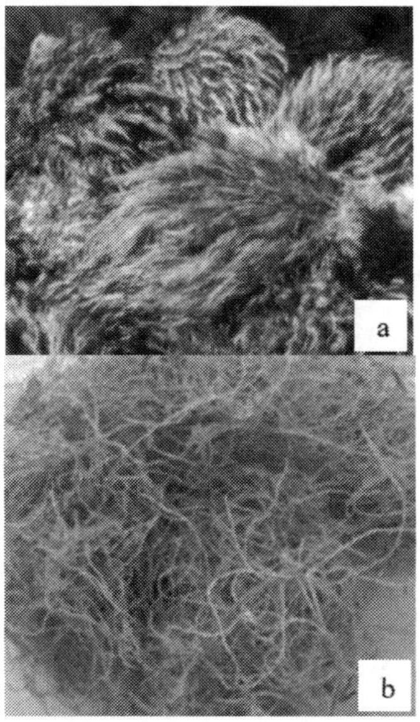

Fig. 1. Empty Fruit Bunch waste (a). EFB fibre (b)

2.2. Screw press machine

The research process consists of preparing the main ingredients in the form of EFB, then drying to reduce the water content in EFB, and further refinement of the size up to ± 1 mm until 5 mm to facilitate the mold process. The briquette printing tool is categorized as manual and automatic mold, with different advantages and disadvantages of each. Manual tools are usually used with the help of hydraulic with piston system, where to insert material, press and remove the whole material done manually. Pressing briquettes requires a drive that will be adjusted to capacity of the tool used, the system can be screw, piston, hydraulic and other systems, the operator only needs to insert the material to be pressed into the tool, the tool will press until briquettes out through the mold with the shape and size that has been determined. System screw can be used for large capacity because it works continuously but requires a lot of power for its operation.

Fig. 2 is a screw press briquette machine used to mold briquettes with a diameter of 4 mm. The mold angle varies with three variations of 65°, 55°, and 45° in order to obtain a briquette that meets the qualifications according to SNI standard 01-6235-2000 with different mold angles.

Fig. 2. Briquette machine of screw press

Extrusion is a process that combines several processes including mixing, destruction, molding and forming. The extruder consists of a screw (pressurized thread) which presses the raw material into a semi-solid material. The material is pressed out through a limited hole (mold) on the tip of the thread, if the raw material is heated. The main characteristic of the extrusion process is its continuous nature. The extruder is operated in a dynamic equilibrium condition, that is, the input equals the output, the incoming material is equivalent to the product. The extrusion process uses high mechanical energy and thermal energy with high pressure, this will result in the materials in the form of powders and grains changed into more fluid. Therefore, material characteristics such as surface friction, hardness, particle density are important to note.

2.3. Mold of briquettes

Cone-shaped plate is made so that the process of emphasis on the angle of the outer to form a briquette. Occurrence of emphasis resulted from the rotation of the screw shaft into the conical corner mold space. The cone dimensions are D_1 = 133.4 mm and d_2 = 43.4 mm. Variation of a briquette mold angle used in this study as shown in Fig. 3.

Fig. 3. Variation of briquette mold angle (a) 45° (b) 55° and (c) 65°

https://doi.org/10.1051/matecconf/201821501039

3. Result and Discussion

The briquetting process is the process of converting low-density biomass into solid fuel in the form of briquettes with concentrated energy and high density. The preparation of a biomass solid fuel can be said to be an identification process aimed at improving the biomass fuel characteristics. The essential properties of briquettes that affect fuel quality are their physical properties and chemical properties. Physical properties include density characteristics, briquette size, water content, calorific value, and volume unity energy. Briquetting techniques can be divided into three groups categorized based on the amount of pressure.

The experimental results for the test at the 45° angle with 3 kg fiber, in get rotation on the screw shaft of 84.5 rpm, then cutting on the briquette sample produced with a length of 40 mm. Specimens that have been cut off are done by using an oven at 250 °C for 3.5 hours to reduce the moisture content and then specimens are burned to ashes, The length of time the burning of the specimen to ash is obtained for 65 minutes. The same way and process as the above experiment for testing at the mold angle 55° and 65° can be seen and concluded on the Table 1.

Table 1. The angle effect on the length of time of specimen burning

Angle (°)	Time (minutes)
45	65
55	63
65	62

Fig. 4 is a sample of briquettes resulting from the printing process with a briquette machine as shown in Fig. 2. Each sample is made of three pieces to obtain more data and analysis. Fig. 3(b) is a briquette burning test to determine the quality of combustion produced. The analysis shows that the effect of the angle of the mold on the duration of combustion shows the difference in the time value that is not significant between the angles 45°, 55° and 65°.

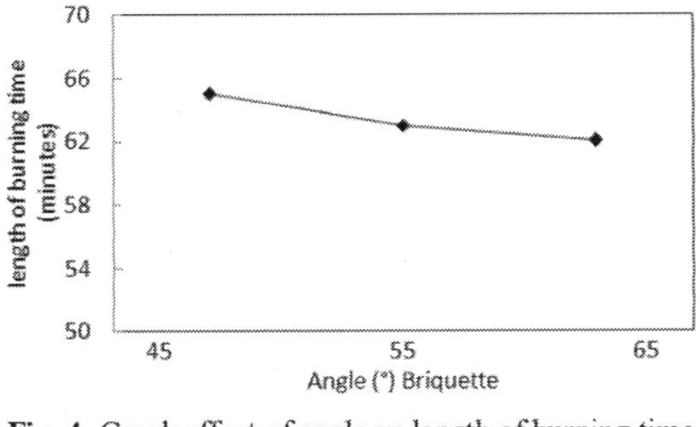

Fig. 4. Graph effect of angle vs length of burning time

The Graph Fig. 5 shows that a specimen using 45° angle of mold produces a briquette burning time of 65° minutes, while at 65° angles the resulting combustion time is only 62 minutes. Seen that the time difference is only 1 to 2 minutes. This is because at the mold angle 45° the resulting briquettes are denser than angles 55° and 65°. The conclusive analysis of this study is that the more dense the briquettes affect the density and physical properties.

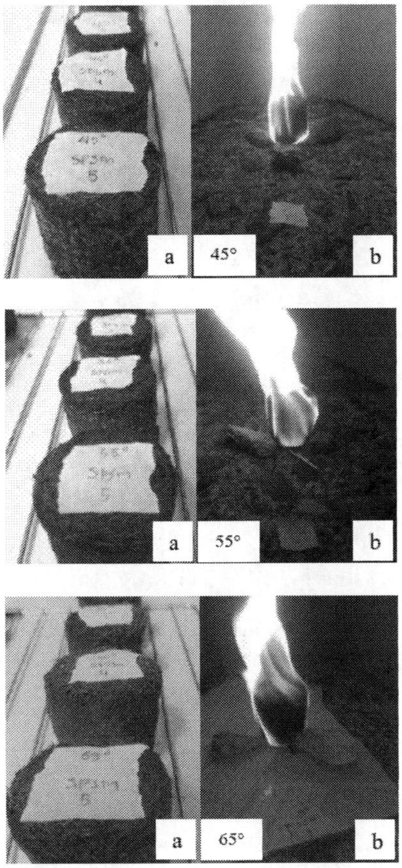

Fig. 5. Samples of 45°, 55° and 65° angle briquettes (a) and the combustion (b)

Fig. 6 Graph shows that rotation on the highest screw shaft at an angle of 65° with a rotation value of 90.6 rpm, while the lowest rotation is produced at an angle of 45° with a value rotation of 84.5 rpm. This indicates that the greater the angle of mold briquette feeding the rotation of the screw axis will be higher and the smaller the angle of mold then the pivot rotation will be lower, this will cause the shaft load to rotate the screw will be greater due to the influence of angle. Difference of rotation value (rpm) between angle 55° and 65° shows no significant difference.

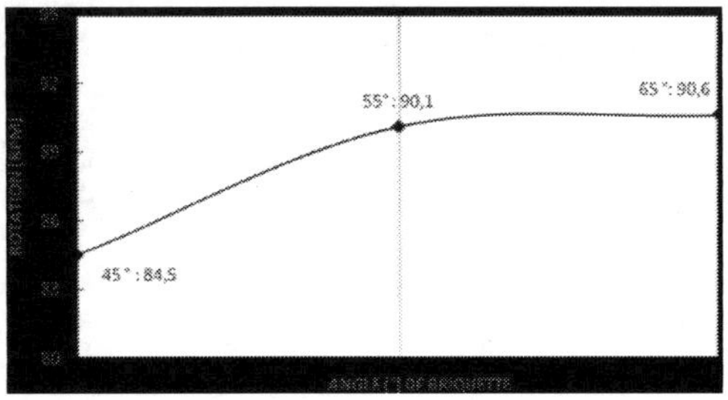

Fig. 6. Graph effect of angle vs rotation of screw shaft

4. Conclusion

1. Effect of the angle of the mold on the duration of combustion shows the difference in the time value that is not significant between the angles 45°, 55° and 65°.
2. The rotation of the screw shaft slows down at an angle of 45° with a round of 84.5 rpm, while the rotation of the shaft has increased in rotation at 65° angle with rotation of 90.6 rpm.
3. Differences in the cone angle affect the value of the burning time of the specimen and the rotation of the screw shaft so that it affects the engine performance

References

[1] N. Handra, IOP Conference Series: Earth and Environmental Science Effect of Binder on Combustion Quality on EFB Effect of Binder on Combustion Quality on EFB Bio-briquettes, (2017).

[2] N. Handra and A. Kasim, Pengaruh Ukuran Partikel Bio-briket TKKS terhadap Nilai Kalor Effect of Particles Size on EFB Bio-briquettes of CalorificValue, vol. 7, no. 1, (2017).

[3] K. H. Khor, K. O. Lim, Z. a Zainal, P. Pinang, and N. Tebal, "Characterization of Bio-Oil: A By-Product from Slow Pyrolysis of Oil Palm Empty Fruit Bunches School of Physics , School of Mechanical Engineering , Engineering Campus," *Am. J. Appl. Sci.*, vol. 6, no. 9, pp. 1647–1652, (2009).

[4] T. Deac, V. Ros, F. Mariasiu, M. Deac, and B. Muncii, "The influence of the sawdust briquettes geometric parameters on the conversion efficiency," vol. 43, no. 103, pp. 306–311, (2011).

[5] P. Wilaipon, The Effects of Briquetting Pressure on Banana-Peel Briquette and the Banana Waste in Northern Thailand., American Journal of Applied Sciences 6 (1): 167-171, (2009).

[6] R.M. Singh, H.J. Kim, Mitsushi. K, and S. Toran, Briquettes-an Alternative Fuel for Sustainable Development, Nepal Journal of Science and Technology 10: pp: 121-127, (2009)

Analysis of Power Loss of 20 kV Power Distribution

Dasman Dasman

Institut Teknologi Padang, Departement of Electrical Engineering, Padang, West Sumatra

Abstract. In the distribution of electrical energy from the plant to the consumer, there is a decrease in quality due to the loss of power (losses). These power losses are caused by a voltage drop across the line and subsequently producing a power loss on the line. This power loss can be classified into two types based on its line parameters, i.e., active power loss and reactive power loss. The line's active power loss generates losses of power/losses so that the active power reaches the load on the receiving end is always less than the productive power of the sender side. Power losses in the electrical system must exist and cannot be reduced to 0% (zero percent). According to SPLN No. 72 of 1987, the permitted distribution network's power loss should not be higher than 10%. This paper investigates the magnitude of the voltage loss and the line active power losses on the 20 kV distribution line. The calculation conducted through case study and simulation of Etap 12.6 program on an electrical power distribution system that is 20 kV distribution line in PT. PLN (Persero) Rayon Muara Labuh. In the distribution line 20 kV, there is IPP (Independent Power Plant) PLTMH PT SKE used to improve the stress conditions in Rayon Muara Labuh. Therefore the loss of power will be calculated in 3 terms, i.e., before and after IPP PT. SKE with 20 kV distribution lines as well as on feeder load maintenance (as a repair action plan). The simulation results show the highest voltage drop and the highest power losses continue generated during IPP. PT SKE has not done synchronized with the distribution line of 20 kV with a significant voltage drop of 1,533 kV percentage of 7.93% and power loss of 777.528 kWh percentage of 7.69%.

1 Introduction

Given the importance of electrical energy for people's lives and for national development, a power system must be able to serve customers well both in terms of continuity and quality. However, in the distribution of electrical energy from the generator up to the consumer, a decline in quality due to the emergence of power losses (losses). The power loss caused by the voltage drop on the line and then produces power losses in the line. Drop voltage itself occurs from two components namely I. Rs is the voltage drop due to line resistance and I.Xs is the voltage drop due to line reactance. The voltage drop due to passage resistance will cause a loss of active power while the voltage drop due to line reactance will cause reactive power losses [1].

Power losses in the electrical system must exist and can not be reduced to 0% (zero percent). According to SPLN No. 72 of 1987, the permitted distribution network's power loss should not be greater than 10%. This study was conducted to analyze the power losses account for a large line with a line voltage drop through a case study on the distribution lines distribution line (feeder) 20 kV PT. PLN (Persero) Rayon Muara Labuh. In the 20 kV distribution line, there are IPPs (Independent Power Plant) MHP PT SKE used to improve voltage conditions in Muara Labuh Rayon. Therefore for the initial stages, the power loss will be analyzed in two conditions namely before IPP PT SKE interconnection and after IPP PT SKE interconnected with 20 kV distribution line owned by PLN. While the method used is by the method of direct calculation (study formula) and by using the program Etap 12.6 [2]

After large power loss is obtained, then the prepared work plan and an action plan to reduce the power loss. One of the steps that can be done is to solve the load on 2 or more existing feeders. This stage is a stage-3 in calculating the power loss of 20 kV distribution line Rayon Muara Labuh [3-6].

2 Review of The Literatures

The distribution line is illustrated by an equivalent model by taking the circuit parameters on a per phase basis. Terminal voltage is described from one line to neutral, the current phase of the line so that the three-phase distribution system is reduced to an equivalent single-phase distribution system. The distribution line model is used to calculate the voltage, current and power flow that is influenced by line length. The distribution line model is obtained by multiplying the impedance of the long unity line with the line length

* Corresponding author: dasman@gmail.com

$$Z = (r + j\omega L)l \ldots\ldots (1)$$

$$Z = R + jX \ldots\ldots (2)$$

Where r and L represent the resistance and the per-phase inductance of the length, and l is the channel length The distribution channel model on a per phase basis is shown in fig. 1. and the voltage and current at the end of the shipping channel, and the voltage and current at the receiving end of the channel.

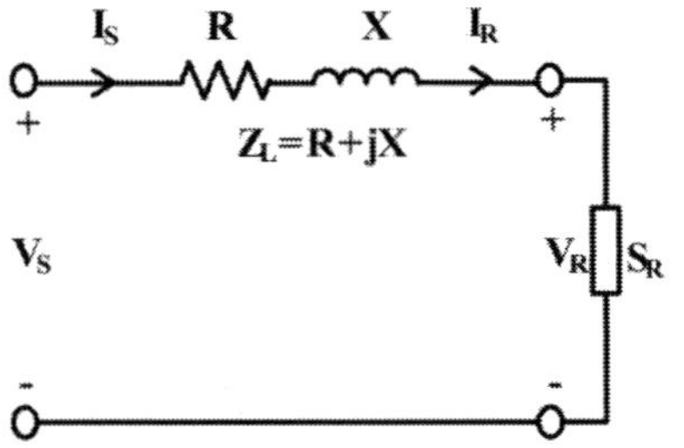

Fig. 1. Distribution Channel Model

If the three-phase apparent power is distributed to the load at the receiving end, the sender's end current is obtained through

$$I_S = \frac{S_{S\,(3\phi)}}{3V_S} \ldots\ldots (3)$$

Where:

$S_{S\,(3\phi)}$ = three-phase visible power at the sender side (MVA)

Vs = voltage sender side (kV)

Therefore, the circuit current distribution channel is a series connection which channel shunt capacitance is ignored, the current source end and the receiving end is the same,

$$I_S = I_R \ldots\ldots (4)$$

Drop voltage (voltage drop) is the difference between the send voltage and the receive voltage due to impedance and channel current in the conductor. Drop channel voltage can be determined,

$$V_Z = I_S \,.\, Z_L \ldots\ldots (5)$$

$$= I_S \,.\, (R + jX_L) \ldots\ldots (6)$$

Where :

ZL = channel impedance

In the calculation, the value of the channel reactance can be ignored so that the equation becomes:

$$V_Z = I_S \,.\, R \ldots\ldots (7)$$

The receiving-side voltage or the voltage reaching to the load is the receiving side voltage less the channel drop voltage,

$$V_R = V_S - V_Z \ldots\ldots (8)$$

Based on channel equivalent circuit shown in Figure 1, and the description of equation (1) to (8) can be described phasor diagrams of current and voltage to the load with a lagging power angle (lagging) as shown in Figure 2.

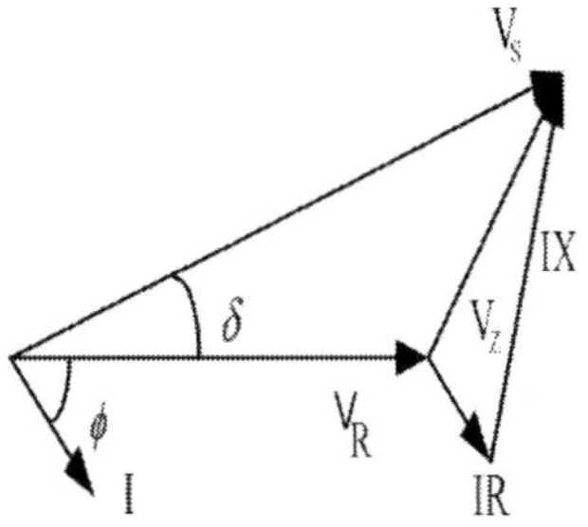

Fig. 2 Phasor Channel of Distribution Channel

with a large percentage value (%) voltage drop is,

$$\%\,V_{rugi} = \frac{V_Z}{V_S}\, X\ 100\,\% \ldots\ldots (9)$$

Based on Figure 2, the channel power loss arises because of the channel resistance and reactance components in the form of active and reactive power losses. The current flowing on the channel will produce a visible loss of power channel,

$$S_{Z(3\emptyset)} = 3.\,V_Z I_S^{*} \ldots\ldots (10)$$

The visible power loss generated on the line consists of active power loss and reactive power loss written in the form of complex numbers in which the active power loss as real numbers and reactive power losses as imaginary numbers,

$$S_{Z(3\emptyset)} = P_{Z(3\emptyset)} + jQ_{z(3\emptyset)} \ldots\ldots (11)$$

Based on the phasor diagram of Figure 2.2, the active power loss per phase can be determined from the variable current, voltage and angle of the phase difference of the voltage drop and current of the channel,

$$P_Z = V_Z I_S\, COS\, \emptyset \ldots\ldots (12)$$

The phase difference angle between the voltage drop and the line current, cos is also called the power angle of the channel or power factor.

 https://doi.org/10.1051/matecconf/201821501040

3. Result and Discussion

From the single line diagram of distribution channel 20 kV Rayon Muara Labuh can be seen that distribution channel Rayon Muara Labuh has 3 pieces Exp. Feeder among others Exp. Feeder Muara Labuh, Exp. Feeder Lubuk Gadang and Exp. Feeder SKE. Besides Exp. Feeder there are also 5 pieces of Feeder services include Feeder Muara Labuh, Feeder City, Feeder Partners, Feeder Lubuk Malako, and Feeder Mark.

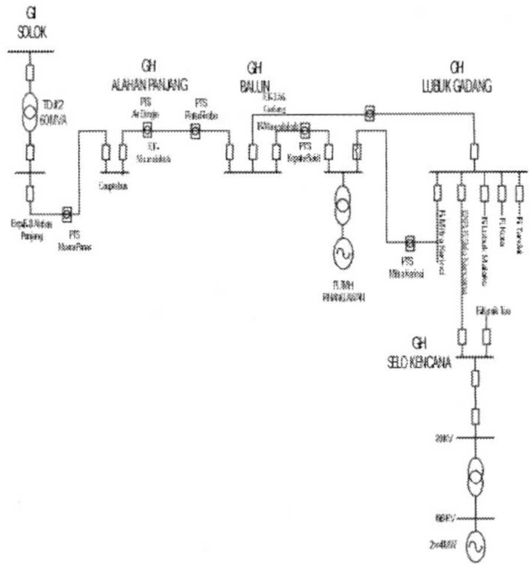

Fig. 3 Single Line Channel Distribution Diagram 20 kV Rayon Muara Labuh

Table 1 Network Length per Feeder

NO.	FEEDER NAME	CONDUCTOR A3C (kms)			
		240 mm²	150 mm²	70 mm²	35 mm²
1	EXP. FEEDER MLBH	0,000	27,117	20,684	4,300
2	MUARA LABUH	0,000	0,000	43,146	0,637
3	EXP. FEEDER LBGD	0,000	44,900	0,000	0,000
4	EXP. FEEDER SKE	10,495	0,000	0,000	0,000
5	KOTA	0,000	0,000	20,169	5,700
6	MITRA	0,000	0,000	39,600	0,000
7	TANDAI	0,000	29,700	11,769	0,000
8	LUBUK MALAKO	1,100	66,200	12,500	0,000
Sum		**11,595**	**167,917**	**147,868**	**10,637**

Table 2 Impedance Conductor A3C By SPLN 64 1985

a (mm²)	r (Ω)	jX (Ω)	Z (Ω) ∠ Θ (°)
16	1,9550	0,40506	1,9965∠11,70
25	1,1830	0,38966	1,2455∠18,23
35	0,9217	0,379	1,0322∠21,86
55	0,6650	0,37296	0,7624∠29,28
70	0,4608	0,3572	0,5830<37,78
95	0,3550	0,38442	0,5232∠47,28
110	0,2930	0,37729	0,4777∠52,167
150	0,2250	0,38966	0,4499∠59,997
185	0,1830	0,38442	0,4257∠64,54
240	0,1370	0,35488	0,3804∠68,89

The load data used in this calculation can be seen in table 3.

Table 3 Feeder Load at Peak Load Time

NO	FEEDER NAME	LOADS WBP (A)
1	EXP. FEEDER MLBH	18,0
2	MUARALABUH	86,6
3	EXP. FEEDER LBGD	152,3
4	EXP. FEEDER SKE	283,6
5	KOTA	46,3
6	MITRA	34,0
7	TANDAI	2,6
8	LUBUK MALAKO	59,3
JUMLAH		**682,70**

The data obtained during the research were analyzed using ETAP simulation. Starting from Single Line Diagram data, Rayon Muara Labuh Asset data, as well as Load Measurement data, then simulated using ETAP 12.6.

Network length data per Feeder is grouped by type and area of cross section. The data can be seen in table 1. Network length data are grouped per section in accordance with Feeder service area. The resistance value (r) and reactance (X) of the carrier is obtained from the standard contained in SPLN 64 Year 1985. The data can be seen in Table 2 as follows: Manual calculations should be added to calculations when 20 kV PLN system has not been in sync with IPP PT. SKE. But it can not be done because it is constrained by the absence of load data. The steps performed in calculating the value of voltage drop and power loss are as follows:

a. Calculates channel resistance value according to table data (1) and table (2).
b. Calculate the voltage drop value according to equation (7).
c. Calculate the value of power loss according to equation (12).

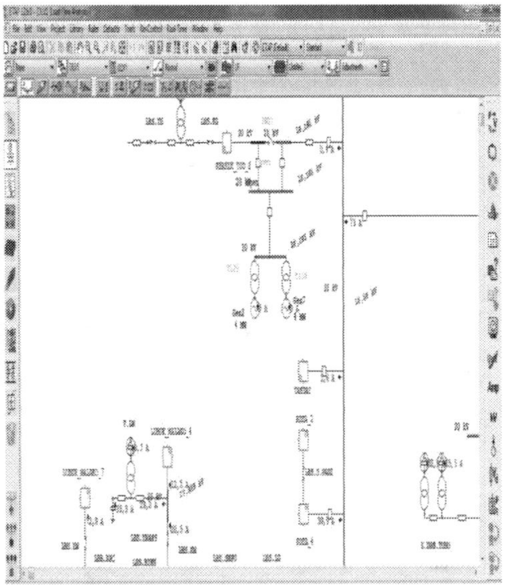

Fig. 4 Etap Simulation Before IPP PT. SKE Interconnection

From result of simulation Etap obtained value of voltage drop equal to 1,535 kV with percentage of 7.93% and power loss value equal to 1079,9 kW with percentage of 7,69%.
When the power loss is changed in units of electrical energy equivalent to:

$$E = P.\,T$$
$$= 1079.9 \text{ kW} \times 24 \text{ hours} \times 30 \text{ days}$$
$$= 777.528 \text{ kWh}$$

After the previous IPP PT. SKE is not connected to the 20 kV distribution channel owned by PLN, then in this discussion IPP PT. SKE we connect with 20 kV system so that icon T129 and T234 which was blurred, start seen clearly as in fig 4.

After the feeder load is broken, a new shrinkage difference is obtained. Stages performed to solve the feeder load equal to the stages when done manual calculations.

From the results of the simulation Etap obtained voltage drop value of 0.822 kV with 4.10% percentage and power loss value of 514.4 kW with 4.20% percentage.
When the power loss is changed in units of electrical energy equivalent to:

$$E = P.\,T$$
$$= 514.4 \text{ kW} \times 24 \text{ hours} \times 30 \text{ days}$$
$$= 370.368 \text{ kWh}$$

4. Conclusions

From the calculation that has been done, either manually or simulation, can be concluded as follows:

1. From the condition of IPP PT. SKE has not been interconnected with distribution channel 20 kV, for simulation calculation, obtained voltage drop equal to 1,533 kV with percentage of 7.93% and power loss equal to 777.528 kWh with percentage of 7,69%.
2. Difference of power loss from manual calculation and simulation calculation, at condition 2 and 3, 1,305 kWh with percentage 0.0001%.

References

1. Kadir, A. Power Distribution and Utilities. Jakarta: Universitas Indonesia Press (2006)
2. SPLN No.72: Design Specification For Medium Voltage Network and Low Voltage Network, Jakarta, PT. PLN (Persero). (1987)
3. Akbar, A.A. Calculation of Power Shuts On Medium Voltage Distribution System of Air and Cable Channels. (2007).
4. Elisa Lubis,. Study of Loss Loss Energy Loss on Melon 20 KV Repeaters". (2008)
5. Muhdar, Isla. Juniarti and Suherman Yunus. "Drop Voltage Evaluation In Medium Voltage Network 20 KV Feeder Bojo PT. PLN (Persero) Rayon Mattirosi. (2013)
6. Riski, Aldi. The Influence of Adding Networks to Drop Voltage at SUTM 20 kV Grade Feeder Tuo Rayon Kersik Tuo Kerinci District. (2013)

Collective Intellectual Right? A Case on Protected Geography Indicated

Firmansyah David[1,*], *Wahyudi* David[2]

[1]Institut Teknologi Padang, Department of Information Technology, Padang Indonesia,
[2]Universitas Bakrie, Department of Food Science and Technology, Indonesia,

Abstract. Many literature in the collaboration of innovation have suggested inventors should avoid the join ownership of intellectual property. However, in a special case the intellectual right can be assigned to a product. Our paper addresses the issues and challenges of shared intellectual right in the context of Protected Geography Indicated (PGI). The PGI recognizes such products based on their originality (in term of geography), not based on who have been invented them. This highlights that the right is belong to a community, not to individuals. In practice, this is problematic in which individuals in a community may or able to claim the right on the product. To illustrate how policy makers in developing country deal with this situation, we use secondary data from Indonesian Agency on Intellectual Property and case studies on indigenous food products. We approached the cases using theory of resolving potential conflict in community. The discussion in our contribution is taking aim at identifying of problems of which may be occurred during the process of Intellectual Right application. Further, we propose recommendations for individual, communal, and policy levels to resolve potential problems in the future.

1 INTRODUCTION

The knowledge economy has emerged by the greater utilization of intellectual capital than the exploitation of natural resources [21]. This era highly depends on 'knowledge workers' who play a prominent role to 'produce' and disseminate knowledge [8]. Knowledge workers in the regime of 'Open Innovation' (OI) tend to co-operate with multiple-actors and groups in the process of increasing the values of new ideas and knowledge [11][1]. Indeed, the OI has triggered inventors to share the ownership of Intellectual Properties (IPs). European Patent Office shows that the number of co-ownership of IPs is dramatically increased in the last two decades [10]. Nevertheless, despite of success stories of the co-ownership of IPs, the conflict between shared and private IPs were remained problematic. These two situations contradict to each other [3]. Whilst OI naturally nurtures inventors to collaborate in the i.e. technological invention, the co-ownership of IPs may put inventors in a dilemma - either protecting their inventions by private IPs or let others developing the inventions by sharing the co-ownership - all of which resulted with profit consequences.

The co-ownership of IPs recorded by the EPO were mostly originated from developed countries and advanced knowledge institutes [10]. Our contribution in this paper discusses the issues of co-ownership of IPs in a case of developing countries. The developing nations emphasize their effort fostering innovation particularly in Small and Medium Enterprises and small groups of business [13]. The study in this paper uses a framework of Protected Geography Indicated (PGI) to illustrate how the knowledge economy that requires collaboration and sharing has collided with protection on geographical indication products. Our paper aims to exhibit the phenomenon of conflict in the (co) shared IPs and potential conflict among the IP holders. One of the main challenges in PGI the IPs is fully owned by a community, not to individuals, which this might lead to conflict and complex resolution. Moreover, this paper majorly discusses the implication of OI for developing countries particularly its effect for PGI and potential co-ownership of IPs in PGI.

The paper is arranged as follows. The next section is review on issues in co-ownership of IPs and its challenges if it is implemented in the PGI framework. The third section illustrates problems of co-ownership of IPs using PGI cases in Indonesia as a case study. The last section is conclusion and recommendation for future study.

2 Co-ownership of IPs versus PGI

* Corresponding author: firman@itp.ac.id

The co-ownership of IPs is originated from the co-invention and co-operation among institutions or individuals. It was firstly practiced as 'knowledge spill over' that allows knowledge flows or 'circulates' from knowledge institutes to nearby industries [15]. Indeed, the traditional industries hold on their competitive advantage to win competition by preserving technical and informal know how [24]. In the era of OI, instead of competing, companies in an innovation cluster co-invented products or services in a localized district or geography in the way to strengthen their competitive advantage [21]. In the inter-institutions co-operation, the co-ownership of IPs is not only established among companies but also majorly resulted from university and business co-operation [18]. Since the proximity (in the distant) is an important incentive in the formation of co-invention, however in an innovation cluster, inventors in the companies tend to co-operate with scientists from reputable universities rather than with low reputable universities [16].

As the industries grow, the collective inventions become proliferated. For instance, an OI is the incentive for fostering Open Source Software (OSS) development [25]. The open source platform is developed based on collective inventions and co-operation [22]. Thus, the co-operation platform is the incentive for knowledge sharing which created an open forum for inventions. Using co-operation platform, technical know-how is 'updated' suggesting innovation has been fostered. This indicates the OI is on the right track [12].

Since the Bayh-Dole Act has enacted in the US in the late eighties, the regulations regarding Intellectual Property and Patents have been emulated by many countries [19]. Nevertheless, collective invention and co-operation in an innovation Eco-system remained complex and problematic [5]. When a common property is converted to a private property, there will be too many IPs which led to too many owners – this may trigger conflict and complexity in getting rights [4]. Open Source Software (OSS) communities play a role in foundation of common property, however, it is vulnerable due to the development of patent legislation [20].

Based on the studies above, the co-ownership of IPs seems to have advantages for groups and individuals which each of them can take benefits. The co-invention may save resources such as R&D costs, and duration for invention. In the other hand, the PGI concerns on the protection of commodities in a region or a nation. PGI has an objective to leverage a region or a nation economy. In this circumstance, PGI will protect commodities/products of which being commercialized in a certain region [6][14]. Furthermore, PGI will protect such commodities from misuse and violation from other individuals or groups.

However, in the knowledge-based economy where innovation becomes the driven factor, PGI can be a solution to protect the indigenous products but it can inhibit for further innovation. The status to which member of a community can hold the right remains ambiguous. With the two streams that literature shown above, we interested to discuss the intertwined between co-ownership of IPs and PGI. We propose that these two conditions may strengthen to each other and thus may be weaken to each other.

3. Case Study: Protected Geography Indicated

Most of the agriculture products is strongly related to their region of origin. The distinctive characteristic of an agricultural product is resulted from the area's factors such as climate, soil conditions, know-how and local breeds [9]. Based on their uniqueness, these products were sold using their origin names as their commercial names, which consumers are then remembered. To avoid the misuse of well-known names on the imitated products, many countries develop a regulation to protect the geographical indication using two different designations, namely Protected Geographical Indication (PGI) and Protected Designation of Origin (PDO) [23]. The originality of a product includes quality parameters, characteristics and certain direct or indirect reputation. In the market perspective, PGI allows an opportunity for local 'brands' or 'product' to be recognized as it is and allow consumers/costumers get the 'feeling' from of originality of the "brand or "product".

Indonesia is known for its diversity of culture and agricultural products. Indonesia has adopted this protection since 2011. PGI or in Indonesia known as Geography Indication (GI) defines as an intellectual right which given to protect the name of a product in a certain area (area, locality or even country) which assigned a product to be recognized as their origin. The story of locality of the GI products is the main 'selling point' for the producers. Consumer mostly perceives the story of locality compared to the quality of product itself. For instances, Coffee Gayo from Aceh, Lada Putih Muntok and Madu Sumbawa. Based on Direktorat Jendral Kekayaan Intelektual (DJKI), up to 2017 there are 35 products has been registered and recognized as GI product. The beneficial of GI is not only to protect the local's right but also to promote local origin and to be exposed to the global market. Most of the time GI products are listed to be a premium product because of their originality. In the other hand the trace-ability of a product can bring transparent information for consumer and can increase the "trust" of the consumers. The challenges of the GI system is that the right is belong to communal, not individual, therefore to maintain the trust it should be commitment of many stakeholders.

Over 100 years, Indonesia has given protection for PGI. Data from DJKI recorded at least 102 PGI commodities are registered.

Table 1. List of registered PGI commodity in Indonesia - Source DJKI, 2018

Varieties	Number
Coffee	27
Fish	4
Rice	5

Tea	1
Sweet Potato	1
Pepper	3
Honey	1
Milk	1

To illustrate of a PGI commodity we take an example of the Kintamani Arabica Coffee. This product has been registered in 2007 and will be reserved until 2017. The product was proposed by the Society of PIG of Kintamani Coffee in Bali. The Kintamani Coffee is planted from Arabica Coffee growth in the highland of Kintamani village, the Province of Bali, the altitude above 900 above sea level. The area is surrounded by Batur volcano and comprised of soils such as Entisol and Inceptisol (Regusol). With the dry and chill weather with precipitation is 1867 mm/year with average temperature 17.8 C. This 'special' arabica is the breed of arabica varieties. This coffee is planted under a shelter and is combined with other plantation and given organic fertilizer. As the results, this kind of coffee has a unique citrus fragrant with low acidity. The red coffee beans were selected and were fermented over 12 - 36 hours and later naturally dried. As the results, the flavour of this arabica consistent with citrus fragrant and in low viscosity. This is a unique flavour for an arabica coffee.

4 Discussions

The study was aimed to illustrate the conflict and recommendation of co-ownership of IPs. Using PGI as a case, we synthesize of which problems that might be occurred in the situation when PGI of intellectual right is applied. The main question is that who will have the claim to the right? Do the rights go to an individual or groups in the community or can it be for individuals outside the geographical boundary? It is remained unclear. According to the Law on PGI that right goes to community not to individuals since the proposals are done based on community in a certain geographical boundary. However, if there is a member who runs their business on PGI product outside the geographical 'area', will this violate the right? The main question is - how to guarantee the right of a product packed is originated from PGI place or possibility of guarantee that there is no fraud or 'labelling and packaging'.

The PGI products may acquire a guarantee such certification or an existing certification e.g. fair trade or even organic agricultural certification. If there is a certificate upon this product and where and who will be the IPs belong to? It has attached on the brand or product? When will a product be a part of PGI? If products such as coffee with same varieties planted in the different area, according to PGI can be a different product. If PGI only allows limitation on geographical boundary this will cause problem related to IP (not individuals but communal). In terms of violation, PGI do no set the sanction to be given for the frauds.

To protect the PGI right, the certification system can be an alternative for assuring the genuine and trace-ability of PGI product. This system requires assurance institution (third party) similar to fair-trade and organic form. This system further needs "norms" or "rules" which should be followed by producer and the third party has common standard with the producer. If PGI follows this system then there is no IPs anymore since it is not even exclusive right for everyone since they can use certification. This remains problematic for PGI.

References

1. Antikainen, M., Mäkipää, M., & Ahonen, M. Motivating and supporting collaboration in open innovation. European Journal of Innovation Management, 13(1), 100-119. (2010)
2. Belderbos, R., Cassiman, B., Faems, D., Leten, B., & Van Looy, B. Co-ownership of intellectual property: Exploring the value-appropriation and value-creation implications of co-patenting with different partners. Research Policy, 43(5), 841-852. (2014).
3. Chesbrough, H., & Ghafele, R.. Open innovation and intellectual property. New Frontiers in Open Innovation, 191. (2014).
4. Colangelo, G. Avoiding the tragedy of the anticommons: collective rights organizations, patent pools and the role of antitrust. (2004).
5. David, F., & van der Sijde, P.. University–Business Co-operation in Indonesian Higher Education for Innovation. In New Technology-Based Firms in the New Millennium (pp. 187-200). Emerald Group Publishing Limited. (2015)
6. Deselnicu, O. C., Costanigro, M., Souza-Monteiro, D. M., & McFadden, D. T. A meta-analysis of geographical indication food valuation studies: what drives the premium for origin-based labels?. Journal of Agricultural and Resource Economics, 204-219. (2013).
7. Direktorat Jenderal Kekayaan Intelektual Indonesia. http://www.dgip.go.id/
8. Drucker, P. F. Knowledge-worker productivity: The biggest challenge. California management review, 41(2), 79-94. (1999).
9. European Commission. https://ec.europa.eu/chafea/agri/
10. European Patent Office. https://www.epo.org/index.html
11. Fichter, K. Innovation communities: the role of networks of promotors in Open Innovation. R&d Management, 39(4), 357-371. (2009).
12. Garriga, H., Von Krogh, G., & Spaeth, S. How constraints and knowledge impact open innovation. Strategic Management Journal, 34(9), 1134-1144. (2013).

13. Hadjimanolis, A. Barriers to innovation for SMEs in a small less developed country (Cyprus). Technovation, 19(9), 561-570. (1999).
14. Irawan, C. Pendaftaran Indikasi Geografis sebagai Instrumen Perlindungan Hukum dan Peningkatan Daya Saing Produk Daerah di Indonesia. Proceeding SENDI_U. (2017).
15. Jaffe, A. B., Trajtenberg, M., & Henderson, R. Geographic localization of knowledge spillovers as evidenced by patent citations. the Quarterly journal of Economics, 108(3), 577-598. (1993).
16. Laursen, K., Reichstein, T., & Salter, A. Exploring the effect of geographical proximity and university quality on university–industry collaboration in the United Kingdom. Regional studies, 45(4), 507-523. (2011).
17. Lundvall, B. Å. National innovation systems—analytical concept and development tool. Industry and innovation, 14(1), 95-119. (2007).
18. Motohashi, K., & Muramatsu, S. Examining the university industry collaboration policy in Japan: Patent analysis. Technology in Society, 34(2), 149-162. (2012).
19. Mowery, D. C., & Sampat, B. N. The Bayh-Dole Act of 1980 and university–industry technology transfer: a model for other OECD governments?. The Journal of Technology Transfer, 30(1-2), 115-127. (2004).
20. Osterloh, M., & Rota, S. (2007). Open source software development—Just another case of collective invention?. Research Policy, 36(2), 157-171.
21. Powell, W. W., & Snellman, K. The knowledge economy. Annu. Rev. Sociol., 30, 199-220. (2004).
22. Schrape, J. F. Open Source Communities: The Sociotechnical Institutionalization of Collective Invention. In Collectivity and Power on the Internet (pp. 57-83). Springer, Cham. (2018).
23. Sukartiko, A. C. Geographical Origin Characterization and Evaluation of Selected Quality Parameters of Potato Tubers. Cuvillier. (2012).
24. Tallman, S., Jenkins, M., Henry, N., & Pinch, S. Knowledge, clusters, and competitive advantage. Academy of management review, 29(2), 258-271. (2004).
25. West, J., & Gallagher, S. Challenges of open innovation: the paradox of firm investment in open-source software. R&d Management, 36(3), 319-331. (2006).

Literature Review on Relationship Building for Community-academic Collaboration in Health Research and Innovation

Choiwai Maggie Chak [1]

[1]Science-to-Business Marketing Research Centre, FH Münster

Abstract In response to European Commission Horizon 2020's call for 'science-for-and-with-community', scholars have recognized the need to conduct 'responsible research and innovation' and engage more with communities to combat today's complex health challenges. Hence, higher priority has been placed to cooperate with communities in health research and innovation development to better match societal values, needs and expectations. Accordingly, the approach of community-based participatory research (CBPR), the 'gold standard' within the community-engaged research spectrum, is the most widely discussed. However, it is seldom achieved in reality, as it requires establishment and maintenance of open, transparent, trustful and ongoing relationships between community partners and academia to succeed. Paradoxically, despite of the significance of quality collaborative relationship to the quality and success of community-academic collaboration, the key elements to achieve it were seldom discussed.Herein, the literature review aimed to (1) discuss the previous experiences and challenges in building and sustaining community-academic collaborative relationships; (2) examine the relationship building strategies for quality collaborative relationships; and (3) identify the potential research gaps for future research.Focusing on the area of health research and innovation, peer-reviewed articles, books and grey literature related to building and sustaining relationships in community-academic collaboration published between 1998 and 2018 were identified using the Web of Science, PubMed and Google Scholar bibliographic databases and Google search engine. Literature available in full-texts and English language with a focus on relationship aspects of community-academic collaboration were examined. Previous literature suggested thatacademics and community members encountered common challenges in experiencing inequitable relationships, distrust, divide between academia and community, uncommon norms of power sharing, dissemination of results and lack of resources for maintaining long-term relationships. Two approaches of relationship building: (1) personal qualities and competence, and (2) actions for relationship building from the beginning to the end stages of collaborative relationship were discussed. Literature revealed that the ways that academics approach, collaborate, communicate with and maintain in the community had significant impact on both current and future collaborative relationships. In addition, academics differed in acceptance and readiness towards community engagement, which could be attributed to the differences in personal qualities and competence. Future research should target on identifying the factors contributing to such individual differences and compare its impact on the quality of relationship with community, so as to better cultivate individuals' readiness and capacity towards community engagement and effective relationship building with community. KEYWORDS: LITERATURE REVIEW, RELATIONSHIP BUILDING, RESPONSIBLE RESEARCH AND INNOVATION, COMMUNITY-ACADEMIC COLLABORATION, HEALTH

1 Introduction

1.1 Research Background

In response to European Commission Horizon 2020's call for 'science-for-and-with-community', academia have recognized the need to conduct 'responsible research and innovation' via engaging with communities to combat today's complex health challenges(Jacob, 2013). Hence, universities have given higher priority to community engagement in the aim of better aligning health research and innovation development to meet the societal values, needs and expectations (Trencher *et al.*, 2017; van Hove and Wickson, 2017).

Accordingly, community-engaged research, a collaborative approach which addresses health inequities via engaging community stakeholders as partners in health research process (Ross *et al.*, 2010; Wang *et al.*, 2017), has been increasingly valued in health research and innovation (Israel *et al.*, 2006;

Provan, Harvey and Zapien, 2005). Community-based participatory research (CBPR), which is the 'gold standard' among the whole community-engaged research spectrum, is the most widely discussed approach over the last two decades (LaVeaux and Christopher, 2009; Winterbauer *et al.*, 2016). It emphasises equal partnerships with equitable involvement, equal authority and responsibility between academia and community partners at all stages of research process (Israel *et al.*, 1998; Israel, 2005; Katz, 2003; Minkler, 2005; Ross *et al.*, 2010), which addresses power imbalances across the whole spectrum of community engagement (Wallerstein *et al.*, 2005).

1.1 Knowledge gap

Despite the emerging discussions on its importance and availability of case studies, an immaculate CBPR is seldom achieved in reality (Blumenthal 2011), as it demands (1) mutual understanding and respectful trust between community partners and academia; (2) commitment to partnership development and sustainability; (3) acknowledgement and reduction of power imbalances and tension in relationships and (4) operationalization of equity among partners(Winterbauer and Myers, 2013), all of which must be built upon quality, cooperative and sustainable relationships between community partners and academics (Mayan and Daum, 2016; Wang *et al.*, 2017).

Hence, establishing and sustaining open, transparent, trustful and ongoing relationships between community partners and academia is highly essential for CBPR(Ahmed *et al.*, 2016; Israel *et al.*, 1998; Lemacks, Landry and Wenzler, 2018; Rothman and Gass, 2000). It helps partners to understand each other's concerns, interests, and needs and incorporating them into the development agenda (Minkler *et al.*, 2017), to implement strategies responsive to the needs, priorities, and values of the community (Huang, Lipman and Daniel Mullins, 2017) and to obtain synergy from all partners (CDC, 2011; Lasker, Weiss and Miller, 2001). It is also a key driver to university-community collaboration quality and success (Ahmed *et al.*, 2016; Bahraminejad *et al.*, 2015; Christopher *et al.*, 2008; Serrell *et al.*, 2009).

However, despite quality collaborative relationships are fundamental for the success of community-academiccollaboration, there are limited discussions on how to achieve them in literature (Mayan and Daum, 2016; Netshandama, 2010), such as ways to strengthen understanding of stakeholders' relationship objectives, responsiveness of coordination, access and service to community needs, and to ensure relationship sustainability (Netshandama, 2010).

Hence, the questions are: how well did academia and community stakeholders establish and maintain collaborative relationships in community-academic collaboration? What challenges did they face in such relationships? What approaches could be adopted to strengthen the bridging and alignment of goals between the stakeholders? Answering these questions will provide us the insights to facilitate quality collaborative relationships essential for better collaborative outcomes for health research and innovation.

1.2 Aims of research

In response to the questions, the aims of this literature review are to: (1) discuss the previous experiences and challenges in building and sustaining community-academic collaborative relationships; (2) examine the relationship building strategies for quality collaborative relationships; and (3) identify the potential research gaps that should be discussed in future research.

2 Methods

The search of literature was performed with the use of the Web of Science, PubMed and Google Scholar bibliographic databases and Google search engine to identify peer-reviewed articles, books and grey literature including organisational reports, case reports over the last two decades (between 1998 and 2018). The scope of literature review covered topics regarding to relationship aspects for health research and innovation in community-academic collaboration contexts, including responsible research and innovation (RRI), community-academic partnership (CAP), university-community collaboration (USC), community-based participatory research (CBPR), and community-engaged research (CEnR).

Articles included in the review were the literature that mainly focused on describing the relationships between universities or academics with community stakeholders in partnerships or collaboration for community-engaged health projects. Only full-texts studies in English languages were included and examined in the review. Nevertheless, they were not limited to geographical locations, so as to gain a better picture of the global situation.

3 Results

3.1 Challenges in establishing and sustaining collaborative relationships between academics and community

Despite the goodwill of engaging the community in research and innovation development, a number of literature suggested that establishing and sustaining quality collaborative relationships between academia and community depicted by CBPR could be easier said than done (Blumenthal, 2011; Council of Higher Education, 2004; Eden, Jirotka and Stahl, 2013). The followings are the prominent challenges reported from both sides:

3.1.1 Inequitable relationship

Achieving a collaborative and equitable relationship is one of the biggest challenges in realising CBPR. This is attributed to academics' common perception of community engagement as an '*add-on, nice-to-have and philanthropic act*'(Council of Higher Education, 2004). The educational expertise provided academics the scientific privilege, legitimacy and power in research (Cherry and Shefner, 2004; Davies *et al.*, 2009). Consequently, academia often assumed that its knowledge exceeded the community's understanding of its own needs, subsequently reassured their expertise in identifying the community's 'problems', providing 'solutions' by treating the community as inferior ones (Katz, 2003; Tippins, Bell and Lerner, 1998). One example was the labelling of the communities that participated in the community-engaged programs and research as 'low-income', 'at risk' or 'marginalised'(CDC, 2011; Fletcher *et al.*, 2013). As a result, academics tended to play a dominating and paternalistic position in collaborative relationships (Provan, Harvey and Zapien, 2005), prioritizing their interests over those of the community (Netshandama, 2010),and controlling the research process ranging from resources, methods, to dissemination of results (Winterbauer *et al.*, 2016; Winterbauer and Myers, 2013). Such power imbalance in community-academic relationships was not uncommon and often lead to distrust, disrespect and impeded willingness to collaborate in community, and subsequently, tensions and conflicts in projects (Dempsey, 2010; Netshandama, 2010).

3.1.2 Uncommon norms ofpower sharing

Power sharing advocated in community engagementis a significantly different norm compared to conventional research. Adopting community engagementimplies thatacademicsmustlet down some or evenly distribute their power to community stakeholders(Rothman and Gass, 2000).Therefore, community engagement could be seen as beneficial to researchers but also a dilution of return in contribution and investment (Grand *et al.*, 2015).Certain academics found their standard modes of operation and primary professional obligation of producing publishable resultsmore comfortable and achievable than venturing into community engagement with more dispersed goals(Dempsey, 2010; Miller *et al.*, 2015). Recent research also supported that some scholars were still cautious or reluctant towards community engagement, suggesting the conventional notions and norms of science were still vivid (Petrescu, 2017; van Hove and Wickson, 2017).

Even when academics desired to engage community or recognised the necessity of power shift to genuinely collaborate with community in projects, many of them found it difficult to or were uncomfortable about releasing the control, working and sharing credits, responsibility and ownership of research with the community (Staley, 2009),particularly because academics' professional identities as experts have been long built upon years of knowledge, skills and craft development, which was highly important among academia (Staley, 2009), as their professional value depended on theexclusive possession of expertise (Ahmed *et al.*, 2004)and control of ideas, data and intellectual property(Grand *et al.*, 2015).

Likewise, the conventional perceptionofbeing the passive recipients of knowledge and technology transfer still had significant influences on the community side, which madecommunity stakeholders uncomfortable in expressing their needs and priorities to academic partners in a collaboration(Allen *et al.*, 2011).

3.1.3 Distrust between partners

Even when scholars incorporated community into their research, it was often that they did not truly work 'with' the community partners as defined by CBPR approach, rather conducted a community-based research 'in' the community where community members were served as passive participants (García-Rivera *et al.*, 2017; Horowitz, Mimsie Robinson and Seifer, 2009). This resulted in debatable extent of genuine reciprocity and dialogue in community engagement (Horst and Michael, 2011) that could be detrimental to the relationship between partners.One indicator was that there was a general distrust among academia to involve the public in any processes of decision-making, despite they agreed on the contribution to public good as the purpose of research funding allocation (Eden, Jirotka and Stahl, 2013).

Equally, Netshandama (2010) reported coherent distrust from community stakeholders' view towards university-community partnerships. Community members found scholars untrustworthy, as they seldom devote time to maintain the collaborative relationships or show commitments to improve the communities' well-being(Netshandama, 2010). Instead, theyused 'community engagement' to address their own needs andto justify their political correctness in spite of undermining community's voice in actual discussions (Netshandama, 2010). Consequently, most community members and leaders could not see any value in establishing collaborative relationships with academics who did not put the community's interests in mind and were non-differential to community needs (Ahmed *et al.*, 2004; Gass, 2005).When conventional paternalistic, manipulative and exploitativeresearch approach was applied to community engagement, it could erode community's trust to partner with academics (Netshandama, 2010).

3.1.4 Divides between academia and community

Ideally, academia should integrate themselves withthe communityincollaborative partnerships. Paradoxically, academia often perceived themselves to be divided from their wider community (Dempsey,

2010; Minkler, 2004). Hence, academics who participated in community engagement often got into the community looking for research support but quitted its relationship withthe community once the research was completed without any gratitude or even left without ensuring the project could be successfully continued in community(Netshandama, 2010). Such boundary-dividing approach made communities feel disempowered and dependent. It also further distanced the communities from academia (Netshandama, 2010).As a result, community underwent these unfavourable experiences often held the perception of being manipulated by academia rather than being involved (Davis, Cook and Cohen, 2005; Katz, 2003; Netshandama, 2010), which often resulted in distrust in relationships and avoidance of future collaboration with academics who considered themselves as the 'outsiders' of a community.

3.1.5 Knowledge Dissemination

It is reported that academics sometimes offered the community no information about the results nor direct benefits for their participation(Ahmed *et al.*, 2016; Davis, Cook and Cohen, 2005; Grand *et al.*, 2015; Huang, Lipman and Daniel Mullins, 2017; Netshandama, 2010).On the other hand, when academics collaborated with industry for the commercialization of health innovations and products, itgave rise to the concern of conflicts of interest (Miller *et al.*, 2015),as academic patenting could indirectly cause constraints on the free flow of information with community members (Miller *et al.*, 2015), such thatacademics were unwilling to disclose all information about their community projects. Withholding information also damage the reciprocity and trust in the relationship between community and academics.

3.1.6 Lack of resources for maintaining long-term relationships

Academics often experienced significant challenges in securing long-term funding and resources. Not only did the funding typically vulnerable to political changes (Miller, 2001), compared to traditional research initiatives, research with community engagement often required increased time, resource burdens and extra efforts in planning identification of additional resources and relationship building, which lead to lower access and competitiveness in grant applications (García-Rivera *et al.*, 2017). As a result, previous research literature not only reported lack of access to community, but also lack of funding, time, and opportunities and resources to effectively engage community and sustain relationships(Lemacks, Landry and Wenzler, 2018). For example, research targeting hard-to-reach communities required more time for relationship development (Lemacks, Landry and Wenzler, 2018). Limited resources for relationship building could reduce relationship building activities. Otherwise, academics must support at their personal expenses(Lemacks, Landry and Wenzler, 2018).

3.2 Relationship building approaches

Existing literature, however, suggested that community-academic relationships could be built and sustained in two ways: (1) personal qualities such as skills, attributes, virtues of academics on nurturing relationships with community members(Mayan and Daum, 2016; Pinto, 2009; Pinto, McKay and Escobar, 2008) and competence (Shineha *et al.*, 2017), as well as (2) actions targeted on relationship building (Huppert, 2000; Mayan and Daum, 2016).

3.2.1 Personal qualities and competence

Literature reporting successful casesalso highlighted the essential social skills and attributes of academics such as friendliness, honesty, caring, empathy, compassion, concern, and commitment and openness (Pinto, McKay and Escobar, 2008; Pinto, 2009) in facilitating relationship building for partnerships. For instance, certain academics succeeded in maintaining good relationships with community partners as they were great listeners, open-minded, culturally competentand respectful to all partners (Christopher *et al.*, 2008), whom were later framed as the '*boundary spanners*'(Weerts and Sandmann, 2010). It refers to individuals who often engage themselves in sustaining effective personal relationships with other circles and arehighly motivated to collaborate with different stakeholders for mutually beneficial outcomes(Weerts and Sandmann, 2010).

Apart from personal qualities, academics' competence for interdisciplinary or intersectoral collaboration could also be cultivated via provision of rapid and intense crash courses, workshops and trainings on community engagement and relationship building with community members, such as the basic languages and approaches used in other fields and sectors (van Hove and Wickson, 2017). This could support and promote academics'cultural competence and readiness for establishing effective community-academic collaboration relationships(Andrews *et al.*, 2012; Shineha *et al.*, 2017).

3.2.2 Actions targeting on relationship building

Previous literature suggested a number of actionsthat facilitate relationship building at different stages of collaboration to enhance equity, transparency and eliminate power imbalance and hierarchy in relationships, which could be categorised into (1) actively approaching the community before collaboration, (2) early stage of establishingtrustful, collaborativerelationships, (3) facilitating smoother relationships during collaboration, and (4) sustaining relationships after collaboration.

3.2.2.1 Actively approaching community before collaboration

In order to effectively engage the community, academics must first gain entry to the community and build trust with the community stakeholders before establishing collaborative relationships (Caine, Davison and Stewart, 2009; Mayan and Daum, 2016; Pinto, McKay and Escobar, 2008). One way of connecting to and becoming the 'insider' of the community is by paying visits to the community (Huppert, 2000; Pinto, McKay and Escobar, 2008)and participating in community tours led by community leaders before approaching the community for collaboration. The aim isto first understand, respect and valuetheir operational norms and cultures (Huppert, 2000). These acts not onlyencourageinformal conversations andfoster academics' interests and understanding to community issues, but also show goodwill to the potential community partners and increase the chance of success and effectiveness of establishinga new collaborative relationship with a proposal that meet their needs(Mayan and Daum, 2016). In addition, establishing informal relationships (such as participating in community events or informal lunch meetings) and casual conversations with community could also help academics reduce hierarchy and get into the community more easily (Christopher *et al.*, 2008).

3.2.2.2 Early stage of establishingcollaborative relationships

To establish a trusting and quality collaborative relationship, honesty, reciprocity and transparency between partners are essential. Upon the start of collaborative relationships, all partners should(1) make their needs and goals explicit and establish a common ground(Stilgoe, Owen and Macnaghten, 2013); (2) be committed to the project goals(Huang, Lipman and Daniel Mullins, 2017); (3) establish a communication plan to remain well-informed in the research process(Andrews *et al.*, 2012;Roberts *et al.*, 2013; Huang, Lipman and Daniel Mullins, 2017); (4) maintain the flexibility to negotiateand revise changes in the project's goals or strategies (Huang, Lipman and Daniel Mullins, 2017); and(5) be willing to work through disagreement and maintain mutual respect when consensus are not reached(Katz, 2003).

To achieve this, having an open dialogue with community partners is a prerequisite (Minkler, 2004).All partners should (1) explain the reasons for interest in establishing a relationship and the timeline in clarity and honesty, (2) negotiate each other's formal roles and expectations (Huppert, 2000; Winterbauer *et al.*, 2016); and (3) be committed to disclose and share information and results to community members (García-Rivera *et al.*, 2017).

Both parties should understand the fact that there may not be adequate resources and capacity to address all needs. Thus, the interests, priorities, possibilities and limitations between partners should be openly and clearly discussed at early stage of partnerships, since community stakeholders highly valued the openness(García-Rivera *et al.*, 2017).

In terms of formal roles and expectations, each member should indicate their ways of participation and expected levels of effort. One way to eliminate power imbalance and hierarchies in partnership is to ensure a proportional representation in meetings (e.g. balanced number of community stakeholders and academics) and a rotation of leadership and task assignment (e.g. designating different leaders at each study phase)between academia and community stakeholders to ensure that a diversity and equity of voices (Provan, Harvey and Zapien, 2005).To assure all members understand their formal roles and responsibilities in partnerships, tools such as Memoranda of Agreement, contracts stating the scope and standard of work, or signed letters of understanding could promote the formalization of discussions and agreements (Huppert, 2000).

Despite the potential presence of conflicts of interests where academics may not be able to disclose all information to the community members, academics should address the issue at the beginning of collaboration and negotiate with members on which information to share and be committed to disclose them to community members(Banks *et al.*, 2013).

Afterwards, a comprehensive needs assessment should be conducted to identify partners' needs and priorities of the communities served (Gwede *et al.*, 2010; Luque *et al.*, 2011; Simmons *et al.*, 2015), and acknowledge and accommodate different timelines, goals and be flexible in negotiating the priorities with community.

Meanwhile, offering seed funding for projects was proved to be essential for community stakeholdersto support their time and foster commitment to the project(Allen *et al.*, 2011; Luque *et al.*, 2011; Shineha *et al.*, 2017), hence it could be beneficial to the early relationship building stage.

3.2.2.3 Facilitating smoother relationships during collaboration

During collaboration or partnership, the communication frequency and quality between partners should be regular, otherwise infrequent communication would give the community members an impression that one only gets in touch when something is needed from them (Huppert, 2000). Regular dialogue via meetings, phone calls, e-mails provide updates on the progress of project could ensure academics get updated information from the community, keeps partners engaged and offer renewal of relationships(Huppert, 2000; Luque *et al.*, 2011).

In terms of communication language, academicsshould avoid theoretical, impersonal terms and jargons, as they are found to be intimidating to community stakeholders (Huang, Lipman and Daniel Mullins, 2017). Hence, communication channels

 https://doi.org/10.1051/matecconf/201821502002

including local presentations, group discussions, and newsletters should be in common and culturally appropriate language and storytelling approach (García-Rivera *et al.*, 2017; Luque *et al.*, 2011). Meetings organised within the community and active listening could allow community stakeholders to be physically and psychologically stay in the community (Cherry and Shefner, 2004) and be more comfortable to express their views (Trench, 2008).

It is alsohighly important to recognise and reward the efforts of both community and academic stakeholders, as in many situationsthe participation of members in partnerships were voluntary or underpaid. For example, community members who helped generate the intellectual property rights or knowledge (Netshandama, 2010)should beincluded as co-authors or in acknowledgement of abstracts, posters or manuscripts to maintain trust and respect in collaborative relationships (García-Rivera *et al.*, 2017).

Another approach is to recognise partners'leadership and contribution with an award or a featurestory in the local media to honourtheir accomplishments(del Pino *et al.*, 2016). Partners could take action to write a nomination letter for a community award, or introduce one's great work to the media to promote the experiences of community collaboration and honourtheir roles as local agents of change in health and well-being of community(del Pino *et al.*, 2016; García-Rivera *et al.*, 2017).

If possible, compensating academics or community partners with certificate or coupons to a restaurant or bookstore as a gesture of contribution recognition is also be appreciated(Huppert, 2000). Otherwise, positive reinforcement measures such as giving a letter of congratulation or praise from the dean could also help maintain good relationships via demonstratinggratitude to partners' contribution and effort (Huppert, 2000).

3.2.2.4 Sustaining relationshipsafter collaboration

Quality partnerships requires long-term relationship building among stakeholders to maintain commitment and interests during and after the collaboration period.To ensure sustainability, academics should slowly pace out by empowering community to monitor the results and offer assistance at the end of the project instead of leaving the community alone immediately. To avoid the impression of manipulation and exploitation, academics should stay engaged in the community via continue getting involved in community life(Staley, 2009). Such practices could be supported on organisational level. For instance, instead of evaluating academics purely based on their academic publications, higher education policymakers could also include public outreach work (such as engagement and dissemination work in addition to teaching and research) as the evaluation criteria for employment and promotion in scientific positions (Shineha *et al.*, 2017) to provide motivation for academics to sustain their relationships with community.

4 Conclusions and recommendations

Nowadays, academics are undeniably more expected to step out of their 'ivory tower', extend their boundaries to bridge with their wider community in order to achieve better and more accepted research and innovation outcomes.Accordingly, the purpose of this literature review is to offer academics and community stakeholders insights on the common situations, challenges and pitfalls in building and maintaining community-academic collaborative relationships and to demonstrate ways to build stronger collaborative relationships.

From literature it is clear that the ways how academics approach, collaborate, communicate with and stay in the community demonstrated significant impact ontheir relationships, which could eventually influence not only the quality, processes, impact and sustainability of the existing collaborations or partnerships, but also the potentials of future collaborations. Hence it is extremely crucial for academics to acknowledge and be well-prepared of the pitfalls and be capable to deal with the potential tensions and conflicts that may arise before initiating collaborative relationships with community members. CBPR has offered a valuable insight to achieve that via establishing an equitable, transparent, trustful relationship with community. Although there is still plenty of room for improvement in practice, a huge progress has been made over the last two decades.

Moreovoer, it is worth notice that literature has offered valuable insights to the effect of individual differences towards relationship building for community engagement. Apparently, some academics were more open-minded while some were still reluctant to accept or had concerns about community engagement, or some started community engagement activities despite of the lack of enough knowledge about its true essence. Accordingly, they faced various types of challenges, ranging from starting a new collaborative relationship to sustaining an existing relationship. Therefore, future research may consider to explore the differences of acceptance and readinessamong academics towards community engagement andidentify the factors contributing to such differences. Given personal qualities and competence could be a unique approach for relationship building, comparing how academics' individual qualities and competence may affect the quality of relationship with communitycould also benefit thecultivation of their readiness and capacity in promoting community engagement andeffective relationship building with community.

5 Reference list

[1] Ahmed, S.M. et al. (2004) 'Overcoming Barriers to Effective Community-Based Participatory

Research in US Medical Schools', Education for Health (Abingdon, England), 17(2), 141–151. doi: 10.1080/13576280410001710969

[2] Ahmed, S.M. et al. (2016) 'Opening the Black Box: Conceptualizing Community Engagement from 109 Community-Academic Partnership Programs', Progress in Community Health Partnerships : Research, Education, and Action, 10(1), 51–61. doi: 10.1353/cpr.2016.0019

[3] Allen, M.L. et al. (2011) 'A Capacity Building Program to Promote CBPR Partnerships between Academic Researchers and Community Members', Clinical and Translational Science, 4(6), 428–433. doi: 10.1111/j.1752-8062.2011.00362.x

[4] Andrews, J.O. et al. (2012) 'Partnership Readiness for Community-based Participatory Research', Health Education Research, 27(4), 555–571. doi: 10.1093/her/cyq050

[5] Bahraminejad, N. et al. (2015) 'Partner's Engagement in Community-based Health Promotion Programs: a Case Study of Professional Partner's Experiences and Perspectives in Iran', Health Promotion International, 30(4), 963–975. doi: 10.1093/heapro/dau043

[6] Banks, S. et al. (2013) 'Everyday Ethics in Community-based Participatory Research', Contemporary Social Science, 8(3), 263–277. doi: 10.1080/21582041.2013.769618

[7] Blumenthal, D.S. (2011) 'Is Community-Based Participatory Research Possible?' American Journal of Preventive Medicine, 40(3), 386–389. doi: 10.1016/j.amepre.2010.11.011

[8] Caine, K.J., Davison, C.M. and Stewart, E.J. (2009) 'Preliminary Field-work: Methodological Reflections from Northern Canadian Research', Qualitative Research, 9(4), 489–513. doi: 10.1177/1468794109337880

[9] Center for Disease Control and Prevention (ed.) (2011) Principles of Community Engagement. 2nd edn. USA: National Institutes of Health.

[10] Cherry, D.J. and Shefner, J. (2004) 'Addressing Barriers to University-Community Collaboration', Journal of Community Practice, 12(3-4), 219–233. doi: 10.1300/J125v12n03_13

[11] Christopher, S. et al. (2008) 'Building and Maintaining Trust in a Community-based Participatory Research Partnership', American Journal of Public Health, 98(8), 1398–1406. doi: 10.2105/AJPH.2007.125757

[12] Council of Higher Education (2004) Chapter Seven: Community Engagment. [online] available from https://innerweb.ukzn.ac.za/scer/Council%20on%20Higher%20Education/SA_HE_10years_Nov2004_Chapter7.pdf [09 June 2018].

[13] Davies, S.R. et al. (2009) 'Discussing Dialogue: Perspectives on the Value of Science Dialogue Events that Do Not Inform Policy', Public Understanding of Science, 18(3), 338–353.

[14] Davis, R., Cook, D. and Cohen, L. (2005) 'A Community Resilience Approach to Reducing Ethnic and Racial Disparities in Health', American Journal of Public Health, 95(12), 2168–2173. doi: 10.2105/AJPH.2004.050146

[15] del Pino, H.E. et al. (2016) 'Integrating Community Expertise into the Academy: South Los Angeles' Community-Academic Model for Partnered Research', Progress in Community Health Partnerships: Research, Education, and Action, 10(2), 329–338. doi: 10.1353/cpr.2016.0028

[16] Dempsey, S.E. (2010) 'Critiquing Community Engagement', Management Communication Quarterly, 24(3), 359–390. doi: 10.1177/0893318909352247

[17] Eden, G., Jirotka, M. and Stahl, B. (2013) Responsible Research and Innovation: Critical Reflection Into the Potential Social Consequences of ICT.Proceedings of the IEEE 7th International Conference on Research Challenges in Information Science (RCIS). Held May 29-31, 2013 at Paris, France :1-12.

[18] Fletcher, F. et al. (2013) 'Needs and Readiness Assessments: Tools for Promoting Community-university Engagement With Aboriginal Communities', Gateways: International Journal of Community Research and Engagement, 6(1), 131. doi: 10.5130/ijcre.v6i1.3219

[19] García-Rivera, E.J. et al. (2017) 'Building Bridges to Address Health Disparities in Puerto Rico: the "Salud para Piñones" Project', Puerto Rico Health Sciences Journal, 36(2), 92–100.

[20] Gass, E. (2005) 'The Path to Partnership: A New Model for Understanding University-Community Partnerships', Professional Development-Philadelphia, 8, 12–23.

[21] Grand, A. et al. (2015) 'Mapping Public Engagement With Research in a UK University', PloS One, 10(4), e0121874. doi: 10.1371/journal.pone.0121874

[22] Gwede, C.K. et al. (2010) 'Strategies for Assessing Community Challenges and Strengths for Cancer Disparities Participatory Research and Outreach', Health Promotion Practice, 11(6), 876–887. doi: 10.1177/1524839909335803

[23] Horowitz, C.R., Mimsie Robinson, R. and Seifer, S. (2009) 'Community-Based Participatory Research from the Margin to the Mainstream: Are Researchers Prepared?' Circulation, 119(19), 2633–2642. doi: 10.1161/CIRCULATIONAHA.107.729863

[24] Horst, M. and Michael, M. (2011) 'On the Shoulders of Idiots: Re-thinking Science Communication as 'Event'', Science as Culture, 20(3), 283–306. doi: 10.1080/09505431.2010.524199

[25] Huang, J., Lipman, P.D. and Daniel Mullins, C. (2017) 'Bridging the Divide: Building Infrastructure to Support Community-academic Partnerships and Improve Capacity to Conduct Patient-centered Outcomes Research',

Translational Behavioral Medicine, 7(4), 773–782. doi: 10.1007/s13142-017-0487-z

[26] Huppert, M.E. (2000) 'Principle 6: Roles, Norms, and Processes for the Partnership Are Established with Input and Agreement of All Partners', Partnership Perspectives, 1(2), 47–55.

[27] Israel, B.A. (2005) Methods in Community-based Participatory Research for Health. San Francisco, CA: Jossey-Bass [online] available from http://site.ebrary.com/lib/alltitles/docDetail.action?docID=10304499 [09 June 2018].

[28] Israel, B.A. et al. (1998) 'Review of Community-based Research: Assessing Partnership Approaches to Improve Public Health', Annual Review of Public Health, 19, 173–202. doi: 10.1146/annurev.publhealth.19.1.173

[29] Israel, B.A. et al. (2006) 'Challenges and Facilitating Factors in Sustaining Community-Based Participatory Research Partnerships: Lessons Learned from the Detroit, New York City and Seattle Urban Research Centers', Journal of Urban Health : Bulletin of the New York Academy of Medicine, 83(6), 1022–1040. doi: 10.1007/s11524-006-9110-1

[30] Jacob, K. (2013) Options for Strengthening Responsible Research and Innovation: Report of the Expert Group on the State of Art in Europe on Responsible Research and Innovation. Luxembourg: Publications Office of the European Union.

[31] Katz, D.L. (2003) 'Representing Your Community in Community-based Participatory Research: Differences Made and Measured', Preventing Chronic Disease, 1(1).

[32] Lasker, R.D., Weiss, E.S. and Miller, R. (2001) 'Partnership Synergy: A Practical Framework for Studying and Strengthening the Collaborative Advantage', The Milbank Quarterly, 79(2), 179–205. doi: 10.1111/1468-0009.00203

[33] LaVeaux, D. and Christopher, S. (2009) 'Contextualizing CBPR: Key Principles of CBPR meet the Indigenous research context', Pimatisiwin, 7(1), p. 1.

[34] Lemacks, J., Landry, A. and Wenzler, P. (2018) 'Formative research to identify community partnerships and foster relationships for health promotion research in South Mississippi', Public Health. doi: 10.1016/j.puhe.2018.01.023

[35] Luque, J.S. et al. (2011) 'A Social Network Analysis Approach to Understand Changes in a Cancer Disparities Community Partnership Network', Annals of Anthropological Practice, 35(2). doi: 10.1111/j.2153-9588.2011.01085.x

[36] Mayan, M.J. and Daum, C.H. (2016) 'Worth the Risk? Muddled Relationships in Community-Based Participatory Research', Qualitative Health Research, 26(1), 69–76. doi: 10.1177/1049732315618660

[37] Miller, F.A. et al. (2015) 'Citizen Expectations of 'Academic Entrepreneurship' in Health Research: Public Science, Practical Benefit', Health Expectations : an International Journal of Public Participation in Health Care and Health Policy, 18(6), 2356–2374. doi: 10.1111/hex.12205

[38] Miller, S. (2001) 'Public Understanding of Science at the Crossroads', Public Understanding of Science, 10, 115–120.

[39] Minkler, M. (2004) 'Ethical Challenges for the "Outside" Researcher in Community-Based Participatory Research', Health education & behavior : the official publication of the Society for Public Health Education, 31(6), 684–697. doi: 10.1177/1090198104269566

[40] Minkler, M. (2005) 'Community-based Research Partnerships: Challenges and Opportunities', Journal of Urban Health : Bulletin of the New York Academy of Medicine, 82(Suppl 2), ii3-ii12. doi: 10.1093/jurban/jti034

[41] Minkler, M. et al. (2017) Community-based Participatory Research for Health : Advancing Social and Health Equity [online] available from http://www.myilibrary.com/?id=1041315 [09 June 2018].

[42] Netshandama, V. (2010) 'Quality Partnerships: the Community Stakeholders' View', International Journal of Community Research and Engagement, 3(0), 70. doi: 10.5130/ijcre.v3i0.1541

[43] Petrescu, A.M.A. (2017) 'Ways of Valorizing The Public Engagement In Responsible Research And Innovation', 2nd Central and Eastern European LUMEN International Conference - Multidimensional Education and Professional Development. Ethical Values, 2016: Cognitive-crcs, 617–622. doi: 10.15405/epsbs.2017.07.03.72

[44] Pinto, R.M. (2009) 'Community Perspectives on Factors That Influence Collaboration in Public Health Research', Health Education & Behavior : The Official Publication of the Society for Public Health Education, 36(5), 930–947. doi: 10.1177/1090198108328328

[45] Pinto, R.M., McKay, M.M. and Escobar, C. (2008) '"You've Gotta Know the Community": Minority Women Make Recommendations About Community-Focused Health Research', Women & Health, 47(1), 83–104. doi: 10.1300/J013v47n01_05

[46] Provan, K.G., Harvey, J. and Zapien, J.G. de (2005) 'Network Structure and Attitudes Toward Collaboration in a Community Partnership for Diabetes Control on the Us-mexican Border', Journal of Health Organization and Management, 19(6), 504–518. doi: 10.1108/14777260510629706

[47] Roberts, C.B. et al. (2013) 'Lessons Learned From Building an Infrastructure for Community-engaged Research', International Public Health Journal, 5(1), 7–16.

[48] Ross, L.F. et al. (2010) 'The Challenges of Collaboration for Academic and Community Partners in a Research Partnership: Points to Consider', Journal of Empirical Research on

Human Research Ethics : JERHRE, 5(1), 19–31. doi: 10.1525/jer.2010.5.1.19
[49] Rothman, N.L. and Gass, D.L. (2000) 'A Successful Community-based Partnership: Formation and Achievements.', Metropolitan Universities, 11(2), 59–62.
[50] Serrell, N. et al. (2009) 'An Academic-community Outreach Partnership: Building Relationships and Capacity to Address Childhood Lead Poisoning', Progress in Community Health Partnerships : Research, Education, and Action, 3(1), 53–59. doi: 10.1353/cpr.0.0056
[51] Shineha, R. et al. (2017) 'Science Communication in Regenerative Medicine: Implications for the Role of Academic Society and Science Policy', Regenerative Therapy, 7, 89–97. doi: 10.1016/j.reth.2017.11.001
[52] Simmons, V.N. et al. (2015) 'Participatory Evaluation of a Community-academic Partnership to Inform Capacity-building and Sustainability', Evaluation and Program Planning, 52, 19–26. doi: 10.1016/j.evalprogplan.2015.03.005.
[53] Staley, K. (2009) Exploring Impact: Public Involvement in NHS, Public Health and Social Care Research. Eastleigh.
[54] Stilgoe, J., Owen, R. and Macnaghten, P. (2013) 'Developing a Framework for Responsible Innovation', Research Policy, 42(9), 1568–1580. doi: 10.1016/j.respol.2013.05.008
[55] Tippins, P., Bell, M. and Lerner, S. (1998) Building Relationships Between University and Community Paths to Partnership. Boulder and Littlefield: Rowman and University and Community as Learners in Interprofessional Education.
[56] Trench, B. (2008) 'Towards an Analytical Framework of Science Communication Models', in:'Communicating Science in Social Contexts: New Models, New Practices'. ed. by Cheng, D. Dordrecht Springer, 119–135.
[57] Trencher, G. et al. (2017) 'Implementing Sustainability Co-Creation between Universities and Society: A Typology-Based Understanding', Sustainability, 9(4), 594. doi: 10.3390/su9040594
[58] van Hove, L. and Wickson, F. (2017) 'Responsible Research Is Not Good Science: Divergences Inhibiting the Enactment of RRI in Nanosafety', NanoEthics, 11(3), 213–228. doi: 10.1007/s11569-017-0306-5
[59] Wallerstein, N. et al. (eds.) (2005) Developing and Maintaining Partnerships With Communities. San Francisco: John Wiley (Methods in community-based participatory research for health).
[60] Wang, K.H. et al. (2017) 'Using Community-based Participatory Research and Organizational Diagnosis to Characterize Relationships Between Community Leaders and Academic Researchers', Preventive Medicine Reports, 7, 180–186. doi: 10.1016/j.pmedr.2017.06.007
[61] Weerts, D.J. and Sandmann, L.R. (2010) 'Community Engagement and Boundary-Spanning Roles at Research Universities', The Journal of Higher Education, 81(6), 632–657. doi: 10.1080/00221546.2010.11779075
[62] Winterbauer, N.L. and Myers, C. (2013) 'Pracademics as Culture Brokers in Practice-based Participatory Research'. Proceedings of the Keeneland Conference,'Public Health Services & Systems Research'. Held April 2018. Lexington, KY.
[63] Winterbauer, N.L. et al. (2016) 'Applying Community-Based Participatory Research Partnership Principles to Public Health Practice-Based Research Networks', SAGE Open, 6(4), 215824401667921. doi: 10.1177/2158244016679211

MATEC Web of Conferences **215**, 02003 (2018) https://doi.org/10.1051/matecconf/201821502003
ICTIS 2018

Linkage between Flexibility and SMEs Performance: Does Improvisation Matter?

Darwina Arshad, *Nazlina* Zakaria, *Kadzrina* Abdul-Kadir and *Norzieiriani* Ahmad

School of Business Management, College of Business, Universiti Utara Malaysia, Malaysia

Abstract. Small Medium Enterprises (SMEs) has become significant in today's economic growth. To gain and sustain the SMEs performance, one of the ways the organization should do is to be flexible and improvise in its business activities. The link between flexibility, improvisation and SMEs performance is still vague, thus this paper aims to investigate the effect of improvisation as a mediator between organizational flexibility and SMEs performance. Three hypotheses are put forward to achieve the aforementioned research goal. Obtaining on a survey data from 202 manufacturing SMEs in Malaysia, the findings of the study confirmed that all hypotheses have a positive significant association. Theoretically and in practice, this study denotes rich addition to the vocabulary of business and management.

1 Introduction

Today, Small Medium Enterprises (SMEs) has become one of the key competitive sectors in emerging economies and has been said as constant environmental changes. In Malaysia, the SMEs' contribution to overall gross-domestic product (GDP) in 2015 was reported at 35.9% [1]. In gaining and sustaining the best company performance and competitive advantage, firms under SMEs need to be flexible, require moving creatively and quickly to adapt to changing conditions. Development on the most appropriate plan and taking into strategic decisions and actions in the new challenging environment are not an easy process in organizations. Improvisation is one of the business actions that entrepreneurial firms need to consider as it can diverge from strategic plans to instantaneously respond to opportunities when they emerge [2].

In the meantime, previous scholars have proved that improvisation may lead to business performance [3-6]. This appears that improvisation is significant to produce distinct business performance. However, the empirical evidence on this association is still scarce in management and business research. Henceforth, the aim of this study is to put forward three important objectives: to examine (1) the association between flexibility and improvisation, (2) the relationship between improvisation and performance; and (3) the mediating role of improvisation on the link between flexibility and SMEs performance.

We examine our objectives using survey data generated from SMEs manufacturing sector. This sector was chosen because SMEs manufacturing sector is considered as fast-moving setting where flexibility and improvisation are more likely to happen in their business practices. Further, according to Savita, Dominic and Ramayah (2016), Malaysia offers a cost-competitive avenue for investors to capitalize in manufacturing the technological and advanced products. This sector is the second largest contribution to overall GDP with 7.8% after SMEs service sector [1]. SMEs manufacturing companies are significant contributors to Malaysia's economic growth (MIDA, 2012), therefore there is a need to investigate this setting.

2 The Hypotheses

Flexibility and Improvisation

Flexibility in general means an ability to adapt or change. In organizational approach, flexibility is suggested to enable organizations to manage uncertain and 'fast-occurring' markets effectively and provide a capability to promptly generate and grasp upon creativities and opportunities [7]. Scholars stated that flexibility is one of the elements of improvisation. Improvisation is an action involved in real time situations in which it tangled a high degree of spontaneity and creativity in convergence of plan and implementation by individuals, groups, or the whole organization [8-9]. Improvisation is a conscious choice rather than something that occurs by chances [5, 10-11]. Organizational improvisation has been said to create value added to the organization [12]. Organizations need to understand how organizational flexibility can affect improvisation in the business. Flexibility is essentially considered as a basic 'infrastructure' that facilitate improvisation.

Organizational flexibility appears from the outcome of an interaction between the responsiveness of the

* Corresponding author: darwina@uum.edu.my

organizational and managerial capabilities [13]. Managerial capabilities can be individuals or team of the firms. In organization, flexible individuals or team are believed to be able to explore in an extensive range of approaches to a problem without misleading their overall goal. This is unlike to less flexible individuals or team who are more obsessed with stability, direction, and precision and are more possible to suffer considerable stress and loss of control when threatened with changing environments. In some circumstances, flexible individuals or team within organizations could generate a greater flexible management systems and means of operating, strategizing and hence, decision making. The managerial flexibility will thus collectively would create the capacity of organizational flexibility. Thus, the hypothesis is as follows:

Hypothesis 1: Firms with high levels of flexibility exhibit greater levels of improvisation.

Improvisation and Performance

Improvisation is defined as an action taken in real time situations where it encompasses a high amount of spontaneity and creativity [4, 9]. Crossan (1997) posits that improvisation is the ability to plan and perform actions concurrently in organization where it may help providing superior performance and better innovative results. In early investigations, improvisation has typically relied on artistic metaphors such as jazz and theatre settings. While recent studies have proved that scholars much focus improvisation in organizational settings such as study on new product development [9, 14], export decision making [5-6] and firm performance [3-4] However,the study is still in infancy stage where only few studies available in the business management research.

In strategic management research, firm performance has long been agreed as an outcome in organizational phenomena. Prior researches have investigated several variables such as strategic planning and strategic making process [15-17], business-level, or corporate-level strategy [18-20], organizational structure and capabilities [19, 21], choice of environmental domains as well as organizational characteristics [4] on various performance. Such efforts have emphasized substantial consideration on the importance of improvisation at individual, group [22] and organizational performance. The study by Moorman and Miner (1998), Akgun and Lynn (2002) and Vera and Crossan (2005) disclose new product development as a result of team improvisation [9, 23]; Leybourne and Sadler-Smith (2006) study on the link between improvisation and the project performance [12]; Souchon and Hughes (2007) emphasis on export performance as an outcome of export improvisation [6]; and Hmieleski and Corbett (2008) reveal venture performance as an outcome of entrepreneurial improvisational behavior [25]. Only little studies have sought to deem and prove the relationship between organizational improvisation and firm performance (*see* Arshad and Hughes, 2009; Arshad et al. 2015). Therefore, this study is hypothesized as below:

Hypothesis 2: The stronger the organizational improvisation, the better the firm performance of Malaysia manufacturing of SMEs.

The Relationship between Flexibility and Performance through Improvisation

Flexibility can be a mechanism of improvisation in which it endows the capacity of the organization to improvise. Greater organizational flexibility could help organizations to plan and execute simultaneously (improvisation) in a conscious manner. Whilst organizations seek to enhance their feasible performance in a rapid change environment by performing actions through improvisation [11]. This scenario is thus reflected that organizational improvisation can be the mediator that could enable organizations to proactively flexible to strengthen their performance. However this study is still empirically very limited proof, thus it is proposed in this study as below:

Hypothesis 3: through organizational improvisation as a mediator between flexibility and performance.

3 Research method

3.1 Research setting and Sample Size

The setting for this research is a stratified random of manufacturing SMEs which divided into three areas includes northern, southern, and central part of peninsular Malaysia. The target population of this research was the owner or entrepreneur or manager or top management of the manufacturing SMEs who directly involved with overall operation, routine and performance of the firm. Top managers were selected because they were the one who responsible for managing, making decisions as well as striving to reach competitive advantages. This study is limited to only examine the organizational flexibility, organizational improvisation and SMEs performance among Malaysian manufacturers.

According to Hair et al. (2010), the ratio of observations to independent variable should not fall below five (5:1) [25]. This study was used 24 items in exploratory factor analysis and structural equation modeling; therefore, it required a minimum sample size of 120 respondents.

3.2 Data collection method

This study was used on a nationwide-scale data collection involving the Malaysian Manufacturing SMEs as the central subject. Data was collected via a developed structured questionnaire. The questionnaire is a well-established method for social science research to obtain information about social characteristic of respondents, past and present behavior, standards of attitudes or behavior, and their reason for action with

https://doi.org/10.1051/matecconf/201821502003

respect to the topic that being reviewed. The questionnaires were randomly distributed to SMEs based on directory of SME Corporation website. The questionnaire was delivered through e-mails or personally distributed by hand directly to the respondents. The respondents were given reasonable time to answer the questionnaires. The time period that the researchers took to deliver and collect all the questionnaires was two month through three major areas. The researchers were able to collect a total of 202 completed questionnaires to be analyzed in this study; in which it passes the minimum requirement of a sample size of 5:1 ratio.

3.3 Measurement of variables and Data Analysis

SMEs performance construct consists of flexibility are adapted from Jones, Rafferty, and Griffin (2006) with nine construct items. Whereas, organizational improvisation construct consists of seven items adapted from Vera and Crossan (2005); and five items adapted from the work of Ahmad, Wilson, and Kummerow (2011) was used for SMEs performance measures. The items for each construct and their scale of measurements are listed in Table I.For the data analysis, this study used the Partial Least Squares (PLS) approach using the SmartPLS3 to analyze the data. Bootstrapping method (500 resamples) was employed to determine the significance levels for loadings, weights, and path coefficients [26].

4 Results

4.1 Demographic profile of respondents

Results reveals that the majority of the manufacturing SMEs that participated in this study had been operating their business more than 20 years (27.2%), followed by 5 to 10 years (23.3%),11 to 15 years (20.3%) and 16 to 20 years (16.8%), while those operating under 5 years accounted for 12.4%. The table also shows the majority (74.3%) of the responding firms were small-sized firms (5 to 75 employees), and only 25.7% were medium-sized firms (75 to 200 employees).

4.2 Measurement model

There are two-staged processes involved in the analysis. Firstly, the assessment of the reliability and validity of the measurement model, and secondly, the assessment of the structural model. The research model of this study is depicted in Figure 1, which exhibits the loading for each item for this study.

To assess the measurement model, the researchers verified both reliability and validity. Reliability was measured through composite reliability and validity was assessed via convergent validity (as shown in Table 1) and discriminant validity (see Table 2). The analyses was done to confirm that the construct measurements are reliable and valid before evaluating the links in the structural model. Convergent validity can be proven if the loadings are larger than 0.5, composite reliability (CR) greater than 0.7 and the average variance extracted (AVE) is greater than 0.5 [27].

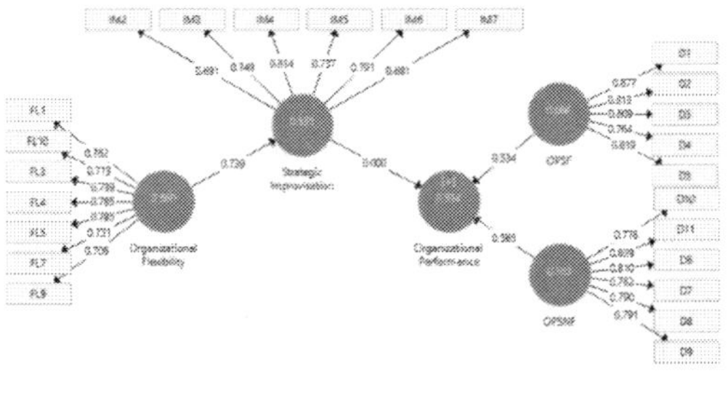

Fig. 1: Research model of the study

Table 1. Results of Measurement Model

First Order Construct	Second Order Construct	Scale Type	Item	Loadings/ weights	AVE/ VIF	CR/ t-value
Satisfaction Financial Performance		Reflective	D1	0.877	0.688	0.909
			D2	0.813		
			D3	0.809		
			D4	0.764		
			D5	0.819		
Satisfaction Nonfinancial Performance		Reflective	D6	0.810	0.583	0.893
			D7	0.762		
			D8	0.790		
			D9	0.791		
			D10	0.776		
			D11	0.639		
	SMEs	Formative	OPSF	0.534	1.780	26.599**
	Performance		OPSNF	0.565	2.163	26.400**
Organizational Flexibility		Reflective	FL1	0.762	0.560	0.899
			FL10	0.713		
			FL3	0.739		
			FL4	0.795		
			FL5	0.785		
			FL7	0.731		
			FL9	0.706		
Organizational Improvisation		Reflective	IM2	0.691	0.555	0.882
			IM3	0.749		
			IM4	0.814		
			IM5	0.737		
			IM6	0.791		
			IM7	0.681		

First Order Construct	Second Order Construct	Scale Type	Item	Loadings/ weights	AVE/ VIF	CR/t-value
Satisfaction Financial Performance		Reflective	D1	0.877	0.688	0.909
			D2	0.813		
			D3	0.809		
			D4	0.764		
			D5	0.819		
Satisfaction Nonfinancial Performance		Reflective	D6	0.810	0.583	0.893
			D7	0.762		
			D8	0.790		
			D9	0.791		
			D10	0.776		
			D11	0.639		
	SMEs	Formative	OPSF	0.534	1.780	26.599**
	Performance		OPSNF	0.565	2.163	26.400**
Organizational Flexibility		Reflective	FL1	0.762	0.560	0.899
			FL10	0.713		
			FL3	0.739		
			FL4	0.795		
			FL5	0.785		
			FL7	0.731		
			FL9	0.706		
Organizational Improvisation		Reflective	IM2	0.691	0.555	0.882
			IM3	0.749		
			IM4	0.814		

IM5	0.737
IM6	0.791
IM7	0.681

Note: AVE = (summation of the square of the factor loadings)/ {(summation of the square of the factor loadings) + (summation of the error variances)}; CR = (square of the summation of the factor loadings)/ {(summation of the square of the factor loadings) + (summation of the square of the error variances)}

From the result of the study, the loadings range from 0.639 to 0.877 in which showed more than half of the variance in the observed variable was explained by the constructs. The CR values explained the degree to which the construct items represent the latent, which were in the range of 0.882 and 0.909. The AVE measures "the degree to which a latent construct explains the variance of its items" (Hair et al., 2014, p.114), which was in the range of 0.555 and 0.688. In this study, SMEs performance was modeled as second-order formative constructs. Three steps were involved in measuring formative measures: (i) test for weight significant; (ii) test for multi-collinearity; and (iii) test of the correlation of the indicators with the latent construct.

This study found that the statistical significance of weights implies the relative importance of indicators in forming a latent construct. The analysis also demonstrated that all items had VIF of less than 5, indicating no threat of multi-collinearity between the different indicators [28]. Finally, the correlation of the indicators with the latent construct was tested to find out their absolute contribution. Result revealed that all items had a significant weight and were correlated to the latent constructs. Consequently, all items in the formative construct were retained for further analysis. From Table 1, the results prove that all the three construct, flexibility, performance and improvisation are valid measures of their respective constructs based on their parameter estimates and statistical significance [29].

Discriminant validity (see Table 2) was tested using the Fornell and Lacker (1981) criterion which proposes that more variance is shared by a latent construct with its own indicators than with other latent construct in the structural model [30]. Table 2 illustrates that all the square root of the AVE values was larger than other correlation values among the latent variables, indicating that several constructs used in the model belong to distinct entities. In essence, the measurement model displayed good discriminant validity among constructs.

Table 2: Fornell-Lurker Criterion

	OPSF	OPSNF	Organizational Flexibility	Organizational Improvisation
OPSF	**0.817**			
OPSNF	0.656	**0.763**		
Organizational Flexibility	0.506	0.669	**0.748**	**0.745**
Organizational Improvisation	0.457	0.59	0.739	

Note: Diagonals (in bold) represent the square root of AVE while the other entries represent the correlation

4.3 Structural model

As this study calls for the measurement of both reflective and formative in the same model, the two-stage approach were used to test the hypothesis (Hair et al., 2014). The results are presented in Figure 1andTable 3. The R^2 values of 0.546 and 0.357 which propose that flexibility and improvisation contributed 54.6 and 35.7 percent of the variance in the respective dependent variables. As shown in Table III, all hypotheses were fully supported which was confirmed a positive and significant association between flexibility and improvisation ($\beta = 0.739$, $t = 17.267$, $p < 0.01$) and organizational improvisation and performance ($\beta = 0.597$, $t = 12.370$, $p < 0.01$). The bootstrapping analysis also showed that the indirect effect ($\beta = 0.441$) was significant with t-value of 8.204. Also, as indicated by Preacher and Hayes (2008), the indirect effect 95% Boot CI: [LL = 0.325, UL = 0.535], did not straddle a 0 in between, indicating there is mediation. Thus, the result revealed that the mediation effect of organizational improvisation on the relationship between organizational flexibility and SMEs performance was statistically significant ($\beta = 0.441$, $t = 8.204$, $p < 0.01$).

Table 3: Path Coefficients and Hypotheses Testing

H	Relationship	Beta	SE	t-value	Bootstrapped Confidence Interval (Boot CI) 95% LL	95% UL	Decision
H1	Flexibility -> Improvisation	0.739	0.043	17.267*	-	-	Supported
H2	Improvisation ->SMEs Performance	0.597	0.048	12.370*	-	-	Supported
H3	Flexibility -> Improvisation ->SMEs Performance	0.441	0.054	8.204**	0.325	0.535	Supported

Note: *P<0.05 (1.645), **P<0.01 (2.33)

5 Implications and Contributions

Our primary contributions of this paper is to provide theoretical and practical research gaps. This study explores the understanding on the significant element of improvisation which are based upon organizational flexibility, as well as to provide empirical evidence on whether the flexibility could exist an effect on performance through organizational improvisation. Improvisation in the business is believed that it could generate a good outcome, which is to lead to superior performance. The finding of this study implies that top managers or decision-makers of companies need to consider implementing improvisational practice in their organizations in order to gain and sustain superior firm performance. In addition, flexibility is assumed as a desired outcome of improvisation as it is also apparent here that flexibility is a necessary condition for improvisation to occur. The finding thus indicates that organizational flexibility provides the ability to improvise organizational activities by committing resources to new courses of actions in response to those changes and therefore affect better performance return. This organizational flexibility enables organizations to recognize and improvise promptly to respond to various demands and opportunities existing in a dynamic and uncertain competitive environment in gaining and sustaining best firm performance.

The study also emphasized several essential areas that some parties need to be concerned. Concerning on the improvisational activities that add on the business practice in organization, firms are believed to be more competence to survive in its business. In the condition of limited resources and with fast and rapid environmental change, firms need to be decided and acted strategically. Therefore, element of improvisation is significant as it could gain and sustain the growth and survival of the firms, specifically in SMEs setting.

6 Conclusion

SMEs should be flexible to enable a creative and spontaneous move to respond on the frequent changing environment. Taking decisions out of the traditional planning process by creating improvisational practice is still scarce in the organizations' management system. The pursuit investigation on the relationships between the aforementioned three hypotheses is reasonable given that improvisation normally involves creative and spontaneous decisions and actions which enabling the alteration of pre-planned activities or semi-structured work processes; organizational flexibility can be the element that affect improvisation; while firm performance is the firms' business success.

References

1. SME Corporation Malaysia, SME Statistic, http://www.smecorp.gov.my/index.php/en/policies/2015-12-21-09-09-49/sme-statistics
2. Hughes, P., Hodgkinson, I., Hughes, M., & Arshad, D. Explaining the entrepreneurial orientation–performance relationship in emerging economies: The intermediate roles of absorptive capacity and improvisation. *Asia Pacific Journal of Management, in press.* (2017).
3. Arshad, D. & Hughes, P. (2009). Examining organizational improvisation: the role of strategic reasoning and managerial factors International. *Journal of Social, Behavioral, Educational, Economic and Management Engineering*, 3(6), 948-954.
4. Arshad, D., Julienti, L., Ahmad, H. &Hafizi, S. (2015). Unraveling the Link between Environmental Factors and Organizational Improvisation. In *E-Proceeding of the International Conference on Social Science Research, ICSSR 2015*, 647–655.
5. Nemkova, E., Souchon, A. L., Hughes, P., &Micevski, M., Does Improvisation Help or Hinder Planning in Determining Export Success? Decision Theory Applied to Exporting. *Journal of International Marketing*, 23, 41–65.
6. Souchon, A.L. and Hughes, P. (2007). Improvising export decisions: A contingency theory perspective. International and Cross-cultural Marketing, Track 8.
7. Dunford, R. (2013). "Flexibility" as the rationale for organizational change: a discourse perspective. *Journal of Organizational Change Management*, 26, 83–97.
8. Moorman, C., & Miner, A. S. (1998). The convergence of planning and execution: Improvisation in new product development. *Journal of Marketing*, 61, 1-20.
9. Vera, D. & Crossan, M. (2005). Improvisation and Innovative Performance in Teams. *Organization*
10. Arshad, D. (2011). Understanding organisational improvisation: foundations and performance implications. PhD Thesis, Loughborough University.
11. Arshad, D., Razalli, R., Julienti, L., Ahmad, H., & Mahmood, R. (2015). Exploring the Incidence of Strategic Improvisation: Evidence from Malaysian Government Link Corporations. *Asian Social Science*, 11, 105–112.
12. Leybourne, S. (2006). Improvisation within the Project Management of Change: Some Observations from UK Financial Services. *Journal of Change Management*, 6, 365-381.
13. Michielsens, E., Bingham, C., & Clarke, L., Managing diversity through flexible work arrangements: management perspectives. Employee Relations, 36(1), 49–69.
14. Kyriakopolous, K. (2011). Improvisation in product innovation: the contingent role of market information sources and memory types. Organizational Studies, 32(8), 1051-1078.
15. Rogers, P.R., Miller, A., and Judge, W.Q. (1999). Using information-processing theory to understand planning/performance relationships in the context of strategy. Strategic Management Journal, 20(6), 567-577.
16. Brews, P.J. and Hunt, M.R. (1999). Learning to plan and planning to learn: Resolving the planning school/learning school debate. Strategic Management Journal, 20(10), 889-913.
17. Slotegraaf, R.J. and Dickson, P.R. (2004). The paradox of a marketing planning capability. Journal of the Academy of Marketing Science, 32(4), 71-385.
18. Porter, M. E. (1980). Competitive Strategy: Techniques for Analyzing Industries and Competitors. New York, NY: The Free Press, 1980.
19. Miller, D. (1998). Relating Porter business strategies to environment and structure: Analysis and performance implications. The Academy of Management Journal, 31(2), 280-308.

20. Liao, Y.S. (2005). Business strategy and performance: The role of human resource management control. Personal Review, 34(3), 294-305.
21. Burns, T. and Stalker, G.M. (1961). The management of innovation. Oxford: Oxford University Press.
22. Kamoche, K., Cunha, M., & Cunha, J. (2002). Organizational Improvisation. London: Routledge.
23. Akgün, A.E., Lynn, G.S., Byrne, J.C. (2006). Antecedents and consequences of unlearning in new product development teams. *Journal of Product Innovation Management*, 23, 73-88.
24. Hmieleski, K.M. and Corbett, A.C. (2008). The contrasting interaction effects of improvisational behaviour with entrepreneurial self-efficacy on new venture performance and entrepreneur work satisfaction. Journal of Business Venturing, 23(4), 482-496.
25. Hair, J. F., Sarstedt, M., Hopkins, L., & Kuppelwieser, V. G. (2014). Partial least squares structural equation modeling (PLS-SEM): An emerging tool in business research. *European Business Review,* 26(2), 106-121.
26. Chin, W. W. (2010). How to write up and report PLS analyses. In V. E. Vinzi, W. W. Chin, J. Henseler& H. Wang (Eds.), *Handbook of Partial Least Squares: Concepts, Methods and Applications* 2(28), 655-690. New York: Springer Heidelberg Dordrecht.
27. Hair, J. F., Hult, G. T. M., Ringle, C. M., &Sarstedt, M. (2014). *A primer on partial least squares structural equation modelling (PLS-SEM)*: SAGE Publications, Inc.
28. Luk, C. L., Yau, O. H. M., Sin, L. Y. M., Tse, A. C. B., Chow, R. P. M., & Lee, J. S. Y. (2008). The effects of social capital and organizational innovativeness in different institutional contexts. *Journal of International Business Studies,* 39(4), 589-612.
29. Chow, W. S., & Chan, L. S. (2008). Social network, social trust and shared goals in organizational knowledge sharing. *Information & Management,* 45(7), 458–465.
30. Fornell, C., & Larcker, D. F. (1981). Evaluating structural equation models with unobservable variables and measurement error. *Journal of Marketing Research (JMR),* 18(1), 39-50.

Multi Criteria Decisions Making approach to choose 'Integrators' in Malaysian local broiler industry

Hendrik Lamsali and Ahmad Shabudin Ariffin

School of Technology Management and Logistics,Universiti Utara Malaysia, Kedah, Malaysia

Abstract. The Malaysian broiler industry is an integral component of the agriculture sector that generates sustainable food supplies to almost 30 million populations in the country. The industry comprises of conventional and commercial farms for which the latter is more sustainable with contract farming schemes and involvement of major integrators and growers. The survival of local growers as one of the important players within broiler's supply chain hierarchy is largely depending on the integrators. Hence, this study aims to identify important factors that local growers consider when selecting their integrators. Specifically, the objectives are to prioritize integrators' selection factors and to determine the critical ranking of each factor that will be beneficial to the local growers. A MCDM approach in the form of Analytical Hierarchy Process (AHP) is employed to evaluate and rank the importance of the said factors based on inputs from selected broilers' representatives. Five main criteria are considered in the AHP analysis that include relationships, reliability, logistics, input and price. The result indicates that reliability had the highest priority, followed by pricing factor, input criteria, relationships with the integrator, and finally the logistics facility. For overall sub-criteria, supplied quantity is ranked number one, followed by price of raw materials, availability of day-old chick, quality conformance, technology sharing, and in-house logistics facility. At the end of the study, future research avenues are suggested.

1 Introduction

The Malaysian broiler industry is an important part of the agriculture sector providing employment and producing useful animal protein food for the population, estimated at 28 million people and also to about 4 million people in Singapore. According to Ali (2003), Malaysia has one of the highest per capita consumption of chicken in the world. Broiler industry in Malaysia comprises of commercial farms and conventional farms; commercial farms that run business on contract farming basis with integrator and conventional farms that belong to independent entrepreneurs. According to Ariffin, Lamsali and Mohtar (2012), the contracting scheme is therefore more likely to sustain. In 2009 there were 3,300 farms in operation carrying a standing population of nearly 186 million broiler chickens. Of these farms, 22.9% are large farms with more than 50,000 broilers per cycle. Ariffin, Lamsali and Mohtar (2013) also highlighted that the states of Johor, Sarawak and Perak alone were producing 52% of total national production. For local broiler industry, main players normally have a vertical integrated supply chain as well as operating as an integrated producer. Two parties in a typical contract farming arrangement include the grower and the company (Integrator). Integrators recruit growers to rear broiler chickens for meat based on a predetermined contractual guideline. This contract farming scheme is also helping the growers to mitigate risks related to fluctuations of input prices and provide a secure market demand for their product. Most integrators in Malaysia participated in contract farming with growers for broiler production. Hence, the integrators are always actively involved in almost every stage of production. While the important role of integrators is well documented, empirical evidence suggesting which factor to consider when selecting integrators remain limited and inconclusive. The need to identify and to prioritize integrators' selection factors is timely to both growers and integrators. It is a high time for relevant parties such as the integrators to understand the 'survival' need of the growers and to seek further improvement. Hence, the objective of this study is to determine factors that are critical when selecting potential integrators. In particular, the study aims to prioritize and rank the criteria (selection factors) using the Analytical Hierarchy Process (AHP) method. The remaining part of this paper is organized as follows: *Section 2* presents overview of the current broiler industry followed by *Section 3* on the AHP method and *Section 4* on the determination of the main criteria and sub-criteria. *Section 5* discloses the computational works in which the results and sensitivity analysis are discussed. Finally, *Section 6* concludes the paper with discussion and recommendation of the study.

2. The Broiler Industry

Broiler contracting involves the use of improved and standardized technology and production practices. This involves supply of inputs, close contact and training of the contract grower. Main players normally have a vertically integrated supply chain, operating as integrated producer, owning the majority of all breeding, feed, slaughtering and processing facilities as well as operate with a wide variety of distribution channels, ranging from super and hyper markets to distributors, restaurants, wet markets and groceries. Vertical production chains consist of a single company controlling all aspects of each stage of production. Hatcheries, farms, feed companies processing plants, harvesting team, distribution, and markets can all be integrated into a single corresponding supply system. Many producers are shifting their production further into these types of vertical systems. In Malaysia, there are some concerns of a few large integrated systems controlling the broiler sector.

The term "contract farming" generally refers to situations in which a farmer raises or grows an agricultural product for a vertically integrated corporation. There are two parties in a typical contract farming arrangement: the grower and the company (Integrator). Broiler contracts consist of outsourcing the growing stage. Integrators recruit large farms (growers) to rear broiler chickens for meat according to contractual guidelines. Farming contracts can also help growers mitigate risks posed by fluctuations of input prices and provide a secure market outlet for their product. The latter is especially important because of the limited facilities that process chickens raised by independent farmers. While current trends are moving producers toward vertical integration, there remain many farms currently under contract or with unused infrastructure from past contracts. Most integrators in Malaysia participate in contract farming with growers for broiler production. Coordinating mechanisms along a vertical supply chain include contracts and integrated ownership and operation. Vertical agreements may either foster competition by generating efficiency gains, or they may inhibit competition through vertical market foreclosure or by facilitating collusive activities at any level of the supply chain (Vaidya, Omkarprasad and Kumar, 2006).

3 The AHP Method

The Analytical Hierarchy Process (AHP) is a multi-criteria decision making method developed by Thomas L. Saatyin 1970s. One can refer to many of his previous studies on hierarchies, prioritization of decision making factors and the AHP method (Saaty, 1979; Saaty, 1990; Saaty, 1994; Saaty, 2000; Saaty, 2008). The method has been used extensively in many different sectors such as government, manufacturing, services, engineering and management (Opasanon, Santhaporn and Lertsanti, 2013). According to Vaidya et al., (2006), AHP has been widely employed to decision making in areas such as resource allocation planning. It was also pointed out by Sipahi and Timor (2010) that manufacturing sector had been the biggest user of the AHP method. The applications of AHP method in agribusiness was illustrated by Sigueira, da Silva and Aguiar (2008) in which the method had been used to rank the commodities in terms of the feasibility prospects with the intention of introducing milk futures contracts in Brazil. Study by Garcia, Almeida, Caldara, Naas, Pereira and Ferreira (2012) investigated the usage of AHP for selecting the most suitable bedding material for broiler production in Brazil. In Indonesia, Febransyah and Simangunsong (2015) had examined supply chain competitiveness in local food industry using a combination of the AHP and ANP methods. In the meantime, Yakovleva, Sarkis and Sloan (2012) had used AHP method to determine importance ratings and overall index of sustainability of food supply chains. Hitherto, there had been very limited applications of the AHP-related methods in livestock or poultry industry. This research utilized both primary and secondary data collection methods to get insight into the broiler industry. Primary data were gathered from interviews with four senior officers from local growers with positions ranging from managing director to chief business officer. Special briefing to all selected respondents had been conducted prior to the fulfillment of the questionnaire. The pairwise comparisons were developed based on key information in the secondary data and input from an experienced chief business officer of a local grower. Table 1 depicts the measurement scale that is used in this study and is adopted from Saaty (2000).

Table 1: Measurement scales of the level of importance

Importance Level	Denotation	Definition
1	Equally preferred	Both factors in consideration are of equal importance
3	Moderately more preferred	Experience and judgement shows a slightly more preference of one factor than the other
5	Strongly more preferred	Experience and judgement strongly favor one factor over another
7	Very strongly more preferred	An activity is favored very strongly over another; its dominance demonstrated in practice

9	Extremely more preferred	The evidence favoring one activity over another is of the highest possible order of affirmation
2,4,6,8	Intermediate values	When compromise is needed. Judgments can reveal an evenly matched preference between the levels of importance

Source: Saaty (2000)

The AHP method is based on three key steps in which are (1) decomposition, (2) comparative judgment, and (3) synthesis of priorities (Korpela and Tuominen, 1996). The first step involves breaking down problem and creating hierarchical structure of several elements. The hierarchy comprises of goal, criteria, sub-criteria and alternatives. The second step is to determine the relative importance of each element via pairwise comparison. Then, the third step is to assess the composite weight of each decision alternative (Opasanon, Santhaporn and Lertsanti, 2013). Figure 1 shows the AHP procedural steps as highlighted by Saaty (2000):

The summary of the steps to carry out the AHP method is as follows:

1. Develop the hierarchy of the problem comprising of the decision goal, the alternatives, and the criteria for evaluating the alternatives.

Fig.1. The analytic hierarchy process algorithm

2. Establish priorities among the elements of the hierarchy by using the pairwise comparisons analysis. Hence, pairwise comparison matrix should be developed for each decision alternative for each criterion.
3. Synthesize these judgments to generate set of overall priorities for the hierarchy. This can be done by computing the normalized matrix, followed by developing the preference vector, determining overall score for each decision alternative, and finally rank the decision alternatives.
4. Check the consistency of the judgments. This can be done by determining the degree of consistency for the pairwise comparisons in the decision criteria matrix using the following formula:

$$\frac{CI}{RI} < 0.1$$

Where CI = Consistency Index and RI = Random Index

Attributes	1	2	3	4	5	6	7	8	9	10
RI	0	0	0.52	0.39	1.11	1.25	1.35	1.40	1.45	1.49

5. Make a final decision. In overall steps or stages to be followed for determining priorities and the best alternative are shown in the following Figure 2.

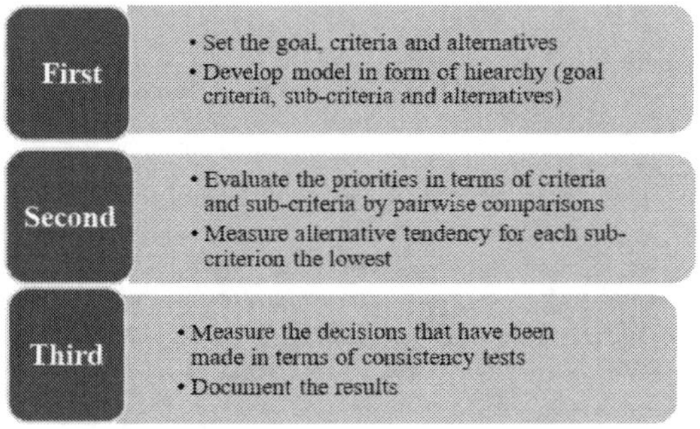

Fig. 2: Steps used in this study for prioritising alternatives

4. Determination of main and sub-criteria

Two approaches had been employed to determine main and sub-criteria that growers consider when selecting local integrators. First, secondary data gathering from relevant articles and journals were carried out in which relevant factors for selection of integrators had been identified. Then, an interview with a chief business officer from a local grower establishment had been conducted to further verify the aforementioned factors and to determine important criteria and the sub-criteria. The following Figure 3 illustrates the main criteria and the sub-criteria. Table 2 defines the operational definition for all criteria.

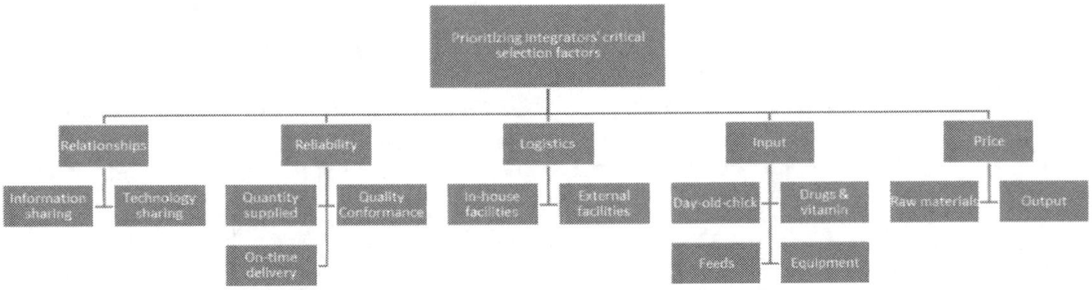

Fig. 3: Hierarchy of main and sub-criteria

Table 2: Definitions of the criteria and the sub-criteria

No	Criteria/Sub-criteria	Definition
1	Relationships	The extent of which integrator is willing to foster closer relationships with the grower in terms of sharing of information and technology
2	Reliability	Measured by how reliable is the integrator in terms of quality conformance, accuracy of quantity order fulfillment and on-time delivery
3	Logistics	Refer to whether Integrator has available in-house logistics facilities or external 3rd party logistics (3PL)
4	Input	Relevant input factors of which are offered in the form of chicks, drugs and vitamin, type of feeds, and equipment.
5	Price	Price of the raw materials (input from integrator) and output (buyback price)
6	Information sharing	Willingness of the integrator to share relevant information with the grower
7	Technology sharing	Willingness of the integrator to share the technology and assist the grower how to use them
8	Quantity supplied	Ability of the integrator to supply to grower's demand in terms of quantity
9	Quality conformance	Ability of the integrator to supply quality inputs based on predetermined standards
10	On-time delivery	Ability of the integrator to deliver grower's orders on-time
11	In-house facilities	Capability of the integrator to provide in-house logistics support and facilities to the grower
12	External facilities	Integrator favors the usage of a 3rd party logistics provider to deliver grower's orders
13	Day-old chick	Ability of the integrator to supply 'a day-old chick' to the grower
14	Drugs & vitamins	Types of drugs and vitamins that the integrator use to breed chicks
15	Feeds	Integrator's types of feeds given to the chicks
16	Equipment	Types of equipment and technology that integrator used to breed chicks
17	Raw materials price	The price of chicks and other relevant raw materials the grower has to pay
18	Output price	The buyback price the integrator is willing to pay to the grower

Table 3: Weights and priorities of each criteria

	Weight of each main criteria with respect to the Goal					
Respondent (P) *Criteria*	P1	P2	P3	P4	average	**Rank**
Relationships	0.468	0.044	0.045	0.061	0.098	**4**
Reliability	0.222	0.458	0.441	0.358	0.406	**1**
Input	0.147	0.127	0.186	0.140	0.168	**3**
Price	0.075	0.291	0.246	0.351	0.232	**2**
Logistics	0.089	0.079	0.083	0.091	0.096	**5**

5 The Computational Works

The analysis had been conducted using decision making software, the Expert Choice. For the pairwise comparisons, purposive sampling was employed. Input from four (4) important respondents were gathered and analyzed. The selected respondents were key representatives from four different local growers. Geometric means were then calculated to determine group judgment. At the end of the analysis, consistency test was carried out. The result in Table 3 indicate that reliability had been given the highest priority followed by pricing factor, input criteria, relationships with the integrator, and finally the logistics facility. Both reliability and pricing factors were dominantly important, accountable for 63.8% from overall weight with respect to the goal. The least important factor was the logistics. For the overall sub-criteria, Table 4 show that reliability in terms of supplied quantity had been ranked number one, followed by price of raw materials, availability of day-old chick, quality conformance, technology sharing, and in-house logistics facility. The bottom half of the ranking saw on-time delivery made it as the seventh important sub-criteria, followed by type of feeds, buyback price, information sharing, drugs and vitamins, the equipment used, and finally the 3rd party logistics provider. The results show that reliability in terms of quantity supplied, the price of raw materials, and availability of day-old chick are the top three most important factors that growers consider when selecting integrators. Quality conformance, technology sharing and in-house logistics facility made up the next three high prioritized factors. At the other end, external 3rd party logistics provider, type of equipment used, and type of drugs and vitamins had been ranked as the three least important factors by the growers.

Overall inconsistency for decision maker P1 is 0.08, P2 is 0.07, P3 is 0.08, P4 is 0.09, while for the group judgment (combined geometric mean) the inconsistency is 0.05. In the meantime, sensitivity analysis had been carried out to measure how changes in certain criteria or decision maker's priority influence the prioritization of other criterion or the alternatives hierarchy. Using the Expert Choice software, both performance and dynamic sensitivity analysis had been performed. Figure 4 and Figure 5 below illustrated the hierarchy and the prioritization order. Figure4 illustrated the weights and the prioritization order of each sub-criterion with respect to the main criterion. In Figure 5, it is highlighted that technology sharing, quantity supplied, availability of day-old chick, in-house logistics facility, and raw materials prices were given the highest weights for each main criteria. Nonetheless, the prioritization order may change upon changes in decision makers' preferences.

If closer relationships with integrator is given the highest priority (let assumes an increase of 21.3% for the weight of the relationships criteria from 9.8% to 31.1%), then technology sharing becomes a number two alternative closely behind quantity supplied but way ahead of other factors. Technology sharing will become the most important alternative if the weight of the relationships factor increases to more than 32%. Had a decision maker given more priority to the input factor, the prioritization order will change accordingly. For instance, an increase of weight for the input factor from 16.8% to 35.9% will push the availability of day-old chick into the summit of the prioritization order. Performance sensitivity analysis had indicated that when the price factor increases from 23.2% to 40%, the price of raw materials becomes the most important factor in the prioritization ranking, followed by quantity supplied and output prices. However, it is also worth noting that only with substantial changes in one criteria or decision maker's priority can affect the prioritization order.

Table 4: Synthesized results of sub-criteria

	Synthesized results with respect to the Goal					
	P1	P2	P3	P4	Average*	**Rank**
Relationships						
• Information sharing	0.71	0.006	0.007	0.008	0.033	**10**
• Technology sharing	0.10	0.029	0.028	0.041	0.065	**5**
Reliability						
• Quantity supplied	0.296	0.305	0.277	0.239	0.271	**1**
• On-time delivery	0.080	0.067	0.053	0.046	0.058	**7**
• Quality conformance	0.055	0.116	0.121	0.104	0.092	**4**
Input						
• Availability of day-old chick	0.122	0.085	0.117	0.093	0.112	**3**
• Drugs & vitamins	0.048	0.018	0.031	0.027	0.032	**11**
• Type of feeds	0.032	0.049	0.048	0.044	0.047	**8**
• Equipment used	0.017	0.015	0.017	0.014	0.018	**12**
Price						
• Raw materials	0.169	0.194	0.155	0.234	0.154	**2**
• Output (buyback)	0.019	0.049	0.077	0.078	0.040	**9**
Logistics						
• In-house facilities	0.070	0.053	0.052	0.060	0.064	**6**
• External 3PL	0.009	0.013	0.017	0.012	0.014	**13**

**the average is calculated using geometric mean formula*

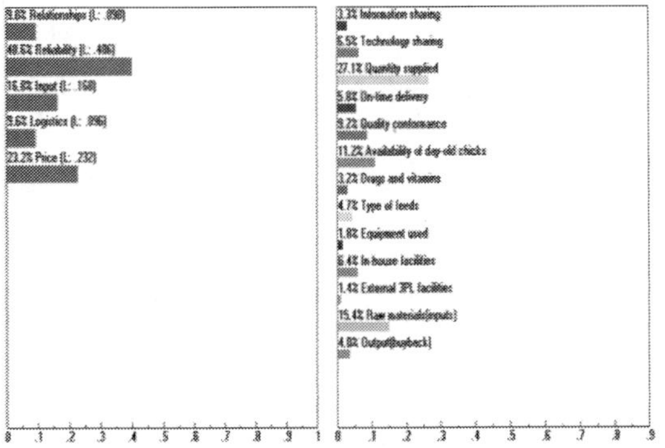

Fig. 4. Dynamic sensitivity analysis for the criterion and sub-criterion

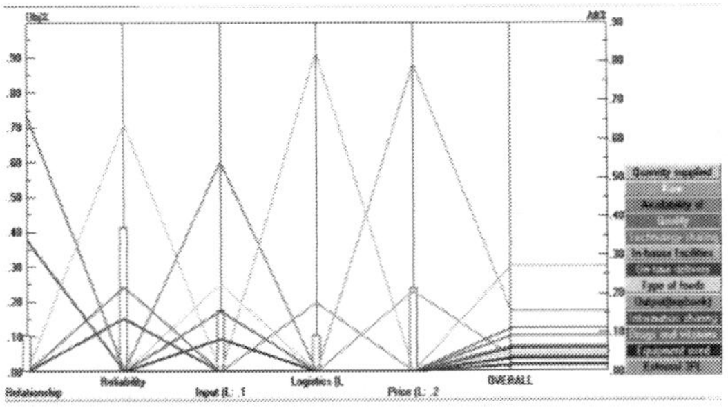

Fig. 5. Performance sensitivity analysis for the criterion and sub-criterion

5. Conclusion and The Way Forward

The study aims to facilitate local growers' selection of integrators by determining and prioritizing relevant important factors. Selecting competent and reliable integrators is crucial to the survival of growers in which one is expected to assist the latter in terms of raw materials, equipment and technology, feeding and hatchery, logistics and other support services. The findings show that reliability, followed by price had been given the highest priority when selecting potential integrators. Apparently, having reliable supplies (accuracy in terms of quantity), reasonable and competitive raw materials' prices, and consistent availability of day-old chick had been identified as the top three most important factors. The result, however, may not be generalizable due to small number of respondents. From all four selected respondents, only one stated that relationships were the most important factor when selecting potential integrator. It is therefore predicted that growers prefer a fully integrated partner that has both vertical and horizontal supply chain capabilities. Nonetheless, the extent of which a grower has actually had the luxury to 'select' reliable integrator instead of the integrator choosing its preferable grower remains debatable as the latter has more bargaining power (as well as resources). Hence, avenue for further research may include investigation over integrators' view for grower selection criteria. In terms of contribution, this study presented an attempt to establish a more holistic supply chain perspective of Malaysian local broiler industry. The study can also be generalized by getting more respondents from local broiler industry to participate in the survey. This may include key officers from both integrators and growers.

7. References

1. Ali, A. H. M., (2003). Poultry Industry in Malaysia: Issues and Challenges. Knowledge Transfer Programme (KTP) Workshop on Business Model for Broiler Industry in Malaysia. Penang.
2. Ariffin, Ahmad Shabudin Bin, Hendrik Lamsali, and ShahimiMohtar, (2013). 'Linkages between Integrator, Grower Involvement and Business Performance: An Excerpt from Preliminary Findings', International Journal of Supply Chain Management, 2.3: 47-52.
3. Ariffin, Ahmad Shabudin, Hendrik Lamsali, and ShahimiMohtar, (2012). 'Linkages between supplier, customer involvement and business performance: A green supply chain investigation in the poultry industry', 2012 International Conference on Green and Ubiquitous Technology (GUT), IEEE, Bandung, 41-44.
4. Febransyah, A., and Simangunsong, E., (2015). 'Supply chain competitiveness in food industry: An Indonesian case, Supply Chain Design and Management for Emerging Markets', Springer International Publishing, 147-175.
5. Garcia, R. G., Almeida Paz, I. C. L., Caldara, F. R., Nääs, I. A., Pereira, D. F., and Ferreira, V. M. O. S., (2012). 'Selecting the most adequate bedding material for broiler production in Brazil', RevistaBrasileira de CiênciaAvícola, 14.2: 121-127.
6. Korpela, J., and Tuominen, M., (1996). 'A decision support system for strategic issues management of logistics', International journal of production economics, 46: 605-620.
7. Opasanon, Sathaporn, and PattarakamolLertsanti, (2013). 'Impact analysis of logistics facility relocation using the analytic hierarchy process (AHP)', International Transactions in Operational Research, 20.3: 325-339.
8. Saaty, T. L., (1979). Mathematical modeling of dynamic decisions; priorities and hierarchies with time dependence, Mathematics and computers in Simulation, 21.4: 352-358.
9. Saaty, T. L., (1990). 'How to make a decision: the analytic hierarchy process', European journal of operational research, 48.1: 9-26.
10. Saaty, T. L., (1994). 'Highlights and critical points in the theory and application of the analytic hierarchy process', European journal of operational research, 74.3: 426-447.
11. Saaty, T. L., (2008). 'Decision making with the analytic hierarchy process', International journal of services sciences, 1.1: 83-98.

12. Saaty, T.L., (2000). 'Fundamentals of decision making and priority theory with the analytic hierarchy process', Rws Publications, 6.
13. Sipahi, Seyhan, and Mehpare Timor, (2010). 'The analytic hierarchy process and analytic network process: an overview of applications', Management Decision, 48.5: 775-808.
14. Siqueira, K. B., da Silva, C. A. B., and Aguiar, D. R., (2008). 'Viability of introducing milk futures contracts in Brazil: a multiple criteria decision analysis', Agribusiness, 24.4: 491-509.
15. Vaidya, Omkarprasad S., and Sushil Kumar, (2006). 'Analytic hierarchy process: An overview of applications', European Journal of operational research, 169.1: 1-29.
16. Yakovleva, N., Sarkis, J., and Sloan, T., (2012). 'Sustainable benchmarking of supply chains: the case of the food industry', International Journal of Production Research, 50.5: 1297-1317.

 https://doi.org/10.1051/matecconf/201821502005

Absorptive capacity in low-tech industry: Case Study of Indonesian Manufacturing Companies

Lutfah Ariana[1], Indri Juwita Asmara[2]

[1,2]Research Center for Science and Technology Development, Indonesian Institute of Sciences

Abstract. Innovation has widely recognized as an important factor for driving competitiveness of many firms. In order to generate innovative performances, firms need to improve their capabilities in absorbing knowledge and technology from external sources, which is so called absorptive capacity. This paper will analyze what kind of sources of innovation in manufacturing sectors especially for low tech industries. Focusing on innovation activities, this paper aims to identify what kind of determinants in influencing the difference of absorptive capacity in low tech industries. The source of data is derived from Innovation Survey 2011 held by Center for Science and Technology Development Studies. The survey conducted for 1360 firms in manufacturing sector, in which most of the distribution is mainly consisted of low technology sectors. Instead of quantitative approach, the result is also supported by in depth interview from selected firms observed in 2013. This paper addresses multiple case studies as the qualitative approach, including firms in food and beverages, and jewelry art and design. According to the results, most of low tech companies searched their external sources of knowledge from their market, and customers were the main driver for their innovation output. In respond to this situation, this paper proposes an idea of open innovation for enhancing industrial competitiveness. As policy insights, the sources of competitive advantage in an open innovation setting will encourage the firm to the internal organizational processes that allow a firm to recognize, assimilate and exploit knowledge.

Keywords: absorptive capacity, source of innovation, low tech, manufacturing, companies

1 Introduction

To support the company's sustainability, competitiveness becomes an important key in its success. A company that has a competitive advantage will be able to use existing resources efficiently and effectively. One of the driving forces of competitive advantage that is believed in today's business world is innovation. The company's ability to innovate is highly dependent on good sources of information about markets, technologies and other strategic resources that can be an advantage in competition.

Creating innovation is an important factor for increasing productivity and competitive advantage in the manufacturing industry. How innovation activities revealed in manufacturing industry can be seen through innovation survey 2011 conducted by Pappiptek LIPI. This survey provided an overview of the application of science and technology to produce goods and services benefited for the fulfillment of societal needs and to generate competitive advantage for domestic and export markets. This survey was categorized in term of technology intensity, whereas: Low Technology, Medium-Low Technology, Medium-High Technology, and High Technology. As can be seen in Figure 1, innovations to create products from both high-tech industries and low-technology industries have almost the same level ranging from 60% to 67%.

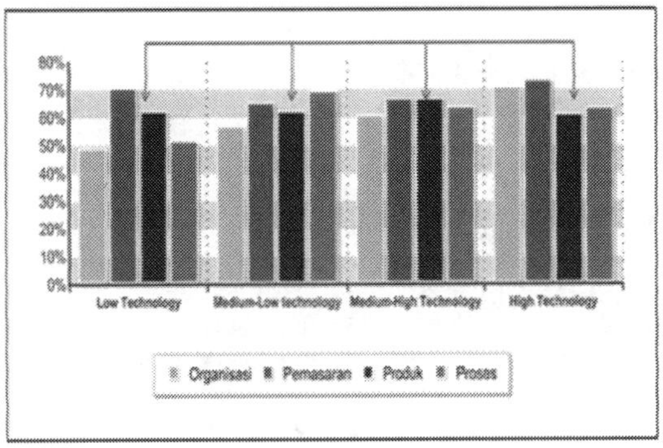

Figure 1. Product innovation in manufacturing sectors based on intensity of technology

Based on data obtained from the same survey, low technology manufacturing industries are also able to absorb technology to create new products in the market higher than firms in medium-tech and high technology intensity areas. This result is shown in the following Figure 2.

https://doi.org/10.1051/matecconf/201821502005

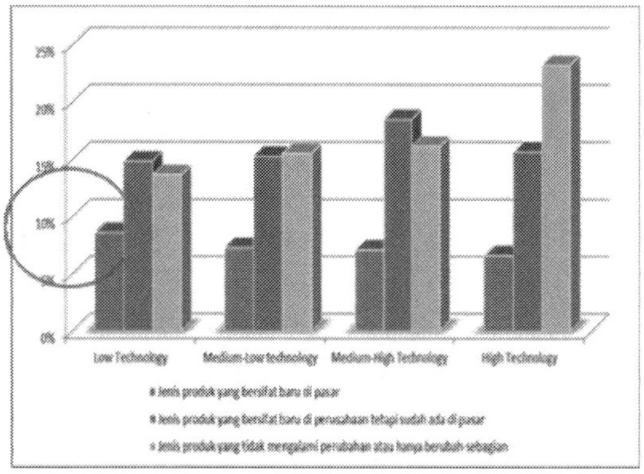

Figure 2. Technology absorption in manufacturing sectors based on technology intensity

This result was interesting, because the low-tech manufacturing industry contributed greatly to the economic development in Indonesia, especially the food and beverage industry. The food and beverage industry was the largest populations compared to other industries, as shown in the following Figure.

Source : Innovation Survey Pappiptek (2011)

Figure 3. Distribution of the number in manufacturing companies by ISIC

According to the survey result, in Indonesia, nearly 80% of manufacturing industry was dominated by food and beverage sectors. This industry is also including the non-oil and gas industry with the most contribution to GDP of 73.65% in 2011 by total employment amounted for 715,648 in 2010 (BPS). The value added increased from Rp 34,733 billion in 2001 to reach Rp 166,012 billion in 2010. Through this data it can be said that low-tech manufacturing industries such as food and beverage industry have played an important role in the positive economic growth rate. Creation of innovations with low technology intensity environments is generated through the process of information absorption into useful knowledge for the company. Therefore, absorptive capacity in low technology manufacturing industry becomes interesting to be studied.

Some previous studies widely recognized that non-technological forms of innovation have also contributed in upgrading a firm's performance (Piva and Vivarelli, 2002; OECD, 2005 and Arundel et al., 2008). In other words, innovation performance in a firm can be identified as an activity occurring in low and medium tech sectors (e.g. Kirner et al., 2009). Jensen et al. (2007) considered two different modes of innovation, "Science, Technology and Innovation" and "Doing, Using, Interacting" (DUI). The interesting mode of Doing, Using and Interacting is mostly occured in low tech sectors and it relied on processes and experience-based know how. This kind of learning may not require formal R&D programmes, but incremental problem solving and experimentation are significantly improved the production performances. However, there is still little evidence on innovation activities in low tech sectors.

In fact, the contribution of low and medium tech sectors is more than 90% to the economy of the EU (see Robertson et al., 2003), while a large number of industrialized OECD countries has a significant contribution to employement for more than 60%. In addition, the importance of low-medium tech sectors in a firm is very crucial since this kind of sectors have innovation capability to create product development (Hirsch-Kreinsen, 2008). Therefore, this paper attempts to understand the innovation activities of low-medium tech sectors and its relation to absorptive capacity to identify the key determinants for pursuing sustainability of their competitiveness in long term period.

Absorptive Capacity and Innovation Performance

Absorptive capacity is a functional concept, and in practice it is based on an interdependent foundation of capabilities, structures, routines and policies, and is largely situation-specific. For this reason it is not possible to develop a set of reliable standard indicators of absorptive capacity.

Absorptive capacity is the company's ability to absorb knowledge from various sources of information used to generate innovation within the company. The absorptive capacity within a company depends heavily on the company's ability to receive information as a source of knowledge. Some literature described the various processes that occur in absorbing knowledge. The concept of absorptive capacity was first introduced by Cohen &Levinthal (1990) in his book Absorptive capacity: a new perspective on learning and innovation. Cohen &Levinthal (1990) mentioned "Absorptive capacity, the ability of a firm to recognize the value of new, external information, assimilate it, and apply it to commercial ends is critical to its innovative capabilities." Katz, J. Corbett, A. C. (1995) and Camisón & Forés (2010) formulated four dimensions: acquisition, assimilation, transformation and exploitation. The result of these four dimensions is an innovative output, as shown in the following figure.

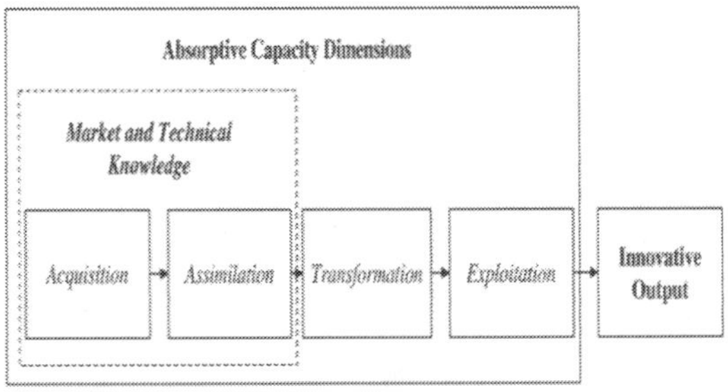

Figure 4. Dimensions of absorptive capacity

According to Lane et al., (2006, p.849) absorptive capacity contributes to increase the speed, frequency and magnitude of an innovation. The improvement of innovation capability is strongly supported by the absorptive capacity that provides an in-depth understanding of the various domains or sources of knowledge in accordance with the core competencies of the company (Van den Bosch et al., 1999). Innovation that focuses on the content of knowledge generated by the company can be in the form of patents and new products.

The absorptive capacity is began by recognizing the value of external information that the company might use, this information is then assimilated into a knowledge then used for commercial purposes. The process of recognize, assimilate and apply is a series of activities that are linear. In addition, Zahra & George (2006) suggests that there are four dimensions in absorptive capacity: acquisition, assimilation, transformation and exploitation, then they further stated that the four processes are divided into two components: Potential Absorptive Capacity (PACAP) means acceptable and acceptable external knowledge opportunities, and Realized Absorptive Capacity (RACAP) means external knowledge that has effectively been exploited by the company. In their seminal works, it described that there is an interrelated relationship between PACAP and RACAP, both of which are different but interdependent with each other. RACAP is unlikely to be executed without the process of acquiring information and assimilating the information into new knowledge of the company, and vice versa.

Some research emphasizes the role of strategy or action orientation as a key factor in the success of absorptive capacity. This is confirmed by Liao et al (2003) who conducted a survey of several companies, and found that in the process of acquiring new knowledge, the more innovative a company would be the greater the company's commitment to action against existing opportunities. Therefore, the absorptive capacity and innovation capabilities within the company are closely related and interdependent. The absorptive capacity is a dimension of innovation capability, in the process of identifying, assessing, acquiring and integrating external knowledge into competitive advantage is an asset for innovation.

Van den Bosch also considers absorptive capacity as a key contributor to organizational performance outcomes (Van den Bosch, 2003), such as:

- Competitive advantage, financial performance, in-company knowledge flow and knowledge transfer
- Innovative performance and new product development
- Learning within organizations and international co-operation
- Establishment of expectations, proactive strategies, strategic renewal, diversification and adaptation of the organization;

Therefore, it can be described that the increase in absorptive capacity is directly proportional to the improvement of innovation capability within the company. The better the absorptive capacity of a company, the more innovative the company will be.

PACAP consists of the dimensions of acquisition and assimilation, while RACAP consists of transformation and exploitation. Figure 5 shows a general picture of PACAP and RACAP conditions in low technology sectors in Indonesia. The most densely areas are indicated by red. Thus, it can be seen that most of the low technology industries in Indonesia have a higher PACAP index than the RACAP index.

Furthermore, to see the absorptive capacity can also be seen from the efficiency of absorptive capacity. The efficiency of absorptive capacity is the ratio between RACAP and PACAP indexes. The higher the resulting efficiency value, it means the RACAP index is much higher than the company's PACAP index. That is, the company is able to transform all the knowledge absorbed into a concrete form. The efficiency of absorptive capacity has a range of values between ∞ and 0, where value 1 is a state of equilibrium. The value of absorptive capacity efficiency of 1 means the PACAP index is balanced with the RACAP index. In other words, the company can change all the knowledge absorbed into a concrete form with a balanced.

Results and Discussions

The result of this study found that low technology sector in Indonesia is a typical labor-intensive industry and less intensive in applying technology. Another result showed that most of innovation type in low technology sector is a kind of radical change. The idea of innovation in the low-tech industry is largely determined by market demand, rather than science push. These ideas were derived from various sources of information or knowledge ranging from competitors, suppliers, partners, customers, various media information, expertise to owners of expert knowledge. Figure 5 shows that the red area is below the diagonal line. Thus, the efficiency of absorptive capacity in low technology industry firms is generally relatively low (below 1). That is, the company has been doing the process of assimilation and knowledge acquisition but it is difficult to manage the process of transformation and exploitation that is comparable with assimilation and acquisition.

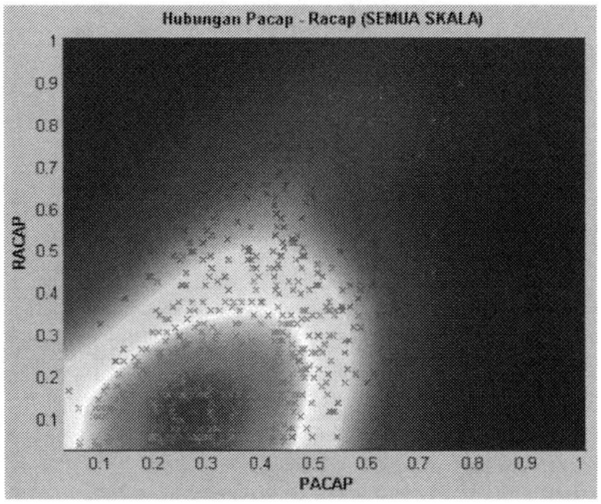

Source : Asmara et. al (2013)

Figure 5. Relationship between PACAP and RACAP in low tech sectors

Based on the regional mapping of the potential of absorptive capacity and the realization of absorptive capacity, it can be described as follows. Low technology sectors in Indonesia tend to be in potentially low absorptive capacity positions and have not achieved high factor efficiency. According to the scale of the business (the amount of labor), the pattern of absorptive capacity indicated the dominance of low-tech mid-scale industry compared to large-scale manufacturing industry.

In this case, large-scale group companies have a more specific pattern, which is closer to the factor efficiency line, meaning that large-scale industries are more efficient at converting the potential absorptive capacity into higher realization or innovative performance than middle-scale enterprise groups.For export activities, the group of exporting companies expressed a pattern of distribution of absorptive capacity that tends toward a factor efficiency line with a relatively high realization rate.In terms of capital ownership (capital status), group companies that conduct joint ventures tend to have a pattern of distribution of absorptive capacity close to the line of factor efficiency and the level of realization of higher absorptive capacity.

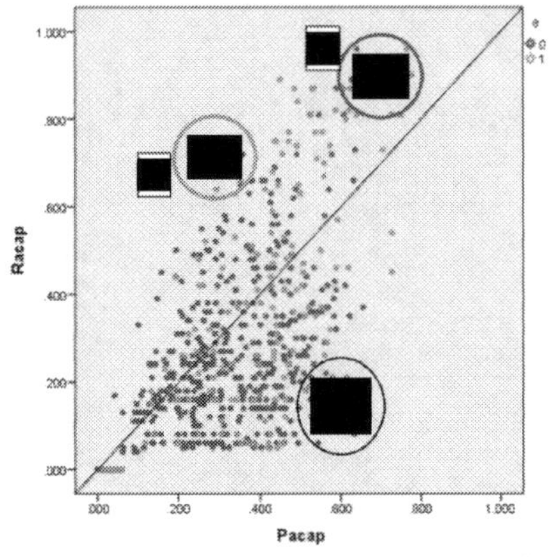

Source : Asmara et. al (2013)

Figure 6. Distribution of companies in low tech sectors by efficiency factor

This study also analyzes the relationship of potential absorptive capacity (PACAP) and its realization (RACAP). Based on Figure 6, the highest efficiency level is Area B, it could be considered as the best case in realizing absorptive capacity. Most of the low technology industry in Indonesia is dominated by industries located in Region C and Region D characterized by importing machinery, equipment or software to produce product and process innovation, conduct its own R & D activities (intramural), the percentage of labor with undergraduate > 5%, the percentage of labor involved in R & D activities > 5%, Joint Venture ownership status, percentage of export value > 50%, average sales value per year > Rp 1 billions.

In order to describe how absorptive capacity in specifically implemented in firm level, this paper investigated two case studies in low tech sectors (region A and region B), selected from the survey result.

Case study 1: A bottled drinking water company

Company A operated since 2003, with main production was mineral water packaged. As food and beverages company, this company has expanded its business to similar products such as tea drink, fruit juice, energy drink, and other canned beverages. One of the recent innovation product was mineral water in gallon package with easy-handle and made from non-poly carbonate, which has been based on eco-friendly technology.

This company has a wide range of production line starting from downstream up to upstream units, including the packaging materials produced as in house/in site. In order to support the technological capability of the company and to control the quality of final products, a set of machinery supports was imported from Germany. In 2013, Company A has developed 11 plants supported by integrated procurement, packaging and final product control sites. For its efforts, this company has been awarded an achievement in 2008 for ISO 22000: 2005 for high quality standard and production standard process.

In an effort to generate innovation, the company explored information from various sources, mainly from visiting international exhibitions held every 3 years. These visits were mostly conducted by representatives of the board of directors, as the main decision maker for strategic purposes. By engaging in this expo, the company had opportunities to obtain new information on advance technology products provided by most leading suppliers from various countries, especially manufacturing technology, packaging materials (plastic), and machineries.

In addition to this information, the company also investigated new product ideas by having market survey, benchmarking from product's competitors, examining emerging trends of product development, and tracing information about technology suppliers and new packaging materials by internet supports.

This company searched relevant information and then assimilated the significant knowledge for creating idea for product innovation. In addition, other important information such as how to reduce production cost, the changing trend of bottle-to-bottle product packaging, or information about the trend of change in the bottle net content of 330 ml is now a 295 ml net bottle size. From the various information, representatives from companies usually represented by the director of the company and other teams about 8 people discuss together to find new ideas that will be the future product development plan at the company.

The ideas of product innovation are reviewed and conducted in special research to know the product content in detail and the feasibility of developing the new product as needed. The selection of innovation ideas was discussed in special meetings at the managerial level and further explored to finalize the existing concepts.

Transformation process in the dimension of absorption capacity focuses on integrating information from external sources into the capabilities already owned by the company. In this case, the company has developed special research, for example for developing new packaging of mineral products that has been decided as the potential innovation. When the company has got the idea of innovation for lab scale, they put some efforts to find the appropriate supplier. Information about the supplier itself has been collected from the exhibition, then they will communicate and analyze some feasibilities of purchasing materials. For example, a company needs a robotic packer to manufacture its new packaging material, then the company will contact directly to the supplier for planning the input. If there is unclear and insufficient information regarding product and technology specifications, then the company invites suppliers to explain more about it.

When the new design has been generated, it will be executed by the Operational Division. For laboratory-scale execution, the company will put an investment for a new machine or a new technology. As for mass production, the company firstly developed its ideas and further reviewed the feasibility of production both in terms of cost and the prospect of sustainability of the product in the long run. In this case, the company admitted not buying a new machine, but making its own machine by having consultation with the manufacturer. If needed, a high support in operating production facilities wil be encouraged for improving the capacity of the human resources by distributing trainings and workshops.

The dimension of exploitation in this case is understood as the company's efforts in developing innovation ideas into commercialization activities that generate economic benefits. In addition to good innovations in the form of new products and new packaging, the company also developed co-branded products with other companies. Co-branding products are a product with two brands which are preferred for low-end products and affordable price for consumers. As sharing partners, this company focused on packaging innovation, and the partner has the potential for distribution networks of marketing and wide distribution of products through their outlets. Cooperation of both is quite capable to accelerate the process of commercialization of new products.

To maintain and continue the development of innovation products, the company implemented a Balance Score Card system where innovation performance was evaluated according to its Key Performance Indicator (KPI). The evaluation was done twice a year. While routine evaluation was applied every month for each factory. The achievement of this company is a form of company commitment to expand product distribution network in various regions.

As its commitment to be sustain in domestic market, the company put a high concern for being a cost leadership. For example, it can be seen from the product packaging made with the lowest gramation per cup. Since 2005, this company has produced the lightest cup capacity in Indonesia. In addition, the company also continues to seek new innovations in packaging such as gallons of water refill handled with BPA free raw material. With these breakthroughs, the company tried to meet the demand of consumers at the lowest price level. In addition to product innovation, the company also focuses on economical and environmentally friendly products without neglecting added value to end customers.

Case study 2: Company B and the jewelry products

At the beginning of its establishment, Company B is a type of home industry producing jewelry since 1958. As a family business, the company expanded her products market through several gold shops run independently. In the late 1990s to 1998 the company began building small factories to produce its own jewelry products.

Information as a source of innovation was largely derived from market survey activities, especially those related to jewelry trends based on customer preferences. To meet the diverse demands of the market, the company identified several important aspects, including: demographic factors, motivation of consumption, fashion trends in different periods, geographical factors (consumers in the village and town), and so on. To improve the company's performance, Company B has changed the management that was initially family-based into professional management. In addition, the company also conducted outsourcing human resources e.g experts in the field of art and design to provide new ideas in jewelry and feedback on organizational management. The existence of professionals in the organization of the company has provided learning organization that focused on way of thinking to run a professional organization that put forward high quality innovation. With such professional management, the company admitted that it has adapted many working systems of professional organizations and new technologies that can support the company's sustainability in the future.

How the market knowledge that will determine the product innovation produced by the company can be explained through several dimensions of absorption capacity as follows.

Acquisitions. Before deciding the jewelry design for the production focus, the company identified the consumer preference as explored from market survey. With the rapid development of technology, the company analyzed the consumer behaviors where accessability to information is widespread; not only coming from consumer based design, but also arising from complex issues that affect the motivation of consumers to buy. Therefore, to create product innovation, companies need to study the external value elements of a new idea, so that the product of the innovation can be a trend leader.

Based on the various informations that have been reviewed in this acquisition phase, it will be further preceded by the R & D unit. This unit needed to be supported by market survey for providing evidences before it is produced in large scale. The typical manufacturing condition of the jewelry company lies in the high value of the raw material, so the possibility of a defect should be avoided (to a minimum). To make a piece of jewelry is a simple thing, but if the company will do mass production process for 300 jewelry then the production process will be very different. This also applies to the marketing process, where on a small scale the company does not experience any obstacles but for large scale requires separate consideration because it involves the transfer of process from research to industry.

The R & D team consists of 6 people, with two functional groups: drawing team and team translating the image. Since this company started from a home industry company with a non-designer background, the company's consulting experts provided training from different ways of thinking, how to work better, how to understand research and ideas diverse and understanding "meanings" (meaning an idea).

The internalization process of this new understanding was given intensively by the experts because to produce a new design was a new challenge for organizational change. Moreover, a fundamental understanding of the mindset for professional management of the company was also directed by the expert, in addition to efforts to build corporate image from core company to core design.

At the beginning of this transition process, the company has to create a window of opportunity in managing product, including how to sell the product. Since the product of jewelry is unique and very specific, a new concept and innovative idea are the key in developing product innovation. For the purpose, one of innovative organizational change has been actualized through presentation media for conducting sales in various concepts. This is to provide a better understanding of sales which previously have traditional ways of thinking, especially in convincing consumers as to why their products are better than other jewelry products, both in terms of design and in terms of image. With this transition process, the company capable to build a new image as a leading jewelry company in Indonesia. Therefore, company B is committed not to imitate competitors' products and prioritize differentiation strategies for innovation.

After the new design of the R & D team built, it will be preceded to a more technical production process. In this case, the control of the production process is led by the expert to monitor whether the product with the design drawings is appropriate or not. If the production process has any trouble, the company will look for solutions to find ways to achieve the most efficient new targets. In addition, how to manufacture it if there is a design change so as not to change the intensity. This is because the manufacturing process in the production process of jewelry products is very different from the process of making craft products (craft), so that required a process called rough manufacturing. The process of change may be an adaptation of a new technology, or process change so that its design should be changed even if it is only 1%.

For the company purpose, R & D division was responsible to not only creating new concepts of design, but also have to manage how to produce the products with the most efficient methods and what technology is appropriate. To achieve the cost feasibility, the production department also makes changes or modifications to the existing machinaries to expand its work function. Instead of limited information, the company operates the machine and tries to cope how it works and handles including maintainance in case of damage. In order to find a solution to the problem of appropriate technology requirements for a new design production process, the R & D team conducted experiments with some trials or changed some sections to find a solution. Some of the findings from solution-solving problems related to production machinery become company secret.

Discussions

The identification of absorptive capacity in low tech firms shows that the source of information is largely dependent on market demands and these preferences are influenced by the external or environmental conditions of the consumer. To support the company's long-term competitiveness, sustainable capabilities are required in absorbing diverse information. If the company relies on only one source of information, it will be difficult to compete with other companies. In addition, most of technological capabilitiesdepend on technology importsfrom advanced countries also make theirproducts less competitive in the market.

It has been widely recognized that open innovation improves innovation performance. In fact, not every firm benefits equally from tapping into external knowledge in the innovation process. Open innovation contributes to competitive advantage in product innovation and now arguably this might be even more difficult to achieve given that externally access knowledge is typically also available to competitors.
Most scholars shedlight some statement by providing insights into organizational processes that help to explain into firm differences in benefiting from open innovation. This paper provides some empirical evidences that absorptive capacityin low tech sectors can indeed contribute to competitive advantage and product innovation. Some companies have created a way forward by engaging with external partners as a form of open innovation.

As a lesson learned that will become evidence for policy recommendation, the question of open innovation effectiveness is crucial. This is because knowledge and competencies related to product innovation that we are traditionally developed internally are now increasingly accessed from a broad set of external parties and so given this investment in external knowledge sourcing. It is essential to understand whether it actually contributes a competitive advantage so does open innovation lead to higher product effectiveness and higher product efficiency compared to other competitors and to answer this absorptive capacity as a theoretical lens. Both open innovation and absorptive capacity focus on how innovating firms can effectively use external knowledge.

As discussed in the previous section, absorptive capacity consists of three components the capacities to recognize, assimilate, and capacities to recognize, assimilate and exploit external knowledge. These abstract components are embedded in organizational processes, therefore, for example, assimilation capacity should be captured in terms of coordination, integration and knowledge management processes. The underlying measurement items provide concrete organizational activities and systems. In this case, it is important for a company to have a reward and incentive system for actually utilizing external knowledge. Another significant point that should be addressed is the availability of a system for searching, analyzing and filtrating external knowledge, that can generate a company likely to have a higher level of simulation capacity. These components capacity are associated with external technological resource access that is a measure of open innovation and are associated with competitive advantage and product innovation.

Conclusions

This paper attempts to analyze how company in low tech sectors in Indonesia gained their industrial competitiveness by indicating their absorptive capacity from external source of knowledge. Most of the firms are rarely conducted R&D activities, but the activities of research embedded in the production system, and marketing research. For enhancing the technological capabilities, most of the firms experienced some training from the suppliers through technology acquisition and licensing system. These activities are supporting factors for acquiring new technological changes to produce new products and services. It reflected that innovation capabilities of low tech industries in Indonesia are mainly driven by market demand. Therefore, in term of technological capabilities, they still depend on technology import from advanced countries.

In the long term, this dependency will create a lag behind and a new trap for domestic firms to be competitive in global market. Regarding the relationship between potential absorptive capacity and realized absorptive capacity, low tech industries are characterized by process, organizational and marketing innovations, by weak internal innovation capabilities (even to the extent that most lack of R&D facilities) and by strong dependencies on the external provision of inputs, i.e. suppliers.

This paper has important implications for policy makers especially in generating innovating process of non R&D performers which are mainly dominant in low tech sectors. Innovation in product needs R&D activities and university supports, while innovation in process requires a different input of innovation activities. However, for low tech sectors these kinds of resources can be achieved with the idea of open innovation to reinforce firm's internal resources and external knowledge. Therefore, policy makers should pay attention to the fact that innovative performance can be achieved without R& activities, but open innovation will disclose a wide opportunities to access new ideas with cooperation agreements.

Acknowledgements

This paper is partly a result of research activities conducted in 2013, funded by Research Center for Science and Technology Devlopment, Indonesian Institute of Sciences (PAPPIPTEK-LIPI). The authors would like to thank the team in this research for giving supports and comments.

References

[1] Asmara, I.J., Berliana, N.G., Ariana, L., Rahmaida, R., Kusnandar. (2013) 'Studi Analisis Kapasitas Absorpsi pada Industri manufaktur teknologi rendah'. Serial report series of Research Center for Science and Technology Development, Indonesian Institute of Sciences, Jakarta

[2] Camisón C., Forés B. (2010) 'Knowledge absorptive capacity: New insights for its conceptualization and measurement'. Journal of Business Research 63, 707–715.

[3] Cohen, W., Levinthal, D. (1990) 'Absorptive capacity: a new perspective on learning and innovation'. Administrative Science Quarterly, 35, 128-152

[4] Hirsch-Kreinsen, H. (2008) 'Low -technology: a forgotten sector in innovation policy.' Journal of Technology Management & Innovation, 3, 11-20

[5] (2011) 'Innovation Survey' Serial Research Report. Research Center for Science and Technology Development, Indonesian Institute of Sciences (LIPI), Jakarta.

[6] Jensen, M.B., Johnson, B., Lorenz, E., Lundvall, B.A. (2007) 'Forms of knowledge and modes of innovation'. Research Policy, 36 (5), 680-693

[7] Katila, R., Ahuja, G. (2002) 'Something old, something new: a longitudinal study of search behavior and new product introduction'. Academy of Management Journal, 45 (6), 1183-1194

[8] Katz, J. Corbett, A. C. (1995) 'Advances in Entrepreneurship, Firm Emergence and Growth.' Emerald Group.

[9] Kirner, E., Kinkel, S., Jaeger, A. (2009) 'Innovation paths and the innovation performance of low-technology-firms—an empirical analysis of German industry.' Research Policy, 38, 447-458

[10] Liao, J. W., Welsch, H., & Stoica, M. (2003) 'Organisational absorptive capacity and responsiveness: an empirical investigation of growth-oriented SMEs.' Entrepreneurship Theory and Practice, 28(1), 63-85

[11] Lane, P., Koka, P., Pathak, S. (2006) 'The reification of absorptive capacity: a critical review and rejuvenation of the construct.' Academy of Management Review, 31 (4), 833-863

[12] Piva, C., Vivarelli, M., (2005) 'Innovation and employment: evidence from Italian microdata.' J. Econ. 86, 65–83.

[13] Robertson, P., Pol, E., Carroll, P., (2003) 'Receptive capacity of established industries as a limiting factor in the economy's rate of innovation'. In: Paper presented at the PILOT Workshop on Concepts, Theory, Taxonomies and Data. Department of Industrial Economics and Management, Royal Institute of Technology in Stockholm, 26–27 September 2003

[14] Zahra, S.A. George, G. (2002) 'Absorptive capacity: a review, reconceptualization, and extension.' Academy of Management Review, 27, 185-203

 https://doi.org/10.1051/matecconf/201821502006

Influence of Product Quality, Price and Supporting Infrasturcture to Perceived Value and Interest in Buying of Electric Motorcycle

Edwin Sholeh Rahmanullah,[1], Siti Nurjanah [2]

[1]Kalbis Institite, Magister Management, Faculty of Business
[2]Kalbis Institite, Magister Management, Faculty of Business

Abstract. Energy consumption in Indonesia always increase every year. Transportation sector is the highest energy increase among other sector, totally transportation sector consump 35% energy. Motorcycle, especially automatic type is dominate population of vehicle. This research want to know the influence of several factor to the interest of buying electric motorcycle. From research result we can conclude that product quality, price and supporting infrastructure have positive influence to both of perceived value and interest in buying of electric motorcycle. Direct relation between those three factors to interest in buying electric motorcycle is higher than indirect relation when through perceived value. For example comparing direct effect of product quality is 0,147 to indirect effect is 0,04674. Other data from this research, 91% of the respondents can accept if the speed of an electric motorcycle under 100 km / hour. In general most respondents or 97.5% of respondents require mileage > 50 km for one time battery charging. Total 85% of respondents can accept charging time over 1 hour. Total 95% of respondents can accept a price range between 10 - 30 million rupiah for each unit of electric motorcycle. For infrastructure, respondents who want a feature of charging directly (charging) and replacement batteries (swap) on electric motorcycle, desired by more than 86% of respondents.
Keywords : electric vehicle; motorcycle; buying interest; perceived value; product quality; price; supporting infratructure.

1 Introduction

Energy consumption in Indonesia always increase every year. Transportation sector is the highest energy increase among other sector, with 6,46% average. Totally transportation sector consump 35% energy, second highest after industrial sector. This is because of vehicle population increase 13,7% every year.

The bad news is to fulfill this needs Indonesia still depend on gasoline and other non renewable energy. It is very risky for Indonesia's future energy sutainability. Refer to BPS data at 2014, total vehicle population in Indonesia is 104.118.969 vehicles. And the bigest population is Jakarta, with 14.734.601 vehicles. Form this population 75% are motorcycle. Matic type motorcycle is dominate almost 72,9% market share of motorcycle sales in the year of 2016.

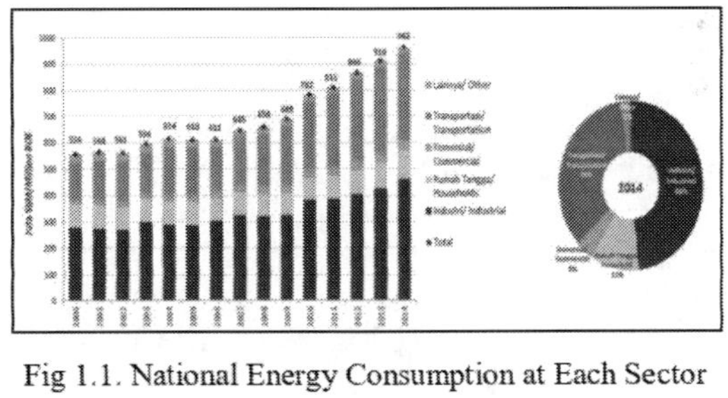

Fig 1.1. National Energy Consumption at Each Sector (Resource : KESDM (2015) Strategic Planning,Ministry of Energy and Mineral Resource 2015-2019, Jakarta.[1])

There is alternative vehicle to overcome from gasoline dependency, we can use electric vehicle. In motorcycle sector there is also electric motorcyle or electric scooter. China is dominate electric motorcycle sales around the world.

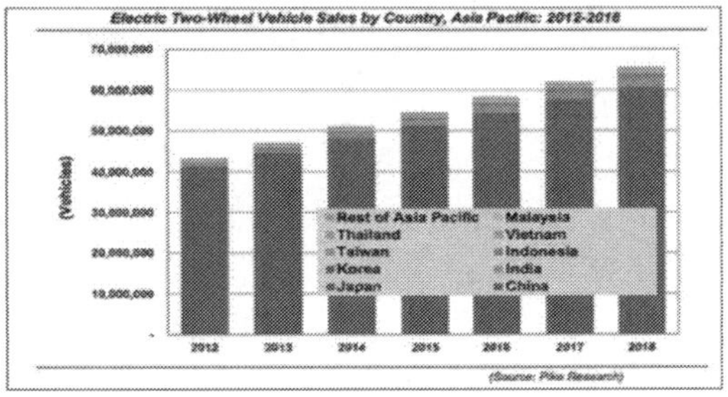

Fig 1.2. Electric 2 wheel Vehicle Sales by Country in Asia (Resource : Pike Research [2])

In Indonesia electric motorcycle sales is at small amount. Refer to National Energy Council target, there is 2.200 units of electric vehicle and 8.000.000 units of electric motorcycle in Indonesia at 2025.

To fulfill this target is not only to develop product, industry and other infrastructure, but need to have a strategy to sale electric motorcycle at Indonesian market. We need to understand what market need and what is market perception to electric motorcycle.

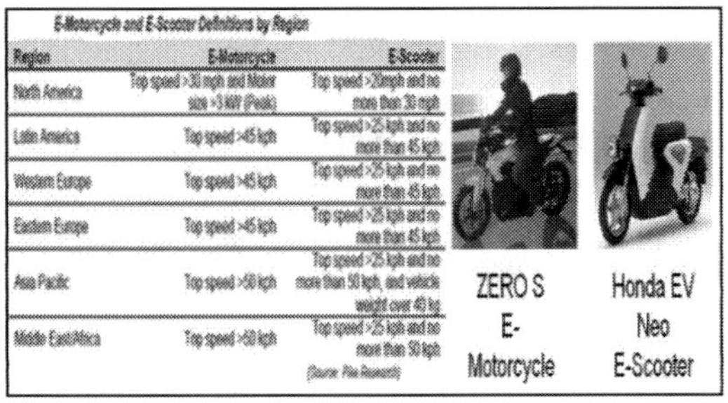

Fig 1.3. Two type of 2 wheel electric vehicle: E-Motorcycle dan E-Scooter

This research want to know the influence of several factor to the interest of buying electric motorcycle. To build interest of buying there is perceived value factor in buyer perception. In the term of electric motorcycle there is 3 dominant factor, refer to previous research at other country, product quality, pice and supporting infrastructure.

1 Research methodology

1.1 Interest in Buying

According to Kinnear and Taylor [3], buying interest is the stage of respondent's tendency to act before the buying decision is actually implemented.

According to Ferdinand [4], buying interest can be identified through the following indicators:

1. Transactional interest, namely the tendency of someone to buy the product.
2. Referential interest, the tendency of a person to reference the product to others.
3. Preferential interest, this interest is describes the behavior of someone who has a primary preference for the product. This preference can only be changed if something happens with its preference product.
4. Explorative interest, this interest describes the behavior of a person who is always looking for information about the product he is interested in and seeking information to support the positive traits of the product.

1.2 Perceived Value

According to Kotler [5] "customer perceived value is the difference between the perspective of customer's evaluation of all benefits and all the costs of an offering and the perceived alternatives".

Sanchez, et al [6], explains that there is a benefit component and sacrifice component in assessing perceived value. Benefit components consist of:

1. Economic benefit: relates to what customers get from the product.
2. Emotional benefit: shows the affective benefits that customers get from the product.
3. Social benefits: show positive recognition of the brand that will recommend to relatives / friends.
4. Relationship benefits: the state where the expectations of customers in accordance with the needs of customers.

For sacrifice component consists of:

1. Price sacrifice: related to monetary costs as perceived by customers.
2. Time sacrifice: relates to the customer in spending time looking for, buying or consuming products / services.
3. Effort sacrifice: related to the energy customers spend to find and buy products / services.
4. Risk: the probability of negative consequences of purchasing products / services.
5. Inconvenience: related to the customer having a bad experience of purchasing products / services.

1.3 Product Quality

In electric motorcycle there is 3 important items related to product quality : vehicle speed, driving range and charging time. As we know there is a worries about vehicle speed of electric motorcycle comparing to gasoline motorcyle, so we need to know this factor influencies for cutomer.

As limitation of battery capacity as energy storage at electric motorcycle, it will take effect to vehicle driving range. Comparing to gasoline motorcycle, electric motorcycle have less driving range. As a consequence of the current technological limitations, only average electric vehicles have a distance of about 160 km for a one-time filling. For electric motorcycle even far below that number. The ability of electric vehicle mileage at this time has not been able to meet the desires of customers. For example, nearly 60% of respondents in a survey that requires a minimum mileage of 160 km. (Deloitte, [7])

For gasoline motorcycle we only need several minute to refueling gasoline. But, for electric vehicle we need several hours to recharge the battery. Therefore, refueling time becomes a more important factor than vehicle mileage. (Segal, [8]). So, we need to know cuctomer perception on these three factors.

1.4 Price

Electric vehicle are still more expensive than gasoline vehicle. Price is important factor influencing customer on interest in buying of electric motorcycle.

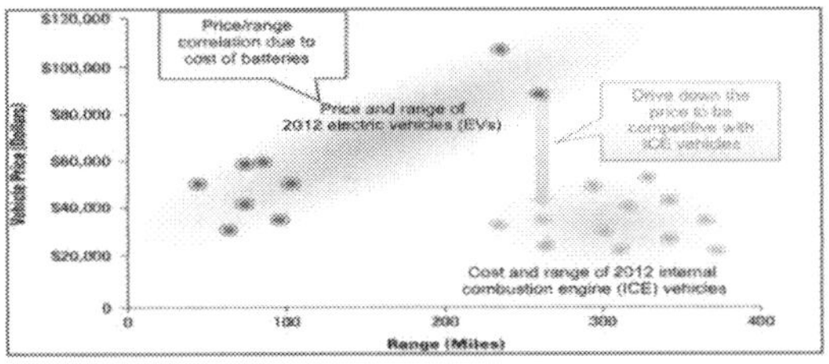

Fig2.1. Price Comparation Electric Vehicle and Internal Combution Engine (ICE)(Resource: Ping Liu, et al (2015) Long-range, Low-cost Electric Vehicles Enabled by Robust Energy Storage, MRS Energy & Sustainability [9])

According to Greene [10] and Mau et al. [11] purchase price is the most important factor in determining purchasing decisions, as all other factors depend on price.

1.5Supporting Infrastructure

Based on the American Public Works Association, infrastructure is defined as the physical facilities developed or required by public agencies for government functions in water supply, electric power, waste disposal, transportation and similar services to Facilitate economic and social objectives.

For electric motorcycle the supporting infratructure is charging infrastructure. There is also another alternative of infrastructure, by swapping the battery. This battery swap station is alternative infrastructure, this method is quicker than charging station.

Fig 2.2. Illustration of Charging Station (left) dan Battery Swap Station (right)

1.6Correlation Between Each Variable Base on Previous Research

Rachmad Dodi Triawan [12] from the Department of Management, Faculty of Economics, State University of Surabaya in a journal entitled: "The Influence of Brand Image and Perception Value Against Motorcycle Buying Purpose Brand Honda Type PCX 150 (Study on Cafe Visitor at Tunjungan Plaza Surabaya), which Published in Journal of Management Sciences Volume 05 Number 01 - Department of Management Faculty of Economics, State University of Surabaya, said that there is a positive relationship between perceived value (purchase perceived value) and purchase intention (buying interest). Where the higher the perception of the value of motorcycle products will increase purchasing intentions against the motorcycle.

Ning Wang and Yafei Liu [13] from the School of Automotive Studies, Tongji University, Shanghai, in his journal entitled "Key factors influencing customers' willingness to purchase electric vehicles in China", citing the results of his research that there is a positive relationship between the readiness of supporting infrastructure Electric vehicle (electric vehicle) with customer buying interest in China.

In the Thesis entitled "Analysis of Factors Influencing Interest in Buying New Yamaha Motorcycles in Semarang City", Agus Sukasman Hidayat [14], from Master Program Management of Postgraduate Program of Diponegoro University of Semarang, said that there is a positive influence on competitive prices with an interest in purchasing a motorcycle.In addition, this study also mentions that there is a positive influence between the quality of motorcycle products with buying interest.

Surya Danu Kusmono [15] from Master Program of Postgraduate Program Management of Widya Mandala Catholic University Surabaya, on his thesis entitled "The Influence of Marketing Mix Against Perceived Value and Purchasing Decision of ACR Brand Energy Saving Lamp Products in Surabaya", stated that there is influence between product , price, promotion and place against perceived value.

William Sierzchula, Sjoerd Bakker, et.al [16] from Delft University of Technology, Faculty of Technology, Policy, and Management, The Netherlands, on his research paper, entitled "The influence of financial incentives and other socio-economic Factors on electric vehicle adoption ", states that charging infrastucture has a positive influence on customer adoption of electric vehicles (electric vehicle).

1.7Research Conceptual Model & Variables

Refer to literature study this research conceptual model refer to Fig 3.1.

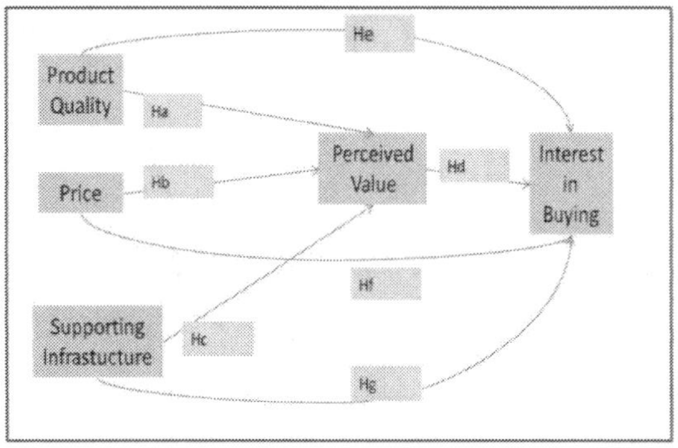

Fig 2.3 Research Conceptual Model

From this conceptual model, there is 4 independent variables : Product Quality, Price, Infrastructure and Perceived Value. Interest in Buying is dependent variable.

This research has 7 hypothesis as follows:

1. Ha: There is a positive influence between electric motor technology with perceived value
2. Hb: There is a positive influence between price and perceived value
3. Hc: There is a positive influence between supporting infrastructure and perceived value
4. Hd: There is a positive influence between perceived value and buying interest
5. He: There is a positive influence between electric motor technology with buying interest
6. Hf: There is a positive influence between price and buying interest
7. Hg: There is a positive influence between supporting infrastructure and buying interest

1.8Unit Analysis, Population & Samples

In this research is determined his unit of analysis is a motorcycle rider in Jakarta.The population of motorcycle users of automatic type in Jakarta in this study can not be known with certainty.

The population of this research is all owners and users of motorcycle type automatic in Jakarta. Because the amount is not known for certain then used sampling technique for infinite population as follows :

$$n = \frac{Z^2}{4(moe)^2}$$

Information:

- N = number of samples
- Z = confidence level
- Moe = Margin of Error

With a confidence level of 95% or Z = 1.96 and a maximal sample error rate that can still be tolerated or moe by 10% then the sample size can be determined as follows:

$$n = \frac{1{,}96^2}{4(0{,}1)^2}$$

$$n = \frac{3{,}8416}{0{,}04}$$

$$n = 96{,}04$$

Based on the above calculation results obtained a good number of samples of the population at least 96.04 people. But to facilitate the calculation and because of the elements of rounding, so that in this study targeted the sample used at least amounted to 100 respondents.

Sampling in this research will use non-probability sampling approach that is sampling technique that does not give equal opportunity or opportunity for every element or member of population to be chosen as sample. The sampling used is purposive sampling technique. In this technique, the writer approached the prospective respondents. Then the authors asked whether the prospective respondent is a motorcycle user type matic and meet the specified sample requirements, in accordance with specific objectives in this study. If true candidate respondents qualify then the author asked the person's permission to become respondents.

1.9 Pre Test & Main Test

1. Validity & Reliability Test

This research tested the validity using product moment correlation, the formula is:

$$r_{XY} = \frac{n\sum X_iY_i - (\sum X_i)(\sum Y_i)}{\sqrt{\left[n\sum X_i^2 - (\sum X_i)^2\right]\left[n\sum Y_i^2 - (\sum Y_i)^2\right]}}$$

Where :

r = Product moment correlation

x = Score of each question

N = total sample

y = total score

Furthermore, by statistical methods, the correlation value obtained must be tested first by stating whether the value is significant or not. The correlation test is done by comparing r obtained with product moment r in table, seen from n = number of respondents with α = 5% or at 95% confidence level, then r table (0,05,30) = 0,361.

Basic decision making:

• If r count> r table, then the questionnaire question is valid.

• If r arithmetic <r table, then the questionnaire question is invalid.

Reliability test is an instrument used to indicate the extent to which a measurement result is relatively consistent if the measuring device is used repeatedly. Of the many techniques to measure reliability, the authors used the Cronbach Alpha technique, the formula is as follows:

$$r_{alpha} = \left[\frac{k}{(k-1)}\right]\left[1-\frac{\sum s_b^2}{\sum s_t^2}\right]$$

Information :

r alpha= instrument reliability

K = Number of questions

Σs_b^2 = Number of grain variants

Σs_t^2 = Total Variant

2. Classic Assumption Test

There is 3 classic assumption test that used at this research : normality test, heterocedasticity test and multicollinearity test.

Normality test is performed to see whether the disturbing or residual variable generated in the regression model is normally distributed or not. A good regression model is a model that has a normally distributed residual. In this study the normality test was measured by testing the non parametric statistical test of Kalmogorov - Smirnov (K - S).

The heterocedasticity test aims to test whether in the regression model there is a variance inequality of the residual one observation to the other. If the residual variant from one observation to another observes remains, then it is called homocedasticity and if different is called heteroscedasticity. A good regression model is homocedasticity or does not occur heterocedasticity. The heteroscedasticity test in this study used Glejser test.

Multicollinearity test aims to determine whether the regression model found a correlation between independent variables (independent). A good regression model should not be correlated between independent variables or multicollinearity.

3. Hypothesis Test

For hypothesis test this research used : multiregression analysis, significant test of coefficients (t test) and path test.

The author uses multiregression analysis because there are more than one independent variable. Significant test of coefficients (t test) used to show how far the influence of one independent variable individually in explaining the variation of the dependent variable. Decision making accept or reject the hypothesis in the study is based on consideration of the coefficient significance of each independent variable to the dependent variable.

Path test is intended to determine the comparison between direct and indirect effects of independent variables on dependent variables if through an intermediate variable (indirect influence) than if not through an intermediate variable (direct influence).

2 Result & Discussion

2.1 Validity & Realiability Test Result

From the validity test conducted through SPSS, with data from 110 respondents, the whole research instrument has r value exceeding r table value at n = 110, ie 0.1874. So, can be concluded that the data on the main test of this study with 110 respondents valid and can be used as data on further analysis. The results of the validity test on the main test can be seen in Table 4.1.

		Total			Total
VAR00001	Pearson Correlation	,598**	VAR00016	Pearson Correlation	,597**
	Sig. (2-tailed)	,000		Sig. (2-tailed)	,000
	N	110		N	110
VAR00002	Pearson Correlation	,535**	VAR00017	Pearson Correlation	,547**
	Sig. (2-tailed)	,000		Sig. (2-tailed)	,000
	N	110		N	110
VAR00003	Pearson Correlation	,220*	VAR00018	Pearson Correlation	,447**
	Sig. (2-tailed)	,022		Sig. (2-tailed)	,000
	N	110		N	110
VAR00004	Pearson Correlation	,447**	VAR00019	Pearson Correlation	,586**
	Sig. (2-tailed)	,000		Sig. (2-tailed)	,000
	N	110		N	110
VAR00005	Pearson Correlation	,621**	VAR00020	Pearson Correlation	,555**
	Sig. (2-tailed)	,000		Sig. (2-tailed)	,000
	N	110		N	110
VAR00006	Pearson Correlation	,447**	VAR00021	Pearson Correlation	,610**
	Sig. (2-tailed)	,000		Sig. (2-tailed)	,000
	N	110		N	110
VAR00007	Pearson Correlation	,482**	VAR00022	Pearson Correlation	,357**
	Sig. (2-tailed)	,000		Sig. (2-tailed)	,000
	N	110		N	110
VAR00008	Pearson Correlation	,487**	VAR00023	Pearson Correlation	,338**
	Sig. (2-tailed)	,000		Sig. (2-tailed)	,001
	N	110		N	110
VAR00009	Pearson Correlation	,508**	VAR00024	Pearson Correlation	,405**
	Sig. (2-tailed)	,000		Sig. (2-tailed)	,000
	N	110		N	110
VAR00010	Pearson Correlation	,481**	VAR00025	Pearson Correlation	,313**
	Sig. (2-tailed)	,000		Sig. (2-tailed)	,002
	N	110		N	110
VAR00011	Pearson Correlation	,439**	VAR00026	Pearson Correlation	,547**
	Sig. (2-tailed)	,000		Sig. (2-tailed)	,000
	N	110		N	110
VAR00012	Pearson Correlation	,600**	VAR00027	Pearson Correlation	,665**
	Sig. (2-tailed)	,000		Sig. (2-tailed)	,000
	N	110		N	110
VAR00013	Pearson Correlation	,514**	VAR00028	Pearson Correlation	,534**
	Sig. (2-tailed)	,000		Sig. (2-tailed)	,000
	N	110		N	110
VAR00014	Pearson Correlation	,576**	VAR00029	Pearson Correlation	,596**
	Sig. (2-tailed)	,000		Sig. (2-tailed)	,000
	N	110		N	110
VAR00015	Pearson Correlation	,637**	Total	Pearson Correlation	1
	Sig. (2-tailed)	,000		Sig. (2-tailed)	
	N	110		N	110

Table3.1Validity TestResult (respondent n=110)

In the test of reliability using SPSS, for the number of respondents 110, obtained the value of Cornbach's Alpha is 0.738 and more than 0.1874, so it can be concluded that the kusioner used is reliable or reliable to be continued as a research instrument. The results of the test reliability on the main test can be seen in Table 4.2.

Reliability Statistics

Cronbach's Alpha	N of Items
,738	29

Table 3.2Reability Test Result (n=110)

2.2 Classic Assumption Test Result

From the normality test results obtained significance value of 0.200 where the value is greater than 0.05, it can be concluded that the research data is normally distributed.

From result of heterocedasticity test of significance variable of Quality (K) equal to 0,488, Price variable (H) equal to 0,099, Infrastructure variable (I) 0,573 and variable Perceived Value (PV) 0,932. The significance value of all variables is greater than 0.05, so it can be concluded that the research data does not occur heterocedasticity.

From the result of multicolinearity test of tolerance value of Quality variable (K) 0,884 and VIF value 1,131, Price variable (H) tolerance value 0,803 and VIF value 1,246, Infrastructure variable (I) tolerance value 0,725 and VIF value 1,379. As for the variable Perceived Value (PV) tolerance value of 0.924 and VIF value of 1.082. The tolerance value of all variables is greater than 0.10 and the VIF value is less than 10.0, so it can be concluded that the research data does not occur multicollinearity.

2.3 Hypothesis Test Result

From regression test result all significancy value is under 0,05, it means that all hypothesis can be accepted that there is positive relationship between each variables.

Coefficients[a]

Model		Unstandardized Coefficients		Standardized Coefficients	t	Sig.
		B	Std. Error	Beta		
1	(Constant)	-2,913	1,882		-1,548	,123
	K	,213	,102	,147	2,078	,039
	H	,287	,069	,277	4,154	,000
	I	,178	,061	,220	2,900	,004
	PV	,116	,039	,205	2,934	,004

a. Dependent Variable: MB

Table 3.3 Regression Test Result with Interest in Buying as Dependent Variable.

Coefficients[a]

Model		Unstandardized Coefficients		Standardized Coefficients	t	Sig.
		B	Std. Error	Beta		
1	(Constant)	2,442	3,893		,583	,485
	K	,585	,191	,228	3,065	,003
	H	,435	,128	,236	3,385	,001
	I	,338	,115	,225	2,946	,004

a. Dependent Variable: PV

Table 3.4 Regression Test Result with Perceived Value as Dependent Variable.

Also form Table 3.3 and 3.4, we can see that T value is over t tabel (n=110) value : 1,65950. So, it can be concluded that all hypothesis can be accepted.

For path analysis test, the direct effect of quality variables on buying interest is 0.147. While the indirect effect of quality variable on buying interest if through perceived value is: 0,228 x 0,205 = 0,04674. So it can be concluded if the direct influence of quality variables on buying interest is more significant if compared indirect influence if through perceived variable value.

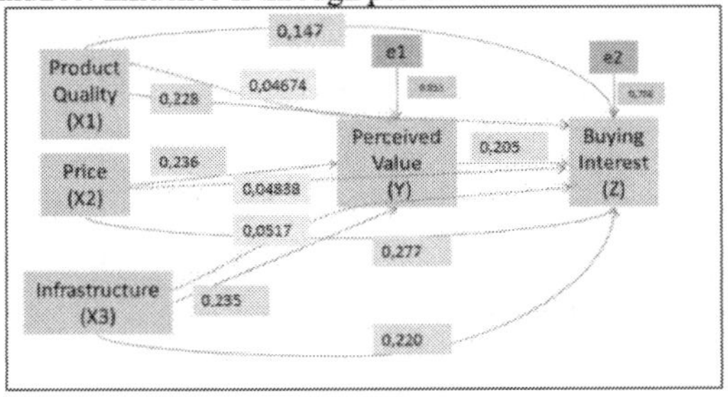

Fig 3.1. Path Analysis Test Result

The direct effect of price variables on buying interest by 0.277. While the indirect effect of price variable on buying interest if through perceived value is: 0,236 x 0,205 = 0,04838. So it can be concluded if the direct influence of quality variables on buying interest is more significant if compared indirect influence if through perceived variable value.

The direct effect of quality variables on buying interest is 0.147. While the indirect effect of quality variables on buying interest if through perceived value is: 0,235 x 0,205 = 0,0517. So it can be concluded if the direct influence of quality variables on buying interest is more significant if compared indirect influence if through perceived variable value.

2.4 Discussion

From hypothesis test we can conclude that all hypotesis can be accepted. For further analysis, this research also ask respondent for the deeper data of independent variables.

1. Product Quality on Customer Perception

• The distance of motorcycle for one battery charge

For the distance from the electric motorcycle, if asked further to the respondents about the acceptable mileage, 37.5% of respondents can accept the distance between 80-100 km. For the distance of 50-80 km and also> 100 km respectively 30% of respondents who can accept it. And the remaining 2.5% of respondents can accept 20 - 50 km. In general most respondents or 97.5% require mileage> 50 km for one battery charge.

No	Mileage Expected	Percentage (%)
1	20 – 50 km	2,5
2	50 – 80 km	30
3	80 – 100 km	37,5
4	> 100 km	30

Table 3.5 Mileage of electric motorcycles expected by costumer

From the results of this survey the possibility of respondents still compare with the ability of a motorcycle with gasoline, which has a distance of up to 232 km for a one-time full tank of gasoline fuel.

However, when compared with the daily needs of motorcycle riders from respondents in the table 4:31, 40% of respondents traveled 5-20 km per day. Or if totaled 79% of respondents daily mileage less than 30 km. Only 21% exceed 30 km.

This means that there is a gap between the desire of the customer with the actual needs of customers. This matter need to be paid attention by automotive motorcycle industry producer so that can do education to society if want to market electric motorcycle.

No	Daily Mileage Use	Percentage (%)
1	< 5 km	19
2	5 - 20 km	40
3	20 - 30 km	20
4	> 30 km	21

Table 3.6 Daily mileage of motorcycle users

• Charge time of battery from empty to full condition

For charging time from empty to full, 40% of respondents can accept charging time between 3 -7 hours. If the total 85% of respondents can still accept charging time over 1 hour. And only 15% of respondents who want time charging under 1 hour.

No	Battery Charging Time Expect	Percentage (%)
1	7 – 9 hours	12
2	3 – 7 hours	40
3	1 – 3 hours	33
4	< 1 hour	15

Table 3.7 Battery charging time that customers expect

Respondents can still accept and understand that electric motorcycles with batteries do take longer in charging. However, it is still necessary to socialize the users of motorcycles if you want to switch to electric motorcycle related recharging habits of energy. Because if it is only 7% of the respondents who fill the gasoline motorcycle every day. 93% of the rest fill gasoline motorcycle 2 days or more.

 https://doi.org/10.1051/matecconf/201821502006

No	Refueling Frequency Habit	Percentage (%)
1	Everyday	7
2	Every 2 days	39
3	Every 3 days	29
4	More than 3 days	25

Table 3.8 Habit of refueling frequency of motorcycle gasoline respondent

If you want to switch to electric motorcycle requires charging energy in this case fill the batteries every day.

No	Refueling Frequency Habit	Percentage (%)
1	Full Tank	50
2	Money Reference (Rupiah)	40
3	Volume Reference (Litre)	4
4	Random	6

Table 3.9 Habits method of refueling gasoline motorcycle respondents

For this energy charging habits 50% of respondents to fill up to full, so this habit will be in line with the habits to be formed on charging electric motorcycle batteries that will tend to fill up to full.

• Maximum speed of electric motorcycle

For maximum speed of electric motorcycle 44% of respondents can accept if the maximum speed of electric motorcycle ranges between 50-80 km / hour. If 91% of the respondents can accept if the speed of an electric motorcycle under 100 km / hour. Only 9% of respondents wanted speeds above 100 km / h.

No	Maximum Speed Expected	Percentage (%)
1	30 – 50 km/h	12
2	50 – 80 km/h	44
3	80 – 100 km/h	35
4	>100 km/h	9

Table 3.10 Maximum speed of electric motorcycle expected

No	Riding Habit Speed	Percentage (%)
1	< 50 km/h	11
2	80 – 100 km/h	24
3	50 km/h	54
4	>100 km/h	11

Table 3.11 The habits of motorcycle riding respondents

The above data is in line with the data of motorcycle driving habits of the respondents where 54% of respondents admitted the maximum speed that has traveled between 50-80 km / hour.
With this data the electric motorcycle manufacturer can set the target of electric motorcycle performance in this case its maximum speed at acceptable level by the customer.

2. Price

If it is experienced further by customer acceptable price on electric motorcycles, 53% of respondents want a price hike between 10-15 million rupiahs, and 42% of respondents can accept price range 15-30 million rupiah. If 95% of respondents can accept a price range between 10 - 30 million rupiah for each unit of electric motorcycle.

No	Acceptable Price (IDR)	Percentage (%)
1	> 50 million	2
2	30 – 50 million	3
3	15 – 30 million	42
4	10 – 15 million	53

Table 3.12. Acceptable Price to customer electric motorcycle

No	Income per Month (IDR)	Percentage (%)
1	< 2.500.000	21
2	5.000.000 – 10.000.000	34
3	2.500.000 – 5.000.000	34
4	> 10.000.000	11

Table 3.13. Income per month of respondents

If this data is linked to monthly income data from the respondents found a close relationship, of which 89% of respondents earn <10 million rupiah. With that income the ability to buy respondents in the price range 10 - 30 million rupiah.

3. Supporting Infratructure

If experienced to respondents mengalam this infrastructure can be seen through the data charging method of electric motorcycle product. Seen from the results of deepening of respondents who want a feature of charging directly (charging) and replacement batteries (swap) on electric motorcycle, desired by more than 86% of respondents.

No	Charging Method	Percentage (%)
1	Charge (direct connected)	11
2	Swap Battery	3
3	Both	86

Table 3.14. Electric motor batteries charging method desired by respondents

Availability of battery replacement location can disiasati automotive industry by exploiting the mushrooming mini market in Indonesia. So it can cover the lack of availability of charging infrastructure by replacing it into a reliable and available replacement battery replacement line across the region.

3 Conclussion

From the data and discussion we can conclude that :

1. Ha hypothesis is acceptable, there is a positive influence between quality with perceived value.
2. Hb hypothesis is acceptable, there is a positive influence between price and perceived value.
3. Hc hypothesis is acceptable, there is positive influence between infrastructure with perceived value.
4. Hd hypothesis is acceptable, there is positive influence between perceived value with buying interest.
5. He hypothesis is acceptable, there is a positive influence between quality with buying interest.
6. Hf hypothesis is acceptable, there is a positive influence between price and buying interest.
7. Hg hypothesis is acceptable, there is a positive influence between infrastructure and buying interest.

From the results of this study there are some suggestions from the author:

1. Suggestions for further research

Because of the limitations of this study only has 110 respondents, according to the authors in the next study should increase the number of respondents so that the accuracy of research is better.

Should also at the time of conducting research with an example of electric motorcycle products that can be tested by respondents in advance so that respondents better understand the statements that exist in the research questionnaire because it can be directly explained through existing products.

In addition it should be considered to conduct research on other variables that may affect both perceived value and on buying interest.

2. Suggestions for industry

From the results of this study can be seen that the quality, price and infrastructure have a good influence on perceived value and the interest in buying electric motorcycles. With the order of its biggest influence is price, then infrastructure and quality.

The price that can be accepted by respondents for electric motorcycle ranges between 10-30 million rupiah. For the desired infrastructure are battery charging facilities and also battery replacement (most respondents want both to exist).

While in terms of product quality, most respondents want the ability of their electric motorcycle: maximum speed 50-80 km / hour, mileage once charging 80 - 100 km battery and battery charging time is 3 - 7 hours.

This is a challenge for the automotive industry in general in order to meet the expectations of consumers.

3. Suggestions for the government

Due to the most influential factor is the price and infrastructure, the authors suggest to the government to consider the existence of a subsidized policy for electric vehicles in order to meet consumer expectations. It also takes the role of government together with industry to provide battery charging infrastructure and battery exchange.

References

[1] KESDM (2015) Strategic Planning, Ministry of Energy and Mineral Resource 2015-2019, Jakarta.

[2] Hurst, Dave and Gartner, John. (2012). Pike Pulse Report: Electric Motorcycles and Scooters Assessment of Strategy and Execution for 12 Leading Electric Motorcycle and Scooter Manufacturers, Pike Research, Columbia USA.

[3] Kinnear, Thomas C. and James R. Taylor. (1995). Marketing Research: An Applied Approach. McGraw Hill Text.

[4] Augusty, Ferdinand. (2006). Metode Penelitian Manajemen: Pedoman Penelitian untuk skripsi, Tesis dan Disertai Ilmu Manajemen. Semarang: Universitas Diponegoro.

[5] Kotler, Philip. (2008). Manajemen Pemasaran, Jilid 1 dan 2, Alih Bahasa Benyamin. Jakarta: PT.Indeks. Kelompok Gramedia.

[6] Sanchez, Javier. et al. (2006). *Perceived Value of the Purchase of Tourism Product*. Elsevier Tourism Management, 394-409

[7] Deloitte.(2011). Unplugged: Electric Vehicle Realities versus Consumer Expectations.

[8] Segal. R.(1995) Forecasting the Market for Electric Vehicles in California Using Conjoint Analysis, in The Energy Journal, vol, 16., no. 3, 89-111.

[9] Ping Liu, et al (2015) Long-range, Low-cost Electric Vehicles Enabled by Robust Energy Storage, MRS Energy & Sustainability

[10] Greene, D. L. (2001). TAFV Alternative Fuels and Vehicles Choice Model Documentation, Centre for Transportation Analysis, Oak Ridge National Laboratory, and Report No. ORNL/TM-2001/134.

[11] Mau, P., Eyzaguirre, J., Jaccard, M. et al.(2008) the Neighbor Effect: Simulating Dynamics in Consumer Preferences for New Vehicle Technologies, in Ecological Economics.

[12] Dodi Triawan, Department of Management, Faculty of Economics, State University of Surabaya, "The Influence of Brand Image and Perception Value Against Motorcycle Buying Purpose Brand Honda Type PCX 150 (Study on Cafe Visitor at Tunjungan Plaza Surabaya), Journal of Management Sciences Volume 05 Number 01 - Department of Management Faculty of Economics, State University of Surabaya.

[13] Ning Wang and Yafei Liu, School of Automotive Studies, Tongji University, Shanghai, "Key factors influencing customers' willingness to purchase electric vehicles in China".

[14] Agus Sukasman Hidayat, "Analysis of Factors Influencing Interest in Buying New Yamaha Motorcycles in Semarang City", Master Program Management of Postgraduate Program of Diponegoro University of Semarang.

[15] Danu Kusmono, Master Program of Postgraduate Program Management of Widya Mandala Catholic University Surabaya, "The Influence of Marketing Mix Against Perceived Value and Purchasing Decision of ACR Brand Energy Saving Lamp Products in Surabaya"

[16] William Sierzchula, Sjoerd Bakker, et.al, Delft University of Technology, Faculty of Technology, Policy, and Management, The Netherlands, on his research paper, "The influence of financial incentives and other socio-economic Factors on electric vehicle adoption ".

 https://doi.org/10.1051/matecconf/201821502007

Internal factors that affect SMEs to export: A case study of Footwear Cluster

Wawan Dhewanto, *Sri* Herliana*, *Donald Crestofel* Lantu, *Nur* Lawiyah

Institut Teknologi Bandung, School of Business and Management, Bandung, Indonesia

Abstract. Cibaduyut is one of the footwear clusters that have a high potential in terms of export. The development of globalization creates new pressures and opportunities in competition for SMEs nationally and internationally; the internal factors, playing an important role for SMEs to export. The purpose of this study is to determine what internal factors affect the decision of SMEs in the cluster to export, how, and what the future recommendations to develop export activities in Cibaduyut cluster. The research method used in this research is by using a quantitative method to 10 respondents that have export experience by using frequency data approach. From the frequency data studied, 10 internal factors that include, strong business capital, skilled workforce, good product made, strategic location, intensive marketing, adequate machine tools, adequate warehouse, attractive packaging, foreign language skills, and availability of raw materials, studied to 10 respondents by using the data frequency approach of the development hypothesis, indicates that only the language factor is rejected in the hypothesis testing.

1 Introduction

The effect of globalization on trade is to open a country's economic gate for export. SMEs have a role as a strengthening of a country's economy. From the SME sector created positive business activities, especially in making jobs and developing other busi-ness potentials such as export activities. Export ac-tivities for SMEs are the gateway to enter the inter-national market. However, in practice not all SMEs dare to export, which of course is based on internal factors and external factors. Cibaduyut is one of the famous footwear clusters in Indonesia. Although it has stood since very long, but the SMEs there still do not have enough courage to do export. They have a very high potential for export, including having good quality products, competitive prices, and having skilled craftsmen. Although they have not dared to export directly, but some SMEs do indirect exports, through overseas customers who come and buy Cibaduyut products directly and through brokers. What are the factors affecting SMEs to export and enter the international market in Cibaduyut cluster. In this study, researchers focused on examining internal factors affecting SMEs in Cibaduyut to conduct and participate in international markets. This research uses quantitative research approach measured from the frequency of respondents to internal factors that researchers mention based on literature support. From this research will be known what are the factors that influence SMEs in Cibaduyut for export, and how the recommendations for the future.

Hypothesis Development:

H1: Strong business capital [1], has a positive impact on export activities in Cibaduyut.
H2: Skilled workforce [2], has a positive impact on export activities in Cibaduyut.
H3: Good product made [1,3], has a positive impact on export ac-tivities in Cibaduyut.
H4: Strategic location [4], has a positive impact on export activ-ities in Cibaduyut.
H5: Intensive marketing [5], has a positive impact on export ac-tivities in Cibaduyut.
H6: Adequate machine tools [1], has a positive impact on export activities in Cibaduyut.
H7: Adequate warehouse [1], has a positive impact on export activities in Cibaduyut.
H8: Attractive packaging [1,3], has a positive impact on export ac-tivities in Cibaduyut.
H9: Foreign language skills [6], has a positive impact on export ac-tivities in Cibaduyut.
H10: Experience of export [1], has a positive impact on export activities in Cibaduyut.

* Corresponding author: sri.herliana@sbm-itb.ac.id

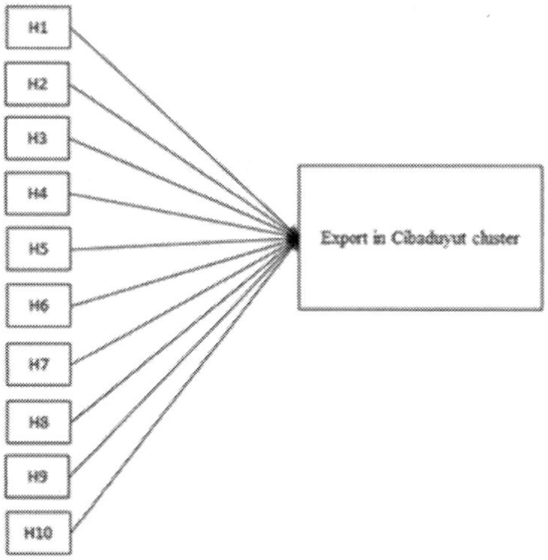

Fig 1. Hypothesis Development

2 Literature Review

2.1 SMEs for export

The development of globalization creates new pressures and opportunities in competition for SMEs nationally and internationally. Opportunities that could be exploited by SMEs in the development of globalization, such as increased productivity and im-proved markets [7]. International expansion has opened the way for SMEs to grow by expanding their customer base to increase profitabil-ity and growth [8]. The willingness, ability, and motivation of the owners / managers in making decisions, often influence the successful ap-plication of international entrepreneurial ideas [9]. However, in practice, the growing international development has made it difficult for small sectors to develop, as they have to face obstacles in order to survive and com-pete in international markets [10]. It makes, the contribution of SMEs in international is still very low compared with their contribution in the country. In fact, many government programs to sup-port SMEs in order to enter the international market [8]. Therefore, SMEs now, should be able to develop competitive ability, innovation, and relationships in order to participate actively in the in-ternational market [10].

2.2 Internal factor for export

Internal factors, playing an important role for SMEs to export, these internal factors include the quality of the products offered, the resources owned, the scale of the company, the management of the enterprise, and the experience of exports [1]. The researcher assumes that internal factors for export are factors related to the condition of the company, such as location, marketing, innovation, skilled labor, and language skills, in addition to the factors mentioned earlier. The company's location factor for SMEs in general has an influence on the company's ability to export, although it is not felt directly [4]. The company's skilled labor is one of the decisive factors for the company to export. Skilled labor is closely related to higher work productivity [2]. The company's commitment to export orientation with innovation has a role to the success of exports [3]. Most of the success of exports comes from the ability of firms to implement marketing strategies effectively [5]. Foreign language skills and abilities are a key factor in the international market in customer relationships. Communication problems that occur in the international market, because they do not understand each other English language used, or use a bad translation [6]

3. Methodology

The research method used in this research is by using quantitative method to 10 respondents that has export experience, to know what internal factors that influences SMEs to conduct and enter into international market or export. The quantitative method uses a frequency approach, which is judged by how many respondents score each variable. Score value using a linkert scale approach that is from 1-5. This study is also supported by literature data from journals, articles, books, electronic newspapers, proceedings, and other sources that support the literature search about export factors and around the cluster Cibaduyut. The purpose of this study is to determine what internal factors affect the decision of SMEs in the cluster Cibaduyut to export and how and what the future recommendations to develop export activities in clusters Cibaduyut.

4 Analysis and Discussion

4.1 Respodent's profile

Profile of respondents in this study to 10 SMEs is 6 respondent's business owners and 4 employees in the field of marketing. Their educational background was 5 respondents who received high school education, 2 respondents received junior high school education, 1 respondent received diploma education, and 2 respondents received bachelor degree. The SMEs age in this study are the oldest was 32 years old and the youngest was 4 years old. The majority of them can export from foreign buyers who come directly to Cibaduyut to buy Cibaduyut products that will be brought to their country and through brokers. The majority of them do not apply price differences between domestic and overseas buyers. There are many

 https://doi.org/10.1051/matecconf/201821502007

competitors and Cibaduyut products are already known as a product with an affordable price. Although this cluster has been established for a long time, but few SMEs have export experience.

4.2 Hypothesis testing by internal factor frequency data

The testing hypothesis based on the frequency data on internal export factor in Cibaduyut cluster can be seen below;

Table 1. Internal factor frequency data affecting export activities in Cibaduyut

Internal Factor Variables	**Hypothesis**	**Data Frequency**					**Total**
		1	**2**	**3**	**4**	**5**	
Strong business capital	H1			1	1	8	10
Skilled workforce	H2	2			2	6	10
Good product made	H3			4	1	5	10
Strategic location	H4	1		5		4	10
Intensive marketing	H5	1	1	1		7	10
Adequate machine tools	H6	3		1	2	4	10
Adequate warehouse	H7	3	1			6	10
Attractive packaging	H8	4				6	10
Foreign language skills	H9	4		2	1	3	10
Experience of export	H10			2	3	5	10

Strong business capital has a positive impact on export activities in Cibaduyut, it is seen from the frequency data shows 8 respondents put the internal factor of this export in the number 5 which means very influential. The strong business capital is needed by SMEs for production and marketing. Moreover, in the case of production, SMEs must order raw materials demanded by customers to ensure raw material stock. If the raw materials run out, there will be no production activities. Therefore, strong business capital is needed by SMEs. Thus, SMEs apply gradual payments or advances to customers or apply cash payments for export activities. (*H1: Strong business capital, has a positive impact on export activities in Cibaduyut is accepted).*

The expertise of the workforce or craftsmen is a major factor in business activities in both production and marketing lines. It is approved by SME respondents in this study, frequency data shows as much as 6/10 respondents strongly agree or put score 5, that the expertise of the workforce to support the export activities. This is in harmony with the condition of Cibaduyut, which is a cluster of footwear with thousands of skilled craftsmen or experts, which makes many overseas buyers or brokers produce and buy products in Cibaduyut to be sent abroad. (*H2: Skilled workforce, has a positive impact on export activities in Cibaduyut is accepted).*

Good product made with innovation has an influence on export activities in Cibaduyut. 5/10 respondents put the quality of products offered in score 5 or very influential. Indeed Cibaduyut products have long been famous for the good products that are made but for the problem of innovation still have many obstacles, based on information from respondents. Therefore, SMEs realize that the good product and innovation are the things that have an influence on export activities in Cibaduyut. (*H3: Good product made, has a positive impact on export activities in Cibaduyut is accepted).*

Cibaduyut is in a very strategic location in Bandung, Cibaduyut's big name makes it easy to access. Large road conditions and located in a very strategic area to make business activities in this cluster is so alive. Plus, business activities from upstream to downstream in the footwear sector or the like are centered in this location. Among the advantages, 4/10 respondents placed the location factor is very influential (score 5) on export activities in Cibaduyut, where the rest or 6/10 are neutral (score 3) to this location factor. This is because, when heavy rains or during peak hours there is always a long traffic jam and sometimes cause flooding when the rain is falling heavily. This also hampers business activities in Cibaduyut. Nevertheless, Cibaduyut's big name and lively location by various business activities make the location factor has a positive influence on export business activities in Cibaduyut. (*H4: Strategic location, has a positive impact on export activities in Cibaduyut is accepted).*

7/10 respondents strongly agree (score 5) that internal factors of marketing have a positive influence on export activities in Cibaduyut. Moreover, the name of Cibaduyut which is already well known as a footwear shopping center in the city of Bandung; Supporting the marketing of the name Cibaduyut itself. Marketing activities must be done by SMEs to get into the international market; especially the international market has a different condition from the domestic market. (*H5: Intensive marketing, has a positive impact on export activities in Cibaduyut is accepted).*

Machine equipment owned to support production needs is very influential on business activities in Cibaduyut, one of them for export. 6/10 respondents stated that adequate machine tools contribute (score 5) to fulfilling the demand of production from customers, by giving effectiveness to the production. (*H6: Adequate machine tools, has a positive impact on export activities in Cibaduyut is accepted).*

Adequate warehouse has an influence on export activity. Products that are finished in production or ready to be shipped and sold should be placed in a safe room so that the product is neat and not damaged. This makes it easy to list products that are ordered or searched by customers. Therefore, 6/10 respondents stated that the internal factor of adequate warehouse is a very influential (score 5) factor and has a positive impact on export business activities in Cibaduyut. (*H7: Adequate warehouse, has a positive impact on export activities in Cibaduyut is accepted).*

From the results of frequency data, 6/10 respondents stated that the interesting packaging has a very high effect on export activities in Cibaduyut (score 5), but 4/10 respondents stated that the interesting packaging has no effect (score 1) on export activity In Cibaduyut. Based on the description of the respondents, overseas buyers who come and shop for products in Cibaduyut not too concerned with attractive packaging, they usually will repackage Cibaduyut product more attractive. So it can reduce costs in purchasing products or product production in Cibaduyut. Nevertheless, from this result the researcher assumes that the attractive packaging has a positive effect on export activity in Cibaduyut. (*H8: Attractive packaging, has a positive impact on export activities in Cibaduyut is accepted).*

Talking about export business activities certainly cannot be separated from the language factor. From the frequency data in this study can be seen that 4/10 respondents stated that the language factor is very no effect (score 1) on export business activities in Cibaduyut. 2/10 respondents are neutral towards this factor. Although SMEs do not have the ability to speak foreign languages or English well, they can still communicate through body language or Indonesian language or with translators brought by overseas buyers. From this data, the researcher assumed that foreign language ability factor had no effect to business activity in Cibaduyut. (*H9: Foreign language skills, has a positive impact on export activities in Cibaduyut is rejected).*

Experience in export activities perceived by SMEs, have a positive impact on business activities in Cibaduyut. Direct experience is felt to provide insight into export activities and new experiences for SMEs to explore the international market. This is consistent with the frequency data obtained, 5/10 respondents stated that experience in export activities has a high influence (score 5) on export activities, where 3/10 respondents also stated this factor has an effect (score 4) on export activities in Cibaduyut. Researchers assume that experience of export activities have a positive impact on export activities in Cibaduyut. (*H10: Experience of export, has a positive impact on export activities in Cibaduyut is accepted).*

5 Conclusion and Recommendation

5.1 Conclusion

From the frequency data studied, 10 internal factors that include, strong business capital, skilled workforce, good product made, strategic location, intensive marketing, adequate machine tools, adequate warehouse, attractive packaging, foreign language skills, and availability of raw materials, studied to 10 respondents by using the data frequency approach of the development hypothesis, indicates that only the language factor is rejected in the hypothesis testing. In fact, the factor of foreign language ability is an important factor for SMEs to be able to conduct export business activities or find out about export opportunities independently. Internal factor is a very vital factor for SMEs to export; internal factors are factors that come from the condition of the company. These internal factors create a powerful motivational drive for exports from within the company or SME. As mentioned in the literature, SMEs have an important role to the economic growth of a country in general, and in particular SMEs can or have the potential to export and develop their line of business internationally. From this study, shows that, SMEs in Cibaduyut have been very aware of internal factors or conditions of the company to conduct or participate in international activities. However, the internal factors studied can be a constraint factor faced by SMEs because they cannot meet the expectations of foreign ldemand caused by one of the internal factors that are not met. SMEs in Cibaduyut can solve the internal factor problems for export by way of their own negotiations, although they are constrained in foreign language abilities.

5.2 Recommendation

Although the internal factor of foreign language proficiency is rejected in the testing hypothesis, it is helpful that a continuous foreign language training program is held in this cluster. In addition to SMEs in Cibaduyut cluster reliable in making products, it is expected they are also reliable in communicating foreign languages that will open more export opportunities. Knowledge and training on exports is also important to SMEs in Cibaduyut to understand how international market conditions are happening today, how to respond to dynamic changes in international markets, and how to provide added value that can increase the selling value of products made in this cluster. The location conditions in the Cibaduyut cluster need to be addressed in terms of road construction in order to provide comfort for domestic and foreign tourists, especially during peak hours.

References

1. L. Su, J Adams, Export capacity impact factors on Chinese SMEs: A survey analysis of Fujian Province. Journal of Chinese Economic and Foreign Trade Studies, **3**(1), 57. (2010)
2. Y. Amornkitvikai, C Harvie, & T. Charoenrat, Factors Affecting The Export Participation And Performance Of Thai Manufacturing Small And Medium Sized Enterprises (Smes). *ICSB World Conference Proceedings* (hal. 10). Washington: International Council for Small Business (ICSB). (2013)
3. M. Dressler, Managing export success - An empirical picture of German wineries' performance. *BIO Web of Conferences*, 2. (2015)

4. J. Freeman, C. Styles, & M. Lawley, Does firm location make a difference to the export performance of SMEs? *International Marketing Review,* **29**(1), 90. (2012)
5. N.A. Morgan, C.S. Katsikeas, & D.W. Vorhies, Export marketing strategy implementation, export marketing capabilities, and export venture performance. Academy of Marketing Science. Journal, **40**(2), 272. (2012).
6. J. Asasongtham, S. Wichadee, The roles of foreign language in export operations of thai smes. International Journal of Entrepreneurship, 43. (2014).
7. D.K. Mutalemwa, Does globalisation impact SME development in Africa? African Journal of Economic and Management Studies, **6**(2), 168. (2015).
8. F. Hashim, SMEs' impediments and developments in the internationalization process: Malaysian experiences. World Journal of Entrepreneurship, Management and Sustainable Development, **11**(2), 101. (2015).
9. N.Z. Kovacevic, J.V. Tankosic, & B. Lazic, The Mechanism Of Smes Internationalization Towards The Eu Single Market Perspective. *Conference Proceedings of the International Scientific Conference* (hal. 44-45). Pula: Sveuciliste Jurja Dobrile u Puli, Odjel za Ekonomiju i Turizam "Dr. Mijo Mirkovic". (2015).
10. T. Husain, Spatial Composition of Indian Small and Medium Enterprises' Export. Journal of International Economics, **7**(2), 71, (2016).

The Constraints of Agricultural Credit and Government Policy Strategy

Sri Herliana*, *Acip* Sutardi, *Qorri* Aina, *Qonita* Himmatul Aliya, *Nur* Lawiyah

Institut Teknologi Bandung, School of Business and Management, Bandung, Indonesia

Abstract. Low access to credit in the agricultural sector is also caused by problems of agricultural sector actors (especially farmers) and financial institutions. Farmers are still having difficulty in accessing credit (accessibility and unbankable) and the limited financial institutions that channel credit to the agricultural sector. Therefore, the government must issue a policy in growing the agricultural sector, especially in anticipation of access credit constraints by farmers. The agricultural sector as a high-risk business, therefore formal institutions are less interested in financing the agricultural sector on the grounds of high transaction costs, asymmetric information, low profits, lack of collateral, education of farmers is relatively low. In addition, most banks do not want to finance agriculture due to fluctuating production and uncontrolled price risk. While the constraints of the farmers in obtaining formal credit is a complex procedure, there should be collateral as well as high payment delay fees, long distances and less information about capital.

1 Introduction

Agricultural Sector (viewed from production), based on data from the Central Bureau of Statistics [1](BPS, 2017) is the second most influential sector of economic growth, after processing industry. For the second quarter of 2017, the agricultural sector in a broad sense accounted for 13.92 percent, while in the first quarter of 2017 it contributed 13.59 percent. Compared to the previous quarter (q to q), the agricultural sector became the highest growth sector, at 8.44 percent. This increase is obtained from the increased production of a number of plantation crops such as coffee and sugar cane and from horticulture. Based on data from Indonesian Banking Statistics as of January 2017, credit distribution to agriculture, hunting and forestry sector amounted to Rp278 trillion (6.45%) while credit to the fishery sector was only Rp9.14 trillion (0.21%). The NPLs in both sectors reached Rp6.04 trillion (2.17%) and Rp384 billion (4.21%), respectively. Total bank credit until January 2017 reached Rp4,313 trillion. The credit distribution to the agricultural sector from the Bank is still small compared to other sectors. This is because credit risk to the agricultural sector has a high risk among others because it is directly related to nature. So that the banks remain cautious in holding public funds, and keep the credit given does not become a credit problem (non-performing loan / NPL). Low access to credit in the agricultural sector is also caused by problems of agricultural sector actors (especially farmers) and financial institutions. Farmers are still having difficulty in accessing credit (accessibility and unbankable) and the limited financial institutions that channel credit to the agricultural sector. Therefore, the government must issue a policy in growing the agricultural sector, especially in anticipation of access credit constraints by farmers.

2 Literature Review

2.1 The Constraints of Agricultural Credit

Agricultural credit constraints according to Minh Chau Tran et al (2016) there are some problems or constraints in access to agricultural credit. Agricultural credit problems will be related to the condition of a region or country. Credit as an important source to improve the welfare and production of farm households. But in the process, it is almost the same as incidence in many other developing countries, in rural Vietnamese agricultural households accessing credit to formal financial institutions is exempt due to high transaction costs and information asymmetries, lack of guarantees, weak credit contract enforcement and underdevelopment of insurance services make formal financial managers unable to serve the market this [2]. Another problem in accessing credit is the different treatment in the ease of obtaining credit. The distinguishing factors are the characteristics of head of household (age, sex and education), household characteristics (factors related to physical capital, factors related to human capital, social capital related factors and factors related to the economy), factors geographical factors (distance to markets or formal

* Corresponding author: sri.herliana@sbm-itb.ac.id

lenders increase the transaction costs of households, the livelihood of local credit institutions and the development of local production.

Pavel Ciaian et al (2012) examines the impact of credit constraints on agricultural behavior in CEE transition countries. Based on the theoretical model shows that with the existence of binding credit limits, increased access to credit can lead to increased productivity, agricultural output and input use. With symmetric credit constraints, the eradication of agricultural credit constraints increases the use of all inputs [3]. However, if asymmetrically limited, increased access to credit may result in restricted credit input substitution to provide unlimited input. The results of empirical testing on the hypothesis show that the farm in CEE is restricted credit. Access to credit increases TFP up to 1.9 per cent EUR 1,000 of additional credit. Agriculture in CEE is primarily limited by credits involving variable inputs and capital investments, as variable inputs and capital investments increase respectively to 2.3 and 29 per cent per 1,000 EUR of additional credit. On the other hand, land and labor are not limited to credit. This could be due to the relatively high abundance of land and the high employment of agricultural labor in the CEE transition countries, especially in Poland, Slovenia and the Baltic countries. So the results showed that agriculture can address the problem of land financing and workforce with better than the input and investment variables. Family farms mainly use their own labor in production, which reduces the need for pre-financing. Family labor can overcome credit problems by delaying household consumption until the last period, when revenues from production sales are collected (after harvest at the end of the season). Similar to land. Agriculture can increase land use through the rental market.

The problems that occur in some developing countries in agricultural credit policy are similar to those in Indonesia. Based on Farida Siregar et al (2015) shows the result that the KUR Program was launched by the government to realize inclusive financing, especially for micro businesses to fund working capital and investment from formal bank loans. Of 332 respondents from household micro enterprises, 46.7% of respondents had access to KUR and the rest did not use KUR to fund their businesses. The results of this study indicate a determinant factor that significantly affects the access of household micro enterprises to KUR. Gender plays an important role in accessing KUR in household micro enterprises, including men, have a higher chance of accessing KUR than women. Property and property ownership in the name of the husband reduces the role of wife in getting a loan. Women have no interaction with formal institutions and sign loan contracts because they have little experience or low level of education. The longer business tenure and accessibility to alternative funding sources are factors that adversely affect their accessibility to KUR. The main reason is that capital needs are met without the need for KUR access from banks. Another case if the barriers faced by households due to limitations of micro-marketing, economies of scale low, so KUR is not the right solution [4].

With the constraints in accessing credit, it will certainly affect the production activities and welfare levels of farmers. Mamudu Abunga Akudugu (2016) examined the relationship between agricultural productivity and credit in a paper entitled "Agricultural productivity, credit and farm size in Ghana: a case study of Ghana. Overall, the results show that formal and informal credits have a positive and significant effect on agricultural productivity. The impact of formal credit on agricultural productivity is lower than that of informal credit. Although the size of the land is found not to be a linearly significant determinant of agricultural productivity of farm households, the quadratic term is. The implication of the results of this study is that efforts to promote agricultural productivity in Africa in general and Ghana in particular should focus on finding the right size of agricultural land for farmers taking into account the context in which farmers operate to be able to produce so as to produce at optimal pareto. Therefore, in making policy interventions in increasing agricultural productivity in Africa and Ghana in particular should be in accordance with the size of land owned by farmers. This is to ensure that farmers operate within the appropriate range of farm sizes that will make them economically viable. In addition, pre-harvesting contracts that are used as a proxy for market access have an insignificant effect on agricultural productivity. This suggests that interventions aimed at improving agricultural productivity should not focus on providing pre-harvest market contracts as this may lead to a decrease in productivity [5].

2.2 Government Policy on Agricultural Credit

The role of government in supporting the farmer's economy and overcoming the capital problem faced by farmers is by the inclusive financial system which among the programs is low interest credit and how to make the bankable farmers and get complete information about the capital. Some researchers have analyzed programs that have been done by the government. Here are presented research results in several countries as a comparative study.

Amruth Prasad Reddy and Venkata Subbaiah (2012) in his research results show that agricultural credit is a key factor to accelerate agricultural development in India. Farmers' credit needs are three kinds. First, farmers need short-term credit to finance agricultural operations such as purchasing seeds, pesticides and fertilizers. Secondly, they need medium-term credit for the purchase of plows, farm equipment, tractors and other tools to cultivate their land with the help of modern tools Third, they need it for long-term agricultural development such as land improvement, border development and horticulture. To increase agricultural production, they have to borrow more credit. This paper examines the impact of agricultural credit on the working generation of farmers by age, education, caste, size, occupation in the delta and non delta regions of Nellore district of Andhra Pradesh [6].

Roy, Tuhin Narayan (2017) in his research, trying to quantitatively review the current scenario of access to agricultural credits by small and marginal farmers and their performance under the priority lending sector policy (PSL) in India from various secondary sources of information w.e.f. 2001 [7]. The objective of the PSL program is to ensure adequate credit for vulnerable economic sectors such as agriculture. Agricultural credit, in India, increased by 15.78 percent from FY10 to FY15. Despite various policy efforts to lend priorities to poor farmers, very little progress has been made. Nearly 51.9 percent of Indian farmers and 85 percent of marginal and small farmers are under debt but the formal credit provided to them is very poor (30%). Only 40 percent of the total farmers have received Kishan Credit Card. Most PSL programs are linked to interest rates. As per the RBI policy, 40 percent of loans must go to the PSL sector where 18 percent will go to agriculture. But, that's only 13 percent by 2015. Due to changes in norms and regulations, PSL coverage already exists. The share of direct agricultural loans to marginal farmers has fallen sharply from almost 23 percent in 2005 to just 4.3 percent in 2013. They are 85.03 percent at no. ownership and 44.5 percent in the operated area. But, the stock is now only 7 percent and 8 percent respectively. Indian agricultural production and credit levels have shown a positive growth rate. But lending to farmers does not encourage an increase in agricultural credit but also the agribusiness sector and companies involved in agriculture. Thus, the delivery and access of agricultural credit to poor farmers under PSL has not been satisfactory. Experts emphasize the government's proactive role and advise that the design and innovation of PSL policies be implemented effectively. Therefore, it is suggested that more efforts can be undertaken such as alternative livelihoods, poverty alleviation, mainstreaming of marginalized groups and promotion of appropriate technologies / inputs for production, income and quality of life of small and marginal farmers.

Joseph Chisasa and Daniel Makina (2015) shows that there is a positive and significant relationship between bank credit, capital formation and agricultural output in South Africa [8]. The empirical results of this study indicate that, in the short term, capital formation has a positive and significant effect on agricultural output. So while credit may have a negative impact on agricultural yields in the short term, long-term adjustment mechanisms which have a rapid positive impact. Based on the Engle-Granger causality test conducted, it is concluded that there is a positive relationship of (1) bank credit to the growth of agricultural output; (2) agricultural products on capital formation; (3) agricultural products for labor; (4) capital formation into credit; (5) the formation of capital for labor, and bi-directional causality between credit and labor.

Swamy, Vighneswara (2010), in the results of his research show that equal growth is important for inclusive growth which in turn can lead to sustainable growth. Access to finance by the poor is a prerequisite for reducing poverty and sustainable economic development. This study has determined that there is a strong need to strengthen the policy approach to finance the priority sector in India because it has a positive impact on inclusive growth. Given the strong relationship between priority sector lending and inclusive growth, it is imperative for policymakers in general and governments in particular to make efforts to encourage banks and financial institutions to increase lending to priority sectors beyond the prescribed conditions. Priority sector lending in India has been heavily influenced by the lending approach of Government policy in India. Priority sector loans over the period of the year in Indian banks have had a positive impact on inclusive growth. Given the strong relationship between priority and inclusive sector lending, it is imperative for policymakers in general and the government in particular to make an effort to motivate banks and financial institutions in increasing priority sector lending beyond the provisions laid down by the Reserve Bank of India banks in India and expanding their businesses exponentially to reach priority sectors in providing fair and equitable financial aid to achieve inclusive growth [9].

3 Results and Discussion

3.1 The Constraints of Agricultural Credit

Based on a review of several papers, farmers' problems in accessing agricultural credit in detail are as follows:

1. Difficulty Fulfilling the Requirements (Unbankable). To access credit from a financial institution or Bank, the common valuation criteria must be met by the customer using 5C analysis. Character is the nature or character of a person; Capacity is an analysis to know the ability of customers in paying credit; Capital is a state of wealth owned by a company managed by a prospective debtor; Condition is an analysis that considers the economic condition seen from prospective business prospects; Collateral is a guarantee provided by a prospective customer both physical and non-physical. However, in reality farmers are still constrained in meeting the requirements of the Bank (unbankable). Reinforced by the results of research Farida, et al (2014) showed that the agricultural sector is the lowest sector that get KUR. Agriculture is considered a high-risk sector, therefore formal institutions avoid financing the sector for the following reasons; high transaction costs, asymmetric information, low profits, lack of collateral, low education and low literacy.
2. Low Return Loan Guarantee. This is because agriculture is considered a high-risk sector, therefore formal institutions avoid financing the sector for the following reasons; high transaction

costs, asymmetric information, low profits, lack of collateral, low education and low literacy. Generally, banks do not want to finance agriculture due to fluctuating production and uncontrolled price risk. It is like the result of Rahmatullah (2010) research that credit granting is still mostly handled by Central Government Bank, Regional Development Bank or small lending bank although the local bank is closer to the government and agricultural credit distribution is still small compared to the distribution to other sectors [10]. Meanwhile, according to Darmawanto (2008), the Bank in lending is always bound by the prevailing law, in the case of credit distribution to the agricultural sector there is a contradiction of interests, on the one hand the Government / Bank Indonesia seeks credit development in the agricultural sector, on the other hand emphasizes the prudential principle in each disbursement with the risk of any credit degradation without special treatment [10].

3. Credit Market Failure. The bargaining position of farmers at this time is generally weak, this is one obstacle in an effort to increase the income of farmers. The weak bargaining position of farmers is due largely to the market structure at the farm level is monopolistic. In this structure, some traders / wholesalers who control market access, market information, and capital adequately deal with many farmers who lack market access, market information and capital are inadequate, so to access credit even farmers are in a position of lack of information and weak in fulfilling the requirements. So the subsidy or low interest credit given by the government is not so much accessible to farmers. In this structure it is assumed that the trader has full power over the commodity sold by the farmer, but the trader is in the pure competitive market structure of the transaction with the aggregate agricultural commodity market (the trader can not affect the aggregate market of agro-commodities, but only the transactions at the farm level). In addition to facilitate the analysis, it is assumed there is no marketing and processing costs so that the price at the trader equal to the price in the market of producer centers. Not all household loan applications in rural areas are approved by the banks although they are willing to pay higher interest rates (incomplete market). With the incomplete market, farmers borrow their capital at informal financial institutions even with high interest rates. This is supported by Minh Chau Tran's (2016) study that informal credit plays an active role in increasing household income that is constrained by credit when it is a sufficient supplement to formal credit. this per capita consumption variable shows that credit-constrained households receiving sufficient credits from informal sources can improve their per capita consumption.
4. Differences Treatment in Accessing Credit. Farida's research, et al (2014) shows that there are several factors that can significantly affect the access of people's business credit programs. This includes gender, length of business, business barriers, bank accounts, spousal working and other sources of lending. Based on the results of the odds ratio, it was concluded that men were 6.56 times more likely to have access to credit than women. People who have bank accounts have a 3.66 times greater chance of getting credit. New ventures facing capital constraints and those whose partners work tend to access KUR. Gender plays an important role in accessing KUR in household micro enterprises, including men, have a higher chance of accessing KUR than women. Property and property ownership in the name of the husband reduces the role of wife in getting a loan. Women have no interaction with formal institutions and sign loan contracts because they have little experience or low level of education. While Minh Chau Tran's research (2016) shows that young and under-educated households with female heads are under-financed from formal financial institutions. Similarly, the size of agricultural land, labor resources and non-agricultural income play an important role in reducing the status of household credit constraints.

4.2 Government Policy Strategy

With the problems faced by farmers in accessing and managing agricultural credits (formal), the agricultural credit policy instruments are prepared, as follows: (1) Launched low-interest agricultural credit, and (2) Implementing an inclusive financial system.

4.2.1 Low-interest agricultural credit

In facing the problems of farmers in the aspect of funding for the sustainability of farming and meet the needs of households, agricultural credits with low interest is needed. But farmers and small businesses often face obstacles in fulfilling credit access requirements and lack of information. Therefore, the government provides assistance by legalizing credit programs for MSMEs in the form of People's Business Credit (KUR). The program was launched to support government programs in efforts to alleviate poverty and reduce unemployment. The program was adopted on 5 November 2007 by President Susilo Bambang Yudhoyono. Businesses financed by KUR include trade, agriculture, communications, restaurants, and others. The KUR program was born in response to Presidential Instruction No. 6 Year 2007 on the Policy of Acceleration of Real Sector Development and Empowerment of Micro, Small and Medium Enterprises. The Presidential Instruction was followed up with the signing of a Memorandum of

Understanding (MoU) between the Government, Guarantee Institution and Banking on October 9, 2007 as amended by addendum on 14 May 2008 on Credit Guarantee / Financing to MSMEs and Cooperatives or more popular with the term of the People's Business Credit Program (KUR). The objective of the KUR program is to accelerate the development of economic activities in the real sector in the context of poverty alleviation and expansion as well as the expansion of employment opportunities. Result of Limited Cabinet Meeting dated June 17, 2015 which decides that the KUR interest rate for debtors is a maximum of 12% effective per annum. At Permenko 6/2015 the sector funded by KUR only covers the agriculture, fisheries, processing industries, and trade sectors related to the three sectors. The expansion of sector in Permenko 8/2015 is the trade sector is not restricted anymore but covers all business in trade sector and some service sector. As the legal basis for the determination of interest rates charged to debtors from 12% to 9% in 2016, issued Permenko 13 of 2015 on December 30, 2015. The interest rate reduction is intended to further encourage micro, small and medium enterprises. In the implementation or implementation of KUR, there are three important pillars: the government that functions to assist and support the implementation of credit provision along with credit guarantee, Guarantee Institution which acts as the guarantor of credit / financing channeled by Banking and Banking as recipient of guarantee functioned to distribute credit to UMKM and cooperatives using their own internal funds. Referring to the KUR legal foundation above, the KUR program scheme is different from either the empowerment / assistance program to the community or with other program credit schemes that have been issued by the government. KUR is a Working Capital Credit or Investment Credit financed entirely from banking funds, provided to MSME and new Cooperative with maximum credit limit of Rp. 500 million / debtors [12].

Subsequent developments in order to support financing for Micro, Small and Medium Enterprises (MSMEs), the Government through the Coordinating Minister for Economic Affairs decided to lower the KUR interest rate in 2018 from the original 9% effective per year to 7%. Effective interest per year. The new KUR interest will be effective starting January 1, 2018. Coordination meeting attended by Minister of Industry Airlangga Hartarto, Head of BPKP Ardan Adiperdana and related ministry / agency representatives also decided to increase the target of KUR distribution in the production sector (agriculture, fisheries, processing industry, construction and production services) in 2018 to a minimum of 50% of the total distribution target of Rp 120 trillion. This is because MSMEs in the production sector (agriculture, fishery, processing industry, construction and production services) are difficult to get credit / financing from Financial Institutions, since the production sector has a relatively higher risk than the trade sector. In order to encourage the acceleration of KUR distribution in the production sector, the Policy Committee has also prepared a new KUR scheme, specifically KUR for the smallholder plantation sector, and community farming. Special KUR is a KUR scheme given to a group of businesses that are managed jointly in cluster form by using business partners for community plantation commodities, and community farms. The Special KUR ceiling is set at Rp 25 million -Rp 500 million for each individual member of the group. In the future, the Policy Committee will set the KUR ceiling for 2018 for each KUR Distributor, taking into account the recommendations of the Financial Services Authority (OJK).

The role of government in supporting the farmer's economy and overcoming the capital problem faced by farmers is by the inclusive financial system which among the programs is low interest credit and how to make the bankable farmers and get complete information about the capital. Some researchers have analyzed programs that have been done by the government. Here are presented research results in several countries as a comparative study.

4.2.2 Inclusive Finance

Inclusive finance is one of the solutions to overcome farmers' barriers to accessing formal financial systems. The Government launched the National Strategy for Inclusive Finance and the National Council for Inclusive Finance with the issuance of Presidential Decree No. 82 of 2016 on the National Strategy for Inclusive Finance. The objective of which is for the public to gain access to wider financial institutions so that they can improve their business activities such as in agriculture, livestock or fisheries. With this inclusive financial system, farmers who have unbankable become bankable and receive financial management assistance.

Inclusive Finance (financial inclusion) is an entire effort that aims to eliminate all forms of barriers that are price and non-price, to access the community in utilizing financial services. This inclusive finance is a national strategy to encourage economic growth through equal distribution of income, poverty alleviation and financial system stability.

In the National Strategy for Inclusive Finance, the inclusive financial strategy is outlined in six pillars: financial education, public finance facilities, financial information mapping, supporting policies / regulations, intermediation and distribution facilities, and consumer protection. Some examples of inclusive financial implications in helping farmers other than KUR are as follows:

1. Digitalization of payment of Business to Person (B2P) and Government to Person (G2P). The financial gap in rural areas is still very large, where most of the small farmers are still untouched by the services and products of banks. Without having a bank account, many small farmers are running their economy in cash, both in receiving payments for

the sale of crops and in receiving social assistance from the government. The digitization of Business to Person (B2P) and Government to Person (G2P) payments in agriculture is evolving into a new opportunity for electronic money service providers to help drive rural growth, in line with their efforts to expand services outside of urban areas and into segments the new one. Digital payments to electronic wallets belonging to smallholders will reduce the time and cost of cash transactions because they no longer require a long journey just to receive and pay in cash. In addition, this has also resulted in increased security and transparency. The digitization of payments will be an entry point for inclusive finance for farmers who have not been touched by banks, where the use of electronic money in agricultural payments will create a financial identity for them and be able to open the door to wider financial services such as savings and loans.

2. Information Systems for Farmers & Fishermen (SIPN). In the agricultural sector there is a need for up-to-date and inaccessible information. The existence of asymmetric information has resulted in bargaining position of farmers and fishermen becoming weak. Therefore, in order to overcome this problem, it is necessary to provide information system for farmers and fishermen, ie input material price such as fertilizer price, seeds, pest medicines, supporting information, such as weather and farming / distribution, and product selling price. Information Systems for Farmers and Fishermen (SIPN) or Mobile Agriculture should be simple, user friendly and at an affordable cost. One model of information dissemination is through mobile phones. This is considering the high number of mobile phone users in Indonesia [13].

4 Conclusion

Credit constraints on the agricultural sector as a high-risk business, therefore formal institutions are less interested in financing the agricultural sector on the grounds of high transaction costs, asymmetric information, low profits, lack of collateral, education of farmers is relatively low. In addition, most banks do not want to finance agriculture due to fluctuating production and uncontrolled price risk. While the constraints of the farmers in obtaining formal credit is a complex procedure, there should be collateral as well as high payment delay fees, long distances and less information about capital.

Government policy on agricultural credit is the strategy of inclusive Finance is a national development strategy to encourage economic growth through equal distribution of income, poverty alleviation and financial system stability. This community-centered strategy needs to target groups experiencing barriers to accessing financial services. The inclusive financial strategy explicitly targets the groups with the greatest or unfulfilled needs for financial services ie the three categories of people (the poor, low-income, working poor / poor and the near-poor) and three cross-categories (migrant workers, women and the population underdeveloped regions). To realize a sustainable inclusive financial program, coordination between Bank Indonesia and the relevant ministries and institutions is required in the framework of developing, prioritizing and implementing the program, and monitoring and evaluating the program. With good coordination is expected to increase the goal of community access to financial services can be achieved. One of the inclusive financial programs needed to address farmers 'problems in terms of funding for sustainability of their farming and to meet their household needs is low-interest agricultural credit is needed such as KUR and farmers' development from unbankable to bankable.

References

1. Central Bureau of Statistics (BPS). https://www.bps.go.id/
2. Minh Chau Tran,Cristopher Gan, Baiding Hu. Credit Constraints and Their Impact on Farm Household Welfare: Evidence from Vietnam's North Central Coast Region. International Journal of Social Economics, 782-803, (2016)
3. Pavel Ciaian, Jan Falkowski d'Artis Kancs, Access to credit, factor allocation and farm productivity: Evidence from the CEE transition economies. Agricultural Finance Review Vol. 72 No. 1, (2012)
4. Farida, F., Siregar, H., Nuryartono, N., & Intan, E. K. Micro Enterprises' Access to People Business Credit Program in Indonesia: Credit Rationed or Non-Credit Rationed? International Journal of Economic Perspectives, 9(2), 57-70, (2015)
5. Mamudu Abunga Akudugu. Agricultural productivity, credit and farm size nexus in Africa: a case study of Ghana. Agricultural Finance Review Vol. 76 No. 2, 2016 pp. 288-308, (2016)
6. Amruth Prasad Reddy, Venkata Subbaiah. Impact of Agricultural Credit on Employment Generation of The Farmers. Journal of Commerce & Accounting Research Volume 1 Issue 1 January (2012)
7. Roy, Tuhin Narayan. Study on Access to Farm Credit by the Small and Marginal Farmers in India under the Policy on Priority Sector Lending (PSL) Economic Affairs; New Delhi Vol. 62(1), 39-45. (2017)
8. Joseph Chisasa. Bank Credit and Agricultural Output in South Africa: Cointegration, Short Run Dynamics and Causality. The Journal of Applied Business Research –31(2), (2015)
9. Swamy, Vighneswar. Financial Development and Inclusive Growth: Impact of Government Intervention in Prioritised Credit. Zagreb International Review of Economics & Business;13(2) 55-72, (2010)

10. Rahmatullah Rizieq. Analisa Dampak Kredit Pertanian pada Pertumbuhan Sektor Pertanian dan Ekonomi. Jurnal Visis Ekonomi, **9** (2), (2010).
11. Darmawanto. Pengembangan Kredit Sektor Pertanian. Program Magister Ilmu Hukum Program Pasca Sarjana Universitas Diponegoro, Semarang, (2008)
12. http://www.bi.go.id/id/perbankan/keuanganinklusif/program/sipn/Contents/Default.aspx
13. http://keuanganinklusif.co.id/artikel/81-pembayaran-di-bidang-pertanian-berbasis-digitalisasi

The Formation of Food Cluster in Indonesia

Donald Crestofel Lantu[1], *Sri* Herliana[2*], *Mia* Rosmiati[1], *Qorri* Aina[1], *Nur* Lawiyah[1]

[1] Institut Teknologi Bandung, School of Business and Management, Bandung, Indonesia
[2] Institut Teknologi Bandung, School of Life Sciences and Technology, Bandung, Indonesia

Abstract. Cluster has an important role in developing the existing resources in an area to be economic value. Companies gain competitive advantage through competing with each other. However, there is now an increased awareness that to ensure survival, it is necessary to balance industrial advocacy and personal interests. Thus, cluster operations are characterized by competition and cooperation, where the role of quadruple helix plays a role in it. SME clusters occur in every country, considering that SMEs are an important element in the economy of the country. Most SMEs in developing countries are located in industrial clusters. Despite the limitations in organizational resources and capacity, the grouping of companies in geographic proximity is capable of improving the performance of the companies within them. Therefore, cluster formation becomes the main attraction for deeper examination, how clusters are formed and how the process and role of elements in it. This study involves two different case studies of the chips and milk dairy clusters, both located in Cimahi, West Java. West Java is one of the provinces that have potential in the development of food and beverage clusters. This research uses qualitative data approach and supported by literature data support. From the analysis result, both clusters have different cluster forming approach, where the formation of clusters of chips, formed spreads and dairy cluster vertically.

1 Introduction

West Java province has potential in the growth of SMEs food-based cluster. Thus, West Java has become one of the government's priorities in developing food clusters [1]. Clusters play an important role in the competitive process in business, where group resources affect the company's internal resources [2]. Among them are increasing the credibility of the company, the products, and the provision of access to the market. Thus, establishing a fair and supportive trade in market information research [3]. The development of successful industrial clusters can be likened to art and science, where the human relationship in it symbolized with art. The symbol of science represents an analysis of industry data available for making key decisions [4]. Cimahi is one city in West Java which has Human Development Index is above the average of West Java province. However, one component of the Human Development Index is the ability of purchasing power turned out to have a low score.

Therefore, the local government is pursuing a strategy of local economic development potential to expand the purchasing power of the pro-poverty [5]. Strategy of local economic potential development by local government is by developing cluster of SMEs in accordance with the existing potential. There are four clusters were developed, namely the food and beverage industry clusters, textile industry and textile products clusters, handicraft industry cluster, and telematics industry cluster. As mentioned before, the potential of West Java is one of them is in the food and beverage industry cluster. Therefore, researchers further examined the case study of food and beverage clusters in Cimahi as the main focus of this study. In this study, researchers examined two types of industrial and food clusters, namely industrial clusters chips in the Pojok Cimahi and dairy cow industry clusters in Cipageran Cimahi. Researchers focused the research area on the process of establishing food and beverage industry clusters, which could represent the process of clustering SMEs in Indonesia. Due to the cluster formation model can help to succeed the local potential economic development strategy.

2 Literature Review

2.1 Forming cluster

Companies gain competitive advantage through competing with each other. However, there is now an increased awareness that to ensure survival, it is necessary to balance industrial advocacy and personal interests. Thus, cluster operations are characterized by competition and cooperation. Where the role of quadruple helix plays a role in it [6]. Policy-based SME cluster formation has been implemented by the Government of Indonesia since the 1970s. Aims to improve their competitiveness; as SMEs become an important engine for national growth [7,8]. In the phase of cluster

* Corresponding author: sri.herliana@sbm-itb.ac.id

formation and growth, where the growth phase consists of 4 phases including agglomeration, emerging, developing, and mature. Transformation can happen anytime, either when a cluster is formed or when it matures. Even the possibility of cluster to disperse always exist in various phases [9]. Each country has a different formation of the cluster initiative. This is due to differences in regional policy, the role of state agencies, and the function of the cluster itself [10]. Government policy is required to perfect existing clusters or develop newly emerging clusters. Adaptation of policies tailored to the important cluster character is done, due to the unique character of the cluster, so universal implementation of the policy cannot be done. There are five most common types of cluster policies that can be applied and adapted, namely; mediation policy, policy of demand stimulation, educational policy, policy of stimulation of external connections, and policy of creation of favorable structural conditions [10]. Based on Tambunan (2005) study, there are four cluster types in Indonesia that is 2rtisanal, active, dynamic, and advanced. Where the type of 2rtisanal is a cluster consisting of Micro enterprises and has limitations in resources. The active type is a cluster consisting of SMEs with expertise and using better technology than the artist type. The dynamic type is a cluster consisting of SMEs that have a wide trading network, have adequate expertise and technology. The advanced type is a cluster type that has been stable in every line of business and form of cooperation and market [11].

2.2 SME's Food and Beverage cluster

Most SMEs in developing countries are located in industrial clusters. Despite the limitations in organizational resources and capacity, the grouping of companies in geographic proximity is capable of improving the performance of the companies within them [8, 12]. Much literature discusses that food and beverage clusters are very closely related to geographic and local potential. In which key organizations are formed to manage and develop clusters [6] As mentioned earlier, the formation of food and beverage clusters can be one of the strategies to improve people's purchasing power. Where in its development can help reduce the poverty rate [5]. Industry clusters stimulate and enable innovation [13], certainly in it there is the product commercialization process. Where the commercialization process requires a lot of strategic marketing activities and decisions and related tactics, it takes a driving force that comes from innovation and understanding of their activities in choosing decisions [14]. The formation and development of clusters cooperate with local government bodies. Including for food and beverage industry clusters, where government agencies and private institutions are adapted to the needs of clusters [15].

3 Methodology

The purpose of this research is to know and analyze how food and beverage clusters are formed. Therefore, this study uses a double case study of two clusters in Cimahi, including the chips cluster in the Pojok and the milk dairy cluster at Cipageran. In collecting the data, the researcher used a qualitative data [16] approach obtained from the in depth unstructured interviews to the SMEs in these two clusters. Secondary data support is obtained from various journals, books, and government agency reports. The selection of these two clusters as primary data sources is due to differences in the process of cluster formation. Especially these two clusters are in the same area, namely Cimahi City.

4 Analysis and Discussion

4.1 Chips's Cluster

Pojok Cimahi is famous as the industrial center of chips. The advantages of chips products produced and sold in this cluster include a wide selection of products, variety of raw materials used, taste choices offered, and affordable and competitive prices. The initial formation of clusters in this cluster is motivated by the success of one SME which is their neighbor. These successful SMEs motivate neighbors to create the same business by imitating its business processes. Although they imitate their business processes, every SME in this cluster is doing a little bit of innovation in its business processes. Thus, they have different target markets as well as with products that are made, due to adjusting to their target market. Based on the data collected and the results of the analysis, it is known that the process of forming this cluster formed by spreading see one of successful SMEs in this cluster. The formation of this naturally chips cluster invites quadruple helix to contribute to the development of clusters. Figure 1 illustrates the process of cluster formation in the chips cluster at Pojok Cimahi.

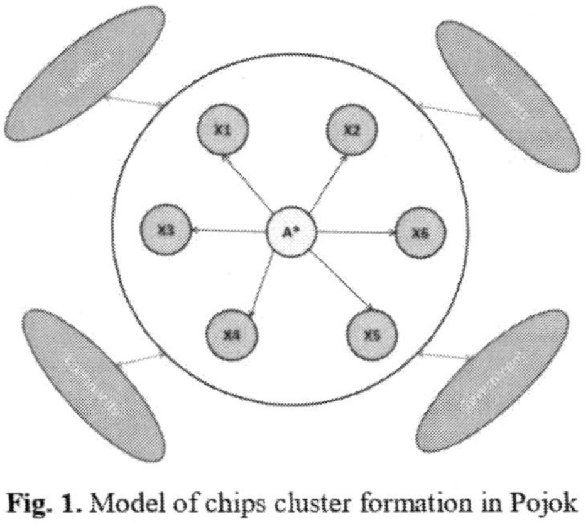

Fig. 1. Model of chips cluster formation in Pojok

Figure 1 illustrates the process of forming the chips cluster in the Pojok Cimahi is spread. Where SME A is portrayed as a successful pioneer of business chips, then neighbors of the surrounding are tempted to do the same business and succeed. Viewed from the cluster type that is formed as described in the study Tambunan (2005), this chips cluster is included in the category of active cluster type, where in this cluster involves specific expertise and the use of technology. The skills required in this type of business are expertise in production and research and development product. Where the use of technology required is for the field of production and marketing. This naturally occurring cluster, invites quadruple helix to give their respective roles directly to the cluster, where the role of government gives its policy to help this cluster develop well. Academia provides a role in the form of training in production and marketing development as well as providing consulting services. The existence of this cluster provides widespread opportunities for cooperation with other business lines, such as raw material suppliers and marketing dealers. The last role of the community is to help introduce the name of Pojok Cimahi as the center of chips industry in Cimahi. The appropriate policy to be applied in this cluster is policy of demand stimulation policy, because this cluster has shaped its market and create stable market demand [10].

4.2 Dairy Milk's Cluster

Just like the previous explanation of the Pojok Cimahi cassava chips cluster, the Cipageran milk cluster may be called a cluster because in it there are many dairy farmers and dairy business groups, which produce a wide variety of dairy-based products, such as milk's soap, milk's chips, milk's seroja, milk's rangginang, milk's dodol, caramel candy, yoghurt, and other products. It cannot be separated from the role of government in seeing the huge potential that this cluster possesses. Together with educational institutions, the government is working together to train the housewives to be made a dairy group, where one of the training coaches finally went directly to the cluster development process in the form of opening a Cipageran milk center store. This store has a role in collecting products of business groups and independent in selling dairy products that will be marketed by this store. In contrast to the cimahi Pojok cassava chips cluster, where cluster formation is formed on personal initiative, this cluster of Cipageran milk centers is formed on the basis of the role of government, educational institutions, and private institutions. Thus, the existence of this Cipageran milk cluster can provide added value to housewives including skill and additional income. For farmers and local people have the advantage that this cluster is more famous because there are many activities that live in it.

The initial formation of this cluster is based on the existing potential of dairy cow breeding potential that produces cow's milk. Nevertheless, the potential of this area cannot be maximized to be named as a cluster, due to the lack of number of SMEs. Then, the municipal government in cooperation with educational institutions provides training and assistance to the majority of housewives to be given skills training in processing milk. The training and mentoring work well until there are many dairy business groups growing in this cluster. They together learn how to entrepreneurship such as in research and develop dairy innovation products, team management in groups and their conflicts, and other challenges. Hence, business groups where it can be said as a container of SMEs get a lot of experience and science valuable in building their entrepreneurial competence. The education gained from the training helped to open the insights of business groups to be creative in interpreting their potential, so that although some groups disbanded. Former executives and members have the initiative to continue the group's business independently. Where the boards and group members have entrepreneurial competence in daring to try new things, innovate, persistent, and never give up in building their business. The description of the process of dairy cluster formation in Cipageran is vertically formed as seen in Figure 2, where initiation of cluster formation is initiated by the local government in collaboration with other quadruple helix elements. An overview of the cluster-based cluster formation process previously described in the Tambunan (2005) study. The difference is the illustration of the process of milk dairy cluster formation is more emphasis on the formation and role of small groups, where each group will form a business unit.

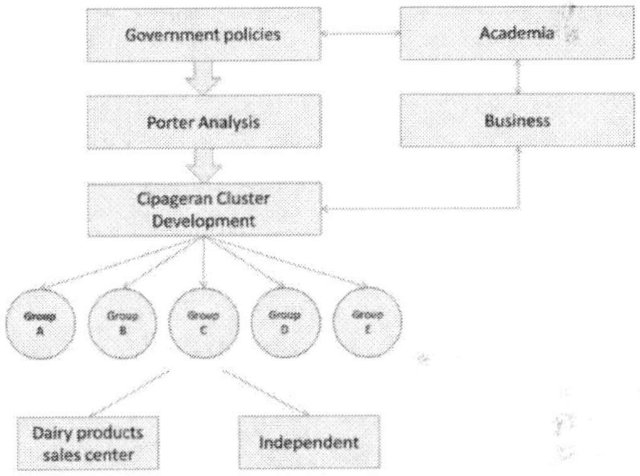

Fig. 2. Model of Dairy Milk's cluster in Cipageran

The formation of this Cipageran milk cluster uses education policy[10]. Where the government cooperates with other quadruple helix makes the curriculum to foster entrepreneurship spirit and to read and learn. The majority of the population has a low level of formal education. Hence, the existence of this business training activities as well as encourage their learning interest. This type of dairy cluster is the same as the chips cluster, which is the active type, where in this cluster involves specific expertise with the use of technology. Expertise in this cluster is in term of caring for cattle to produce quality milk and certain skills in making various dairy products.

5 Conclusion

Clustering has different approaches. This is motivated by the motivation in forming the cluster. These two types of clusters have different formation approaches. Where the cluster of chips stands independently and naturally, a dairy cluster stands on the initiation of local government policy in developing potential. Although the processes in cluster formation are different, these two clusters have been beneficial in the economy even in small geographic areas. At the very least, cluster formation has encouraged people's purchasing power and ability to innovate in product commercialization. The formation of chips clusters was formed due to successful neighboring motivations that then spread to neighboring surrounding areas. This phenomenon actually provides a positive competition. Although their businesses are the same, they are able to develop different target markets between one SME and another. As discussed earlier, the formation of dairy clusters is formed on the initiation of local governments in collaboration with other quadruple helix elements. The formation of small groups with the output of business units helps in developing the capacity and competence of the participants. Although in the process many participants who resigned or dismissed their business, among them some are back to build business independently armed with knowledge and experience in the group. Same as expressed by Handayani et al., (2012), that the transformation of cluster innovation or business dissolution can occur in various phases in clustered. Because the cluster is a merger of art and science, where in solving the problems needed creativity and good analysis so that clusters can survive and develop.

References

1. M. Industri, Pertumbuhan Industri Melampui Target. (Media Industri, 2010)
2. J.E. Fensterseifer, J.L. Rastoin. Cluster resources and competitive advantage: A typology of potentially strategic wine cluster resources. International Journal of Wine Business Research, 25(4), pp.267–284, (2013)
3. M. Tieman, Halal clusters. Journal of Islamic Marketing, 6(1), pp.2–21, (2015)
4. N. Reid, M.C. Carroll, and B.W. Smith, Critical Steps in the Cluster Building Process. EcDevelopment, 6(4), pp.44–53. (2007)
5. Kementerian Pemberdayaan Perempuan dan Perlindungan Anak Republik Indonesia, Manual Model Pelaksanaan Kebijakan Industri Rumahan Melalui Cluster Makanan dan Minuman, (2005)
6. L.P. Dana, K.E. Winstone, Wine cluster formation in New Zealand: Operation, evolution and impact. International Journal of Food Science and Technology, 43(12), pp.2177–2190, (2008)
7. M. Najib, A. Kiminami, Innovation, cooperation and business performance. Journal of Agribusiness in Developing and Emerging Economies, 1(1), pp.75–96. (2011)
8. M.K. Mawardi, T. Choi, and N. Perera, The Factors of SME Cluster Developments in a Developing Country: the case of Indonesian clusters. ICSB World Conference Proceedings, pp.1–28. (2011)
9. N.U. Handayani, A. Cakravastia, L. Diawati, and S.N. Bahagia, A conceptual assessment model to identify phase of industrial cluster life cycle in Indonesia. Journal of Industrial Engineering and Management, 5(1), pp.198–228, (2012)
10. E. Popkova, A. Natsubidze, E. Kukina, V. Urodovskikh, E. Ioda, and N. Neustrova, Problems and perspectives of implementation of cluster initiatives in business in developing countries. European Research Studies Journal, 18(3), pp.187–196. (2015)
11. T. Tambunan, Promoting Small and Medium Enterprises with a Clustering Approach : A Policy Experience. Journal of Small Business Management, 43(2), pp.138–154, (2005)
12. A,K. Singh, R.L. Shrivastava, Critical success factors of rice mills located in a cluster. International Journal of Productivity and Performance Management, 62(6), pp.616–633, (2013)
13. S.A.A. Wijaya, Studi peranan klaster industri, hambatan bisnis, dan kepemilikan asing terhadap intensitas kapital di indonesia. AGORA, 3(2), pp.1–5. (2015)
14. L. Aarikka-Stenroos, and T. Lehtimäki, Commercializing a radical innovation : Probing the way to the market. Industrial Marketing Management, 43(8), pp.1372–1384. (2014)
15. Bank Indonesia, Kegiatan Bank Indonesia Dalam Mendukung Ketahanan Pangan Berbasis Klaster Komoditi Unggulan (Panduan Replikasi). (2014)
16. J.W. Creswell, Qualitative Inquiry and Research Design: Choosing Among Five Approaches. California: Sage Publications, Inc. (2007)

Determinant Factors of Information Technology Adoption in Creative Business and The Result of Its Application: Case of SMEs Cluster in South Bandung

Wawan Dhewanto, *Yuliani Dwi* Lestari, *Sri* Heliana*, *Qonita Himmatul* Aliya, *Nur* Lawiyah

Institut Teknologi Bandung, School of Business and Management, Bandung, Indonesia

Abstract. The expansion of information technology and electronic commerce in Indonesia has provides the opportunities for entrepreneurs to develop their business. It can be seen from the rapid growth of SMEs and creative business in Indonesia increased from year to year. Most SMEs have adopted information technology and electronic commerce (e-commerce) for their business. E-commerce was really famous in today business to be discussed. In general e-commerce is radically changing traditional ways of doing business. The government says ecommerce has huge potential to build the economy of the nation because the large number of internet users increase continuously and become the first factors of adopting technology of ecommerce by the organization. Various research has been analyzed widely the adoption of ecommerce by SMEs. The purpose of this research is to examine determinant factors of adoption of technology ecommerce in SMEs and the impact on their organizational business as a result of level of success. Firstly, empirically investigate the determinants factors in internal and external by conducting interview. Secondly, provide new direction addressing why the business adopt ecommerce and what are concerning factors in adopting ecommerce with a successful. Analysis was done by comparing and analyzing six SMEs in South Bandung in a cluster that have same of types of products and adopt technology ecommerce but have a different in many ways. As the result of this study, limited human resource capacity and skills is the main constrains faced by SMEs when adopting technology ecommerce.

1 Introduction

The growth of SMEs in Indonesia has rapidly increased from year to year. General Secretary of the ministry of cooperatives and SMEs, Agus Muharram said, about 8 million more new SMEs growing in the year of 2016, 10 million more being targeted at the end of 2018 and its predict to continue growing by 5% of population in Indonesia or about 13 million more new SMEs at the end of 2019. It is aligning with the rapid advances in technology that changed the trading system from originally offline being online and create the fast-growing SMEs in this last five years [1]. The expansion of information technology and electronic commerce in Indonesia has provides the opportunities for entrepreneur to develop their business. Most SMEs have adopted information technology and electronic commerce (e-commerce) for their business. Although it has not reached 50% of the total number of SMES, but its growth steadily and significantly increases. Data from the Directorate General of small and medium Industry in 2015, around 40 percent from the number of SMEs who already utilizing the sophistication of information technology to develop its business. However, the sales of ecommerce in Indonesia are extremely high, in 2017 around 98.5 trillion rupiah obtained from the sales in ecommerce [2].

E-commerce was really famous in today business to be discussed. In general e-commerce is radically changing traditional ways of doing business. The government says ecommerce has huge potential to build the economy of the nation. The magnitude of the potential of ecommerce is not separated from the development of the internet users in Indonesia. Large number of internet users in Indonesia increase continuously and become the first factors of adopting technology of ecommerce by the organization. According to kompas.com [3], more than 50 percent or around 143 million people have connected the internet network throughout the 2017. Much increased from the previous two years that reached 93.4 million people. Report from the Association of Internet service provider in Indonesia (2015), the majority of internet users as much as 72.41 percent is urban people. The utilization of internet itself already much further, not only to communicate but also to purchase goods, order a transport, to do business and work. From the total number of internet users in Indonesia, the potential of ecommerce seen in 77% of internet users that used internet for searching information about product and shop online [4].

* Corresponding author: sri.herliana@sbm-itb.ac.id

As a comparison of the benefits of using ecommerce for business growth, SMEs that use the internet or ecommerce can grow 10% over than haven't used it [5]. Given the significance of the utilization of ecommerce in business development of SMEs and in line with the vision of the Ministry of industry to encourage the SMEs in utilize information technology to compete on the global market, an in-depth study need to be done by doing research about the adoption of e-commerce by SMEs and what determinant factors that affected the success of the SMEs. The purpose of this research is to examine determinant factors of adoption of technology ecommerce in SMEs and the impact on their organizational business as a result of level of success. Firstly, empirically investigate the determinants factors in internal and external by conducting interview. Secondly, provide new direction addressing why the business adopt ecommerce and what are concerning factors in adopting ecommerce that brought on the maximal results.

2 Literature Review

Information technology has the potential of helping SME in supporting market research and global marketing. The growth of information technology has helping business owner in tackle their problem with issues such as cost control and accounting, competition, merchandising, and the need for more skilled personnel [6]. Arthur Andersen (1995) found that having computers, upgrade systems, access internet and use an online service were more likely than average of companies that fast growing. Recent media have been a great deal on how small business are using information technology to compete with the huge companies within their industries. Massey (1987) urged small business owners in order to exploit their networking potential they should considering the revenue of generating potential of computers. Customer service, ordering, sales analysis, correspondence, and distributor support are include as suggested application in information technology. Small businesses encounter special problems when implementing information systems, among them lack of experience, cost overruns, and inadequate expert support [7,8]. They run the risk of never "catching up" with larger firms and being bought out by more efficient larger enterprises [9]. There is also concern over the ability of SMEs to benefit from these networks. The empirical evidence suggests that small and medium enterprises are ill-equipped to benefit from these new technologies.

2.1 E-commerce and Small Medium Enterprise

Electronic Commerce (e-commerce) is a concept that is commonly described as the process of buying and selling goods or services on the World Wide Web of the Internet [10] or the process of selling or exchanging products, services and information through the network information including the internet [11]. Laudon and Traver, in Ahmad et al. (2014) defined e-commerce as a set of transaction processing products, services and information exchange using the internet or intranet computer network [12]. Huniati et al. (2009), describe the benefits of ecommerce in particular SME business activities include: providing broader opportunity for perpetrators of SMES to enter the national market and the global market where not previously affordable, increase the intensity of the communication between business, increase the acquisition of access to information, improve and expand marketing and transactions between consumers and suppliers [13]. Purbo and Wahyudi (2001) says companies that use Ecommerce will get a number of benefits, namely [14]: (a) Opening the new revenue stream that is more promising that cannot be found in traditional transaction systems; (b) Increase market exposure; (c) Lower operational costs; (d) Expand the reach, increase customer loyalty, improve supplier management; (e) shorten production time and increase the value chain. The important things in the process of e-commerce business is to build relationships with consumers by providing confidence and guarantee security in the transaction. Brand building activities are key in obtaining a sustainable competitive advantage [15]. According to Anderson and Srinivasan (2003), trust and perceived value is an important determinant in satisfaction on loyalty [16]. Based on the type, e-commerce is divided into 4 categories for this research that are, social media, website, email, and marketplace. Social media in ecommerce is media that frequently used by people to communicate with other then utilized by the business to attract people, it is included Instagram, Facebook, Line@, BBM, Twitter, and Youtube. Some research categories website as social media but on this research, website is separate categories because people doesn't frequently used website to communicate and compare with other social media, in using and creating account of website need more challenging than social media that free account. Marketplace is the media create as an intermediary in business transaction, the seller will not get the payment directly from the buyer but will get the payment from the market place as intermediary after the transaction success with the buyer. Marketplace are included Lazada, Tokopedia, Bukalapak, Shopee, Blibli, Elevenia, Matahari Mall, Zalora, Bhineka, JD.ID and many more [2].

2.2 Factors Influencing IT (e-commerce) adoption in SME

Some researchers have posited the factors that influence the adoption of ecommerce. Olatokun and Kebonye (2010) said, factors influencing SMEs to adopt information technology affected by the pressure of external factors i.e. competitors, consumers, business partners, media and the public [17]. Those factors influence directly or indirectly in the adoption of information technology. Size also affects the adoption of information technology, where the smaller size of business will be the smaller desire to advantage the information technology. This is because of the limitations or resource scarcity, financial constraints, the ability to compete are low, and human resource constraints. According to Hussin and Noor (2005) explained that the factors influence in adoption of e-commerce on SMES in developing countries include [18]: (a) Relative benefits will received by SME adoption of e-commerce such as: cost efficiency, outreach to a wider market (b). Compatibility, that shows how to implement new technology innovations in accordance with the existing business process on SMEs, (c). Complexity that indicates the level of complexity or difficulty faced by SMES by adopting e-commerce, (d) Trialability or the ability to be tested, e-commerce can be tested if it is able to bring a shift or change in business and the existence of support funding to cover the costs to start testing, (e) Observability or can be observed, that shows the ability to see the results of the benefits from the implementation of e-commerce. Other researcher said [19], Factors that affect SMEs in adopting e-commerce in developing countries are follows a) Organizational Factors including: awareness, Business Resources, Owner's Support, Human resources, I.T. Expertise, and Technology Resources. b). External Factors including: Market forces, Government, Supporting industries, and Competitive pressure. c) Innovation Factors including: Relative advantage, Compatibility, Cost, and image. Based on the research above in general, organization, technology and environment are the factors that influenced SMEs in adopting information technology or e-commerce.

The adoption of information technology, on this research is ecommerce, by SMEs can divided into 2 part these are internal and external factors that exist in SMEs. From the studies have been done, all the determinant factors include in three major aspects that are organization, technology and environment [20]. Organization, which is in the internal factor, environment is an external factor, while technology can be internal and external factors that affects SMEs in the adoption of ecommerce. Based on study above, internal factors include; awareness, business resource, owner support, human resource, IT expertise, technology resource, size of business (financial), and innovation factors (compatibility, cost, and image). While external factors included; competitors, competitive pressure, customers, business partner, market forces, government policy, supporting industries, and market trend.

3 Methodology

The method used on this research is descriptive analysis that support for this research to gain deep understanding of the findings and research conduct to create SWOT analysis. Qualitative method also conducts by observing and interviewing the respondents. One of the purposes of this research are to provide direction addressing what are concerning factors in adopting ecommerce to be success. Comparing and analyzing a few SMEs that used ecommerce is a solution. Then the respondents of this research are six SMEs that have same of types of product and adopt technology ecommerce but have a different in many ways. This research was taking the SMEs in south Bandung in the field of fashion textile as an object.

4 Finding Arguments

One of the uniqueness of SMEs compared to large scale business unit is located on the management style. In general, most SMEs rely heavily on intuition the owners, the decision-making process on SME is done centrally [21]. These conditions make the individual context becomes one of special consideration in the adoption of e-commerce [22]. Many people have accepted the innovation as the important of individual's competence. The success of the adoption of e-commerce for SMEs depends on the level of mastery of information technology from the owner, as initiator and determinant business decisions [22,23].

4.1 SWOT analysis of Factor influencing

Based on interview, these are internal and external factors influenced SMEs in adopting ecommerce. Those factors have positive impact but also can bring negative impact for the SMEs in adopting technology. The SME should aware with the possibility that might happen when they are adopting ecommerce. From the internal and external factors, creating SWOT analysis to be more clearly understanding the factors that can be strength, weakness, opportunities, and threat faced by the SMEs when adopting ecommerce.

Table 1. SWOT Analysis of Information Technology

INTERNAL	**STRENGTHS** - Awareness of technology - Owner support to adopt ecommerce - Do not require a lot of cost in operational - Size of business (Small and micro business can run ecommerce) - Fast branding by using ecommerce - Distribution of shipping worldwide	**WEAKNESSES** - Less technology knowledge - Less IT expertise - Unstable management (most of the SMEs) - The complexity on using technology
EXTERNAL	**OPPORTNITIES** - Market trend in using IT - Government policy that support the development of IT (ecommerce) by SMEs - Customer behavior in using internet - Market forces in today's technology - Supporting industries such as logistic company	**THREATS** - Large number of competitors - Competitive pressure (in pricing, quality, branding, etc.) - No barrier entry

Adoption

On the Table 1, internal factors creating strength and weakness for adopting ecommerce, while external factors create the opportunity also threat for SMEs in adopting ecommerce. But the strength and opportunities on Table 1 above can be the positive impact and beneficial to adopt technology by SMEs. The weakness of this factors can be obstacles from adopting technology that are less technology knowledge, limited skill in IT, complexity in exploiting

IT. All the obstacles factors are come from the human resource ability. But human is the fast learning, the weakness can be the strength when the human skill ability in IT are growing. Research conducted by Yulimar and Setiawan (2008) explains that the compatibility, support management, organizational readiness, external factors, and the perceived benefits have influence positively and significantly to the adoption of e-commerce. Those results also show the adoption of e-commerce have positive and significant influence on the company performance [24].

4.2 Concerning factors in adopting ecommerce

In the previous explanation, SWOT analysis was creating to determine the factors in adopting ecommerce by SMEs. What is the strength and weakness in adopting ecommerce also the opportunity and the threat that should be concerned in build the business. The next step after knowing the factors affected SMEs in adopting ecommerce, is how to apply this ecommerce correctly to obtain maximal in results. As the goal in business is to get the highest possible income. As it is known, the adoption of ecommerce has many benefits, but not all SMEs can get the maximal benefit from ecommerce. It can be seen from the achievement of SME after using ecommerce. Because, not a few of SMEs that failed in operating the ecommerce. The existence of other factors that should be concerned by SMEs after adopting ecommerce technology to be successful in the application.

This research was interviewing the respondent to analyze the concerning factors to be success in applying ecommerce. There are 6 respondents who participated in this study, all of which are engaged in the same field and have the similar product that is curtain. Even they sell similar product with only differentiate in several motif design, they have many similarities but also the differences. The companies named by LG, AG, IC, ZN, UG, and GO. LG Company started their operational in 2014, ZN and GO Companies started their operational a year after LG Company in 2015, while other companies that are AG, IC, and UG started their company in 2016. All of the companies are selling curtain and the accessories of curtain itself. From the six companies, only three companies owned an offline store that are LG, IC, and GO Companies. Other three companies only use online sales, because create the offline store takes a lot of cost. But ZN company thinks to have an offline store after collecting the fees, because ZN's owner says have an offline store can increase the credibility and the existence of their business. Five of the six companies have a tagline as their marketing media, only GO company do not have a tagline. Further description can find in the Table 2. Based on the results of study in the Table 2 above, the average of companies started their business in 2015-2016, all of the companies still classified as Startup Company for duration less than 5 years. Those company are located in the same area in South Bandung. They even got the supply of their raw materials from the same distributor. But it can be seen that their market reach is around the nation. All of the companies make the transaction via online or internet, but several company that are LG, IC, and GO provided offline store that can be directly visited by the customers. The six companies selling the similar product with good quality, with the number of varieties that are not significant. The company also has multiple accounts in their media ecommerce with competitive price. The critical differences from this six companies are in the revenue they obtained that become the level of their successful in adopting ecommerce.

Number of percentages of revenue on Table 2 obtained from the company's revenue split with the total revenue of all company. As the result in percentage of revenue on Table 2, shows that LG Company has superior in the revenue compared with other company, while other companies have a percentage that is not much different. This research will analyze the highest and the lowest revenue of the respondents. The lowest revenue obtained by GO Company which founded a year after LG Company. From the six companies, LG Company stand longer and the first in this business on that area based on the interview. AG Company although still under the LG on the revenue only a half of LG Company, but they are growing rapidly outperformed than other companies in fact ZN and GO company that stands before AG's company. The Table 2 also shows the number of accounts of ecommerce owned by the companies. All of companies have more than three accounts in ecommerce media. But LG Company have most multiple accounts followed by AG and IC Company. Only LG and ZN Company who owned their website, as for the others, almost all companies use the same in media e-commerce that are social media, email and marketplace. Based on the interview, all of companies stated their largest in revenue gained from the use of media marketplace. It is the reason why all of the companies joined many marketplaces with multiple accounts. Because they believe having many accounts will enlarge their opportunities to be seen by customers.

Based on the interview result, that are factors influenced the six companies on their successful. The most consideration on the successful in adopting ecommerce that are management of the company itself especially in term of management of its information technology. The concerning factors in adopting ecommerce are summarized below:

1. IT management. It is included human resource and skill capacity in using technology. The owner of LG Company has knowledge and skill in IT more than the other owner. As state before most SMEs are relied heavily on intuition the owners, make the decision-making process is done centrally. It was concluded that the commitment of the business owners was very influential in the success of the process of adoption. Business owners in this matter assessed to have a significant influence and authority against other individuals to accept the changes. Secondly the employee that engaged in the

company also have a big role in adopting technology successfully. Human resource is really important, on this field human resource required is that have skill in using IT. The company need resource of human that want to be learning to develop themselves following the changes of time, the changes of technology.

2. Price. Price become very important by SMEs who adopted ecommerce. Because with using ecommerce, customers can easily compare the price with other competitors. As customer behavior to get the lowest price with the best quality. This is what AG's company implement. They are placing the lowest price than other companies to attract more customers. Somehow lowering the price even only Rp.100, cheaper than other company can be affected. This is call as pricing strategy.
3. Number of accounts of media ecommerce. In term of ecommerce, multiple accounts same as the number of stores or branch owned. The more number of accounts, the more possibility of transaction that will happen. Have multiple accounts also make the product easy to be found by customers. Internet search engine will randomly display the product, the more accounts or online shop the more possibility the product will be display when customer click the keyword. Have many accounts should be coupled with a number of human resources that are able to operate it. On this case ZN Company doesn't have enough resource to operate their ecommerce, and it became one of the reasons ZN's revenue are below AG's and IC's revenue although ZN establish ahead of them but ZN cannot compete with them because of less human resource.
4. Quality of product. Quality of product in ecommerce cannot be ascertained and measured clearly because the customers do not see the product directly in person. The product can only be seen digitally by the photo or video with additional description regarding the product. It makes the photo of the product is very important as a representation of the quality of products as well as the image of the company. The company must be able to display photos of the products as good and interesting as possible without eliminating the authenticity of the original image of the product.

Those are the factors influence the six companies on their successful. It can be the concerning factors for other SMEs when deciding to adopt ecommerce technology to operate ecommerce appropriately.

5 Conclusions

The adoption of information technology by SMEs divided into internal and external factors. Those factors influenced the SMEs in adopting ecommerce, it can give positive impacts but also negative impacts. Then using SWOT analysis to be grouping the factors to find the strength, weakness, opportunity, and threat which can help the SMEs in adopting ecommerce. All the determinant factors include in three major aspects that are organization, technology and environment. Limited of human resource in skill ability of using technology become the weakness also the obstacle in adopting ecommerce, but that can be covered by learning and training. This research proves other studies who stated organization, technology, and environment are the determinants factors influenced in adopting technology. From the three factors, based on the result on this study, organization factor is the most influencing factor to adopting ecommerce successfully. Because the organization who operate the business and will operate the adopting of ecommerce. Operate ecommerce appropriately will bring to expected result. There are four factors in the organization that should be concerned by SMEs in order to get the maximum result in adopting technology ecommerce; a) IT management, it is included human resource and skill capacity in using technology, b) Pricing, c) Number of accounts of media ecommerce, d) Quality of product, can be seen as photo product. The four factors can increase the probability to be success in adopting ecommerce.

References

1. Ministry of Cooperation and Small and Medium Enterprises of the Republic of Indonesia. Data UMKM. Retrieved April 22, 2018 from http://www.depkop.go.id/berita-informasi/data-informasi/data-umkm/
2. katadata.co. (2018). databoks.katadata.co.id. Penjualan e-Commerce Indonesia Mencapai US$ 16 Miliar: Retrieved 2018 from https://databoks.katadata.co.id/datapublish/2018/02/12/2022-penjualan-e-commerce-indonesia-mencapai-rp-16-miliar
3. F.K Bohang, tekno.kompas.com. Jumlah Pengguna Internet Indonesia? Retrieved 2018 from https://tekno.kompas.com/read/2018/02/22/16453177/berapa-jumlah-pengguna-internet-indonesia
4. A.N. Hanum, A. Sinarasri, Analisis Faktor-Faktor Yang Mempengaruhi Adopsi E Commerce dan Pengaruhnya Terhadap Kinerja Umkm (Studi Kasus Umkm Di Wilayah Kota Semarang). 15. (2017)
5. A. Nuvriasari, Peran Dukungan Organisasional, Kompetensi Teknologi Dan Lingkungan Eksternal Dalam Rangka Mendorong Pengadopsian E-Commerce Pada Usaha Kecil Menengah. Siasat Bisnis, 205-217. (2012)
6. C. Nyandoro, Factors Influencing Information Communication Technology (Ict) Acceptance and Use in Small and Medium Enterprises (Smes) In Kenya. Capella University. (2016)
7. M.J. Smith, M.V. Flinders, Quangos, Accountability and Reform: The Politics of Quasi-Government, (Springer, 2016)
8. X. Granell, Multilingual information Management: Information, Technology & Translators, (Chandos Publishing, 2014)

9. .J.Y.L. Thong, C.S. Yap,CEO characteristics, organizational characteristics and information technology adoption in small businesses,Omega, Elsevier, Vol. **23**(4), pages 429-442, (1995)
10. J. Shim, A. Qureshi, J. Siegel, & R. Siegel. The International Handbook of Electronic Commerce. (The Glenlake Publishing Company Ltd, Chicago, 2000)
11. E. Turban, D. King, J.L. Lee, M. Warkentin, H.M. Chung, Electronic Commerce 2002: A Managerial Perspective, (Pearson, 2002)
12. S. Z. Ahmad, A.R. Abu Bakar, T.M. Faziharudean, & K.A.M. Zaki,. An empirical study of factors affecting e-commerce adoption among small and medium sized enterprises in a developing country: Evidence from Malaysia. Information Technology for Development, Vol. **21** No. 4. (2015)
13. Z. Hunaiti, R. Masa'deh, and M. Mansour, Electronic Commerce Adoption Barriers in SMEs in Developing Countries: The Case of Libya, IBIMA Business Review, Vol. **2**, 2009
14. O.W. Purbo, A.A. Wahyudi. Mengenal e-Commerce, (PT. Elex Media Komputindo, Jakarta, 2001)
15. M. Gommans, K.S. Krishnan, & K.B. Scheffold, From Brand Loyalty to E-Loyalty: A Conceptual Framework, Journal of Economic and Social Research, **3**(1), pp. 43-58, (2001)
16. R.E. Anderson, K. Srinivasan, E-Satisfaction and E-Loyalty: A Contingency Framework, Psychology and Marketing, **20**(2), 123-138, (2003)
17. Olatokun, W. et al. e-Commerce Technology Adoption by SMEs in Botswana. International Journal of Emerging Technologies and Society, **8**(1). (2011)
18. Hussin, H. et al. Innovating Business Through E-Commerce: Exploring the Willingness of Malaysian SMEs. *The second International Conference on Innovation in IT*. (2005)
19. K. Salah, B, Irwin. A Structural View of E-Commerce in SMEs In Least Developing Countries. *18th European Conference on Information System*. (2010)
20. Almoawi, A. et al. Applying the Role Model in Determining the E-Commerce Adoption on SME In Saudi Arabia. Asian Journal of Business and Management Service, **1**(7), 12-24. (2010)
21. R.C. Macgregor, M. Kartiwi, Perception of barriers to e-commerce adoption in SMEs in a developed and developing country: a comparison between Australia and Indonesia. Journal of Electronic Commerce in Organizations, **8** (1), 61-82. (2010).
22. R. Rahayu, J. Day, Determinant Factors of E Commerce Adoption by SMEs in Developing Country: Evidence from Indonesia. Procedia-Social and Behavioral Science **195**, 142-150. (2015)
23. E. Cloete, S. Courtney, & J. Fintz. Small businesses acceptance and adoption of e-commerce in the Western Cape Province of South Africa. Electronic Journal on Information Systems in Developing Countries, Vol. **10** No. 4. (2002)
24. V.A. Yulimar, A. Setiawan, Analisis Faktor-faktor yang Mempengaruhi Pengabdosian electronic commerce dan Pengaruhnya Terhadap Kinerja Perusahaan. Journal IST AKPRIND Yogyakarta. (2008)

Table 2. Respondent description

Company	Product	Quality and Price	e-commerce	Percentage of Revenue
LG	It has about 60 types of curtains with a different motif or color. Provide the most choice of motifs and colours.	Provide good quality product with a high price than other companies.	SosMed: Instagram (3), facebook ads, BBM, youtube Website Email MP : Tokopedia (5), Bukalapak (2), Lazada (1), Shopee (6), Blibli (3)	35,7%
AG	It has about 50 types of curtains with a different motif or color.	Provide good quality and medium quality of product with the lowest price than other companies.	SosMed: Instagram, Facebook Ads Email MP: Tokopedia (4), Bukalapak (1), Lazada (1), Shopee (7), Blibli (1)	17.1%
IC	It has about 40 types of curtains with a different motif or color. Provide most complete in accessories of curtain than other	Provide good quality product with a medium lower price.	SosMed: Instagram (3), facebook ads, youtube Email MP : Tokopedia (5), Bukalapak (2), Shopee (5), Blibli (2)	14,3%
ZN	It has about 45 types of curtains with a different motif or color.	They provide good quality product with a medium high price than other.	SosMed: Instagram (3), facebook ads, Website Email MP : Tokopedia (3), Bukalapak (2), Lazada (1), Shopee (4), Blibli (1)	12.2%
UG	It has about 45 types of	Provide good quality	SosMed: Instagram (2), facebook ads	11,4%

	curtains with a different motif or color.	product with a medium lower price.	Email MP : Tokopedia (4), Bukalapak (2), Lazada (1), Shopee (5), Blibli (1)	
GO	It has about 40 types of curtains with a different motif or color.	Provide good quality product with lower price.	SosMed: Instagram (1), facebook ads MP : Tokopedia (4), Bukalapak (2), Lazada (1), Shopee (5), Blibli (1)	9,3%

*SosMed : Social Media MP : Market Place ( ) : number of accounts

Quality Analysis Of Organic Rice Variety Mentik Susu And Sintanur Nutritional Approach

Sri Handayani[1], Muhammad Irfan Affandi[2], Sussi Astuti[3]

[1] *State Polytechnic of Lampung, Departement Economics and Business*
[2] *Lampung University, Departement Agribusiness*
[3] *Lampung University, Departement Agricultural Technology*

Abstract Organic rice production in Indonesia is increasing due to the tendency of consumers who start to consume healthy food and one of them is organic rice. Varieties cultivated by farmers in Lampung Province is mentik susu and sintanur based on high yields and climate suitability. The quality of organic rice can be known through nutritional approach. The purpose of this research is to analyze quality comparison of organic rice of mentik susu and sintanur varieties with nutritional approach. The research methodology used is laboratory research. Data analysis methods used to answer the objective of a proximate test to determine the nutrient content of organic rice in both varieties of mentik susu and sintanur. Nutritional content that is cultivated is carbohydrates, fats, proteins, water, fiber, and ash content. The result of the analysis shows that carbohydrate, protein, and nutrient content of organic rice of mentik susu variety was higher than sintanur varieties. While the fat content, water content, and ash content of organic rice varieties mentik susu is lower than the sintanur varieties. In general it can be concluded that the quality of organic rice varieties mentik susu better than sintanur varieties.
Keywords: Organic Rice, Nutritional Content, Proximate

INTRODUCTION

Food demand is always increasing as population growth increases. The main food ingredients of the community consist of rice, maize, and cassava (Handayani, 2016). As a major food ingredient not only in Indonesia but also in the world, rice has a strategic role in community welfare policy. Indicator of community welfare is the availability of rice both quantity and quality. Increased public awareness for healthy living, starting with a healthy diet. This is in synergy with the increasing amount of organic rice consumption because it has a high nutrient content and free of chemicals. The amount of demand for organic rice in Indonesia reaches 1.1 quintals and always increases every year (Ahmad, 2009). In addition, the benefits of organic rice obtained, among others, is to help improve soil fertility due to reduced application of chemical fertilizers in the soil, minimization of production costs for farmers because only use organic fertilizer / compost, without pesticides, as well as good health benefits for the body.

The main nutrient content in food consists of carbohydrates, proteins, fats, fiber, and water. Carbohydrate is the largest nutrient content in rice and as a source of energy for the body (Hasan & Astuti, 2011). Protein is needed for growth and repair damaged tissues. Fat is one of the important substances but the amount should be limited. Fiber is needed for body digestion, and mineral water functions in the body's metabolism. Each element of nutrients is needed in certain levels for the health of the body. According to Waluyo (2007) in Wahyudin (2008), in his study of differences in organic and non-organic rice, concluded that organic rice has a higher nutrient content than non-organic rice. The content of carbohydrates and proteins in organic rice more easily decompose / digested by the body. While the content of carbohydrates and proteins in non-organic rice does not decompose / is not easily digested by the body. Furthermore, quality of organic rice compared with non-organic rice such as organic rice is relatively safe for consumption because it does not contain chemical residues, rice texture of organic rice more pulen, color and shelf life is better than non-organic rice (Andoko, 2010).

Proximate analysis is performed to determine the main component of a material. For food, the main components generally consist of moisture content, ash, carbohydrate, protein and fat (Hui, 2006). This analysis becomes necessary to do as it provides the main content data of a foodstuff. Another factor is the proximate analysis in the diet with respect to the nutritional content of the foodstuff. Nutritional levels need to be known as they relate to the quality of the food.

Organic rice production in Lampung Province is located in Pringsewu and Lampung Selatan districts. Types of cultivated varieties are Mentik Susu and Sintanur. The reason for the use of this type of variety is because of its resistance to pest and its taste is delicious. This research was conducted to determine the nutritional content and quality of local organic rice of Mentik Susu and Sintanur variety, and organoleptic properties of both varieties. Levels of proximate studied were moisture content, ash content, fat content, protein content, coarse fiber content, and total carbohydrate content.

According to Sari et al. (2014) the end of the quality assessment is how much the level of acceptance / consumer preferences of the product in terms of quality components. In general, food products, the value of subjective quality is more prominent than the nature of objective quality. Based on the description, this study aims to examine the nutritional quality of organic rice varieties of Meentik susu and Sintanur .

METHOD

Tools

Tools that used are Porcelain Grille, Eksikator, Erlenmeyer, Hot Plate, Pumpkin Kjedhal 300ml, Buret 50ml, Electric Oven, a set of distillation apparatus, a set of Soxhlet tools, Electrical furnace, and analytic scales.

Materials

The ingredients that used are alcohol, boric acid (H_3BO_3), Hydrochloric acid (KCl), sulfuric acid (H_2SO_4) Penoftalein indicator, Filter paper, Petroleum ether, NaOH, Organic Rice, varieties of milk and synthetic milk.

Proximate Analysis Procedure

(1) Water content (Method of Oven / AOAC1970, Ranggana 1979)

Weigh the smoothed example 2-5 g. In a porcelain cup that has been known to weigh.

Dry in oven at 105 ° C for 3-5 hours.

Then cool in the Extractor and weigh, reheat in oven for 30 minutes, cool in the Extractor and weigh this treatment repeated until the constant weight (the weighing increment is less than 0.2 mg respectively)

Weight reduction is the amount of water in the material.

$$\% \text{ water} = \frac{B - C}{A} \times 100\,\%$$

A = Sample weight
B = plate + wet sample
C = plate + dry sample

(2) Ash Content

Weigh the smoothed example 2-5 g. In a porcelain cup that has been known to weigh

Burn the cup containing the example on the stove until it is not smoky.

Then spice in the furnace at a temperature of 500-600^{0}C for 3-4 hours (until ash is obtained whitish)

Cool the saucer and ash in the Extract then weigh.

$$\% \text{ Ash} = \frac{B - C}{A} \times 100\,\%$$

A = The weight of the sample (the weight of the cup containing the sample - the empty cup)
B = Grail + Ash
C = empty plate

(3) Crude Fiber

Crude fiber is a residue from food or agriculture after being treated with acid or alkaline boiling, and consists of cellulose with little lignin and pentosan.

Puree the material up through a 1mm diameter sieve.

Weigh 2 grams of dry matter and extraction of fat with soxhlet,

Move in a 600 ml Erlenmeyer flask, add 200 mL of SO_4 H_2 solution to boil (1.25 gr H_2 SO_4 concentrated / 100 ml = 0.255 N H_2 SO_4) and cover with refrigerant, boil for 30 minutes with occasional wobble

Filter suspension through filter paper and residue left on filter paper washed with hot water until it is not acidic anymore (test with litmus paper)

Remove the residue from the filter paper into the erlenmeyer again with a spatula, and the rest cleaned with boiling NaOH (1,25 gr NaOH / 100ml = 0.313 N NaOH) of 200 ml until all the residue goes into the erlenmeyer. Bring to a boil by cooling while sometimes shaking for 30 minutes.

Strain through a filter paper already known by weight or crucified Gooch crucible and known by weight, while washed with K_2SO_4 10 lar solution

Wash again residue with boiling aquades and then with 15 ml Alcohol 95%

Dry filter paper or crucible with its contents at 110^{0}C until constant weight (1-2hour) cool in desiccator and weigh.

Residual weight = rough fiber weight

$$\% \text{ crude fiber} = \frac{B - C}{A} \times 100\,\%$$

A = Weight sample
B = Filter Paper + Fiber
C = Filter Paper

(4) Protein (Gunning Method)

weigh 0.5 to 1.0 gr of mashed material and put in kjeldahl flask, add 1 gr K_2S or anhydrous Na_2SO_4, and 10 - 15 ml of concentrated H2SO4. If the distruction is difficult to be added 0.1 - 0.3 gr $CuSO_4$ and gojok

Then performed distruksi above the electric heater in the fume hood, first with a small fire, after the smoke lost fire raised, the heating is ended after the liquid becomes clear colorless again

Created blank treatments, such as the above treatment without an example.

After cooling add to 100 ml of kjeldahl aquades flask, and 45% NaOH solution until the liquid is base, install the kjeldahl flask immediately on the Distillation apparatus.

Heat the Kjeldahl flask until ammonia evaporates all, the distillate is accommodated in an erlenmeyer containing 25 ml of HCl 0.1N which is given a PhenolPtalein indicator 1% of a few drops. The distillation is terminated after the distillate is reached as much as 150 ml or after the outgoing distillate is not base. Excess of 0.1 N HCl in distillate is titrated with standard base solution (0.1 N NaOH solution) to pink.

% N = (ml blank of NaOH – ml sample of NaOH) X N NaOH X 14,008 / (mgr. sample) X 100

% Protein = % N X conversion factor

(5) Determination of Fat and Oil (Soxhlet Method)

Weigh carefully 2 - 5gr. Examples that have been mashed, wrap with filter paper. insert in the Soxhlet Extraction tube.

Flow cooling water through the condenser.

Install the extraction tube on the Soxhlet distillation apparatus with solvent (Petrolium Benzen, Chloroform, N. Hexan etc.) to taste. The extraction is done for 4-5 hours.

Dry the cup containing the fat on the Oven with a temperature of 100-105^{0}C for 30 minutes.

The residual weight in the fat plate is expressed as the weight of fat and oil

$$\% \text{ fat} = \frac{B - C}{A} \times 100\,\%$$

A = Weight sample
B = Cup + Fat
C = empty plate

(6). Total Carbohydrate Determination

Carbohydrate content is done by using carbohydrate method by difference method. Carbohydrate by difference is obtained from the reduction of the number 100 with the presentation of other components.

RESULT

Rice not only serves as a staple food but also serves as a functional food ingredient that has an active component that is useful for health. Types of organic rice that is widely used are varieties of Mentik Susu and Sintanur. This type of rice contains carbohydrates, fats, proteins, fiber and minerals consumed as a healthy food. Based on descriptive research to know the description of nutrient content in organic rice varieties of Mentik Susu and Sintanur, got the result of examination of nutrient content from Quality Laboratory of Lampung University gave the following result:

Table 1. Result of organic Rice Organic Rice Nutrient

Variabel	Result (%)	
	Mentik Susu variety	Sintanur variety
carbohydrate	80.8079	79.4400
fat	0.8201	1.0761
Protein	5.2475	4.8463
water	12.0900	13.3087
fiber	0.5299	0.6868
Ash	0.5046	0.6421

Based on Table 1, the results of testing of organic rice of Mentik Susu and Sintanur varieties can be explained as follows:

a. Carbohydrate

Proximate test results obtained carbohydrate values for varieties of Milk Milk equal to 80,8079% and Sintanur varieties of 79.4400%. Based on this it shows that carbohydrate content of varieties of milk milk is bigger than Sintanur varieties. Research conducted by Nani Ratnaningsih et al (2010) obtained carbohydrate result of 72,49 - 83,94%. Carbohydrates are a nutrient that serves to produce energy for the human body. In addition, carbohydrates also serve as a sweet giver on food, protein saver, regulator of fat metabolism, helps the expenditure of feces.

b. Fat

Fat content of organic rice varieties of Mentik Susu obtained results of 0.8201% and Sintanur varieties of 1.0761%. This shows that the fat content in the variety of milk milk is smaller than the varieties of Sintanur. Based on the results of laboratory tests of the Industrial Research and Consulting Center Surabaya on March 18, 2004, yielded data that organic rice has a lower fat content than inorganic rice. Although both varieties tested were both organic, the quality of organic rice of Mentik Susu variety was better than that of Sintanur varieties. Fat is an important food substance to maintain the health of the human body. Fat works as a source of energy, dissolves vitamins so that it can be absorbed by the intestine, and prolongs satiety.

c. Protein

Protein content of organic rice varieties of Mentik Susu obtained result of 5.2475% and Sintanur varieties of 4.8463%. This shows that the protein content of Mentik Susu varieties is greater than that of Sintanur varieties. Research conducted by Nani Ratnaningsih et al (2010) obtained the results of protein by 5% -10%. Protein is the main ingredient for plant cells, animals and humans. About ¾ solid body is protein. Proteins function as growth and maintenance, the formation of essential bodily bonds, regulating water balance, maintaining the neutrality of the body, the formation of antibodies, transporting nutrients, and energy sources. Based on the description can be explained that the quality of organic rice nutrition Mentik Susu better than Sintanur varieties.

d. Water

Water content of organic rice of Mentik Susu varieties yielded 12.0900% and Sintanur varieties 13.3087%. Water is the largest component in the structure of the human body. Water serves as a medium for transfortation of nutrients, removes metabolic waste, regulates body temperature during physical activity, and maintains blood volume balance. The result of premium quality standard

(SNI 6128-2015) shows good quality of rice if its water content is less than 14%. Differences in water content in varieties of Mentik Susu and SIntanur can be caused by the process of storage and separation process of rice from different grains, rice separation is not done simultaneously because the process of getting rice varieties following the planting period. Based on the point tersbut can be explained that the quality of organic rice nutrition Mentik Susu better than Sintanur varieties

e. Fiber

The content of organic rice varieties of Mentik Susu obtained by 0.5299% and Sintanur varieties of 0.6868%. The fiber content consists of carbohydrates such as cellulose, hemicellulose, pectin and lignin. This fiber can not be hydrolyzed by digestive enzymes. Materials that contain lots of fiber will accelerate the transit time of food waste in the intestine so that it becomes shorter. The benefits of dietary fiber can lower cholesterol in the blood. According to Kahlon et al (1994), high fiber in rice also affects the mechanism of cholesterol reduction. The mechanisms underlying cholesterol reduction are the ability of lipid-absorbing fibers in the gastrointestinal tract and increased excretion of bile acids. Lattimer et al (2010) revealed that the fat-deprived rice can be used to make the product high.

f. Ash Content

The content of organic rice ash of Mentik Susu varieties obtained by 0,5046% and Sintanur varieties of 0.6421%. Research conducted by Nani Ratnaningsih et al (2010) obtained the ash of 0,71 - 1,69%. Ash content is the residue obtained after the rice oxidation due to heat, ash content as a measure of mineral content in rice. That is, the use of biological fertilizer (compost) which many affect the amount of ash content in organic rice.

CONCLUSIONS

From the results of proximate analysis can be concluded that the carbohydrate content of organic rice Mentik Susu varietiesgreater is 80.8079% compared to Sintanur varieties of 79.4400%. The fat content of organic rice of Mentik Susu varieties is smaller that is 0.8201% compared with Sintanur varieties is 1.0761%. Protein content of organic rice of Mentik Susu varieties is greater that is 5.2475% compared with Sintanur varieties is 4.8463%. Water content of organic rice of Mentik Susu varieties is smaller that is 12,0900% compared with Sintanur variety that is 13,3087%. The content of organic rice of Mentik Susu varieties is smaller, that is 0.5299% compared with Sintanur varieties is 0.6868%. The content of ash of organic rice of Mentik Susu varieties is smaller that is 0,5046% compared with Sintanur varieties that is 0,6421%. In general it can be concluded that the nutrient content of organic rice Mentik Susu varieties better than Sintanur varieties.

REFERENCES

[1] Andoko, Agus. (2010) Budidaya Padi Secara Organik. Penebar Swadaya. Depok.

[2] Handayani, Sri. (2010) Analisis Produktivitas Dan Kinerja Adopsi Teknologi Singkong Sambung (*Grafting Cassava*) *Sebagai Bahan Baku Bioetanol Di Kabupaten Lampung Timur. Tesis. Universitas Lampung.*

[3] Handayani, S. (2016, September). Analisis Keuntungan dan Sensitivitas UMKM Makanan Ringan Berbahan Baku Singkong di Kecamatan Gedong Tataan. In *Prosiding Seminar Nasional Teknologi Pertanian*.

[4] Hasan, V. and Astuti, S., Susilawati. (2011) Indeks glikemik oyek dan tiwul dari umbi Garut (Marantha arundinaceae L.), suweg (Amorphallus campanullatus BI) dan singkong (Manihot atullisima). *J. Tek. Industri dan Hasil Pertanian*, *16*(1), pp.34-50.

[5] Hui, Yiu H. (2006) *Handbook of Food Science, Technology, and Engineering Volume 1*. Taylor & Francis Group. Boca Raton

[6] Lattimer J, Mark D, Haub.NN. (2010) Effect of Dietary Fiber and its Componentson Metabolic Health. Journal of Nutrition.

[7] Ratnaningsih N, Ekawatiningsih P. (2010) Potensi Beras Hitam Sebagai Sumber Antosianin dan Aplikasinya pada Makanan Tradisional Yogyakarta. Bidang MIPA dan Sains.

[8] Sari, D.K., S.A. Marliyati, L. Kustiyah, A. Khomsan dan T.M. Gantohe. (2014) Uji Organoleptik Formulasi Biskuit Fungsional Berbasis Tepung Ikan Gabus (Ophiocephalus striatus). Agritech. Jurnal Teknologi Pertanian. 34 (2): 120-125

[9] Wahyudin, Imam. (2008) Analisis Perbandingan Kandungan Karbohidrat, Protein, Zat Besi Dan Sifat Organoleptik Pada Beras Organik Dan Beras Non Organik. Skripsi. Universitas Muhammadiah Surakarta.

[10] Windani, Isna. (2009) Preferensi Konsumen terhadap Beras Organik di Kota Yogyakarta.Tesis. Universitas Gajah Mada. Yogyakarta.

Indonesian Cultural Preferencein Designing User Interface

Andhika Giri Persada*

Universitas Islam Indonesia, Department of Informatics, Yogyakarta, Indonesia

Abstract. Interface design is the first thing users can see when accessing website. First impression is presented here. If they feel interested, users will continue exploring website. But, if they feel not interested, users will leave website with negative impression. They will be reluctant to access the website in the future, because the first impression is not good. In order to design good and interesting interface design, there is no particular methods can be used to absolutely measure it. Measuring the interface design is closely related with the domain of social behavior. Each user has different perspective, which means has different taste of design. So far, there is no existing method that can be used to measure the taste of interface design accurately. Interface design tend to be measured subjectively. The only way to measure interface design is use usability principles, which is tend to focus on the interaction not to the interface design itself. Indonesia has there are 1331 tribes across the country which are have unique and richness of cultural ornament. Their ornament has known well by people because it had been applied into their various kinds of product, such as carving, clothes, and house. Finally, the purpose of this research aim to provide new idea about cultural preference in order to design the interface. At the end of this research, we offer methods which can be used to ensure the interface design based cultural is met with the usability principles.

1 Introduction

Interface become the first things that users can see when they are interacting with the systems. Unfortunately, users which are accessing systems are come from different socio or cultural background. Therefore, cultural aspect can be considered in the designing user interface [1] In dot net era, there are a lot of information that will be accessed utilizing systems, especially website. Website is special because it can be accessed by heterogeneous peoples, across countries and cultural boundaries. So far, generalizing Interface that is designed do not consider local wisdom yet. In order to introduce something regarding local wisdom, cultural aspects should be considered to be implemented [2]. The reason why cultural-based interface design must be considered to be applied, because different user has different preference of design and perception across the countries [1, 3]. So, it is very interesting to discuss about these issues in the rest of papers. In fact, cultural preference is less considered to be used by designer. Designer may believe that good design should be proven well against the principles of design. Aside from those principles, designer may set aside them. Whereas, several industries such as Electrolux, General Motors, and IKEA had experienced on failed production due to missing the cultural aspect on their products [4]. In this paper, we take examples on the official website of Indonesia local government. Why local government website? Because local government website expected able to represent the diversity of social culture. In Indonesia, there are diverse range of social culture. Each culture has special and unique characteristic. According to BPS (Statistical Center of Indonesia) data in 2016, there are 1331 tribes in Indonesia [5]. Each tribe has its own unique characteristics, such as language, ornament, belief, ceremony, carving, clothes, etc.

Based on that fact, it is interesting to discuss and attempt to relate between tribe characteristics and interface design of website. Specifically, how to apply tribe characteristics into interface design of local government website. Each of Indonesian tribe goods have unique ornament, pattern, and staining, so it isappropriate to be used as case study on this topic of research. Reinecke and Bernstein had revealed on their study, Asian websites contains more multimedia elements, such as animation and staining. Otherwise, European websites contains less multimedia elements, but the information which is presented is more structured [2]. This conclusion shows that each region has potentially different taste of design. There are a lot of website in Indonesia has not implemented cultural preference into their interface design yet. Surely, this not aligned with the richness of tribes in Indonesia. Even though, cultural preference that is implemented into interface design hopefully can attract users feeling. The feeling expected can influences users when measure website. This study aims to provide another point of view about the interface design of website. Each Indonesia tribes has a lot of resource to be implemented into interface

* Corresponding author: andhika.giri@uii.ac.id

design. One of the example, Batik is one of the Indonesian cultural heritage that is famous in this country. Batik has interesting and diverse style in their pattern. It is potential to be used into interface design. If those cultural resources are utilized, it is expected that the local wisdom can be seen by users when accessing website. In 2002, McSweeney criticized about the generalizing of the interface design, which treat them equal in wherever location [6]. Specifically, contribution from this paper is trying to gain another point of view in order to design the cultural-based interface of website.

In the rest of the papers, we divide into several sections. First section, we provide the objectives and limitations of the study. Second, we provide some literature studies which has relation to the issues of the relationship between cultural preferences and interface design. Third, we discuss about the result of the literature studies. Forth, we discuss about the cultural preference that exist in Indonesia and its potential implementation. Last, we provide conclusion based on whole discussion, then it is closed by future works that is give recommendation to increase the empirical evidence related to the results obtained from this study.

2 Objective and Limitation of Studies

This paper is just an early part of the study that should be broader in the future. The scope of study in this paper not specific on the technical discussion, such as what methods to be used to apply cultural preference into the interface design. In this study, focus lies on the ideas about how cultural preference is related to the interface design. In this study, official local government websites are used as case study. Why official government website? Because there are 34 official government websites in Indonesia [5]. Each website represents each province where one or some tribes are living. The discussion of this research begins with the literature studies of previous similar research about the advantages of cultural preferences. Those literature studies can be used to formulate the problems. Next, we discuss about the potential relation between cultural preference and interface design. Indonesian tribes are used as case study. Indonesia is a country that has a lot of tribes. Each tribe has richness of cultural tribe. The richness and potential ornament then discussed and can be applied into interface design. This research hopefully become the initial discussion that is expected to be a trigger on the future study. This study was closed by a brief discussion of the principle of usability. A brief discussion about the principle of usability is used to accommodate the part of doubt regard to the result caused by this study. Usability principles tend to be considered to ensure the usability of website is maintained.

3 Previous Studies

There are a lot of papers discussed about the relation between interface design and cultural preference [1-4, 8-9]. Based on Hostfede (2010), culture can be defined as the collective programming of the mind that distinguishes the member of one group or category of people from others. There are several culture meaning refer to, they are tribes or ethnic group, political or social menegement, and organizational [7]. Indonesian tribes have resources to be used in this study. Based on Lee and Harada, cultural preference can be considered to understand the cultural behaviour of users [8]. So, cultural approach is expected to be used to attract user's attention. Cultural dimension should become necessity to be applied into the theory and practices of interface design strategy [9]. There is similar result about the cultural preference on the interface design conducted from several studies before. All of those studies said that there is relevancy between the cultural aspect and the interface design.Those results are expected to represent results in other similar studies that can not be presented in this papers. So far, there is no existing method that can be used to measure quality of the interface design accurately [10]. Difference culture means difference users behavior. Difference user behavior means difference preference of design [11]. Although it is related, it does not mean it has positive impact on the usability [8]. Only a few studies stated that cultural preference has positive relationship on usability [2]. So, there are still some disagreement about the usabilities impact on the implementation of cultural preference. Moreover, interface which is designed based on cultural preference can perceived as more attractive. Interface based cultural preference can attract users where come from certain regional.

4 Indonesian Culture and Interface Ornament

There are 1331 tribes or ethnic groups in Indonesia. Different regional, linguistic, and country are strongly effect onthe way they measure interface design [3, 4].Those tribes have unique cultural patterns whereas implemented into their carving, ornament, clothes, etc. Such as Batik, one of the most popular cultural heritage in Indonesia. Batik has unique pattern that is implemented in several usage, both formal and informal need. Based on Callahan (2005), provided three cultural aspects of user interface, they are staining, navigational support, and information density [3]. Two of those three aspects, staining and navigational support, can be accomodated when implemented cultural preference on Indonesian tribes. Example of the navigational support adopted from the

Javanese culture can be seen in Figure 3. Javanese is one of tribes in Indonesia. Staining, can be seen in almost all cultural style, such as Batik as we can see in Fig. 1 (credit to www.welovesolo.com/tag/batik/) [12].

Fig. 1. Example Ornament of Batik

In Indonesia, majority of the entire websites, whether private or state, have not implemented their local culture into their websites. On the Table 1, shown the list of the official government website. This data is taken on January 2018.

Table 1. List of Government Website and Its Characteristics

Name of Province	Symbol of Culture	Scenery of Culture
Aceh	No	Yes
Bali	No	No
Banten	No	Yes
Bengkulu	No	No
Gorontalo	No	Yes
Jakarta	No	Yes
Jambi	No	No
Jawa Barat	No	Yes
Jawa Tengah	No	Yes
Jawa Timur	No	No
Kalimantan Barat	No	Yes
Kalimantan Selatan	No	No
Kalimantan Tengah	No	No
Kalimantan Timur	Yes	No
Kalimantan Utara	No	No
Kep. Bangka Belitung	No	Yes
Kep. Riau	No	No
Lampung	No	No
Maluku	No	No
Maluku Utara	Cannot be accessed	
Nusa Tenggara Barat	No	No
Nusa Tenggara Timur	No	No
Papua	No	No
Papua Barat	Cannot be accessed	
Riau	No	No
Sulawesi Barat	No	No
Sulawesi Selatan	No	No
Sulawesi Tengah	No	No
Sulawesi Tenggara	No	No
Sulawesi Utara	No	Yes
Sumatera Barat	No	No
Sumatera Selatan	No	Yes
Sumatera Utara	No	No
Yogyakarta	Yes	Yes

There are three indicators used, they are official government logo, symbol of culture, and scenery of culture. Almost every province places official government logos. Symbol of culture means there are some ornaments, such as logos, buttons, which adopted from cultural aspects. Scenery of Culture means the design implemented cultural preference on their theme, such as background, languange, and sound effect. As we can see in Fig. 2, official website of Jawa Barat who has implemented cultural preference almost comprehesively. It has implemented scenery of culture on its interface design, but has not implemented the symbol of culture perfectly.

Fig 2. Jawa Barat Government Website

In the Fig. 3, the official website of Yogyakarta shows informal impression. They has implemented both symbol of culture and scenery of culture almost comprehensively. As a tourism city, the website of Yogyakarta is already capable of presenting their local culture when access by visitor. Another region also has a lot of cultural richness. There are diverse of ornament that can be used. For example, Jawa Tengah has a lot of cultural ornament that potentially can be used, such as Prambanan Temple or Borobudur Temple. Papua Barat, as an area where is well known for its amazing natural tourist destinations, such as Raja Ampat, they can implement their nature landscape into interface design of their website. Another advantage of the implementation of the cultural preference is to gain tourism purpose. Just by access website, users can feel the impression just like being in the city.

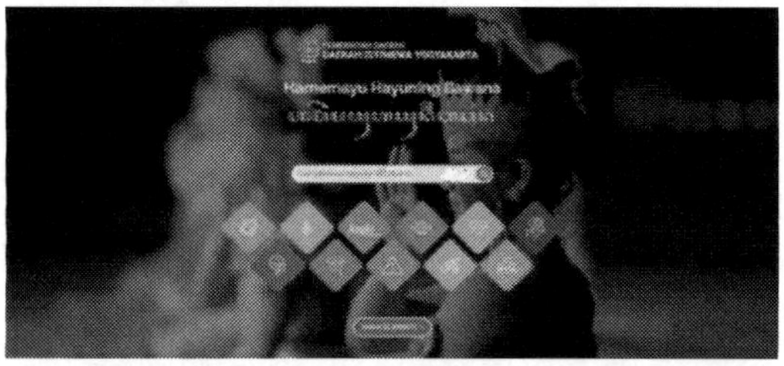

Fig 3. Official Website of Yogyakarta Government

Whereas, there are some cultural preferences that can be applied into the interface design. A Javanese scenery can be implemented to give the impression of local culture on the interface design of the website. For example, this scenary can be used as background of the website. In Fig.4, Javanese alphabet or we can call it *Aksara Jawa* is used to welcome the visitor when homepage is first appeared.

Fig 4. Utilization of *Aksara Jawa* on Interface Design

Some of cultural symbols can be used to replace previous commonly elements. Commonly elements used in website such as *Home*, *Navigation*, and *Back*, can be replaced using ornament based cultural. As shown in Fig. 5 (Credit to https://www.pinterest.com/pin/530510031084835341/) [13], the analogy on the left is *Home* (general) can be replaced by the *Home* on the right (cultural).

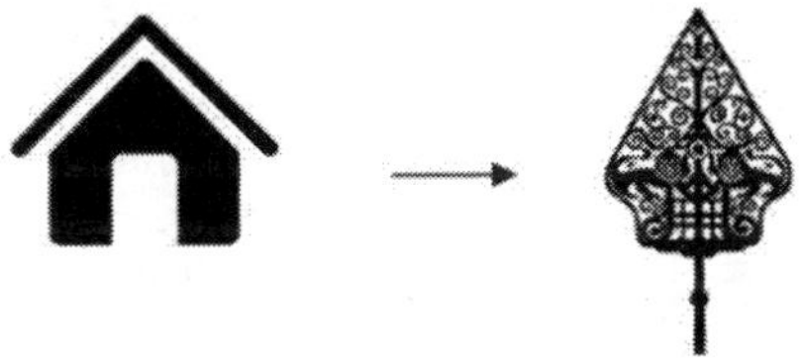

Fig 5. Home Analogy Can Be Replaced By Cultural Ornament

Furthermore, expression of language can be used to enhancethe scenery of culture aspect. In Table 2, we can see example of expression on Javanese language that can be applied into design.

Table 2. Example of Javanese Expression

Conventional	Cultural Based Languange
Welcome	SugengRawuh
Thank You	MaturNuwun

5 Usabilities Issues

In order to apply cultural preference into interface design, usability aspect is a defiance. ISO 9241-11 defined usability as the capability of the system being used by users [14]. Based on previous research, it was said that the implementation of cultural preferences does not guarantee it will improve the usability of website [8]. Therefore, it is important to consider the aspect of usability in order to implement cultural preferences in this study. It is useless, if the cultural aspects are successfully implemented, but the aspect of usability is ignored. In usability study, there are two approach that we can use, they are cognitive walkthrough and heuristic evaluation. In cognitive walkthrough approach, users are the key. Users will always be involved in every design process. Users, in this case are person who understand about the culture who living in place where the cultural preference is located. For example, person who live in certain location with similar culture will communicate in similar language. Daily, they are uses similar language, even though they are using national language (Bahasa Indonesia) in formal business. Furthermore, expert used in heuristic approach are humanist and interaction designer. Humanist actively involved in the design process. He asked to ensuring the ornament remains in line with the intended purpose. He works together with interaction designers to apply ornaments into the interface design. So, it is expected that ornament of the interface design is accordance to the cultural philosophy. In other way, heuristic evaluation can be used to measure the usability of website using design principles. One of the most commonly used is Nielsen's Heuristics [15]. Based on Quinones and Rusu, afterreviewing 73 papers, they have stated following methodology:

(1) Determine specific features of system
(2) Identify existing sets of usability heuristics
(3) Specify new set of heuristic based on standard template
(4) Validate new set of heuristic

Several ordinary elements which are replaced by cultural ornament potentially confuse users. Some ornament may seem unfamiliar with users at the first sight. Design principles can be used to guide interaction designer to design the interface fulfill the usability principles. Cognitive walkthrough and heuristic evaluation model are related closely to user-centered design (UCD). In UCD, observation is very crucial phase. The deeper we understand users, the more we can obtain good result. In this case, the more we understand cultural preferences and its ornament phylosophy, better results hopefully we can obtain. ISO standard divide into several terms as follows [14].

(1) **Goal** - what is the goal to be achieved. Relevant Goal for this research is to replace recent website interface into cultural-based website.
(2) **Personas** - is the person who understand and involved in the design process. Community of person who located in similar culture can be select as cognitive walkthrough respondents. Humanist can be selected as heuristic evaluator to ensure interface design match against the rules.
(3) **Effectiveness** - the accuracy and completeness of Personas while achieving Goal. Cultural-based interface should guarantee users of being not confused. There is some unusual ornament used, so it is potentially confused users.
(4) **Efficiency** - resources expended in order to achieve Goal. There are a lot of cultural ornament potentially used in the interface design. So, the utilization of ornament such as logo and image should be restricted. High quality image will impact on higher size of image.
(5) **Satisfaction** of Personas while interacting with website in order to achieve Goal. Cultural ornament aims to lure users.
(6) **Context of use** – analysis of the tasks, equipment, physical, and social environments.

If those six principles are met, we can say that website has good usability. Cultural preferences do not directly affect usability. Good implementation on cultural-based website does not mean it is good in usability principles. Otherwise, good implementation on cultural-based website does not mean it is bad in usability principles. There are some interesting findings revealed from this study:

(1) Cultural preference is not necessarily in line with the usability of website, but it is recommended to maintain local wisdom on local website.
(2) Difference region has difference preference of design, difference tribe also has difference culture and diverse ornament.
(3) This topic is just the beginning of the potentially bigger, so the concept and discussion in this research can be used as a trigger to the future work.
(4) There are many and various cultural tribes in Indonesia, so it is relevant to be used as sample in this domain of research.
(5) Cognitive walkthrough and heuristic evaluation can be used as guidelines to ensure the cultural-based website stick to the usability principles.

6 Conclusions and Future Works

User interface is the first gate of the interaction between usersand website. Therefore, the design has important role in the way of luringand influencing users to continue using it and help them tounderstand the information that is presented. However, it israre for websites, especially in Indonesia, that implementedtheir local cultural preference into their interface design. In fact, userinterface is potentially capable of luring both beginner andadvanced users. Cultural preference can make interfacedesign more interactive to the users. However, the cultural-based interface design has no absolute relation to theusability. In Indonesia, there are so many websites, both private orgovernment, have not implemented their local cultural preferenceinto their design. Indonesia has richness and diverse of cultural tribes, which are each tribe has special and unique ornament. Some of thesecultural ornament can be implemented to add local wisdom intotheir websites. But, this study has disadvantages, it has notproven empirically that cultural-based interface design can improve the usability of website. In order to implementcultural preference into design, we recommended to use one ofthese two approaches, cognitive walkthrough and heuristicevaluation. There are still so many weaknesses in this paper. This paper is still a small part of the discussion that should be broader. To obtain more comprehensive results, findings on this research can be proven empirically. On the future works, the result of this study can be improved by comparing two conditions. First condition, we can measure conventional design against the users. Second, we can measure cultural-based design against the users. Finally, we can compare the result and provide result empirically, whether positive or negative. Positive means cultural-based design is empirically providing good impact than conventional-based design. Negative means cultural-based design is empirically providing less effective than conventional-based design.

References

1. Z. Ishak, A. Jaafar, A. Ahmad, Interface Design for Cultural Differences,' in *International Congress on Interdisciplinary Business and Social Science* (2012).
2. K. Reinecke, A. Bernstein, Improving Performance, Perceived Usability, and Aesthetics with Culturally Adaptive User Interfaces,' ACM Transactions on Computer-Human Interaction, 8:1-8:29, (2011)
3. E. Callahan, Cultural similarities and differences in the design of university websites,' Journal of Computer-Mediated Communication, (2005)
4. L. Ulvydiene, Psychology of Translation in Cross Cultural Interaction,' in *5th World Conference on Educational Sciences*, (2014)
5. BPS (Badan Pusat Statistik) [online] available from https://www.bps.go.id/KegiatanLain/view/id/127 [30 July 2017]
6. B. McSweeney, Hofstede's Model of National Cultural Differences and their Consequences: A Triumph of Faith - a Failure of Analysis,' Sage Journals, (2002)
7. G. Hofstede, Dimensionalizing Culture: Te Hofstede Model in Context.' IACCP, 1-26, (2011)
8. K. P. Lee, A. Harada, A Study on the Cultural Effects on User Interface Design, in Proceedings of the ACM SIGCHI Conference, (2000)
9. J. Diaz, C. Rusu, C. A. Collazos, Experimental validation of a set of cultural-oriented usability heuristics.' Computer Standards & Interfaces, 160-178, (2017).
10. G. Lingaard, Aesthetics, Visual appeal, Usability and User Satisfaction: What Do the User's Eyes Tell the User's Brain?' Australian Journal of Emerging Technologies and Society, 1-14, (2007)
11. D.A. Norman. Emotional Design: Why We Love (or Hate) Everyday Things. New York: Basic Books, (2004)
12. www.welovesolo.com
13. https://www.pinterest.com/pin/530510031084835341/
14. N. Bevan, J. Carter, S. Harker, Human-Computer Interaction: Design and Evaluation,' Lecture Notes in Computer Science, 9169, 143-151, (2015)
15. D. Quinones, C. Rusu, How to Develop Usability Heuristics: A Systematic Literature Review,' Computer Standards & Interfaces, 53, 89-122, (2017).

MATEC Web of Conferences **215**, 02013 (2018) https://doi.org/10.1051/matecconf/201821502013
ICTIS 2018

Micro Imagination: Imagination with an Alternative Framework in a Chemistry Class

Nurdiana Abdullah[1], Nur Bahiyah Abdul Wahab[2], Taufik Lock Kim Wai[2], Johari Surif[3]

[1]Institute of Teacher Education, Temenggong Ibrahim Campus, In-ServiceTraining Unit
[2]Institute of Teacher Education, Temenggong Ibrahim Campus, Corporate Communication Unit
[3]Universiti Teknologi Malaysia, Department of Educational Science, Mathematics and Multimedia Creative, Faculty of Education

Abstract. The curriculum for the 21st century must be futuristic, flexible and dynamic in order to produce learners with creative and critical thinking. One of the strategies to inculcate creative and critical thinking among students is to train and familiarize learners with the process of generating imagination in teaching and learning. The process of generating imagination corresponds to the characteristics of the subject itself which consists of abstract concepts and complexities. These concepts require students to use their imagination to illustrate concepts, where learners are usually difficult to achieve. Therefore, this study was carried out to identify alternative frameworks in the students' imaginations of the concept of matter at submicroscopic level. A qualitative study with a descriptive study design is implemented to five secondary school students and ten students of institute of teacher education, aged from 18 to 25 years old. Guided imagery interviews and document analysis are used to collect data from selected students by purposive sampling. The data was analyzed using the grounded theory analysis strategy. The findings show that one of the alternative framework categories found in students' imagination is micro imagination. The image of hydrogen gas is the ultimate framework of the micro imagination of the most generated structure by the students followed by hydrogen electrons, collision of hydrogen molecules and the formation of water molecules. In this regard, scientific imagination needs to be enhanced by students with emphasis on the concept of science with effective imagination so that students can master chemical concepts at the sub-microscopic level competently. From the conclusion, the implication of the study suggests that teachers should expose to the students the aspects of generative imagination during teaching and learning sessions so that the desired skills can be improved effectively.

1 Introduction

Chemistry is a subject based on concepts and most of these concepts are abstract [1]. Therefore, it is difficult to master and learn by students. As a result, the literature shows a range of alternatives and difficulties in learning and under-standing of the chemical concept that exists amongst students [2-4]. The alternative frameworks related to matter are parts of the widely studied and widely reported aspects of the literature [5-8]. In fact, the literature also reveals that students have an alternative framework in the key aspects of matter con-cepts such as composition and structure [9-11], physical properties [11,12] and chemical properties [13].

The alternative framework is the existing knowledge that is in conflict with the scientific con-cepts that are concepts that are understood and accepted by scientists and are actual concepts. It is accepted by students through their interaction process with the environment and socialization process before or when in the classroom [14]. The alternative framework is also considered a strong concept, very robust and difficult to change and create obstacles to the next learning [15]. The early concepts of students with the world around them and during chemistry lessons may develop into alternative frameworks and these alternative frameworks that arise from the teaching process referred to as school-made misconceptions [16].

2 Literature Review

One of the factors in the existence of an alternative framework among students is that the chemical concept requires the habitual behavior learning of students with micro particle interactions at the submicroscopic level

* Corresponding author: cdiana818@gmail.com

[6,17-18]. In chemistry, submicroscopic levels are defined as levels that use the arrangement and movement of particles of atoms, molecules and subatoms to explain phenomena and chemical reactions [19] or levels used to describe the visible changes in the interaction between atoms and molecules [20] which form the matter [21. For students, understanding the phenomena and chemical reactions requires submicroscopic ability to visualize interactions between different types of atoms, molecules and other micro particles [6,12,18,22-23]. The existence of various alternative frames at the submicroscopic level is closely related to those levels that are not capable of being achieved by human sensory organs, levels associated with the world of micro particles (atoms, molecules and ions) and can only be achieved through imagination [24]. Hence, the ability of imagination among students, especially science students need to be nurtured and stimulated consistently, so that these skills can help them to understand better the abstract concepts of abstract science. DePorter (2000) defines imagination as the ability to see, hear and feel in mind. Mazur (2003) states that it is one of the ways to create a 'natural home' for something that is in the mind or one of the mental image creations [25]. The definition of imagination is also associated as one of the most important cognitive capabilities and can therefore be seen as a 'tool' to actively in thinking creatively [26-27]. The highlight of the study demonstrates the many positive impacts the students gain from imagination. One of them is that imagination that helps children to understand their world. This situation occurs when children use their imagination to sort and allocate the world into units that they can explore and eventually assimilate the information into their cognitive schemes. Therefore, children can gain control over their symbolic representation system [28]. Other than being applied to understand the world, imaginations can also be used by educators to understand children's understanding of a field because of its ability as a 'diagnostic tool' in the capability of reflecting the level of development of a child [29].

Teacher as a facilitator in the teaching and learning process of a student plays a role in using appropriate imagination based learning strategies for students. This is because the success of the teacher in utilizing the imagination of the student is directly able to enhance the student's learning. The importance of this learning strategy is supported by previous studies such as Tindall-Ford and Sweller (2006) studies that students of Grade 8 who have knowledge about a material and then imagine the material to be learned with accompanying audio / visual teaching can promote better learning than students who only study the material traditionally [30]. Such learning strategies are also in line with grade 4 and 5 students [31]. Glenberg *et al.* (2004) uses an imaginative based learning strategy in his studies and finds that the strategy is effective in improving the learning of grade 2 students as well [32]. Students demonstrate better reading performance when they are asked to visualize the activities in the book as compared to reading the materials alone. The conclusion of a very young age is evidence that students encouraged to participate in the imagination eventually demonstrate the ability to control emotions, have better empathetic skills and sophisticated cognitive skills [33].

As such, it is important for teachers to identify lessons that emphasize intelligence components such as imagination, analytic, practical and creativity as these teaching strategies are more beneficial to students than traditional teaching that relies largely on analytical intelligence. In addition, using a variety of developmental activities that are appropriate for children's imagination, teachers can also develop children's readiness and social skills, enhance their learning and motivation to learn while having fun and creating interrelationship with the school contexts [33]. Realizing the importance of imagination in the education world from this discussion, it creates a spark to these questions: how is the imagination of students on abstract chemical concepts at the submicroscopic level? Is there an alternative framework in the student's imagination of these chemical concepts? and if the alternative framework exists, what are the features of the alternative framework? Therefore, this study needs to be carried out to learn more about the student's imagination of chemical concepts at the submicroscopic level in general and the alternative framework that exists in the imagination in particular.

3 Research Objective

The objective of this study was to identify the alternative frameworks that the students of various levels of age had in their imaginations on the concept of matter at the submicroscopic level. Identifying alternative frameworks that exist among learners is crucial as the alternative framework affects students' learning when they interpret the teacher's teaching using the alternative framework perspective [34]. Hence, it is important to define the student's alternative framework and to develop appropriate teaching strategies to address these problems. This study is based on the following question: How are the alternative frameworks that exist in the students' imaginations of the concept of matter at the submicroscopic level?

4 Methodology

4.1 Research Design

This study was carried out using a descriptive approach in qualitative study as it is appropriate to collect detailed and in depth information on the alternative frameworks that exist in the students' imagination of the concept of matter at the submicroscopic level among the various levels of age. These methods and approaches are appropriate for being able to be the best strategy to answer the research question in this study. In addition, qualitative studies are also capable of explaining the real situation and producing meaningful insights [35-36].

4.2 Samples

The study involved five science stream of form four students (aged 16-17 years) from secondary school and ten first year until the final semester (age 18-19 to 24-25 years) undergraduate students from a selected teachers' education institute through purposive sampling. This technique is used because of its ability to describe in detail and give an in depth understanding of a phenomenon studied [37]. A total of five secondary schools and ten undergraduate students' education institutes in the southern zone of Malaysia were involved in the study. The main factors of student selection are based on three main criteria: (i) the students who have taken the Test of Matter Concept and Understanding at the Submicroscopic Level (SUKKJPAS), (ii) possess good score in SUKKJPAS which is> 50 percent and (3) the category of age focus of this study. The selection of both categories of these students is due to the concept of matter is one of the concepts in their curriculum.

4.3 Data Collection

Qualitative data collection in semi-structured interviews using guided imagery interviews and document analysis is executed after the students has completed the Test of Matter Concept and Understanding at the Submicroscopic Level (SUKKJPAS). Interview techniques are appropriate and accurate to get in depth information and to know what is expressed and implied in a person's mind [38] where the analysis of the document serves to reinforce and prove a statement and to complement the data obtained from other sources [39]. A total of 15 students were interviewed in guided imagery to identify the alternative framework students had in their imaginations on the concept of matter at the submicroscopic level. Each student was interviewed individually for 60minutes to150 minutes. Interviews involved two main sections, which are guided imagery and follow-up questions. Guided imagery activities began with students watching a two-minute video clip of natrium and water reaction to set the students familiar with the reaction. Inthe video clip, a pebblesized sodium is put into a beaker containing 1000ml of water and the reaction produces fire. After watching the video clip, the teacher read studentswith the guided imagery scenario adapted from Al-Balushi (2003) in a closed eye condition for five minutes [40]. After the activity, follow-up questions were posed to the students. The questions in this study focus on four concepts: the concept of hydrogen gas, hydrogen electrons, hydrogen molecule collision and the formation of water molecule.

4.4 Data Analysis

Data analysis began by recording all interviews and then being copied verbatimally. A copy of the completed transcripts were submitted to the studentsfor review purposes which were; to confirm or add or subtract any part of the interview. The transcript was then analyzed using a grounded theory analysis strategy involving three stages: open coding, axis decoding and selected coding with Nvivo Software version 10.0 and ATLAS.ti version 7.0 to understand and compute the large and unorganized data. The data were analyzed based on the four concepts that were asked to the students during the interview sessions. The data obtained were then endorsed by two experts in the field of chemistry education who have more than 30 years of experience.

5 Findings and Discussions

The findings of the study found that micro imaginations were one of the alternative framework categories that existed in the students' imaginations on the concept of matter at the submicroscopic level with a percentage of 15.30 percent from 31.12 percent imagination with an alternative framework (Figure 1). The micro imagination in this study refers to the imagination generated by the students at the submicroscopic level but it is not based on scientific concept and it contains an alternative framework. The details of the micro imaginations on each of the concepts of matter among the students are presented as in Table 1.

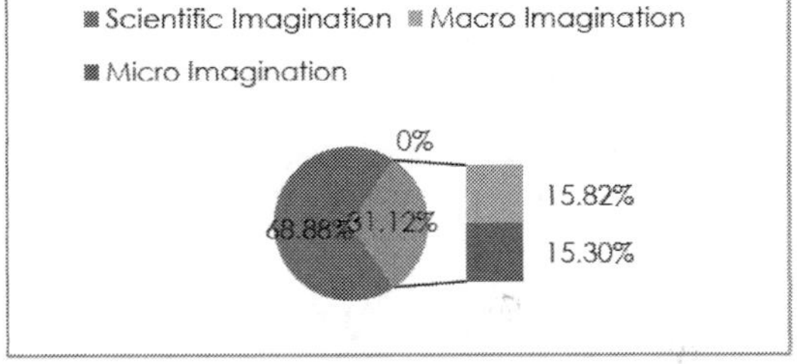

Fig 1. Percentage of scientific imagination, macro imagination and students'micro imagination on the concept of matter

Table 1. Students' micro imaginations on the concept of matter

Micro Imagination	Percentage (%)
Hydrogen gas	7.14
Hydrogen electron	4.08
Hydrogen molecul collision	3.57
Formation of water molecule	0.51
Total	15.30

Table 1 shows the presence of micro imaginations among students on the four concepts of matter studied with the concept of hydrogen gas as the most generated images of students' imagination followed by the concept of hydrogen electrons, collision of hydrogen molecules and water formation.

(1) Micro Imagination of Hydrogen Gas

The study found that among the students' micro imagination of the hydrogen gas concept was to generate the image of hydrogen gas as a circle containing the letter H, the movement of hydrogen gas is going up very slowly and hydrogen gas bondingemerged as if there is a bond in the center of the atom. One example of the students' micro imagination on the form of hydrogen gas is as follows:

Researcher: When I say hydrogen gas is about to form, what do you see?

Student : That's the round hydrogen...

Researcher: [Mmm ...] looks round?

Student: H is round

Researcher: [Mmm ...] Does it look alone round or multiple round to the whole a great extent?

Student : One

P1SK1, 16-17 years old)

In the interview transcript, the students are figuring out the form of hydrogen gas as a circle containing the letter H. This imagination shows the students' confusion on the concept of atoms and molecules for hydrogen gas comprising two hydrogen atoms. Due to the confusion over the term of the particle, students generate micro imaginations that contain an alternative framework. This situation proves the importance of mastering science concepts scientifically in helping students produce scientific imagination. This confusion reveals the existence of long-term integration problems in science education. This means that science students usually learn small pieces of information scattered and cover different concepts by studying different phenomena. Therefore, they are lack of the ability to develop accurate and scientific explanations that incorporate pieces of information that has been learned.

(2) Micro Imagination of Electron Hydrogen

The findings show that the H + black and the charge on letter H are among the micro-imaginations generated by the students on the form of hydrogen electrons. Other than the form, students also generated micro imaginations on the movement of hydrogen electrons, which is to visualize the movement of hydrogen electrons in orbital recip-rocating, static and slow moving circles. Here is an example of a student's micro imagination:

Researcher: So electron hydrogen you imagine H + ... it has no color because it is writing ... so the writing is black?

Student : Ha'a black color

(GP1M1, 24-25 years old)

From the above reponses, it clearly exhibits a student's micro-imagination on an electron shape which implies an electron shape as black H +. This demonstrates the existence of alternative framework in students' imagination. This imagination also proves that the student's confusion about the term electron with the charge that exists in hydrogen atoms. In addition, the H + symbol indicate that a student's imagination is influenced by reading from textbooks. This is due to text illustration is one of the factors that influences the student's imagination when the image of the student's imagination is dominant with text illustration, resulting that only text elements can be activated from past experiences [40].

(3) Micro Imagination of Hydrogen Molecule Collision

Micro imagination to the concept of collision of hydrogen molecules occurs when the student generates collision image in a state of water molecules joined to each other and the hydrogen molecules merge with oxygen molecules. The student describes the following collision situations:

Researcher : Ok when I say, you see the water molecules formed swirling swiftly and collide with the molecules around them, so what do you see?

Students : Water molecules try to join each other ... enforcing their energy to fight with the fire to extinguish the fire

Researcher: [Mmm ...] it moves fast?

Student : [Mmm ...] very fast

(GP4M1, 18-19 years old)

The analysis of the answers indicates the failure of students to comprehend the current situation of water molecule collisions with other molecules around them. Student imag-ine the collision by producing imaginations of water molecules trying to join each other. The reason given to this perspective is to extinguish the fire formed from the sodium and water reactions. Although students were generating images of micro imaginations at first, however, the reason given to extinguish the fire for the dissemination process re-vealed the imagination of students at the submicroscopic level was a combination of macroscopic and submicroscopic levels. This is because students are not able to differ-entiate and separate their physical world with submicroscopic level. This finding is co-herent with the study of Al Balushi (2003) that one of the students imagined some of the water molecules moving in the liquid water. The presence of both these water molecules and water fluids in the student imagination marks the difficulty of students accepting and understanding the concept of macroscopic and submicroscopic levels. This phenomenon is called Raisin Cake Model. This situation occurs when the student accepts the presence of particles in matter but still confused with the concept of matter consisting of discrete particles.

(4) Micro Imagination of the Formation of Water Molecules

The formation of water molecules is the concept that the least image of a micro-imagination is generated by a student. Students only generate images of hydrogen atoms into oxygen orbit when asked to imagine the formation of water molecules. This is evi-dent from the conversation:

Researcher: Ok when I say, now that both hydrogen atoms are combined with oxygen atoms, what do you see?

Student: Looks like a hydrogen atom trying to get in orbit

Researcher: [Mmm ...] the hydrogen atom enters orbit?

Student: Yes ... oxygen orbit

(GP2M3, 22-23 years old)

In this interview transcript, students figure out the concept of molecular combination for the formation of water molecules by generating imagination of hydrogen atoms entering the oxygen orbit. This imagination shows students have an alternative framework for the concept of sharing and electron transfer to form the bond between the particles for the formation of water molecules. On the other hand, no micro imagination is produced by students for the concept of water molecule state. From a positive aspect, no micro imagination image produced by the student on this concept indicates that the student is able to imagine the concept well. However, from a negative aspect, it indicates that the students are less or rarely use the submicroscopic level during their teaching and learning chemistry.

6 Conclusion

In conclusion, the findings revealed that the majority of students produced more micro-imaginations for hydrogen gas images of 7.14 percent compared with other images such as hydrogen electrons (4.08 percent), hydrogen moleculescollision (3.57 percent) and formation water molecules (0.51 percent). The scenario implies the concept of matter at submicroscopic level with the existence of an alternative framework among students not surprisingly due to lack of pedagogy in giving a fair emphasis to submicroscopic levels rather than macroscopic and symbolic levels when designing and planning texts and teaching materials. As a result, such educational systems produce incompetent students to think and use submicroscopic levels for natural phenomena and chemical phenomena. Gabel *et al.* (1987) [41] and Al-Balushi (2003) [40] also revealed the disruption of the situation among students. Compounding to the aforesaid matter, studies by Kokkotas and Vlachos (1998) also show that chemistry teachers have the same alternative frameworks on submicroscopic levels of matter [42]. If teachers are lack of the ability to explain and investigate chemicals phenomenon at the submicroscopic level, then the probability of their students to experience the same condition is high. This situation also encourages students to create imaginative imagery that has an alternative framework despite the fact that students are encouraged to imagine learning abstract science concepts. Thus, existing knowledge plays an important role in the process of generating a student's imagination.

7 Implications

The findings of this study on the imagination of students with alternative frameworks suggest that teachers need to relate the imagination of students to the relevant science concepts so that even though they are imaginative according to their own interests and tendencies, they still maintain a scientific perspective in the course of their imagination. By applying these strategies, students are expected to acquire imaginations that are not only interesting and creative, but also accurate and scientific as the subject of chemistry has great importance in accuracy and scientific concepts. In addition, teachers' exposure to the aspects of imagination generation during teaching and learning sessions among students should also be enhanced. It is important for students to understand a chemical phenomenon more profoundly when the imagination is generated by students according to their own ability and interest without interfering scientific concepts. This situation allows students to imagine in the absence of boundaries yet retaining the concepts of science and chemistry as a foundation and goundwork. For example, when students are figuring out the movement of gas particles, students need to know the basic concept of the gas particle movement, which has the form of Brownian motion. Thus, the imagination generated by the students is based on the basic concepts so that the imagination produced by the students is accurate and scientific.

References

1. M.I. Stojanovska, B.T. Šoptrajanov, V.M. Petruševski. Addressing Misconceptions about the Particulate Nature of Matter among Secondary-School and High-School Students in the Republic of Macedonia.Creative Education. **3**(5): 619-631. (2012)
2. M.H. Chiu. A National Survey of Students' Conceptions of Chemistry in Taiwan.International Journal of Science Education. **29**(4): 421-452. (2005)
3. W.H. Cliff, Chemistry Misconceptions Associated with Understanding Calcium and Phosphate Homeostasis. Advances in Physiology Education. **33**: 323-328. (2009)
4. M. Çalýk, A. Ayas, J.V. Ebenezer. A Review of Solution Chemistry Studies: Insights into Students' Conceptions. Journal of Science Education and Technology. **14**: 29-50. (2005)
5. A. Badrian, T. Abdinejad, A. Naseriazar. A Cross-Age Study of Iranian Students' Various Conceptions About the Particulate Nature of Matter. Journal of Turkish Science Education. **8**: 49-63. (2011)
6. W. Vos, A.H. Verdonk. The Particulate Nature of Matter in Science Education and in Science.Journal

of Research in Science Teaching. **33**(6): 657-664. (1996)
7. K. Skamp. Atoms and Molecules in Primary Science: What Are Teachers to Do? Australian Journal of Education in Chemistry.**69**: 5- 10. (2009)
8. E.J. Yezierski, J.P. Birk, Misconceptions about the Particulate Nature of Matter.Using Animations to Close the Gender Gap.Journal of Chemical Education. **83**(6): 954-96. (2006)
9. D. Benson, M. Wittrock, M. Baur. Students' Preconceptions of the Nature of Gases.Journal of Research in Science Teaching.**30**(6): 587-597. (1993)
10. D. Krnel, S.S. Glazar, R. Watson, The Development of the Concept of "Matter": A Cross-Age Study of How Children Classify Materials. Science Education. **87**(5): 621-639. (2003)
11. D. Krnel R. Watson S.A. Glazar. Survey of Research Related to the Development of the Concept of 'Matter'. International Journal of Science Education. **20**: 257-389. (1998)
12. O. Lee, D.C. Eichinger, C.W. Anderson, G.D. Berkheimer, T.D. Blakeslee, Changing Middle School Students' Conceptions of Matter and Molecules.Journal of Research in Science Teaching. **30**: 249-270. (1993)
13. H.K. Boo, J.R. Watson, Progression in High School Students' (aged 16–18) Conceptualizations about Chemical Reactions in Solution.Science Education. **85**(5): 568-585. (2001)
14. J. Surif. Kajian Perbandingan Pemikiran Saintifik Pelajar Malaysia dengan United Kingdom. Universiti Teknologi Malaysia: Tesis Ph.D. (2010)
15. N. Canpolat. Turkish Undergraduates' Misconceptions of Evaporation, Evaporation Rate, and Vapour Pressure.International Journal of Science Education. **28**(15):1757-1770. (2006)
16. H.D. Barke, A. Hazari, S. Yitbarek. Misconception in Chemistry. (Springer, German, 2009)
17. R. Day, Visual Cognition in Understanding Biology Labs; Can It Be Connected to Conceptual Change? A Paper Presented at the National Association of Research in Science Teaching Conference, Vancouver, Canada. (2004).
18. A.G. Harrison D.F Treagust. Secondary Students' Mental Models of Atoms and Molecules: Implications for Teaching Chemistry. Science Education. **80**(5): 509-534. (1996)
19. V.M. Williamson, M.R. Abraham, The Effects of Computer Animation on the Particulate Mental Methods of College Chemistry Students.Journal of Research in Science Teaching. **32**(5): 521-534, (1995).
20. J.J. Hesse, C.W. Andersson, Students' Conceptions of Chemical Change.Journal of Research in Science Teaching. **29**(3): 277-299. (1992)
21. M.B. Nakhleh, A. Samarapungavan. Elementary School Children's Beliefs about Matter.Journal of Research in Science Teaching. **36**(7): 777-805. (1999)
22. J.D. Bradley, M. Brand, Stamping Out Misconceptions.Journal of Chemical Education. **62**(4): 318. (1995)
23. A.H. Haidar, M.R. Abraham, A Comparison of Applied and Theoretical Knowledge of Concepts Based on the Particulate Theory of Matter.Journal of Research in Science Teaching.**28**(10): 919-938. (1991)
24. B. Bucat, M. Mocerino. Introduction: Macro, Submicro and Symbolic Representations and the Relationship between Them: Key Models in Chemical Education. In: Gilbert, J. K. dan Treagust, D. Multiple Representations in Chemical Education. (Springer, London. 11-29. (2009)
25. B. Mazur, Imagining Numbers (particularly the square root of minus fifteen). New York: Farrar, Straus and Giroux. (2003)
26. B. Gaut, Creativity and Imagination. In: B. Gaut. and P. Livingston. (Eds.). The Creation of Art (pp. 148–173). Cambridge, England: Cambridge University Press. (2003)
27. G. Heath, Exploring the Imagination to Establish Frameworks for Learning.Studies in Philosophy and Education. **27**(2): 115–123. (2008)
28. P. Bouldin, An Investigation of the Fantasy Predisposition and Fantasy Style of Children with Imaginary Companions.The Journal of Genetic Psychology: Research and Theory on Human Development. **167**(1): 17-29. (2006)
29. S.W. Russ. Play and Creativity: Developmental Issues. Scandinavian Journal of Educational Research. **47**(3): 291-303. (2003)
30. S. Tindall-Ford, J. Sweller. Altering the Modality of Instructions to Facilitate Imagination: Interactions between the Modality and Imagination Effects.Instructional Science. **34**(4): 343-365. (2006)
31. W. Leahy, J. Sweller. Interactions among the Imagination, Expertise Reversal and Element Interactivity Effects.Journal of Experimental Psychology: Applied. **11**(4): 266-276. (2005)
32. A.M. Glenberg, T. Gutierrez, J.R. Levin, S. Japuntich, M.P. Kaschak. Activity and Imagined Activity Can Enhance Young Children's Reading Comprehension. Journal of Educational Psychology. **96**: 424–436. (2004)
33. M. Smith, R. Mathur. Children's Imagination and Fantasy: Implications for Development, Education, and Classroom Activities. Research in the Schools. **16**(1): 52-63. (2009)
34. O. Taştan, E. Yalçınkaya, Y. Boz, Effectiveness of Conceptual Change Text-Oriented Instruction on Students' Understanding of Energy in Chemical Reactions.Journal of Science Education and Technology. **17**(5): 444-453. (2008).
35. J.W. Creswell, Qualitative Inquiry and Research Design: Choosing among Five Approaches. 2nd ed. (Sage, London, 2007).
36. N.K. Denzin, Y.S. Lincoln, Y. S. Handbook of Qualitative Research, (Routledge, London. 2004).
37. S.B. Merriam, Qualitative Research and Case Study Application in Education. Revised and Expanded from Case Study Research in Education. (Jossey-Bass Publishers, San Francisco. 2002).

38. M.Q. Patton, Qualitative Research and Evaluation Methods (3rd ed.). (Thousand Oaks Sage, CA: 2002).
39. S. Marican. Kaedah Penyelidikan Sains Sosial. (Pearson Prentice Hall, Selangor. 2005)
40. S.M. Al-Balushi, Exploring Omani Pre-Service Science Teachers' Imagination at the Microscopic Level in Chemistry and Their Use of the Particulate Nature of Matter in Their Explanations. The University of Iowa: Ph.D Thesis. (2003).
41. D.L. Gabel, K.V. Samuel, D. Hunn. Understanding the Particulate Nature of Matter. Journal of Chemical Education. **64**(8): 695-697. (1987)
42. P. Kokkotas, I. Vlachos. Teaching the Topic of Particulate Nature of Matter in Prospective Teachers' Training Courses.International Journal of Science Education. **20**(3): 291-303. (1998)

AUTHOR INDEX

Abdul Halin Izhal.....73
Abdul-Kadir Kadzrina.....218
Abdullah Nurdiana.....281
Abral Hairul.....124
Adiarto Mikhael.....138
Adiarto Tokok.....143
Affandi Muhammad Irfan.....272
Agus.....171, 177
Agustian Punggara Adrian.....13
Ahmad Norzieiriani.....218
Aina Qorri.....254, 261
Al Al.....62
Al-Ajmi Mohammad Shafi.....73
Alfith Alfith.....45
Aliya Qonita Himmatul.....265
Amalia Sitti.....53
Amin Zulkifli.....59
Anisya Anisya.....161
Anthony Zuriman.....120, 124
Antonov Bachtiar.....94
Ariana Lutfah.....231
Ariffin Ahmad Shabudin.....224
Arlianto Jerry A......40
Arshad Darwina.....218
Asmara Indri Juwita.....231
Astuti Sussi.....272
Aulia Putra Handityo.....1
Bandri Sepannur.....79
Bashnjak S. E......87
Chak Choiwai Maggie.....209
Chandra Sonny Hutomo.....143
Dasman Dasman.....201
David Firmansyah.....205
David Wahyudi.....205
Dewi Arfita Yuana.....62, 69, 98
Dhewanto Wawan.....249, 265
Djali Nazwar.....189
Edison Edison.....128
Effendi Asnal.....69, 98
Erhaneli Erhaneli.....120
Fahmi Hendriwan.....197
Fatmawati Akbarningrum.....138
Franozal Alex.....23
Fu Yen-Pei.....133
Gunawan Ika.....157
Hadinata Stephen.....138
Hafni Hafni.....197
Halin Izhal Abdul.....36
Handayani Sri.....272
Handayani Wenda.....18
Handomo Roi.....143
Handra Nofriady.....197
Hapsari Indri.....40
Hartono Markus.....40
Hasan Alizar.....165
Hayati Yulia.....182
Heliana Sri.....265
Herliana Sri.....249, 254, 261
Hidayat Taufal.....62
Himmatul Aliya Qonita.....254
Honesti Leli.....189
Ikhsan Muhammad.....59
Indra Ade.....128
Ismail Fauzan.....69
Kartiria Kartiria.....45
Kozhemyachenko A. V......87
Krisnanda Yohanes R......40
Kurniawan Ruddy.....171
Lamsali Hendrik.....224
Lantu Donald Crestofel.....249, 261
Lawiyah Nur.....249, 254, 261, 265
Lemeshko M. A......87
Lestari Yuliani Dwi.....265
Lidiawati Tuani.....138
Maidiawati.....182
Majid Muhd Zaimi Abd......189
Md Yunus Nurul Amziah.....73
Medriosa Hamdeni.....182
Michishita Koji.....112
Milyardi Roi.....152
Minarni.....8, 18
Mohd Ariffin Mohd. Khairol Anuar B......73
Muchlian Meli.....189
Mustapha Faizal.....73
Nanda Rahmat Rizki.....29
Nazir Refdinal.....124
Nesti Lisa.....83
Ng Wei Choon.....36
Nofrianto Hendri.....128
Nugroho Fajar.....161
Nurjanah Siti.....239
Nurzal.....148
Perdana Mastaryanto.....148
Persada Andhika Giri.....276
Petrosov S. P......87
Pranata Yosafat Aji.....152
Putera Heru Pratama.....148
Putri Melani Novia.....165
Rachman Arfidian.....83
Rahmanullah Edwin Sholeh.....239
Ramadhana Febriyan.....177
Ridwan.....98
Ridwan Muhammad.....171, 177
Rizki Muhammad.....105
Rosmiati Mia.....261
Sapei Lanny.....143
Sofian Andi.....79
Subardi Adi.....133
Sulandari Noek.....152
Surif Johari.....281

AUTHOR INDEX

Sutardi Acip 254
Syofian Andi..49
Syofyan Z...189
Tanjung Jafril 182
Tanubrata Maksum...157
Thomas Thomas...94
Tjahjoanggoro Anton J. 40
Tondok Marselius S. 40
Wahab Nur Bahiyah Abdul 281
Wahab Wilton 193
Wai Taufik Lock Kim...281
Warman Indra 18, 23
Warmi Yusreni..112
Wira Trise Putra Dede 13
Yuhendra 8, 18
Yulianti Eva...29
Yultrisna 49
Yunus Nurul Amziah Md 36
Zaidir 165
Zakaria Nazlina...218
Zulkarnaini Zulkarnaini 79, 105, 120